CINEMA SEWER

THE ADULTS ONLY GUIDE TO HISTORY'S SICKEST AND SEXIEST MOVIES

EDITED BY

ROBIN BOUGIE

VOLUME

7

A FAB PRESS PUBLICATION

CINEMA SEWER VOL. 7

FIRST EDITION PUBLISHED BY FAB PRESS, AUGUST 2020

FAB PRESS LTD
2 FARLEIGH
RAMSDEN ROAD
GODALMING
SURREY
GU7 1QE
ENGLAND.UK

www.FABPRESS.com

A CIP CATALOGUE RECORD FOR THIS BOOK IS AVAILABLE FROM THE BRITISH LIBRARY.

HARDCOVER LIMITED EDITION INCLUDING EXCLUSIVE 64-PAGE BUTTLORDS FULL COLOR COMIC
ISBN 9781913051037
PAPERBACK
ISBN 9781913051044

COVER ART BY THE ALWAYS AMAZING VINCE RUARUS. VISIT HIM AT:
WWW.VENIVIDIVINCE.COM

THIS BOOK IS DEDICATED TO:

STAN RATHBUN, THE OWNER AND OPERATOR OF RATH ART SUPPLIES, WHICH IS DIRECTLY DOWNSTAIRS FROM MY ART STUDIO. YOU KNOW, IT'S ONLY RIGHT TO CREATE THIS BOOK IN HIS HONOUR, SINCE MOST OF IT WAS MADE WITH PENS, PENCILS AND OTHER ART SUPPLIES OBTAINED IN HIS COZY LITTLE SHOP. SUCH A BIG PART OF THE LOCAL ART COMMUNITY, AND YET RARELY ACKNOWLEDGED. I HONESTLY DIDN'T EVEN KNOW HE WAS SICK, EVEN THOUGH HE VERY RECENTLY HAD SOLD THE STORE AND STEPPED AWAY FROM IT. SADLY, WE LOST STAN TO CANCER IN THE SECOND WEEK OF 2020. HE KEPT THINGS CLOSE TO THE VEST, AND NEVER WANTED TO BURDEN OTHER PEOPLE WITH HIS PROBLEMS, EVEN THOUGH HE WAS SO GRACIOUS TO LISTEN TO OURS AND ALWAYS OFFER A KIND WORD. TRULY ONE OF THE <u>GREATS</u>, I WISH I HAD DONE MORE TO LET HIM KNOW HOW IMPORTANT HE WAS TO US.

VISIT ME ONLINE AT MY VARIOUS SOCIAL MEDIA ACCOUNTS, AS WELL AS AT MY BLOG:
BOUGIEMAN. LIVEJOURNAL.COM

CINEMA SEWER VOL. 7

THE SICKEST AND SEXIEST FILMS EVER

WELCOME TO CINEMA SEWER VOL. SEVEN!

BOUGIE

FLIP

THIS HERE BOOK COLLECTS #30 (THE OVERSIZED TWENTY YEAR ANNIVERSARY ISSUE) AND #31 OF THE CINEMA SEWER ZINE, AS WELL AS 80 PAGES OF BRAND NEW NEVER-BEFORE-SEEN CONTENT CREATED JUST FOR THIS VOLUME. THERE ARE SOME CONTRIBUTORS (WHEN APPLICABLE, THEY HAVE BEEN CREDITED AT THE BEGINNING OR END OF EACH ARTICLE), BUT 90% OF THE CRAP IN HERE OOZED OUT OF MY FAT LITTLE FINGERS AS I GLEEFULLY TOILED AWAY IN MY SECOND FLOOR STUDIO SPACE WHICH RESTS ABOVE AN ART SUPPLY STORE, A COMIC SHOP, AND A VEGETARIAN BURRITO PLACE IN THE MOUNT PLEASANT NEIGHBOURHOOD OF VANCOUVER BC, CANADA.

MY NAME IS ROBIN BOUGIE, I'M IN MY MID '40S, I'M MARRIED TO MY HIGH SCHOOL SWEETHEART (ANIMATOR REBECCA DART), I'VE GOT TWO TWIN TUXEDO CATS NAMED HERBIE AND MARVIN, I DRAW A LOT OF PORN COMICS AND I AM OBSESSED WITH THE MORE TAWDRY SIDE OF CINEMA HISTORY. I'M PLEASED TO MEET YOU IF YOU'RE A NEW READER, AND PLEASED TO SEE YOU AGAIN IF YOU'RE NOT!

CINEMA SEWER STARTED IN 1997 AS A LITTLE SELF-PUBLISHED PHOTOCOPIED ZINE WITH A PRINT RUN OF 200 COPIES, GREW AND GREW TO A CIRCULATION OF ABOUT 2000 COPIES -- AS IT TEASED WITH GETTING POPULAR ENOUGH TO GO MAINSTREAM. IN THE WAKE OF A SOCIETY THAT NOW GENERALLY FINDS SLEAZE "PROBLEMATIC", CS HAS SINCE COLLAPSED BACK TO ITS VERY 'UNDERGROUND' ROOTS, BUT THANKFULLY FAB PRESS ARE STILL PLEASED TO PRESENT THESE BEAUTIFUL PUBLICATIONS THAT INFILTRATE BOOK STORES (BOTH ONLINE AND OTHERWISE) AND HELP KEEP THE ZINE FROM FADING INTO RESOLUTE OBSCURITY! FOR THAT, I'M TICKLED PINK.

DID YOU KNOW THAT I'M EATING A GRILLED CHEESE SANDWICH RIGHT NOW? I DON'T THINK YOU DID. I WAS SORT OF NIBBLING AT IT SECRETLY. I DON'T KNOW, I THOUGHT YOU MIGHT TAKE ME MORE SERIOUSLY IF YOU THOUGHT YOU HAD 100% OF MY ATTENTION, BUT THE FACT IS THAT I WAS SHARING THAT ATTENTION WITH THIS VERY PLEASANT SANDWICH. HOPE THAT'S COOL.

NOW, WITH THAT HORSE SHIT OUT OF THE WAY, JOIN ME ON THE NEXT PAGE AS WE STROLL INTO THE CINEMA SEWER WORLD HEADQUARTERS AND GET THE LAY OF THE LAND... →

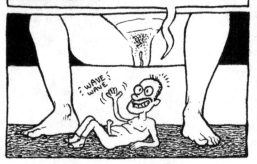

WELCOME TO THE CINEMA SEWER WORLD HQ!

WAVE WAVE

DON'T BE NERVOUS AND DON'T BE SHY! YOU'RE IN **GOOD** HANDS! I'VE BEEN USING COMICS, ILLUSTRATIONS, AND THE HAND-DRAWN AESTHETIC TO TALK ABOUT HISTORY'S SICKEST AND SEXIEST MOVIES FOR OVER 22 YEARS NOW! HERE AT THE CS WORLD H.Q. WE'RE ALL WORKING AROUND THE CLOCK TO REACH INTO THE ABYSS AND PULL OUT THE FINEST IN DEBAUCHERY!

JUST BUG IT.

EACH BOOK AND ZINE WE CREATE IS **BONAFIDE**!

HEH

GRRR

DON'T TOUCH

OR ELSE

CINEMA SEWER

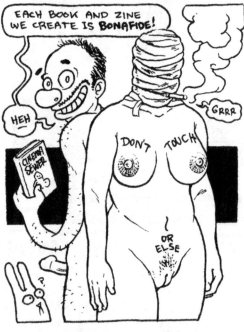

OOOOFF!! ≋PANT≋ IT'S A GREAT PLACE TO COME TO WORK EVERY DAY. WE'RE ALWAYS DOING ALL WE CAN TO KEEP C.S. SLEAZY AND ≋GRUNT≋ INFORMATIVE!

LOOKIT THAT THING!

KEEP UP THE GREAT WORK!

Mmmmm **YESSSSS** YYEEAH

FUCKING CHOKE ON MY PUSSY JUICE, PIG

SO LEAN BACK AND RELAX! LET THE WORLD MELT AWAY AND GET READY TO **ENJOY!!**

LOOK AT THAT!

SEE? REACHING INTO THE **ABYSS!**

I PUT MY HAND RIGHT UP MY ASS!

NEAT!

BOUGIE '19

4

CINEMA SEWER SPOTLIGHT ON: 8mm porn loops

BY: ROBIN BOUGIE · 2019.

THEIR PLACE IN HISTORY IS UNDENIABLE. HARDCORE 8MM STAG FILMS INTRODUCED EXPLICIT HUMAN SEXUALITY TO THE PUBLIC. PREDATING EVERY OTHER MOVIE PICTURE HOME FORMAT, THESE INAUSPICIOUS PRODUCTIONS PROVIDED NOT ONLY A WINDOW TO A WHOLE OTHER WORLD, BUT ALSO IMMEDIATE RELIEF FOR THOSE NOT FORTUNATE ENOUGH TO MAKE THEIR FANTASIES INTO REALITY.

TRADITIONALLY SHOWN AT STAG PARTIES (HENCE THE MONIKER "STAG FILMS") LOOPS WERE ESSENTIALLY A WORDLESS DOCUMENT OF TWO OR MORE PEEPS SATISFYING THEIR MOST URGENT DESIRES. THE LAWS LIGHTENED UP IN THE 1970S, BUT IN THE 1960S AND EARLIER THESE NOW QUAINT-SEEMING UNDERGROUND FILMS WERE RAW, ILLEGAL, AND VERY EDGY. KEEP IN MIND THAT THIS WAS AT A TIME WHEN HOLLYWOOD COULDN'T SHOW A TIT (IT WASN'T UNTIL 1964'S THE PAWNBROKER THAT A PAIR OF BREASTS APPEAR IN A US MOVIE WITH A PRODUCTION CODE SEAL) AND COULDN'T SAY SHIT (LITERALLY: THE 1962 FILM THE CONNECTION WAS BANNED IN NEW YORK STATE FOR UTTERING THE WORD), AND YOU BEGIN TO GRASP THE WEIGHT OF THESE SEEMINGLY INCONSEQUENTIAL LOOPS.

"LOOPS WERE SILENT SHORT FILMS", XXX LEGEND JAMIE GILLIS TOLD ASHLEY WEST'S RIALTO REPORT PODCAST, IN AN INTERVIEW THAT WAS AIRED AFTER HIS 2010 DEATH DUE TO CANCER. "SOMETIMES THEY WERE JUST PEOPLE HAVING SEX, AND SOMETIMES THEY HAD LITTLE STORIES, AND THEY WOULD BE SHOWN IN PEEPSHOW BOOTHS. GUYS WOULD GO IN, AND PUT IN QUARTERS. IT WAS ALWAYS QUARTERS, NEVER LESS OR MORE I DON'T THINK, AND THEY MADE A FORTUNE, JUST IN QUARTERS."

"YOU WOULD HAVE LITTLE SCENARIOS. THEY PUT ME IN A SUPERMAN COSTUME ONCE AND ANOTHER TIME A DRACULA COSTUME. ALL SILENT LOOPS. I THINK IN THE SUPERMAN STORY, SHE'S WITH SOME GUY WHO IS GRABBING HER, AND I THROW HIM ASIDE, AND SHE SUCKS MY DICK IN GRATITUDE. I REMEMBER THERE WAS A POLICE INVESTIGATION FOR SOMETHING OR OTHER, AND A DETECTIVE CAME TO MY DOOR WITH MY SUPERMAN LOOP PICTURE. I OPEN MY DOOR AND HE GOES 'ARE YOU SUPERMAN?' JUST LIKE THAT. DEAD SERIOUS. I DIDN'T THINK I WAS SUPERMAN, BUT YOU KNOW, THAT WAS HIS IMAGE. SO I HAD TO SAY 'YEAH, I AM'".

"THERE WERE SO MANY NORMAL SEEMING PEOPLE, JUST REGULAR PEOPLE, IN (LOOPS) BACK THEN. IT'S HARD FOR PEOPLE TO IMAGINE NOW, BECAUSE THE PACE IS SO MUCH MORE FRENETIC AND

RUNNING AROUND. IT'S ALL FUCKING FUCKING FUCKING. IN THOSE DAYS IT WAS JUST SO MUCH MORE MELLOW. JUST A LOT OF HANGING OUT. I ALMOST REMEMBER THE HANGING OUT MORE THAN ANYTHING ELSE. YOU KNOW, YOU'D HAVE LUNCH, WHATEVER. ORDER OUR CHINESE FOOD. IT WAS LAZY, ALMOST. THERE WAS NO PRESSURE."

JAMIE GOT HIS VERY CASUAL START IN THE BASEMENT STUDIO OF BOB WOLF, ONE OF THE KEY ORIGIN POINTS FOR THE BIRTH OF AMERICAN XXX. IT WAS AN UNASSUMING LITTLE SLEAZE HOT-SPOT ON WEST 14TH AVE IN NYC, NEXT DOOR TO A FUNERAL PARLOUR, THERE, BOB AND HIS ASSISTANT, LARRY REVENE (WHO WOULD GO ON TO BE THE CINEMATOGRAPHER ON MANY OF THE BEST KNOWN XXX THEATRICAL FEATURES OF THE PORNO CHIC ERA) BUILT THE VERY FOUNDATION FOR A MANHATTAN SMUT SCENE THAT WAS STILL IN ITS INFANCY. IF YOU'VE WATCHED ANY NUMBER OF AMERICAN-MADE EARLY SEVENTIES LOOPS, YOU'VE NO DOUBT SEEN AT LEAST A FEW THAT WERE SHOT IN THAT DIRTY LITTLE BASEMENT.

"HIS MOTIVATION WAS GETTING TO MEET GIRLS", LARRY SAID OF HIS BOSS, BOB, WHEN ASKED BY THE RIALTO REPORT PODCAST IN 2013. "HE LIKED THE FACT THAT IT WAS PORNOGRAPHY. HE LIKED THE CLANDESTINE, THE ILLEGAL, THE SURREPTITIOUS, THE ANTI-ESTABLISHMENT ENDEAVOUR HE WAS INVOLVED IN. HE LIKED THAT. HE DIDN'T LIKE THE AIRBRUSHED PLAYBOY GIRLS. HE LIKED FUNKY, REAL PEOPLE."

"I THINK I MADE ABOUT $300 A DAY FOR A SHOOT", LARRY EXPLAINED. "THE PAY SCALE FOR THE TALENT WAS $50 TO $75 BUCKS FOR THE GUYS. THE GIRLS WOULD GET $100 TO $150, WE WOULD SHOOT SIX FILMS IN A DAY. IT WAS VERY PRAGMATIC. A GIRL AND A GUY WOULD COME IN IN THE MORNING. TEN O'CLOCK. WITHIN AN HOUR, IF THE GUY WAS PERFORMING WELL, WE HAD DONE ONE LOOP. RELEASE THE GUY, KEEP THE GIRL. DO TWO GIRLS AND A GUY. THEN THE THIRD FILM WAS WHERE WE WOULD KEEP A COUPLE PEOPLE FROM THE SECOND FILM, AND PUT 'EM INTO AN ORGY WHERE WE HAD PEOPLE THAT WERE GOING TO WORK IN THE AFTERNOON. SO THE ORGY IN THE MIDDLE OF THE DAY WAS DONE SO THAT YOU MIGHT HAVE TWO GIRLS IN THE ORGY THAT ARE FRESH FOR THE DAY, BUT YOU COULD USE THEM IN THE NEXT TWO FILMS. BECAUSE THE GIRLS COULD DO MORE. VERY FEW OF THE GUYS COULD DO MORE THAN ONE FILM."

"(BOB) HAD ALREADY ESTABLISHED LONG BEFORE I EVER SHOWED UP, THE RUNNING OF THE VILLAGE VOICE AD. 'ACTORS WANTED. NO EXPERIENCE NECESSARY. NUDITY REQUIRED.' HE HAD ONE OF THE VERY FIRST ANSWERING MACHINES. IN 1971, THE ANSWERING MACHINE WAS JUST COMING ONTO THE SCENE. WHEN I WOULD GO IN TO EDIT, I WOULD LISTEN TO THE ANSWERING MACHINE STUFF, AND COPY DOWN THE NUMBERS AND SO FORTH."

"THIS WAS ALL IN CONJUNCTION WITH THE SEXUAL REVOLUTION. WE'RE NOT TOO FAR FROM THE '69 WOODSTOCK FESTIVAL. THE PILL WAS RELATIVELY NEW AT THAT POINT. AND THERE WAS A LOT OF EXPERIMENTATION. JUST LIKE TODAY, WHERE YOU SHOW THAT YOU'RE COMMITTED TO YOUR

A TYPICAL 8MM BASEMENT STUDIO SHOOT -- THE KIND THAT BOB WOLF AND LARRY REVENE DID MANY TIMES.

GENERATION, YOU GET TATTOOS, PIERCINGS, YOU KNOW, SHAVE YOUR HEAD. IN THOSE DAYS, IT WAS LIKE PART OF THE THING WITH THE HIPPIES AND FREE LOVE AND SO FORTH. FOR THE MORE DARING, IT WAS DOING IT ON FILM. THERE WAS MONEY INVOLVED, SO THAT WAS AN INCENTIVE."

REVENE IS ABSOLUTELY CORRECT. THE STARS WERE YOUNG PEOPLE WHO WEREN'T MAKING MUCH, BUT THEY WERE HAVING SEX BECAUSE THEY ENJOYED DOING SO, AND THERE WERE GENERATIONAL WALLS OF PURITANICAL SHAME TO TEAR DOWN. THEY WERE TRULY TAKING PART IN A HAPPENING. IT SEEMS ODD TO SAY IT, BUT BECAUSE OF THAT 8MM HARDCORE PORN IS CHARMING. IT REALLY IS, AND I THINK THE LACK OF PRESSURE JAMIE GILLIS REFERRED TO WAS A BIG PART OF WHY THAT WAS. SURE, THESE FILMS WERE CHEAPLY MADE, WITH PATHETIC PRODUCTION VALUES, POOR STAGING, AND UNSOPHISTICATED CINEMATOGRAPHY, BUT THEIR CHARM TODAY LIES IN THE SENSE OF WONDER, INNOCENCE AND FUN IN THEM – EVEN IN THE SOMEWHAT DISTURBING ONES.

THE INNOCENCE I SPEAK OF SHOWED ITSELF ON THE OTHER SIDE OF THE PROJECTOR, AS WELL. THESE MOVIES, PACKED WITH FULL PENETRATION AND SPLAYED HAIRY NETHER REGIONS, ENTERED NORTH AMERICAN HOMES IN THE LATE 1950S, AT A TIME WHEN PLENTY OF MEN DIDN'T EVEN KNOW WHERE A CLITORIS WAS. AT A TIME WHEN ADULT MAGAZINES ON THE NEWS STAND DIDN'T SHOW ANYTHING MORE THAN CLENCHED BUTT CHEEKS AND BREASTS, AND SOMETIMES NOT EVEN THAT. A TIME WHEN MANY SUBURBAN WOMEN DIDN'T EVEN KNOW WHAT THEIR OWN VULVAS LOOKED LIKE. THESE WERE MOVIES THAT ESPOUSED INTEGRATION AND OFTEN HAD INTERRACIAL PAIRINGS AT A TIME WHEN PEOPLE OF DIFFERENT SKIN COLOURS WEREN'T EVEN SHOWN HOLDING HANDS ON THE BIG SCREEN.

BUT LOOPS WEREN'T JUST MADE IN AMERICA, AND RESPONSIBLE FOR AMERICA'S SEXUAL AWAKENING. THEY WERE A WORLDWIDE PHENOMENON. LASSE BRAUN WAS A PIONEER IN THE HARDCORE COLOUR EURO PRODUCTIONS THAT WERE, IN 1961 AND ONWARDS, DISTRIBUTED BY MAKING USE OF HIS RICH FATHER'S DIPLOMATIC PRIVILEGES. BRAUN DIRECTED HIGH QUALITY FULL LENGTH THEATRICAL FEATURES AS WELL, AND BANKROLLED THESE LAVISH PRODUCTIONS WITH THE MOUNTAINS OF PROFIT SECURED WITH HIS 8 TO 10 MINUTE XXX LOOPS.

BUT THE TRUE FAT CATS OF THE EURO SCENE WERE THE THEANDER BROTHERS. WHAT ENDED UP BECOMING THE WORLD'S LARGEST PRODUCER OF PORN STARTED IN COPENHAGEN, DENMARK, ON SEPTEMBER 19TH, 1966. THAT'S THE DAY THE THEANDER BROTHERS BOUGHT A LITTLE ANTIQUE BOOK STORE CALLED "RÅDHUSANTIKVARIATET" IN ORDER TO SELL SMUT OUT OF IT, WHICH THEY WOULD HAVE TO DO ON THE SLY, UNDER THE COUNTER AND WITH THE USE OF CODE WORDS. THIS WAS BECAUSE SMUT WAS STILL ILLEGAL IN DENMARK AT THE TIME, AND WOULD BE FOR ANOTHER COUPLE YEARS. FROM THOSE TINY BEGINNINGS, THE BROTHERS BUILT THE COLOR CLIMAX AND RODOX EMPIRE, WHICH SUPPLIED PORN FOR THE ENTIRE GLOBE.

BRAUN AND THEANDER WENT THOUGH A MAN NAMED REUBEN STURMAN FOR THEIR AMERICAN DISTRIBUTION, AND HE IN TURN SUPPLIED TO NEARLY 60,000 AMERICAN PEEP SHOW BOOTHS LITTERED ACROSS THE COUNTRY. BY THE 1970S THE PROLIFERATION OF COIN-OPERATED MOVIE BOOTHS WAS EVEN MORE WIDESPREAD. STURMAN, A CLEVELAND MULTIMILLIONAIRE, WAS THE BIGGEST DISTRIBUTOR OF 8MM SEX FILMS, PORN MAGAZINES, AND SEX TOYS IN NORTH AMERICA, BUT THE REAL KINGPIN, THE MAN BEHIND THE SCENES OF STURMAN'S EMPIRE, THE MAN GIVING THE ORDERS IN THE AMERICAN XXX WORLD -- WAS BROOKLYN'S OWN ROBERT "DEEBEE" DIBERNARDO.

JUST HOW DID HE GET TO BE KING-SHIT OF FLESH MOUNTAIN? WHO WAS HE? WHY, ONLY ONE OF THE MEN IN CHARGE OF THE GAMBINO CRIME FAMILY. HANDSOME, POLITE, ALWAYS IMPECCABLY DRESSED AND WIDELY FEARED, THE KNOBFATHER HAD A REPUTATION FOR ALWAYS BEING ONE STEP AHEAD OF THE LAW. ROBERT RAN HIS EMPIRE FROM BEHIND CLOSED DOORS.

IN 1965, A 28-YEAR-OLD DIBERNARDO GOT HIS START IN THE SKIN GAME WHEN HE BAILED A BANKRUPT SMUT-PEDDLER NAMED TEDDY ROTHSTEIN OUT AFTER HE'D BEEN CONVICTED ON OBSCENITY CHARGES. THE COST? WHY, ONLY THEO'S PUBLISHING COMPANY, STAR DISTRIBUTORS. THE YOUNG UPSTART GANG-LORD TOLD THE MUCH OLDER ROTHSTEIN TO TAKE A BACKSEAT, AND HE STEPPED IN AS OWNER, VICE PRESIDENT, AND BUSINESS OPERATIONS MANAGER ON HIS WAY TO MAKING THE SMALL DIRTY BOOK PUBLISHER INTO A MASSIVE-ASS PORN CONGLOMERATE -- WITH THE HELP OF MOB BOSSES AROUND THE COUNTRY.

BUT WHEN DIBERNARDO REALLY BEGAN TO MAKE MONEY WAS WHEN HE BRANCHED AWAY FROM PULPS N' PERIODICALS AND INTO 8MM LOOPS, THEIR SALES THROUGH THE MAIL, AND THE PEEP SHOWS THAT DISPLAYED THEM FOR A QUARTER A MINUTE. ALL FIVE OF THE NOW LEGENDARY NEW YORK CRIME FAMILIES WOULD COME TO SHARE IN THE INSANE PROFITS FROM THE FILMS AND THEIR DISTRIBUTION, AND WOULD PAY OUT MONEY TO OTHER SMALLER MOB FAMILIES IN ORDER TO KEEP AN EYE ON THE INDEPENDENT DEALERS IN OUTLAYING TERRITORIES.

IN 1973, THE PRECEDENT OF MILLER V. CALIFORNIA MADE INTERSTATE DISTRIBUTION OF PORNOGRAPHY PROSECUTABLE ACCORDING TO THE STANDARDS OF THE VARIOUS COMMUNITIES THE FILTHY ITEMS WERE SENT INTO. THERE WAS JUST FAR TOO MUCH MONEY TO BE MADE TO CONSIDER CEASING THE PRODUCTION OF PORN FILMS ALTOGETHER, BUT PORNOGRAPHERS WERE ALSO AFRAID TO RISK FEDERAL PENALTIES AND SERIOUS JAIL TIME. THIS LEFT THE CREATORS OF 8MM LOOPS LIKE BOB WOLF AND LARRY REVENE LITTLE CHOICE BUT TO RELY ON ORGANIZED CRIME TO SHIP AND DISTRIBUTE THEIR PRODUCTS.

"THE LABS THAT DID THE ACTUAL (FILM) PRINTING WERE WHERE THE MAFIA WERE HEAVILY INVOLVED, SIMPLY BECAUSE THAT'S THE PAYLOAD," REVENE TOLD ASHLEY WEST'S RIALTO REPORT PODCAST IN 2013. "FIFTY CASES OF FINISHED PRODUCT IS A LOT MORE VALUABLE THAN ONE MASTER THAT YOU HAVE TO PAY FOR. THEY WERE AFTER THAT ASPECT OF IT. THE PERAINOS HAD A LAB OUT IN BROOKLYN. ROTHENBERG'S ARRO LAB WAS ONE IN THE CITY, AS A FRONT THAT COULD PRODUCE THE 8MM CARTOON FILMS, SO THAT WAS THEIR REASON FOR BEING IN EXISTENCE, BUT THE MAJORITY OF THE WORK THAT CAME OUT OF THERE WAS X-RATED STUFF."

"(WE) WOULD SELL TO EDDIE MISHKIN, MAINLY, WHO WAS THE BIGGEST DISTRIBUTOR OF LOOPS IN NEW YORK CITY. EDDIE WAS OLD SCHOOL, HIS RECORDS WENT BACK TO THE '30S. HE WAS FROM THE BRONX. WHEN I FINALLY MET HIM IN THE '70S, HE WAS THE BIGGEST SUPPLIER OF MATERIAL FOR THE WHOLE COUNTRY. HE DEALT WITH EVERYBODY."

MISHKIN HAD LONG BEEN ASSOCIATED WITH RISQUE MATERIAL, STARTING WHEN HE PUBLISHED A BOOK CALLED "NATURAL

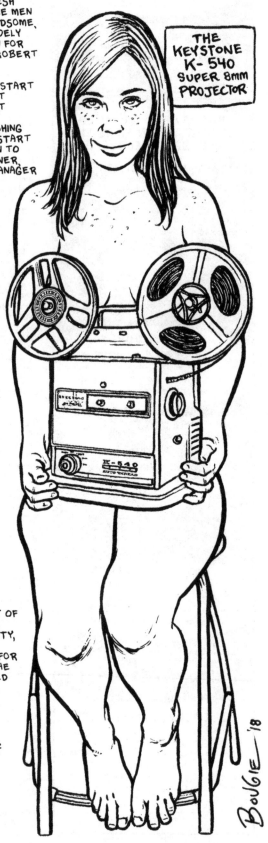

THE KEYSTONE K-540 SUPER 8MM PROJECTOR

BOUGIE — '18

CHILDBIRTH" BACK IN THE '30S. IT WAS AN "EDUCATIONAL PUBLICATION" WHICH EARNED FOR EDDIE WHAT WOULD BE, ADJUSTED FOR INFLATION, MILLIONS OF DOLLARS. HE, ALONG WITH HARRY MOHNEY, MICHAEL THEVIS, AND TEDDY ROTHSTEIN ALL ANSWERED TO DIBERNARDO.

THE ERA OF THE ITALIAN MOB RUNNING THE PORN INDUSTRY ENDED ALONG WITH THE END OF THE 1970S, AT NOON, EASTERN STANDARD TIME, ON FEBRUARY 14TH, 1980. IT WAS CODENAMED "MIPORN", AND ORGANIZED CRIME WAS SUCCESSFULLY ROOTED OUT OF THE SMUT INDUSTRY BY THE INFAMOUS ROUNDUP BY THE FBI ON THAT VALENTINES DAY. THE AGENTS STRUCK AS A UNIFIED FORCE, RAIDING THEATRES, STORES, WAREHOUSES, OFFICES, AND HOMES IN THIRTEEN AMERICAN CITIES (INCLUDING LOS ANGELES AND NEW YORK). CATCHING THEIR FAT PASTA-MUNCHING PREY BY SURPRISE. DIBERNARDO WAS THEN LINKED VIA TELEPHONE RECORDS TO MANY OF THE CRIMINALS ARRESTED, BUT MANAGED TO COVER HIS TRACKS WELL ENOUGH TO EVADE ARREST, AND BEGAN TO MOVE AWAY FROM XXX (WHICH IN THE 1980S WAS RAPIDLY BECOMING FAR MORE LEGAL, THEREBY BECOMING LESS PROFITABLE) AND INSTEAD INTO OTHER LUCRATIVE MONEYMAKING SCHEMES LIKE REAL ESTATE.

HIS DAY WOULD SOON COME, THOUGH. GAMBINO UNDERBOSS SAMMY GRAVANO HAD A SIT-DOWN WITH THE HEAD CAPO JOHN GOTTI, FEEDING HIM A LINE OF BULLSHIT THAT DIBERNARDO WASN'T STAYING TRUE TO THE FAMILY AND WAS GETTING READY TO MAKE A NEFARIOUS MOVE AGAINST IT. IN REALITY, GRAVANO WAS MAD THAT DEEBEE OWED HIM OVER 250 GRAND AND WOULDN'T PAY. KNOWING HE'D BE TAKING OVER HIS JOB, GRAVANO CONSPIRED TO HAVE A FAMILY MEMBER OFFED, WHICH GOTTI WAS RELUCTANT TO DO. NEVERTHELESS, ON JUNE 5, 1986 DIBERNARDO WAS LURED TO THE BASEMENT OFFICES OF GRAVANO'S DRYWALL COMPANY ON STILLWELL AVE IN BENSONHURST N.Y. WHERE ACCORDING TO GRAVANO HE HAD HIS RIGHT HAND TRIGGERMAN, JOE PARUTA, WHACK THE KNOBFATHER OF PORN WITH A SINGLE WELL-PLACED BULLET IN THE BACK OF THE HEAD. HIS BODY WAS NEVER RECOVERED, AND ACCORDING TO ONE FEDERAL AGENT, THERE WAS TALK THAT IT HAD BEEN PUT THROUGH A TREE SHREDDER ON A FARM IN UPSTATE NEW YORK.

"THERE WAS SOMETHING EXCITING ABOUT PORNOGRAPHY," NORMAN MAILER SAID ABOUT THE EARLY SEVENTIES IN THE 2005 DOCUMENTARY INSIDE DEEP THROAT. "IT LIVED IN SOME MID-WORLD BETWEEN CRIME AND ART. AND IT WAS ADVENTUROUS."

THESE GRITTY, LOW BUDGET, DISREPUTABLE FILMS WERE NOT JUST ADVENTUROUS AND DANGEROUS TO MAKE, THEY WERE ALSO A LIFELINE TO THE CURIOUS AND THE DAMNED. IN ORDER TO GRAB THAT LIFELINE, HOWEVER, YOU HAD TO KNOW WHERE TO LOOK FOR IT. 1970S PORN INDUSTRY JOURNALIST, FRANK FORTUNATO, WROTE FOR STROKE MAGAZINES LIKE SWANK AND DETAILED THE EXPERIENCE OF PROCURING AND VIEWING HARDCORE SMUT LOOPS IN NEW YORK IN THE OCTOBER 1979 ISSUE OF SAID MAGAZINE.

"VOYEURISM IS BY FAR THE LARGEST SLICE OF THE 42ND STREET SEX BUSINESS", FORTUNATO WROTE. "IT WASN'T ALWAYS THAT WAY. ABOUT 10 YEARS AGO, PRIOR TO THE HARDCORE EXPLOSION, BUYING PORN

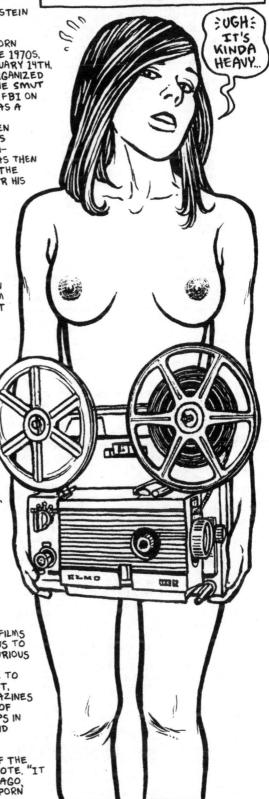

THE ELMO GP-E DUAL 8mm PROJECTOR

UGH IT'S KINDA HEAVY...

HERE WAS SOMETHING LIKE BUYING MILITARY SECRETS. A RECORD STORE CLOSE TO THE CORNER OF 42ND AND 8TH AVE WAS A TYPICAL SET UP. THE PROPRIETOR OF THIS JOINT WOULD INEVITABLY BE FOUND IN QUIET MOMENTS SITTING IN THE BACK OF THE STORE WEARING A PRAYER SHAWL AND YARMULKE AND READING INTENTLY FROM THE TALMUD. WHEN HE SPOTTED YOU, HE WOULD REMOVE THE RELIGIOUS GARMENTS, CLOSE THE TALMUD, AND MOTION YOU TO THE BACK ROOM WHERE HE WOULD DISCUSS YOUR SMUT NEEDS. HE SOLD FILMS IN PAIRS, AND AFTER PAYING A PRICE HE WOULD GIVE YOU THE KEY TO A SUBWAY LOCKER WHERE THERE WERE NEATLY PACKAGED PORN FILMS."

"TODAY, HARDCORE PORN HAS GONE FROM THE COVERT TO THE OVERT IN A BIG WAY, AND LOOP FILMS HEAD THE MONEYMAKING LIST. THE ARITHMETIC IS OBVIOUS. IT COSTS ABOUT $2.00 TO A VIEW A 15-MINUTE LOOP FILM, AND SOME OF THE MULTI-FLOORED MEGA-PEEP JOINTS OFFER SEVERAL HUNDRED FILMS WITH EASILY HALF THE BOOTHS FILLED DURING PEAK-PEEPING HOURS. IT TRANSLATES INTO DAILY PROFITS IN THE THOUSANDS."

"ALWAYS SENSITIVE TO THE NEEDS OF THE PUBLIC, THESE PLACES OFFER A PSYCHOPATHIA SEXUALIS ASSORTMENT OF FILMS. FOR THOSE INTO 'ANIMAL HUSBANDRY', THERE ARE FLICKS FEATURING WOMEN WITH DOGS, DONKEYS, HORSES, PIGS, SNAKES, AND EELS. FRIENDS OF MISCEGENATION CAN CHOOSE BETWEEN BLACK MEN AND WHITE WOMEN, WHITE MEN AND BLACK WOMEN, ORIENTAL WOMEN WITH WHITE MEN AND BLACK DWARFS, AND JUST ABOUT ANY OTHER COLOR COMBO IMAGINABLE. IN FACT, ALL FETISHES ARE AVAILABLE FOR VIEWING HERE, AND THEY ARE ALL 'COLORFULLY' DESCRIBED."

SOMEWHERE ALONG THE LINE IN HUMAN HISTORY, SOME BRAINIAC HUSTLER PUT TWO AND TWO TOGETHER AND FIGURED OUT THAT THE IDEA OF SEX WAS FAR MORE MARKETABLE AND PROFITABLE THAN SEX ITSELF. AND THE ULTIMATE RECEPTACLE FOR IDEAS IS MEDIA — ALL FORMS OF MEDIA. THE MOST VISCERAL AND ATTENTION GRABBING FOR THE COMMON MAN AND WOMEN, OF COURSE, BEING THE MOVING IMAGE, WE RESPOND TO IT.

PORN HISTORIAN/REVIEWER ROBERT RIMMER CLAIMS THE FIRST STAGS WERE MADE IN 1896, AND IN 1915, THE EARLIEST KNOWN SURVIVING AMERICAN STAG FILM WITH HARDCORE SEX WAS MADE. "A FREE RIDE" (AKA "A GRASS SANDWICH") IS 9 MINUTES LONG, AND SHOT IN THE RURAL OUTDOORS. WHILE THE FILMING LOCATION ISN'T KNOWN, MANY HAPPEN TO BELIEVE THAT THIS HISTORIC LOOP WAS SHOT AND PRODUCED IN NEW JERSEY. BEING AS WHAT THEY DID WAS HIGHLY ILLEGAL AT THE TIME (AND REMAINS SO TO THIS DAY WHEN YOU CONSIDER THAT THEY WERE HAVING SEX IN PUBLIC), THE CAST AND DIRECTOR USED PSEUDONYMS AND DISGUISES. THIS DELIBERATE OBSCURING OF IDENTITY HAS PROMPTED TWO CONTRADICTORY THEORIES, WITH VARIOUS SOURCES SUGGESTING THAT THESE WERE LOWLY CRIMINALS AND/OR DRUG ADDICTS, AND OTHERS ASSERTING THAT IT WAS ACTUALLY PRODUCED BY INDIVIDUALS OF A HIGHER SOCIAL CLASS, AND FROM LEGITIMATE BACKGROUNDS.

THE OPENING TEXT OF THE SHORT ESTABLISHES THE SCENE AS "THE WIDE OPEN SPACES, WHERE MEN ARE MEN AND GIRLS WILL BE GIRLS, THE HILLS ARE FULL OF ROMANCE AND ADVENTURE." TWO YOUNG WOMEN WALK TOGETHER ALONGSIDE AN OLD COUNTRY ROAD, AND A WEALTHY GENT PULLS UP ALONGSIDE THEM IN A 1912 HAYNES 50-60 MODEL Y TOURING CAR, AND OFFERS THEM A RIDE. AFTER THEY HOP IN NEXT TO HIM IN THE FRONT SEAT, HE

10

SMOOCHES THEM AND GRABS THEIR TITS. A MOMENT LATER, HOWEVER, HE EXCUSES HIMSELF, AND TAKES A PISS BEHIND A TREE, WHILE THE WOMEN SPY ON HIM. AFTER HIS RETURN, THE WOMEN TAKE THEIR TURN TO EMPTY THEIR BLADDERS IN THE WOODS WHILE THE MAN ALSO SECRETLY WATCHES THEM.

AFTERWARDS, THE GUY AND ONE OF THE LADIES GO IN THE WOODS TOGETHER AND AWKWARDLY MASTURBATE EACH OTHER IN UNISON WHILE STANDING TOTALLY CLOTHED. AGAIN WITH THE VOYEURISM, THE OTHER GIRL SPIES ON THEM, AND PLAYS WITH HER VERY HAIRY CUNT. MEANWHILE, THE COUPLE HAVE NOW PLOPPED DOWN INTO THE DIRT, AND FUCK MISSIONARY POSITION. BEFORE LONG, THE OTHER GIRL JOINS THEM SAYING "CAN I HAVE A LITTLE?", GETS FUCKED DOGGY STYLE, AND THE OTHER CHICK SUBSEQUENTLY GIVES THE GUY SOME HEAD. NONE OF THESE JITTERY BLACK AND WHITE SEX ACTS SEEM TO LAST LONGER THAN ABOUT 20 SECONDS EACH, AND BEFORE LONG THEY HOP UP AND DUST THEMSELVES OFF. "HURRY UP, LET'S GET OUT OF HERE" THE TITLE CARD READS, AND THEY DRIVE AWAY.

PROFESSOR FRANK A. HOFFMANN OF THE UNIVERSITY OF BUFFALO NOTED QUITE ELOQUENTLY THAT DESPITE ITS QUAINT OLD-TIMEY ANTIQUITY AND VASTLY SHORTER COUPLING SCENES THAN MODERN MASTURBATORS ARE COMFORTABLE WITH, A FREE RIDE CONTAINS MANY OF THE KEY ELEMENTS AND SOLID FOUNDATIONS OF PORNOGRAPHIC FILMS AS WE KNOW THEM EVEN TODAY. HE PINPOINTS THESE BASIC CONSTITUENTS AS:

A carefully planned but not complicated state of affairs to provide introductory motivation

Visual stimuli to sexually excite the women

A theme that is generally rare in reality

A straightforward and very quick seduction

Sex acts as the film's central theme

LEGENDARY PORN CRITIC JIM HOLLIDAY'S FAVOURITE EARLY STAG WAS MADE IN 1951, STARRED A GIRL NAMED JUANITA SLUSHER, AND WAS MADE IN A MOTEL NEAR NASHVILLE TENNESSEE. "SHE BECAME KNOWN TO THE WORLD AS CANDY BARR", JIM WROTE IN HIS 1986 BOOK, ONLY THE BEST. "AND SMART ALECK WAS TO BECOME THE BEST KNOWN STAG OF ALL TIME. SHE HAD BREASTS THAT TRACI LORDS WOULD BE PROUD OF, AND SOME ENTHUSIASM FOR HUMPING, BUT NOT FOR PERFORMING ORAL SEX. HER FEMALE FRIEND PROVIDES THAT."

BASIC FUCKING AND SUCKING WAS FINE FOR THE SMOKERS AND STAG LOOPS OF YESTERYEAR, BUT AS THE '70s ROLLED AROUND, THE POPULARITY OF AN 8MM LOOP OFTEN CAME TO DEPEND ON HOW MUCH OF A STORY (OR AT THE VERY LEAST, A NOTEWORTHY SCENARIO) IT COULD PACK IN AMONGST THE BOOT-KNOCKING. THE MOST NOTEWORTHY STORYTELLERS OF THIS SORT WERE DANISH FILMMAKER LASSE BRAUN, HANS SCHLIEGER, KARLA SCHMIDT, AND THE TEAM OF RONALDO AND SWEET. OTHER INNOVATIONS GAVE EXTRA BUCK BANGS AS WELL. FOR GENERATIONS, SEX FILMS WERE ONLY AVAILABLE IN BLACK AND WHITE, BUT THAT DIDN'T MAKE THEM ANY LESS INCREDIBLE FOR VIEWERS.

THE PORNO CHIC ERA NOW GAVE MASTURBATORS THE OPTION TO UPGRADE THE IMAGERY IN THEIR SPANK BANK TO COLOR 8MM, SUPER 8MM, AND 16MM. THERE WERE OTHER INNOVATIONS AND GRABS FOR CASH TOO. THE DOZEN FILMS IN THE WELL-MADE AMERICAN "BLUE MOVIE" SERIES FROM 1974 HAD SUBTITLES TO GIVE A NARRATIVE PLOT A FRONT SEAT IN THE PROCEEDINGS

WHEN MOST LOOPS WERE DOING IT MIME-STYLE. SWEDISH EROTICA EVEN STARTED HIRING WRITERS TO ADAPT THEIR POPULAR 8MM FILMS INTO FULL LENGTH NOVELS, WHICH WERE PUBLISHED THROUGH "SWEDISH HOUSE", A SUBSIDIARY OF ART PUBLISHERS INC IN SANTA MONICA CALIFORNIA. HOW ABOUT THE FEW SELECT LOOPS THAT EVEN CAME WITH AN ACCOMPANYING PHONOGRAPH RECORD? THAT WAY YOU COULD ACTUALLY HAVE A FUNKY SOUNDTRACK AND DIALOG -- HIGH TECH STUFF, MAN! PRIVACY WOULD HAVE BEEN AN ISSUE CONSIDERING YOU WOULD HAVE HAD TO CRANK THAT SHIT UP PRETTY LOUD TO HEAR IT OVER THE LOUD WHIRRING PROJECTORS OF THE ERA, BUT THAT'S WHAT SOUND-ABSORBING WOOD PANELING IN A BASEMENT RUMPUS ROOM WAS FOR, RIGHT?

THESE BELLS AND WHISTLES WERE ONLY AS GOOD AS WHAT WAS ACTUALLY MADE AVAILABLE TO THE PUBIC-OBSESSED PUBLIC, HOWEVER, AND CUSTOMERS DIDN'T ALWAYS GET WHAT THEY THOUGHT THEY WERE PAYING FOR. IT WAS "BUYER BEWARE" OUT THERE ON THE MEAN STREETS, AND THIS WAS NEVER SO APTLY PROVEN AS IT WAS IN AN ACCOUNT BY NEW YORK RAUNCH REPORTER FRED LESLIE IN THE AUGUST 2ND 1976 EDITION OF SCREW MAGAZINE.

"MY WIFE, MYSELF, AND FOUR OTHER FRIENDS HAD JUST LEFT THE JERRY LEWIS ANNUAL MUSCULAR DYSTROPHY TELETHON AT THE AMERICANA HOTEL AND WALKED DOWN 6TH AVE TO 42ND STREET ON OUR WAY TO THE TIMES SQUARE SUBWAY STATION. ON A LARK, WE DECIDED TO MAKE A QUICK STOP AT ONE OF THE MANY NOVELTY SEX SHOPS IN THE NEIGHBOURHOOD."

"AS WE LOOKED AROUND THE SHOP, THE NIGHT MANAGER MUST HAVE SENSED THAT WE WEREN'T FINDING ANYTHING THAT SPARKED OUR INTEREST. WITH A SLIGHT GESTURE OF HIS HAND, HE MOTIONED FOR ME TO JOIN HIM IN A REMOTE CORNER OF THE SHOP, WHERE HE PRODUCED A REEL OF 8MM FILM THAT HE SAID WAS GUARANTEED TO DRIVE US ALL UP THE WALL WITH PASSION AND EXCITEMENT. THE BOX WAS UNMARKED AND UNLABELLED, BUT I WAS ASSURED THAT THE FILM DEPICTED A JAPANESE GIRL EXERCISING SOME RATHER STRANGE EROTIC SEXUAL PRACTICES WITH HER LOVER. THE MANAGER WENT ON TO DESCRIBE THE FILM IN MORE LIVID TERMS."

"I WAS DROOLING AS I PAID SEVEN $5 BILLS FOR THIS MASTERPIECE OF EROTICA. THE TRAIN RIDE HOME WAS FILLED WITH GROWING ANTICIPATION AND ANXIETY. WHEN WE REACHED MY PLACE, I PUT THE FILM ON MY TRUSTY PROJECTOR, THEN FOR 14 SOLID MINUTES THE SIX OF US PATIENTLY WATCHED THIS YOUNG ORIENTAL GIRL TAKE OFF HER SHOES AND STOCKINGS AND WALK BAREFOOT ACROSS THE BARE BACK OF HER LOVER, SQUEEZING HIS FLESH WITH HER TOES, AND RUBBING HER HEELS INTO THE BACK PART OF HIS RIB CAGE. AND THAT WAS IT, THE WHOLE THING. THERE AND THEN I VOWED THAT NO ONE WOULD NEVER BE ABLE TO RIP ME OFF AGAIN IN A SIMILAR FASHION."

MANY BOOKS, ESSAYS, AND ACADEMIC PAPERS HAVE BEEN WRITTEN ON THE SUBJECT. CRITICS, FANS, PORN HISTORIANS, AND UNIVERSITY SCHOLARS HAVE POINTED TO THE POLITICAL AND SOCIAL SIGNIFICANCE OF PORN THEATRES AND THE FILMS THAT PLAYED IN THEM, PARTICULARLY IN RELATION TO QUEER CULTURE. AND YET THE PEEP SHOW BOOTHS AND THEIR LOOPS CONTAINED WITHIN REMAIN FORGOTTEN WITHIN THIS GROWING WORLD OF LEGITIMATE PORN STUDIES. VERY LITTLE HAS BEEN SAID.

THIS EXCLUSION ISN'T ON PURPOSE OR BECAUSE THE FILMS ARE CONSIDERED IRRELEVANT, IT'S MUCH MORE OF A RESULT OF THE DIFFICULTIES INVOLVED IN THE RESEARCHING OF PEEP SHOWS AND THEIR CONTENT. PRIOR TO THE BURGEONING LEGALITY OF "OBSCENE MATERIAL" PRODUCERS AND DISTRIBUTORS OF LOOPS

12

WERE OFTEN CONNECTED TO THE MOB, AND WERE LOATHE TO MAINTAIN ARCHIVAL RECORDS OR LEGIT BOOKS. THE MACHINES USED TO SHOW THE FILMS OPERATED ON SMALL CHANGE. NOW, WHILE THIS SORT OF COINAGE WAS AWKWARD TO CARRY TO THE BANK (IT WAS ACTUALLY CARRIED AROUND IN WHEELBARROWS AND WEIGHED RATHER THAN COUNTED BACK IN THE PROFITABLE HEYDAY OF PEEP) IT WAS VERY SIMPLE FOR OWNERS TO MASK THE REVENUE NUMBERS AND COOK THE BOOKS.

MORE SO THAN THAT, THESE FETID DENS OF INIQUITY WERE RARELY PHOTOGRAPHED (SHY CUSTOMERS PREFERRED PRIVACY), AND UNLIKE REGULAR PORN THEATRES, SHOWTIMES AND PLAY DATES WERE NOT ADVERTISED IN LOCAL PAPERS. NO ONE REMEMBERS SPECIFICALLY WHICH LOOPS WERE INVOLVED, AND THERE ARE OFTEN FEW CLUES WHETHER CERTAIN LOOPS WERE EVER SHOWN IN A PEEP BOOTH OR A 'BLACK BOX'. THERE IS A VERY SHORT PAPER TRAIL AND A LOT OF MYSTERIES LEFT TO REVEAL ABOUT THE BRICK AND MORTAR LOCATIONS THEMSELVES, LEAVING WHAT LITTLE RESEARCH HAS BEEN ATTEMPTED TO HAVE BEEN FOCUSED UPON THE LOOPS THEMSELVES.

ONE EXCEPTION IS AN ARTICLE (A COVER STORY, NO LESS) WRITTEN BY JAMES POETT FOR THE MAY 1ST 1978 EDITION OF NEW YORK'S THE VILLAGE VOICE. ENTITLED "DEEP PEEP", POETT KNEW HE COULD SELL PAPERS BY ALLOWING NEW YORKERS TOO NERVOUS ABOUT VISITING TIMES SQUARE THEMSELVES, TO HAVE A LOW DOWN DIRTY EXPERIENCE VIA HIS WRITING — TO LIVE VICARIOUSLY THROUGH HIS WORDS.

ONE PART OF HIS ARTICLE DETAILS HIS VISIT TO THE PEEP SHOW BOOTHS IN THE EAST AVENUE — TIMES SQUARE AREA (EATSA FOR SHORT), A PLACE HE IS SURPRISED TO REPORT IS RATHER QUIET. IT'S NOT A PEACEFUL QUIET, BUT A "FEELING THAT SOME SORT OF INTENSE CONCENTRATION IS GOING ON, AND THAT SOUNDS LIKE QUIET, THE WAY THE CALM BEFORE THE STORM ISN'T REALLY CALM, BUT A SENSE OF IMMINENT RIOT THAT'S GOING TO BREAK LOOSE AT ANY MOMENT."

"THE 25-CENT PRIVATE VIEWING BOOTHS HAVE BEEN MULTIPLYING FOR THE LAST TWO OR THREE YEARS", POETT REPORTS AS HE DESCRIBES ONE OF THE MOST LEGENDARY TIMES SQUARE PEEPSHOW VENUES. "PEEPLAND IS THE LARGEST AND ONE OF THE NEWEST PORN SHOPS. ON ITS TWO FLOORS IT HAS ABOUT 200 BOOTHS AND OLD STYLE BOXES. THE CLASSY BOOTHS UP FRONT ON THE GROUND FLOOR SHOW HEADLINERS SUCH AS 'ENEMA', 'WILD HOG', AND 'THE NUN AND THE DONKEY'. DOWNSTAIRS THE BASEMENT IS CRAMMED FULL OF BOOTHS UP FRONT, AND THE OLD

BOXES, MEN MILLING AROUND — ONE GUY THERE, PROBABLY IN HIS FORTIES, A SHORT MAN WITH A BRIEFCASE IN HIS RIGHT HAND AND A COAT FLUNG OVER HIS ARM, WAS STARING INTENTLY INTO A BLACK BOX ENTITLED 'SPANKING'.

"THERE ARE SEEDIER PLACES", HE CONTINUES. "THE WINDOWS UNDER THE SIGN 'SHORTY'S SPAGHETTI HOUSE' HAVE BEEN PLASTERED OVER TO KEEP OUT THE LIGHT AND, INSIDE, THE AIR, WHICH RUNS A CLOSE SECOND TO THE BREEZE OVER THE URINALS IN PENN STATION, IS DIM ENOUGH TO GET ALONG WITH THE DARK BLUE BOOTHS. THERE IS A STILL PICTURE FROM THE MOVIE AVAILABLE IN EACH BOOTH POSTED OUTSIDE BESIDE EACH DOOR. MOSTLY A WOMAN GIVING A MAN A BLOW JOB OR OF THE TWO OF THEM FUCKING, OR SOMETIMES A CLOSE UP. IN THE BACK, A CORRIDOR LEADS TO ANOTHER ROOM WITH THE GAY STUFF. A BLACK DUDE WAS BACK THERE, LEANING UP AGAINST THE WALL, RUBBING A LUMP IN HIS PANTS WHILE A WHITE GUY IN A BLUE BLAZER WENT FROM BOOTH TO BOOTH INVOLVED AS INTENSELY AS IF HE WERE PERFORMING SOME POLLINATION RITE."

BACK DOWN THE STREET POETT GOES, UNTIL HE ENDS UP AT BLACK JACKS ON 42ND. "IT USED TO BE A BOOK AND MAGAZINE STORE BEFORE THE BOOTHS BEGAN TO CATCH ON WITH THE ADVENT OF THOUSANDS OF CHEAP 8MM FILMS", HE RECOUNTS. "NOW THE PLACE HAS ABOUT 50 BOOTHS ON THE GROUND FLOOR AND ANOTHER 20 AROUND THE LIVE SHOW UPSTAIRS. FROM NOON UNTIL NIGHT, THE PLACE AVERAGES ABOUT 15 OR 20 IN CONSTANT USE. YOU CAN TELL AS THERE IS A RED LIGHT ABOVE THE DOOR WHEN A BOOTH IS RUNNING . . . ONE MAN GOING INTO ONE OF THE BOOTHS BALKED WHEN HE SAW A SPLASH OF WHITE LIQUID ON THE FLOOR ABOUT THE SIZE OF A COUPLE OF QUARTERS. THE GUY WITH THE MOP AND BUCKET WAS STILL PRETTY FAR DOWN THE AISLE."

NOW IT'S OFF TO SHOW WORLD, WHICH POETT TELLS US IS RIGHT ACROSS THE STREET. "OF ALL THE PORN SHOPS IT SEEMS TO DO THE BEST BUSINESS", HE INFORMS US. "BIG YELLOW LIGHTS SPIN AROUND THE MARQUEE. THE PLACE IS ALIVE. OF THE 50 BOOTHS ON THE GROUND FLOOR, 24 ARE GOING. I'D GOTTEN INTO THE HABIT OF COUNTING THE RED LIGHTS OVER THE DOORS. IF A DOOR IS CLOSED BUT THE LIGHT ISN'T ON, A MANAGER WILL COME OVER AND POUND ON THE DOOR, TELLING WHOEVER IS INSIDE TO PUT IN ANOTHER QUARTER OR GET THE HELL OUT."

BUT IF YOU DIDN'T LIVE IN NEW YORK, BOSTON, CHICAGO, PHILADELPHIA, OR ANY OTHER MAJOR CITY THAT HAD THOSE MUSTY AND DISREPUTABLE PORN SHOPS PACKED WITH HOT LITTLE MINI-MOVIES THAT PLAYED IN THE ALMOST 60,000 PRIVATE "PEEP SHOW" BOOTHS LOCATED IN ADULT STORES IN MOST MAJOR CITIES, YOU ORDERED OUT OF THE BACK OF YOUR FAVOURITE STROKE MAGAZINE.

THERE YOU WERE LURED BY THE PERVY PROMISE OF EXOTIC SIGHTS UNAVAILABLE ANYWHERE ELSE. THAT WAS HOW YOU ROLLED IF YOU WEREN'T LUCKY ENOUGH TO LIVE NEAR A RED LIGHT DISTRICT. SURE HOPE THAT ORDER YOU PLACED CAME IN A PLAIN UNMARKED PACKAGE -- YOU WOULDN'T WANT THE COUPLE LIVING ACROSS THE HALL (OR YOUR PARENTS, DEPENDING HOW OLD YOU WERE) SUSPECTING WHAT A DEGENERATE THEY WERE LIVING AMONGST.

YES, THE MAJORITY OF AMERICANS PROCURED THESE FILMS FROM MAIL ORDER SERVICES, AND ENJOYED THEM IN THE PRIVACY OF THEIR OWN HOMES. COUNTLESS RECTANGULAR ADS IN THE BACK

SECTIONS OF MEN'S MAGAZINES PROVIDED A SINFUL SHOPPING CATALOG OF CARNAL DELIGHTS – CATERING TO DOZENS OF FETISHES AND INTERESTS. "OPENLY POSED! AS YOU LIKE THEM – IN INTIMATE HARDCORE BEDROOM ACTION!"

FLASH FORWARD 20 YEARS, AND YOU HAVE A YOUNGER GENERATION DISCOVERING THE DUSTY AND FADED OLD 8MM MOVIES THEIR PARENTS FURTIVELY ENJOYED AFTER THEY HAD GONE TO BEDDIE-BYE, RESPLENDENT IN FOOTY PAJAMAS AND BLISSFULLY IGNORANT OF THE CARNAL FILTH PROJECTED BY THE OLD BELL AND HOWELL UPON THE LIVING ROOM WALL DOWNSTAIRS. IT'S A DISCOVERY MANY OF US HAVE MADE, BUT WAS ELOQUENTLY DESCRIBED BY BILL MARQUEZ IN A 2001 PIECE HE CALLED 'HARDCORE SCORE'.

"RECENTLY, WHILE CLEANING OUT OUR GARAGE, I STUMBLED UPON SOME EPHEMERA FROM MY WONDER YEARS: THE FAMILY FILM PROJECTOR STILL IN THE BOX", WROTE MARQUEZ. "DAD'S GONE NOW AND ONLY HE KNEW HOW TO GET EVERYTHING TO WORK, SO I WAS ABOUT TO DUMP IT UNTIL I DISCOVERED MORE THAN A MARY POPPINS REEL INSIDE. JOHN HOLMES, SWEDISH EROTICA #57, AND EVEN A DONKEY FLICK WERE IN THEIR ORIGINAL BOXES. THERE WERE TWENTY OF THEM."

"I PLUGGED IN THE MACHINE AFTER IT HAD LAID DORMANT FOR ALMOST TWO DECADES. THE GEARS STARTED CRANKING AND THE LIGHT STILL WORKED. BACK IN THE DAY, I USED TO THINK THAT THE MACHINE TOOK AN EXPERT TO GET IT GOING, BUT IN REALITY, DAD MADE IT LOOK HARD. FOR ME, THE FILMS LOADED EASILY, EVEN THOUGH I SAW THAT DAD MUST HAVE HAD A FEW PROBLEMS SINCE THE LEADERS WERE TORN UP.

"THE FIRST FILM FEATURED SOME IN-AND-OUT BETWEEN A BLACK GUY AND A WHITE WOMAN. AT THE TIME, THIS MUST HAVE BEEN A HOT ONE. THEN I SAW JOHN HOLMES'S MONSTER ROCKET AND SOME WHITE WOMAN – I FELT SORRY FOR HER, BUT SHE GOT PAID. ONE EVEN HAD AN ASIAN WOMAN DOING A WHITE GUY. THIS WAS A RARE FIND FEATURING BELL BOTTOM JEANS, AND AN UGLY DUDE WHO COULD HAVE BEEN A CREAM ROADIE. THE FILM WAS SIMPLE, NO WEIRD POSITIONS, NO SOUND, AND A LOT OF LONG HAIR."

"BUT THE ONE THING I DIDN'T KNOW IS THAT DAD MUST HAVE BEEN RICH. THE BOX COVERS OF MOST OF THE FILMS HAD PRINTED PRICE TAGS OF $49.95 AND $69.95, WITH THE DONKEY ONE MARKED DOWN FROM $50 TO $30! TWENTY FILMS AT $50 EACH WAS A THOUSAND BUCKS, AND IN THE MID '70S, THAT COULD HAVE BOUGHT A CAR! IT'S FUNNY THAT WHEN YOU'RE LIVING AT HOME, YOU THINK YOU KNOW WHAT IS GOING ON IN EVERY ROOM, BUT THIS SHIT WAS CRAZY. THE HANDWRITTEN 'GOOD' AND 'BAD' ON THE BOXES SERVED AS A RATING SYSTEM MY DAD MUST HAVE THOUGHT UP ON HIS OWN."

"I THINK IT'S COOL THAT HE HID SOMETHING FROM US FOR YEARS, AND WAS NOW SMILING DOWN AT ME SINCE I FOUND HIM OUT. PORNO WAS PROBABLY THE ONE THING HE COULD HAVE HIDDEN THAT MADE ME APPRECIATE HIM MORE: THE BOX OF FLICKS MADE ME THINK THAT DAD WASN'T SUCH A

SQUARE AFTER ALL. HE WAS AN OG HARDCORE PORN FAN, AND EVEN HAD AN OPINION ABOUT EACH FLICK. I'LL ASSUME HE KEPT EVERYTHING IN GOOD CONDITION FOR ME TO SEE, THINKING THAT MORE ADVANCED TECHNOLOGY AND BETTER LOOKING PEOPLE WOULD NEVER EXIST.

FINDING MY OWN FATHER'S PORN STASH GAVE ME SIMILAR FEELINGS TO THE ONES BILL MARQUEZ HAD IN HIS STORY, ALTHOUGH I WAS A LOT YOUNGER, AND DAD WASN'T DEAD. BUT THERE AGAIN WAS THAT UNDENIABLE "PASSING OF THE TORCH" FEELING, A WAY TO UNDERSTAND THAT YOUR FATHER AND YOUR GRANDFATHER WEREN'T JUST THAT ALIEN KNOWN AS "PARENT" AND "GRANDPARENT", BUT ALSO REGULAR GUYS, WITH DESIRES AND FANTASIES JUST LIKE EVERY OTHER MAN THAT HAS WALKED THIS PLANET DURING THEIR SHORT STAY UPON IT. FOR THE MYRIAD OF EVILS THAT PORN IS SUPPOSED TO BE GUILTY OF, IT'S WORTH NOTING THAT EROTICA DOES ALLOW PEOPLE TO UNDERSTAND EACH OTHER BETTER AND MAKE US FEEL NOT SO ALONE AND WEIRD, AND THAT FACT SIMPLY DOESN'T GET SPOKEN OF ENOUGH.

LOOPS MAY HAVE BEEN MISSING THE LARGER BUDGETS AND THE MORE COMPLEX PLOTS, BUT THEY HAD QUALITIES FOR THOSE WHO APPRECIATED THEM. THAT DIRTY AND WHOLLY UNPRETENTIOUS FEEL THEY GAVE OFF IS PRECISELY WHY SO MANY VIEWERS WERE DRAWN TO THEM. AND ALSO BECAUSE THEY OFTEN FEATURED GIRLS ONE COULDN'T SEE ANYWHERE ELSE. THIS, MY FRIENDS, WAS THE 1970S PORN INDUSTRY'S GROUND ZERO, THE TESTING GROUND FOR NEW TALENT COMING INTO THE SCENE.

WHEN A NEW GIRL (OR STUD) CAME TO TOWN, AGENTS LIKE JIM SOUTH AND REB SAWITZ WOULD OFFER THEM A SEAT, FLASH A CHESHIRE CAT SMILE, MAKE A COUPLE OF DUMB JOKES TO EASE THE TENSION, AND CALMLY LOWER THE NEW FISH INTO THE SCUMMY WATER WITH A DAY SHOOT ON A LOOP. YOU KNOW, TO SEE IF SHE/HE COULD FEEL COMFORTABLE ENOUGH TO PERFORM WHEN THE STAKES WERE HIGHER ON A BIGGER BUDGET SHOOT DOWN THE ROAD. INDEED, MANY OF THE PERFORMANCES YOU'LL WITNESS IN VINTAGE 1970S XXX 8MM LOOPS ARE CHERRY-BUSTERS ; SPUNK STARLETS TAKING THEIR FIRST ON-SET LOADS. SOME WOULD GO ON TO BECOME SOME OF THE BEST KNOWN PORN PERFORMERS OF THE ERA, AND OTHERS WOULD RUN SCREAMING BACK TO NEW HAMPSHIRE, OREGON, AND NORTH DAKOTA, NEVER TO BE SEEN IN THOSE SINFUL FUCK FILMS EVER AGAIN.

THE BIGGEST PRODUCERS OF 8MM FOR MANY YEARS WERE THE AFOREMENTIONED THEANDER BROTHERS OF DENMARK, AND TO GIVE YOU AN IDEA OF HOW BIG THE 8MM INDUSTRY GOT -- BY THE TIME THE FORMAT HAD BECOME NEARLY OBSOLETE IN 1980, THEY'D PRODUCED 8 MILLION PRINTS. AS THE INDUSTRY MOVED ON FROM 8MM AS THE ERA OF VHS BLOSSOMED AND IT SIMPLY DIDN'T MAKE ANY GODDAMN SENSE TO GO THROUGH ALL THE TROUBLE OF THREADING FILM THROUGH A PROJECTOR AND WATCHING AN EXPENSIVE 10 TO 12 MINUTE SILENT FILM WHEN 2 (AND EVEN 6 HOURS IN EP MODE) HOUR VHS TAPES WERE NOW AVAILABLE, AND COMPLETE WITH SOUND - ADMITTEDLY ONE OF THE SEXIEST ASPECTS OF MATING AND PORNOGRAPHY. FROM VHS THEN DVD TOOK OVER, AND HERE WE NOW RESIDE IN THE DIGITAL AGE OF PORN, WHICH SEEMS EVEN FURTHER DIVORCED FROM THE EARLIEST DAYS OF THE STAG FILM.

THE 8MM LOOP WAS NOW DEAD, AND FOR MANY IT HAS BEEN FORGOTTEN. IT WAS A VERY DIFFERENT TIME DURING THE 8MM GOLDEN AGE, AND AS THE LATE MR GILLIS NOTED IN THAT RIALTO REPORT INTERVIEW, THE WHOLE PROCESS OF WATCHING 8MM WAS VERY TACTILE, AND THAT IS CERTAINLY SOMETHING MISSING IN AN AGE OF DOWNLOADS AND INSTANT STREAMING.

"I HAD THIS OLD 8MM PROJECTOR" GILLIS NOTED. "IT HAD THIS WONDERFUL SOUND TO IT. YOU KNOW? AND THE ADVANTAGE TO THE PROJECTORS WAS THAT YOU COULD PROJECT. SO I REMEMBER SOMETIMES BRINGING A NAKED GIRL INTO MY APARTMENT AND PUT HER AGAINST THE WALL, AND HER BODY WOULD BE THE SCREEN. I THINK THOSE OLD 8MM PROJECTORS WERE MUCH SEXIER IN A WAY. THERE WAS SOMETHING ABOUT THEM . . . IT WAS LIKE UNDRESSING A GIRL. THERE WAS A TEASE TO THEM, GETTING THE FILM READY."

⬦━━━━━━━━━━━━━━━━━⬦

LARGE PARTS OF THIS SPOTLIGHT ON 8MM SMUT WERE ACCUMULATED FROM THE ESSAY SERIES I WROTE FOR THE LINER NOTES OF THE FIRST 13 VOLUMES OF THE 42ND STREET FOREVER: PEEP SHOW COLLECTION DVD PUT OUT BY IMPULSE PICTURES STARTING IN 2013. IF YOU WANT TO READ AND SEE MORE, PICK THOSE DISCS UP, MY PALS, WITH 15 VINTAGE LOOPS PER DISC, THEY ARE A GREAT STARTING POINT FOR YOUR 8MM COLLECTION. CONSIDERING THAT WE'RE NOW IN AN ERA WHERE VERY FEW PEOPLE OWN A WORKING 8MM PROJECTOR, 99% OF YOU WILL HAVE TO SEE THEM THAT WAY, ON DVD.

REQUIEM FOR A DREAM IS ONE OF THOSE MOVIES (LIKE DANCER IN THE DARK, DOGVILLE, MARTYRS, SCHINDLER'S LIST, COME AND SEE, AND GRAVE OF THE FIREFLIES) WHERE IT'S A TOTALLY FANTASTIC MOVIE, BUT I DON'T REALLY NEED TO OWN IT BECAUSE IT'S JUST TOO MUCH OF A **BUMMER** TO WATCH RECREATIONALLY. BUT THAT "ASS TO ASS" SCENE -- THAT PART GIVES ME SUCH A WEIRD BONER! WEIRD, BECAUSE THE SCENE IS SUCH A **GRIM NIGHTMARE.**
— ART BY AARON LANGE. 2017—

THE BEETLEJUICE WE NEVER SAW

The original script of Tim Burton's spooky comedy Beetlejuice (1988) was actually a scary horror film. It was written by Michael McDowell in 1985 with help by pulp novelist Larry Wilson, who Burton then had replaced by Warren Skaaren, whose drastic overhaul of their work was used for the final version of the film.

Much like artist Joe Coleman, Michael McDowell specialized in collecting death memorabilia, an odd and extensive collection that packed over 75 boxes, and went on display at Chicago's Northwestern University in 2013. He co-wrote "The Jar" (which was the 1986 episode of the TV series "Alfred Hitchcock Presents" which helped get Tim Burton's career kickstarted), an earlier draft of the Nightmare Before Christmas, and sadly died of AIDS in 1999. Only 49 years old, his final project (which he never completed before his death) was a sequel to Beetlejuice. An accomplished novelist, McDowell was once described by Stephen King as "the finest writer of paperback originals in America today".

As we know, Beetlejuice eventually became a dark comedy (it begins with the deaths of the main characters), but what's really interesting about McDowell's original version of this cult classic was how much bleaker, gorier, scarier, and off-putting it was. It featured Beetlejuice – not as a wise-cracking, mischief-making, con-man entity, but as a winged, homicidal reptile-demon whose main human form was a small

MICHAEL McDOWELL

shifty-lookin' middle eastern guy. He's not really interested in scaring the Deetzes, or giving them the heebie-jeebies, as much as he's taken with abusing them and trying to murder them.

The god daughter of Timothy Leary, Winona Ryder's Lydia Deetz is the goth teenager character that put her career on the map, but it was originally turned down by Jennifer Connelly, Diane Lane, and Sarah Jessica Parker. That all sort of makes sense now when you note that in this earlier version she isn't nearly as important a character. Instead her six-year-old sister Cathy Deetz (whom Beetlejuice mauls after turning into a rabid squirrel) is the one who can see the ghostly Maitland couple and moves the plot along.

The shapeshifting is far more manipulative here, as the villain takes on the guise of various people that the Deetz family find off-putting – an IRS agent for Charles (a jerky penny-stock trader in this draft), a clumsy old woman for Delia, and a rock star rapist (named "Danny Death") for Lydia. Danny Death plays a neon violin, is described as a "demonic Bruce Springsteen", and makes a somewhat chilling effort to straight-up rape 16-year-old Lydia in her bedroom.

This climactic rape attempt (which includes a moment where dirty old Beetlejuice has a

TIM BURTON

18

DICK-SHAPED VERSION OF HIMSELF SHOOT OUT OF HIS CHEST RIGHT INTO LYDIA'S FACE) NOW MAKES THE PLOT ELEMENTS IN THE FINAL FILM WHERE MICHAEL KEATON'S CHARACTER SURPRISINGLY WANTS TO "MARRY" THE YOUNG WOMAN (EVEN THOUGH HE WANTS TO TORMENT EVERYONE ELSE) MAKE A LOT MORE SENSE, AND ARE NOW RESOUNDINGLY EXPOSED AS A THINLY VEILED METAPHOR FOR HIS ATTEMPT AT FORCED SEXUAL CONQUEST. AND I DO MEAN VERY THINLY VEILED.

ALL THIS, AND I DIDN'T EVEN GET AROUND TO MENTIONING THE WHOLE SUB PLOT WITH PROSTITUTES AND A "WHOREHOUSE", BEETLEJUICE'S DEMISE VIA EXORCISM, AND THE FAR MORE INTENSE VERSION OF THE MAITLANDS' CAR ACCIDENT WHERE GEENA DAVIS' CHARACTER'S ARM GETS MUTILATED IN GRAPHIC DETAIL. NO KIDS, THIS IS CERTAINLY NOT THE BEETLEJUICE YOU GREW UP WITH.

ALL SAID, IT'S NOT A VERY GOOD SCRIPT, AND THE TONE CHANGES BY BURTON AND SKAAREN WERE CERTAINLY THE RIGHT CALL. ONCE A PG-13 SCREENPLAY WAS IN PLACE, BURTON NOW HAD BIGGER PROBLEMS, NAMELY: THE STUDIO. WARNER BROS. EXECS WERE NOT AT ALL FOND OF THE NAME BEETLEJUICE, AND PUSHED HARD TO HAVE BURTON CHANGE IT TO "HOUSE GHOSTS". BURTON HATED THE NEW TITLE, AND JOKINGLY SUGGESTED THAT EVEN "SCARED SHEETLESS" WOULD BE BETTER. BURTON WAS REPORTEDLY GOBSMACKED WHEN WARNER BROS TOOK HIS GAG AT FACE VALUE, AND NEARLY TOOK HIM UP ON IT.

MAN, I LOVED THIS MOVIE SO MUCH WHEN I WAS FIFTEEN!

WINONA RYDER

MICHAEL KEATON

DID YOU KNOW?

ALL THE PEOPLE IN THE NETHERWORLD WAITING ROOM ARE IN THE SAME DISTURBING CONDITION AS WHEN THEY DIED AS A COMEDIC WAY TO REVEAL THEIR DEATHS. HOWEVER, THE MAITLANDS, WHO WERE DROWNED, ARE NOT WET. THIS IS NOT A FLUB, BUT RATHER AN ARTISTIC DECISION SO THAT THE POOR ACTORS WOULD NOT HAVE TO CONSTANTLY WEAR SOPPING WET CLOTHING ON SET FOR THE DURATION OF THE MONTH LONG SHOOT.

MIRROR GOOFS! WHEN ADAM AND BARBARA MAITLAND FIRST GET TO THEIR HOUSE AFTER DYING, WE CAN SEE THEIR REFLECTION IN A MIRROR IN A HALLWAY TO THE LEFT OF THEM. A COUPLE SHOTS AFTER THAT WE FIND OUT THEY'RE NOT SUPPOSED TO HAVE REFLECTIONS, BECAUSE THEY'RE GHOSTS. LATER, THEY HAVE REFLECTIONS AGAIN IN A MIRROR IN THE ATTIC.

DESPITE BEING CREDITED AS THE STAR, MICHAEL KEATON ONLY SPENDS 17 AND A HALF MINUTES ON SCREEN IN THIS MOVIE, OUT OF A 92-MINUTE RUNTIME. HE IMPROVISED MANY OF HIS MOST FAMOUS LINES OF DIALOG, WITH THE ENTHUSIASTIC APPROVAL OF DIRECTOR TIM BURTON.

"DAY-O (THE BANANA BOAT SONG)" IS ICONIC MUSIC FROM THE MOVIE, BUT THE SONG PLAYING DURING THE DINNER SCENE WAS ORIGINALLY PLANNED TO BE 1930S DOO-WOP POP FROM THE INK SPOTS. STAR CATHERINE O'HARA SUGGESTED THAT CALYPSO WOULD BE WAY MORE INTERESTING FOR THE SCENE, AND BURTON AGREED THAT THIS WAS A GODDAMN GREAT IDEA.

HER NAME WAS BOND... RENE BOND

☆ ROBIN BOUGIE 2018

(THIS IS PART TWO OF MY SERIES OF ARTICLES ON MISS RENE BOND. FOR PART ONE POP ON BACK TO CINEMA SEWER VOL 3 -- PAGE 163, AND WE'LL MEET YOU BACK HERE WHEN YOU'RE DONE CATCHING UP.)

"THERE WAS A SENSE IN THE BIZ THAT HARDCORE WAS LIKELY TO HAPPEN... SOON", WROTE LEGENDARY PORN INDUSTRY PHOTOGRAPHER PAUL JOHNSON ON HIS WEBSITE, PAULSFANTASY.COM. "WHEN THINGS BROKE LOOSE AFTER I SHOT 'SEX IN MARRIAGE', WE LOST SOME GOOD MODELS BUT MUCH OF THE SLACK WAS TAKEN UP BY SWINGERS GETTING INTO THE BIZ, NOW THAT THEY COULD HAVE REAL SEX WHILE MODELLING. ONE DAY REB SAWITZ HANDED ME A POLAROID OF A CUTE NEW SWINGER WHO HE HAD JUST BOOKED WITH TWO OF HER FRIENDS, A SWINGING COUPLE, INTO THEIR FIRST SHOOT WITH ME. . . REB BOOKED NEARLY EVERY NEW MODEL WITH ME FIRST BECAUSE HE WANTED THEIR FIRST SHOOT TO BE A GOOD EXPERIENCE. I BROKE IN THE MOST NEW MODELS IN THOSE EARLY DAYS."

"THIS SEXY LITTLE SWINGER WAS RENE BOND. THIS WAS NOT ONLY HER FIRST PORN BUT ALSO THE FIRST TIME SHE HAD SEX WITH ANOTHER WOMAN, SO SHE HAD TWO FIRSTS IN ONE DAY. SHE CERTAINLY LIKED IT AS SHE WENT ON TO BECOME ONE OF OUR FIRST PORN STARS. RENE'S FIRST PORN SHOOT EVER CAN BE FOUND IN RESPONSE VOL. 1, #2 BY ACADEMY PRESS."

RENE RUTH BOND WAS BORN ON OCTOBER 11TH, 1950 IN SAN DIEGO, AND DESPITE BEING RAISED BAPTIST, DIDN'T GET ANY FLACK FROM HER PARENTS WHEN SHE PAIRED UP WITH HER BOYFRIEND, RIC LUTZE (THEY WOULD APPEAR TOGETHER THROUGHOUT MUCH OF BOND'S FILMOGRAPHY), AND BECAME QUITE POPULAR IN THE BURGEONING ADULT FUCK BIZ. LUTZE, FOR HIS PART, DRESSED LIKE A PIMP AND ALSO APPEARED WITHOUT RENE, NOT ONLY IN A DOGFUCK LOOP, BUT IN OTHER LESS OUTRAGEOUS SEX FILMS AS WELL. HE WAS VERY COMFORTABLE STROKING HIS ERECTION WITH A BUNCH OF PEOPLE AWKWARDLY STANDING AROUND WATCHING, SOMETHING IN VERY HIGH DEMAND ON ADULT SETS IN A PRE-VIAGRA ERA.

"THEY WERE EXTREMELY COMFORTABLE WITH EACH OTHER AND WITH ME" PAUL JOHNSON NOTED. "THEY HAD SOMETHING GOING I HAD NEVER SEEN ELSEWHERE. RENE AND RIC LIKED TO TAKE SMOKE BREAKS RIGHT IN THE MIDDLE OF SEX SCENES. THIS WORRIED ME, AS A LOT OF UP AND DOWN CAN WEAKEN A GUY, MAKING IT HARDER TO GET THE SCENE MOVING AGAIN. NOT WITH THIS COUPLE. THEY WOULD GO BACK TO WHEREVER THEY WERE LAST AND RENE WOULD WHISPER INTO RIC'S EAR AND HIS COCK WOULD RISE WITHOUT BEING TOUCHED; THEN THEY WOULD GO RIGHT TO WHERE THEY LEFT OFF."

RENE ADORED ANIMALS SO MUCH!

"I WAS PETRIFIED, SCARED TO DEATH", RENE TOLD THE SACRAMENTO BEE IN THE MAY 3RD 1975 EDITION. "I NEEDED THE MONEY VERY BADLY, BUT I GRADUALLY GREW MORE RELAXED AND WENT FROM THERE. MOST PEOPLE START OUT VERY SCARED, I GUESS."

RENE WASN'T JUST ADORABLE WITH HER PETULANT SMIRK AND EVER-GROWING CONFIDENCE BEING NAKED IN FRONT OF CAMERAS, SHE COULD ALSO ACT QUITE DECENTLY AND WASN'T OUT OF HER ELEMENT DOING EITHER DRAMATIC SCRIPTS OR FUNNY STUFF, AND THE FACT THAT SHE COULD REMEMBER HER LINES AND DELIVER THEM REASONABLY WELL MEANT THIS CURVY BRUNETTE WAS SOON SO BUSY IN THE INDUSTRY THAT SHE HAD TO TURN DOWN WORK. SOME OF

HER MOST ENDEARING PHOTO MODELLING WAS DONE FOR LEGENDARY FOOT/STOCKING PHOTO-FETISHIST, ELMER BATTERS, AND SHE ALSO APPEARED IN CALENDARS, ON ALBUM SLEEVES, AND ON DOZENS OF MAGAZINE COVERS.

SHE'D GO FROM MAKING $100 (OR OFTEN LESS) PER SCENE IN THE LATE 1960S TO $2000 TO $5000 A MOVIE IN 1973. AT THAT TIME SHE WAS LIVING IN BURBANK CALIFORNIA, OFF A SIDE STREET NEAR THE PICKWICK DRIVE-IN ON ALAMEDA AVENUE. ONE OF HER FAVOURITE THINGS TO DO ON WARM SUMMER EVENINGS WAS TO GO OUT ON HER PORCH WITH A CUP OF HOT CHOCOLATE AND WATCH WHAT WAS PLAYING ON THE BIG SCREEN AT THE DRIVE IN.

MISS BOND STARS IN ONE OF MY ALL TIME FAVOURITE ADULT FILM SCENES, THE INFAMOUS "BLOWJOB COMMENTARY" SCENE IN 1973'S TEENAGE FANTASIES. I THINK ONE HAS TO SIT THROUGH A LOT OF EARLY 1970S SMUT TO RECOGNIZE HOW SPECIAL IT WAS FOR RENE TO SPEAK DIRECTLY TO THE VIEWER AS SHE SMILES AND STROKES THE COCKS OF EACH OF HER FIVE ANONYMOUS MALE CO-STARS. THIS IS NOT JUST GONZO PORNOGRAPHY (BEFORE IT WAS EVEN INVENTED), IT'S CINEMA VERITE. WHEN SHE COOS "MY FANTASIES ARE MOSTLY ORAL. I ENJOY GIVING HEAD. I ENJOY MAKING MEN CUM", YOU FEEL EVERY GODDAMN SYLLABLE TICKLE THE UNDERSIDE OF YOUR MARBLE BAG. IT'S AN ELECTRIFYING SCENE THAT ALSO PROMPTED THE END OF A FRIENDSHIP, TOO. AUTHOR IRVING PODOLSKY (HIS BOOK SERIES ABOUT HIS LIFE AND EXPERIENCES IS AVAILABLE AT IRVSODDSSEY.COM) WROTE ABOUT THAT EXPERIENCE IN 2013.

"Our relationship started like others do outside the sex business. Two people meet and they like each other. Rene was sweet and kind. Everyone thought so. She was also cute but not gorgeous, confident but not pushy, personally open but not really nosy about you or me. And she was married, sort of, to Ric Lutze, who doubled as her on-camera lover in most of her early films and clips."

"As I got to know Rene, I got to know Ric too and I liked him. The three of us became pals. About once a week I'd drop over to their pad after work for some weed, pizza and "free-love" with their friends. Still, I had never seen either Ric or Rene in any sex scene and I had no intentions of seeking that out. It happened anyway."

"I was working for a porn distributor at the time (one of my many fill-in gigs) and I had to screen prints before they got shipped. Anyway, there she was, Rene Bond in dazzling 16mm, doing what she did best. Just like everyone said, Rene was an awesomely alluring pixie. And although I wasn't turned on, (didn't want to be) I was definitely impressed with her technique. At the end of the scene she looked into the camera and whispered, 'Who could be next? You?'"

"I guess I wanted to be next 'cause two nights later, sitting beside Ms. Bond while puffing her husband's stash, I said something about that sex scene. I can't remember my words but it wasn't brash. It was a whimsical flirt that could go places if she wanted it to. She didn't."

"Oh my God, the walls iced. I'll never forget that look. It said, 'Not you too…'. Then she got up and silently left the room."

"With a few stupid words I had cleaved our connection. I had become a fan with fantasies like the other boys who wanted her bad. She could never again trust my reasons for friendship. In two seconds that all became clear. I had misjudged her intentions. I thought I was just another guy in her world of admirers – an okay chum for chatting but nothing special. My God, she was like, the Marilyn Monroe of porn! She had tons of "special" people buzzing around, including producers wanting private time. Where was I in all that?"

"Her stare…that look said it all. With me, 'special' was the freedom to be Plain Rene – a no-makeup gal like my sister and yours. She wanted a sanctuary of confidence and a best friend far from the sex. And that's what we were shaping until I raped her refuge with three words: '…great tongue moves!'"

THE PRICE OF FAME IS YOU'RE NEVER TRULY SURE WHO YOUR REAL FRIENDS ARE. AND WITH FAME, RENE TOOK MORE INITIATIVE IN MAKING A LIVING OFF HER NAME. SHE BEGAN SELLING PHOTOS, SLIDES, AND USED UNDERWEAR THROUGH A MAIL ORDER COMPANY THAT WOULD ADVERTISE IN THE BACKS OF ADULT MAGAZINES LIKE JAGUAR AND CAVALIER. SOME PORN HISTORIANS CITE RENE AS THE VERY FIRST XXX GIRL TO EVER FORM HER OWN FAN CLUB.

AS NOTED IN PART ONE OF THIS SERIES ON RENE, SHE WAS INFAMOUS FOR WORKING ON THE SIDE AS A STRIPPER AND BURLESQUE PERFORMER AT THE LEGENDARY IVAR THEATER IN LOS ANGELES, WHICH CAN BE SEEN IN THE 1980 JODIE FOSTER MOVIE FOXES, AND IS SUNG ABOUT BY TOM WAITS IN HIS 1975 SONG, "EMOTIONAL WEATHER REPORT". "IT'S COLD OUT THERE", STATES THE RASPY-VOICED CROONER. "COLDER THAN A TICKET TAKER'S SMILE AT THE IVAR THEATRE ON A SATURDAY NIGHT". IT WAS A SLEAZY DIVE, BUT THE SOULFUL, BRASH KIND I WISH WERE EASIER TO FIND IN TODAY'S SANITIZED, GENTRIFIED, COMMODIFIED URBAN SPRAWL. FOR THE SUM OF $3.50 YOU GOT A FREE BREAKFAST (IF YOU SHOWED UP BEFORE NOON), AND THEN YOU GOT A NAKED SONG AND DANCE SHOW FROM RENE.

"SHE WAS A CUTIE", NOTED BUZZ ANDERSON, AN AVID IVAR CUSTOMER. "I WAS FORTUNATE TO HAVE MET HER. WHEN I SAW

HER DANCING AT THE IVAR SHE WAS WEARING THIS SPECTACULAR ORANGE SEQUINED GOWN FOR HER ACT. SHE WAS THE FIRST WOMAN I EVER SAW SHAVED, AND I WAS SITTING NEAR THE FIRST ROW BY THE RUNWAY. MET HER AFTERWARDS AND GOT HER AUTOGRAPH, BUT LOST IT YEARS AGO. I HAD MEANT TO FRAME IT AND NEVER GOT AROUND TO IT. . . AFTER THAT SHOW I PRETTY MUCH GOT ALL MY GIRLFRIENDS AND EVENTUALLY MY WIFE TO SHAVE AND THAT WAS IN THE '70S. GLAD TO SEE IT FINALLY CAUGHT ON."

"I WORKED WITH RENE AS AN EXOTIC DANCER IN THE MID'70S AT THE IVAR IN HOLLYWOOD", DIXIE VAN ZUILEN TOLD CHRISTOPHER ELAM IN 2018. "SHE WAS SO NICE TO EVERYONE. WE HUNG OUT WITH HER ON OUR OFF DAYS AT HER HOUSE IN SILVER LAKE. . . SHE WAS SO SWEET AND PATIENT WITH HER FANS. ESPECIALLY ONE NAMED BOB THAT WOULD PASS OUT DIFFERENT COLORED OSTRICH FEATHERS TO THE GIRLS. HE TOTALLY LOVED RENE. SHE ALWAYS MADE THEM FEEL LIKE THEY WERE HER BIGGEST FAN."

DESPITE HAVING A LOVELY PAIR OF BREASTS, UNFORTUNATELY RENE WAS ONE OF EARLIEST ADULT FILM STARS TO GET BREAST AUGMENTATION, AND SADLY THIS WAS AT A TIME WHEN IT WASN'T ALL THAT SAFE AND CERTAINLY DIDN'T LOOK THAT AUTHENTIC. HER FIRST SURGERY DIDN'T MANGLE THEM UP TOO MUCH, BUT SHE PRESSED HER LUCK WITH YET ANOTHER TIT JOB.

"I RECALL HOW THEY LOOKED LIKE TWO COCONUTS", NOTED DIXIE. "WE JOKED ABOUT IT. . . SHE'D TAKEN TIME OFF DANCING AT THE IVAR TO HAVE EVEN LARGER IMPLANTS PUT IN BEFORE HER NEXT MOVIE. WHEN SHE GOT BACK SHE WAS SO MAD BECAUSE THEY DIDN'T PAY HER THE AMOUNT THEY SAID THEY WOULD, AND THERE WAS NOTHING SHE COULD DO ABOUT IT. SHE WAS A PROFESSIONAL, AND GENUINE."

ONCE THE 1970S WERE OVER, SO WAS RENE'S PORN CAREER. IT WASN'T UNTIL SHE SHOWED UP AS A CONTESTANT (WINNING $9000 IN CASH AND PRIZES) ON SEVERAL CONSECUTIVE EPISODES OF THE TV GAME SHOW BREAK THE BANK IN 1986 THAT THE PUBLIC SAW HER AGAIN. SHE WAS INTRODUCED AS A "BANKRUPTCY SPECIALIST" AND HAD A NEW HUSBAND NAMED LONNIE LEVINE THAT SHE APPEARED ALONGSIDE. IT WAS AN APPEARANCE THAT WENT TOTALLY FORGOTTEN UNTIL A FAN OF THE GAMESHOW (THAT HAD NO CLUE WHO RENE BOND EVEN WAS) UPLOADED THE APPEARANCE TO YOUTUBE FROM AN OLD VHS TAPE HE'D COPIED OFF TV DECADES EARLIER. A LUCKY BREAK FOR BOND FANS.

ON JUNE 2ND, 1996, AT THE AGE OF 45, RENE BOND TRAGICALLY DIED OF CIRRHOSIS OF THE LIVER, LEAVING BEHIND TWO CHILDREN. A CHARTER MEMBER OF THE XRCO'S HALL OF FAME IN 1985, RENE WAS POSTHUMOUSLY INDUCTED INTO THE LEGENDS OF EROTICA HALL OF FAME IN 2000, AND HAS SINCE BEEN NAMED TO THE AVN HALL OF FAME AS WELL.

— BOUGIE

LIFE LONG PALS:

Interviewing Rene's best friend, Joan Tyer
BY ROBIN BOUGIE (2016)

ROBIN: HEY JOAN, THANK YOU FOR SPEAKING WITH ME. YOU GREW UP WITH RENE BOND, THAT'S CORRECT?

JOAN: YES, RENE WAS MY LIFELONG BEST FRIEND. MY DAUGHTER AND MY GRANDDAUGHTER BOTH HAVE THE MIDDLE NAME 'RENE' BECAUSE OF HER. WE MET IN 7TH GRADE BACK WHEN CANYON COUNTRY, CA WAS SIMPLY SAUGUS, CALIFORNIA. OUR MOTHERS KNEW IF THEY FOUND ONE OF US, THEY WOULD FIND THE OTHER. WE WERE INSEPARABLE.

R: LOSING HER MUST HAVE BEEN TERRIBLE. I NEVER KNEW HER, BUT OF COURSE ALL FANS FEEL LIKE THEY KNOW

THEIR IDOLS ON SOME LEVEL. RENE IS MY ALL-TIME PERSONAL FAVOURITE ADULT FILM STAR.

J: YOU KNOW, EVEN AS LONG AS SHE'S BEEN GONE, THE WOUND IS STILL VERY TENDER. I HAD A DREAM THAT REPEATED OVER AND OVER — THAT SHE REALLY WASN'T DEAD. BUT OF COURSE SHE WAS, AND AFTER A WHILE THE DREAM FINALLY CEASED. I MISS HER SO MUCH.

R: SHE DIED OF LIVER PROBLEMS? IS THAT RIGHT?

J: THERE ARE INCORRECT STORIES OUT THERE. RENE DID NOT HAVE AIDS AS SOME HAVE SAID, AND HER PREMATURE DEATH DUE TO LIVER PROBLEMS WAS BECAUSE OF LEAKING SILICONE BREAST IMPLANTS POISONING HER.

R: HORRIBLE. YES, SHE HAD ONE OF THE EARLIER BOOB JOBS KNOWN OF IN THE HARDCORE PORN INDUSTRY, BACK WHEN THEY WERE NOT SAFELY DONE, UNFORTUNATELY. I THINK IT'S TESTAMENT TO JUST HOW INCREDIBLY SPECIAL SHE WAS THAT SHE COULD HAVE SUCH A FOLLOWING EVEN NOW WITH SUCH RESOLUTELY UNSPECTACULAR FAKE BOOBS.

J: YES. YOU KNOW, I'M CURIOUS. . . I WOULD LIKE TO KNOW WHAT MADE YOU A FAN.

R: MY INITIAL FANDOM OF RENE CAN REALLY JUST BE ATTRIBUTED TO A SCHOOLBOY CRUSH. I WAS RECENTLY GRADUATED FROM HIGH SCHOOL AT THE TIME THAT I DISCOVERED HER OLD FILMS, AND THIS WAS JUST A COUPLE YEARS BEFORE SHE PASSED AWAY. SPECIFICALLY, THERE WAS SOMETHING IN HER FACE IN PARTICULAR THAT GRABBED MY ATTENTION AND MADE ME WANT TO SEEK MORE OF HER MATERIAL OUT. HER EYES TWINKLED, AND SMILED, YOU KNOW? THERE IS A KINDNESS EMANATING FROM HER THAT IS VERY PALPABLE, AND ALSO. . . AN APPROACHABILITY, FOR LACK OF A BETTER TERM. I'M SURE THAT ASPECTS OF THAT PERSONA WERE JUST PUT ON FOR THE CAMERAS, BUT EVEN THEN THAT JUST SPEAKS TO HER TALENTS AS A MODEL AND PERFORMER, AND MAKES ME LIKE HER ALL THE MORE.

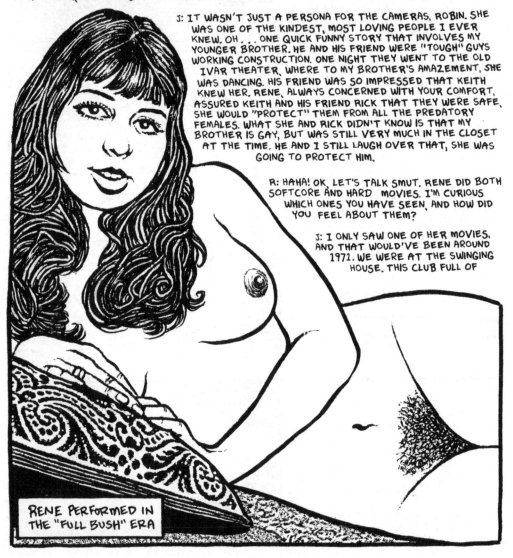

J: IT WASN'T JUST A PERSONA FOR THE CAMERAS, ROBIN. SHE WAS ONE OF THE KINDEST, MOST LOVING PEOPLE I EVER KNEW. OH . . . ONE QUICK FUNNY STORY THAT INVOLVES MY YOUNGER BROTHER. HE AND HIS FRIEND WERE "TOUGH" GUYS WORKING CONSTRUCTION. ONE NIGHT THEY WENT TO THE OLD IVAR THEATER, WHERE TO MY BROTHER'S AMAZEMENT, SHE WAS DANCING. HIS FRIEND WAS SO IMPRESSED THAT KEITH KNEW HER. RENE, ALWAYS CONCERNED WITH YOUR COMFORT, ASSURED KEITH AND HIS FRIEND RICK THAT THEY WERE SAFE. SHE WOULD "PROTECT" THEM FROM ALL THE PREDATORY FEMALES. WHAT SHE AND RICK DIDN'T KNOW IS THAT MY BROTHER IS GAY, BUT WAS STILL VERY MUCH IN THE CLOSET AT THE TIME. HE AND I STILL LAUGH OVER THAT. SHE WAS GOING TO PROTECT HIM.

R: HAHA! OK, LET'S TALK SMUT. RENE DID BOTH SOFTCORE AND HARD MOVIES. I'M CURIOUS WHICH ONES YOU HAVE SEEN, AND HOW DID YOU FEEL ABOUT THEM?

J: I ONLY SAW ONE OF HER MOVIES, AND THAT WOULD'VE BEEN AROUND 1971. WE WERE AT THE SWINGING HOUSE. THIS CLUB FULL OF

RENE PERFORMED IN THE "FULL BUSH" ERA

24

SWINGERS THAT SHE USED TO LIVE IN. SHE WAS SHOWING IT AT A BIRTHDAY PARTY FOR HERSELF.
I JUST REMEMBER BEING LOADED AND LAUGHING AT HOW DIRTY THE BOTTOMS OF HER FEET
WERE IN THE FILM. THIS ALWAYS MAKES ME SAD. . . THAT SHE WAS DRESSED UP IN A "LITTLE
GIRL'S DRESS", YOU KNOW. . . ALL FLUFFY AND FRILLY WITH A LARGE BOW IN HER HAIR. I GUESS I
WAS NEVER REALLY COMFORTABLE WITH WHAT SHE CHOSE AS A CAREER. I'M NOT A PRUDE, I
WAS A FREE LOVE HIPPIE (EVEN AFTER I GOT MARRIED) BUT I JUST COULDN'T RECONCILE DOING
IT FOR OTHER PEOPLE'S ENTERTAINMENT. SHE ALSO TOLD ME THE MONEY REALLY WASN'T ALL
THAT GOOD. I KNOW SHE WANTED TO BE A "REAL" ACTRESS, BUT I THINK ONCE SHE GOT INTO
PORN THAT DREAM WAS SHATTERED.

R: YEAH, PORN IS NOT FOR EVERYONE. I GUESS WE WON'T TALK SMUT IF IT'S NOT REALLY YOUR
THING, BUT IF YOU DIDN'T GET TO SEE HER MOVIES I THINK YOU SHOULD HEAR FROM SOMEONE
WHO HAS THAT SHE REALLY BROUGHT A LOT OF EXUBERANCE AND LIFE TO HER ROLES. AND
JUDGING BY THE FACT THAT SHE'S NOW NOTHING SHORT OF A LEGEND. . . I MEAN, WE'RE STILL
TALKING ABOUT HER TODAY BECAUSE OF THE AURA AND PASSION SHE HAD UP THERE ON THAT
SCREEN. . . IT'S SAFE TO SAY THAT SHE'S A GOOD EXAMPLE OF THE BEST OF WHAT ADULT
ENTERTAINMENT HAS TO OFFER, REGARDLESS IF ONE LIKES PORNOGRAPHIC CONTENT OR NOT.
SHE'S GOT A LOYAL FOLLOWING OF FANS THAT JUST GROWS MORE EVERY DECADE. SO SETTLE
SOMETHING ONCE AND FOR ALL: RENE BOND WAS HER REAL NAME?

J: RENE'S FATHER'S NAME WAS PETER BOND, HER MOTHER'S RUTH'S MAIDEN NAME WAS SMALL.

R: WHAT DID RENE'S DAD DO? WAS HE REALLY A POLITICIAN? THERE ARE RUMOURS THAT HIS
INFLUENCE KEPT THE HEAT OFF RENE? I HAVE SEEN A COUPLE OF THINGS SUGGESTING THAT
THE L.A. COPS (WHO WERE NOTORIOUSLY HARD ON PORN INDUSTRY PEOPLE) OFTEN LOOKED THE
OTHER WAY WITH RENE.

J: I REMEMBER MEETING PETER BOND ONLY ONCE, I DO NOT KNOW IF HE WAS A POLITICIAN, BUT
DIDN'T LIVE IN LA AND I CAN'T IMAGINE HIM HAVING ANY INFLUENCE OVER LAPD. I THINK THAT
STORY ORIGINATES BECAUSE RENE KNEW SEVERAL
OFFICERS THROUGH HER DANCING AT THE IVAR AND
THEY KEPT AN EYE OUT FOR HER.

R: AH, THAT MAKES SENSE. SO. . . (SHOWS PHOTO) NOW,
WAS THIS MAN RENE'S FATHER? SHE USED TO DO
A LEGENDARY NUMBER DURING HER SHOWS DOWN AT
THE IVAR THEATER/STRIPCLUB CALLED "MY
HEART BELONGS TO DADDY", AND THIS FUNNY
OLDER GUY WOULD COME OUT TOWARDS
THE END AND SHE WOULD SING TO HIM, AND
IT ALWAYS BROUGHT THE HOUSE DOWN.
I'M 90% SURE IT WASN'T HER REAL
DAD, BUT IT'S WORTH ASKING.

J: NO, I DON'T BELIEVE IT WAS
PETER WHOM SHE SANG TO.
THERE WAS ANOTHER OLDER MAN
IN HER LIFE AT THAT TIME,
MAYBE THIS WAS HIM?

R: AN OLD SUGAR DADDY?
JUST AN OLDER DUDE
WORKING AT THE
IVAR, IS WHAT IM
THINKING. SO NOW I
GUESS MY NEXT
OBVIOUS QUESTION

I THINK
I DREW
RENE
A LITTLE
TOO
SKINNY
HERE,
BUT FUCK
IT. . . I
LIKE HOW
THE
DRAWING
TURNED
OUT.

WHAT A GAL!

I'M A MORON

25

HAS GOTTA BE: HOW DID THE TWO OF YOU MEET, JOAN?

J: RENE'S PARENTS HAD BEEN DIVORCED FOR MANY YEARS WHEN RENE AND I MET. IT WAS BACK IN 1962 WHEN BOTH OUR FAMILIES HAD MOVED TO SAUGUS, CA (NOW CANYON COUNTRY) INTO BRAND NEW COOKIE CUTTER HOMES IN THE NORTH OAKS TRACT. HER HOME WAS ON STILLMORE STREET. RENE AND I MET FOR THE FIRST TIME IN 1963 AT THE SCHOOL BUS STOP. WE WOULD TAKE THE BUS INTO NEWHALL TO PLACERITA JUNIOR HIGH WHERE WE ATTENDED 7TH AND 8TH GRADES. 9TH GRADE WAS AT THE BRAND NEW JR. HIGH, SIERRA VISTA, WHICH WAS WITHIN WALKING DISTANCE. WE WOULD HAVE TO TAKE THE BUS AGAIN INTO NEWHALL TO ATTEND WM. S. HART HIGH. RENE'S FAMILY AT THAT TIME CONSISTED OF HER MOM AND STEP-DAD, AN OLDER STEP-SISTER, JAMIE AND A YOUNG BLOOD SISTER NAMED LAURIE.

R: VERY INTERESTING STUFF. I MYSELF USED TO LIVE IN VENTURA CALIFORNIA, AND THANKS TO FELLOW RENE BOND MEGA-FAN CHRISTOPHER ELAM'S SEARCHING THROUGH OLD NEWSPAPER ARCHIVES, I SEE THAT RENE HAS A CONNECTION TO OXNARD, WHICH IS RIGHT ACROSS THE 101 FREEWAY FROM MY OLD VENTURA STOMPING GROUNDS.

J: YES. RENE'S FATHER'S FAMILY LIVED IN OXNARD. SHE HAD A HALF BROTHER STEVE. THERE WAS ANOTHER SIBLING, KATHY BOND, I BELIEVE SHE WAS A HALF SIBLING AS WELL. RENE'S RELATIONSHIP WITH HER MOTHER WAS CONTENTIOUS IN HER TEEN YEARS, AND SHE MOVED TO HER FATHER'S HOME IN 1967. SHE ATTENDED/GRADUATED FROM OXNARD HIGH IN 1968.

R: YUP. THAT SOUNDS RIGHT. OH MAN, I'M SO TICKLED TO FINALLY GET A BETTER PICTURE OF THIS STUFF. YOU HAVE NO IDEA HOW MUCH BULLSHIT CIRCULATES ONLINE, AND HOW MUCH OF IT JUST BECOMES FACTS AFTER GETTING REPEATED SO MANY TIMES. SHE DIED BEFORE THE INTERNET WAS REALLY A THING. . . SHE DIED BEFORE ANYONE EVER REALLY HAD A CHANCE TO INTERVIEW HER PROPERLY ABOUT HER LIFE. THE FEW PORN INTERVIEWS SHE DID WERE . . . YOU KNOW. . . PORN INTERVIEWS. "HOW OFTEN DO YOU CUM?" STUFF LIKE THAT. THEY WEREN'T ALL THAT IN-DEPTH. THERE IS A GOOD ONE THAT APPEARED IN AN OLD SEX PAPER CALLED SAN FRANCISCO

RENE RELAXING AT THE "SWINGERS HOUSE."

BALL, THOUGH. OK, I'M BABBLING HERE. . . . SO THEN SHE MOVED OFF TO LOS ANGELES AND GOT INTO THE SKIN TRADE. THAT'S A BIG LEAP.

J: SHE WAS ALREADY LIVING IN LOS ANGELES WHEN SHE BEGAN HER FILM CAREER. SHE AND HER FIRST HUSBAND WERE RENTING ONE OF MY FATHER'S HOUSES IN ENCINO, CA. AROUND THE SUMMER OF 1967 HER MOTHER WAS MANAGING AN APARTMENT COMPLEX. YOU KNOW, I'M NOT SURE IF SHE DIVORCED RENE'S STEP-DAD OR HE DIED. RENE AND HER SISTER LAURIE WERE THERE. STEP SISTER JAMIE HAD MARRIED AND WAS ON HER OWN.

R: AND YOU WOULD TRAVEL TO SEE HER?

J: YES, I VISITED THERE MANY TIMES, MY FAMILY HAD MOVED BACK TO THE SAN FERNANDO VALLEY AS WELL. I REMEMBER HER MOTHER HAD A PET MONKEY, BUT WOULD NOT ALLOW RENE TO HAVE A KITTEN. RENE MOVED TO OXNARD FOR HER SENIOR YEAR AFTER MY PARENTS SAID NO TO HER LIVING WITH US.

R: A PET MONKEY? SWEEEEEET. AND THERE ARE RUMOURS ABOUT HER SPENDING HER FINAL YEARS WITH HER MOM IN LAS VEGAS. DOES THAT SOUND RIGHT?

S: NO, RENE, TO MY KNOWLEDGE, NEVER LIVED IN LAS VEGAS.

R: BUT SHE DID GO THERE FOR VACATIONS QUITE A BIT. RENE AND TONY GOT MARRIED THERE. SO I'M TRYING TO ESTABLISH A TIMELINE OF HER RELATIONSHIPS. SO FIRST OFF IN OXNARD THERE WAS RAYMOND ACEBO JR. JUST OUT OF HIGH SCHOOL, AND THAT WAS A NEAR MISS WITH MARRIAGE I BELIEVE? IT DIDN'T HAPPEN? I THINK IF SHE DID MARRY ACEBO JR, IT MUST HAVE BEEN ANNULLED, BECAUSE THE FIRST MARRIAGE RENE HAS ON RECORD IS 1970. HER FIRST MARRIAGE WAS TO MICHAEL J. GILLEN, I BELIEVE. WAS THAT THE REAL NAME OF PORN STAR RIC LUTZE,

OR A DIFFERENT GUY? BECAUSE WHILE SOME OF HER FANS SWEAR SHE WAS MARRIED TO LUTZE, I'M QUITE SURE THEY WERE ONLY DATING. I ASSUME IT WAS A DIFFERENT GUY, BECAUSE IN AN INTERVIEW SHE ONCE SAID "WHAT FIRST GOT ME IN (TO ADULT MOVIES) AT FIRST WAS THE MONEY. I WAS MARRIED THEN, BUT MY HUSBAND WASN'T. . . WELL, WE NEEDED MONEY. MY FIRST HUSBAND, I MEAN."

J: SHE MET RAY IN HIGH SCHOOL: THEY DATED QUITE AWHILE. HE WAS VIOLENT. HE HIT HER. I HATED HIM. SHE ACCEPTED AN ENGAGEMENT RING FROM HIM. I DON'T REMEMBER WHAT HAPPENED, BUT THANK GOD THE MARRIAGE DID NOT HAPPEN. I DATED HIS BEST FRIEND FOR A WHILE, RANDY WESTBERRY, AND THEY WOULD DRIVE DOWN TO THE SAN FERNANDO VALLEY FROM OXNARD. HE BROKE UP WITH ME BECAUSE HE DECIDED I WAS TOO LOOSE. . . I FUCKED HIM ON OUR FIRST DATE. HE TRIED TO GET BACK TOGETHER. HIS LOSS, I'D ALREADY MOVED ON. I DON'T REMEMBER HOW MUCH LONGER SHE AND RAY STAYED A COUPLE.

R: SO WHO WAS HER FIRST MARRIAGE TO, THEN?

J: HER FIRST MARRIAGE WAS TO MICHAEL GILLEN. I WAS 8 MONTHS PREGNANT AND SERVED AS HER MATRON-OF-HONOUR. SHE WAS GODMOTHER TO BOTH MY KIDS, AND MY DAUGHTER'S MIDDLE NAME IS RENE. I DON'T REMEMBER HOW THEY MET, SHE WAS LIVING WITH HER MOM IN GLENDALE THEN. HE WAS A SLACKER. THEY RENTED ONE OF MY DAD'S PROPERTIES IN ENCINO, STOPPED PAYING RENT AND LEFT A MESS - BUT WE NEVER BLAMED RENE FOR THAT. IT WAS WHILE LIVING THERE THEY GOT INVOLVED WITH A GROUP OF SWINGERS AND THEY EVENTUALLY MOVED INTO THE SWINGERS' HOUSE - I THINK IT WAS IN THE HILLS OF STUDIO CITY, NOT SURE. I VISITED HER THERE SEVERAL TIMES AND I BELIEVE THAT IS WHERE SHE MET RIC LUTZE AND GOT INVOLVED IN THE PORN BUSINESS. THAT WAS THE ONE AND ONLY TIME I MET RIC, AND I'M PRETTY SURE HE WAS ONE OF THE RESIDENTS THERE.

R: RIC DID SHITLOADS OF PORN WITH HER. THE LARGE MAJORITY OF HER HARDCORE SCENES IF SHE'S WITH A GUY, WERE DONE WITH RIC. HER HUSBAND THAT SHE MOVED TO THE LOS ANGELES AREA DIDN'T GET INTO PORN TOO, DID HE? MAYBE THAT'S WHY THEY BROKE UP.

J: I DON'T REMEMBER HER HUSBAND DOING ANY FILMS. THEY DIVORCED WHILE LIVING THERE. THE FIRST TIME I WENT THERE WITH HER (IT WAS BEFORE SHE AND MIKE HAD MOVED THERE), SHE KNOCKED ON THE DOOR AND THE HEAD SWINGER OPENED IT, STARKERS. I HAD TO LAUGH OUT LOUD BECAUSE HE QUICKLY COVERED HIS DICK WITH A NEWSPAPER. HE WAS ONLY EXPECTING RENE.

R: IN ANOTHER INTERVIEW SHE SAYS THAT HER SECOND HUSBAND "MISREPRESENTED HIMSELF AS A BIG-DEAL MOVIE MAN". NOW THIS WAS A GUY NAMED TONY MAZZIOTTI. SOME HAVE SAID HE WAS A "FREELOADER" AND SHE WAS "SUPPORTING HIM". SOUNDS LIKE A REAL CLASS ACT, THIS FELLA. DO YOU KNOW THAT NAME OR REMEMBER HIM?

J: I NEVER GOT OVER THE SHOCK OF HER PHONE CALL TELLING ME ABOUT TONY, HUSBAND #2. SHE MET HIM ON A FLIGHT TO LAS VEGAS - AND THEY GOT MARRIED THAT VERY WEEKEND. I NEVER MET HIM. I GOT ANOTHER SHOCKING PHONE CALL FROM HER, THEY WERE LIVING IN HOLLYWOOD. TWO MEN SHOWED UP LOOKING FOR TONY WHO OWED THEM QUITE A BIT OF MONEY. HE WASN'T HOME AT THE TIME AND SO THEY RAPED AND BEAT HER. I BEGGED HER TO REPORT IT BUT SHE WOULDN'T. I DON'T KNOW IF SHE WAS AFRAID OF TONY OR THE PEOPLE HE OWED MONEY TO.

R: HOLY CRAP. AWFUL. SO YEAH, OK, NOW, AFTER THAT SHE WAS DATING VARIOUS BROS. . . I KNOW CULT FILM DIRECTOR JIM WYNORSKI WAS AMONG THEM. THIS WAS IN THE MID 1970S, AND THIS WAS AFTER SHE SHOWED MAZZIOTTI THE DOOR. GOOD RIDDANCE TO THAT FUCKIN' GUY.

27

J: I REALLY DON'T KNOW ANY OF THE MEN SHE MAY HAVE DATED AFTER TONY. WE LOST TOUCH FOR A BIT. I WAS MARRIED WITH 2 KIDS AND LIVING IN MOORPARK, AND RENE WAS BUSY WITH HER CAREER. I REMEMBER TWO OF THE GUYS SHE DATED WHEN WE ATTENDED HART HIGH – JIM DOOLITTLE AND RICK SLOCUM! WE ALWAYS HAD GREAT LAUGHS OVER HIS NAME. HE WAS THE ONE WHO TOOK HER CHERRY.

R: SLOCUM GOT THE JOB DONE, REGARDLESS OF HOW SLOW HE CAME! (PROCEEDS TO LAUGH AT OWN JOKE) SO LET'S WRAP UP THE ROUGES GALLERY, HERE, FINALLY THERE'S HER LAST HUSBAND, LONNIE, WHICH IS WHO SHE APPEARS ON THE BREAK THE BANK GAME SHOW WITH IN 1986. YOU MENTIONED THAT HE WAS WELL-TO-DO, AND THAT THEY HAD TWO CHILDREN VIA SURROGACY? LONNIE LAVINE.

J: I DON'T REMEMBER HOW OR WHERE SHE MET LONNIE. I HAVE A VAGUE MEMORY OF MAYBE THEY MET WHILE SHE WAS DANCING AT THE IVAR THEATER. HE WAS YOUNGER BY SEVERAL YEARS, AND ADOPTED BY RICH JEWISH PARENTS. LONNIE WAS VERY PROUD OF HIS MONEY. SHE CONVERTED TO JUDAISM FOR HIM, AND ACTUALLY BECAME A BETTER JEW THAN HE WAS. I ATTENDED THEIR WEDDING, WHICH WAS ALL PAID FOR BY HIS MOTHER. I WOULD HOUSE AND PET SIT FOR THEM WHEN THEY TOOK TRIPS, AND RENE SHE WAS BREEDING YORKIES THEN. SHE WAS SUCH A SOFTIE... THERE WAS ONE WHO WAS BORN BADLY DEFORMED. SHE REFUSED TO PUT HIM DOWN AND KNEW HE COULD NOT BE SOLD. HE HAD A FOREVER HOME WITH HER. THE LITTLE YORKIE'S NAME WAS BILL, AND HE BECAME MY FAVORITE TOO, SIMPLY BECAUSE HE HAD NO IDEA HE WAS SO HIDEOUS.

R: BILL: THE FREAKY YORKIE WITH NO SELF AWARENESS. HA HA!

J: HAHA! I THINK THEIR FIRST HOUSE WAS IN VAN NUYS, BUT I HONESTLY DON'T REMEMBER. I WAS LIVING IN RESEDA AT THE TIME AND IT WAS ONLY A FEW MILES FROM ME. THEY WERE TRYING TO GET PREGNANT. SHE HAD MANY MANY INVITRO PROCEDURES, BUT THEY NEVER TOOK. RENE ONLY HAD 1/4 OF AN OVARY. WHEN WE WERE IN HIGH SCHOOL SHE HAD SURGERY TO REMOVE SEVERAL OVARIAN CYSTS AND SADLY THEY HAD TO TAKE THE OVARIES TOO, LEAVING ONLY A PARTIAL SO SHE WOULDN'T GO INTO MENOPAUSE AT 15. LONNIE TRAVELED QUITE A BIT FOR BUSINESS, DON'T REMEMBER WHAT THAT WAS.

R: WERE THEY HAPPY TOGETHER? LONNIE AND RENE?

J: RENE CONFIDED IN ME THAT SHE WAS POSITIVE HE WAS GAY, AND HAD MARRIED HER AS A BEARD. THEY RARELY HAD SEX, HE HUNG OUT A LOT WITH CERTAIN. . .MALE FRIENDS. HE PROBABLY WOULD HAVE BEEN DISOWNED BY HIS MOTHER IF HE CAME OUT. BACK THEN IT WAS SO HARD TO BE OPENLY HOMOSEXUAL. HE HAD A RED PORSCHE, AND WOULDN'T LET RENE TOUCH IT. HE RESENTED ME AND THE CLOSE FRIENDSHIP RENE AND I SHARED. I DON'T KNOW WHY, BUT I'VE NEVER FORGIVEN HIM FOR NOT CALLING ME WHEN RENE FELL ILL THAT WEEKEND. HE WAITED UNTIL SHE DIED TO PHONE ME. YOU KNOW, MAYBE IT'S BECAUSE HE WAS AWARE THAT SHE CONFIDED EVERYTHING TO ME. THAT MADE ME THREATENING TO SOMEONE WITH SECRETS. SHE WANTED ME TO GO TO LAS VEGAS WITH THEM ONCE – IT WAS AN ANNIVERSARY TRIP, BUT SHE KNEW SHE'D BE SPENDING IT MOSTLY BY HERSELF. HE PHONED AND FLAT OUT TOLD ME HE DIDN'T WANT ME TO GO, SO I DIDN'T. I WISH NOW I HAD.

R: YIKES. AND THEY HAD TWO KIDS EVEN THOUGH SHE WAS BARREN?

J: THEY FINALLY WENT THE SURROGATE ROUTE AND HAD TWO LOVELY LITTLE BOYS WHOM RENE ADOPTED AND LONNIE WAS THE BIOLOGICAL DAD. THEY TRAVELED A LOT, THEY ALWAYS TOOK THE BOYS WITH THEM. THEY HAD MOVED TO A LOVELY HOME IN SEPULVEDA. SHE SWITCHED FROM BREEDING YORKIES TO BREEDING PERSIAN CATS. I NEVER HAD A MEAL THERE WITHOUT CAT

HAIR MAKING AN APPEARANCE ON MY PLATE! GOOD THING I LOVE CATS. RENE WAS SO LOVING AND SO GENEROUS. FOR MY DAUGHTER'S HIGH SCHOOL GRADUATION, SHE GAVE HER A MINK JACKET (WHICH SHE STILL HAS). AFTER HER WINNING STREAK ON THAT GAME SHOW, SHE AND LONNIE WENT CAMPING WITH US AT PISMO BEACH IN HER NEW SAMURAI JEEP, WHICH WAS A PRIZE SHE WON.

R: SOUNDS AMAZING.

J: WE HAD A WONDERFUL TIME, BUT IT ENDED ON A BUMMER. THEY STOPPED SOMEWHERE ALONG HIGHWAY 101 TO EAT, AND WHILE THEY WERE IN THE RESTAURANT SOMEONE STOLE EVERYTHING THEY HAD IN THE BACK OF THE CAR, NOT REAL SECURE. THE PLASTIC ROOF WAS CHEAP AND SIMPLY SNAPPED ON AND OFF WITH NO WAY TO LOCK IT. BUT SHE SMILED AND SAID "IT'S ONLY STUFF". I THINK LON FELT VIOLATED THOUGH. MATERIAL THINGS WERE ALWAYS REALLY IMPORTANT TO HIM. HE EVEN BRAGGED ABOUT THEIR BEING WELL OFF WHEN EULOGIZING RENE! I WAS APPALLED.

R: CLASSY OL' LONNIE.

J: DON'T GET ME WRONG, HE WAS AN OKAY GUY AND FOR THE MOST PART VERY GOOD TO RENE, SHE WASN'T UNHAPPY, BUT NEITHER WAS SHE 100% HAPPY. THAT CHANGED SOMEWHAT WHEN THEY HAD THE BOYS. SHE WAS A DEVOTED MOTHER AND HER WHOLE LIFE WAS FOR THEM. I OFTEN WONDER HOW THEY ENDED UP. . .

THE FOLLOWING FEATURE APPEARED IN THE UNDERGROUND NEWSPAPER SAN FRANCISCO BALL #156. A DATE STAMP INDICATES IT WENT ON SALE NOVEMBER 22, 1974. AUTHOR BOB EARLTON ALSO WROTE A PORN NOVEL IN THAT SAME YEAR CALLED "THE SECRET GIRL WATCHERS", WHICH WAS PUBLISHED BY BARCLAY HOUSE). IT IS ONE OF ONLY THREE FULL LENGTH RENE BOND INTERVIEWS THAT HAVE AS OF YET SURFACED, AND IS THE MOST INFORMATIVE OF THE BUNCH CONCERNING HER ENTRY INTO THE INDUSTRY. THANK YOU TO CHRISTOPHER ELAM FOR TRACKING IT DOWN.

RENE BOND: SWINGING INTO PORN
How an information operator for Ma Bell became the star of over 200 porno movies and still remains a nice girl.

PROBABLY EVERY PERSON WHO HAS EVER GONE TO A PORNO MOVIE HAS WONDERED WHAT IT WOULD BE LIKE TO BE IN ONE. PURSUING THAT THOUGHT A LITTLE FURTHER, THE NEXT OBVIOUS QUESTION IS, HOW DOES ONE GET STARTED IN THE BUSINESS? RENE BOND, WHO HAS NOW APPEARED AS A STAR OR FEATURED PLAYER IN OVER 200 MOVIES, GOT HER START AT THE

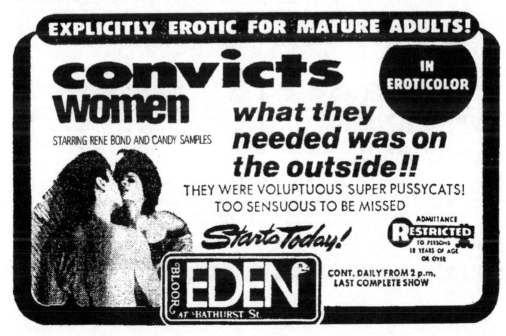

TELEPHONE COMPANY AS A DIRECTORY ASSISTANCE OPERATOR. SHE WAS NINETEEN AT THE TIME, THE PRODUCT OF A MIDDLE-CLASS HOME, SEXUALLY INHIBITED AND IN HER OWN WORDS, "NOT A VERY GOOD LAY."

DURING THE COURSE OF HER WORKING DAY, SHE WOULD COME ACROSS MANY UNUSUAL LISTINGS, AND BEING A CURIOUS GIRL, SHE WOULD SOMETIMES CALL THESE NUMBERS ON HER BREAKS. ONE OF THE NUMBERS SHE CALLED WAS THE COLLEGE DATING SERVICE, WHICH BY THEN HAD BEEN TRANSFORMED INTO THE 101 CLUB, PROBABLY THE BIGGEST AND NICEST SWING CLUB IN LOS ANGELES AT THE TIME. TOMMY, THE OPERATOR OF THE CLUB, AND RENE, THE INFORMATION

WHAT LED NICE GIRLS LIKE THESE INTO DARK ALLEYS AT NIGHT?

THEY HAD BEEN RAVAGED AND NOW IT WAS TIME FOR REVENGE!

VIOLATED!

METROCOLOR
RELEASED BY THE FANFARE CORPORATION

OPERATOR, STRUCK UP A FRIENDSHIP OVER THE PHONE THAT RESULTED MANY MONTHS LATER IN HER BECOMING AN EMPLOYEE OF 101.

BY THEN RENE WAS MARRIED TO HER FIRST HUSBAND, AND IT WAS HE WHO FINALLY ACCEPTED AN INVITATION FOR THEM BOTH TO ATTEND A SWING PARTY AT THE CLUB. "NOW, BY THIS TIME I WAS JUST CURIOUS ENOUGH, BUT PETRIFIED OF GOING. BUT I TOLD MY HUSBAND, 'OKAY, BUT IF I DON'T LIKE IT, WE'RE SPLITTING QUICK.' HE SAID, 'RIGHT, RIGHT, RIGHT,' BECAUSE HE HADN'T DONE ANYTHING LIKE IT BEFORE EITHER. BUT HE HAD THE MALE CHAUVINIST DREAM OF NAKED WOMEN RUNNING AROUND, EACH OF THEM AVAILABLE. HE WAS LIKE A KID IN A CANDY STORE. WELL, WE WENT AND HAD A GREAT TIME. THE PEOPLE WERE NICE AND RELAXED, NOBODY FORCED YOU TO DO ANYTHING. IT WAS A NICE CLUB."

FOLLOWING THAT FIRST EXPERIENCE, RENE AND MICHAEL RETURNED A FEW TIMES AND WERE SOON INTO THE SCENE. RENE WAS FED UP WITH ALL THE RULES AT THE PHONE COMPANY AND ALREADY HAD AMBITIONS TO BECOME A MODEL. SO WHEN SHE WAS OFFERED A JOB MANAGING THE CLUB, SHE QUIT HER JOB WITH MA BELL AND MOVED INTO THE CLUB WITH HER HUSBAND AND TWO OTHER RESIDENT MANAGERS. NOW THEY WERE IN A POSITION WHERE THEIR ROOM AND BOARD WAS PROVIDED, BUT NEITHER OF THEM HAD AN OUTSIDE JOB (HUSBAND MICHAEL HAD DROPPED OUT TO ENJOY THE SWINGING SCENE AND WAS DETERMINED TO DO NOTHING ELSE) AND NO SPENDING MONEY.

ENTER THE PORN BUSINESS. THE TWO OTHER MANAGERS OF THE CLUB WERE ALREADY HEAVILY INVOLVED IN THE BUSINESS AS MODELS AND ACTORS. "THIS SOUNDS TERRIBLY STUPID, BUT I DIDN'T REALIZE THAT THERE WERE SIMULATED MOVIES! I KNEW THAT THERE WERE STAG FILMS, THAT PEOPLE MADE ACTUAL LOVE FOR THE CAMERA, BUT THAT WAS ALL I KNEW ABOUT THE BUSINESS. SO BUD AND MARCIE WOULD COME HOME ALL EXCITED. THEY'D SAY, 'OH WOW, BUD GOT THE LEAD IN THIS FEATURE.' IT SOUNDS GOOD, IMPORTANT, RIGHT? HE WAS GETTING $100 FOR THE DAY. THAT SOUNDS LIKE A LOT OF MONEY WHEN THE MOST YOU'VE EVER MADE WAS $2.25 AN HOUR FOR THE PHONE COMPANY."

"BUT I WAS STILL VERY HUNG UP ABOUT SEX. SEX WAS SOMETHING MEN DID TO YOU. I WAS SCARED OF MEN. I WASN'T SATISFIED. I FELT I WAS BEING USED. IF A MAN I DIDN'T KNOW CAME UP AND TALKED TO ME I DIDN'T KNOW WHAT TO SAY, AND THIS WAS AFTER I HAD BEGUN WORKING AT THE CLUB. I DID AN AWFUL LOT OF RUNNING AWAY, ANSWERING THE DOOR, DOING THIS, DOING THAT, AND NOT SWINGING VERY MUCH AT ALL, UNLESS IT WAS WITH SOMEONE I ALREADY KNEW. I HAD A LOT OF MEN TELL ME I WASN'T VERY GOOD IN BED, WHICH DOESN'T DO MUCH FOR ANYBODY'S EGO. BUT I KNEW THEY WERE RIGHT. I WAS AFRAID TO MAKE ANY NOISE, AFRAID TO REACH OUT, TO BE ANY KIND OF AGGRESSOR. I HAD BEEN TAUGHT AND CONVINCED THAT IF YOU WERE UNINHIBITED, THAT YOU WERE IN SOME WAY BAD, A HUSSY. MY GRANDFATHER CALLED ME A HARLOT WHEN WE MOVED INTO THE CLUB. IT TOOK ME A MONTH TO GO IN THE POOL AT NIGHT WITH NO CLOTHES ON."

"FINALLY, WE GOT SO BROKE THAT WE COULDN'T AFFORD TO BUY KOTEX — THE CLUB DIDN'T SUPPLY THAT. I HAD TO DO SOMETHING. WELL, BUD AND MARCIE HAD BEEN TRYING TO GET ME TO

WORK WITH THEM AND I FINALLY AGREED. BUD GOT ME BOOKED TO DO A CHEESECAKE LAYOUT AND A SIMULATED SHOOTING WITH ANOTHER GIRL AND A GUY. THE PHOTOGRAPHERS AND THE COUPLE I WORKED WITH WERE REALLY NICE, THEY TOLD ME EVERYTHING I HAD TO DO AND REALLY HELPED ME A LOT. THE DAY AFTER I DID THOSE TWO JOBS I WAS BOOKED FOR A HARDCORE FILM WITH BUD AND MARCIE THAT WAS TO BE SHOT AT THE CLUB. I WAS PETRIFIED. IF I WASN'T ANY GOOD, IT WAS RIGHT THERE ON FILM. SO I GOT STONED. THE CAMERAMAN WAS UNDERSTANDING AND JUST TOLD US TO DO IT AND HE'D MOVE AROUND US, WHICH DOESN'T HAPPEN VERY OFTEN."

"WELL, IT WENT PRETTY WELL. I THOUGHT TO MYSELF, 'GEE, THAT'S NOT SO BAD. IF I'M AT THE CLUB DOING IT FOR FREE AND IT DOESN'T FEEL GOOD, THEN GEE, I MIGHT AS WELL GET PAID FOR IT.' SO I STARTED DOING WORK AND GOING AROUND TO THE AGENCIES.

WHY HAS RENE BOND BEEN SUCH A SUCCESS IN HER FIELD? WHY DOES SHE WORK CONSTANTLY IN A BUSINESS WHERE FACES COME AND GO, USUALLY OVERNIGHT? "THERE'S SOMETHING ABOUT THE WAY I WORK, I GUESS. I'VE STUDIED MYSELF ON THE SCREEN, WATCHED WHAT I DO. I DON'T THINK MY BODY IS EXQUISITE AND I DON'T THINK THAT I'M BEAUTIFUL. I THINK THAT I'M VERY ATTRACTIVE. I THINK THAT I'M APPRECIATED, BUT I DON'T THINK I'M EXQUISITE."

"PEOPLE LIKE ME. I WORK VERY HARD AND DO THE BEST I CAN. MY FIRST LEAD WAS IN A ONE DAY QUICKIE CALLED LOLLYPOP. EVEN THOUGH IT WAS A HARDCORE FILM, I THOUGHT I WAS A STAR. I MEAN I LEARNED MY LINES BY HEART AND I REALLY TRIED TO GIVE IT EVERYTHING I HAD."

THE ROAD TO SEX STARDOM STILL WASN'T AN EASY ONE. IT WAS A LONG TIME AFTER THAT FIRST FLICK THAT SHE GOT HER FIRST LEGITIMATE ACTING JOB IN A REGULAR, FEATURE LENGTH FILM. BEFORE THAT WERE SCORES OF HARDCORE FILMS AND EVEN BREAKING INTO THE SIMULATED SEX PICTURE FIELD WASN'T EASY OR CHEAP.

"SIMULATED PEOPLE WOULDN'T HIRE ME BECAUSE THEY HAVE THIS BIG IDEA THAT YOU WON'T SELL A PICTURE IF YOU DON'T HAVE BIG BOOBS. THE NORTH AMERICAN BREAST FETISH IS JUST UNBELIEVABLE, THEY HAVE GOTTEN AWAY FROM IT A LITTLE NOW. PENTHOUSE AND OTHER MAGAZINES HAVE SHOWN THAT THERE IS MORE TO A WOMAN THAN JUST HAVING BIG MAMMARY GLANDS. SO I FINALLY SAVED SOME MONEY AND HAD SILICONE IMPLANTS PUT IN MY BREASTS. I REALLY DID IT BECAUSE ALL THE PEOPLE WHO YOU WORK WITH GET YOU CONVINCED THAT YOU'VE GOT SMALL BOOBS SO THEREFORE YOU'RE NOT ALL YOU COULD BE. 'IF YOU HAD BIG BOOBS, BOY, YOU WOULD BE TERRIFIC!' WELL, I DIDN'T WANT TO DO HARD-CORE FOREVER BECAUSE I REALLY LIKED THE ACTING PART OF FILMS AND YOU DON'T GET MUCH OF AN OPPORTUNITY TO ACT IN HARDCORE. IT'S ALL HURRY UP, HURRY UP AND SAY YOUR LINES AND DO THIS AND DO THIS. IT'S JUST DIALOGUE TO GET INTO THE SEX SCENES."

"I REALLY WANTED TO DO THE ACTING, BUT I TRIED TO DO THE SEX SCENES WELL, TOO, BECAUSE I KNEW WHAT THE PEOPLE WANTED. EVEN IF IN MY PRIVATE LIFE I WASN'T TERRIFIC IN BED, I KNEW WHAT THE AUDIENCE WANTED TO SEE, SO I WORKED VERY HARD. DURING A SCENE, YOU'LL HAVE A DIRECTOR SAYING 'OKAY HONEY, WE'RE ON YOUR FACE, YOU'RE COMING, YOU'RE COMING!' AND YOU'RE SUPPOSED TO GO INTO THESE WILD, ECSTATIC EMOTIONS, BIG AND LOUD. AND I'D NEVER CUSSED BEFORE I WENT INTO FILMS. SO IT WAS REALLY ACTING EVEN THEN, BECAUSE HARDCORE FILMMAKERS THINK YELLING 'FUCK ME, FUCK ME' IS EROTIC. I KNOW IT ISN'T, AND SO DO THE PEOPLE WHO GO TO THE FILMS. I GET LETTERS FROM FANS, EVEN THOUGH I'M NOT A HOUSEHOLD WORD LIKE LINDA LOVELACE, AND THEY'VE TOLD ME THE SAME THING. BUT YOU DO WHAT YOU'RE TOLD TO DO, AND I'VE WORKED STEADILY FOR THE PAST FOUR YEARS ALTHOUGH I HAVEN'T DONE ANY HARDCORE FOR A LONG TIME NOW."

RENE STILL WORKS IN SEX FILMS (HER LATEST RELEASE WAS PANORAMA BLUE) BUT TODAY SHE APPEARS IN MORE AND MORE LEGITIMATE FILMS AND TELEVISION SHOWS. ALTHOUGH WITH SOME PRODUCERS SHE CAN'T LIVE DOWN HER PAST WORK

AND IT IS DIFFICULT TO GET JOBS, SHE PERSEVERES. SHE IS NOT ASHAMED OF WHAT SHE HAS DONE. SHE FEELS IT IS HONEST, HARD WORK AND THAT SHE HAS LEARNED A LOT FROM IT.

"I TOLD YOU HOW I WAS WHEN I STARTED. I WENT THROUGH A LOT OF SHIT BECAUSE I WAS SO TIMID. BUT IT TAUGHT ME SO MUCH. IT MADE ME VERY SURE. I KNOW EXACTLY WHO I AM. I KNOW WHO I WANT TO BE. I KNOW WHAT KIND OF MAN I CAN LIVE WITH. I DON'T NEED TO DATE A LOT OF PEOPLE BECAUSE I CAN MEET SOMEONE AND KNOW IF THEY HAVE WHAT I NEED AND IF I CAN GIVE THEM SOMETHING. AND SEXUALLY, I'M ABOUT 5 MILLION PERCENT BETTER IN BED THAN I WAS. I'VE LEARNED TO COMMUNICATE WITH MY LOVER. IF YOU WANT SOMETHING DONE TO YOU, YOU HAVE TO LET THE OTHER PERSON KNOW. YOU HAVE TO BE ABLE TO COMMUNICATE WITH ANYBODY WHETHER YOU'RE TALKING ABOUT POLITICS OR SEX OR LOVE OR ANYTHING. AND I'M GOING TO GO ON COMMUNICATING UNTIL I ACHIEVE EVERYTHING I WANT. AND THAT'S A LOT."

RENE BOND: implants VS. au naturel

THIS LIST INCLUDES BOTH FILMS AND LOOPS, AND WAS PUT TOGETHER BY MARTIN BROOKS IN LATE 2018. IT'S NOT COMPREHENSIVE (SHE ESTIMATED SHE HAD MADE NEARLY 300 FILMS AND LOOPS) BUT IT IS USEFUL REFERENCE FOR THOSE THAT PREFER TO SEE HER WITHOUT THE IMPLANTS THAT ULTIMATELY KILLED HER.

Pre-Implants

Bad Bad Gang
Below the Belt
Brute Therapy (aka Sex Asylum)
Cameo
City Women
A Clockwork Blue
Country Cuzzins
Devil's Little Acre
Ensanada Pickup
Flesh Gordon
Girl in a Basket
The Heist
Hot Pistols
I'm No Virgin
The Jekyll and Hyde Portfolio (cameo)
Journal of Love
Kidnapped!
Kim Comes Home
Lollipops for Judy (aka Lollypop. Rene's 1st)
My Little Sister
Naked Encounters
Necromania
Never Enough
Private Private
Refinements in Love
Rendezvous in Hell
Sessions of Love Therapy
The Sexpert
Shot on Location
Teenage Lovers
Teenage Fantasies
Three for One
Touch Me
Your Wife Or Mine

Post-Implants (she had multiple surgeries, but the first was in March 1972)

The Adult Version of Jekyll & Hide
Angel Above, The Devil Below
Beach Blanket Bango
Betrayal (TV movie)
The Class Reunion
The Cocktail Hostesses
Convicts Women (aka Bust Out)
Country Hooker
Cream Rinse

Danish Connection, The
Diary of a Schizo aka Sexophrania
Dicktator, The
Did Baby Shoot Her Sugardaddy?
Disco Lady (cameo)
Do You Wanna Be Loved?
Fantasm
Frankie and Johnnie... Were Lovers
French Love Secret, The
Fugitive Girls aka Five Loose Women
Godchildren aka Hawaiian Split
Guess Who's Coming This Weekend
High School Fantasies
Honey Buns
Jiggling Jugs (loop)
Les Chic
Lesbian Seduction (loop)
Love and the Great Grunt
Mary! Mary!
Mermaid, The
Mirage (loop)
My Sister's Boobs aka Boobs (loop)
Panty Party
Partnership, The
Playmates, The
Please Don't Eat My Mother
Porno Mondo
Princess and the Horny Toad (loop)
Renee (loop)
Renee and Her Mirror Trick (loop)
Runaway Hormones
Saddle Tramp Women
School Girl (short), The
Sex Dolls (loop)
Sexy Shooting (loop)
Teaser, The
Teenage Fantasies Part 2
Teenage Jailbait
Teenage Sex Kitten
Topless Service (loop)
Violated!
Women of Vengeance
World of Peeping Toms aka Peek-A-Boo

THE HAIDA THEATER

BY ROBIN BOUGIE '16

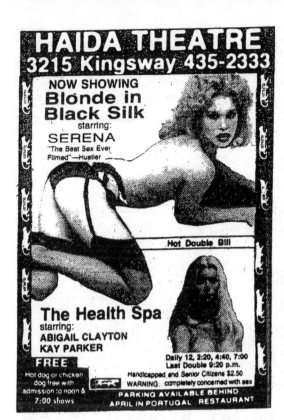

CINEMA SEWER MAGAZINE IS CREATED AT MY ART STUDIO ON KINGSWAY AVE HERE IN VANCOUVER. ACROSS THE STREET IS THE OLD FOX THEATER (WHICH I'VE WRITTEN ABOUT PLENTY IN THESE PAGES) BUT FURTHER UP KINGSWAY, AT 3215, THERE USED TO BE ANOTHER PORN MOVIE HOUSE — A 375 SEAT VENUE CALLED THE HAIDA. IT GOT ITS NAME FROM THE TRIBE OF ABORIGINAL PEOPLE WHO ORIGINALLY OCCUPIED THE COASTAL BAYS AND INLETS OF BRITISH COLUMBIA BEFORE WHITEY MOVED IN.

THESE DAYS THE NORTHERN PART OF KINGSWAY AVENUE (WHERE I AM SITUATED) IS QUITE GENTRIFIED, BUT KINGSWAY HAS ENJOYED A LONG HISTORY OF BEING A HOTSPOT OF VICE AND SIN IN VANCOUVER. THROUGH EACH DECADE THIS WINDING AVENUE (ORIGINALLY A WAGON TRAIL) OPERATED AS A HAVEN FOR BROTHELS, MASSAGE PARLOURS, BURLESQUE HOUSES, AND STRIP CLUBS. EVEN TODAY, THE SOUTHERN PARTS OF KINGSWAY ARE ONE OF THE FEW PLACES YOU CAN STILL SEE STREETWALKING PROSTITUTES (LADIES, THERE IS THIS AMAZING THING CALLED THE INTERNET, LOOK INTO IT), ALTHOUGH THESE DAYS AN ESTIMATED 95 PERCENT OF THE SEX TRADE IN VANCOUVER HAPPENS INDOORS.

IN 1939 THE VENUE AT 3215 KINGSWAY ORIGINALLY TOOK BLOOM AS THE KINGSWAY THEATER, WHICH OPERATED AS A MAINSTREAM HOLLYWOOD MOVIE HOUSE UNTIL 1965, WHEN IT CLOSED. IT WAS REMODELLED IN 1966, SUBSEQUENTLY RENAMED THE HAIDA, AND THEN BEGAN SHOWING SEXPLOITATION MOVIES AND OTHER GENRE FILMS. VANCOUVER PUNK ICON BILLY HOPELESS NOTES THAT HE DISCOVERED ROCK AND ROLL MUSIC AT THE HAIDA AS A KID "WHEN THEY WERE SHOWING BEATLES MOVIES AT THE MATINEES".

ON MAY 30TH 1982, THE HAIDA REOPENED AS A PORNO PALACE AND BEGAN SHOWING XXX ADULT FILMS. ITS VERY FIRST PORNO MOVIE WAS AN EXTENSIVELY EDITED VERSION OF GERARD DAMIANO'S DEEP THROAT. NO VAGINAL OR ANAL PENETRATION, NO EJACULATION, AND NO DEPICTIONS OF VIOLENCE WERE ALLOWED. THE BRITISH COLUMBIA FILM CLASSIFICATION BRANCH SAW TO THAT, AND EACH PORN MOVIE WOULD HAVE TO PASS THROUGH THEIR ACTIVE SCISSORS. ONLY ORAL SEX, NUDITY, AND SIMULATIONS OF SEXUAL INTERCOURSE WOULD BE ALLOWED, AND THOSE RULES WOULD STAND FOR THE REST OF THE 1980S UNTIL CENSORS RELAXED THE RULES.

THE NEW OWNERS WERE A COUPLE OF FRIENDLY EASY-GOING EAST INDIAN DUDES IN THEIR 30S NAMED KARTAR SINGH AHLUWALIA AND ANDY AULAKA. KARTAR WAS THE MANAGER, AND HAD COME TO CANADA FROM INDIA IN 1967, AND FIRST WORKED AT A SAWMILL BEFORE HE GOT THE IDEA TO OPEN HIS OWN MOVIE HOUSE. HE HAD ENJOYED SOME NOTORIETY AS A GOLD MEDAL WINNING RUNNER IN THE 400, 800, AND 1500 METRES IN THE INDIAN NATIONAL CHAMPIONSHIPS. ANDY CAME TO CANADA IN 1972 WHEN HE WAS ONLY 17, AND LATER WROTE THE PROVINCIAL EXAM TO BECOME A CERTIFIED PROJECTIONIST.

BEING SMUT-MONGERS WASN'T THE PLAN AT THE OUTSET. NOT AT ALL.

INITIALLY THE PAIR SHOWED EAST INDIAN FILMS, WITH SOME PORNO ON THE SIDE TO PAY THE BILLS. THEN IT BECAME PORN FOR MOST OF THE WEEK, AND THE BOLLYWOOD STUFF ON THE WEEKENDS. "MORE PEOPLE TURNED UP EXPECTING TO SEE PORNO ON WEEKENDS THAN WANTED TO SEE EAST INDIAN FILMS", AHLUWALIA TOLD VANCOUVER PROVINCE REPORTER, PETER WILSON, IN 1983. "WE DECIDED THEN TO GO FULL TIME WITH THE PORNO."

AT FIRST, CUSTOMER COMPLAINTS ROLLED IN -- NUMEROUS AND OUTSPOKEN DISPARAGING REMARKS FROM MEMBERS OF THE COMMUNITY WHO HAD NEVER HAD A PORN THEATER IN THEIR MIDST BEFORE, AND CERTAINLY DIDN'T LIKE THE IDEA, CENSORED MOVIES OR NOT. "NOW WHAT WE GET ARE SUGGESTIONS" KARTAR NOTED, A YEAR LATER. "WE KNOW OUR REGULAR CUSTOMERS. WE'RE LIKE A FAMILY NOW. THEY TELL US WHAT THEY WANT, AND WE TRY TO GET IT FOR THEM. WE HAVE FREE HOT DOGS OR CHICKEN DOGS AT THE NOON AND 4:30 SCREENINGS."

DISPLAYED PROUDLY ON THE MARQUEE OF THE BUILDING, AS WELL AS IN EVERY ADVERTISEMENT THE HAIDA EVER RAN FOR THEIR SCREENINGS, WAS THE FOREBODING "RESTRICTED COUGAR" LOGO, FIRST INTRODUCED IN THE 1960S BY THE B.C. FILM CLASSIFICATION BOARD AS A WAY TO WARN THEATER GOERS. BUT ADULT VENUES LIKE THE NIGHT AND DAY (LATER KNOWN AS THE VENUS), THE FOX, AND THE HAIDA WOULD CONFOUND THE BOARD BY USING THE WARNING PROUDLY AND LOUDLY, TO DRAW THE PUBLIC IN. THEY HAD TAKEN WHAT WAS DESIGNED TO BE A SCARLET LETTER, AND MADE IT INTO A CALLING CARD. EVEN TODAY THE BC RESTRICTED COUGAR IS RECOGNIZED AROUND THE WORLD, AND WAS HONOURED BY QUENTIN TARANTINO IN HIS 2007 FILM, DEATH PROOF.

IN SEPTEMBER 1983, KARTAR AND ANDY EXCITEDLY CONTACTED THE MEDIA TO LET THEM KNOW OF A NEW ATTRACTION THAT WOULD BE MAKING ITS DEBUT IN THEIR BALCONY SECTION. 34 TWO-PERSON "LOVESEATS" HAD BEEN INSTALLED, PROMPTING ONE SUSPICIOUS REPORTER TO ASK IF THE BOYS WERE TRYING TO ENCOURAGE THEIR HORNY CUSTOMERS TO FUCK EACH OTHER IN A PUBLIC PLACE -- AN ILLEGAL ACT IN BRITISH COLUMBIA FOR SURE.

"HEAVENS, NO!" AN INCREDULOUS KARTAR REPLIED WHILE SMILING. "WE DON'T EXPECT THAT FROM OUR CUSTOMERS! THEY ARE VERY CIVILIZED, EDUCATED PEOPLE. DOCTORS, LAWYERS, PROFESSORS." HE ALSO ADDED THAT THERE WAS CERTAINLY NOTHING HE COULD DO TO STOP PEOPLE FROM "KISSING AND HUGGING", AND THAT HE WAS EXPECTING TO HAVE TO START A RESERVATION SYSTEM FOR THE POPULAR "CUDDLER'S COUCHES".

IN 2012 I SPOKE TO A GUY IN HIS 50S THAT WENT THERE A FEW TIMES. WE MET ON AN ESCORT MESSAGE BOARD THAT VANCOUVER JOHNS USE TO REVIEW, RATE AND DISCUSS THE SERVICES AND SKILLS (OR LACK THEREOF) OF LOCAL PROSTITUTES. NOT SURPRISINGLY, HE ASKED TO GO ANONYMOUS AND HAD THIS TO SAY WHEN I ASKED HIM ABOUT HIS EXPERIENCES:

"THE HAIDA WAS A GOOD PORN THEATER. CLEAN, AND NO ONE WOULD MESS WITH YOU. NO DRAMA, WHICH I APPRECIATE. THIS WAS BACK WHEN THE PORN HAD STORIES, SO MOST OF THE MOVIES WERE PRETTY GOOD. WE USUALLY WENT TO MY OLD APARTMENT BACK THEN, BUT ON TWO DIFFERENT OCCASIONS THAT I CAN REMEMBER I TOOK A WORKING GIRL TO THE HAIDA FOR A BLOWJOB. THE ONE I RECALL THE BEST WAS A REAL FRIENDLY BRUNETTE IN A DENIM

JACKET, WITH WHAT LOOKED LIKE A YELLOW DANCERS LEOTARD UNDERNEATH. YOU KNOW, THEY'RE SKINTIGHT. SHE HAD THESE GREAT STILETTO HEELS, AND I'M REALLY INTO LEGS AND SHOES, SO I REMEMBER THOSE FOR SURE. I DON'T REMEMBER WHICH DOUBLE BILL WE SAW, BUT I KNOW WE DIDN'T STAY FOR THE WHOLE THING. SHE HAD TO GET BACK TO WORK, AND I HAD TO GET TO BED. I WAS WORKING LONG HOURS IN CONSTRUCTION BACK THEN."

AT ITS PEAK THE HAIDA SHOWED FIVE DOUBLE BILL SHOWS, SEVEN TIMES A WEEK, WITH A WEEKLY AVERAGE OF 2000 CUSTOMERS, EACH OF WHOM WERE PAYING $5 EACH, OR $9 FOR A COUPLE. IF A BILL DID FEWER THAN 1200 A WEEK, KARTAR AND ANDY WOULD PULL IT AND MOVE ON TO NEWER RELEASES, WHICH WERE SUPPLIED BY STEKO FILMS OUT OF MONTREAL. RECEIPTS I'VE OBTAINED FROM PORN HISTORIAN DIMITRIOS OTIS SHOW THAT KARTAR WAS PAYING STEKO $300 TO $400 TO RENT EACH DOUBLE BILL.

DOUBLE BILLS I SEE NOTED IN THESE RECEIPTS ARE: ECSTACY GIRLS/HERE COMES THE BRIDE, V: THE HOT ONE/THE OTHER SIDE OF JULIE, BAD PENNY/ MONA Q, COMING OF SEKA/SEX ROULETTE, BABY FACE/MORE THAN SISTERS, DESIRES WITHIN YOUNG GIRLS/ NAKED AND FREE, LAURA'S DESIRES/CARNAL GAMES, PUSSYCAT RANCH/ZETA ONE, INSATIABLE/ CONFESSIONS, SENSATIONAL JANINE/PRETTY PEACHES, -- AMONG MANY OTHERS.

ANDY AULAKA, FRESH-FACED PROJECTIONIST OF THE HAIDA THEATER IN 1983.

20 YEARS BEFORE LUSH THEATER VENUES LIKE THE ALAMO CHAIN WERE INSTALLING DELUXE SEATING, VANCOUVER'S HAIDA WAS DOING JUST THAT.

KARTAR WOULD LATER BUY THE FOX PORN THEATER ON MAIN STREET, AND ALSO PURCHASE OUTRIGHT THE 35MM PRINTS OF MANY OF THE FILMS HE'D BEEN RENTING FROM STEKO FILMS. COMPLAINTS FROM PORNOGRAPHERS LIKE CECIL HOWARD BRING UP THE FACT THAT STEKO SELLING OFF THESE MOVIES WAS VERY MUCH AGAINST THE DISTRIBUTION RULES, AS 35MM PRINTS ARE ALWAYS MEANT TO BE RETURNED TO THE ORIGINAL RIGHTS HOLDER OR INDIVIDUAL PRODUCER AFTER THEY COMPLETE THEIR THEATRICAL RUN, AND NOT SIMPLY SOLD OFF TO WHOMEVER MIGHT WANT THEM.

AGAIN, THE DUSTY RECEIPTS I'VE LOOKED AT SHOW THAT THE 1970S AND 1980S ADULT MOVIES WERE SOLD OUTRIGHT IN 1987, FOR $400 A POP. BY 1988, THE PRICE HAD DROPPED TO $250 A FILM, AND KARTAR BOUGHT A SHITLOAD OF THEM. THESE 35MM PRINTS WERE LATER ILLEGALLY DISPOSED OF (TOSSED IN GARBAGE BINS DURING CLANDESTINE NIGHT-TIME RUNS UP AND DOWN THE ALLEYWAYS OF MAIN AND CAMBIE STREET) WHEN THE FOX PORN THEATER WAS SOLD AND RENOVATED INTO A BAR AND LIVE MUSIC VENUE IN 2013. A SCANT FEW WERE RESCUED FROM THE BINS, (STILL IN THEIR LARGE OCTAGONAL STEEL SHIPPING CANISTERS) BY 'THEY LIVE VIDEO' OWNER, BEN JACQUES. EVENTUALLY THEY WERE BOTH SOLD AND GIVEN AWAY TO APPRECIATIVE COLLECTORS WHEN THEY LIVE WENT OUT OF BUSINESS IN 2015.

THE HAIDA PORN THEATER EVENTUALLY SHUT DOWN IN 1991. IN 1992, IT BECAME THE RAJA, AND STARTED SHOWING EAST INDIAN BOLLYWOOD MOVIES TO THE NOW LARGE EAST INDIAN COMMUNITY IN THE AREA. AFTER THAT, IT BECAME A SHORT-LIVED THEATER CALLED THE COLLINGWOOD, AND IN 2013

IT SHUT DOWN FOR GOOD, AND HAS REMAINED EMPTY SINCE THEN.

IN 2015, THE BUILDING WENT UP FOR SALE. THE REALTOR AD READ: "A RARE OPPORTUNITY TO OWN A MOVIE THEATRE! CENTRALLY LOCATED ON KINGSWAY WITH AMPLE TRAFFIC AND EXPOSURE. LOCATED ACROSS FROM SIR GUY CARLETON ELEMENTARY SCHOOL. RENOVATED ABOUT 3 YEARS AGO WITH NEW ROOF, SEATS, FLOORING, DOLBY SOUND SYSTEM, AIR-CONDITIONING AND MUCH MORE. TOTAL 375 SEATS: MAIN LEVEL WITH 300 SEATS AND BALCONY WITH 75 SEATS. LOT 49.59' x 104'14' (5,164 SQFT). CAN BE CONVERTED INTO A PERFORMANCE THEATRE. C-2 ZONING WITH THE POTENTIAL TO DEVELOP INTO CONDO/RETAIL MIX USE. DON'T MISS OUT ON THIS RARE INVESTMENT OPPORTUNITY!"

SO HEY, IF YOU'RE LOOKING TO RUN AN OLD VINTAGE PORN THEATER, THE OLD HAIDA IS READY AND WAITING FOR YOU!

— BOUGIE

CINEMA SEWER'S 30 FAVOURITE FILMS OF 2015

WELL, MY PALS N' GALS -- NO MATTER HOW YOU STACK IT, 2015 WAS A FANTASTIC YEAR FOR MOVIES. BECAUSE NO ONE ASKED, HERE ARE MY PERSONAL FAVOURITES. CHECK OUT THE RELEASES YOU DIDN'T GET A CHANCE TO SEE, AND SEE IF YOU AGREE.

1. Mad Max: Fury Road (Australia/USA)
2. It Follows (USA)
3. Hateful Eight (USA)
4. Turbo Kid (Canada/New Zealand)
5. What Happened Miss Simone? (USA)
6. Chappie (USA)
7. The Look of Silence (Denmark/Indonesia)
8. April and the Extraordinary World (Canada/France)
9. The Seven Five (USA)
10. What We Do in the Shadows (New Zealand)
11. Cop Car (USA)
12. Star Wars: The Force Awakens (USA)
13. Sicario (USA)
14. White God (Sweden)
15. Amy (UK/USA)
16. H. (USA/Argentina)
17. Meru (India/USA)
18. Ex Machina (UK)
19. Circle (USA)
20. Bone Tomahawk (USA)
21. Kingsman: The Secret Service (UK)
22. Nina Forever (UK)
23. The Revenant (USA)
24. When Marnie Was There (Japan)
25. Cartel Land (Mexico/USA)
26. Orion: The Man Who Would Be King (USA)
27. Scherzo Diabolico (Mexico)
28. Spectre (UK)
29. Chuck Norris VS Communism (Romania/UK)
30. A Most Violent Year (USA)

DISAGREE?! PLEASE ALLOW ME THIS REBUTTAL

(JUST KIDDING, KIDS! YOU'RE TOTALLY ALLOWED TO DISAGREE WITH MY LIST!)

SPLAT

OW!

YOU HAVE SHOWN ME THE ERROR OF MY TASTES!

SPOOO

FOOT JOBZ

FEET AREN'T REALLY MY THING, PERSONALLY, BUT I KNOW THEY'RE A VERY FETISHIZED PART OF A WOMAN'S ANATOMY. DON'T YOU THINK IT IS A LITTLE ODD THAT THE "FOOTJOB" IS ALMOST NONEXISTENT IN OUR XXX PORN? I MEAN, ASIDE FROM FOOT FETISH VIDS THAT ARE SPECIFICALLY ABOUT THAT, I'M JUST NOT SEEING IT. CONSIDERING SOME OF THE TRE' WEIRD SHIT THAT IS ROUTINELY PART OF MAINSTREAM SMUT, YOU WOULD THINK THERE WOULD BE ROOM FOR THE OCCASIONAL HARMLESS FOOTIE.

LUBE UP THEM SWEET FOOTSIES, LADIES! I'M WAITIN' FOR YA!

☆☆☆ How's this for a glitch in the matrix? ☆☆☆

FILMED IN 1958, THERE WAS AN EPISODE OF THE AMERICAN TV SERIES "TRACKDOWN" ABOUT A CONMAN NAMED "TRUMP" WHO COMES TO TOWN AND TAKES ADVANTAGE OF THE IGNORANCE OF THE TOWNSFOLK. THE EPISODE HAS A LESSON ABOUT GROUPS OF PEOPLE NEEDING TO BE WEARY OF SNAKE-OIL SALESMEN LYING TO THEM AS THEY WHIP UP FEAR AMONGST THE PUBLIC IN ORDER TO PROFIT AND FILL THEIR OWN POCKETS. AS THE PLOT UNFOLDS, TRUMP CONVINCES THE PEOPLE THAT ONLY HE CAN SAVE THEM, AND IF THEY DON'T BUILD A PROTECTIVE WALL, THE WORLD WILL BE DESTROYED.

Narrator: The people were ready to believe. Like sheep they ran to the slaughterhouse. And waiting for them was the high priest of fraud.

Trump: I am the only one. Trust me. I can build a wall around your homes that nothing will penetrate.

Townperson: What do we do? How can we save ourselves?

Trump: You ask how do you build that wall? You ask, and I'm here to tell you.

THE EPISODE IS CALLED "THE END OF THE WORLD". HOLY FUCK-NUGGETS SO WEIRD.

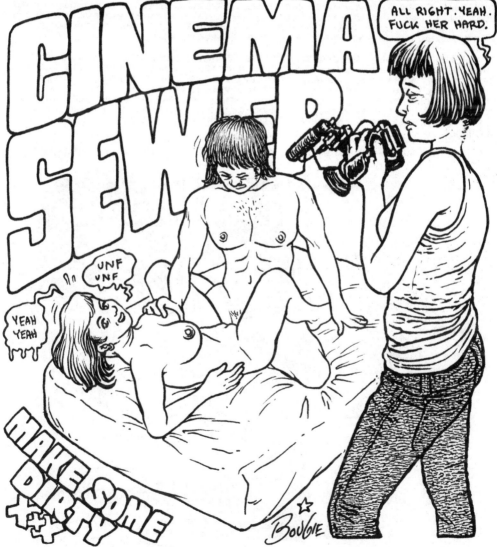

37

POLICE SQUAD: TOO GOOD TO EXIST ON NETWORK TV?

IT'S DUMB, BUT MY FAVE JOKE FROM THE MID 1980S ZUCKER BROS. POLICE SQUAD! SERIES IS:

Captain Ed Hocken: "We sent the ransom note down to the lab for analysis. They want a million dollars"
Detective Frank Drebin: "Where does the lab get off asking for a million dollars?"

IT'S KIND OF INCREDIBLE THAT THIS GREAT SHOW GOT CANCELLED AFTER ONLY 4 EPISODES AND ONLY GOT TO MAKE 6. THE HEAD OF THE NETWORK TOLD ZUCKER/ABRAHAMS/ZUCKER THAT HE FELT THE REASON IT DIDN'T DO WELL IS THAT AUDIENCES ACTUALLY HAD TO PAY ATTENTION AND WATCH IT TO BE ENTERTAINED, WHEREAS THE OTHER POPULAR COMEDIES OF THE ERA COULD JUST BE SOMETHING ON IN THE BACKGROUND. THEY SAY ON THE COMMENTARY TRACK THAT THE THING THAT INFLUENCED THEIR HUMOUR THE MOST WAS THE OLD MAD MAGAZINE COMICS, THE ONES BY WILL ELDER AND HARVEY KURTZMAN. THAT MAKES A LOT OF SENSE.

SPEAKING OF THE ACTOR WHO PLAYED DREBIN, LESLIE NIELSON, HERE'S ANOTHER THOUGHT: WAS NIELSON THE ONLY SINGLE FUCKING PERSON ON EARTH THAT DIDN'T REALIZE HE WAS (PERFECTLY) CAST BY THE ZUCKER BROS BECAUSE HE'S THE QUINTESSENTIAL 'STRAIGHTMAN' – AN ESSENTIAL INGREDIENT OF THEIR STYLE OF HUMOUR? BECAUSE JUDGING BY THE MOVIES HE MADE AFTERWARDS, IT WAS BECAUSE HE THOUGHT HE WAS SOME KIND OF ZANY COMIC GENIUS.

ANOTHER GREAT JOKE EVERY EPISODE WAS HOW THE TITLE CARD PROCLAIMING THE NAME OF THE EPISODE WAS ALWAYS SOMETHING TOTALLY DIFFERENT THAN THE NARRATOR WOULD SAY OUT LOUD. "I WORKED AT ABC DURING THE FINAL PRINT-CHECKING PROCESS", KRIS GILPIN TOLD ME IN 2019. "WE'D ALWAYS MAKE A NOTE ON THE TELECINE PAPERWORK LIKE: 'NOTE: THE TITLE ON THE PRINT WILL NOT MATCH UP WITH THE VOICEOVER, THIS IS NOT A MISTAKE!'. BUT EVERY WEEK THE LAZY OLD GUY IN TELECINE WOULD CALL US UP & FRANTICALLY YELL 'YOU SENT US THE WRONG PRINT!!' AND WE'D ALWAYS YELL BACK, 'READ YOUR PAPERWORK, DAMMIT!'"

AT THE END OF THE DAY, HOWEVER, ZUCKERS AND ABRAHAMS WERE ULTIMATELY RELIEVED THAT THE SHOW WAS CANCELLED. NOT BECAUSE THEY DIDN'T WANT TO KEEP MAKING IT, BUT SIMPLY BECAUSE THEY DIDN'T HAVE THE ABILITY TO KEEP COMING UP WITH ENOUGH QUALITY MATERIAL IN THE TIME ONE IS GRANTED TO PRODUCE CONTENT FOR NETWORK TELEVISION. INSTEAD, A HANDFUL OF YEARS LATER THEY SAVED UP A CINEMATIC-SIZED LOAD OF POLICE SQUAD GAGS, AND RELEASED IT IN THE FORM OF A COUPLE OF NAKED GUN MOVIES (1989 AND 1991), WHICH GAVE US ABSOLUTELY UNFORGETTABLE SCENARIOS – ONE OF WHICH BEING THE AMAZING "CONCRETE PENIS" SEQUENCE.

HERE IT IS, RECREATED FOR YOU BY ONE OF MY FAVOURITE ILLUSTRATORS, DANNY HELLMAN:

THE FUNNIEST SCENE IN THE HISTORY OF CINEMA

BORN ANDREA PARDUCCI IN JANUARY OF 1960, SHE STARTED AS A NUDE MODEL IN 'BIG TIT' MAGS LIKE FLING IN 1979, AND FOUND HER FAME IN THE EARLY 1980S PORN FILM SCENE AS "LITTLE ORAL ANNIE". SO NAMED FOR HER LEGENDARY COCK-SUCKING AND DEEP-THROATING ABILITIES, ANNIE ROSE TO FAME WHEN SHE WAS WIDELY FEATURED IN THE SWEDISH EROTICA LOOP SERIES (WHICH WAS MADE IN CALIFORNIA, NOT SWEDEN) AND FILMS LIKE AUNT PEG GOES HOLLYWOOD (1981), SUCCULENT (1983), INSIDE LITTLE ORAL ANNIE (1984) AND I LIKE TO WATCH (1984). RON JEREMY NOTES THAT ANNIE'S TRICK WAS THAT SHE WOULD PUT A GLOP OF VASELINE ON THE ROOF OF HER MOUTH BEFORE SHE GAVE HEAD, WHICH HE CLAIMS FELT "INCREDIBLE" AND GAVE HER THE ABILITY TO DEEP THROAT FAR MORE VIGOROUSLY.

LATER IN HER ADULT CAREER SHE WOULD APPEAR IN MORE FETISH-THEMED CONTENT, TAKING BOTH DOM AND SUB ROLES IN BDSM VIDEOS, AND WAS REALLY INTO SPANKING AND HAVING HER FLOPPY TITS ROPED UP. SHE ALSO APPEARED IN SOME GODDAMN GREAT 'APARTMENT WRESTLING' (TRACK DOWN THE 2001 TASCHEN 'EXQUISITE MAYHEM' BOOK) AND CATFIGHTING FETISH SERIES FOR COMPANIES LIKE TRIUMPH STUDIOS AND TAO PRODUCTIONS.

ANDREA OFTEN REFERRED TO HERSELF AS "AN ILLUSIONIST", AND MARRIED OLDER MUSICIAN BUDDY OWEN (HIS CAREER IN DO-WOP, COUNTRY AND BLUES GOES BACK TO THE 1950S) WHOM SHE STARTED DATING WHEN SHE WAS ONLY 18. BUDDY FUCKED HER IN FRONT OF THE CAMERAS IN SOME OF THOSE EARLY HARDCORE PORN MAGAZINE LAYOUTS, TOO. TODAY ANDREA IS A BEAUTIFUL VENERABLE HIPPIE LIBERAL WHO SMILES A LOT, AND LIVES IN BOLINAS, CALIFORNIA.

TANGERINE (1979. USA. Dir: Gary Graver)

☆☆☆☆☆☆

An Extraordinary Woman...

Tangerine

...An Unforgettable
Adult Motion Picture
Experience.

A MARK CORBY PRODUCTION

RATED X	Starring CECE MALONE	IN COLOR

☆☆☆☆☆☆

TANGERINE IS A QUIRKY LITTLE PORN FILM. IT WAS MADE IN 1979 BY GARY GRAVER (AS ROBERT MCCALLUM) AND PRODUCER JAY FINEBERG (AS MARK CORBY). IT WAS FINEBERG'S FIRST MOVIE, AND FOR HIS PART GRAVER WOULD GO ON TO MAKE FAR BETTER ADULT MOVIES AND WOULD EVEN GO ON TO WORK AS ORSON WELLES' CINEMATOGRAPHER IN THE HOLLYWOOD LEGEND'S LATER YEARS. IT'S NOT THE BEST VINTAGE AMERICAN XXX MOVIE BY A LONG SHOT, BUT IT IS QUITE WATCHABLE, AND THE STORIES BEHIND THE MAKING OF IT ARE WORTHWHILE.

TANGERINE (JENNIFER WEST, HERE BILLED AS 'CECE MALONE') IS A MYSTERIOUS WOMAN WHO LIVES IN AN ELEGANT HOME BY THE SEA. AS THE FILM OPENS, SHE'S HOSTING A SUNDAY BRUNCH ATTENDED BY IMPECCABLY DRESSED GUESTS AS WELL AS HER THREE DAUGHTERS (PLAYED BY HOLLY MCCALL, LORI BLUE, AND ANGEL DUCHARME). THE FIRST SHOT OF THE MOVIE HAS THE CAMERA SLOWLY PANNING OVER TANGERINE'S CROWDED LIVING ROOM, AND WE EVENTUALLY SEE THAT SHE'S ENTERTAINING HER GUESTS BY JERKING OFF A GERMAN SHEPHERD. IN THE EDIT OF THE MOVIE I'VE SEEN, THIS BIZARRE ACT IS NOT SHOWN GRAPHICALLY, BUT IT'S QUITE OBVIOUS WHAT IS HAPPENING. NEEDLESS TO SAY, WE'RE OFF TO THE RACES HERE. VRoooom.

EACH OF TANGERINE'S LOVELY OVER-SEXED DAUGHTERS ARE PIMPED OUT BY THEIR PERVERSE MOTHER, AND ARE MADE TO SEDUCE CERTAIN MALE GUESTS WHO HAVE THE GREEN STUFF THAT MOMMY WANTS. HOLLY MCCALL (HERE GIVING OFF A STRONG JUDY GARLAND VIBE) IN PARTICULAR IS VERY FUCKING CUTE, AND STEALS THE WHOLE SHOW TO SOME EXTENT. NOT ONLY IS SHE ADORABLE, BUT SHE'S VERY PROUD OF HER LONG, FLAPPY LABIA, AND YANKS ON THEM AND TWISTS THEM AROUND MUCH TO THE DELIGHT OF ONE BEARDED SUITOR (MICHAEL MORRISON) STARING UP FROM HIS POSITION ON THE BATHROOM FLOOR. I GUESS GOOD OL' VERI KNOTTY (AND HER TWISTED, BUT CONGENIAL GENITALS) WASN'T THE ONLY SAUCY ON-SCREEN SLUT WHO COULD PULL OFF THAT TRICK BACK IN THE DAY! HOLLY MCCALL NEEDS MORE PROPS, IF YOU ASK ME. SHE'S BARELY KNOWN AMONGST PORN NERDS, AND THAT NEEDS TO BE RECTIFIED. (OR SHOULD THAT BE ERECTIFIED? I DUNNO. WHATEVER)

PLOT-WISE, THE REAL GOAL HERE IS BLACKMAILING THE HORNY MEN IN EXPENSIVE SUITS WHICH IS HOW TANGERINE MAKES THE SORT OF COIN SHE NEEDS TO LIVE IN A MANSION AND THROW THE SORT OF CLASSY, LAVISH PARTIES YOU WOULD INVITE A GERMAN SHEPHERD TO. YOU WOULD THINK WORD WOULD QUICKLY GET AROUND AMONGST THE FABULOUSLY WEALTHY POLITICIANS AND BUSINESSMEN WHO KEEP FALLING FOR THE EXTORTION SCHEME, BUT MAYBE I'M EXPECTING A LITTLE TOO MUCH REALISM FROM THE PLOT OF THIS LIGHT, SLEAZY FLUFF. AS PUSSY IS BANGED AND BONERS ARE SUCKED, THE ELEGANT "SLEEPY SHORES" BY JOHNNY PEARSON (THE ELDERLY BRITISH COMPOSER WHO LED THE TOP OF THE POPS ORCHESTRA FOR SIXTEEN YEARS) TINKLES ON THE SOUNDTRACK.

THE ACTING IS PRETTY TERRIBLE RIGHT ACROSS THE BOARD, WITH STAR JENNIFER WEST AND THE TUBBY MICHAEL MORRISON BEING THE MOST CRINGEWORTHY OFFENDERS IN MY OPINION. EVEN PERFORMERS LIKE JULIET ANDERSON AND KEN SCUDDER, WHO ARE USUALLY PRETTY RELIABLE, ARE EITHER TOTALLY FLAT OR OVERACT. THE DIALOG IS CHALLENGING AND THESE PERFORMERS JUST SIMPLY AREN'T UP TO THE TASK OF MAKING IT COME OFF IN A BELIEVABLE WAY, ALTHOUGH THE TERRIBLE LINE READING ACTUALLY BECOMES PRETTY ENTERTAINING SIMPLY BY HOW WOODEN IT IS.

JENNIFER WEST WAS A PERENNIAL BEAUTY PAGEANT WINNER IN HER LATE TEENS BACK IN THE 1960S, AND STARTED HER PORN CAREER IN 1975 AT THE AGE OF 28, JUST DOING MAGAZINE LAYOUTS. AS IT OFTEN GOES, SHE THEN GRADUATED TO MAKING XXX FEATURES IN 1976 WHEN THE PRINT WORK DRIED UP. SHE WORKED PRETTY STEADILY UNTIL 1983, AND THEN FOCUSED MORE ON MAGAZINES AGAIN, EXCEPT NOW IT WAS WITH A SPECIAL EMPHASIS ON KINKY BONDAGE SLICKS WHERE SHE WAS BOTH TIED UP, AND PORTRAYING A DOMINANT LEATHER BITCH — DEPENDING ON WHICH MAGAZINE IT HAPPENED TO BE. OFTEN SHE WORKED FOR HARMONY CONCEPTS, A BONDAGE MAGAZINE PUBLISHER RUN BY ROBERT Q HARMON OUT OF A SMALL OFFICE IN VAN NUYS CALIFORNIA. IN MANY FANS' EYES, THIS IS WHERE JENNIFER REALLY EXCELLED DURING HER SMUT CAREER. "JENNIFER WEST WAS THE MOST NATURAL BONDAGE MODEL OF ALL TIME — IT JUST LOOKED RIGHT ON HER", WROTE HARMON ON HIS WEBSITE, WHICH IS AT HARMONYCONCEPTS.COM.

"I SPENT SOME TIME IN JENNIFER DURING THE MAKING OF SUPERWARE PARTY IN 1979.", BILL MARGOLD INFORMED ME WHEN I ASKED HIM ABOUT MISS WEST. "SHE WAS A HAPPY GO LUCKY LADY WHO BROUGHT A CONSIDERABLE AMOUNT OF SINCERE SEXUALITY TO THE SET. A RUMOUR CIRCULATED THAT SHE HAD BEEN A PRO FOOTBALL CHEERLEADER, AND THAT SHE WAS ALSO THE MISTRESS OF A HOLLYWOOD CELEBRITY. SHE WAS ALSO FEATURED AS THE GREEK CHORUS IN ONE OF MY FAVOURITE (AND MOST VILE) PERFORMING ATTRACTIONS: WEEKEND FANTASIES (1980). SHE ALSO RETURNED TO THE SAME HOLLYWOOD HILLS LOCATION TO APPEAR WITH ME IN THE RATHER ODD LOVE GODDESSES (1981)."

"WEST HAD ONE OF THE FUNNIEST, MOST UNFLATTERING PORN NOM DE PLUMES FOR A FEW OF HER MOVIES IN THE NAME 'SALLY BALLGARGLE', CLEARLY GIVEN TO HER BY A TOTALLY WISEASS PRODUCER. "SHE WAS ALSO KNOWN IN SOME CIRCLES, AS THE ORIGINAL BIONIC BIMBO" INDUSTRY VET HART WILLIAMS TOLD ME IN LATE 2014. "THAT WAS BECAUSE OF AN EARLY, BUT PRETTY GOOD BOOB JOB. SHE WAS A HAPPY PERSON, WITH A REAL NAME THAT SOUNDED MORE PORNY THAN HER 'JENNIFER WEST' STAGE NAME."

HOWIE GORDON (AKA RICHARD PACHECO) WASN'T AS PLEASED WITH THE IMPLANTS AS WILLIAMS WAS. MEETING JENNIFER WAS HIS EARLIEST INTRODUCTION TO, WHAT WAS THEN, THE LATEST IN BODY MOD TECHNOLOGY. "I WAS NOT OVERLY IMPRESSED", HE WROTE IN HIS 2013 BOOK, HINDSIGHT. "IT WAS ALL DOWNHILL FROM THERE. THE BREASTS WERE AS HARD AS BASEBALLS AND

JENNIFER WEST

DIDN'T SEEM TO DO TOO MUCH IN THE WAY OF AROUSAL FOR EITHER THE TOUCHER OR THE TOUCHEE. AND THEY JUST DIDN'T MOVE, NOT EVEN IF THE OWNER DID JUMPING JACKS OR STOOD ON HER HEAD."

"(JENNIFER) WAS TALLER THAN ME", RECALLED HOWIE. "WHEN SHE PUT ON HER HIGH HEELS, IT WAS RIDICULOUS. TO COMPENSATE, I HAD TO WEAR PLATFORM SHOES THAT MADE ME FIVE INCHES TALLER. IT WAS LIKE SPENDING THE WHOLE DAY ON STILTS. NO DOUBT BORIS KARLOFF WORE A SIMILAR PAIR WHEN HE PLAYED THE FRANKENSTEIN MONSTER. IT WAS A LOT OF FUN TO BE TALLER, BUT IT SOON TOOK ITS TOLL. AFTER A COUPLE OF HOURS IN THOSE SHOES, MY LEGS WOULD START TO TREMBLE. I WOULD CRAMP UP AND GET SHOOTING PAINS. PERIODICALLY, I WOULD HAVE TO PARACHUTE BACK TO EARTH WHERE I DIDN'T GET NOSEBLEEDS. THERE WAS A SCENE IN THIS MOVIE WHERE (JENNIFER) WAS SUPPOSED TO HAVE SOME KIND OF SEX WITH A DOG. HE WAS A BIG GERMAN SHEPHERD AND HE WAS NOT INTERESTED IN HAVING SEX AT ALL! POOR BASTARD JUST SAT THERE WHIMPERING TO BE SAVED AS SHE STROKED HIS COCK IN A VAIN EFFORT TO AROUSE HIS ARDOR. OH, MAN, THE DOG LOOKED TOWARD HIS MASTER WITH BEGGING IN HIS EYES TO BE FREED FROM THIS INDIGNITY, BUT THE OWNER MADE HIM STAY."

"WE WERE NOT A GREAT COUPLING AND TANGERINE WAS FAR FROM A GREAT MOVIE. I DID ENJOY MEETING HOLLY MCCALL ON THAT ONE. MOSTLY CECE (JENNIFER) SEEMED TO BE INVOLVED WITH THE PRODUCER ALL THE TIME, A GUY NAMED JAY FINEBERG, WHO ACTUALLY WENT TO THE SAME HIGH SCHOOL I DID IN PITTSBURGH. WE SANG THE ALMA MATER ON THE SET. ANYWAY, THOSE TWO WERE ALWAYS HUDDLING IN A CORNER TALKING TO EACH OTHER. I JUST HIT MY MARKS AND DID MY LINES AND GOT THROUGH IT."

Crocodile (1979. Thailand. Directed by Sompote Sands)

GODZILLA PLUS JAWS EQUALS CROCODILE, AND THE PLOT GOES SOMETHING LIKE THIS: A GIANT MUTATED CROCODILE IS CREATED BY ATOMIC FALLOUT AND UNLEASHED UPON MANKIND BY A HURRICANE. A DOCTOR AND A UNIVERSITY PROFESSOR ARE KEEN TO AVENGE THE DEATH OF COUNTLESS VICTIMS, SO THEY MEET UP WITH A BUFF FISHERMAN WHO CAN HELP. HE'S GOT A TATTOO OF A BIG OL' EAGLE ON HIS CHEST, AND HE'S ALSO GOT A FISHING VESSEL THAT THEY CAN USE TO TRACK DOWN THE MONSTER REPTILE.

FROM THE SLIMY DEPTHS OF THE OCEAN... NATURE EXPLODES WITH SAVAGE FURY!

CROCODILE

THE ONLY GOOD PART IS THE CROWDED TOURIST-FILLED VILLAGE GETTING TORN APART BY THE HUGE CROC. I LOVED THE MINIATURES GETTING SMASHED TO PIECES, THE GIANT CROCODILE PUPPET TAIL, MOUTH, AND CLAWS PROVIDING CRAZY CARNAGE, AND ALL THOSE EXTRAS TRYING IN VAIN TO ESCAPE THE COLLAPSING BUILDINGS AS THE MONSTER TEARS THEM INTO BLOODY CHUNKS. THE EFFECTS ARE AWFULLY PRIMITIVE, SURE, BUT IT'S A VERY ENTERTAINING, HIGH-ENERGY, STUNT-FILLED SEQUENCE.. IT'S LIKE THE MOVIE POSTER COME TO LIFE! THAT 7 MINUTE SCENE IS ABOUT AS GOOD AS IT GETS THOUGH, BECAUSE THE REST IS A SLOG. IT'S POORLY DIRECTED, WHILE BEING REALLY BADLY FRAMED, LIT, AND EDITED. THE CROC IS (DEPENDING ON THE EFFECT BEING USED) SOMETIMES THE SIZE OF A HOUSE, AND OTHER TIMES THE SIZE OF A BICYCLE. EVEN SADDER IS THAT DESPITE THE DIRECT PLAGIARISM OF JAWS IN THE FINAL ACT, DIRECTOR SOMPOTE SANDS CAN'T SEEM TO GET HIS SHIT TOGETHER ENOUGH TO GET WHERE HE NEEDS TO GO — EVEN AFTER SPIELBERG HAS PROVIDED HIM WITH A ROADMAP, A FULL TANK OF GAS, AND A DRIVER. DID OUR HEROES DEFEAT THE CREATURE? DID ANYONE SURVIVE? I HAVE NO FUCKING CLUE. WHAT A MESS.

THE PASSION OF JOHN RAMBO

✝✝✝✝ BY JOSH SIMMONS ✝✝✝✝✝✝✝✝✝

"IF THE WORLD HATES YOU, REMEMBER THAT IT HATED ME FIRST."

RAMBO AND THE PASSION OF THE CHRIST MAKE A SPECTACULAR AND PUNISHING DOUBLE BILL FOR THE CURRENTLY UNFOLDING SUPREME ANXIETY ERA.

THE PASSION OF THE CHRIST CAME OUT IN 2004 TO A GOOD AMOUNT OF CONTROVERSY REGARDING ITS DEPICTION OF JEWISH PEOPLE AND WAAAYYY OVER-THE-TOP VIOLENCE. DIRECTED BY MEL GIBSON, IT IS PRIMARILY CONCERNED WITH THE FINAL 12 HOURS OF JESUS CHRIST'S LIFE. IN THE FIRST HOUR OR SO HE CHILLS IN A GARDEN AT NIGHT AND TALKS TO GOD, IS CAPTURED AND PUT ON TRIAL; WE ALSO GET A SMATTERING OF GUEST APPEARANCES BY SATAN AND DEMONS, AS WELL AS SOME VIOLENCE. IN THE 2ND HOUR, WE GET THE LURID AND EXPLICIT TORTURE AND DISASSEMBLAGE OF A HUMAN BEING TO RIVAL CANNIBAL HOLOCAUST. GOD IS A HUGE PAIN FREAK, APPARENTLY.

IN 2008'S RAMBO, CO-WRITTEN, DIRECTED BY AND STARRING SYLVESTER STALLONE, THE TITULAR CHARACTER IS LIVING IN THAILAND ON THE BORDER WITH MYANMAR. RAMBO AND A BUNCH OF MERCENARIES JOURNEY INTO MYANMAR TO RESCUE A GROUP OF CHRISTIAN AID WORKERS FROM A MURDEROUS ARMY. MAYHEM ENSUES, HUNDREDS ARE ANNIHILATED AND RAMBO SAVES THE DAY IN HIS INIMITABLE MANNER (THAT IS, BY SLAUGHTERING DOZENS OF HUMAN BEINGS).

WATCHING THE ROYALTY OF THE 1980s AMERICAN DREAM MACHINE SPIRAL INTO WEIRDNESS, DEPRAVITY AND SCANDAL HAS BEEN ONE OF THE ODD CONSTANTS OF THE INTERNET AGE. AS CULTURE AND ATTENTION SPANS HAVE BECOME MERCILESSLY FRAGMENTED BY THE WEB, WE'VE SEEN THE LIKES OF BILL COSBY AND MICHAEL JACKSON CRASH AND BURN IN SPECTACULAR, SICKENING FASHION. GIBSON HAS GOTTEN OFF RELATIVELY EASY IN COMPARISON, WITH HIS ALCOHOL-INDUCED RACIST AND MISOGYNISTIC TIRADES. STALLONE EASIEST OF ALL, WITH HIS ARREST FOR BRINGING HUMAN GROWTH HORMONE INTO AUSTRALIA PREVIOUS TO FILMING RAMBO BEING THE BIGGEST (SUBSTANTIATED) STAIN ON HIS REPUTATION.

STILL, ON THE ONE HAND WE HAVE THE DISCONNECT FROM CONVENTIONAL LIFE OF BEING MEGA FAMOUS AND WEALTHY PUSHING SUPEREGOS INTO KOO-KOO LAND. COMBINE THAT WITH DECENT BUDGETS AND A CERTAIN AMOUNT OF CYNICAL PANDERING TO AUDIENCE EXPECTATIONS AND WHAT WAS TRENDY AT THE TIME IN FILMMAKING, AND IN THESE TWO MOVIES WE GET SOMETHING CLOSER TO EXPERIMENTAL, CULT CINEMA THAN WHAT THESE TWO WERE KNOWN FOR IN THE 1980s AND '90s. THESE MOVIES ARE WONKERS.

ON THE BRITISH TALK SHOW PARKINSON IN 2007, GIBSON INTRODUCED HIS ALTER EGO, BJÖRN. HIS CRAZED SIDE, HE SAID BJÖRN CAME OUTA LOT IN HIS 20s. HE WENT ON TO EXPLAIN THAT DOCTORS HAD RECENTLY DISCOVERED THAT HE HAS A RARE CONDITION WHERE HIS KIDNEYS ARE FUSED INTO ONE, HORSE SHOE-SHAPED SUPER KIDNEY. LOOKING WIDE-EYED CRAZED AND DOWNRIGHT RIGGS-IAN, GIBSON BLAMED THIS FOR THE

MANIC ENERGY HE OFTEN DISPLAYED IN HIS YOUTH, ALTHOUGH A MORE RECENT DIAGNOSIS OF MANIC DEPRESSION MIGHT HAVE MORE TO DO WITH IT. EITHER WAY, HE WENT TO GREAT LENGTHS TO DROWN OUT HIS MANIA WITH ALCOHOL, WHICH IN PART LEAD TO HIS SCANDALS JUST A FEW YEARS LATER. AT ANY RATE, THIS ALL CLEARLY HELPED CONTRIBUTE TO HIS BI-POLAR/GOD FREAK/SOBER GUY/OCD/DEATH-OBSESSED LEANINGS AS A FILM-MAKER, FOR WHICH I AM GRATEFUL!

SYLVESTER STALLONE ON THE OTHER HAND, HAS BEEN KNOWN POST-COITUS, TO REFER TO THE SEX ACT AS THE "BAM HAM SLAM."

IN THE POST-MATRIX AND POST-HOSTEL MOVIE LAND OF THE '00S, BOTH FILMS HAVE THE STRIPPED DOWN COLOR PALETTE AND FETISHISTIC FOCUS ON VIOLENCE AND GORE. RAMBO HAS THE SHAKY CAM HYPER CRISP DIGITAL LOOK, PASSION HAS THE WEIRD SLO-MO BULLET TIME OF THE MATRIX, WHICH ADDS TO THE OFF-PUTTING AND DISCORDANT QUALITIES IN THIS TELLING OF THE JESUS STORY.

BOTH FILMS FEATURE PSYCHOTIC VIOLENCE, LOVINGLY PHOTOGRAPHED LIKE A LURIDLY SATURATED SPREAD FROM A 1980S ISSUE OF FANGORIA. RAMBO MOSTLY FEATURES CGI GORE, BUT PUT TO SUCH SPECTACULAR USE AS SEEING AN ENTIRE TRUCKBED FULL OF HUMAN BEINGS DISINTEGRATE INTO A BLOODY MIASMA DUE TO JOHN RAMBO'S HEAVY MACHINE GUN FIRE. PASSION HAS FANTASTIC OLD SCHOOL PROSTHETIC EFFECTS COMBINED WITH CGI, CREATING IN OUR NEW MILLENNIUM'S JESUS A FLAYED MONSTER TO RIVAL DRACULA AND FREDDY.

IN KEEPING WITH THE TRADITION OF SO MUCH AMERICAN-MADE ENTERTAINMENT, BOTH FILMS ARE PRETTY MUCH SEX-LESS. IN THESE MOVIES, THE VIOLENCE IS THE SEX. OR THE SEX IS SUBLIMATED SO HARD IT SURFACES IN THE PER-VERT VILLAINS. IN BOTH THESE FILMS (AS WELL AS IN GIBSON'S OTHER DIRECTORIAL EFFORTS), THE VILLAINS ARE DEPICTED AS SEXUAL DEVIANTS, CODED AS DECADENT HOMOSEXUALS ON ONE END, IF NOT DEPRAVED PEDOPHILES ON THE OTHER. IN RAMBO, THE LEADER OF THE CORRUPT ARMY IS SHOWN TO HAVE A PASSION FOR BOYS. IN PASSION, KING HEROD WEARS MAKE UP AND IS FLAMBOYANT.

THEN THERE'S PASSION'S SATAN, THE ULTIMATE ANDROGYNOUS SEX BEAST. COOLER THAN BOWIE. MAYBE THE SEXIEST DEPICTION OF SATAN IN FILM EVER, REVEALING GIBSON'S SUBCONSCIOUS LONGING AS WITH 2015'S THE WITCH, THE SATAN TRAIN IS SHOWN TO BE THE MOST FREEING AND FUN TRAIN ON THE TRACKS. HOP ON BOARD AND SIGN ME UP!

THE FOCUS AND TONE OF BOTH FILMS IS CLOSER TO THE NOISE DRONE OF POWER ELEC-TRONICS BANDS LIKE WHITEHOUSE THAN THE KIND OF CROWD-PLEASING PRODUCTIONS STALLONE AND GIBSON WERE PREVIOUSLY KNOWN FOR. YET THEY ADHERE PRETTY FAITH-FULLY TO THE BELOVED COWBOY AESTHETIC AND "RUGGED INDIVIDUALIST" OF SO MUCH AMER-ICAN-MADE CINEMA. TOGETHER THEY MAKE FOR A FANTASTIC EVENING'S DOUBLE BILL CONCOCTION OF SADISM AND MASOCHISM, BEAUTIFULLY DESIGNED TO PUMMEL THE MODERN AMERICAN PSYCHE, EMBEDDED, CURLED UP AND TERRIFIED, INSIDE A DISINTEGRATING EMPIRE.

THEY'RE A SADOMASOCHIST'S WET DREAM; RAMBO FULFILLS THE SADISTIC SIDE, AND PASSION IN-DULGES IN GIBSON'S LONGING TO BE WHIPPED INTO AN ECSTATIC STATE. RAMBO WILL PROVIDE THE CHEAP AND NASTY JOLT TO YOUR LIZARD BRAIN. PASSION IS OSTENSIBLY ABOUT A CHRIST-IAN GOD AND SALVATION FOR SINNERS AND MANKIND OR WHATEVER, BUT LET'S BE HONEST, IT'S REALLY ABOUT ROLLING AROUND IN VISCERA AND NAILING YOUR CONTROL FREAK ALCOHOLIC TENDENCIES DOWN INTO A WORK OF ART FOR THE WORLD TO CONSUME. PLOP THEM ONTO YOUR FLAT SCREEN TV AND TRAUMATISE YOURSELF INTO SUBMISSION WITH THESE TWO NUTSO, WELL-CRAFTED, HYPER-VIOLENT POP FANTASIAS. YES, FRIENDS, MAKE YOURSELF NICE AND NUMB FOR THE COMING NEW DARK AGE.

JHS 2016

SONS AND MOTHERS (1972)

Director: Roman Nicholson

(Sam Weston aka Samuel Weinstein aka Anthony Spinelli)

Review and ad-mats supplied by: Martin Brooks

PUNNINGLY-TITLED AFTER D. H. LAWRENCE'S NOVEL SONS AND LOVERS, SAM WESTON'S SONS AND MOTHERS IS A PSEUDO 'WHITE-COATER' PORTRAYING A SERIES OF DISPARATE HETEROSEXUAL COUPLINGS, ALL STITCHED TOGETHER THROUGH A NARRATIVE PLACEHOLDER IN THE FORM OF A GROUP THERAPY ENCOUNTER. A SIMILAR CINEMATIC TROPE WAS ALSO USED BY WESTON IN ANOTHER FILM HE MADE IN 1972 ENTITLED MEMOIRS OF A MADAM.

BORN IN CLEVELAND, OHIO AS SAMUEL WEINSTEIN, SAM WESTON WAS THE YOUNGER BROTHER OF VERSATILE ACTOR JACK WESTON AND PRODUCED HIS FIRST FILM IN 1958 — THE UNITED ARTISTS' WESTERN GUN FEVER. HE PLAYED BIT PARTS IN A NUMBER OF TV SERIES UNTIL WESTON AND HIS DIRECTOR-FRIEND LARRY PEERCE MADE THE ACCLAIMED RACIAL DRAMA ONE POTATO, TWO POTATO IN 1964, AFTER WHICH HE ENDED UP SELLING ENCYCLOPEDIAS DOOR-TO-DOOR. IN 1971 HE WATCHED A 16MM XXX FEATURE ON HIS SALES' ROUND AND DECIDED HE COULD DO BETTER, MAKING HIS FIRST HARDCORE FEATURE DIARY OF A NYMPH. ONE OF THE MOST ACCLAIMED DIRECTORS OF THE GOLDEN AGE, WESTON MADE OVER 120 ADULT FILMS BEFORE HIS DEATH FROM PNEUMONIA AT THE AGE OF 73 IN 2000.

AN ORIGINAL ACOUSTIC SIGNATURE SONG, 'SONS AND MOTHERS', PLAYS OVER THE TITLE CREDITS, JARRINGLY JUXTAPOSED AGAINST AN ANIMALISTIC SEX-ORGY WHERE ALL THE PARTICIPANTS WEAR ANIMAL MASKS AND FERAL SCREECHING AND GRUNTING NOISES BLAST OUT FROM THE SOUNDTRACK. WE EVENTUALLY CUT TO A WHEELCHAIR-BOUND PSYCHOTHERAPIST (THE SAME ACTOR ALSO APPEARED IN WESTON'S THE LOVER AKA THE TRAINING OF BONNIE, WITH BRIGITTE MAIER), WHO EXTOLS THE POSITIVE EFFECTS OF ENCOUNTER GROUP THERAPY ON SEXUAL NEUROSES. HE INTRODUCES THE FIRST COUPLE UNDER THE PROBLEM MICROSCOPE: JOHN AND MARY ALEXANDER, A MIXED RACE MARRIED COUPLE.

JOHN CAN ONLY GET IN THE SWING OF THINGS BY BEING RACIALLY ABUSED AND DOMINATED BY HIS BLACK WIFE (THE 'SHAFT' INSTRUMENTAL PLAYS ON THE SOUNDTRACK). HE ALSO LIKES TO SNIFF COWBOY BOOTS, FANTASIZE ABOUT HIS WIFE WITH OTHER MEN AND WEAR LADIES' BLOOMERS OVER HIS PANTS! HE LATER REVEALS TO THE GROUP THAT HE'S A LATENT HOMOSEXUAL. DUO NUMBER TWO COMPRISES OF JOSEPH AND JOANNE SCHERING (PLAYED BY KINKY RED BOOTS HERSELF, NINA FAUSE). AGAIN, THE MALE SIDE OF THIS RATHER STRAINED RELATIONSHIP HAS ISSUES. JOSEPH WOULD RATHER WATCH THE BALL GAME THAN TEND TO HIS WIFE'S CARNAL CRAVINGS, THINKING HER SEXUAL IDEAS ARE DISGUSTING. THIS SEQUENCE FEATURES SOME CLEVER EDITING: JOANNE FANTASIZES THAT THEY ARE IN SEXUALLY EXPLICIT CONGRESS, BUT THE REALITY IS QUITE THE OPPOSITE. THE FILM CUTS BACKWARDS AND FORWARDS BETWEEN HER IMAGINATION AND STARK ACTUALITY.

THE FINAL TWOSOME IS AN ALCOHOLIC HUSBAND AND HIS SUFFERING PARTNER (RICK AND CAROL SPINELLI). HE'S A BRUTE WHO ROUGH-HOUSES HIS WIFE INTO ONE-SIDED DRUNKEN SEX. NOTE THE SURNAME USED FOR THE CHARACTERS HERE, WESTON REUSED IT FOR HIS DIRECTORIAL MONIKER FROM A PORTRAIT OF SEDUCTION (1976) ONWARDS.

THIS IS A RARITY, AND SADLY THE VERSION USED FOR THIS REVIEW HAD A MUDDY VISUAL QUALITY AND SUFFERED FROM ECHOEY SOUND THROUGHOUT. IT ALSO APPEARED TO BE HEAVILY TRUNCATED WITH AN EARLIER SEQUENCE REPEATED AT THE END, PROBABLY JUST TO PAD OUT THE RUNNING TIME. IF IT SOUNDS LIKE THERE'S NO APPARENT REASON IT'S ACTUALLY CALLED SONS & MOTHERS, TAKE NOTE THAT THE CREDITS HAVE "LADY ELENORE SPENCER AS THE MOTHER", AND THE VERSION I VIEWED WAS MISSING THAT CHARACTER AND THAT STORY ELEMENT ENTIRELY.

REGARDLESS, THIS IS AN ENTERTAINING HIDDEN GEM IN WESTON'S EARLY STOREFRONT FILM PORTFOLIO.

ADDITIONAL MUSIC FEATURED:
THE BLUES MAGOOS - MAGOO'S BLUES
RAYMOND LEFEVRE - TIME ALONE WILL TELL
WAGNER'S THE RIDE OF THE VALKYRIES

THIS IS MARTIN BROOKS' FIRST TIME CONTRIBUTING TO C.S! THANKS FOR JOINING IN, PAL!

AND NOW: HOW ABOUT A LITTLE COMIC?

— BOUGIE '18

ON THE RECORD!!

with AARON LANG

EWOK CELEBRATION, 1983
MECO (MECO MONARDO)

DISCO FEVER MET THE **STAR WARS** FLU IN 1977, WHEN SYNTH-POP IMPRESARIO MECO RELEASED HIS SOON-TO-BE PLATINUM RECORD, **STAR WARS AND OTHER GALACTIC FUNK**. THE SPACE DISCO SINGLE, **STAR WARS THEME/CANTINA BAND**, SPENT TWO WEEKS AT NUMBER ONE AND MECO WOULD SPEND MUCH OF HIS CAREER CHASING THIS HIGH LIKE A WANING COCAINE RUSH. HE RETURNED IN 1980 WITH THE OBSCURE 10" **MECO PLAYS MUSIC FROM THE EMPIRE STRIKES BACK** AND **CHRISTMAS IN THE STARS: STAR WARS CHRISTMAS ALBUM**. HOT ON THE HEELS OF **RETURN OF THE JEDI**, DESPITE A MORIBUND DISCO SCENE, MECO RETURNED WITH **EWOK CELEBRATION** IN 1983. THE TITULAR SONG, POPULARLY KNOWN AS **'YUB NUB'** RANKS AS ONE OF THE

STRANGEST IN WHAT IS A LONG LIST OF **STAR WARS** NOVELTY RECORDINGS, CULMINATING IN THE 'EWOK RAP' PERFORMED BY HIP-HOP LEGEND DUKE BOOTEE. TRACK TWO IS A WEIRD RENDITION OF **LAPTI NEK** WITH THE 'HUTTESE SOLO' BY CHIC BACK UP SINGER DIVA GRAY. THE A-SIDE'S THIRD AND FINAL TRACK IS A MEDLEY OF MECO-IZED THEMES FROM **STAR WARS**. THE B-SIDE CONTAINS VARIOUS MECO RENDITIONS OF '80s FILM AND TELEVISION SCORES INCLUDING **MANIAC**, FROM **FLASHDANCE**, FEATURING A YOUNG KENNY G ON SAX. YOU'LL EASILY RECOGNIZE THIS DISC IN ODDITY AND DOLLAR BINS BY ITS OFF PUTTING COVER ART— A BACKLIT EWOK PAW HOLDING UP A CHAMPAGNE FLUTE IN A TOAST TO THE STARS. ON THE BACK YOU'LL SEE TEXT FROM MECO HIMSELF, WISHING 'TO AKNOWLEDGE THE UNFAILING COOPERATION OF THE GALACTIC COUNCIL, IN PARTICULAR THE TELE-CON DTZ 88.4, CLY VE2 DAY VIS.' LAPTI NEK INDEED!

STARMAN, 1984
JACK NITZSCHE

JOHN CARPENTER'S LOW KEY ROMANTIC SCI-FI ADVENTURE, **STARMAN**, ISN'T AS CELEBRATED AS HIS OTHER FILMS

(CONT.)

LIKE **HALLOWEEN** AND **THE THING**, BUT IT HAS STOOD THE TEST OF TIME WELL. THE FILM'S APPEAL RESTS CHIEFLY ON THE CHEMISTRY OF ITS TWO STARS. JEFF BRIDGES PLAYS A STRANDED ALIEN AND RECEIVED AN ACADEMY AWARD NOMINATION FOR HIS EFFORTS, AND DIMPLE-CHINNED FRECKLE-FACED KAREN ALLEN BROUGHT HER TOMBOY CHARMS TO THE ROLE OF JENNY. ROMANCE IS SELDOM EMOTIONALLY RESONANT IN GENRE FILMS, BUT **STARMAN** AND **THE FLY** ARE TWO NOTABLE EXCEPTIONS FROM THE DECADE. BRIDGES AND ALLEN ARE GIVEN AN ABLE ASSIST BY THE SIMPLE YET ROUSING SYNTH SCORE BY JACK NITZSCHE. NITZSCHE BEGAN HIS CAREER WITH PHIL SPECTOR AND EVENTUALLY MOVED ON TO WORK CLOSELY AS A KEYBOARD PLAYER FOR THE ROLLING STONES AND NEIL YOUNG. THE '70s WERE DIFFICULT FOR NITZSCHE AS HE WAS PLAGUED WITH DEPRESSION AND SUBSTANCE ABUSE DEMONS. IN 1979 NITZSCHE BROKE INTO THE HOME OF NEIL YOUNG'S FORMER GIRLFRIEND, ACTRESS CARRIE SNODGRESS (WHOM NITZSCHE HIMSELF HAD BEGUN SEEING) AND

RAPED HER WITH THE BARREL OF A GUN. NITZSCHE WAS ABLE TO WORK HIS VOODOO AND WIGGLE OUT OF THE CHARGES, BUT HIS ROCK AND ROLL DAYS WERE BEHIND HIM. HE SOLDIERED ON SUCCESSFULLY IN A CAREER SCORING FILMS. HIS MAIN THEME TO **STARMAN** DRIVES LIKE AN UNHOLY SYNTH-WAGNER AND SERVES AS AN EXCELLENT RESPONSE TO JOHN WILLIAMS ANODYNE SCORE TO THE SIMILARLY THEMED **E.T.** FROM TWO YEARS PRIOR. THE B-SIDE OF THE RECORD OPENS WITH NITZSCHE'S SCORE BUT QUICKLY TAKES A LEFT TURN INTO BRIDGES AND ALLEN'S DUET OF **ALL I HAVE TO DO IS DREAM**. THIS NUMBER REMINDS ME OF ALLEN'S TURN IN **ANIMAL HOUSE** AS KATY AND HER STONED, GIGGILY DUET WITH 'BOON' OF **HEY PAULA**. KAREN ALLEN IS TOPS AND I WISH SHE HAD BROUGHT HER WIDE TOOTHPASTE-COMMERCIAL-SMILE TO MORE FILMS. ON AN END NOTE, IN THE 1990s JACK NITZSCHE APPEARED ON AN EPISODE OF THE TELEVISION PROGRAM **COPS** FOLLOWING AN INCIDENT WHERE HE DRUNKENLY BRANDISHED A GUN. ALL WE HAVE TO DO IS DREAM.

HALLOWEEN III: SEASON OF THE WITCH, 1982 (REISSUED 2014) JOHN CARPENTER AND ALAN HOWARTH

LIKE THE **HALLOWEEN** FRANCHISE ITSELF, VINYL RECORDS REFUSE TO DIE- SALES ARE THE HIGHEST THEY'VE BEEN IN DECADES. A SMALL POR-TION IS DUE TO THE NICHE OF FILM SOUNDTRACKS REISSUED IN DELUXE EDITIONS. **DEATH WALTZ** IS CERTAINLY A LEADER IN THIS FIELD AND THEIR CANDY-ORANGE-COLORED RELEASE OF **HALLOWEEN III** SERVES AS AN EXCELLENT EXAMPLE OF THEIR WORK. REMASTERED AND FEATURING SIX UNUSED CUES, THE RECORD ALSO COMES WITH A POSTER AND SLIM BOOK WITH LINER NOTES. THRILL TO THE ALCOHOLIC GRUMBLINGS OF TOM ATKINS AS HE BATTLES AN OCCULT IRISH TOY MANUFACTURER. THIS HEAD-ACHE INDUCING DENTIST DRILL OF A SOUNDTRACK WILL HAVE YOU SINGING "HAPPY, HAPPY HALLOWEEN" UNTIL SNAKES AND BUGS POUR OUT YOUR EARS. [AL]

TOM ATKINS DIET

25 UNDER APPRECIATED HORROR SEQUELS

BY DAVID HINDS

SEQUELS, BY DEFINITION, ARE INFERIOR TO THEIR ORIGINATORS. THEY ARE DESIGNED TO IMITATE THE ORIGINAL CONCEPT WHILST ADDING A FEW NEW WRINKLES TO THE FORMULA TO AVOID COMPLETE REPETITION, BUT STILL DRAW IN THE SAME CROWD. IF A MOVIE GENERATES A HANDSOME PROFIT AT THE BOX OFFICE, OR ON HOME VIDEO, IT STANDS TO REASON THAT PRODUCERS WITH DOLLAR SIGNS FLASHING IN THEIR EYES WILL ATTEMPT TO RECREATE THAT SUCCESS BY OFFERING MORE OF THE SAME.

THE LONGER A FRANCHISE RUNS, THE SILLIER, AND OFTEN CHEAPER, THE INSTALMENTS BECOME UNTIL THEY REACH SELF-PARODY. THE FRIDAY THE 13TH AND A NIGHTMARE ON ELM STREET FRANCHISES ARE GOOD EXAMPLES WITH THE DREADFUL FREDDY'S DEAD AND JASON X. WHEN IT COMES TO ART VERSUS COMMERCE, BY THEIR VERY DEFINITION, SEQUELS FALL INTO THE LATTER. TAKING THIS INTO ACCOUNT, IT'S EASY TO SEE WHY HIGHBROW CRITICS DESPISE SEQUELS, BUT THE BOTTOM LINE FOR ME IS SIMPLE: IS IT ENTERTAINING? DID THIS MOVIE KICK MY ASS? ANYTHING ELSE IS SEQUEL SNOBBERY.

THE HORROR GENRE HAS BECOME SYNONYMOUS WITH SEQUELS AND FRANCHISES, AND THE 1980S WAS THE GOLDEN ERA OF THE SEQUEL. THIS IS THE DECADE THAT SAW FREDDY KRUEGER, JASON VORHEES AND MICHAEL MYERS TAKE ON CELEBRITY STATUS AND TERRIFY AUDIENCES AROUND THE GLOBE, AND I'VE ALWAYS FOUND SOME COMFORT KNOWING THERE'S ANOTHER HALLOWEEN OR PUPPET MASTER SEQUEL IN THE WORKS. I _LOVE_ SEQUELS AND WILL ALWAYS FIGHT THE GOOD FIGHT IN THEIR DEFENCE.

FOR THIS ARTICLE I WANT TO HIGHLIGHT A SELECTION OF SEQUELS THAT HAVE BEEN UNDESERVEDLY SHUNNED OVER THE YEARS. YOU WON'T FIND EVIL DEAD II, DAWN OF THE DEAD OR ALIENS IN THE REVIEWS BELOW, BECAUSE THOSE ARE CLASSICS THAT HAVE EARNED AN INCREDIBLE AMOUNT OF RESPECT AND ADULATION ALREADY. NO, THESE ARE 25 MOVIES THAT DESERVE GREATER RECOGNITION AND RESPECT, AND I'M HERE TO ENCOURAGE BOTH NEW FANS AND THOSE WHO HAVE SEEN THEM ALREADY TO GIVE THEM ANOTHER CHANCE. HOORAY FOR REPETITION!

Amityville II: The Possession (1982, Dir. Damiano Damiani)

FEW THEATRICAL HORROR SEQUELS ARE AS DELIBERATELY SICK AND DOWNBEAT AS AMITYVILLE II. NOT ONLY IS THIS A GREAT SEQUEL, IT'S ACTUALLY BETTER THAN THE FIRST FILM, WHICH SUFFERS FROM POOR PACING AND A TEDIOUS FINAL HALF HOUR. CREEPING STEADICAM PHOTOGRAPHY AND LALO SCHIFRIN'S HAUNTING SCORE HELP TO CREATE A MENACING, EERIE ATMOSPHERE AS WE WITNESS A TEENAGE BOY BECOME POSSESSED BY DEMONIC FORCES. THE SEQUENCE WHERE HE STALKS FROM ROOM TO ROOM, MURDERING HIS FAMILY, IS SUPERBLY EXECUTED FOR MAXIMUM TENSION BY DIRECTOR DAMIANO DAMIANI. THROW IN SCENES OF INCEST, DOMESTIC ABUSE, ATTEMPTED RAPE, DEMONIC POSSESSION, WEIRD BODY HORROR AND SOME GRUESOME SPLATTER AND YOU'VE GOT A DOWNRIGHT NASTY TREAT WHICH IS EASILY THE BEST THIS FRANCHISE HAS TO OFFER. BURT YOUNG'S (PAULIE IN THE ROCKY FILMS) PERFORMANCE IS OUTSTANDING AS THE GREASY, ABUSIVE FATHER.

Blair Witch (2016, Dir. Adam Wingard)

AFTER THE PEDESTRIAN BLAIR WITCH 2: BOOK OF SHADOWS I CAN'T SAY I HELD MUCH HOPE FOR ADAM (YOU'RE NEXT) WINGARD'S NEW INSTALMENT. I WAS WRONG. WHEREAS THE FIRST BLAIR WITCH PROJECT IS ABOUT A GROUP OF PEOPLE GETTING LOST IN THE WOODS AND ARGUING IN THE WOODS, THIS SEQUEL IS ESSENTIALLY ABOUT A GROUP OF PEOPLE BEING CHASED THROUGH THE WOODS AND SCREAMING FOR THEIR LIVES. THE CRISP HI-DEF PHOTOGRAPHY AND THE ADDITION OF A RAINSTORM GENERATE A GROWING SENSE OF UNEASE. I HAD A GENUINE SENSE OF DREAD EVERY TIME THE CAMERA MOVED TO POTENTIALLY REVEAL SOMETHING OUT IN THE DARKNESS. THE USE OF A DRONE-CAM IS ALSO AN INTERESTING TOUCH HERE. WINGARD'S FILM IS SERIOUS AND FAST PACED AND THE SHOCKS ARE EXPERTLY TIMED. GLIMPSES OF HORRIBLE THINGS IN THE WOODS LINGER LONG AFTER THE CREDITS HAVE ROLLED. THIS IS A VERY EFFECTIVE, FRIGHTENING EXPERIENCE. ENSURE YOU CRANK UP THE VOLUME AND SWITCH OFF THE LIGHTS FOR MAXIMUM IMPACT.

Bride of Frankenstein (1935, Dir. James Whale)

ALTHOUGH THIS HORROR CLASSIC ISN'T CRITICALLY UNLOVED, IT ALWAYS SURPRISES ME HOW MANY MODERN HORROR FANS STILL HAVEN'T ACTUALLY SEEN IT. ITS VINTAGE MIGHT PUT OFF SOME CONTEMPORARY VIEWERS BUT THIS IS ESSENTIAL VIEWING AND WAY AHEAD OF ITS TIME. WITH ITS FAST PACING, GREAT PERFORMANCES, PERVERSE CONCEPT AND ICONIC IMAGERY THERE IS PLENTY TO ENJOY HERE. BORIS KARLOFF, WHO SWEATED OFF 20 POUNDS DUE TO THE HEAVY MAKE-UP, ALSO DISLOCATED HIS HIP DURING THE INFAMOUS WINDMILL SCENE. ELSA LANCHESTER'S ICONIC HAIRDO HAD TO BE KEPT IN SHAPE BY A WIRE HORSEHAIR CAGE AND SHE REMAINED TRUSSED IN BANDAGES FOR DAYS, AND THANKS TO HER FINGERS BEING TIGHTLY WRAPPED-- SHE COULDN'T EVEN FEED HERSELF. WHEN THE FILM WAS PREVIEWED IN APRIL 1935, AUDIENCES WERE SHOCKED. THE FILM'S PRODUCER CARL LAEMMLE, JR. IMPOSED EXTENSIVE RE-EDITING TO TONE DOWN THE MORE EXCESSIVE ELEMENTS, WITH SEVERAL SCENES DELETED IN THEIR ENTIRETY AND MANY OTHERS TRIMMED. THE BODY COUNT WAS REDUCED FROM 21 ON-SCREEN DEATHS TO ONLY 10. THE EXCISED FOOTAGE HAS NEVER BEEN SEEN SINCE.

Captured For Sex 2 (1986, Dir. Gô Ijuuin)

THIS EXTREMELY RARE AND UNFORGETTABLE TORTURE THEMED S+M SICKIE FROM JAPAN IS ONE OF THE MOST DERANGED SLEAZE FILMS EVER MADE AND CATALOGUES AN ASTONISHING ASSORTMENT OF SEXUAL DEPRAVITY AND TORTURE. SORDID DELIGHTS ON OFFER HERE INCLUDE SOME KINKY CULINARY DELIGHTS, HOT WAX AND NEEDLE TORTURE, PUBIC SHAVING, AN ENEMA, FETISHY FLAGELLATION, SEVERAL RAPES, FORCED LESBIANISM AND AN UNFORGETTABLE SCENE IN WHICH A WOMAN IS FORCED TO EXPEL RED WINE AND MARBLES FROM HER ANUS. THEN COMES THE TRULY AWE-INSPIRING FINALE IN WHICH THREE WOMEN ARE TORTURED BY FIRE WHILST BOUND IN GIANT ROPE COBWEBS THAT MUST BE AMONGST THE MOST ELABORATE ROPE BINDING TO BE SEEN IN A JAPANESE FETISHFLICK. THIS CREEPY AND INTENSE LITTLE HORROR-PINKU HYBRID IS A MUST SEE FOR ANYONE INTERESTED IN THE DARKER SIDE OF ASIAN CINEMA. ALL KNOWN PRINTS CONTAIN OPTICAL BLURRING TO OBSCURE GRAPHIC GENITAL CLOSE-UPS AND PENETRATION. THE CREDITED DIRECTOR IS ACTUALLY A PSEUDONYM FOR RYUICHI HIROKI, HITOSHI ISHIKAWA & GENJI NAKAMURA.

Cold Prey II (2008, Dir. Mats Stenberg)

THIS NORWEGIAN SLASHER MOVIE DOESN'T MESS ABOUT AND GETS STRAIGHT DOWN TO BUSINESS. AS SOON AS SURVIVING CHARACTER JANNICKE IS ADMITTED TO A HOSPITAL FOLLOWING THE TRAUMATIC EVENTS OF PART ONE, BONES START BREAKING AND THE BLOOD BEGINS TO FLOW. OF THE VERY SMALL NUMBER OF SLASHER FILMS SET WITHIN THE CONFINES OF A HOSPITAL (HALLOWEEN 2, VISITING HOURS, HOSPITAL MASSACRE), COLD PREY 2 IS THE BEST OF THE BUNCH. IT'S ALSO A STEP UP FROM ITS PREDECESSOR IN TERMS OF PACING AND HORROR SET-PIECES. WHEREAS THE FIRST INSTALMENT LACKED ANY BRUTAL PAY-OFFS, THIS SEQUEL DELIVERS SOME PLEASINGLY NASTY KILL SCENES.

Daughter of Darkness 2 (1994, Dir. Lai Kai-ming)

FANS OF CATEGORY III HONG KONG SHOCKERS WILL FIND PLENTY OF MAYHEM TO ENJOY HERE. THIS DEMENTED IN-NAME-ONLY SEQUEL IS ABOUT AS SCHIZOPHRENIC AS MOVIES COME. CONSTANTLY SHIFTING GEARS BETWEEN GOOFY SLAPSTICK COMEDY AND EXTREME NASTINESS. THE MOST HARROWING SCENE INVOLVES A YOUNG WOMAN ATTEMPTING TO ABORT HER OWN BABY WITH A COAT HANGER - STANDING LEGS APART IN THE SHOWER WE GET A BLOODY SHOT FROM BEHIND OF HER TEARING APART HER INSIDES AND BLOOD FLOWING DOWN HER QUIVERING LEGS. THIS MOVIE IS ONE OF THE MOST INSANE EXAMPLES OF HONG KONG'S TRADITION FOR MIXING INAPPROPRIATE COMEDY WITH DEEPLY DISTURBING SUBJECT MATTER. DOD2 UPS THE ANTE IN TERMS OF SEX AND VIOLENCE AND THE FINALE, SET IN A RAINSTORM, OFFERS PLENTY OF CRIMSON SPILLS FOR PLASMA LOVERS. THERE IS ALSO A COMEDY SCENE WITH A POLICE OFFICER DEMANDING A ROOM FULL OF MALE MURDER SUSPECTS JERK OFF IN FRONT OF HIM TO PROVIDE SEMEN SAMPLES. <u>TOTAL INSANITY</u>!

Day Of The Dead (1985, Dir. George A. Romero)

ROMERO'S THIRD ENTRY IN HIS LIVING DEAD SERIES HAS GAINED SOME CRITICAL APPRAISAL IN RECENT YEARS BUT STILL REMAINS A SHAMEFULLY UNDERRATED HORROR CLASSIC. AT THE ELEVENTH HOUR ROMERO LOST A CONSIDERABLE AMOUNT OF FUNDING AND HAD TO SCALE BACK HIS EPIC, APOCALYPTIC VISION. DESPITE THIS FACT, THE FILM DOESN'T SUFFER AND FOCUSES MORE ON THE MENTAL AND SOCIAL BREAKDOWN OF THE CHARACTERS RATHER THAN EXPENSIVE SET-PIECES. THIS CLAUSTROPHOBIC, NIHILISTIC NIGHTMARE FEATURES GREAT PERFORMANCES, AN INCREDIBLE FINAL HALF HOUR AND AN EXHILARATING, EMOTIONAL SCORE BY JOHN HARRISON (WHO LATER DIRECTED *TALES FROM THE DARKSIDE: THE MOVIE*). TOM SAVINI DELIVERS THE BEST SPECIAL EFFECTS OF HIS CAREER WITH SOME OUTSTANDING ZOMBIE MAKE-UP AND REVOLTING GORE SET-PIECES THAT INCLUDES FLESH RIPPING, EYE GOUGING, HORRIFIC MEDICAL EXPERIMENTS ON ZOMBIES AND A MAN BEING RIPPED IN HALF, SPILLING HIS INTERNAL ORGANS AS HE SCREAMS "CHOKE ON EM!" THE MOST DISTURBING SPLATTER SEQUENCE SHOWS A SOLDIER HAVING HIS HEAD SLOWLY TORN FROM HIS BODY— AS HIS THROAT TEARS, STRETCHING HIS VOCAL CHORDS, HIS SCREAMS BECOME HORRIBLY HIGH PITCHED. THIS FILM TIES WITH DAWN OF THE DEAD FOR ME AS THE BEST ZOMBIE MOVIE EVER MADE. RIP GEORGE.

The Devil's Rejects (2005, Dir. Rob Zombie)

IT STILL SURPRISES ME THAT THIS FILM RECEIVED A MAINSTREAM THEATRICAL RELEASE IN THE USA AND UK. EASILY ONE OF THE NASTIEST FILMS OF ITS DECADE, THE DEVIL'S REJECTS IS A SINCERE LOVE LETTER TO GRINDHOUSE HORROR AND SUPERIOR ON EVERY LEVEL TO ITS PREDECESSOR, HOUSE OF 1000 CORPSES. PACKED WITH INTENSE SCENES OF VIOLENCE, TORTURE, MUTILATION AND AN INCREDIBLY UNPLEASANT SEXUAL ASSAULT (UNUSUAL IN MODERN THEATRICAL HORROR) IN A MOTEL, THE DEVIL'S REJECTS PULLS NO PUNCHES. BILL MOSELEY, WILLIAM FORSYTHE AND SID HAIG ARE ON THE TOP OF THEIR GAME AND GIVE FEVERISH PERFORMANCES - PARTICULARLY FORSYTHE AS A LOATHSOME, VENGEFUL SHERIFF. THE REST OF THE CAST INCLUDES KEN FOREE, MICHAEL BERRYMAN, DANNY TREJO, SUPER SEXY SHERI MOON ZOMBIE, AND CLINT EASTWOOD REGULAR GEOFFREY LEWIS. ADD TO THIS A GREAT RETRO SOUNDTRACK, GRUESOME SPECIAL EFFECTS, AND SEVERAL SLAM BANG SET-PIECES AND YOU'VE GOT ONE OF THE BEST HORROR FILMS OF THAT DECADE. THE MOST INTERESTING ASPECT IS THE FACT THERE ARE NO GOOD GUYS TO ROOT FOR. EVERYONE IN THIS FILM IS A VILE SCUMBAG. IT INVITES THE AUDIENCE TO CHEER ALONG WITH THE SICKNESS AND FEEL SYMPATHY FOR THE SERIAL KILLERS WHEN THEY ARE HUNTED DOWN AND BLEAKLY BRUTALISED. BE SURE TO SEEK OUT THE UNCENSORED VERSION FOR MAXIMUM IMPACT.

Dracula A.D. 1972 (1972, Dir. Alan Gibson)

HAVING RETURNED AGAIN AND AGAIN TO GOTHIC PERIOD SETTINGS IT WAS TIME FOR HAMMER TO TRY SOMETHING DIFFERENT, UPDATING THEIR FRANCHISE TO THE THEN PRESENT DAY - THE EARLY 70S. THRILL-SEEKING CHELSEA TEENS RESURRECT COUNT DRACULA IN THE RUINS OF A DILAPIDATED CHURCH AND THE EVIL COUNT CUTS A BLOODY SWATHE THROUGH SWINGING LONDON. THE FUSION OF TRENDY LONDON BARS, HIP DIALOGUE, THE CONTEMPORARY ACID INFUSED ROCK AND THE GOTHIC DERELICT CHURCH SEQUENCES MAKE THIS A DELIRIOUS, PLAYFUL TREASURE TROVE OF CAMP THRILLS AND ONE OF THE MOST MEMORABLE MOVIES TO EMERGE FROM THE HAMMER CANNON. ENGLISH BEAUTIES CAROLINE MUNRO AND STEPHANIE BEACHAM BRING SOME EYE CANDY TO THE PROCEEDINGS, WHILST CHRISTOPHER LEE AND PETER CUSHING REPRISE THEIR ICONIC ROLES WITH GUSTO. THIS FILM IS A TREMENDOUS AMOUNT OF FUN AND MOVES AT A CRACKING PACE - MY PERSONAL FAVOURITE OF THE SERIES.

Exorcist III (1990, Dir. William Peter Blatty)

ONE OF THE MOST OVERLOOKED MAINSTREAM HORROR SEQUELS EVER MADE, EXORCIST III IS A VERY CLASSY AND INCREDIBLY CREEPY MOVIE WITH A DISTURBING SCORE BY BARRY DEVORZON. THIS IS THE TRUE SEQUEL TO FRIEDKIN'S MASTERPIECE. BLATTY'S MASTERFUL FILM WAS A COMMERCIAL AND CRITICAL FAILURE DUE TO STUDIO INTERFERENCE. THE ORIGINAL VERSION, TITLED LEGION, WAS RE-CUT AND NEW SCENES WERE ADDED, INCLUDING AN OVERBLOWN EXORCISM SEQUENCE FOR THE FINALE. THE NEW ENDING IS SO AWKWARDLY CROW-BARRED IN AND EXCESSIVE IT FAILS TO GEL WITH THE SUBTLE, DELIBERATE PACING THAT PRECEDES IT. IN ITS ORIGINAL DIRECTOR'S CUT FORM, BLATTY EXPERTLY

CREATES A CHILLING ATMOSPHERE RIGHT FROM THE OPENING SCENE AND SUSTAINS THIS UNTIL THE FINAL SHOT. ONE SCENE IN PARTICULAR, INVOLVING A HEADLESS STATUE AND A PAIR OF SURGICAL SHEERS IS HEART STOPPING - COMPRISED OF ONE PROTRACTED WIDE SHOT, THE DIRECTOR TOYS WITH THE AUDIENCES EXPECTATIONS AND PATIENCE TO CONJURE ONE OF THE MOST STARTLING MOMENTS IN HORROR CINEMA. THIS MOVIE REALLY FUCKIN' CREEPS ME OUT, AND I WOULD SERIOUSLY NOT WANT TO WATCH IT ALONE! SHOUT FACTORY RECENTLY RELEASED A STUNNING BLU-RAY SPECIAL EDITION IN THE USA THAT FEATURES BOTH THE THEATRICAL CUT AND THE SUPERIOR DIRECTOR'S CUT.

Food of the Gods II (1989, Dir. Damien Lee)

FOOD OF THE GODS II (AKA. GNAW IN THE USA) IS AN IN-NAME-ONLY SEQUEL THAT IMPROVES ON THE ULTRA LOW BUDGET SCARES OF THE ORIGINAL BERT I. GORDON DRIVE-IN FAVOURITE. MAKE NO MISTAKE ABOUT IT, THIS IS EIGHTIES VIDEO RENTAL TRASHOLA AT ITS FINEST. A LAB EXPERIMENT INVOLVING A SERUM DESIGNED TO CREATE SUPER SIZE FRUIT AND VEGETABLES TO FEED THE POOR GETS WAY OUT OF HAND WHEN A HOARD OF RATS DEVOUR SOME OF THE MUTATED PRODUCE. THE RATS GROW TO THE SIZE OF WOLVES AND THEN PROCEED TO CLAW, GNAW AND TEAR THEIR WAY THROUGH THE CITY. THE FINALE SEES A SWARM OF HUGE RATS ATTACK THE ONLOOKERS AT A SWIMMING COMPETITION - PURE GOLD! THE GORE EFFECTS ARE PLENTIFUL, THE GIANT RATS LOOK PRETTY DECENT, AND THE PACING IS SPOT ON IN THIS GOOFY THRILL RIDE. MOST MEMORABLE IS A SCENE WHERE A GUY HAS SEX WITH A WOMAN AFTER INJECTING THE SUPER-GROW SERUM. SUDDENLY HE GROWS TEN FEET TALL. HIS DICK GROWS INSIDE HIS PARTNER GIVING HER A THRILL, UNTIL SHE REALISES A HAND THE SIZE OF A SPACE-HOPPER IS CARESSING HER FACE. INSANE! WORTH THE PRICE OF ADMISSION FOR THIS SCENE ALONE!

Friday the 13th: The Final Chapter (1984, Dir. Joseph Zito)

THIS FILM IS THE EPITOME OF THE SLASHER FILM AND STANDS AS THE HIGH WATERMARK FOR QUALITY IN 1980s TEENAGE BUTCHERY. THIS ENTRY WAS DIRECTED BY JOSEPH ZITO WHO ALREADY HAD HIS SLASHER MOVIE CREDENTIALS IN CHECK HAVING HELMED THE ULTRA GRISLY *THE PROWLER* IN 1981. ZITO APPLIES THE SAME COLD, UNFRIENDLY ATMOSPHERE AS THE FORMER FILM ESCHEWING ANY COMIC VIOLENCE. WITH ZITO AT THE HELM EVEN THE WOODS LOOK CREEPY IN THE DAYTIME AND THERE IS A PERVASIVE SENSE OF DANGER. ANOTHER BONUS HERE ARE THE LIKEABLE CHARACTERS WHICH INCLUDE DEAD FUCK JIMBO (THE ECCENTRIC CRISPIN GLOVER) AND TEDDY BEAR (LAWRENCE MONOSON FROM CHER'S MASK). I ALWAYS FEEL GENUINELY SAD WHEN THESE GUYS GET BUTCHERED. THE SPECIAL EFFECTS BY TOM SAVINI ARE A GRISLY JOY TO BEHOLD AND THE MURDER SET-PIECES ARE EXPERTLY PLAYED FOR MAXIMUM SUSPENSE AND VIOLENT PAYOFF. THE BEST IS SAVED FOR JASON'S DEMISE BY MACHETE TO THE FACE. ZITO ALSO DELIVERS THE BEST INCARNATION OF JASON IN THE ENTIRE FRANCHISE, GOING FOR A MORE REALISTIC APPEARANCE RATHER THAN THE INFLATED MUSCLE MAN LOOK THAT WOULD FOLLOW IN LATER INSTALMENTS. HEAVILY BUTCHERED BY THE MPAA ON ITS ORIGINAL RELEASE, THIS GOLDEN AGE SLASHER HAS YET TO BE RELEASED IN ITS UNCUT FORM, BUT A FAN-MADE COMPOSITE CAN BE FOUND ONLINE THAT EDITS IN THE GRAPHIC GORE.

Halloween III: Season Of The Witch (1982, Dir. Tommy Lee Wallace)

THIS IN-NAME-ONLY SEQUEL ALWAYS GETS A HARD TIME BECAUSE IT DOESN'T FEATURE MICHAEL MYERS AND ISN'T A SLASHER FILM. MY ADVICE? GET PAST THE MICHAEL MYERS HANG UP. THIS IS A GHOULISH HALLOWEEN TREAT FULL OF MACABRE DELIGHTS IN THE VEIN OF *INVASION OF THE BODY SNATCHERS* - ONLY MORE DEMENTED AND OUTRAGEOUS. THE SCORE BY JOHN CARPENTER IS EXCELLENT, THE SCOPE PHOTOGRAPHY IS A PLEASURE TO BEHOLD, AND TOM 'MOUSTACHE' ATKINS GIVES ONE OF HIS BEST PERFORMANCES. THIS CREEPY MOVIE HAS A FUN CONCEPT AND ONE OF THE MOST EDGE OF YOUR SEAT, CHILLING CLIFFHANGER ENDINGS THAT THE GENRE HAS TO OFFER. DIRECTOR TOMMY LEE WALLACE WOULD GO ON TO DIRECT STEPHEN KING'S IT AND THE EXCELLENT FRIGHT NIGHT 2, WHICH ALMOST MADE THIS LIST.

Hellbound: Hellraiser II (1988, Dir. Tony Randall)

HELLBOUND FOLLOWS ON SEAMLESSLY FROM ITS ORIGINATOR, AND TAKES THE GRUESOME VIOLENCE TO ANOTHER LEVEL. THIS IS NASTY STUFF AND FEATURES AN INCREDIBLE CENOBITE BATTLE AS WELL AS INTRODUCING THE TENTACLE FINGERED DR CHANNARD - A TRULY EVIL CREATION. IN ITS UNCUT FORM THIS IS EASILY AMONGST THE NASTIEST AND MOST MEAN SPIRITED STUDIO FILMS TO EMERGE FROM THE EIGHTIES. THE MOST HARROWING SCENE OF CARNAGE

DEPICTS A RAVING LUNATIC COVERED IN MAGGOTS WHO SLICES HIMSELF TO RIBBONS WITH A RAZOR BLADE. REVOLTING! THIS FILM IS THE PERFECT SUCCESSOR, ACHIEVING THE SAME GRITTY TONE AS BARKER'S ORIGINAL AND DEVELOPING THE PINHEAD MYTHOS IN A WORTHY DIRECTION (BEFORE THE FRANCHISE WENT INTO SPACE!). WATCH THIS BACK TO BACK WITH THE ORIGINAL FOR AN EVENING OF MAXIMUM HELL!

Henry: Portrait of a Serial Killer Part 2 - Mask of Sanity (1996, Dir. Chuck Parello)

THAT TITLE IS A MOUTHFUL, ISN'T IT? JOHN MCNAUGHTON'S SURPRISE INDIE-HIT HENRY WAS SO RESPECTED THAT ANY SEQUEL WAS DESTINED TO MEET WITH CRITICAL DISDAIN, AND THAT'S EXACTLY WHAT HAPPENED. GRANTED, IT ISN'T AS GOOD AS THE ORIGINAL BUT IT IS STILL ONE HELL OF A GRITTY, GRIMY, DEPRESSING SERIAL KILLER FILM AND AN EXTREMELY SOLID EFFORT. BY DAY HENRY CLEANS OUT PORT-A-LOO'S, BY NIGHT HE AND HIS BUDDY KAI DRIVE AROUND AND MURDER RANDOM PEOPLE. ALTHOUGH THIS IS ESSENTIALLY MORE OF THE SAME (EVEN DOWN TO ITS SERIOUSLY BLEAK FINALE) THE DARK TONE AND SERIOUS INTENTIONS MAKE THIS A WORTHY SEQUEL. NEIL GIUNTOLI REPLACES MICHAEL ROOKER IN THE LEADING ROLE AND DELIVERS A COLD, CALCULATED PERFORMANCE, AND DIRECTOR CHUCK PARELLO WOULD DIRECT TWO MORE SERIAL KILLER FILMS AFTER THIS: THE RATHER DULL ED GEIN (2000) AND THE ULTRA NASTY HILLSIDE STRANGLER (2004).

Howling II : Stirba - Werewolf Bitch (1985, Philippe Mora)

SYBILL DANNING REPEATEDLY BEARS HER HEAVING ASSETS IN THIS CRUDE, ENDLESSLY FUN, ODDBALL WEREWOLF MOVIE. A HIGH WATERMARK OF '80S SPLATTER TRASH, FEATURING PLENTY OF GORE, NUDITY AND CHEESY ROCK MUSIC - THE BAND BABEL PERFORM THEIR SUPER CATCHY SONG 'THE HOWLING'. THE HILARIOUSLY EXCESSIVE END CREDITS MONTAGE REPEATS AN IMAGE OF SYBIL DANNING TEARING HER BLOUSE OFF TO REVEAL HER BREASTS SEVERAL TIMES IN PERFECT TIMING TO THE MUSIC. PLUS YOU GET TO SEE A DWARF'S EYES EXPLODE IN A SHOWER OF GORE! WHAT MORE COULD YOU ASK FOR? CHRISTOPHER LEE, WHO HAS A SIZEABLE AMOUNT OF SCREEN TIME HERE, WAS INCENSED WITH THE FINAL PRODUCT. OUTRAGEOUS AND MINDLESS ENTERTAINMENT.

Inferno (1980, Dir. Dario Argento)

DARIO ARGENTO'S FOLLOW-UP TO SUSPIRIA IS ANOTHER MIND BENDING ASSAULT ON THE SENSES. CANDY COLOURED LIGHTING, STUNNING COMPOSITIONS, AND SEVERAL CRACKING MURDER SET-PIECES DELIVER THE GOODS IN SPADES. THE OPENING SEQUENCE IN PARTICULAR IS A CHILLER FEATURING EURO BABE IRENE MIRACLE TAKING A SWIM IN AN UNDERWATER BALLROOM AND ENCOUNTERING A MOULDY CORPSE. LIKE ITS PREDECESSOR, INFERNO ISN'T INTERESTED IN RATIONAL THINKING OR LOGICAL CHARACTER MOTIVATIONS - THIS IS A MOVIE DRIVEN BY ITS IMAGERY AND NIGHTMARISH ATMOSPHERE. THE FIRST TIME I WATCHED THIS I DIDN'T GET IT AT ALL. I FOUND IT FRUSTRATING AND MESSY. BEING AN AVID ARGENTO FAN I KEPT GOING BACK TO IT AND ULTIMATELY FELL IN LOVE WITH THIS REWARDING (IF YOU GIVE IT A CHANCE) MOVIE. IT HAS A MESMERISING LYRICAL QUALITY ACCOMPANIED BY A UNIQUE SCORE BY KEITH EMERSON OF EMERSON, LAKE AND PALMER. ESSENTIAL VIEWING FOR ARGENTO FANS.

Jaws 2 (1978, Dir. Jeannot Szwarc)

COME ON - WHAT'S NOT TO LIKE HERE? THIS IS NO CHEAP CASH-IN. FOR ME THIS IS A GREAT SEQUEL THAT IS FAITHFUL TO THE ORIGINAL. FEATURES PREDOMINATELY THE SAME CAST, FAMILIAR LOCATIONS AND A COMPARABLE TONE. THE SHARK ATTACK SCENES ARE BRILLIANTLY CHOREOGRAPHED - THE BEST BEING THE PURSUIT AND KILLING OF A WATER SKIER. THE INCLUSION OF REAL GREAT WHITE SHARK FOOTAGE SHOT BY RON AND VALERIE TAYLOR (WHO ALSO PROVIDED UNDERWATER FOOTAGE FOR SPIELBERG'S ORIGINAL), CLEVERLY EDITED INTO THE ATTACK SEQUENCES BRINGS A GENUINE SENSE OF DANGER TO THE PROCEEDINGS. ROY SCHEIDER GIVES ANOTHER GREAT PERFORMANCE AS THE LIKEABLE HERO, DESPITE THE FACT HE DIDN'T WANT TO REPRISE HIS ROLE AS CHIEF BRODY AND ONLY DID SO IN ORDER TO ESCAPE FROM HIS CONTRACT WITH UNIVERSAL PICTURES. THE ONLY NEGATIVE ASPECT HERE IS THAT WE SEE TOO MUCH OF THE FAKE SHARK - SOME TIGHTER EDITING ON THIS FRONT WOULD SERVE THE PICTURE BETTER.

Maniac Cop 2 (1990, Dir. William Lustig)

THE FIRST MANIAC COP TURNED OUT TO BE A SUBSTANTIAL STRAIGHT-TO-VIDEO HIT, AND MANIAC COP 2 DELIVERS MORE OF THE SAME BUT WITH A TIGHTER PLOT AND INCREDIBLE ACTION SET-PIECES. IF YOU WANT EXPLOSIVE, BLOODY GUN FIGHTS AND DANGEROUS STUNTS, BUT DON'T HAVE A LOT OF BUDGET, THEN LOOK TO WILLIAM LUSTIG. MANIAC COP 2 IS PACKED WITH OUTRAGEOUS SET-PIECES, ONE OF WHICH FEATURES A WOMAN HANDCUFFED TO THE OUTSIDE OF A CAR AS IT MOVES DOWN A BUSY HIGHWAY. WE ALSO GET SOME CHAINSAW VIOLENCE AND SOME DANGEROUS FIRE STUNTS, AND THE SCENE IN WHICH

ZOMBIE COP MATT CORDELL LAYS WASTE TO A NEW YORK POLICE STATION IS EXHILARATING AND REMINISCENT OF THE POLICE STATION MASSACRE IN *THE TERMINATOR*. THIS HAS A DARKER OVERALL TONE THAN THE FIRST FILM AND INTRODUCES AN INTERESTING CONCEPT WITH CORDELL WORKING WITH A SERIAL KILLER THAT TARGETS HOOKERS (PLAYED WITH SLEAZY RELISH BY LEO ROSSI).

Nekromantik 2 (1991, Dir. Jorg Buttgereit)
THE ORIGINAL NEKROMANTIK IS SO GROSS AND NAUSEATING ONE WONDERS HOW ON EARTH YOU WOULD FOLLOW IT. NEKROMANTIK 2 IS SOMEHOW EVEN MORE REPULSIVE, THANKS TO A HANDSOME BUDGET (FOR THIS KIND OF FILM) AND THE UPGRADE FROM SUPER 8MM TO 16MM PHOTOGRAPHY. THE BEAUTIFUL MONIKA M IS EXCELLENT AS A NECROPHILE WHO KEEPS ROTTING COCKS IN HER REFRIGERATOR. TO ADD TO THE GROSS OUT FACTOR THERE IS SOME VERY UNPLEASANT SEAL CULLING FOOTAGE. NEKROMANTIK 2 ALSO HAS ONE OF THE MOST PERVERSE, JAW DROPPING FINALES IN CINEMA HISTORY. AS REPULSIVE AS THE SUBJECT MATTER IS BUTTGEREIT HANDLES IT WITH SOME ARTISTIC BEAUTY AND PATHOS – THE BEAUTIFUL, MELANCHOLY PIANO SCORE BRINGS A TOUCH OF CLASS TO THE PROCEEDINGS. THIS FILM TREADS A FINE LINE BETWEEN ART-HOUSE AND EXPLOITATION AND AFTER A SLOW FIRST HOUR IT GOES RIGHT FOR THE JUGULAR. THE SLIMY NECROPHILIA SCENES ARE UTTERLY REVOLTING THANKS TO THE EXCELLENT SPECIAL EFFECTS WORK. EVERYTHING IN NEKROMANTIK 2 IS BRIGHTLY LIT AND COLOURFUL IN CONTRAST WITH THE MORBID, GRAINY GLOOM OF THE ORIGINAL. BOTH THIS FILM AND THE ORIGINAL WERE CONFISCATED BY THE AUTHORITIES IN BUTTGEREIT'S NATIVE GERMANY ON CHARGES OF OBSCENITY AND GLORIFYING VIOLENCE. BUTTGEREIT FOUND HIMSELF IN COURT DEFENDING HIS WORK AND ULTIMATELY WON.

A Nightmare On Elm Street Part 2: Freddy's Revenge (1985, Dir. Jack Sholder)
THIS IS SET SEVERAL YEARS AFTER CRAVEN'S ORIGINAL AND SHARES SOME SIMILARITIES WITH ANOTHER FILM ON THIS LIST, AMITYVILLE II, WITH A PLOT THAT FOCUSES ON THE TERRORISATION AND POSSESSION OF A TEENAGE BOY. THIS HAS AN ODDBALL SENSIBILITY THAT MAKES FOR A UNIQUE VIEWING EXPERIENCE. WRITER DAVID CHASKIN DELIBERATELY FILLED HIS SCRIPT WITH HOMOEROTIC SUBTEXT BUT DIRECTOR JACK SHOLDER (*ALONE IN THE DARK*) WAS UNAWARE OF THIS, RESULTING IN A VERY ECCENTRIC MOVIE THAT IS PACKED FULL OF SURPRISING HOMOEROTIC IMAGERY – AN S&M INSPIRED NIGHTMARE SCENE, A LEATHER BAR, EMPHASIS ON SWEATING MALE PHYSIQUES, AND AN EFFEMINATE HERO. SHOLDER'S FILM MAINTAINS A MACABRE SENSIBILITY AND FREDDY IS STILL A TERRIFYING CREATION HERE, OPPOSED TO THE WISECRACKING COMIC VILLAIN IN LATER ENTRIES. THE OPENING NIGHTMARE SEQUENCE FEATURING A SCHOOL BUS BEING DRIVEN STRAIGHT INTO HELL BY FREDDY IS BRILLIANTLY REALISED. THIS ALSO HAS A UNIQUE SCORE BY CHRISTOPHER YOUNG (*HELLRAISER*) WHICH REALLY BOLSTERS THE FEVERED DREAM SEQUENCES.

Night Of The Seagulls (1975, Dir. Amando de Ossorio)
THIS IS THE FOURTH AND FINAL INSTALMENT IN THE BLIND DEAD SERIES AND PROBABLY THE LEAST TALKED ABOUT. THIS CREEPY ENTRY TAKES PLACE IN A PICTURESQUE COASTAL VILLAGE WHERE VIRGIN SACRIFICES ARE MANDATED EVERY SEVEN YEARS TO KEEP THE EVIL TEMPLAR ZOMBIES FROM DESTROYING THE TOWNSHIP. THE LOCATIONS AND PHOTOGRAPHY ARE QUITE STUNNING HERE AND THE EERIE SCORE ADDS GENUINE MENACE TO THE PROCEEDINGS AS POTENT SLOW MOTION IMAGES OF THE SKELETAL TEMPLARS RIDING THEIR HORSES SEND CHILLS DOWN THE SPINE. OSSORIO THROWS IN PLENTY OF GORE AND NUDITY FOR GOOD MEASURE, WITH MORE EXPLICIT NUDITY FILMED FOR EXPORT VERSIONS. (A STANDARD FOR OSSORIO'S BLIND DEAD FILMS). NIGHT OF THE SEAGULLS ALMOST BECAME A VIDEO NASTY IN THE UK IN THE EARLY '80S WHEN IT APPEARED ON GREATER MANCHESTER POLICE'S HIT LIST OF TITLES FOR SEIZURE, BUT WAS EVENTUALLY DROPPED FROM THE DIRECTOR OF PUBLIC PROSECUTIONS SECTION 3 LIST.

Phantasm III: Lord of the Dead (1994, Dir. Don Coscarelli)
PICKING UP DIRECTLY WHERE PART TWO FINISHED, THIS THIRD INSTALMENT IN THE SERIES IS PROBABLY THE MOST IMAGINATIVE IN ITS DEVELOPMENT OF THE PHANTASM MYTHOS. SOME OLDER QUESTIONS ARE ANSWERED BUT COSCARELLI WEAVES SEVERAL MORE TEASING NARRATIVE STRANDS SO AS NOT TO REVEAL TOO MUCH OF THE MYSTERY THAT MAKES THIS FRANCHISE SO FASCINATING. I COULD LOSE SOME OF THE COMEDIC ELEMENTS IN THIS ENTRY BUT OVERALL THIS IS AN INCREDIBLY CREATIVE, KINETIC MOVIE. COSCARELLI DELIVERS SOME GREAT IMAGERY HERE -- WE GET TO SEE A ROOM FULL OF DEADLY FLYING SPHERES, A SPECTACULAR HEARSE CRASH, SPLATTERIFIC VIOLENCE FROM A MODIFIED FOUR BARREL SAWN-OFF SHOTGUN, AND WE LEARN WHAT MAKES THOSE FLYING SPHERES TICK IN A GRUESOME SURGERY SCENE. BEST OF ALL THOUGH IS A LARGE GOLDEN SPHERE THAT EMERGES FROM THE TALL MAN'S HEAD TO SMASH A PERFECTLY CIRCULAR HOLE IN A ZOMBIE'S FACE – MIND BLOWING! AFTER A TROUBLED PRODUCTION HISTORY PHANTASM III ENDED UP GOING DIRECT TO VIDEO - A REAL SHAME AS THIS WOULD HAVE BEEN AWESOME ON THE BIG SCREEN.

Stripped to Kill 2: Live Girls (1989, Dir. Katt Shea)

A PSYCHO SLASHER STALKS DANCING GIRLS AT STRIP CLUBS AND SLASHES THEM UP WITH A RAZOR. SOUND FAMILIAR? THAT'S BECAUSE IT'S VIRTUALLY THE SAME AS THE FIRST INSTALMENT. ORIGINALITY ASIDE, THIS IS INCREDIBLY ENTERTAINING STUFF AND WILL CERTAINLY APPEAL TO THOSE WITH SLEAZIER TASTE BUDS. ALTHOUGH THE VIOLENCE ISN'T GRAPHIC HERE, THE SHEER VOLUME OF STRIPTEASES, BARE BREASTS AND LINGERIE DANCE NUMBERS BOLSTERS THE GREASY SLEAZE FACTOR RIGHT OFF THE SCALE. STRIPPED TO KILL 2 IS A DEFINITE IMPROVEMENT ON THE ORIGINAL THANKS TO TIGHTER EDITING AND NO-NONSENSE NARRATIVE. MARIA FORD IS ALSO SMOKING HOT AND GIVES A SOLID PERFORMANCE AS THE QUEEN OF STRIPLAND. THIS IS AN OBSCURE TREAT FROM THE DAYS OF '80S RENTAL VIDEO THAT DESERVES A CULT FOLLOWING.

Texas Chainsaw Massacre Part 2 (1986, Dir. Tobe Hooper)

CANNON FILMS EAGERLY ANTICIPATED SEQUEL TO HOOPER'S MACABRE MASTERPIECE HAD A TOUGH TIME AT THE BOX OFFICE AND MANY FANS DISMISSED IT WHICH IS A REAL SHAME. IF YOU'RE WANTING MORE OF THE SAME THEN THIS ENTRY IS LIKELY TO DISAPPOINT AS HOOPER GOES FOR A DEMENTED OVER-THE-TOP COMIC SPLATTER VIBE RATHER THAN THE GRITTY REALISM OF THE FIRST FILM. CHAINSAW 2 IS ONE OF THE MOST EXCESSIVE AND ECCENTRIC HORROR FILMS OF ITS DECADE, FEATURING PROLONGED SCENES OF MUTILATION AND TORTURE, WHILST DELIVERING SOME OUTRAGEOUS BLACK HUMOUR AND LUNATIC PERFORMANCES FROM THE CAST. TEXAS MARSHALL DENNIS HOPPER HOLSTERS UP SOME MINI-CHAINSAWS, BILL MOSELEY IS A DERANGED VIETNAM VET WHO PICKS THE SCABS FROM HIS HEAD WOUND AND EATS THEM, JIM SIEDOW REPRISES HIS ROLE AS THE PSYCHOTIC COOK, AND 'SCREAM QUEEN' CAROLINE WILLIAMS IS FANTASTIC AS A TERRORISED RADIO SHOW HOST. THIS FULL-THROTTLE MOVIE IS REALLY SICK IN THE HEAD, AND FEATURES SUPERB FX BY TOM SAVINI.

Honourable Mentions:

MANIAC 2 : MR ROBBIE
PROM NIGHT II: HELLO MARY LOU
BLOODSTONE: SUBSPECIES II
FRIGHT NIGHT PART 2
CHILD'S PLAY 3
SLEEPAWAY CAMP II
POLTERGEIST III
INSIDIOUS 2
HALLOWEEN 4
CHILDREN OF THE CORN IV

ARTICLE BY: **DAVID HINDS** ☆
DAVID IS THE AUTHOR OF 'FASCINATION: THE CELLULOID DREAMS OF JEAN ROLLIN' (HEADPRESS). AND THE DIRECTOR OF 'THE HOUSE ON CUCKOO LANE' AND 'THE NIGHTMARE CHAMBER'.
—BOUGIE

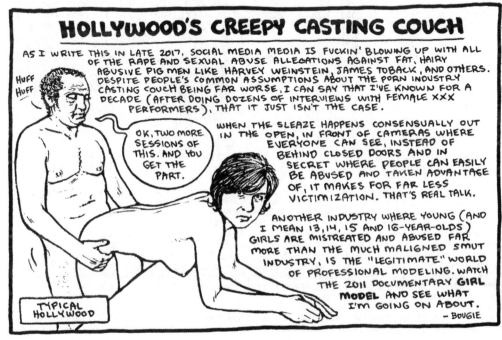

HOLLYWOOD'S CREEPY CASTING COUCH

AS I WRITE THIS IN LATE 2017, SOCIAL MEDIA MEDIA IS FUCKIN' BLOWING UP WITH ALL OF THE RAPE AND SEXUAL ABUSE ALLEGATIONS AGAINST FAT, HAIRY ABUSIVE PIG MEN LIKE HARVEY WEINSTEIN, JAMES TOBACK, AND OTHERS. DESPITE PEOPLE'S COMMON ASSUMPTIONS ABOUT THE PORN INDUSTRY CASTING COUCH BEING FAR WORSE, I CAN SAY THAT I'VE KNOWN FOR A DECADE (AFTER DOING DOZENS OF INTERVIEWS WITH FEMALE XXX PERFORMERS), THAT IT JUST ISN'T THE CASE.

Huff Huff

OK, TWO MORE SESSIONS OF THIS. AND YOU GET THE PART.

WHEN THE SLEAZE HAPPENS CONSENSUALLY OUT IN THE OPEN, IN FRONT OF CAMERAS WHERE EVERYONE CAN SEE, INSTEAD OF BEHIND CLOSED DOORS AND IN SECRET WHERE PEOPLE CAN EASILY BE ABUSED AND TAKEN ADVANTAGE OF, IT MAKES FOR FAR LESS VICTIMIZATION. THAT'S REAL TALK.

ANOTHER INDUSTRY WHERE YOUNG (AND I MEAN 13, 14, 15 AND 16-YEAR-OLDS) GIRLS ARE MISTREATED AND ABUSED FAR MORE THAN THE MUCH MALIGNED SMUT INDUSTRY, IS THE "LEGITIMATE" WORLD OF PROFESSIONAL MODELING. WATCH THE 2011 DOCUMENTARY **GIRL MODEL** AND SEE WHAT I'M GOING ON ABOUT.
— BOUGIE

TYPICAL HOLLYWOOD

PORN'S POLITICIANS

☆ ☆ ☆ ☆ ☆ By MICHAEL WALSH ☆ ☆ ☆ ☆ ☆

WE WERE WARNED.

TWELVE YEARS BEFORE AMERICANS ELECTED THEIR FIRST ACTOR-PRESIDENT -- FORMER GENERAL ELECTRIC PITCHMAN RONALD REAGAN -- FILMMAKER BARRY SHEAR EXPLORED THE NOTION OF A POP STAR IN THE WHITE HOUSE. HIS 1968 POLITICAL FANTASY WILD IN THE STREETS WAS BASED ON THE IDEA THAT CELEBRITY WAS A QUALIFICATION FOR HIGH OFFICE. (IT HAD WORKED FOR REAGAN, WHO IN 1966 HAD BEEN ELECTED GOVERNOR OF CALIFORNIA) IN SHEAR'S PICTURE, ROCK REBELS DEMANDING "POWER TO THE (YOUNG) PEOPLE" PROMISE TO LOWER THE VOTING AGE. THEIR SLOGAN: "FOURTEEN OR FIGHT!"

A BOXOFFICE HIT FOR DOUBLE-FEATURE DISTRIBUTOR AIP, I BLAME WILD IN THE STREETS FOR INSPIRING THE BIG SCREEN'S MOST INCREDIBLE CANDIDACY, 1975'S LINDA LOVELACE FOR PRESIDENT. MARKETED AS A COMEDY, IT TRADED ON ITS STAR'S NOTORIETY AS A PORN PERFORMER. HER CAMPAIGN SLOGAN: "A VOTE FOR LINDA IS A BLOW FOR DEMOCRACY."

IN THE YEARS SINCE, WE'VE SEEN DOZENS OF AMERICAN ENTERTAINERS FOLLOW REAGAN'S EXAMPLE AND SEEK PUBLIC OFFICE. THE SUCCESSFUL ONES HAVE SERVED AS CITY MAYORS (JACK KELLY, CLINT EASTWOOD), STATE GOVERNORS (JESSE VENTURA, ARNOLD SCHWARZENEGGER) AND IN THE U.S. CONGRESS (FRED THOMPSON, SONNY BONO, AL FRANKEN). NOW, THERE IS REALITY TV STAR DONALD J. TRUMP, AMERICA'S CURRENT (AT THE TIME OF THIS WRITING) PERFORMER-PRESIDENT.

IT SHOULD COME AS NO SURPRISE THAT A NUMBER OF ADULT FILM STARS HAVE DONE THE SAME. THIS ISSUE OF CINEMA SEWER SALUTES SIX WOMEN WHO WENT ALL THE WAY, NO MERE SIMULATIONS OF POLITICAL PARTICIPATION. THEIR CAMPAIGNS WERE EXPLICIT ACTS OF ELECTORAL DEMOCRACY. THEIR

CICCIOLINA

REAL NAMES APPEARED ON OFFICIAL BALLOTS, AND THE RESULTS ARE A MATTER OF PUBLIC RECORD.

****

1. CICCIOLINA (ITALY; 1987): "DOWN WITH NUCLEAR ENERGY, UP WITH SEXUAL ENERGY"
THE GOLDEN AGE OF PORN'S BEST KNOWN INTERNATIONAL STAR, CICCIOLINA WAS BORN ELENA ANNA STALLER ON NOVEMBER 26, 1951 IN BUDAPEST, HUNGARY. BETWEEN 1970 AND 1994, SHE PERFORMED IN SOME 40 FEATURE FILMS. AS ILONA STALLER, SHE WAS A FOUNDING MEMBER IN 1979 OF LA LISTA DEL SOLE (SUN PARTY), ITALY'S FIRST GREEN PARTY. IN 1985 SHE SWITCHED TO THE PARTITO RADICALE, CAMPAIGNING FOR HUMAN RIGHTS AND AGAINST NUCLEAR ENERGY, ITALIAN NATO MEMBERSHIP AND WORLD HUNGER.

PERHAPS INSPIRED BY DELACROIX'S CLASSIC PAINTING "LIBERTY LEADING THE PEOPLE," THE TAKE-CHARGE BLONDE OFTEN DELIVERED HER POLITICAL SPEECHES BARE-BREASTED. IN THE 1987 ELECTION

(HELD JUNE 14-15), SHE WON A FULL FIVE-YEAR TERM TO THE ITALIAN PARLIAMENT, DURING WHICH SHE CONTINUED TO APPEAR IN HARDCORE FEATURES.

THE REPRESENTATIVE OF THE LAZIO DISTRICT OF ROME (1987-1992), HER 20,000 VOTE TOTAL MADE HER THE SECOND MOST POPULAR RADICAL PARTY CANDIDATE, AFTER THE PARTY'S LEADER. AMONG ITALY'S MOST COLOURFUL PROGRESSIVE POLITICIANS -- IN 1990, DURING THE RUN UP TO THE GULF WAR, SHE SAID "I AM AVAILABLE TO MAKE LOVE WITH SADDAM HUSSEIN TO ACHIEVE PEACE IN THE MIDDLE EAST" -- CICCIOLINA HAS BEEN COLLECTING A €39,000 ($47,940 US) PARLIAMENTARY PENSION SINCE SHE TURNED 60 IN 2011.

2. JODIE MOORE (AUSTRALIA: 2001) "QUEENSLAND I'LL PROMOTE IT."
BORN JODIE ANN KLASSEN ON APRIL 11, 1976 IN BRISBANE, AUSTRALIA, JODIE MOORE MADE TWO LIFE-CHANGING DECISIONS IN 2001. HAVING ACHIEVED REGIONAL FAME AS A STRIP-TEASE DANCER AND MEN'S MAGAZINE MODEL, SHE MADE HER DEBUT AS AN ADULT FILM ACTOR. (DURING A SIX-YEAR CAREER, SHE STARRED IN MORE THAN 60 FEATURES.) THAT SAME YEAR, SHE STOOD AS AN INDEPENDENT PARTY CANDIDATE IN QUEENSLAND'S FEBRUARY 17 STATE ASSEMBLY ELECTION. RUNNING IN BRISBANE'S WOOLRIDGE CONSTITUENCY, MOORE PLACED FIFTH IN A FIELD OF FIVE, RECEIVING 1,057 (OR 5.1 PER CENT) OF VOTES CAST.

MARY CAREY

CAUCUS, ANYONE?

A MONTH LATER, SHE RAN IN THE MARCH 17 BY-ELECTION FOR A SEAT IN AUSTRALIA'S FEDERAL PARLIAMENT. IT WAS NEWS WHEN A BILLBOARD FEATURING NUDE PHOTOS OF THE SENATORIAL CANDIDATE FOR BRISBANE'S RYAN CONSTITUENCY WAS TAKEN DOWN BY THE CITY'S ROADS DEPARTMENT. ALTHOUGH MORE PEOPLE VOTED FOR HER IN THE LARGER FEDERAL DISTRICT -- SHE GOT 1,351 (OR 1.79 PER CENT) OF THE VOTES -- SHE CAME IN SIXTH IN A FIELD OF NINE.

SUCCESS IN POLITICS ELUDED HER, BUT THE TINY BLONDE AUSSIE USED HER FAME IN THE INTERNATIONAL PORN INDUSTRY TO FULFILL THE PROMISE OF PROMOTING HER HOMELAND. FOR MANY YEARS HER WEBSITE COMBINED ADULT HARDCORE CONTENT WITH PERSONAL POLITICAL COMMENTARY.

3. MARY CAREY (UNITED STATES: 2003) "I'LL BE A KICK-ASS GOVERNOR."
CLEVELAND, OHIO-BORN MARY ELLEN COOK WAS INTO THE SECOND YEAR OF HER 10-YEAR-LONG ADULT FILM CAREER WHEN CALIFORNIA GOVERNOR GRAY DAVIS WAS FACED WITH A RECALL ELECTION. BORN JUNE 15, 1981, THE ALL-AMERICAN ACTRESS WAS ONE OF A NUMBER OF SHOW BUSINESS CELEBRITIES ON THE HUGE BALLOT FACED BY GOLDEN STATE VOTERS ON OCTOBER 7, 2003. RUNNING ON A CICCIOLINA-LIKE PLATFORM OF SOCIAL REFORMS-- SHE PROMISED TO "RECRUIT FELLOW PERFORMERS FROM THE ADULT VIDEO INDUSTRY AS AMBASSADORS OF GOOD WILL" FOR THE STATE -- SHE RECEIVED 0.1 PER CENT OF THE VOTES CAST.

CRITICS OF HER CANDIDACY SUGGESTED THAT SHE WAS NOT VERY BRIGHT AND THAT SHE WAS LYING ABOUT HAVING A NATURALLY BIG BUST. IT'S NOT CLEAR WHETHER THE IMPLANTS CONTROVERSY WON OR LOST VOTES FOR THE FULL-FIGURED BLONDE.

YES, SHE LOST TO MAINSTREAM MOVIE ACTOR ARNOLD SCHWARZENEGGER (WITH 4,158,194 VOTES), BUT

MARY CAREY DID MANAGE TO COME IN A RESPECTABLE 10TH IN A FIELD OF 135 CANDIDATES. ALTHOUGH HER CANDIDACY WAS CALLED A PUBLICITY STUNT, CAMPAIGN PROMISES SUCH AS LEGALIZING SAME-SEX MARRIAGE, A GUN-CONTROL PROGRAM AND ADDRESSING THE AIDS EPIDEMIC MADE SENSE TO 11,179 VOTERS.

4. DOLLY BUSTER (CZECH REPUBLIC: 2004) "POLITICS DOES NOT HAVE TO BE HELL"
HER CALMLY REASSURING CAMPAIGN SLOGAN REFLECTED THE YEARS OF SOCIAL AND CULTURAL CHANGE THAT SHAPED NORA BAUMBERGEROVÁ'S POLITICAL PERSONA. BORN KATERINA BOCHNICKOVA ON OCTOBER 23, 1969 IN PRAGUE, SHE LEFT THE SOVIET SATELLITE STATE AT 14 FOR AFFLUENT WEST GERMANY. IN 1989, SHE MADE HER DEBUT AS DOLLY BUSTER, PARLAYING A DOMINATING PRESENCE INTO MAJOR STARDOM DURING A 12-YEAR CAREER IN REUNIFIED GERMANY'S ADULT FILM INDUSTRY.

IN 1993, HER NATIVE CZECHOSLOVAKIA SPLIT INTO SLOVAKIA AND THE CZECH REPUBLIC. IN 2004, THE YEAR THEY JOINED THE EUROPEAN UNION, THE SOCIALLY-ACTIVE ACTRESS RETURNED TO PRAGUE. SHE STOOD AS THE INDEPENDENT EROTIC INITIATIVE PARTY'S CANDIDATE FOR A DEPUTY'S SEAT IN THE EUROPEAN PARLIAMENT, CAMPAIGNING ON A PLATFORM OF SEXUAL FREEDOM AND ANIMAL RIGHTS.

SHE EARNED JUST UNDER 7,000 VOTES, OR 0.72 PER CENT OF BALLOTS CAST DURING THE JUNE 11-12 ELECTION. THOUGH THE BLONDE BUSTER -- THE NAME CELEBRATED HER SURGICALLY-ENHANCED BREASTS -- WAS NOT A WINNER, SHE REMAINED ENTREPRENEURIAL. BRANCHING OUT FROM FILM PRODUCTION TO RESTAURANT MANAGEMENT. RECENTLY, SHE WAS INDUCTED INTO DAS SYNDIKAT (GERMANY'S ASSOCIATION OF MYSTERY WRITERS) FOR HER SERIES OF CRIME NOVELS FEATURING LILLY DELIGHT, A PORN STAR TURNED AMATEUR DETECTIVE.

5. MARILYN CHAMBERS (UNITED STATES: 2004) "DON'T WRITE US OFF - WRITE US IN!"
IF AMERICA'S "PORNO CHIC" MOMENT BEGAN WITH LINDA LOVELACE'S DEBUT FEATURE, THE 1972 SEX-CLINIC COMEDY DEEP THROAT, IT REACHED ITS ARTISTIC HIGH POINT WITH MARILYN CHAMBERS'S FIRST ADULT FEATURE, THE SEX-CLUB FANTASY BEHIND THE GREEN DOOR (ALSO 1972). WITH HER ATHLETIC FIGURE AND WHOLESOME GOOD LOOKS -- SHE WAS THE ALL-AMERICAN GIRL ON EVERY BOX OF IVORY SNOW SOAP FLAKES SOLD IN 1971 -- HER CHOICE TO BECOME A PORN STAR WAS THE ULTIMATE ACT OF BOOM-GENERATION REBELLION.

WHILE THE WORKING-CLASS LOVELACE PLAYED A PRESIDENTIAL CANDIDATE IN THE MOVIES, SUBURBAN PRINCESS MARILYN CHAMBERS TAYLOR WENT ON TO BE THE REAL-LIFE RUNNING MATE OF THE LIBERTARIAN PERSONAL CHOICE PARTY'S CHARLES JAY ON THE NOVEMBER 2, 2004 ELECTION BALLOT IN UTAH.

BORN MARILYN ANN BRIGGS ON APRIL 22, 1952 IN PROVIDENCE, RHODE ISLAND, HER 35-YEAR PERFORMING CAREER BRED IN HER THE LIBERTARIAN VALUES REPRESENTED IN HER POLITICS. SHE WAS PRO-CHOICE AND FOR FREE SPEECH, PRIVACY RIGHTS AND PERSONAL RESPONSIBILITY, AND AGAINST LEGISLATING MORALITY AND HIGH TAXES. THE PCP TICKET RECEIVED 946 (OR 0.1 PER CENT) OF UTAH VOTES, TO COME IN SIXTH BEHIND MAINSTREAM PARTY CANDIDATES GEORGE W. BUSH/DICK CHENEY (THE REPUBLICANS WHO WON) AND DEMOCRATS JOHN KERRY/JOHN EDWARDS.

MIMI MIYAGI

6. MIMI MIYAGI (UNITED STATES: 2006) "I'M BARE AND HONEST AT ALL TIMES."
PORNOGRAPHY, AN ESTABLISHED FILM GENRE, HAD JUST BEGUN ITS MIGRATION TO THE INTERNET WHEN MIMI MIYAGI MADE HER SCREEN DEBUT IN 1990. BORN MELODY DAMAYO ON JULY 3, 1973 IN DAVAO CITY, PHILIPPINES, SHE MADE NO SECRET OF HER 14 YEARS AS AN ADULT PERFORMER WHEN SHE RAN IN THE 2006 REPUBLICAN PRIMARY RACE TO CHOOSE THE PARTY'S NEVADA GUBERNATORIAL CANDIDATE. IN ADDITION TO BEING A REGISTERED REPUBLICAN, SHE WAS A CARD-CARRYING MEMBER OF THE NATIONAL RIFLE ASSOCIATION.

SHE ALSO REPRESENTED THE NEW AMERICAN DIVERSITY. A DIMINUTIVE ASIAN, SHE HAD THE FORTHRIGHT MANNER OF A TIGER MOM, AND HER CAMPAIGN ISSUES INCLUDED SCHOOL REFORM, REDUCING THE STATE'S CRIME RATE AND RAISING THE MINIMUM WAGE. SHE CAME IN FOURTH IN A FIELD OF FIVE ON THE AUGUST 15 BALLOT, RECEIVING 1,651 VOTES (OR 1.17 PER CENT). AFTERWARDS, MIYAGI FOLLOWED THE EXAMPLE OF MARILYN CHAMBERS (WHO HAD CO-OWNED A LAS VEGAS GUN SHOP IN THE 1980S), AND JOINED HER STATE'S LIBERTARIAN PARTY.

****

AT LEAST TWO QUESTIONS ARE RAISED BY THE BRIEF NOTES ABOVE. WHY IS IT THAT THE HISTORY OF PORN STAR POLITICIANS IS ESSENTIALLY A HER-STORY? WHY IS IT THAT THE PLATFORMS OF THE EUROPEAN PERFORMERS ARE SOCIALLY PROGRESSIVE (OR LEFT-WING), WHILE THE AMERICANS SKEW TO THE RIGHT? THESE ARE SUBJECTS FOR FURTHER STUDY, TO BE SURE.

CARJACKING

IT MAY SEEM LIKE THE TERM "CARJACKING" HAS BEEN AROUND FOREVER, BUT IT WAS ACTUALLY COINED IN 1991 BY EJ MITCHELL, AN EDITOR WITH THE DETROIT NEWS. HE FIRST USED THE TERM IN A 1992 REPORT ON THE MURDER OF 22-YEAR-OLD RUTH WAHL, A DRUGSTORE CASHIER WHO WAS MURDERED IN DETROIT WHEN SHE WOULD NOT SURRENDER HER SUZUKI SIDEKICK. MY PERSONAL FAVE CAR-JACKING SCENES IN MOVIES APPEAR IN RABID DOGS (1974), THE BOYS NEXT DOOR (1985), COMMANDO (1985), MENACE II SOCIETY (1993), RESERVOIR DOGS (1992), THE BRADY BUNCH MOVIE (1995), NOTHING TO LOSE (1997), TRANSPORTER 2 (2005), AND CHAPPIE (2015).

THE EXECUTIONER (DIRECTED BY TERUO ISHII -- 1974 · JAPAN)

THE MEANEST CHIBA MOVIE YET!

CHIBA... IS BACK—

more deadly than any weapon!

SONNY CHIBA IS THE 'EXECUTIONER'

THIS KARATE CRIME THRILLER IS STACKED AND SOLID. I MEAN, THERE'S SOME GREAT SHIT IN THIS, AND I CAN BEST ILLUSTRATE THAT POINT BY NOTING A FIGHT SCENE I ESPECIALLY LIKED, WHERE STAR SONNY CHIBA ACCIDENTALLY DUMPS OVER A COUPLE OF CANS OF PAINT, AND SEEING AN OPPORTUNITY TO BE CREATIVE, STEPS ONE FOOT INTO THE SPILLED YELLOW, AND ONE FOOT INTO THE BLUE, AND PROCEEDS TO PAINT HIS FOES FACES VIA INSANE AND OUTLANDISH HEAD KICKS. HE EVEN GOES SO FAR AS TO ENJOYING KICKING FANCIFUL MIXTURES OF THE TWO COLORS, VIA REPEATED KICKS TO THE SAME SPOT WITH DIFFERENT FEET. CAN YOU BEAT THAT?

A FEW MOMENTS LATER, IN FRONT OF A NIGHT TIME BACKDROP OF NEON SIGNS, CHIBA DOES CINEMA HISTORY'S GREATEST FLYING TWO-LEGGED STOMACH STOMP ON A PRONE VILLAIN, WHO IS LAYING FLAT ON HIS BACK LIKE A WIDE-EYED HELPLESS TURTLE. IF THAT WASN'T ENOUGH, SONNY PROCEEDS TO DO WHAT ALMOST LOOKS LIKE A LITTLE TAP DANCE ON THE POOR GUY'S TUMMY, ALL WHILE DOING HIS PATENTED HIGH PITCHED MONKEY SCREAMS.

THAT'S RIGHT: MONKEY SCREAMS. GOOD OL' CHIBA DOES THESE HILARIOUS LITTLE WAILS AND SCREECHES WHILE KICKING BUTTOCKS, ALL OF WHICH ARE CLEARLY INSPIRED BY WHAT BRUCE LEE WAS DOING IN HIS MOVIES AT THE TIME. AND YET CHIBA'S WAILS ARE EVEN COOLER SOMEHOW, JUST BY VIRTUE OF HOW OVER-THE-TOP THEY ARE!

TERUO ISHII IS A GODDAMN FANTASTIC DIRECTOR. HE'S THE GUY WHO GAVE US SUCH GREAT JAPANESE GENRE FILM STANDOUTS AS: THE ABISHIRI PRISON SERIES, THE JOY OF TORTURE, ORGIES OF EDO, HORRORS OF MALFORMED MEN, FEMALE YAKUZA TALE, BLIND WOMAN'S CURSE, CODE OF THE FORGOTTEN EIGHT, DETONATION: VIOLENT GAMES, AND JIGOKU.

—BOUGIE

I RARELY COVER MOVIES MADE PAST 1993 IN THE PAGES OF CINEMA SEWER, NOT BECAUSE THERE AREN'T ANY THAT ARE DESERVING, BUT BECAUSE THE THEME OF CS FITS VINTAGE GENRE FILMS MUCH BETTER, AND THERE ARE ALREADY A HOST OF MEDIA OUTLETS THAT SURROUND US THAT ARE FULLY DEDICATED TO REPORTING ON MODERN ERA MOVIES. BUT YOU KNOW... EVERY ONCE IN A WHILE I SEE A PICTURE THAT WILL PROMPT ME TO MAKE AN EXCEPTION.

ALMOST ALL OF THE GREAT CAR FILMS WERE MADE IN THE 1970S AND '80S, BUT IF I WAS MAKING A FILM FEST OF NOTEWORTHY NEW MILLENNIUM MUSCLE CAR CINEMA, THERE ARE STILL A HANDFUL OF DECENT CHOICES. MOST PEOPLE WOULD PROBABLY ASSUME THE FAST AND FURIOUS MOVIES WOULD BE FRONT AND CENTRE, AND WHILE A COUPLE OF THEM ARE REALLY COOL ACTION MOVIES, I THINK THE MOVIES I WOULD ACTUALLY LIKE TO SHOW WOULD BE MORE LIKE DEATH PROOF, DRIVE, BABY DRIVER, AND NIGHTCRAWLER.

NIGHTCRAWLER IN PARTICULAR IS A 2014 MOVIE PUT TOGETHER BY THE GILROY BROS. WE HAVE DAN GILROY (WRITER AND FIRST TIME DIRECTOR), TONY GILROY (PRODUCER), AND JOHN GILROY (EDITOR) -- A REAL FAMILY PROJECT. IT'S ONE THAT ORIGINATED WITH DAN, WHO WAS INITIALLY INSPIRED BY AN INFAMOUS AND LEGENDARY CRIME PHOTOGRAPHER FROM THE 1930S NAMED ARTHUR "WEEGEE" FELLIG. I HAVE A COUPLE BOOKS OF HIS PHOTOS, AND THEY'RE STARKLY FASCINATING.

"HE WAS THE FIRST PERSON TO PUT A POLICE SCANNER IN A CAR AND DRIVE AROUND TO CRIME SCENES", DAN NOTED ON THE AUDIO COMMENTARY FOR THE FILM. "HE SOLD THESE PHOTOS TO TABLOIDS IN NEW YORK IN THE 1930S, AND I THOUGHT IT WAS A VERY INTERESTING INTERSECTION BETWEEN COMMERCE AND CRIME. BEFORE I COULD DO ANYTHING WITH THE IDEA THOUGH, JOE PESCI MADE A FILM CALLED THE PUBLIC EYE, AND I MOVED TO LOS ANGELES. THEN, A NUMBER OF YEARS AGO I LEARNED ABOUT THE MODERN EQUIVALENT... WHICH ARE THESE PEOPLE CALLED NIGHT CRAWLERS."

"AT TEN O'CLOCK AT NIGHT, 7 DAYS A WEEK, 365 DAYS A YEAR, THEY GET INTO CARS -- THERE ARE ROUGHLY 2 DOZEN OF THEM -- AND THEY TRAVEL AROUND THE 800 SQUARE MILES OF LOS ANGELES AT EXTRAORDINARILY HIGH SPEED, LISTENING TO POLICE SCANNERS, AND TRYING TO FILM GRAPHIC, LURID IMAGES WHICH THEY THEN TRY TO SELL TO THE NEWS."

"THIS WAS A JAKE NOBODY HAD EVER SEEN BEFORE."

WHEN DAN GILROY WROTE THE SCRIPT, HE KNEW HE WOULD WANT TO DIRECT IT, AND THE FIRST PERSON HE SHOWED IT TO WAS HIS BROTHER, SUCCESSFUL PRODUCER/DIRECTOR TONY GILROY, WHO'D ALREADY HAD A HIT WITH MICHAEL CLAYTON (2007) AS WELL AS DUPLICITY (2009) AND THE BOURNE LEGACY (2012). TONY INITIALLY THOUGHT HIS BROTHER JUST WANTED SOME FEEDBACK, BUT AFTER READING THE SCRIPT IN ONE NIGHT, HE WAS STRUCK BY HOW ORIGINAL AND EXCITING IT WAS, AND TOLD HIS BROTHER THE NEXT MORNING THAT THEY HAD TO WORK ON IT TOGETHER, GET A WELL KNOWN ACTOR INVOLVED, AND USE THAT STAR POWER TO GET THE MOVIE INTO PRODUCTION. THEY WERE OFF TO THE RACES.

"I'VE NEVER SEEN A SCRIPT THAT GOT THIS FAST TRACKED", TONY GILROY STATED ON THE FILM'S AUDIO COMMENTARY. "FROM ITS INCEPTION -- FROM THE MOMENT IT WAS SPRUNG ON THE WORLD -- IT ATTRACTED A GREAT ACTOR AND OTHER GREAT TALENT, AND IT WAS LIKE... IN PREPRODUCTION VERY VERY QUICKLY. IT WAS AMAZING."

JAKE GYLLENHAAL WAS THAT ACTOR, AND BEING A METHOD ACTOR, HE LOST 28 POUNDS AFTER HE DECIDED HE WANTED TO REPRESENT A THIN, GAUNT COYOTE, PROWLING AROUND LOS ANGELES. THIS WAS NOT SOMETHING THE GILROYS WANTED OR PLANNED FOR, BUT SINCE THIS PARTICULAR ACTOR WAS THEIR ACE IN THE HOLE, THEY REALIZED THEY HAD TO RECIPROCATE AND TRUST JAKE.

JAKE GYLLENHAAL

NIGHTCRAWLER

"IT'S TERRIFYING AS A FILMMAKER WHEN YOUR LEAD ACTOR SAYS HE'S GOING TO TRANSFORM HIMSELF THAT WAY. . . WE DIDN'T DISCUSS HOW MUCH WEIGHT WOULD BE LOST, BUT WHEN IT STARTED TO BECOME APPARENT HOW MUCH WEIGHT HE WAS LOSING, AND WE STARTED DOING SCREEN TESTS, IT WAS OBVIOUS THAT THIS WAS A JAKE NOBODY HAD EVER SEEN BEFORE. THE SHAPE OF HIS FACE, THE ANGULAR LOOK WAS SCARY. . . IT WAS VERY RISKY TO PRODUCERS. WE DIDN'T HAVE VERY MUCH MONEY OR VERY MUCH TIME, AND WE HAVE AN ACTOR WHO REALLY FEELS COMMITTED TO THIS. . . IDEA."

JAKE'S MAIN CHARACTER (LOUIS BLOOM) IS AN UNBLINKING SOCIOPATH, BUT INSTEAD OF PLAYING HIM GRIM AND STONE-FACED, GYNLLENHAALL MADE IT SO THAT YOU ARE ACTUALLY ABLE TO GET BEHIND HIM. A CHARACTER ARC AND A MORAL LABEL THAT ALLOWS THE AUDIENCE TO BE JUDGMENTAL OF THE MAIN CHARACTER IS IGNORED BY THE FILMMAKERS, DESPITE THE FACT THAT BLOOM IS IMMORAL AND DOES PRETTY DISTURBING STUFF IN HIS QUEST TO BE SUCCESSFUL. THE FILMMAKERS REFRAIN FROM TELLING US HOW TO FEEL, AND JUST LET US EXPERIENCE WHAT IT IS TO DRIVE AROUND LOS ANGELES AT NIGHT WITH THIS STRANGE MAN, WHO HAS THIS STRANGE, FUCKED UP JOB.

THE OTHER REALLY INTERESTING CHARACTER IS THE FEMALE LEAD IN THE MOVIE, NINA ROMINA, WHO IS PLAYED BY A 60-YEAR-OLD RENE RUSSO. I MAKE A POINT OF SPECIFYING HER AGE, BECAUSE OF HOW UNUSUAL IT IS FOR A MIDDLE AGED WOMAN TO GET TO PLAY THIS CHARACTER, DESPITE THE FACT THAT IN REAL LIFE, THE FEMALE HEAD OF A TV STATION'S NEWS DEPARTMENT WOULD MOST LIKELY BE IN HER 50S OR 60S. AND WHILE A REALITY LIKE THAT WOULD CERTAINLY BE ADHERED TO IF THE CHARACTER WERE MALE, AS WE KNOW -- ONLY YOUNG WOMEN IN HOLLYWOOD GET TO PLAY THE MIDDLE-AGED FEMALE ROLES.

IT'S SOMETHING I'D REALLY LIKE TO SEE GET CHANGED, THE FACT THAT ONCE YOU TURN 45, YOU NO LONGER GET BIG SCREEN ON-CAMERA WORK IF YOU DON'T HAVE A PENIS. UNLESS YOU HAPPEN TO BE MERYL STREEP, YOU GET RELEGATED TO TV PARTS OR VOICE ACTING. SO I LIKE TO MAKE A POINT OF STATING WHAT A BREATH OF FRESH AIR IT IS TO SEE A WOMAN LIKE RENE RUSSO GET A JUICY IMPORTANT ROLE LIKE THIS, EVEN THOUGH THE SAD FACT IS THAT SHE LIKELY WOULD NOT HAVE EVEN GOTTEN A SHOT AT IT IF HER HUSBAND WERE NOT THE DIRECTOR. CYNICAL, BUT TRUE.

"THE REASON I WROTE THIS ROLE FOR RENE, MY WIFE, IS BECAUSE HER ROLE COULD EASILY HAVE BEEN REDUCED TO SOME HARD-NOSED CORPORATE BITCH", DAN GILROY POINTED OUT IN THE FILM'S AUDIO COMMENTARY. "AND WHILE SHE CERTAINLY EMBODIES SOME OF THOSE QUALITIES, RENE HAS THE ABILITY TO TRANSMIT A VULNERABILITY."

NIGHTCRAWLER HAS THE VISUAL QUALITY AND PRODUCTION VALUES OF A BIG-TIME HOLLYWOOD FILM WHICH MAKES A LOT OF PEOPLE ASSUME IT'S A MAJOR STUDIO MOVIE, BUT IT WASN'T. THIS WAS A LOW BUDGET INDEPENDENT MOVIE, AND OFTEN THEY WERE SHOOTING WITH A VERY SMALL CREW AND DIDN'T EVEN HAVE BLOCKED SETS. ASIDE FROM IN THE CRAZIEST CAR CHASE ACTION SCENES, THE TRAFFIC AND PEOPLE WALKING AROUND IN THE BACKGROUND AREN'T EXTRAS, THEY'RE JUST CITIZENS OF LOS ANGELES.

"WE MADE THIS WITH

NO MONEY", TONY GILROY SAID. "IT SHOULD HAVE COST TWICE WHAT WE SPENT ON IT. IT'S A VERY VERY LOW BUDGET MOVIE, BUT EVEN SO... YOU DON'T JUST WANT YOUR FILM TO LOOK GOOD, YOU NEED TO HAVE A BATTLE PLAN THAT HAS EVERY SINGLE POSSIBLE EFFICIENCY BUILT INTO IT."

BUDGETARY CONSTRAINTS MEANT THE MOVIE WAS MADE IN 28 NIGHTS, WITH THE DAYTIME STUFF SHOT ON FILM, AND THE NIGHT SHOOTING ALL DONE WITH ALEXIA DIGITAL. LIKE OTHER SUCCESSFUL GENRE FILMS MADE FOR PEANUTS -- SUCH AS 2017'S GET OUT (COST 5 MILL. MADE 252 MILL.), 2016'S MOONLIGHT (COST 1.5 MILL. MADE 55 MILL.), AND 2013'S THE PURGE (COST 3 MILL. MADE 89 MILL.) -- NIGHTCRAWLER WAS MADE FOR 8 MILLION DOLLARS AND MADE 50 MILLION.

WHAT I TRULY LIKE THOUGH ABOUT THIS ONE, AND WHY I MADE AN EXCEPTION FOR IT WHEN I'VE IGNORED SO MANY OTHER NEWER MOVIES IN THESE PAGES, IS BECAUSE OF HOW ORIGINAL IT IS. THINK ABOUT HOW WE'VE BEEN INUNDATED WITH CRIME MOVIES SINCE THE GANGSTER AND FILM NOIR HEYDAY OF THE LATE 1930S AND '40S. THINK OF THE TENS OF THOUSANDS OF CRIME FILMS FROM THE POINT OF VIEW OF HOODS, CON MEN, COPS, PRIVATE EYES, GAMBLERS, DETECTIVES, JOURNALISTS, PROSTITUTES, ETC ETC. YOU NAME IT AND WE'VE SEEN 20+ VARIATIONS OF IT. BUT TO DO A CRIME FILM FROM THE PERSPECTIVE OF OF A CRIME SCENE PHOTOGRAPHER IS SO INNOVATIVE AND FRESH. IT'S SO RARE WHEN YOU CAN SAY THAT WHEN IT INCREASINGLY FEELS LIKE EVERYTHING HAS BEEN DONE TO DEATH.   —BOUGIE

RENE RUSSO

StarCrash (Italy/USA 1979 Dir: Luigi Cozzi)

BASED ON WHAT I READ IN OTHER REVIEWS OF STARCRASH, PRETTY MUCH EVERYONE THINKS THIS WAS A CRUDDY STAR WARS RIP OFF. WHILE IT CERTAINLY HAS NODS TO THAT FILM HERE AND THERE (LOOK, LIGHTSABERS!), THE FACT IS THAT STAR CRASH WAS ALREADY FULLY DESIGNED AND IN DEVELOPMENT WHEN GEORGE LUCAS BROUGHT OUT HIS SPACE OPERA SPECTACULAR THEATRICALLY IN 1977.

ITS ORIGIN COMES FROM SOMETHING FURTHER BACK, AS DIRECTOR LUIGI COZZI WAS A HUGE FAN OF RAY HARRYHAUSEN, AND THOUGHT THE MOVIE WORLD COULD USE MORE OF THAT KIND OF MAGIC. HOPING TO MAKE A SORT OF "SINBAD GOES TO SPACE" FILM, COZZI MADE SURE TO SWASH AS MANY BUCKLES AS POSSIBLE, AND ALSO CALLED FOR LOTS OF MINIATURES AND CRAZY STOP MOTION EFFECTS FROM HIS ITALIAN AND AMERICAN FX CREWS. LUIGI WAS ADAMANT THAT CAROLINE MUNRO WOULD BE HIS LEAD, THE RAVISHING AND SCANTILY-CLAD SPACE SMUGGLER, "STELLA STAR". MUNRO WAS NOT ONLY A BOND GIRL, BUT APPEARED AS THE SLAVE WOMAN "MARIGANA" IN THE 1973 HARRYHAUSEN EFFECTS FILM, THE GOLDEN VOYAGE OF SINBAD.

WITH A WORKING TITLE OF "THE ADVENTURES OF STELLA STAR", AND GIVEN ONLY TEN DAYS TO WRITE IT, COZZI COBBLED TOGETHER SOME CRAZY SHIT. WHAT HE ENDED UP WITH WAS SOMETHING LIKE A NEON DISCO PARTY IN OUTER SPACE, WHERE THE ONLY PEOPLE INVITED ARE ALIENS, ROBOTS, AND OTHER WEIRDOS. SHOOTING TOOK OVER SIX MONTHS AND WAS BROUGHT TO A HALT DUE TO FINANCING PROBLEMS ON A REGULAR BASIS.

BRITISH THESPIAN CHRISTOPHER PLUMMER DIDN'T GIVE A SHIT. HE WAS JUST HAPPY TO GET HIS PASTY ASS TO ITALY. "GIVE ME ROME ANY DAY," PLUMMER CROWED. "I'LL DO PORNO IN ROME, AS LONG AS I CAN GET TO ROME. GETTING TO ROME WAS THE GREATEST THING THAT HAPPENED TO ME IN THAT FOR ME. I THINK IT WAS ONLY ABOUT THREE DAYS IN ROME ON THAT ONE."

ALONG WITH PLUMMER AND MUNRO, THE MOVIE ALSO STARS FORMER CHILD EVANGELICAL PREACHER MARJOE GORTNER, JOE SPINELL, DAVID HASSELHOFF, A ROBOT FROM TEXAS, AND THEN YOU'VE GOT THE INFAMOUS SALVATORE BACCARO YET AGAIN PLAYING A NEANDERTHAL. SPEAKING OF THE HOFF, DAVID MANAGED TO CONTRACT FOOD POISONING DURING THE SHOOT, AND A PRODUCTION ASSISTANT HAD TO FILL IN FOR A BUNCH OF HIS SCENES. BUT DON'T WORRY, HE MADE IT BACK TO SET IN TIME TO DO SOME OF HIS OWN STUNTS AND ACCIDENTALLY KNOCK AN ITALIAN STUNTMAN'S TEETH OUT. DID I MENTION THAT JOE SPINELL'S SPACE SHIP IS A GIANT HAND THAT CLENCHES INTO A FIST WHEN HE GETS ANGRY? THERE'S TOO MUCH INSANE SHIT GOING ON IN THIS MOVIE FOR ONE SHORT CINEMA SEWER REVIEW.

GIVEN THE OPPORTUNITY TO COMPOSE THE FILM'S SCORE, THE LEGENDARY ENNIO MORRICONE TURNED THE MOVIE DOWN FLAT, LEAVING THE LATE JOHN BARRY TO DO THE MUSIC. AND HE WASN'T THE ONLY ONE TO RAISE AN EYEBROW AT THE FINISHED PRODUCT. ORIGINALLY PRODUCED FOR AMERICAN INTERNATIONAL PICTURES (WHO DECLINED TO HAVE ANYTHING TO DO WITH IT AFTER SEEING THE FINAL CUT), COZZI HAD TO KNOCK ON ROGER

Super weapons can't stop the enemy starships. Now is the time for SUPER-HEROES!

STAR CRASH

with MARJOE GORTNER — CAROLINE MUNRO — CHRISTOPHER PLUMMER
NADIA CASSINI . JOE SPINELL   JUDD HAMILTON . DAVID HASSELHOFF and ROBERT TESSIER
Written and directed by LEWIS COATES . Produced by NAT and PATRICK WASHSBERGER
Music by JOHN BARRY   □□ DOLBY STEREO

CORMAN'S DOOR AND PLEAD WITH NEW WORLD PICTURES TO RELEASE IT, INSTEAD. AND THEY DID.

WHEN THE MOVIE WAS INITIALLY RELEASED IN MARCH OF 1979, THE MONTHLY FILM BULLETIN STATED THAT IT DISPLAYED "MEDIOCRE SPECIAL EFFECTS AND A CLUMSILY PROTRACTED FINALE", AND VARIETY WAS EVEN LESS KIND. IS IT A BAD MOVIE? IN A WAY. LIKE MESSAGE FROM SPACE (THE 1978 JAPANESE MOVIE THAT MAKES A PERFECT DOUBLE BILL WITH THIS), IT'S POORLY ACTED, HAS INTENSELY CHEESY DIALOG, CARDBOARD SETS, AND IS HAPHAZARD IN VARIOUS TECHNICAL WAYS.

AND YET THERE ISN'T A SINGLE BORING MOMENT IN STARCRASH. RATHER, YOU END UP CLAPPING AND LAUGHING LIKE A FUCKING IDIOT WHEN YOU'RE REVELLING IN THE ABSURDITY OF IT ALL, AND THAT, TO ME, CONSTITUTES A CINEMATIC SUCCESS. IT REALLY IS THAT RARE TYPE OF TRASH GEM THAT A CINEPHILE CAN GET OBSESSED ABOUT, AND THOSE GEMS ARE FAR TOO RARE TO EVER BE THOUGHT OF AS "BAD".

— BOUGIE '16

PLAYBOY'S ROLLER DISCO AND PAJAMA PARTY

BY: ROBIN BOUGIE · 2016

ON NOVEMBER 23, 1979, ABC-TV AIRED A SPECIAL UNLIKE ANY OTHER. IF IT WASN'T 1979, WITH ALL ITS HEDONISTIC, COKE-SNIFFING AND TERRI-CLOTH AND POLYESTER DEBAUCHERY, IT SIMPLY WOULD NOT HAVE AIRED ANYWHERE OTHER THAN CABLE OR PAY-TV, BUT THIS WAS A MOTHERFUCKING HOUR LONG PRIMETIME SPECIAL ON NETWORK TV! CAN YOU DIG IT, BOPPERS?

IN GLITTERING NEON LASER LETTERING THE TITLE SHOOTS ACROSS THE SCREEN AS ONE OF THOSE 1970S TV ANNOUNCERS (REMEMBER THEIR DISTINCTIVE INSINCERE EDDIE ANDERSON-ESQUE VOICES?) CALLS OUT: "IT'S PLAYBOY'S ROLLER DISCO AND PAJAMA PARTY!" HOSTED BY FAMILY FEUD'S RICHARD DAWSON, THIS SENSATIONAL SPECIAL TOOK PLACE ENTIRELY AT THE PLAYBOY MANSION ON A SUNNY CALIFORNIA DAY (AND THEN A PAJAMA-CLAD NIGHT) IN 1979, AND FEATURED APPEARANCES BY HUGH HEFNER, JAMES CAAN, JIM BROWN, THE VILLAGE PEOPLE, CHUCK MANGIONE AND HIS BAND, ROBERT CULP, A BIKINI-CLAD DOROTHY STRATTEN, AND MANY OTHER FAMILIAR FACES AS WELL.

ABC WOULD AIR ONE OTHER PLAYBOY-THEMED SPECIAL, ALTHOUGH IT WAS QUITE A BIT MORE STODGY AND PEDESTRIAN IN ITS EXECUTION, SERVING AS A DOCUMENTARY ABOUT HUGH HEFNER AND THE MAGAZINE'S HISTORY UP UNTIL THEN. IT WAS NARRATED BY GEORGE PLIMPTON, AND BOTH SPECIALS PULLED DOWN FANTASTIC RATINGS. SEX SELLS.

WHEN A LOCAL ABC NEWS AFFILIATE IN SAINT PAUL, MINNESOTA CUT IN TO THE ROLLER DISCO PAJAMA PARTY TO LET PEOPLE KNOW WHAT WAS COMING UP ON 'EYEWITNESS NEWS' THAT NIGHT, A SNARKY NEWSCASTER, RON MAGERS, GAVE YOU AN INKLING HOW READY MIDDLE AMERICA WAS FOR THIS KIND OF WILD SCENE. THE CHANNEL WAS KSTP-TV, AND THEY HAD ONLY BEEN AN ABC AFFILIATE FOR FIVE SHORT MONTHS. MAGERS WAS 4 YEARS INTO HIS JOB AS A NEWS ANCHOR -- A 50-YEAR CAREER THAT WRAPPED IN MAY OF 2016.

"I ASSURE YOU THAT WE HAVE NOTHING WHATSOEVER TO DO WITH THE PLAYBOY ROLLER DISCO PAJAMA PARTY, AND THERE IS MORE TROUBLE IN IRAN. THE CRISIS CONTINUES THERE", MAGERS GLOWERED, BEFORE FINISHING WITH "FOR THOSE OF YOU WHO HAVE TURNED OFF YOUR TELEVISION IN DISGUST, YOU CAN WAIT ABOUT A HALF AN HOUR, BECAUSE THAT'S WHEN WE'LL BE BACK WITH THE NEWS."

40 YEARS LATER, MAGERS WAS STILL PISSED. "I CAN JUST HEAR THIS STUPID CONVERSATION SOME EXECUTIVE GROUP HAD, AND THEY PUT THIS SHOW ON THE AIR AND IT'S IRRITATING ME, SO I GET IN THE MIDDLE OF THIS NEWS BRIEF. AND I JUST SAID WHAT I WAS THINKING," HE REMEMBERED ABOUT THE INCIDENT. "I DID GET IN A LITTLE TROUBLE. THE OWNER OF THE STATION WASN'T REALLY HAPPY THAT I DID THAT."

"I KNOW IT JUST SEEMS SILLY NOW, BUT THIS SHOW REALLY DID FEEL LIKE SOFTCORE PORN BY THE STANDARDS OF NETWORK TELEVISION IN 1979", JOURNALIST DENNIS HARVEY POINTED OUT. "I WROTE A HUMOROUS ARTICLE FOR A MIDWESTERN NEWSPAPER ABOUT IT AFTERWARD AND THEY DIDN'T PUBLISH IT. THEY THOUGHT EVEN DESCRIBING THE SHOW WAS TOO RISGUE FOR THEIR READERS."

THE WHOLE THING WAS JUST SOAKING IN DISCO MUSIC, BEGINNING TO END (SEE THE PLAYLIST AT THE END OF THIS ARTICLE), AND THE HAPHAZARD EFFORT PUT INTO A SCRIPTING OR A NARRATIVE GAVE THE IDEA THAT A WHOLE LOT OF COKE WAS SNORTED DURING THE PLANNING AND EVENTUAL FILMING. IT'S REALLY LIKE THEY JUST STUCK A WHOLE SHITLOAD OF PLAYBOY BUNNIES AND FAMOUS PEOPLE WHO WERE OFTEN AROUND THE MANSION TOGETHER AND FILMED THE RESULTS, FIRST PERSON, WHILE SMARMY WHITE-HAIRED HOST RICHARD DAWSON MUMBLED AND BUMBLED AND PRETENDED LIKE HE WAS SHOWING YOU AROUND.

"IS THIS YOUR FIRST TIME HERE? YOU'RE GONNA HAVE THE TIME OF YOUR LIFE." A TURTLENECKED DAWSON SAYS TO THE CAMERA AS IF WE JUST CAME IN THE DOOR. "WHEN HEF THROWS A PARTY, HE REALLY THROWS A PARTY. HAVE A GOOD TIME, MINGLE! I'LL BE AROUND."

RICHARD SAID "MINGLE", SO LET'S MINGLE. LOOK THERE, IT'S ACTOR JAMES CANN. HE'S GOT A SQUIRREL ON HIS SHOULDER. OOPS, NOW IT'S HIDING BETWEEN SOME GIRL'S TITS AND A DOG JUST JUMPED INTO HIS ARMS. NOW HERE COME SOME FLAMINGOS. WHAT THE FUCK? LOOK OVER THERE: WHAT ARE THE VILLAGE PEOPLE DOING OVER THERE WITH THOSE PARROTS? EVERYONE IS EATING HOTDOGS. DON'T LET THAT PUPPET FALL IN THE POOL! CHUCK MANGIONE, OF COURSE, IS WEARING A STUPID HAT AND HIS BAND ARE PLAYING LIVE. LUSCIOUS GIGGLING GIRLS WITH BARELY ANYTHING ON ARE DANCING, MINGLING, GOOFING AROUND, AND SWIMMING IN THE GROTTO. SHIT, I DON'T EVEN HAVE TIME FOR A BONER, THERE IS TOO MUCH GOING ON!

ONE OF THE PLAYMATES PROMINENTLY FEATURED IS DOROTHY STRATTEN, WHO WAS ONE OF HEFNER'S FAVOURITES DURING THE LATE 1970S. FAR LESS OF AN AIRHEAD THAN SOME OF THESE BUBBLY CHICKS, DOROTHY LOOKS UTTERLY RADIANT WHENEVER THE CAMERA IS BLESSED ENOUGH TO CATCH HER, HERE. SADLY, SHE WAS RAPED AND MURDERED BY HER JEALOUS HUSBAND/SUITCASE PIMP JUST NINE MONTHS AFTER THIS SPECIAL AIRED. IT WAS A BRUTAL CRIME REENACTED IN THE 1983 BIOPIC, STAR 80, AND ONE THAT PREMATURELY HALTED THE PROMISING CAREER OF THE GENUINELY SWEET AND KIND WOMAN, MODEL, AND ACTRESS.

ILLUSTRATION BY BEN NEWMAN: BENNEWMANART.BLOGSPOT.COM

HER NOT-SO-SECRET LOVER, DIRECTOR PETER BOGDANOVICH (WHOSE EXISTENCE WAS THE CLEAR IGNITION POINT FOR THE DRAMA THAT LED TO DOROTHY'S MURDER) CAN BE SEEN CHATTING WITH HEFNER IN A LONG SHOT DURING ONE OF THE ROLLER-SKATING SCENES. DESPITE BEING A PLAYBOY MANSION MAINSTAY IN THE 1970S, THE TWO HAD A HUGE FALLING-OUT AFTER BOGDANOVICH BLAMED HEFNER FOR STRATTEN'S MURDER IN HIS BOOK, 'THE KILLING OF THE UNICORN,' AS A WAY TO ABSOLVE HIMSELF OF GUILT. THIS WAS A CLEARLY CALLOUS AND IDIOTIC PASSING OF BLAME THAT FANNED ANIMOSITY BETWEEN THE TWO MEN.

"THIS SUMMER, HEF CONVERTED HIS TENNIS COURTS INTO A SKATING RINK, TO SATISFY THE ROLLER DISCO CRAZE!", DAWSON GAMELY NARRATES, AND SUDDENLY THE ROLLER SKATING ELEMENT TO THE PARTY GETS INSANELY AMPED UP, AND I GET VERY HAPPY. EVERYONE IS IN SKATES AND BOOGIEING THEIR BUTTS ALL OVER THE DAMN PLACE WHILE DONNA SUMMER'S "BAD GIRLS" BLARES. JAMES CAAN LOOKS UTTERLY MORONIC SKATING AROUND IN DENIM OVERALLS, BUT HE'S JAMES FUCKING CAAN, SO NO ONE MINDS AT ALL.

DAWSON CORNERS HEF, AND DEMANDS TO KNOW WHY THE TENNIS COURT ISN'T BEING USED FOR TENNIS, AND FURTHERMORE WHY ISN'T BILL COSBY PLAYING? "COZ IS A REGULAR ON THE COURT HERE", HEFNER PROUDLY STATES, AND FOOTAGE OF BILL PLAYING AROUND WITH HIS TENNIS RACKET IN A PREVIOUSLY RECORDED CELEBRITY GAME WITH SUPERMODEL CHERYL TIEGS IS TROTTED OUT AS PROOF. COSBY JUMPS OVER THE NET DURING THE GAME, AND THE CROWD WATCHING ERUPTS INTO LAUGHTER. THIS SURELY WAS HIS HEYDAY. ALL THE COZ HAD TO DO WAS LOOK SIDEWAYS AND HE GOT A MASSIVE LAUGH OF SUPPORT JUST FOR MOVING HIS HEAD.

"BILL COSBY WAS ONE OF THE FIRST PEOPLE I MET AT THE MANSION, SHORTLY AFTER I MET HEF IN 1968", BARBI BENTON, TOLD THE DAILY MAIL IN 2016. "IT WAS UNUSUAL FOR A FAMILY MAN TO BE AT THE MANSION, ESPECIALLY AS REGULARLY AS COSBY WAS", REMEMBERED THE FAMOUS PLAYBOY CENTERFOLD AND SINGER, WHO ORIGINALLY MADE HER NAME AS A REGULAR ON THE INSIPID TV VARIETY SHOW, HEE HAW, BEFORE DEVOTING HERSELF TO HEFNER. SHE DATED HIM FROM 1968 TO 1976, BEFORE MARRYING A REAL ESTATE DEVELOPER IN 1979, A FEW WEEKS BEFORE THIS SPECIAL AIRED.

BENTON MADE IT CLEAR THAT IT WAS HARD FOR SINGLE MEN TO GET INVITATIONS TO THE LEGENDARY TUDOR-GOTHIC MANSION, BUT THAT BILL COSBY WAS INDEED AROUND, TO THE EXTENT THAT HE HAD A REGULAR PLAYBOY BUNNY GIRLFRIEND THAT HE WOULD SHOW UP AND FUCK, AND JUST FOUR YEARS INTO HIS MARRIAGE TO LONG-SUFFERING WIFE, CAMILLE. BUT EVEN THAT WASN'T ENOUGH FOR RAPEY MCRAPEFACE. NO BUNNY WAS SAFE.

SEVERAL WOMEN WHO ACCUSED COSBY OF RAPE HAD DIRECT CONNECTIONS TO THE PLAYBOY ORGANIZATION (JUDY HUTH HAS SUED COSBY SAYING HE RAPED HER AT THE PLAYBOY MANSION WHEN SHE WAS JUST 15) AND EX-BUNNY P.J. MASTEN SAID SHE KNOWS OF TWELVE FORMER BUNS WHO COSBY MOLESTED. FOR HER PART, COSBY INVITED MASTEN TO DINNER ONE NIGHT AND HE GAVE HER A COCKTAIL. THAT WAS THE LAST THING SHE REMEMBERED BEFORE WAKING UP NAKED AND BRUISED IN HIS BED. "I KNEW I WAS RAPED", SHE TOLD CNN.

WELL, WE'RE HIGH AS HELL AND SWEATY FROM DANCING ALL NIGHT, BUT IT'S TIME TO GO, AND RICHARD DAWSON MAKES SURE WE'RE LEAVING IN STYLE IN A LIMO, BUT NOT BEFORE SHOWING OFF THAT HE GETS TO KISS DOROTHY STRATTEN WHILE SHE PRETENDS TO LIKE HIM. FUCK YOU, RICHARD! FUCK YOU, COSBY! FUCK YOU, PISSY NEWS ANCHOR RON MAGERS! AND A FINAL FUCK YOU TO TIME, FOR MAKING THE AMAZING 1970S FURTHER AND FURTHER AWAY FROM US EVERY PASSING DAY.

— BOUGIE

Music playlist:
"Pinball Playboy Theme" by Cook County
"Sunset People" by Donna Summer
"Feels So Good" by Chuck Mangione
"Have a Cigar" by Pink Disco Queen
"Bad Girls" by Donna Summer
"Ring My Bell" by Anita Ward
"Pump It Up" by Fever
"Move On Up" by Destination
"Come to Me" by France Joli
"Come to Me" by France Joli (Instrumental)
"Heaven Must Have Sent You" by Bonnie Pointer
"Rock & Roll Is Back Again" by Village People
"Makin' it" by David Naughton
"Happy Radio" by Edwin Starr
"Ready for the 80's" by Village People
"Land of Make Believe" by Chuck Mangione

(NOTE: IN A WEIRD TWIST OF FATE, HEFNER SOLD THE PLAYBOY MANSION TO HIS NEXT DOOR NEIGHBOUR, DAREN METROPOULOS (THE OWNER OF HOSTESS TWINKIES AND PABST BLUE RIBBON BEER), ON THE DAY THAT I WROTE THIS REVIEW, ON JUNE 7TH, 2016. THE 20,000 SQUARE FOOT, 29 ROOM MANSION WENT FOR 120 MILLION DOLLARS, WHICH WAS 80 MILLION LESS THAN THE ASKING PRICE BUT STILL MORE THAN ANY OTHER RESIDENTIAL HOME HAD EVER SOLD FOR IN THE HISTORY OF LOS ANGELES. THE 90-YEAR-OLD MAVEN UNLOADED THE PROPERTY WITH THE AGREEMENT THAT HE BE ALLOWED TO LIVE COMFORTABLY IN THE MANSION UNTIL HIS DEATH.)

☆☆☆ ROLLER BOOGIE ☆☆☆

(USA. 1979) Directed by Mark L. Lester -- who also graced us with: Truck Stop Women (1974), Bobbie Jo and the Outlaw (1976), Class of 1984 (1982), Firestarter (1984), Commando (1985), Class of 1999 (1990), and Showdown in Little Tokyo (1991).

I KNOW WHAT I WANT.

I WANNA BE JUST LIKE LINDA BLAIR IN ROLLER BOOGIE!

ROLLERSKATE

LINDA BLAIR WAS ON TOP OF THE WORLD IN THE MID 1970s. HER CAREER WAS MADE FOR HER WHEN SHE STARRED IN THE EXORCIST (1973), ONE OF THE MOST SUCCESSFUL FILMS OF THE DECADE, AND SHE WAS A YOUNG ACTRESS THAT CRITICS AND THEATER-GOERS ALIKE WERE VERY ENTHUSIASTIC ABOUT. BUT AN EMBARRASSING ARREST IN FLORIDA FOR COCAINE POSSESSION (WITH AN INTENT TO SELL) RUINED HER HOLLYWOOD CAREER, REDUCING HER LEADING ROLES TO GRIMY, TRASHY EXPLOITATION AND INDIE HORROR MOVIES THAT SHE HATED. THE SAME KIND THAT DEGENERATES LIKE YOU AND I, SIMPLY ADORE.

HER LAST CHANCE TO SALVAGE HER CAREER IN THE STUDIO SYSTEM CAME WITH A ROMANTIC, MUSIC-FILLED VEHICLE FOR UNITED ARTISTS DESIGNED TO CASH-IN ON THE POPULARITY OF ROLLER SKATING IN THE LATE 1970s, AND IT WAS SET IN THE MECCA FOR THAT FAD: VENICE BEACH, CALIFORNIA. IT WAS CALLED ROLLER BOOGIE, AND AFTER PRINCIPAL PHOTOGRAPHY FINISHED, LINDA WOULD HAVE TO FLY BACK TO FLORIDA TO FACE HER DRUG POSSESSION COURT DATE.

OVER 3000 YOUNG ROLLER SKATING ENTHUSIASTS WERE SEEN AND AUDITIONED DURING CASTING CALLS HEADED BY PRO SKATING TRAINER BARBARA GUEDEL, WHO NARROWED THE GROUP DOWN TO JUST UNDER 50 THAT WOULD APPEAR ON SCREEN. SHE ALSO USED THIS GROUP OF FRESH-FACED FREE-WHEELERS TO FLESH OUT THE ROLLER SKATING EXTRAS IN ANOTHER VENICE BEACH SET EPIC, XANADU, WHICH WAS RELEASED A YEAR LATER IN 1980. FOR HER PART, LINDA BLAIR GOT THREE WEEKS OF TRAINING IN BEFORE THE 8-WEEK SHOOT STARTED, AND DID ALMOST ALL OF HER OWN ROLLER SKATING, WITH GUEDEL STEPPING IN AS A STUNT DOUBLE FOR SOME OF THE MORE COMPLEX TRICKS.

BLAIR'S CO-STAR WOULD BE 19-YEAR-OLD JIM BRAY, A NON-ACTOR WITH SILKY, FEATHERED SCOTT BAIO HAIR WHO HAD ALREADY AMASSED NEARLY 300 TROPHIES ON THE COMPETITIVE ROLLER SKATING CIRCUIT, AND WOULD APPEAR IN TEEN CRUSH MAGS LIKE BANANAS, TEEN, AND TIGER BEAT BECAUSE OF HIS ONLY THEATRICAL STARRING ROLE. ORIGINALLY HE WAS HIRED TO BE THE STAND-IN FOR WHOMEVER WOULD BE CAST AS BLAIR'S LEADING MAN, BUT PRODUCERS AT UNITED ARTISTS COULDN'T FIND AN ACTOR THEY LIKED WHO WAS ALSO A GOOD SKATER, SO YOUNG BRAY GOT HIS SHOT AT THE BIG TIME -- DRESSED IN A PAIR OF NUT-HUGGING SHORTS.

WHICH IS NOT TO SAY THAT ROLLER BOOGIE WAS ANY KIND OF HIT. NO, UNFORTUNATELY FOR LINDA AND JIM, THE DISCO ERA WAS ALREADY COMING TO A CLOSE BY THE TIME DECEMBER 1979 CAME AROUND, AND A PLANNED SEQUEL TO BE SET IN MEXICO ENTITLED 'ACAPULCO ROLLER BOOGIE' WAS SCRAPPED.

"I'VE BEEN TO THE BOARDWALK AT VENICE, AND IT IS, INCREDIBLY, VERY MUCH AS IT'S DEPICTED HERE" WROTE ROGER EBERT ON HIS WAY TO GIVING THE MOVIE A 'THUMBS DOWN'. "THERE ARE, GOD HELP US, REAL TEENAGERS LIKE THE ROLLER BOOGIE GANG, AND THERE ARE SOME SENSES IN WHICH ROLLER BOOGIE IS A DOCUMENTARY."

LOOK, ROLLER BOOGIE IS JUNK, AND I MEAN THAT IN THE NICEST POSSIBLE WAY. THE PLOT, SUCH AS IT IS, IS QUITE SIMPLISTIC, THE ACTING AIN'T GREAT, THE CHARACTERS ARE ONE-DIMENSIONAL... AND NONE OF THAT MATTERS AT ALL IN TERMS OF YOUR POTENTIAL VIEWING ENJOYMENT. THIS MOVIE IS A FEAST FOR THE SENSES. RIDICULOUSLY SHORT SHORTS ON EVERY BOY, TIGHT LYCRA BATHING SUITS AND LEOTARDS ON EVERY GIRL, AND SHIMMERING GLITTERY RAINBOW MIRROR BALL LIGHT SPLASHING ALL OVER EVERY GROOVY SKATING TRICK. IF YOU WANT TO EXPERIENCE AN ALTERNATE UNIVERSE WHERE DISCO PLAYS 24-7 AND EVERYONE HAS A CRAZY-EYED MANIA FOR ROLLER SKATING AND SUSPENDERS, LOOK NO FURTHER.

"IT'S LINDA BLAIR THAT REALLY MAKES ROLLER BOOGIE SOAR", WROTE TORONTO CULT FILM ENTHUSIAST, 'YUM YUM', ON HER BLOG, HOUSEOFSELFINDULGENCE.COM. "YOU'D HAVE TO HAVE BEEN BORN WITHOUT GENITALS OR BE A COMPLETE MORON TO NOT RECEIVE ANY ENJOYMENT FROM THE SIGHT OF LINDA BLAIR SKATING AROUND IN TIGHT-FITTING

OUTFITS OF EVERY COLOR IMAGINABLE; HER GLIMMERING, DELICIOUSLY SUBSTANTIVE THIGHS BASKING IN THE WARM CALIFORNIA SUN."

ROLLER BOOGIE WENT LARGELY FORGOTTEN FOR 25 YEARS UNTIL A DVD WAS RELEASED IN 2004 WHICH IS WHEN I WAS TAKEN WITH ITS CHEESY CHARMS AND DISCOVERED WHAT A DELIGHTFUL DISCO ERA TIME CAPSULE IT IS. I WASN'T THE ONLY ONE.

"WE BECAME OBSESSED WITH (ROLLER BOOGIE)", MATTHEW SWENSON, AMERICAN APPAREL'S FASHION MEDIA DIRECTOR TOLD THE ASSOCIATED PRESS IN JULY OF 2007. "WE MADE A LOT OF PIECES THAT WERE INSPIRED BY IT. IT WAS A WHIM AND OBSESSION WITH THAT FILM, AND THE ITEMS HAVE SOLD. THE GOLD AND SILVER LAMÉ FABRIC LEGGINGS TOOK OFF."

SWENSON SAW TO IT THAT ROLLER BOOGIE PLAYED IN HEAVY ROTATION IN STORE DISPLAY WINDOWS FOR THE CLOTHING CHAIN IN 2006, AND BUYERS FOR MACY'S, THE WORLD'S LARGEST DEPARTMENT STORE, ALSO CITED ROLLER BOOGIE AS ONE OF THE TWO MAIN INFLUENCES FOR THEIR DISPLAYS OF SHORTS, ROMPERS, BODYSUITS, AND TUBE TOPS IN EARLY '80s COLORS LIKE WATERMELON, TURQUOISE, CORAL AND YELLOW. MILLENNIALS ABSOLUTELY LOVED WHAT THEY SAW.

"THE STYLE OF THE LATE '70S AND EARLY '80S IS NOW APPEALING TO A YOUNGER CROWD BECAUSE IT COMES FROM A TIME THAT IS PERCEIVED AS EXUDING CONFIDENCE AND EXPRESSION", WROTE A.P'S SAMANTHA CRITCHELL WHILE TRYING TO EXPLAIN WHY XANADU AND ROLLER BOOGIE, MOVIES MOSTLY IGNORED BY AUDIENCES DURING THEIR ORIGINAL RELEASE, HAD SEEN A CULT MOVIE RESURGENCE AND HAD PROVEN TO BE AN UNEXPECTED INFLUENCE ON MODERN FASHION.

UPDATED VERSIONS OF VINTAGE FASHION ARE KNOWN TO PICK AND CHOOSE WHAT IS TO BE ADAPTED. HOWEVER. NOTHING IS EVER SIMPLY TRANSLATED VERBATIM. THAT MEANS,-- AT LEAST FOR THE TIME BEING-- YOU WON'T HAVE TO DEAL WITH TEENS ROLLER BOOGIE-ING AROUND IN FUCKING SUSPENDERS.

BOUGIE .2017.

DECONSTRUCTING FANDOM
☆ ROBIN BOUGIE '17 ☆

ARE YOU READING THIS COVER TO COVER, OR DID YOU JUST FLIP AROUND AND CHECK OUT ALL THE REVIEWS OF THE MOVIES YOU HAD ALREADY SEEN, FIRST? I ALWAYS DO THAT WHEN I READ MOVIE ZINES AND FILM REVIEW BLOGS FOR THE FIRST TIME, BECAUSE IT'S LIKE A BOROMETER.

IF I KNOW WHERE SOMEONE STANDS ON A MOVIE I'VE SEEN AND HAVE A SOLID STANCE ON, I CAN GET AN IDEA OF HOW SERIOUSLY I SHOULD TAKE THEIR RAMBLINGS, AND IF I CAN TRUST THEIR OPINIONS ON MOVIES I HAVE NOT YET SEEN. I WANT TO SEE IF THEY'RE ON MY 'TEAM' OR IF THEY ARE AN OUTSIDER THAT DOESN'T GET IT -- DOESN'T HAVE ENOUGH EXPERIENCE WITH THAT GENRE TO BE ABLE TO DIGEST AND ACCURATELY PARSE WHAT THEY'VE SAT DOWN AND WITNESSED.

AND YOU KNOW WHAT THAT IS? THAT'S TRIBALISM. THAT'S THE BASIS FOR RELIGION, PATRIOTISM, AND FANDOM OF ALL SORTS. HUMANS JUST NATURALLY WANT TO SURROUND THEMSELVES WITH LIKE-MINDED INDIVIDUALS THAT CAN VALIDATE THEIR LIFE EXPERIENCE BY REFLECTING THEM BACK TO THEMSELVES.

USUALLY WHEN IT'S ARTICULATED LIKE THAT, IT'S ALWAYS CATAGORIZED AS A NEGATIVE (DUE TO THE SHIT-TONNE OF WRONG-HEADED, MINDLESS, BIGOTED AND INHUMANE ACTS THAT HAVE RESULTED FROM TRIBALISM AND WARRING SIDES), BUT REFRAIN FROM SEEING IT THAT WAY IF YOU CAN, BECAUSE THIS BASIC HUMAN PSYCHOLOGY IS NOT GOOD OR BAD UNTIL YOU ACT UPON IT. IT JUST IS.

NOW THAT'S NOT TO SAY THAT YOU'RE DEAD TO ME IF YOU DON'T LIKE THE SAME ENTERTAINMENT I LIKE, NOT AT ALL. I'LL ALWAYS RESPECT A DIFFERING OPINION IF IT IS PRESENTED INTELLIGENTLY, PASSIONATELY, AND WITH A BASIS IN RATIONAL THOUGHT THAT IS DEVOID OF FEAR. THAT'S THE CRUX OF A GOOD DEBATE, AND WHAT'S BETTER THAN THAT?! BUT ONLY A TRUE FILM FAN, A STUDENT OF THE ARTFORM WHO HAS PUT IN THE HOURS AND A LOT OF THOUGHT INTO WHY SOMETHING WORKED OR DID NOT IS EQUIPPED TO VOCATIONALLY BATTLE WITH ONE WHO HAS. ALL OF THE OTHERS ARE JUST THAT: OTHERS. THEY AREN'T IN OUR TRIBE.

SORRY, IS THIS IMAGE OFF-TOPIC FOR THIS LIL' RANT? YEAH PROBABLY. BUT I DIDN'T FEEL LIKE DRAWING MY BIG DUMB FACE YET AGAIN.

DEFIANT YET 'OPEN' POSE

SEASON OF THE WITCH (1972)
Review by Ian Jane ☆

JOAN MITCHELL (JANINA WHITE) IS A MISERABLE WOMAN APPROACHING MIDDLE AGE FASTER THAN SHE'D LIKE TO BE, AND ON TOP OF THAT, SHE'S STUCK IN A DULL MARRIAGE. SHE LIVES OUT IN THE SUBURBS WITH HER BORING (AND AT TIMES VERY ABUSIVE) HUSBAND, JACK (BILL THUNHURST), AND THEIR SAD-SACK TEENAGE DAUGHTER, NIKKI (JOEDDA McCLAIN) WHO IS MORE INTERESTED IN GETTING LAID AND GETTING OUT OF THE HOUSE AS SOON AS POSSIBLE. JOAN WANTS A CHANGE IN HER LIFE. JOAN WANTS SOMETHING MORE EXCITING THAN THE LACK-LUSTER EXISTENCE SHE'S BEEN TOILING THROUGH DAY IN, DAY OUT, FOR THE LAST TWO DECADES.

AT FIRST, JOAN HAS AN AFFAIR WITH A YOUNGER MAN, AN ACQUAINTANCE OF HER DAUGHTER, BUT THIS PROVES TO BE REALLY NOTHING MORE THAN JUST A PASSING DIVERSION. EVENTUALLY, THE HOUSEWIFE IN QUESTION FINDS EXACTLY WHAT SHE'S LOOKING FOR WHEN SHE DECIDES TO PAY A VISIT TO MARION HAMILTON (VIRGINIA GREENWALD), A WOMAN IN TOWN WHO MAKES HER LIVING AS A TAROT READER. WHAT JOAN DOESN'T KNOW, BUT SOON FINDS OUT, IS THAT MARION IS ALSO THE LEADER OF A COVERT WITCHES COVEN WHO DABBLES IN THE BLACK ARTS. WHEN JOAN LEARNS OF THIS, SHE BRUSHES UP ON WITCHCRAFT A BIT AND BECOMES QUITE TAKEN WITH IT, SOON JOINING UP TO PRACTICE WITCHCRAFT HERSELF WITH MARION AND HER FELLOW MISTRESSES OF THE DARK.

HER INVOLVEMENT IN WITCHCRAFT SOON PROVES TO BE A VERY UNHEALTHY DIVERSION FOR JOAN. THE MORE SHE RETREATS INTO

caviar in the kitchen
nothing in the bedroom

HUNGRY WIVES

with an appetite for diversion

IT, THE MORE IT IS ALMOST AS IF SHE'S LIVING IN HER OWN LITTLE WORLD. HER FAMILY STARTS TO NOTICE, BUT SHE JUST PULLS MORE AND MORE INTO HER STRANGE SHELL, AND THEN THINGS START TO GET REALLY BAD FOR EVERYONE INVOLVED.

SHOT AS 'JACK'S WIFE' AND THEN RELEASED THEATRICALLY AS 'HUNGRY WIVES,' GEORGE ROMERO'S SEASON OF THE WITCH IS AN INTERESTING MOVIE, IF A VERY FLAWED ONE. THE FIRST THING THAT BECOMES OBVIOUS IS THAT THIS ONE WAS MADE FAST AND CHEAP. THE PRODUCTION VALUES ARE NOTICEABLY POOR AND THE PERFORMANCES, ASIDE FROM WHITE IN THE LEAD AND A FEW OF THE SUPPORTING CAST MEMBERS (LOOK FOR BILL HINZMAN IN A SMALL ROLE) ARE NOTHING TO WRITE HOME ABOUT. THE PACING ALSO DRAGS IN A FEW SPOTS AND DESPITE AN INTERESTING OPENING SCENE IN WHICH JOAN SEES HERSELF IN THE MIRROR AS A WRETCHED LOOKING OLD WOMAN, IT TAKES A WHILE TO GET GOING.

ONCE THE MOVIE PICKS UP THOUGH, SEASON OF THE WITCH EVENTUALLY BECOMES AN INTERESTING AND ATMOSPHERIC FILM WITHOUT A LOT OF FLASH. ROMERO, AS USUAL, PACKS SOME POLITICS INTO THE FILM THAT GIVE IT AN INTERESTING METAPHORICAL CHARACTERISTIC. ANYONE EXPECTING A MOVIE ON PAR WITH ANY OF HIS INFAMOUS 'DEAD' FILMS, HOWEVER, WILL BE SORELY DISAPPOINTED, AS THIS ONE IS SLOWER AND MORE METHODICAL IN ITS APPROACH.

BLACK CHRISTMAS (1974. DIR: BOB CLARK)

IN 1974 BOB CLARK RELEASED BLACK CHRISTMAS UPON AN UNSUSPECTING AND UNAPPRECIATIVE PUBLIC. OVER THE YEARS, THIS CANADIAN CLASSIC HAS GARNERED A VERY STRONG CULT FOLLOWING AND IS WIDELY CONSIDERED BY MANY TO BE THE INSPIRATION FOR A LOT OF CLASSIC SLASHER MOVIES, JOHN CARPENTER'S HALLOWEEN IN PARTICULAR. THE FILM ALSO BENEFITED FROM ONE OF THE BEST TAG LINES EVER: "IF THIS MOVIE DOESN'T MAKE YOUR SKIN CRAWL. . . IT'S ON TOO TIGHT!"

A SLICK AND VERY SUSPENSEFUL LOW BUDGET HORROR THRILLER, BLACK CHRISTMAS MAY SOUND CLICHÉ TO TODAY'S AUDIENCES AS THE THEMES HAVE BEEN EXPLOITED COUNTLESS TIMES, BUT RARELY HAVE THEY BEEN USED SO SUCCESSFULLY. BOB CLARK'S DIRECTION IS SPOT ON IN THIS FILM AND HE USES HIS SETS AND THE OMINOUS SHADOWS THEY CREATE FOR MAXIMUM EFFECT. THE SORORITY HOUSE IS BIG AND CREEPY, OFFERING PLENTY OF SHADOWY ATMOSPHERE AND IT PROVES TO BE THE PERFECT CENTRAL LOCATION FOR THE FILM TO BE BASED AROUND, AND THE CINEMATOGRAPHY FROM REGINALD H. MORRIS (WHO WORKED WITH CLARK ON PORKY'S AND A CHRISTMAS STORY AND ALSO SHOT THE CANUXPLOITATION SCI-FI CULT CLASSIC THE SHAPE OF THINGS TO COME!) IS QUITE POLISHED AND HELPS TO RAMP UP THE TENSION WITH SOME CLEVER CAMERA ANGLES AND EFFECTIVE LIGHTING.

BLACK CHRISTMAS IS ALSO A GREAT CHANCE TO SEE A NOW FAMOUS CAST IN THEIR YOUTH. SCTV STALWART ANDREA MARTIN, A YEAR AFTER SHE STARRED IN IVAN REITMAN'S CANNIBAL GIRLS IS REALLY SOLID. LIKEWISE, OLIVIA HUSSEY AND MARGOT KIDDER HAVE PROMINENT ROLES HERE A FEW YEARS BEFORE THEIR RESPECTIVE CAREERS WOULD TAKE OFF. JOHN SAXON TURNS IN A LIKEWISE EXCELLENT PERFORMANCE AS TOP COP FULLER, BEFORE WE'D SEE HIM IN CLASSICS SUCH AS CANNIBAL APOCALYPSE, A NIGHTMARE ON ELM STREET AND DARIO ARGENTO'S TENEBRAE.

OFTEN IMITATED BUT RARELY DUPLICATED, BLACK CHRISTMAS REMAINS A TESTAMENT TO LOW BUDGET HORROR MOVIE MAKING AT ITS BEST. IT STANDS AS A PRIME EXAMPLE OF HOW SUSPENSE CAN BE CREATED WITH MOOD, LIGHTING AND ATMOSPHERE FAR MORE SUCCESSFULLY THAN IT CAN WITH BLOOD AND GUTS.

-IAN JANE ROCKSHOCKPOP.COM

EURO INTERNATIONAL FILMS

SENZA RAGIONE

FRANCO NERO   TELLY SAVALAS
MARK LESTER
SENZA RAGIONE

REDNECK (aka Senza Ragione)
Director: Silvio Narizzano (Italy 1973)

SILVIO NARIZZANO (OF FANATIC) DIRECTS TELLY SAVALAS (VIOLENT CITY, KOJAK) AND FRANCO NERO (DJANGO, HITCHHIKE) IN THIS RATHER UNUSUAL ITALIAN ACTION/THRILLER FEATURING A SUPPORTING ROLE BY MARK LESTER OF ALL PEOPLE, THE LITTLE KID WHO PLAYED THE LEAD IN THE 1968 VERSION OF OLIVER!

MEMPHIS (SAVALAS) AND MOSQUITO (NERO) ARE TWO THUGS WHO ROB A JEWELRY STORE IN ROME AND HOPE TO GET ACROSS THE FRENCH BORDER BEFORE THE COPS NAB THEM. MOSQUITO'S GIRLFRIEND MARIA (ELY GALLEANI OF BABA YAGA AND FIVE DOLLS FOR AN AUGUST MOON) IS ALONG FOR THE RIDE, BUT UNBEKNOWNST TO THE THREE OF THEM, SO IS A KID NAMED LENNOX DUNCAN (LESTER) WHO HAPPENS TO BE HIDING IN THE BACKSEAT OF THE CAR THEY JUST HIJACKED.

IT TURNS OUT THAT LENNOX IS THE SON OF A PROMINENT MEMBER OF THE UNITED NATIONS AND THAT HIS MOTHER, WHO WAS IN THE CAR WITH HIM UNTIL THEY STOLE IT, IS ABLE TO ID THE TWO HOODLUMS. THIS PUTS THE GROUP AT THE TOP OF THE POLICE'S WANTED LIST AND THE CHASE IS ON.

AS THINGS GET TENSE AND THEY DISCOVER JUST WHO LENNOX REALLY IS, MEMPHIS STARTS TO GRADUALLY SNAP AND HIS BEHAVIOUR BECOMES MORE AND MORE ERRATIC. WHEN HE STARTS VICIOUSLY KILLING PEOPLE AND BLAMING IT ON EVERYONE ELSE, MEMPHIS AND MOSQUITO ARE TURNED AGAINST EACH OTHER WITH LENNOX'S LIFE HANGING IN THE BALANCE.

REDNECK WOULD PROBABLY WORK REALLY WELL AS A SERIOUS AND GRITTY CRIME DRAMA IF NOT FOR TWO THINGS — FRANCO NERO SPENDING THE LAST TWENTY MINUTES OF THE MOVIE IN A WOMAN'S FUR COAT LOOKING LIKE A PIMPED UP DRAG QUEEN, AND TELLY SAVALAS IN A PERFORMANCE SO OVER THE TOP THAT IT TRULY HAS TO BE SEEN TO BE BELIEVED. ADD TO THE FACT THAT SAVALAS SPORTS ONE OF THE STRANGEST SOUTHERN ACCENTS I'VE EVER HEARD, AND A SCENE IN WHICH A FAR TOO YOUNG MARK LESTER DISROBES IN AN ATTEMPT TO EMULATE NERO'S CHARACTER AND REDNECK BECOMES ALMOST DELIRIOUSLY EXPLOITATIVE.

TAKE THOSE ODD ELEMENTS OUT OF THE PICTURE THOUGH AND YOU'VE GOT A FAIRLY STRAIGHTFORWARD CRIME MOVIE THAT MOVES ALONG AT A QUICK PACE AND HAS SOME NICELY EXECUTED MOMENTS OF TENSION AND ACTION. NERO IS SLICK AS ALWAYS, EXCEPT WHEN HE LOOKS LIKE HE'S IN DRAG, AND THE STORY, DESPITE BEING SEMI FAMILIAR, IS A FUN ONE WITH A COUPLE OF UNEXPECTED TWISTS AND TURNS ALONG THE WAY. GALLEANI IS FUN TO LOOK AT, EVEN IF SHE ISN'T GIVEN MUCH TO DO HERE, AND THE CAMERAWORK KEEPS THE PICTURE LOOKING GOOD FROM START TO FINISH.

REDNECK IS A PRETTY WACKY FILM. SAVALAS SPARES NO EXPENSE IN CHEWING THROUGH ALL OF HIS SCENES LIKE A MANIAC AND HIS 'GOOD OL' BOY' ACCENT PROVIDES A WHOLE LOT OF UNINTENTIONAL HILARITY.

REVIEW BY IAN JANE -- (ROCKSHOCKPOP.COM)

The Love Merchant (1966. Dir: Joe Sarno)

I WATCHED JOE SARNO'S THE LOVE MERCHANT (1966) FOR THE FIRST TIME TONIGHT, AND I GOTTA TELL YOU THAT IT WAS PRETTY GODDAMN GREAT. LOOK, THERE WERE ONLY LIKE TWO GLIMPSES OF BOOBS (WHICH IS CRAZY-LIGHT FOR A SEXPLOITATION MOVIE) BUT AS WITH SO MANY SARNOS, I DIDN'T EVEN NOTICE THE NUDITY WAS MISSING BECAUSE I GOT SO WRAPPED UP IN THE UNSETTLING SEXUAL MELODRAMA. YOU WILL TOO, IF YOU PAY ATTENTION.

IT'S LIKE A WARPED, LOW BUDGET, BLACK AND WHITE INDECENT PROPOSAL, AND ACTOR JUDSON TODD PLAYS "KENDALL HARVEY THE THIRD", A RICH PRICK WITH AN ETERNALLY COCKED EYEBROW WHO HAPPENS TO LOOK, SOUND, AND BEHAVE LIKE A THINNER, CREEPIER, CITIZEN KANE-ERA ORSON WELLES. KENDALL USES A MOD BIKER NAMED CLICK (LOUIS WALDON) AND A DOMINEERING LESBIAN NAMED POLLY FIELDS (PATTI PAGET) TO HUNT DOWN THE BEST BITCHES FOR HIM TO BALL, AND IF A FEW PEOPLE GET HURT ALONG THE WAY, WHO CARES? SUCH ARE THE LIFESTYLES OF THE RICH AND FAMOUS. CHAMPAGNE WISHES AND VAGINAL DREAMS.

SURE, HE BOUNCES HIS SKIN MARBLES OFF THE ASS OF A DIFFERENT BITCH EVERY NIGHT, BUT HE ONLY ENDS UP FEELING LONELY AND DEEPLY UNFULFILLED. THAT IS, UNTIL THE DAY HE MEETS PEGGY JOHNS (PATRICIA MCNAIR), THE CLASSY-ASS, VERY HAPPILY MARRIED WIFE OF A LOCAL ADVERTISING EXECUTIVE (PLAYED BY GEORGE WOLFE). DESPITE ROLLING AROUND IN PUSSY CONSTANTLY, IT'S THE SEEMINGLY UNATTAINABLE PEGGY THAT BECOMES KENDALL'S OVERWHELMING OBSESSION.

THE PLOT TWISTS YOUR NIPPLES AND KICKS INTO HIGH GEAR WHEN PEGGY'S HUSBAND'S BUSINESS FALLS ON HARD TIMES AND HE STARTS TO DRINK HIMSELF INTO ALCOHOLIC OBLIVION. SEEING HIS 'IN', KENDALL USES THE OPPORTUNITY TO TRY TO BRIBE WORRIED LITTLE PRINCESS PEGGY WITH HIS OH-SO-VERY INDECENT PROPOSAL: I'LL MAKE YOUR HUSBAND'S BUSINESS SUCCESSFUL AND BRING THE POOR BOY BACK FROM THE BRINK IF YOU AGREE TO SPEND 48 HOURS AS MY PERSONAL FUCK-SLAVE.

WILL SHE DO IT? WHAT PART DO THE SMARMY BIKER AND THE SALTY DYKE HAVE TO PLAY? WHAT'S WITH THE GO-GO DANCING GIRLS IN THE CAGE MADE OF STRING? WAIT, IS THAT JUNE ROBERTS? I WON'T GIVE ANYTHING AWAY HERE, YOU'LL JUST HAVE TO SEE IT!

"SARNO BALANCED HIS FILMS BETWEEN TWO PHILOSOPHIES: SEX AS A HEALING FORMULA, OR SEX AS A DESTRUCTIVE FORCE", WROTE SLEAZE HISTORIAN CASEY SCOTT IN HIS REVIEW OF THE MOVIE AT DVDDRIVE-IN.COM. "THE LATTER IS THE THINKING BEHIND MOST OF HIS '60S OUTINGS, INCLUDING THE LOVE MERCHANT, WITH LUST RUINING A MARRIAGE AND LEAVING HARVEY FEELING EMPTY AND LONELY. THE LAST LINE, "SHE'S RIGHT, YOU'RE ALL SICK!" IS ALMOST SPOKEN DIRECTLY INTO THE CAMERA, AIMED SQUARELY AT THE 42ND STREET AUDIENCE EXPECTING MORE TITS AND ASS."

A LADY BY DAY... BY NIGHT A WOMAN OBSESSED

No Children "EX A WOMAN"

NOW IN

"LOVE MERCHANT"

SHOWING TONITE ADULTS ONLY

Hi-Way Drive-In U.S. #1 South Ft. Land. at Airport

MORE HAPPENS IN THE 79 MINUTES OF THE LOVE MERCHANT THAN IN A HALF DOZEN OTHER SUBSTANDARD SEXPLOITATION KNOB-POLISHERS OF THE ERA, AND YET IT DOES ACTUALLY MANAGE TO DRAG IN A COUPLE SPOTS. ALSO: DO KINDLY REMEMBER THAT IT SPORTS THE $89.95 COSTUME AND SET BUDGET ONE SHOULD COME TO EXPECT FROM THE GENRE. KEEP YOUR EXPECTATIONS LOW, AND YOUR DOGGED THIRST FOR NUDITY LOWER, AND YOU'LL FIND THE LOVE MERCHANT TO BE A TRULY SATISFACTORY AND TAWDRY TREASURE IN SARNO'S FINE FILMOGRAPHY OF FLAGRANT INFIDELITY. WE ARE ALL SICK, INDEED.

— BOUGIE '19

THE LOVE MERCHANT
THE BRUTAL AND REALISTIC STORY OF A MAN SEEKING LOVE

The Millionairess (1974) Dir: Leonard Kirtman

PLAYING A CHARACTER THAT HAS HIS SAME NAME, BISEXUAL HEROIN JUNKIE AND VINTAGE PORNO SUPERSTUD MARC STEVENS APPEARS AS A JOURNALIST IN A SOUTHERN TEXAS PRISON. HE'S THERE TO INTERVIEW INCARSERATED BIMBO, CLAIRE LEE (PLAYED BY ANDREA TRUE) THE DAUGHER OF A HOUSTON OIL TYCOON WHO HAS BEEN JAILED FOR "EXPOSING HERSELF AT THE ASTRODOME IN FRONT OF 24,000 FANS". SHE PROCEEDS TO TELL MARC ABOUT HER VARIOUS SEXUAL EXPLOITS (WHICH ARE TOLD IN FLASHBACK) SO THAT HIS READERS CAN GET THEIR JOLLIES, AND LATER IN THE PICTURE SHE'LL PROCEED TO BOFF THE HECK OUT OF HIM WHILE THEY BOTH IMPROVISE SOUTHERN ACCENTS AND COLLOQUIALISMS.

THAT EVENING ANDREA SEDUCES HER SNARKY SOUTHERN FRIED PRISON GUARD (JACK WEBB) WHOSE RATHER UNEXCEPTIONAL COCK SHE SUCKS RIGHT THROUGH THE BARS OF HER CELL. "HOW'S THAT FOR A SOUTHERN BITCH?" SHE SMILES AS SHE LICKS HIS CUM GLAZE FROM HER LIPS. THE ROLLING STONES' "BROWN SUGAR" STARTS BLASTING OUT AS HE ENTERS THE CELL AND PROCEEDS TO LAP AWAY AT THE REDHEAD'S HAIRY BEAVER, WHICH YOU CAN BE SURE WAS NEVER PROPERLY OR LEGALLY LISCENSED. VINTAGE PORN FLIES BY THE SEAT OF ITS PANTS WHEN IT COMES TO MUSIC RIGHTS.

THEN ANDREA TELLS MARC ABOUT A TIME WHEN A BLACK GUY (DARYL SPANGLER) IN A DUMB STRIPED HAT AND VEST BROKE INTO HER BEST FRIEND'S PLACE AND PROCEEDED TO RAPE HER. THE BEST FRIEND IS PLAYED CONVINCINGLY BY THE UNDERRATED, BUCK-TOOTHED, SHORT-HAIRED, PALE-SKINNED JUDY CRAVEN (THE SHELLEY DUVALL OF 1970S PORN), WHO I ALSO REALLY ENJOYED IN ANGEL NUMBER 9 (1975), AND SHAUN COSTELLO'S XXX KIDNAPPING MOVIE FROM THE SAME YEAR, THE TYCOON'S

DAUGHTER. SHE'S NOT "PRETTY" IN ANY CONVENTIONAL SENSE, BUT I LOVE THE AWKWARD NERD GIRLS, AND JUDY QUALIFIES. UNFORTUNATELY THIS SCENE IS REALLY UNCONVINCINGLY AND AWKWARDLY DUBBED WITH VOICE ACTORS IN POST PRODUCTION, A PRACTICE THAT DIRECTOR LEONARD KIRTMAN WAS KNOWN FOR. SIGH.

THAT'S RIGHT, THIS WAS DIRECTED BY NEW YORK-BASED SMUT-MAVEN, LEONARD KIRTMAN, WHO, IN A RECENT POLL OF CINEMA SEWER READERS, RANKED 3RD ON A "WORST VINTAGE PORN DIRECTORS" POLL, AFTER ONLY CARLOS TOBALINA AND JOSEPH F. ROBERTSON. (ROUNDING OUT THE TOP 5 WERE RAY DENNIS STECKLER UNDER HIS CINDY LOU SUTTERS AKA, AND RIK TAZINER). KIRTMAN, AS CS FAN CHRISTOPHER ELAM POINTED OUT, "IS ONE OF THE MOST FRUSTRATING PORN DIRECTORS, BECAUSE THEY HAVE THE POTENTIAL TO BE AT LEAST OK, AND THEN HE DOES DIPSHIT STUFF LIKE DUBBING IN FAKE MOANING IN A CONSTANT LOOP, OR SCORING A SCENE WITH A KAZOO OR ELEPHANT SOUNDS".

DISSATISFACTION WITH KIRTMAN DOESN'T JUST END WITH HIS AUDIENCE. HIS CAST AND CREW ALMOST UNIVERSALLY DISLIKED THIS CLOWN, TOO. AS I NOTED IN MY BOOK, GRAPHIC THRILLS 2, "KIRTMAN (AKA LEON GUCCI) WORKED AS A CAB DRIVER IN NEW YORK IN THE MID 1960S BEFORE FOUNDING KIRT FILMS. KNOWN TO SHOOT 4 TO 5 FILMS IN THE SAME WEEKEND ON THE SAME LOCATION, 'LECHEROUS LENNY' WAS LEGENDARY FOR BEING A CHEAP BASTARD, EXTORTING SEX FROM HIS FEMALE CAST MEMBERS, AND WEARING BERMUDA SHORTS."

LENNY ★K★ AINT GOT NO SWAY

HYAPATIA LEE

LEGENDARY 1980s ADULT FILM STAR HYAPATIA LEE WAS BORN 'VICKI LYNCH' IN HAUGHVILLE, INDIANA TO TEENAGE PARENTS IN 1960. SHE IS OF IRISH AND CHEROKEE DESCENT, HAS THREE CHILDREN, IS CURRENTLY ON HER SECOND MARRIAGE, AND PERFORMS IN THE BAND W4IK, WHOSE ALBUM "DOUBLE EUPHORIC" CAME OUT IN 1994. SHE'S ALSO SELF PUBLISHED TWO BOOKS: "THE SECRET LIFE OF HYAPATIA LEE", AND "NATIVE STRENGTH: THE FIRST STEP ON THE PATH OF INDOMITABLE LIFE". SHE IS AN AVID POT SMOKER AND GROWER, AND IN RECENT YEARS HAS BEEN THE AUTHOR OF THE "STONER SEX" COLUMN AT HIGH TIMES MAGAZINE.

THIS INTERVIEW WAS CONDUCTED BY JOHN HUSON IN 1998, AND SEES PRINT HERE FOR THE FIRST TIME.

Q: What was it like the day it came to shoot your first sex scene in an adult movie?

A: I WAS NERVOUS. MY HUSBAND AND I WERE ARGUING, AND THE DIRECTOR MADE IT EVEN WORSE. HIS NAME WAS EDDIE BROWN, AND HE WAS A JERK. HE MADE IT REALLY HARD. THE GUY I WORKED WITH WAS COOL AND HE WAS GREAT TO MY HUSBAND, SO THAT MADE IT A LITTLE EASIER. THE FIRST TIME IS ALWAYS THE HARDEST, AND I WAS TERRIFIED.

Q: You got creative control over your movies pretty quickly. That was pretty unusual for the time, wasn't it?

A: YES, VERY MUCH SO. THE GUY I GOT STARTED WITH WAS HARRY MOHNEY, THE GUY WHO USED TO DO THE GAIL PALMER MOVIES. I HAD WON THE NUDE MISS GALAXY CONTEST TWICE, AND HE WAS THE GUY WHO ASKED ME IF I WANTED TO GET INTO THE BUSINESS. AND ACTUALLY, HE'S THE GUY WHO NOW OWNS ALL THE DEJA VU STRIP CLUBS. HE WAS GREAT TO US. THERE WERE SCRIPTS THAT I WROTE, AND HE SAID "OH, THIS IS A GOOD ONE. I'D LIKE TO SHOOT TWO OF THESE BACK TO BACK, SO WHY DON'T YOU WRITE ANOTHER ONE CALLED 'BODY GIRLS". I SAID "OK, WHAT'S IT ABOUT?", AND HE SAID "I DON'T KNOW, YOU HAVEN'T WRITTEN IT YET, BUT I LIKE THE TITLE 'BODY GIRLS', SO WRITE A MOVIE CALLED 'BODY GIRLS'".

Q: That seems to be the oldest of your films that you can still find fairly easily in video stores.

A: THE FIRST MOVIE I DID WAS CALLED "NAUGHTY GIRLS NEED LOVE TOO", AND THAT ONE'S STILL AROUND. AFTER THAT, I DID "THE YOUNG LIKE IT HOT", AND THAT WAS A GOOD ONE. IT WAS WITH SHAUNA GRANT AND

KAY PARKER. AT THE SAME TIME WE SHOT THAT WE ALSO SHOT "SWEET YOUNG FOXES", WHICH WASN'T REALLY THAT GOOD OF A MOVIE.

Q: What do you remember about "Let's Get Physical", which featured you in a long dance sequence?

A: THAT WAS FUN TO DO. AND PAUL THOMAS WROTE A SONG JUST FOR THAT ONE SEQUENCE — WHERE HE PLAYED ON PIANO AND I DID BALLET. I ENJOYED WORKING WITH PAUL THOMAS AS AN ACTOR. AT FIRST WHEN HE STARTED DIRECTING HE WAS A VERY GOOD DIRECTOR, THEN AS TIME HAS GONE ON HE HAS GOTTEN FRUSTRATED WITH THE BUSINESS AND THE CONFINES OF THE SMALL BUDGETS. HE'S FEELING LIKE HE'S JUST CRANKING THEM OUT NOW AND IT'S LIKE, "OH, WHO CARES, IT'S JUST A PORNO MOVIE, GET IT DONE WITH," WHICH IS VERY DISAPPOINTING, BECAUSE THAT ATTITUDE CAN PERMEATE THE SET AND MAKE THINGS VERY HARD.

Q: One thing I noticed about the films you had control over was that there were lots of interesting casting choices. You don't see the parade of all the same familiar faces that seem to be in every other film.

A: WELL THAT'S GOOD TO HEAR. I TRIED, ESPECIALLY WHEN I WAS AT CARIBBEAN FILMS. THEY WERE A LOT MORE LIABLE TO GIVE SOMEBODY A CHANCE, WHEREAS SOME OF THE OTHER COMPANIES WERE LIKE "TIME IS MONEY, AND WE WANT TO GO WITH SOMEBODY WHO'S PROVEN THEY CAN PERFORM ON CUE".

Q: One other early film that I have to ask about is "The Ribald Tales of Canterbury", which I thought was just fantastic.

A: OH, THAT WAS MY FAVORITE! THAT WAS THE BIGGEST BUDGETED X-RATED FILM I EVER SHOT. WE SPENT OVER THREE HUNDRED THOUSAND DOLLARS.

Q: It looks like a lot more.

A: THE ONLY REASON IT WAS LESS WAS THAT WE GOT THE COSTUMES FROM UNIVERSAL'S LOT THAT WERE LEFT OVER FROM "CAMELOT", OR SOME SIMILAR FILM. THEY HAVE A LOT WHERE THEY RENT COSTUMES, AND WE DID THAT FOR SEVERAL MOVIES, BUT THAT MOVIE WAS THE ONE WHERE WE REALLY COULDN'T HAVE LIVED WITHOUT THEM. MOST OF MY FILMS WEREN'T PERIOD PIECES, SO YOU COULD GO OUT AND GET COSTUMES ON THE STREET OR BORROW SOMEBODY'S WARDROBE. HOW COULD WE REPLACE THOSE COSTUMES? THEY WERE FABULOUS.

Q: Was that a tough shoot, with all the outdoor and location stuff?

A: YEAH, AND MOST OF THE TIME IT WAS VERY, VERY COLD, SO UNDERNEATH THAT LONG DRESS, AS I'M RIDING THAT PRETTY WHITE HORSE, I'VE GOT A SWEATER ON, I'VE GOT ON JEANS, I'M WEARING SOME REALLY CUTE

KNEE HIGH MOCCASINS. AND THE SEX SCENES WERE VERY HARD. THERE'S ONE SCENE WHERE DON HART AND THE GIRL WHO PLAYED THE MONK ARE IN A BARN. WHEN THEY WERE SHOOTING THAT SCENE YOU COULD SEE THE STEAM COMING OFF OF THEIR BODIES BECAUSE IT WAS SO COLD. REALLY HARD TO PERFORM.

Q: You all really earned your money on that one.

A: YEAH, ESPECIALLY THE GUYS!

Q: What was it like working with Colleen Brennan on that one?

A: SHE'S WONDERFUL! I LOVED WORKING WITH HER. FOR A WHILE SHE WAS DOING THE 900 NUMBER LINES. SHE WAS INVOLVED WITH ⟨NAME REDACTED⟩ OF SPECTATOR MAGAZINE, AND THEY HAD A DAUGHTER, WENT THROUGH A CUSTODY BATTLE, AND SHE WAS ON A MILK CARTON FOR A WHILE, BUT THEY FOUND HER. SHE WENT THROUGH SOME REAL SHIT FOR A WHILE, BUT SHE IS A SWEETHEART AND A SURVIVOR AND I LOVE HER DEARLY. SHE'S A VERY SMART LADY. SMART AS A WHIP.

Q: What was it like for you when the shift from film to video hit?

A: IT WAS SO DISAPPOINTING. WHEN THE SHIFT FIRST HAPPENED I WAS UNDER CONTRACT AT ESSEX FILMS, ALONG WITH BARBARA DARE. ESSEX, BEING THE RESPECTED BIG COMPANY

THAT IT WAS, EVEN THOUGH THE FORMAT WAS DIFFERENT, THEY STILL TRIED TO PUT AS MUCH IN FRONT OF THE CAMERA AS THEY DID BEFORE, AND THEY STILL GAVE US CONTROL. THE THING THAT WAS SO DISAPPOINTING TO ME WAS THAT INSTEAD OF SHOOTING FOR FIVE TO SEVEN DAYS, ALL OF A SUDDEN WE WERE SHOOTING FOR THREE DAYS. THEY USED TO CALL THEM THREE-DAY WONDERS. THEN IT WAS LIKE "WELL, WE'RE SHOOTING TWO MOVIES TODAY".

Q: That must have been quite a downer for you, after you put so much time and effort into your earlier movies.

A: EXACTLY. I CAN REMEMBER WHEN IT WAS LIKE "OH, THIS IS JUST A CHEAP, $75,000.00 MOVIE," AND NOW IT'S LIKE "THIS IS A BIG BUDGET. WE'RE SPENDING $35,000.00 ON THIS."

Q: You were still living in Indiana through all of your movies. How hard was it to commute back and forth like that?

A: THE MOST DIFFICULT THING ABOUT IT IS THAT IT WAS NOT ORGANIZED. IF THEY SAID "WE'RE GONG TO START SHOOTING ON THE FIRST," AND YOU GET THERE THE NIGHT BEFORE, SUDDENLY IT'S "WELL, WE'VE HAD SOME PROBLEMS, SO WE'RE NOT GOING TO START UNTIL THE THIRD." AND SO HERE I AM, SITTING OUT THERE IN LOS ANGELES GOING "GUYS, THE HOTEL BILLS ARE REALLY RACKING UP HERE AND I'M NOT MAKING MONEY. WHAT'S GOING ON?"

Q: So expenses were not paid for you?

A: NO, BECAUSE OF THE LAW, THE MANN ACT. IF IT WERE A MOVIE WHERE I WERE GETTING KILLED

IN FRONT OF THE CAMERA IT WOULD BE PERFECTLY LEGAL TO PAY MY AIRFARE, BUT SINCE I'M BEING MADE LOVE TO IN FRONT OF THE CAMERA IT'S ILLEGAL.

Q: For a while there it seemed you were the unofficial spokesperson for the adult film industry to the mainstream media. How did this all come about?

A: I'M NOT EXACTLY SURE HOW IT HAPPENED. I SUPPOSE IT WAS FROM A FEW INTERVIEWS I DID HERE AND THERE. SOME OF THE PEOPLE IN THE BUSINESS, NAMELY BILL MARGOLD AND THE FREE SPEECH COALITION, HAD SEEN THOSE AND THOUGHT I DID A GOOD JOB. SO THEY PAID FOR MYSELF, NINA HARTLEY, AND GLORIA LEONARD TO GO TO A THREE DAY SEMINAR IN LOS ANGELES AT A PLACE CALLED ON CAMERA, WHERE THEY TEACH YOU HOW TO DO INTERVIEWS, AND THEY WORK WITH YOU, SIT YOU IN FRONT OF A CAMERA, AND SAY "DO THIS, NOW DO THAT. OK, NOW LOOK AT IT, AND SEE WHAT YOU DID WRONG NOW, SO DO IT THIS WAY." THAT WAS REALLY NICE, THAT THEY PAID TO HELP US HONE THOSE SKILLS. AFTER THAT, THEY TRIED THEIR BEST TO GET ME AND NINA AND GLORIA IN FRONT OF THE PUBLIC, TO PUT A GOOD REPRESENTATIVE OUT THERE AND TO TRY TO GET OUR POINTS ACROSS. IT WAS FUN. I REALLY ENJOYED DOING ALL OF THOSE SHOWS, EXCEPT FOR "GERALDO". THAT WAS REALLY... WELL, AS YOU WOULD EXPECT.

Q: Did Geraldo really tear into you guys?

A: WELL, HE BROUGHT THE BIBLE-THUMPERS OUT. AND IT WASN'T LIKE THEY JUST HAPPENED TO BE IN THE AUDIENCE. HE HAD INVITED THEM AND THEY WERE IN THE GREEN ROOM BACKSTAGE, AND IT WAS ALL SET UP TO BE THIS BIG RELIGIOUS WITCH BURNING.

Q: So the deck was stacked before you ever got started.

A: KIND OF. I UNDERSTAND THE NEED FOR CONTROVERSY AND TO PLAY THE DEVIL'S ADVOCATE, BUT I WOULD MUCH RATHER HAVE DEBATED SOMEBODY ABOUT THE DANGERS TO SOCIETY OR SOMETHING, BECAUSE TO ME RELIGION IS SOMETHING THAT IS VERY EASILY DISMISSED. I'M NOT OF THAT VARIETY. I'M NATIVE AMERICAN. I AM OF THE NATIVE AMERICAN CHURCH. MY RELIGIOUS BELIEFS FEEL THERE IS NOTHING WRONG WITH SEX, SO IT'S A FREE COUNTRY. NEXT QUESTION! I'M SITTING THERE GOING "THAT'S THE END OF THE RELIGIOUS DISCUSSION, AND YOU'VE GOT ANOTHER SIXTY MINUTES TO FILL, GERALDO. HOW COME WE'RE STUCK ON THIS RELIGIOUS STUFF?"

Q: And I know those folks always have to ask about what your kids think about it.

A: THEY'RE CHILDREN. THEY DON'T KNOW ANYTHING ABOUT IT. I'M NOT GOING TO SIT THERE AND GO "LOOK AT THE MOVIE I MADE."

Q: You retired from adult films about five years ago. What was the last one you made?

A: I THINK "OBSESSED" WAS THE LAST ONE WE MADE, FOR THOMAS PAINE.

Q: What was the final straw that pushed you to stop?

A: THE AIDS ISSUE. FOR SO MANY YEARS I HAD WORKED WITH CONDOMS. ONE OF THE NEW GIRLS WHO GOT INTO THE BUSINESS, SHE GOT HER AIDS TEST ON FRIDAY, WORKED OVER THE WEEKEND, AND MONDAY HER TEST RESULTS CAME BACK POSITIVE. THEY WENT AHEAD AND LET HER WORK WITHOUT SEEING THE RESULTS, SO EVERYBODY SHE WORKED WITH WAS EXPOSED TO THE VIRUS, AND EVERYONE THEY HAD SEX WITH BEFORE THEY KNEW WAS EXPOSED TO THE VIRUS. SO ALL THE PERFORMERS IN THE INDUSTRY SUDDENLY SAID "WE ALL WANT TO USE CONDOMS," AND THE INDUSTRY AS A WHOLE DECIDED THAT IT WOULD COST TOO MUCH MONEY AND TAKE TOO MUCH TIME TO PUT CONDOMS ON THE GUYS. I SAID, "THIS IS RIDICULOUS. THIS INDUSTRY DOESN'T EVEN CARE ABOUT PEOPLE'S LIVES."

Q: Speaking of the industry, do you see any money from repackaging of your films, for instance, if a clip turns up in a "Best of" compilation?

A: NO. I GOT PAID WHEN I DID THEM, AND THAT'S ABOUT IT. IN FACT, I GET MORE IN ROYALTIES FROM MY MUSIC CAREER. WHEN I HEAR OF THE SALARIES THAT GIRLS ARE MAKING MOVIES FOR NOWADAYS, LIKE FOUR OR FIVE HUNDRED DOLLARS, IT'S LIKE "NO, NOT FOR ME!"

Q: Do you remember any projects that you turned down?

A: OH, TONS! IT WAS ALL CRAP! SHORT LITTLE SCRIPTS WITH NO PLOT AND NO CHARACTER DEVELOPMENT AND NO MOTIVATION FOR THE SEX SCENES. I REMEMBER A GANG BANG SCENE THEY WANTED ME TO DO, AND I WAS LIKE "NO THANKS." THERE WAS LOTS OF STUFF I TURNED DOWN, I NEVER DID ANAL SCENES, AND THERE WERE LOTS OF OTHER THINGS THAT I JUST WOULDN'T DO. I TRIED TO PATTERN MY CAREER AFTER MARILYN CHAMBERS, AND SHE JUST DID A HANDFUL OF MOVIES, AND THE LAW OF SUPPLY OF DEMAND WORKS IN ENTERTAINMENT AS WELL AS EVERYWHERE ELSE.

Q: Since then, you've been in a few mainstream projects. Have you run into any prejudice about your past when you're out there looking for jobs?

A: THERE'S SOME PREJUDICE AGAINST MY PAST, BUT THERE'S ALSO THE FACT THAT I DON'T LIVE IN LOS ANGELES. FOR INSTANCE, I DID AN AUDITION FOR "WALKER, TEXAS RANGER", BUT IN ORDER TO DO IT I GOT THE SCRIPT, DID MY AUDITION IN FRONT OF A VIDEO CAMERA, AND FEDEXED THE VIDEO IN. YOU KNOW, THAT'S NOT A GOOD WAY TO AUDITION, AND IT'S REALLY KIND OF HOLDING ME BACK. RIGHT NOW THOUGH, MY MAJOR DESIRE IS TOWARD THE MUSIC, AND WORKING ON THE NEXT CD.

Q: When you go out on the road with your band, do you draw crowds looking to hear the music, or do you get fans of your earlier work?

A: IT'S MORE OF A MUSIC CROWD, ALTHOUGH THERE ARE SOME DIED IN THE WOOL FANS THAT BRAVE THE ROCK AND ROLL MUSIC JUST TO SEE ME. I FIND THERE'S A LOT OF CROSSOVER BETWEEN FANS OF EROTICA AND FANS OF ROCK AND ROLL.

SELECTED FILMOGRAPHY (XXX)

Native Tongue (1993)
Truth or Dare (1993)
Snakedance (1993)
Full Moon Bay (1993)
Centerfold (1993)
Hyapatia Obsessed (1993) (V)
Indian Summer 2: Sandstorm (1992)
Telesex (1992)
Bratgirl (1992)
Indian Summer (1991)
Lust in the Woods (1990)
Heavenly Hyapatia (1990)
One Wife to Give (1989)
Saddletramp (1988)
The Insatiable Hyapatia Lee (1987)
Naughty Girls Need Love Too (1986)
Secret Dreams (1986)
The Red Garter (1986)
Tasty (1985)
The Ribald Tales of Canterbury (1985)
Let's Get Physical (1983)
Body Girls (1983)
Sweet Young Foxes (1983)
The Young Like It Hot (1983)

WEE, HA HA!!!

HELLO THERE, MODEST READER! I'M ROBIN BOUGIE'S PINK DINGUS! PLEASE BE SURE TO DO YOURSELF A FAVOR AND PEEP SOME OF HYAPATIA'S MOVIES!

CINEMA SEWER READERS POLL:
THE BEST 1980s LIVE ACTION SCI-FI FILMS

IN AUGUST 2018, I ASKED CINEMA SEWER READERS FOR THEIR TOP FIVE LIVE ACTION 1980S SCI-FI. EACH ENTRY WAS GIVEN AN EVEN VOTE, AND THESE ARE THE RESULTS.

1. Robocop (58 votes)
2. Aliens (50 votes)
3. Blade Runner (49 votes)
4. The Thing (47 votes)
5. Terminator (40 votes)
6. Star Wars: The Empire Strikes back (31 votes)
7. Videodrome (25 votes)
8. They Live (24 votes)
9. Repo Man (21 votes)
10. Predator (19 votes)
11. Lifeforce (18 votes)
12. Dune (17 votes)
13. Back to the Future (16 votes)
14. Star Trek: The Wrath of Khan (14 votes)
15. Escape from New York (13 votes)
16. The Hidden (12 votes)
tied with The Fly (12 votes)
18. Brazil (11 votes)
tied with Buckaroo Banzai (11 votes)
20. Scanners (10 votes)

(JUST MISSING OUT ON BREAKING INTO THE TOP 20 WERE: THE LAST STAR FIGHTER, FLASH GORDON, AND ENEMY MINE). NOW, COMPARE THAT LIST TO THE TOP EARNING 1980S LIVE ACTION SCI-FI FILMS:

1. ET ($435 million)
2. Star Wars: Return of the Jedi ($309 million)
3. Star Wars: Empire Strikes Back ($290 million)
4. Ghostbusters ($238 million)
5. Back to the Future ($210 million)
6. Gremlins ($148 million)
7. Honey I Shrunk the Kids ($130 million)
8. Back to the Future 2 ($118 million)
9. Ghostbusters 2 ($112 million)
10. Star Trek: The Voyage Home ($110 million)
11. Superman 2 ($108 million)
12. Aliens ($85 million)
13. Star Trek: The Wrath of Khan ($78 million)
14. Star Trek: The Search For Spock ($76 million)
15. Cocoon ($76 million)
16. Superman 3 ($59 million)
17. Predator ($59 million)
18. The Abyss ($54 million)
19. Robocop ($53 million)
20. Star Trek: The Final Frontier ($52 million)

I FIND IT INTERESTING THAT THERE ARE ONLY 6 FILMS THAT APPEAR ON BOTH LISTS, AND VERY FEW OF THE MOST POPULAR NOW, WERE ALSO THE MOST POPULAR AT THE TIME – BACK IN THE 1980S. IT GOES TO SHOW YOU THAT SOME FILMS, NO MATTER HOW POPULAR THEY ARE AT THE TIME, DON'T HAVE THE STAYING POWER NEEDED TO BE LEGENDARY.

RANDOM TRIVIA

A CREW-MEMBER ON THE SET OF ELI ROTH'S CABIN FEVER (2002) NAMED ROBERT JONES WAS NEARLY SHOT BY POLICE AFTER A DAY OF FILMING WHEN HE DECIDED TO TAKE HOME A DEAD BODY FX AS A SOUVENIR. "SO, I WAS RIDING THROUGH DOWNTOWN THOMASVILLE ABOUT 11 AT NIGHT WITH THIS HEADLESS CORPSE SITTING IN THE BACK SEAT," JONES RECALLED. "NEXT THING I KNOW THE THOMASVILLE POLICE DEPARTMENT IS PULLING ME OVER." AT THAT POINT A SCREAMING COP WITH HIS WEAPON DRAWN COMMANDED FOR JONES TO STEP OUT OF HIS CAR WITH HIS HANDS IN THE AIR, AND LAY DOWN ON THE GROUND. "WE ALL HAD A GOOD LAUGH WHEN THEY REALIZED I WASN'T SOME SERIAL KILLER," JONES NOTED. "BUT MAN, THAT WAS SCARIER THAN ANYTHING IN THE MOVIE."

JAIME

LEGENDARY ALTERNATIVE COMIC ARTIST JAIME HERNANDEZ, BEST KNOWN FOR HIS WORK ON THE LONG RUNNING LOVE AND ROCKETS SERIES, HAD A CAMEO AS AN AMBULANCE DRIVER IN THE 1986 MOVIE, RIVER'S EDGE. HIS BIG SCENE WAS SADLY LEFT ON THE CUTTING ROOM FLOOR DURING THE EDITING PROCESS. DIRECTOR TIM HUNTER SAID IT WAS A REALLY GOOD ELEMENT IN THE FILM, BUT THE MOVIE CUT TOGETHER BETTER WITHOUT IT, AND SO IT WAS JUNKED.

ALUMNI THAT CINEMA SEWER READERS MIGHT CARE ABOUT THAT WENT TO PACIFIC PALISADES HIGH SCHOOL, IN LOS ANGELES: JENNIFER JASON LEIGH (THE HITCHER), ELIZABETH ARLEN (BACHELOR PARTY), JEFF BRIDGES (THE FISHER KING), FOREST WHITAKER (GHOST DOG), ERIN GRAY (THE 1970S BUCK ROGERS TV SERIES), SUSANNA HOFFS (LEAD SINGER OF THE BANGLES), MICHAEL MEDVED (FILM CRITIC), THOMAS NEWMAN (FILM SCORE COMPOSER), AND KATEY SAGAL (MARRIED WITH CHILDREN). ALSO PORN STAR LITTLE ORAL ANNIE, BUT NOT JANIS ADAMS. SHE WAS A TEACHER THERE WHO WAS FALSELY IDENTIFIED AS A PORN STAR IN THE STUDENT NEWSPAPER IN 2000, AND SHE SUCCESSFULLY SUED THE SCHOOL FOR FAILING TO PROTECT HER FROM SEXUAL HARASSMENT BY STUDENTS.

The Dirty Mind of Young Sally
(1973. DIR: BETHEL BUCKALEW)

SALLY (REDHEADED SEXPLOITATION GODDESS SHARON KELLY) LEADS A DOUBLE LIFE. SHE WORKS AS A RECEPTIONIST AT A LOCAL RADIO STATION AND SHE ALSO HOSTS HER OWN FILTHY PIRATE RADIO SHOW, A SEX-THEMED BROADCAST "DIRTY SALLY McGUIRE" SHE DOES 3 TIMES A DAY WITH THE HELP OF PAL TOBY ('BUCK' FLOWER) FROM THE BACK OF HIS VAN. SALLY PUMPS UP THE VOLUME AND LOCAL BONERS AS SHE FEATURES EVERYTHING FROM SEX ADVICE TO HER MASTURBATING LIVE ON THE AIR (WHICH TURNS LOCAL LISTENERS ON LIKE CRAZY). SGT. DIMWITTE (NORMAN FIELDS) IS A LOCAL SHERIFF THAT SPENDS HIS DAYS SEARCHING FOR THE ELUSIVE SALLY AND HER MOBILE STUDIO, AND HE DOESN'T PLAN ON LETTING HER GET AWAY WITH THAT KIND OF AUDIO OBSCENITY. NO SIREE BOB.

THE PLOT IS FLIMSY AND SOME OF THE ACTING IS FEEBLE AT BEST, BUT THIS IS PRETTY GOL-DANG ENTERTAINING. THE SEX SCENES ARE SEMICORE (MEANING: ABOUT AS HARDCORE AS SOFTCORE GETS, WITH PLENTY OF FULL FRONTAL) AND PERHAPS TOO PLENTIFUL SINCE IT RUNS A VERY LONG 96 MINUTES (WHICH IN SEXPLOITATION RUNTIME IS BASICALLY WAR AND PEACE). KELLY IS VERY WATCHABLE IN HER FEATURE FILM DEBUT, WHICH ALSO FEATURES BLONDE PIXIE SANDY DEMPSEY AND ANGELA CARNON (WHO WAS ACTUALLY A PRETTY GOOD ACTRESS). ALSO LOOK FORWARD TO A THEME SONG RECORDED BY SOME COUNTRY-ROCK GROUP WITH SHARON ACTUALLY RIGHT IN THERE RECORDING IN THE STUDIO WITH THEM.

IN 2016, SHARON KELLY (WHO IS VERY MUCH STILL ALIVE, AND NOW RESIDES IN KENTUCKY) TOLD ME ABOUT MAKING THE FILM. "IT WAS THE FIRST MOVIE I WAS EVER IN, A BETHEL BUCKALEW MOVIE. BEFORE THE FIRST SCENE HE LEANED IN AND GAVE ME ALL THE ACTING LESSON HE WANTED ME TO HAVE. HE POINTED AND SAID, 'THAT'S THE MICROPHONE, AND THAT'S THE CAMERA. DON'T LOOK INTO THE CAMERA.' I NEVER DID."

"AND JUST A LITTLE SHOUT OUT TO THE MEMORY OF MY FRIEND, BUCK FLOWER", SHARON ADDED, SPEAKING OF HER CO-STAR IN THE FILM. "HE WAS PRETTY FOND OF MY TITS."

THE HOWLING:
AN ENCOUNTER AT LE SEX SHOPPE)
BY: ROBIN BOUGIE
WWW.CINEMASEWER.COM

KAREN WHITE (PLAYED BY DEE WALLACE) WALKS THE STREETS OF THE CITY OF ANGELS IN ONE OF THE VERY EARLIEST SCENES IN JOE DANTE'S 1981 HORROR FILM, THE HOWLING. SHE'S AWASH IN WHAT WINGS HAUSER'S CHARACTER IN 1982'S VICE SQUAD WOULD CALL "THE NEON SLIME". KAREN IS A LOS ANGELES TV NEWS PERSONALITY AND GOING TO WESTERN AVENUE TO MEET EDDIE QUIST, THE MAIN SUSPECT IN A SERIES OF BRUTAL KILLINGS. ADULT BOOK STORES, PROSTITUTES, PIMPS, AND OTHER MALCONTENTS LITTER THE MOONLIT STREETS, AND THERE IN A PHONE BOOTH SHE TALKS TO EDDIE.

"ARE YOU WEARING WHAT I ASKED YOU TO?" THE SERIAL MURDERER SAYS WITH A CREEPY TONE. A RENDEZVOUS POINT IS DECIDED UPON. SHE CONTINUES UP THE AVENUE, TRAVELLING FURTHER UPSTREAM IN THE RIVER OF SLEAZE.

SHE PASSES THE SIN-O-RAMA PEEP SHOW PALACE WHICH IS NEXT DOOR TO THE SULTAN ROOM, A LITTLE DIVE BAR (WHICH TODAY IS A YOGA STUDIO) DOWNSTAIRS FROM THE ST. FRANCIS HOTEL, NOW KNOWN AS THE GERSHWIN APARTMENTS. THE SULTAN WAS ROUTINELY FREQUENTED BY JAMES EARL RAY WHILE HE WAS LIVING IN THE ST. FRANCIS IN THE LATE 1960S JUST A FEW WEEKS BEFORE HE GOT AROUND TO ASSASSINATING MARTIN LUTHER KING DOWN IN MEMPHIS ON APRIL 4TH 1968. "MANY HAVE DIED AND COMMITTED SUICIDE THERE," SAYS FORMER MANAGER CRYSTA LYNCH. "THE GERSHWIN IS VERY HAUNTED, AND EVERYONE THERE KNOWS IT."

SHE ALSO PASSES THE TIKI THEATER "XYMPOSIUM". AFTER THE DEMISE OF THE PUSSYCAT CHAIN THE TIKI REMAINS TODAY THE ONLY VENUE CURRENTLY SHOWING STRAIGHT PORN IN THE GREATER METROPOLITAN LOS ANGELES AREA. IT ALSO HAPPENS TO BE THE LAST THEATRE IN LA WITH A TURNSTILE ENTRANCE. THE 50 SEAT TIKI IS ESPECIALLY HARSH THESE DAYS. IT'S NOT AN EXPERIENCE FOR THE FAINT OF HEART, AS THE SCUMMY, SMELLY LITTLE BUILDING IS TROLLED BY MOUTHY STREETWALKING CRACK WHORES DESCRIBED TO ME AS LOOKING LIKE "JOE NAMATH IN DRAG". LONG GONE ARE THE DAYS OF 35MM OR 16MM PROJECTION, AND THE TIKI NOW SCREENS DVDS ON A POSTAGE STAMP SIZED SCREEN -- ALTHOUGH IT WAS BIG ENOUGH TO SATISFY COMEDIAN FRED WILLARD, WHO WAS ARRESTED WHEN HE WAS SPOTTED IN THE THEATER WITH HIS "PENIS IN HIS HAND" BY VICE COPS ON JULY 18TH 2012.

I'M SURE HE WASN'T HARD TO SPOT, AS THE TIKI IS INFAMOUS AS THE BRIGHTEST PORN THEATER ANYONE I KNOW HAS EVER SET FOOT IN. THE HOUSE LIGHTS STAY UP CONSTANTLY AND THE TINNY VOLUME ON THE VIDEOS PLAYED IS HEADACHE-INDUCING. IT'S WORTH NOTING THAT IN THE LATE 1970S MONSTER COCKSMAN JOHN HOLMES UTILIZED THE ADDRESS NEXT DOOR TO THE TIKI (5466 SANTA MONICA BLVD.) AS HIS BUSINESS MAILING ADDRESS. THAT SPOT IS CURRENTLY A ROUGH LOOKING "99 CENT" DISCOUNT STORE, BUT WAS LIKELY A BUSINESS OFFERING A POST OFFICE BOX SERVICE BACK WHEN JOHNNY WAS DIPPING HIS DICK INTO EVERY OTHER BUBBLY BLONDE IN CALI.

"FUNNY MAN" FRED WILLARD

KAREN ENTERS A PORN STORE CALLED LE SEX SHOPPE AT 5507 HOLLYWOOD BLVD AND WESTERN AVENUE. FAMOUS POET, NOVELIST AND SHORT STORY WRITER CHARLES BUKOWSKI LIVED A BLOCK OVER ON CARLTON WAY, AND DURING THE MID-70s TO LATE 1970S WHEN HE WAS WRITING THE OCCASIONAL SHORT STORY FOR HUSTLER AND OTHER SKIN MAGAZINES TO MAKE ENDS MEET, HE WAS KNOWN TO FREQUENT THIS LITTLE GRIMY PORN STORE. REPORTEDLY, HE MADE FRIENDS WITH THE MANAGER, AND WOULD OFTEN DROP IN TO SEE HIS FRIEND AND CHAT. HE LIKED RUBBING ELBOWS WITH THE PROSTITUTES AND OTHER CUSTOMERS THAT WOULD REGULARLY FREQUENT THE UNASSUMING FLESH EMPORIUM. THE GUTTERS OF LOS ANGELES WERE HUGELY IMPORTANT TO THE WRITING OF BUKOWSKI, AND HE DIED IN THAT CITY IN 1994.

IN AN INTERVIEW IN LONDON MAGAZINE IN 1974, HE SAID, "YOU LIVE IN A TOWN ALL YOUR LIFE, AND YOU GET TO KNOW EVERY BITCH ON THE STREET CORNER AND HALF OF THEM YOU HAVE ALREADY MESSED AROUND WITH... SINCE I WAS RAISED IN LA, I'VE ALWAYS HAD THE GEOGRAPHICAL AND SPIRITUAL FEELING OF BEING HERE. I'VE HAD TIME TO LEARN THIS CITY. I CAN'T SEE ANY OTHER PLACE THAN LA."

ONE OF BUKOWSKI'S GOOD FRIENDS NAMED GEORGE LIVED NEXT DOOR TO LE SEX SHOPPE. GEORGE WAS AN UNDERGROUND COMIX ARTIST AND PUBLISHER, AND HAD PRODUCED A LITTLE SEEN COMIC WITH HIS EX-GIRLFRIEND LAURIE ANDERSON, WHO IS BETTER KNOWN TODAY AS A WORLD-FAMOUS PERFORMANCE ARTIST. HE WAS NOT ONLY PALS WITH CHARLES, BUT ALSO LSD GURU TIMOTHY LEARY, BEAT POET ALLEN GINSBERG, AND CARTOONIST ROBERT CRUMB. IN A LAST DITCH EFFORT TO SAVE HIS MARRIAGE, GEORGE WOULD HAVE A SON WITH HIS WIFE WHILE LIVING THERE IN THAT SQUALID APARTMENT IN 1974. A SON NAMED LEONARDO DICAPRIO, WHO WOULD GO ON TO BECOME ONE OF HOLLYWOOD'S MOST FAMOUS AND BELOVED ACTORS.

PAINTINGS OF GIRLS IN BIKINIS ADORN THE FRONTAGE OF THE GARISH BUILDING, AND STORE SIGNAGE TRUMPETS THAT "MARITAL AIDS" ARE AVAILABLE WITHIN. THE INTERIOR HAS THOSE DISTINCTIVE FAKE "RUMPUS ROOM" WOOD PANELLED WALLS EVERY DIRTY BOOK STORE OF THE ERA HAD. NOT TO MENTION THE BROWN RATTY CARPET, RACKS OF STROKE MAGAZINES, AND POSTERS ADVERTISING THE INFAMOUS "SWEDISH EROTICA" LINE OF 8MM FILMS. AN INDICATION THAT VHS IS JUST ABOUT TO TAKE OVER THE INDUSTRY RESIDES IN A SMALL FLYER BLEATING OUT THRILLS OF "VIDEO ENCOUNTERS OF THE HOTTEST KIND".

AS KAREN WALKS IN WE SEE A SELECTION OF SAID SWEDISH EROTICA 8MM LOOPS (WHICH DESPITE THE NAME WERE NOT MADE IN SWEDEN, BUT RATHER CALIFORNIA) BEHIND GLASS AT THE FRONT COUNTER. $50 TO $80 WAS NOT AN UNUSUAL PRICE TO PAY FOR A TEN TO TWELVE MINUTE 8MM ADULT FILM REEL BACK THEN, WHICH ADJUSTED FOR INFLATION IS $145 TO $220 AMERICAN DOLLARS. KEEP IN MIND THAT THESE RIBALD LOOPS IN THEIR SMALL, FLIMSY CARDBOARD CASES WERE 10 TO 12 MINUTES AND TOTALLY SILENT. TODAY'S YOUNGER GENERATION OF MASTURBATORS TRULY HAVE NO IDEA HOW GOOD THEY HAVE IT.

WITH THE ADVENT OF THE HOWLING RELEASE ON BLU RAY, THE TITLES AND THE COVERS OF THE "SLICKS" (A TYPE OF 1970S/1980S PORN MAGAZINE THAT WAS FAR MORE GRAPHIC THAN PLAYBOYS OR PENTHOUSE, AND SO NAMED FOR THEIR SLICK GLOSSY PAPER) SITTING ON THE SHELVES IN THE BACKGROUND OF THIS SCENE ARE NOW FINALLY VISIBLE FOR THE FIRST TIME SINCE THE MOVIE SCREENED THEATRICALLY. AS A COLLECTOR OF VINTAGE PORNOGRAPHY SOME OF THE TITLES ARE FAMILIAR, AND OTHERS ARE RARITIES: CHOCOLATE PUSSY, MILK, SUPER BOOBS, PEPPER, BOTTOM SPECIAL, REAR VIEW, AND BRA-BUSTERS. OH, AND LOOK -- THERE'S MATURE MYSTIQUE, WOMEN IN COMMAND, GIGANTIC TITS, SHAVED DOLLS, KING-SIZED, FANNY, SKIN, CAPTURED, TRANSVESTITE TREATS, AND BITCH GODDESS.

THE BOOTHS THEMSELVES IN THE BACK OF THE SHOP, PAST SOME BEADED DRAPERY IN A DOORWAY, ARE JUST AS YOU'LL SEE THEM IN THE VARIOUS DOCUMENTARIES THAT EXIST ABOUT THE PORN INDUSTRIES OF

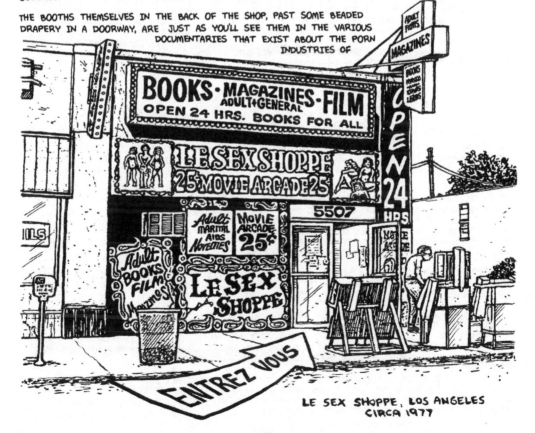

LE SEX SHOPPE, LOS ANGELES
CIRCA 1977

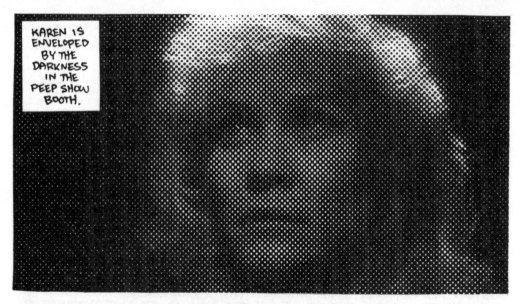

NEW YORK AND LOS ANGELES OF THE 1970S AND EARLY 1980S. EACH SMALL WOODEN DOOR HAS A PANEL THAT IS DECORATED WITH DESCRIPTIONS AND COVER ART FOR THE 8MM FILMS THAT RESIDE WITHIN. VARIOUS FETISHES AND SEXUAL ACTS ARE CATERED TO, WITH LOUD HAND-DRAWN SIGNAGE THAT PROMISES THAT "SATISFACTION IS GUARANTEED".

KAREN IDENTIFIES THE CORRECT BOOTH BY A YELLOW 'SMILEY FACE' EDDIE HAS LEFT ON THE OUTSIDE OF THE DOOR, AND HESITANTLY ENTERS THE SMALL PITCH BLACK ROOM, WITH THE FULL ASSUMPTION THAT THE MEETING IS BEING RECORDED VIA A POLICE WIRE SHE'S WEARING, AND THAT ARMED HELP IS MERE SECONDS AWAY. WHAT SHE DOESN'T REALIZE IS WHAT WE THE AUDIENCE ARE WELL AWARE OF, THAT THOSE NEON LIGHTS OF HOLLYWOOD BOULEVARD HAVE BROKEN THE TRANSMISSION, AND THE POLICE HAVE, FOR ALL INTENTS AND PURPOSES, "LOST HER" FOR THE TIME BEING.

KAREN SITS DOWN IN THE BOOTH, CLEARLY FRIGHTENED AND DISORIENTATED. BEHIND HER, FROM OUT OF THE DARKNESS, A HAND WITH A QUARTER IN IT FEEDS THE COIN OPERATED MACHINE, AND THE PROJECTOR CLUNKS AND WHIRS INTO ACTION. THE 8MM FILM BEGINS TO PLAY ON THE SMALL SCREEN. IT WAS MADE FOR THE FILM, BUT IT LOOKS VERY AUTHENTIC, AND JOE DANTE SHOULD BE ADMIRED FOR HIS ATTENTION TO DETAIL REGARDING SUCH A SMALL AND SEEMINGLY MINOR ELEMENT. DANTE HIMSELF NOTES THAT MAKING THE PEEP SHOW FOOTAGE IN HIS GARAGE WAS THE "LEAST EROTIC EXPERIENCE" OF HIS LIFE, AND HE FELT "DIRTY AND EMBARRASSED" ABOUT IT AFTERWARD.

"HELLO, EDDIE."

"I KNEW YOU'D COME, KAREN."

SHE TRIES TO TURN AND LOOK, TO SEE WHO HE IS AS HER EYES STRAIN TO ADJUST TO THE DARKNESS. HE TOWERS OVER HER, HANDS ON HER SHOULDERS, PRESSURING HER TO LOOK FORWARD AT THE SMALL SCREEN IN THE BACK OF THE CLOSET THEY'RE CROWDED IN TOGETHER, TO WATCH THE ROUGH FORCED-SEX GANG-BANG FOOTAGE PLAYING BEFORE THEM. "JUST WATCH" HE SAYS, BREATHING HEAVILY. "I WATCH YOU ON TV. AND I KNOW HOW GOOD I CAN MAKE YOU FEEL. I'M GOING TO LIGHT UP YOUR WHOLE BODY, KAREN."

ENVELOPED IN THE DARKNESS AND THE THICK BLEACHY STENCH THAT EVERY PORN SHOP JERK-OFF BOOTH CONTAINS, EDDIE'S VOICE BEGINS QUAVERING AND TRANSFORMING, BUT JUST BEFORE HE'S ABOUT TO ADVANCE UPON HER AND DO SOMETHING (WE DON'T KNOW WHAT, BUT WE KNOW IT'S GOING TO BE HORRIBLE), SHE SCREAMS AND THE COPS FINALLY BUST IN AND BLOW THE KILLER AWAY THROUGH THE RICKETY WOODEN DOOR. KAREN WILL SPEND THE ENTIRE FIRST ACT OF THE FILM OBSESSING ABOUT THIS EXPERIENCE AND THE MENTAL TRAUMA SHE SUSTAINED.

WHEN ASKED BY CRAVEONLINE.COM IN 2012 ABOUT WHAT SHE THOUGHT OF SHOOTING THE PEEP SHOW BOOTH SCENE, ACTRESS DEE WALLACE REPLIED "IT FREAKED ME OUT. I WAS THIS YOUNG GIRL FROM KANSAS SO ALL THAT STUFF CREEPED ME OUT EVEN MORE."

LE SEX SHOPPE WAS STILL THERE AS LATE AS 2013, THE LAST STANDING BUILDING ON HOLLYWOOD AND WESTERN THAT PAID DIRECT HOMAGE TO A BYGONE SLEAZY ERA OF HOLLYWOOD EAST THAT IS NOW ALL BUT FORGOTTEN. IT HAD A NEW NAME AND NEW SIGNAGE AS THE "X-SPOT", BUT IT WAS STILL THE SAME LAYOUT, AND STILL HAD THOSE SAME BOOTHS IN THE BACK WHERE KNOWLEDGEABLE HOWLING FANS COULD GO AND HAVE THEIR OWN PEEP SHOW EXPERIENCE IF THEY WERE SO INCLINED.

TODAY, WITH THE NEIGHBOURHOOD MORE GENTRIFIED AND UPSCALE, IT HAS BEEN TORN DOWN AND IN ITS PLACE THERE IS A PETCO PET SUPPLY SUPERMARKET. IF YOU HAPPEN BY ONE DAY, DO ME A FAVOUR AND BRING A YELLOW 'HAPPY FACE', AND STICK IT SOMEWHERE INSIDE THE STORE. YOU NEVER KNOW WHO YOU MIGHT RUN INTO WHEN YOU GO TO PICK UP DOG FOOD.

—BOUGIE 2016

MilkyCat 17: Human Condom Woman
☆ (2005 · JAPAN · XXX) ☆

AS HUMAN CONDOM WOMAN BEGINS WE SEE OUR STAR, YURI KOIZUMI, AND A LARGE COLLECTION OF SHOES BY THE FRONT DOOR OF A MODEST JAPANESE APARTMENT. A LOT OF DUDES HAVE DROPPED BY TO BE IN A PORNO WHERE SHE'S THE STAR, AND IN AN ADJACENT ROOM THAT APPEARS TO BE AN OFFICE (COMPLETE WITH A BLACKBOARD), ANOTHER WOMAN HAS BEEN HIRED AS A FLUFFER. NOW THIS IS A VERY RARE APPEARANCE OF A POSITION WHICH IS MOSTLY AN URBAN LEGEND IN XXX, AND SHE IS PREPPING THE GUYS, WHO ALL HAVE THEIR FACES DIGITALLY BLURRED. DESPITE WHAT SHE'S DOING I DON'T REALLY KNOW IF YOU CAN REALLY CONSIDER THIS GAL AN ACTUAL FLUFFER THOUGH, SINCE SHE'S ON-SCREEN AND PART OF THE SCENE, WHICH MAKES HER MORE OF A CO-STAR. IF WE'RE GOING TO BE TECHNICAL, A TRUE FLUFFER IS SOMEONE WHO DOESN'T ACTUALLY APPEAR AS PART OF THE CAST, BUT JUST AS A MEANS TO KEEP THE MALE PERFORMERS READY FOR SHOW-TIME.

YURI IS QUIETLY PENETRATED FROM BEHIND (ALMOST NINJA-LIKE) AS SHE'S WATCHING THE OTHER GAL GIVING OUT HAND JOBS LIKE THEY WERE HALLOWEEN CANDIES, AND IS HANDED A LARGE RUBBER SUIT THAT IS A LIGHT YELLOW IN COLOR. THE FLUFFER PUTS HER CLOTHES BACK ON, STANDS IN THE CORNER POLITELY AND QUIETLY, AND OUR STAR GETS JIZZED ON BY A HANDFUL OF MEN. THERE IS NO MUSIC OR SOUNDTRACK AS THEY SILENTLY STAND AROUND AND JERK OFF, CUMMING ON HER LEGS, HER FEET, HER BUTT, THIGHS, STOMACH, TITS, ARMPITS, ARMS, AND BACK. THE IDEA SEEMS TO BE THAT THEY ARE LUBRICATING HER ENTRY INTO HER SUIT. THAT'S RIGHT: THIS SEX SUPERHEROINE IS THE HUMAN CONDOM WOMAN, AND HER HUMAN-SIZED CONDOM SUIT IS GOING TO BE FILLED WITH JIZZ! YAY?

BEFORE SHE CAN GET HER WEIRD FLOPPY OUTFIT ON, SHE'S PRESENTED WITH A BOTTLE OF SOMETHING. SHE GINGERLY DRINKS SOME OF IT, PONDERS THE FLAVOR, AND THEN POURS IT INTO THE SLEEVE OF HER BODY SUIT BEFORE SLIDING HER ARM IN AFTER IT. THE GUYS HAVE BEEN SAVING THEIR CUM IN BOTTLES JUST FOR THIS OCCASION! NOW THAT'S PLANNING.

THE SUIT HAS A ZIPPER OPENING AT THE CROTCH, A MOUTH-HOLE FOR BREATHING, AND A RUBBER TUBE CONNECTED TO THE TOP OF HER FOREHEAD SO MORE CUM CAN BE SHOT IN THERE WHILE SHE'S COCOONED, BUT OTHER THAN THAT, THE POOR GIRL IS ENTIRELY AND CLAUSTROPHOBICALLY ENCASED IN THE FULL BODY SUIT. MORE BOTTLES OF MAN-MILK APPEAR AS IF BY MAGIC, AND ARE POURED IN THE NECK OPENING BEFORE SHE'S SEALED UP. SINCE IT'S SEMI-TRANSPARENT, WE CAN SEE ALL THE CUM SLOSHING AROUND IN THERE WITH HER, WHICH IS BOTH TOTALLY REVOLTING AND UTTERLY FASCINATING IN EQUAL MEASURES.

CUT TO A NEW SCENE, AND IT'S THE FLUFFER GIRL WORKING SOME DICKS LIKE SHE WAS WHEN WE CAME IN, AND THIS APPEARS TO HAVE BEEN SHOT EARLIER IN THE DAY WHEN THE ENERGY WAS UP AND EVERYONE WAS IN A MORE CHIPPER MOOD. "HEY, IT'S ALMOST LIKE GETTING JERKED OFF BY YOUR SISTER!" THEY SEEM TO SAY. SHE SMILES AND THEY LAUGH AND CHUM AROUND. THE MEN'S VIBE HERE IS SO MUCH DIFFERENT THAN IT IS WITH YURI IN THE REST OF THE MOVIE.

JUMP BACK AHEAD, AND WE'RE BACK WITH MISS KOIZUMI AS SHE'S TAKING A BREAK TO HAVE A BENTO BOX LUNCH WHILE STILL IN HER SPUNKY SAUNA-SUIT. SHE SITS ALONE ON THE FLOOR WHILE SOMEONE TAKES PICTURES OF HER MUNCHING AWAY WITH HER CHOPSTICKS. LATER, SHE GETS UP, WALKS THROUGH A LIVING ROOM AREA, AND OUT ONTO AN OUTDOOR PATIO WHERE SHE SITS AWKWARDLY ON A PATIO CHAIR FOR AWHILE, LOOKING AT THE DIRECTOR FOR HER NEXT CUE.

INSIDE, ABOUT 50 CONDOMS THAT THE JAPANESE DUDES HAVE BROUGHT FROM HOME (THEY'VE BEEN FILLED WITH SEMEN AND THEN

TIED OFF) ARE PRESENTED TO OUR STAR ON A SILVER PLATTER, AND SHE GETS OUT A PAIR OF SCISSORS AND SNIPS THEM OPEN AND POURS THEIR GOOEY CONTENTS INTO A LARGE GLASS VASE. SHE POSITIONS THIS UNDER HER CHIN, OPENS HER MOUTH, AND A LINE OF GUYS START JIZZING ONTO HER TONGUE, WHICH THEN DRIPS OFF INTO THE VASE.

IF THAT WASN'T ENOUGH SHE HOLDS OPEN HER EYES, TILTS HER HEAD BACK, AND A BUNCH OF THE GUYS SQUIRT THEIR SPUNK INTO HER OPEN EYES. THIS IS EASILY THE HARDEST TO WATCH SCENE (I HATE ANYTHING TO DO WITH EYEBALLS), BUT SHE DOESN'T SEEM AT ALL STRESSED ABOUT IT, AND DOESN'T EVEN SO MUCH AS REGISTER A GRIMACE. CONTENT AS A FUCKING COW. A TRUE PROFESSIONAL, I GUESS. IT NEVER FEELS LIKE SHE'S BEING "TALKED INTO" ANYTHING LIKE YOU SEE IN A LOT OF AMERICAN GONZO SMUT WITH EXTREME CONTENT, AND SHE'S VERY ORDERLY IN THAT TYPICAL JAPANESE WAY, EVEN WHEN SHE'S STARING AT THE CEILING THOUGH A THICK LAYER OF SPUNK.

THE CUMMING-IN-THE-EYES-ON-PURPOSE FETISH IS SOMETHING THAT WAS INVENTED BY JAPANESE PORNOGRAPHERS, AND WHILE STILL VERY FRINGE, HAS REMAINED FAIRLY PREVALENT AS AN EXTREME FETISH SUBGENRE WITHIN THEIR BUKKAKE CONTENT FOR THE LAST 15 YEARS. THE EARLIEST EXAMPLE OF IT THAT I'M AWARE OF WAS IN SOFT ON DEMAND'S SEMEN MANIAC (2002), STARRING NANAMI NANASE.

EVENTUALLY YURI IS SEALED UP IN HER SUIT AGAIN, WAY MORE GOOEY CUM IS POURED IN, AND THEN THE CUNT ZIPPER IS OPENED AND SHE LAYS ON HER BACK AND GETS HUMPED FOR ABOUT 10 MINUTES. THIS CHAPTER ON THE DVD IS APTLY ENTITLED "FUCK". WEARILY, SHE STANDS UP AT THE END OF IT, AND THE CROWDED ROOM (WHICH HAS BEEN UTTERLY SILENT FOR THE PREVIOUS 2 HOURS OF RUNTIME), EXPLODES INTO APPLAUSE. WEARILY, OUR STAR TAKES OFF THE HOOD, SMILES, AND DOES THE LITTLE TWO-FINGER "PEACE" THING THAT JAPANESE CHICKS DO, AND IT'S THE END.

I DON'T EVEN KNOW IF IT NEEDS TO BE SAID: BUT HOLY FUCK JAPAN, ARE YOU EVER **WEIRD**. I JUST FEEL LIKE I WATCHED ALIENS TAKE PART IN SOME BIZARRE MATING RITUAL. I HALF EXPECTED HER TO SPROUT WINGS, EAT THE HEADS OFF THE MALES, VOMIT BRAINS ALL OVER THE FLOOR, AND THEN FLY OUT THE WINDOW. SKREEEX!!! (THAT'S HER ALIEN SCREAM)

THE DVD COMES WITH A 15-MINUTE "BEHIND THE SCENES" SHORT. LIKE THE MOVIE, NONE OF THIS IS IN ENGLISH AND THERE ARE NO SUBTITLES, BUT UNLIKE THE MOVIE (WHICH ALMOST HAS NO DIALOG) I'M SORT OF LEFT WONDERING WHAT'S BEING SAID. WE SEE YURI GETTING HER MAKE-UP DONE, POSING FOR STILLS THAT WILL BE USED ON THE DVD PACKAGING AND PROMO MATERIAL, AND SOME OTHER ALTERNATE CAMERA ANGLES OF THE STUFF WE SAW IN THE FEATURE. THERE'S ALSO A SHORT INTERVIEW WITH ONE OF THE GUYS FROM THE SCENE, WHO HAS HIS FACE BLURRED OUT. HE FUCKS YURI AFTER SHE'S DONE THE SHOOT AND CLEANED UP AND WEARING A BIG WHITE ROBE, AND THEN ALSO PRESENTS HER WITH A BIG BOUQUET OF BEAUTIFUL FLOWERS.

IN CASE YOU'RE WONDERING, MILKY CAT IS A SERIES OF BUKKAKE-THEMED JAPANESE PORN DVDS, WITH EVERY VARIATION YOU CAN IMAGINE. FROM NOSE HOOK BUKKAKE, TO GOKKUN (CUM SWALLOW) BUKKAKE AND EVERY VARIATION IN BETWEEN. OVER AT THEIR OFFICIAL WEBSITE, THEY STATE THAT THIS 17TH INSTALMENT IS "YURI'S FINAL VIDEO. SHE HAS A LOT OF CRAZY FANS AND ONE OF THEM REQUESTED THAT WE MAKE HER AS MESSY AND AS DEGRADED AS POSSIBLE, SO WE MADE THIS! WE SOAKED HER ENTIRE BODY INSIDE THIS SPECIAL SUIT FOR 8 HOURS, WITH CONTINUOUS CUMMING. COMPLETELY UNIQUE."

YEAH, I'LL SAY. GODDAMN.

— BOUGIE '16

MILKYCAT ILLUSTRATIONS: BEN NEWMAN BENNEWMANART. BLOGSPOT.CA/

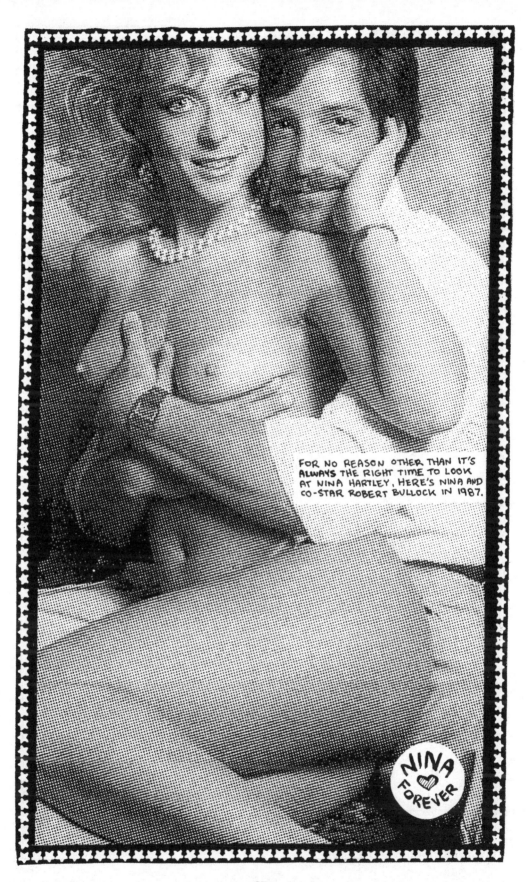

FOR NO REASON OTHER THAN IT'S ALWAYS THE RIGHT TIME TO LOOK AT NINA HARTLEY, HERE'S NINA AND CO-STAR ROBERT BULLOCK IN 1987.

NINA FOREVER

FIFTY movie titles that sound like XXX videos

Hard Candy
Fun with Dick and Jane
Dark Passage
Space Balls
Men in Black
The 400 Blows
Three Men and a Little Lady
The Bone Collector
Anaconda
Nuts
Freejack
Let the Right One in
Dirty Harry
Pacific Rim
Inside Llewyn Davis
Wreck-It Ralph
The Banger Sisters
Stand and Deliver
Blown Away
Inside Man
Naked Lunch
Sister Act
The Jerk
Big
Free Willy
The Crying Game
Monster's Ball
The Harder They Come
In the Line of Fire
The Gay Divorcee
Teaching Mrs Tingle
Big Daddy
The Naked City
Black Snake Moan
Stop! Or My Mom Will Shoot
Grizzly Man
Hannah and Her Sisters
Stroker Ace
Snatch
Blow
Supersize Me
In Too Deep
Splash
Fist of Fury
The Black Hole
Die Hard
Fast and Furious
Enter the Void
Sudden Impact
A Boy and His Dog

HOT RODS: FIVE OF CINEMA SEWER'S FAVE CUSTOMIZED CARS

5. THE 1925 T-BUCKET ROADSTER IN THE CHOPPERS (1961)
CREATED AND OWNED BY ACTOR, AND DRAG RACING LEGEND, TOMMY IVO, THIS CONVERTIBLE IS ARCH HALL JR'S CAR IN THE MOVIE, AND ALSO MAKES AN APPEARANCE IN DRAG STRIP GIRL. IVO CREATED THIS RIGHTEOUS ROADSTER AFTER SEEING THE WORK THAT FELLOW ACTOR, NORM GRABOWSKI, DID ON HIS MUCH MORE FAMOUS "KOOKY KAR" ROADSTER, THAT CAPTURED LOTS OF ATTENTION AS A CUSTOM HOT ROD REGULARLY SEEN ON THE TV SERIES, 77 SUNSET STRIP.

4. THE MACH 5 IN SPEED RACER (2008)
WHILE SOME MIGHT HAVE ASSUMED THAT THIS AWESOME WHITE CUSTOM RACING CAR WAS ENTIRELY COMPUTER GENERATED (LIKE MUCH OF THE REST OF THIS RATHER UNEXCEPTIONAL "LIVE ACTION" RENDITION OF THE CLASSIC JAPANESE ANIMATED TV SERIES) THE MACH FIVE WAS AN ACTUAL WORKING VEHICLE, EVEN THOUGH IT WASN'T DRIVEN FOR REAL, HERE. INSTEAD, IT WAS HUNG FROM A CRANE AS IT WAS FILMED, AND THEN HAD ITS DRIVING FX AND THE ROAD/BACKGROUNDS ADDED IN POST PRODUCTION.

3. PROJECT X IN THE HOLLYWOOD KNIGHTS (1980)
PROJECT X, A GORGEOUS YELLOW CUSTOMIZED 1957 CHEVY IS ARGUABLY THE MOST FAMOUS HOT ROD OF ALL TIME, AND HAS GRACED MANY A COVER OF POPULAR HOT RODDING MAGAZINE, AMONG OTHERS. IT ALSO MADE A MAJOR APPEARANCE IN THIS AMERICAN GRAFFITI RIP OFF, AS THE CAR THAT TONY DANZA'S CHARACTER CRUISES AROUND IN.

2. MILNER'S 1932 FORD 5-WINDOW IN AMERICAN GRAFFITI (1973)
HOTROD.COM ONCE WROTE "IN 200 YEARS PEOPLE WILL STILL WATCH THIS MOVIE TO KNOW WHAT IT MEANT TO GROW UP IN AN AMERICA OBSESSED WITH HOT RODS. AND THEY'LL STILL WANT TO DRIVE MILNER'S '32", WHILE NAMING IT THE GREATEST CAR MOVIE OF ALL TIME. WHILE I DON'T KNOW IF I'D GO THAT FAR, THIS MOVIE AND HOT ROD ARE CERTAINLY AWESOME ENOUGH TO BE ON THIS LIST.

1. THE GIGAHORSE IN MAD MAX: FURY ROAD (2015).
AS J.P. HUFFMAN AT CAR AND DRIVER MAGAZINE WROTE, "TAKE ONE 1959 CADILLAC COUPE DEVILLE BODY AND SPLIT IT OPEN DOWN THE MIDDLE. THEN INSERT ANOTHER COUPE DEVILLE BODY INTO THE FIRST ONE AND WELD LIKE MAD. THE RESULT WILL BE SOMETHING THAT LOOKS LIKE TWO HUMPING LAS VEGAS CONDOMINIUMS. FINALLY, ALL THAT IS MOUNTED TO A HUGE TRUCK CHASSIS AND POWERED BY TWO TURBO ENGINES MOUNTED ALONGSIDE EACH OTHER." CHARGED V-8

GRRRNNNN!

RROAARRR

BOUGIE · 2016 · ☆

HAW

ATTACK OF THE BEAST CREATURES

REVIEW BY NATHAN HILL · ART BY THE KING, ☆ BEN NEWMAN ☆ LETTERING BY ROBIN BOUGIE!

THIS IS A LITTLE GEM THAT GOT LOST AT THE TIME OF ITS THEATRICAL RELEASE ONLY TO BE REDISCOVERED ON VHS IN THE OLD MOM N' POP RENTAL SHOPS ALL ACROSS NORTH AMERICA BACK IN THE DAY. SHOT ON A DEFINITE SHOE STRING BUDGET IN 1985, DIRECTOR MICHAEL STANLEY BROUGHT TOGETHER A SMALL BAND OF PEOPLE TO MAKE A CLASSIC TALE OF MAN VS MAN, MAN VS NATURE, AND MAN VS SUPERNATURAL. THE RESULT IS AN EIGHTY MINUTE TALE OF SURVIVORS ON AN ISLAND INHABITED BY SMALL CANNIBALISTIC BEAST CREATURES. IF THEY DON'T KILL ONE ANOTHER OR THEMSELVES TRYING TO ESCAPE, THE BEAST CREATURES WILL...

IT OPENS UP SOMEWHERE IN THE NORTH ATLANTIC IN MAY 1920, WITH SURVIVORS OF A SHIPWRECK FLOATING IN A LIFEBOAT. EVERYONE IS PANICKING; SCREAMING; IT'S TOTAL CHAOS! WHEN THEY BEGIN DRIFTING AWAY FROM THE OTHER LIFEBOATS (NONE OF ARE VISIBLE ANYWAY), THEY END UP ON THE SHORES OF AN ISLAND. FIVE MEN AND THREE WOMEN. ONE OF THEM IS WOUNDED, AND THE GROUP DECIDES TO LEAVE HIM ON THE BEACH SO THEY CAN FIND WATER AND FOOD. IT'S NOTED BY ONE OF THE CHARACTERS THAT THE ISLAND SURE SEEMS TROPICAL CONSIDERING THEY WERE TRAVELING ON THE NORTH ATLANTIC (THE FILM WAS ACTUALLY SHOT IN FAIRFIELD, CONNECTICUT. HARDLY A TROPICAL STATE, OR AN ISLAND FOR THAT MATTER).

AFTER SOME EXPLORING, ONE OF THE MORE THIRSTY SURVIVORS DIES A GORY DEATH WHEN HE DECIDES TO BEND DOWN, FACE FIRST INTO A POND AND THINK, "OF COURSE IT'S WATER, WHY WOULD IT BE ACID?" ONLY TO DISCOVER IT IS, IN FACT, ACID. HIS TORSO FALLS APART IN GORY PIECES AS HIS SCREAMS SLOWLY MUFFLE INTO NOTHING. THERE'S SOME MINOR HYSTERIA FROM THOSE WHO WITNESSED THE HORROR, AND THEY HEAD BACK TO THE BEACH ONLY TO DISCOVER THE SKELETAL REMAINS OF THEIR WOUNDED FRIEND. WHAT IS GOING ON HERE?! WHAT IN THE HELL DID THIS?!?

THE BEAST CREATURES, THAT'S WHO!!!

WITH THEIR GLOWING GOOGLY WHITE EYES, RAZOR SHARP TEETH, LONG BLACK HAIR, THESE LITTLE TWO FOOT TALL CANNIBAL MANIACS ARE VICIOUS ORANGE-SKINNED PUPPETS TO BE RECKONED WITH. THEY JUMP OUT OF TREES AND BITE AND NIBBLE AWAY AT THEIR VICTIMS UNTIL THERE IS NOTHING LEFT. HUNTED, STALKED, AND TERRORIZED AT EVERY TURN, THE EVER SHRINKING NUMBER OF SURVIVORS SQUARE OFF WITH THESE BASTARDS, BUT FOR EVERY BEAST CREATURE THEY KILL, FIVE REPLACE IT.

I FOUND MYSELF CHEERING THE HAIRY LITTLE FUCKERS ON. KILL THOSE TRESPASSERS! HOW DARE THEY INVADE YOUR ISLAND!? YOU WILL TOO, BECAUSE THEY HAVE INCREDIBLE COMBAT AND BOOBY TRAPPING SKILLS. ONE OF THE CHARACTERS IS BEING CHASED BY THE BEAST CREATURES, TRIPS ON A LITTLE ROPE AND IMPALES HIMSELF ON A STICK! GAME OVER, BAHD! YOU SHOULD HAVE FOUGHT THEM AND DIED LIKE A MAN.

EVENTUALLY THE GROUP OF SURVIVORS MAKE THEIR WAY UP A SMALL CLIFF, AND DISCOVER HUNDREDS OF THESE HUNGRY DUDES IN THE MIDDLE OF A FIELD WORSHIPPING A GIGANTIC STATUE. IS IT A GOD? DOES IT GIVE THEM STRENGTH? IT'S NEVER EXPLAINED WHAT THE STATUE IS OR WHY IT'S THERE, BUT SEEING ALL OF THE BEAST CREATURES HYPNOTIZED BY THIS MASSIVE FIGURE IS MORE THAN ENOUGH REASONS FOR THE GROUP TO GET AS FAR AWAY AS POSSIBLE. MORE CHASING AND FIGHTING, SCREAMING, AND NIBBLING ENSUES RIGHT UP UNTIL THE VERY END OF THE MOVIE.

THE SPECIAL EFFECTS MIGHT BE CHEAP, BUT I HAD NO QUALMS SEEING THE SAME SKELETON BEING USED FOR MULTIPLE CHARACTERS. EACH GORY AND BRUTALLY ENTERTAINING DEATH PUSHED THE MOVIE FORWARD, AND AS THREATENING AS THE BEAST CREATURES ARE, NOT ALL OF THE DEMISES WERE BY THEIR HAND. THIS ADDED AN FLAIR OF THE UNPREDICTABLE TO THE MOVIE, AS WELL AS A BIT OF AN EDGE. THAT'S ALWAYS A PLUS.

SURE THE SCRIPT AND LINE-READING WAS PRETTY CORNY, BUT THE PHYSICAL ACTING HERE WAS ACTUALLY FAIRLY IMPRESSIVE, ALL THINGS CONSIDERED. THERE ARE WIDE SHOTS WITH THE WHOLE CAST RUNNING AROUND WITH BEAST CREATURES ATTACHED TO THEM. DESPITE CONVENTIONAL WISDOM, IT TAKES TALENT TO RELENTLESSLY SCREAM AND FLAIL YOUR ARMS AROUND LIKE THOSE INFLATABLE ARM WAVY-LOOKING STANDOUTS AT USED CAR DEALERSHIPS. AND MAKING THE FEAR OF BEING EATEN BY TWO FOOT DOLLS SEEM LEGITIMATE IS EVEN MORE PRAISE-WORTHY.

AND WHO COULD FORGET ALL THE ACTORS' HAIRSTYLES BEING DONE BY DJ'S HAIR INN? OK, I DIDN'T NOTICE ANYTHING PARTICULARLY NOTEWORTHY ABOUT THE HAIR IN THE MOVIE, AND YET THE PRODUCERS FELT IT WAS IMPORTANT ENOUGH TO ADD DJ'S INTO THE OPENING CREDITS. DJ'S MUST HAVE BEEN A GREAT PLACE TO GET YOUR HAIR DONE BACK IN THE '80S IN FAIRFIELD, CONNECTICUT. I CAN SEE ALL OF THE CAST SITTING IN THEIR HOUSECOATS GETTING THEIR HAIR DONE, AND TALKING TO DJ ABOUT THEIR NEXT SCENE. I WONDER WHAT DJ IS DOING NOW? MAYBE HE/SHE IS SITTING IN AN OLD WATERING HOLE RELIVING THE GLORY DAYS OF 1985, TELLING ANYONE WHO WILL LISTEN ABOUT THE TIME ALL THOSE WOULD-BE HOLLYWOOD STARS CAME IN TO GET THEIR HAIR DONE FOR THAT "ATTACK OF THE HEAT SEEKERS" MOVIE.

ATTACK OF THE BEAST CREATURES IS NOT WITHOUT ITS SHORTCOMINGS. IT LACKS A BIG PAY OFF AT THE CLIMAX, AND THE MOVIE IS ALL OVER THE PLACE EMOTIONALLY, WITH THE CHARACTERS BEING A LITTLE TOO GOOD AT COMPARTMENTALIZING THE TRAUMA THEY EXPERIENCE. THEY GO FROM WITNESSING GORY ACID BATHS TO COMPLIMENTING EACH OTHER'S STICK SHARPENING ABILITY. THEY GO FROM BEING ATTACKED AND BEING EATING ALIVE TO ENJOYING LAUGHS AND A LITTLE WATER SPLASH FIGHT IN A POND. HONESTLY, THE FILM FEELS LIKE TWO MANIC DEPRESSED PEOPLE AT OPPOSITE EXTREMES PLAYING TUG OF WAR -- WITH THE VIEWER SUBSTITUTING AS THE ROPE.

THE MUSIC THAT SERVES AS THE SOUNDTRACK ONLY ADDS TO THIS ODD FEELING. A SYNTHESIZER WAS SUCCESSFULLY UTILIZED IN SUCH A WAY THAT ALMOST MADE ME WISH THAT THEY'D NEVER BEEN INVENTED, AND RESULTED IN A SCORE THAT IS LIKELY SIMILAR TO THE REPETITIVE NOISES IN THE HEAD OF A LOBOTOMY PATIENT.

SOME OF THE ACTORS WHO APPEAR IN THE FILM ALSO SERVED AS CREW MEMBERS BEHIND THE CAMERA. IT'S ALSO INTERESTING TO NOTE THAT MOST OF THE POOR FOLKS WHO WORKED ON BEAST CREATURES DECIDED TO GIVE UP ON THE HOLLYWOOD DREAM SHORTLY THEREAFTER. PERHAPS BEAST CREATURES WAS A LIL' COLLEGE FILM AND THE ACTORS WERE DOING THE DIRECTOR A FAVOR, OR MAYBE THE EXPERIENCE ON SET WAS SO HARROWING AND DISCOURAGING THAT THEY DECIDED A FULL TIME JOB AT K-MART WAS FAR MORE SUITABLE. I SHUDDER TO THINK THAT PERHAPS THE BEAST CREATURE PUPPETS MAY HAVE LEFT IRREPARABLE MENTAL TRAUMA. DIRECTOR MICHAEL STANLEY TOOK A TWENTY-THREE YEAR BREAK BEFORE DOING ANOTHER MOVIE.

EVEN WITH ITS PREDICTABLE LOW BUDGET SHORTCOMINGS, I STILL ENJOYED THIS FUN, BRAINLESS, GORY LITTLE GEM. CHECK IT OUT!

-2017- —NATHAN HILL

AAiEE!

THE EXORCIST

DID YOU KNOW ONE OF THE MOST LEGENDARY HORROR MOVIES OF ALL TIME, WILLIAM FRIEDKIN'S THE EXORCIST, HAS A REAL SERIAL KILLER APPEARING ON SCREEN DURING ITS RUNTIME, AND NO ONE KNEW UNTIL YEARS LATER? HE'S THERE, KILLER PAUL BATESON, IN THE UNNERVING SCENE WHERE REGAN (LINDA BLAIR) GETS A CAROTID ANGIOGRAPHY TO DETERMINE IF SHE HAS BRAIN DAMAGE.

THREE YEARS AFTER THE EXORCIST WAS A SMASH HIT, SIX DISMEMBERED BODIES OF GAY MEN, WRAPPED IN BLACK TRASH BAGS, WASHED UP - ONE AFTER ANOTHER - IN NEW YORK'S HUDSON RIVER. IT WASN'T UNTIL THE CORPSE OF FILM CRITIC ADDISON VERRILL WAS FOUND IN HIS APARTMENT, STABBED FULL OF HOLES, THAT POLICE WERE ABLE TO PUT THE CASE TOGETHER AGAINST PAUL BATESON, AN X-RAY TECHNICIAN IN HIS THIRTIES.

FRIEDKIN HAD FILMED THE SCENE IN QUESTION AT NYU MEDICAL SCHOOL WITH A REAL NEUROPSYCHIATRIC SURGEON AND HIS TEAM, AND BATESON (THE SURGEON'S ASSISTANT) CAN CLEARLY BE SEEN PREPARING THE LITTLE GIRL FOR THE PROCEDURE. SHOCKED, FRIEDKIN CALLED UP HIS LAWYER AND ARRANGED FOR AN INTERVIEW WITH THE KILLER, ONE THAT WOULD PROVIDE THE INSPIRATION FOR HIS NEXT MOVIE, CRUISING, STARRING AL PACINO AS A COP THAT GOES UNDERCOVER IN LEATHER GEAR TO CATCH A KILLER WHOSE DISTURBING CRIMES WERE BASED ON BATESON'S.

MOMMY HIDES THE SALAMI
JEWEL DE'NYLE AND HER PORN STAR MOTHER FACE OFF

JEWEL DE'NYLE (REAL NAME: STEPHANY SCHWARZ) IS BISEXUAL, WAS BORN IN 1976, AND STARTED DOING PORN IN 1998 AT THE AGE OF 22. AT THE HEIGHT OF HER FAME, SHE WAS 5'2" 115LBS, WITH BLACK SEXY HAIR AND 34D-26-31 MEASUREMENTS. HER ANCESTRY IS SPANISH, SICILIAN, AND BLACKFOOT INDIAN. THE WEBSITE ADULTFYI.COM DID A LITTLE INTERVIEW WITH HER BACK IN 2005. HERE'S WHAT SHE SAID:

Q: Where are you from and how did you get into the business?

JEWEL: I'M FROM COLORADO AND I MOVED TO CALIFORNIA WHEN I WAS 20 YEARS OLD, AND WAS A DANCER. SELENA STEELE DISCOVERED ME DANCING AND HOOKED ME UP WITH THE PORN WORLD.

Q: What do you think is your best asset?

JEWEL: MY BEST ASSET IS MY ASS. I'VE BEEN TOLD I'M THE NEXT NINA HARTLEY, WHICH IS A REALLY NICE COMPLIMENT.

Q: What part of being in the adult entertainment business do you like the most?

JEWEL: I LIKE BEING A DIRECTOR MORE THAN ANYTHING BECAUSE I DON'T HAVE SOME FAT FUCK THAT'S SITTING BEHIND A CAMERA WHO'S NEVER BEEN ON FILM BEFORE TELLING ME HOW TO FUCK. LIKE I NEED ANY HELP. SO, WHEN I DIRECT IT'S MY WAY, WHICH IS NASTY, JUST THE WAY IT SHOULD BE.

Q: What do you like the least about having sex in front of a camera?

JEWEL: I HATE HAVING SEX WITH THESE CHICKS WHO ARE "GAY FOR PAY". IF SHE DOESN'T WANT A CHICK TO FUCK HER, THEN DON'T DO GIRL/GIRL. I HATE THOSE BITCHES!

Q: What is the wildest thing you've done in a movie?

JEWEL: THE WILDEST THING I'VE EVER DONE IN A MOVIE IS WITH ROCCO. I ATE SHIT OUT OF HIS ASSHOLE. ANY MORE QUESTIONS?

Q: What's the wildest thing you've done in your personal life?

JEWEL: IN MY PERSONAL LIFE, I DRINK PISS AND I LOVE IT.

Q: What question are you tired of being asked?

JEWEL: "HOW CAN I GET INTO PORN?" DON'T FUCKING ASK ME THIS SHIT IF YOU'RE A GUY, BUT IF YOU'RE A GIRL, AND HOT, I'LL HELP YOU. THE GUYS CAN FIGURE IT OUT FOR THEMSELVES. THERE'S NO FREE RIDE FOR THEM — THEY MUST PAY THEIR DUES BEFORE FUCKING ME.

Q: Have you ever gotten into a fist fight in the industry?

JEWEL: I DON'T THINK ANYONE'S EVER WANTED TO FIGHT ME. I WOULDN'T WANT TO FIGHT ME. I'M MEAN, I WAS A KICKBOXER FOR FOUR YEARS. I FOUGHT IN VEGAS. I HAVE THAT NATURAL FIGHTING INSTINCT. I JUST HAVE NO FEAR. YOU COULD BE 200-POUNDS AND 6' TALL AND BE A MAN AND IF YOU WANT TO SAY SOMETHING TO ME, I'LL GO OFF ON YOU. THAT HAPPENED AT CES. I HAD A BIG GUY COME UP TO ME, SAID SOMETHING SMART-ASS, AND SPILLED BEER ON ME. I TOOK HIS BEER AND THREW IT AT HIM. I WAS SCREAMING AT HIM. I GREW UP A TOMBOY. I PLAYED FOOTBALL. I WAS A ROUGHNUT. I GREW UP AROUND GUYS. MAYBE THAT'S WHY I HAVE A GUY MENTALITY. MAYBE THAT'S WHY I AM IN PORN, BECAUSE I THINK LIKE A GUY. IN HIGH SCHOOL I WAS A JOCK AND A ROCKER. I HAVE A PERSONAL TRAINER AND I WORK OUT FIVE DAYS A WEEK.

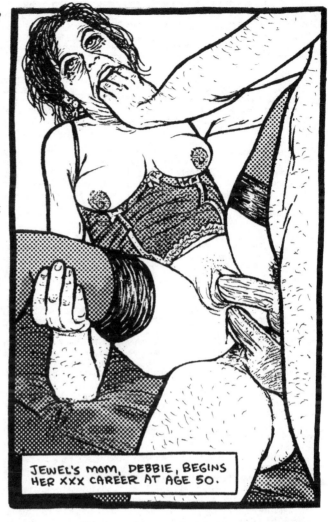

JEWEL'S MOM, DEBBIE, BEGINS HER XXX CAREER AT AGE 50.

SINCE DE'NYLE RETIRED FROM PORN IN 2006, THERE HASN'T BEEN THAT MUCH NEWS ABOUT HER, BUT THE MEMORY OF HER THAT STANDS OUT THE MOST FOR ME WAS NOT ANY NASTY SEX SHE HAD ON SCREEN, BUT RATHER WHEN SHE HAD A VERY NASTY PUBLIC FIGHT WITH HER MOTHER, DEBBIE SCHWARZ, ON THE INTERNET. IT ALL WENT PUBLIC IN 2006, WHEN SOMEONE ON ADULTDVDTALK, A MESSAGE BOARD JEWEL REGULARLY POSTED ON, ASKED HER IF SHE'D EVER HAD "TEARS OF JOY" AT ANY POINT IN HER LIFE. SHE REPLIED: "YES, WHEN I CUT ALL TIES TO MY MOTHER, WHO LOOKS LIKE A CRACK WHORE. I COULDN'T BE HAPPIER WASHING MY HANDS OF HER, AND I HAD TEARS OF JOY."

"I DON'T THINK I LOOK LIKE A CRACK WHORE!" RESPONDED JEWEL'S INDIGNANT MOM, WHO HAD RECENTLY MOVED TO CALIFORNIA AND BEGUN DOING HARDCORE PORN UNDER THE NAME DE'BELLA. "THE PRODUCERS FROM HOWARD STERN SHOW HAVE ASKED JEWEL AND ME TO BE ON THE SHOW. I JUST WANT TO MAKE PEACE AND GET IT ALL OUT IN THE OPEN. IT REALLY HURTS TO HEAR MY DAUGHTER IS SAYING BAD THINGS ABOUT ME. I HAVE ALWAYS SUPPORTED HER THROUGHOUT HER CAREER AND I LOVE HER WITH ALL MY HEART...ALL I WANT IS SUPPORT GIVEN TO ME LIKE I SUPPORTED HER DURING HER ACTING CAREER, AND HOW I SUPPORT HER NOW."

JEWEL'S RESPONSE LEFT NOTHING TO QUESTION. "I WILL NOT BE GOING ON THE SHOW WITH MY MOM, NOR WILL I EVER HAVE ANYTHING TO DO WITH HER AGAIN. SHE'S DEAD TO ME. I WAS FINE WITH HER DOING PORN UP UNTIL SHE STARTED THROWING IT IN MY FACE AND TALKING TO ME ABOUT HER SCENES. THAT IS NOT RIGHT, AND IT'S SOMETHING SHE SHOULD OF KEPT TO HERSELF. THEN I WOULD OF BEEN MORE CARING. BUT RIDING MY COAT TAILS MAKES HER LOOK PLAIN STUPID, AND WHAT SHE DOESN'T REALIZE IS PEOPLE AREN'T LAUGHING WITH HER, BUT AT HER. GET A CLUE, BITCH, AND STOP USING MY NAME TO GET ATTENTION. POOR EXCUSE OF A MOTHER. I WISH SHE WERE DEAD."

"AND AS FOR MY STEPFATHER (LARRY SCHWARZ), WELL HE'S BEEN MADE A FOOL AND IS A TOTAL WIMP. WHEN IT COMES TO MY MOM HE HAS NO BACKBONE AND I CANNOT RESPECT THAT. HE LOST HIS JOB IN POLITICS THAT I TOOK THE LIBERTY OF TRYING TO COVER UP FOR HIM BECAUSE HE SLEPT WITH HIS 16-YEAR-OLD ADOPTED DAUGHTER (JEWEL'S STEP-SISTER) AND IT WAS FOUND OUT

AMONG HIS COLLEGES. THEY RAIDED THEIR HOME AND TOOK EVERYTHING INCLUDING HIS QUESTIONABLE PORN. SO I STARTED PXP TO GIVE THEM BOTH A JOB TO AVOID THE SCANDAL THEY WERE FACING BACK IN COLORADO AND PUT ALL MY SAVINGS INTO A COMPANY TO GET THEM BACK ON THEIR FEET. AND THIS IS MY PAYBACK? TOTAL LOSERS IN MY EYES, THE BOTH OF THEM, AND I'M NOT GOING TO SUPPORT OR PROTECT THEM ANYMORE. HE'S A CHILD MOLESTER AND SHE'S A LAUGHING STALK DRUG USER. SORRY, BUT THE TRUTH HURTS."

THE CIRCUS SIDESHOW CONTINUED ON THE MESSAGE BOARD, AS D'BELLA REPLIED WITH AN OPEN LETTER TO HER DAUGHTER, WHICH CONCLUDED WITH: "I AM DETERMINED TO NOT CHANGE BECAUSE ANYONE ELSE THINKS I SHOULD LIVE MY LIFE DIFFERENTLY. I HAVE "JEWEL" PICTURES IN MY OFFICE, ALONG WITH A SIGN THAT SAYS "PROUD PARENTS OF A PORN STAR", AND BRAG ABOUT HER TO ALL WHO WILL LISTEN. THERE ARE ALSO A LOT OF ADDITIONAL PICTURES OF OUR DAUGHTER IN HAPPIER TIMES. THEY WILL REMAIN THERE, AND SHE IN MY HEART FOREVER, UNTIL I DO IN FACT DIE."

"PLEASE DO ME A FAVOR AND PULL THE TRIGGER, BITCH", RESPONDED JEWEL. "I'VE DONE ALL I CAN FOR MY FAMILY, AND I CAN DO NO MORE, AS IT'S DONE NOTHING BUT BACKFIRE ON ME. I LOST MY FAMILY AND MY COMPANY THAT I PUT ALL MY HARD EARNED CASH AND SOUL INTO. I'VE CRIED A RIVER OF TEARS AND MY HEART IS BROKEN, NEVER TO BE REPAIRED. I'M BITTER AND BEYOND EVIL AT THIS POINT. I WISH THIS NIGHTMARE WOULD END. I'D RATHER MY PARENTS BE DEAD THEN TO LIVE WITH WHAT THEY BESTOW UPON ME. THEY ARE DEAD TO ME, NEVER TO RETURN OR TO BE APART OF MY LIFE."

LARRY SCHWARZ SERVED AS A REPUBLICAN FROM 1995 TO 1997 IN THE COLORADO STATE LEGISLATURE REPRESENTING HOUSE DISTRICT 44, AND WAS THEN APPOINTED TO A SEAT ON THE COLORADO STATE PAROLE BOARD. WHEN A THERAPIST WENT TO THE POLICE IN 2001, AND EXPLAINED THAT SCHWARZ HAD MOLESTED ONE OF HER CLIENTS, AND NOTED THAT SHE'D LEARNED THAT TWO OTHER MEMBERS OF HIS FAMILY HAD ALSO BEEN VICTIMIZED, THE POLICE RAIDED THE SCHWARZ HOME.

MANY BOXES OF SMUT WERE SEIZED (MANY OF THEM WITH CONTENT FEATURING JEWEL), AND AMONGST THEM WERE PUBLICATIONS THAT WERE ALLEGED TO DEPICT CHILDREN HAVING SEX. LARRY AVOIDED CRIMINAL CHARGES, BUT WAS FIRED FROM HIS JOB ON THE PAROLE BOARD AND DUMPED FROM THE CONSERVATIVE REPUBLICAN ARENA. SO HE MOVED TO CALIFORNIA, AND SET HIS WIFE UP WITH A PORN CAREER IN THE COMPANY, PLATINUM X, WHICH JEWEL FUNDED WITH HER LIFE SAVINGS IN ORDER TO GIVE BOTH OF HER PARENTS JOBS. THIS WAS WHEN, AT THE AGE OF 50, DEBBIE BEGAN DOING XXX, WHICH INCLUDED DOUBLE PENETRATION SCENES, AND ANAL FUCKING.

NOT LONG AFTER THEIR PUBLIC SPAT, A DISGUSTED AND DISAPPOINTED JEWEL DE'NYLE RETIRED FROM PORN, AND MOVED TO LONG ISLAND NEW YORK, WHERE SHE MARRIED A COP. IN 2008, HER MOM DEBBIE DIVORCED HER FATHER LARRY, AND ANNOUNCED ON XXXPORNTALK.COM THAT "THE COWARD AND PEDOPHILE QUIT HIS JOB AND IS FLEEING TO THAILAND TO AVOID THE COURT ORDERS WHEN THEY DID NOT GO HIS WAY."

"I WILL HAVE HIM SERVED IN THAILAND THROUGH THEIR EMBASSY", DEBBIE WROTE. "HE THINKS HE'S STILL A CONGRESSMAN OR PAROLE MANAGER. HE'S JUST A LIAR AND COWARD...I RECEIVED THE OFFICIAL TRANSCRIPTS AND POLICE REPORTS FROM COLORADO THIS WEEK. IT IS FROM THE COVERT AND TAPED TELEPHONE CALL LARRY HAD WITH HIS DAUGHTER "DEBBIE". LARRY ADMITTED ON TAPE TO HAVING A SEXUAL RELATIONSHIP WITH HER WHEN SHE WAS UNDER AGE. HE CALLED IT "TRAINING LIKE THE AFRICAN PRINCES' DO WITH THEIR DAUGHTERS". HE ALSO ADMITTED WHEN SHE CONFRONTED HIM ABOUT HAVING A DOG INVOLVED WITH THE SEXUAL ENCOUNTER. YES A DOG. HE ADMITTED THAT HE HAD SEX WITH HIS OTHER DAUGHTER LESA WHEN SHE WAS UNDER AGE. I WATCHED HIM BURN SEVERAL 8MM REELS, DVDS AND MAGAZINES WITH YOUNG CHILDREN HAVING SEX WHEN SOCIAL SERVICES WAS ON THE WAY TO THE HOUSE IN COLORADO. THE ONE AND ONLY REASON FOR THEM NOT PROSECUTING LARRY WAS THE STATUE OF LIMITATIONS HAD EXPIRED. THEY HAD PLENTY OF EVIDENCE TO PROSECUTE. LARRY HAD ME SCARED AND INTIMIDATED TO SAY ANYTHING THEN. WHAT YOU DON'T KNOW IS THAT LARRY KEPT ME IN A STATE OF FINANCIAL SERVITUDE AND MADE ME BELIEVE I COULD GO TO JAIL."

WITHOUT THE POISONOUS LARRY AROUND, JEWEL MADE UP WITH HER MOM SHORTLY AFTER, AND FORGAVE WHAT SHE CALLED "ALMOST UNFORGIVABLY BAD BUSINESS DECISIONS".

"NOW WE ARE GOOD, AND I WISH HER THE BEST", JEWEL TOLD THE ADULT INDUSTRY PRESS. "IT'S NICE HAVING A MOM WHO UNDERSTANDS YOU AND SUPPORTS WHAT YOU DO. IT MAKES LIFE A WHOLE LOT EASIER."

THE LICKERISH QUARTET (1970)

WRITTEN AS "HIDE AND SEEK", AND FILMED AS "MIND GAMES", RADLEY METZGER'S THE LICKERISH QUARTET IS A MUST-SEE FOR SEXPLOITATION FANS. AS MONDODIGITAL.COM NOTED IN 2013 "EVEN IF DIRECTOR RADLEY METZGER HAD ONLY MADE THE LICKERISH QUARTET AND NOTHING ELSE, HE WOULD STILL BE A CRUCIAL NAME IN CULT FILMMAKING."

METZGER AND SCREENWRITER MICHAEL DEFORREST CRAFTED THE FILM ON PAPER WHILE LIVING IN THE LOCATIONS THEY'D BE FILMING IN. THE CASTLE OF BALSORANO IN THE ABRUZZI MOUNTAINS IN ITALY WAS UNUSED AT THE TIME OF PRODUCTION, BUT IS NOW A POPULAR TOURIST ATTRACTION, AND THIS UNIQUE FOUNDATION FOR THE MOVIE GAVE THE CREATORS A WONDERFUL OPPORTUNITY TO TAILOR THE SCRIPT TO MATCH THE UNUSUAL SPACES THAT THE CASTLE PROVIDED. METZGER WOULD LATER SAY THAT HE LOVED THE ENTIRE EXPERIENCE OF CREATING THE MOVIE FROM START TO FINISH, CALLING THE PROCESS "A SERIES OF IDEALIZED CONDITIONS."

BEFORE TAKING UP AS A DIRECTOR, HE TIRELESSLY IMPORTED SEXY EURO CINEMA THROUGH HIS COMPANY, AUDUBON, AND WAS KNOWN TO RECUT, REDUB AND EVEN SOMETIMES SHOOT NEW FOOTAGE TO ADD TO SAID FILMS. AND WHEN METZGER HIMSELF FINALLY BEGAN DIRECTING EROTICA, HE CHAMPIONED THE VISUAL STYLE, SOPHISTICATION OF THOSE FOREIGN PRODUCTIONS, RATHER THAN MAKE THE MORE PREDICTABLE CHOICE OF APING THE GRINDHOUSE/DRIVE-IN EXPLOITATION SLEAZE OF HIS AMERICAN COUNTRYMEN.

ON SCREEN, AN ODD FAMILY TRIO OF JADED ARISTOCRATS (THEY ARE NAMELESS, WHICH IS FITTING FOR A FILM WHERE IDENTITY IS SO CONSISTENTLY FLUID) RESIDE ALONE IN A REMOTE ITALIAN CASTLE. AS WE MEET THESE THREE, THEIR RELATIONSHIP ISN'T ENTIRELY OBVIOUS, BUT IT'S SOON REVEALED THAT THEY ARE HUSBAND (FRANK WOLFF), WIFE (ERIKA REMBERG) AND SON (PAOLO TURCO), AND TONIGHT THEY'RE GOING TO SIT DOWN WITH A 16MM PROJECTOR AND WATCH AN OLD BLACK AND WHITE PORN FILM TOGETHER.

RIGHT OFF THE BAT IT'S PRETTY OBVIOUS THAT THE HUSBAND AND WIFE ARE FAR MORE INTO THE CONCEPT OF LOUNGING AROUND AND WATCHING FILTHY STAG FILMS THAN THEIR SON, WHO FINDS THE ENTIRE ENDEAVOUR OFF-PUTTING AND FRUSTRATING. HE STAYS AND WATCHES REGARDLESS, AS SMIRKING DISCUSSIONS TAKE PLACE REVOLVING AROUND THE PRODUCTION OF "THESE FILMS", AND WHERE THEIR PRODUCERS MIGHT PROCURE THE SHAMELESS WOMEN WHO BARE ALL IN THEM. ONE OF THEM MOCKINGLY DESCRIBES THE TWO GIRLS SEXING EACH OTHER UP ON SCREEN AS "THERESE AND ISABELLE", A NONE-TOO-SUBTLE REFERENCE TO METZGER'S FIRST THEATRICAL SUCCESS.

Beyond the physical edge...

"The Lickerish Quartet"

AN EROTIC DUET FOR FOUR PLAYERS

WITH SILVANA VENTURELLI, FRANK WOLFF, ERIKA REMBERG, PAOLO TURCO. IN EASTMAN COLOR.

Distributed by Audubon Films

Persons under 18 not admitted

LATER THAT NIGHT, THIS ODD FAMILY ATTEND A LOCAL CARNIVAL (ERECTED JUST FOR THE MOVIE) AND WITNESS A GLORIOUSLY FILMED MOTORCYCLE STUNT ACT KNOWN AS "THE WALL OF DEATH", AND THIS IS WHEN THE STORY REALLY REVS INTO GEAR. A LOVELY DAREDEVIL (SILVANA VENTURELLI) DRESSED IN A UNIQUE FORM-FITTING WHITE LEATHER RIDING SUIT TAKES HER HELMET OFF, AND WITH JUST A QUICK REVEAL OF HER FACE INSTANTLY CONVINCES OUR THREE LEAD CHARACTERS THAT SHE IS THE STAR OF THE FILTHY MOVIE THEY JUST GOT FINISHED CHORTLING AT. IN AN AUDIO COMMENTARY CONVERSATION WITH INTERVIEWER MICHAEL BOWEN, METZGER REVEALED THAT WHEN HE WAS 12 YEARS OLD, HE FLEETINGLY GLIMPSED A BEAUTIFUL WOMAN IN AN ALL-WHITE COSTUME AT A CARNIVAL, VERY SIMILAR TO THE ONE HE EVENTUALLY CLOTHED VENTURELLI IN.

INTRIGUED, THE HUSBAND INSISTS THAT HE MUST LURE THIS STUNNING LADY OF ILL REPUTE BACK TO THE CASTLE SO THEY CAN PLAYFULLY CONFRONT HER WITH HER SINFUL AND SEXUALLY EXCITING PAST, BUT AS THE SCRATCHY FILM RUNS THROUGH THE PROJECTOR, SOMETHING IS WRONG. SOMETHING IS DIFFERENT. ASTONISHED, THEY FIND THAT THE FILM THEY JUST WATCHED EARLIER IN THE EVENING HAS CHANGED AND THE WOMAN THEY'VE INVITED HOME IS NO LONGER THE PERSON ON SCREEN. IMPOSSIBLY, SHE'S BEEN REPLACED BY ANOTHER ACTRESS.

THIS STRANGE AND MYSTERIOUS VISITOR IS SEX INCARNATE, AND SEDUCES EACH MEMBER OF THE FAMILY, ONE AT A TIME. VENTURELLI IS AN UTTER KNOCKOUT, NOT TO MENTION A CONFIDENT IN-CHARGE PRESENCE IN EACH SCENE SHE SPEARHEADS. SHE'S ALSO A BLANK SLATE, A FACT THAT METZGER CLEARLY INTENDED BY DESIGN. LIKE A CLEAN SHEET OF PAPER, BOTH THE FILMMAKER AND HIS CHARACTERS DRAW THE OBJECTS OF THEIR DESIRES AND FANTASIES UPON HER. SHE'S A SORT OF OPEN-ENDED PERSONAL THERAPIST WHO PROVIDES HEALING IN EACH OF HER SURREAL AND SEDUCTIVE ROMPS, BUT VENTURELLI IS ALSO THE CONTRADICTION OF INNER PEACE AND THE UPSET OF FAMILIAL BALANCE.

THE LICKERISH QUARTET IS A PUZZLING HALL OF MIRRORS. IT'S NOT A PLOT-DRIVEN STORY BUT EVERY SOFTCORE COPULATION SCENE UNEARTHS MORE ABOUT EACH CHARACTER, AND WHAT THEY REPRESENT. THE HUSBAND, AN EX-GI WITH HIS SIGNATURE OF MALE DOMINANCE, THE WIFE, A PORTRAIT OF THE STRUGGLE TO DEAL WITH SOCIETY'S MOTHER-WHORE STEREOTYPE, AND THEIR MAGIC-OBSESSED SON, THE LIVING EMBODIMENT OF THE OEDIPUS COMPLEX. THEY ALL NEED THIS VISITOR TO MOVE ON TO THEIR NEXT STAGE OF BEING, BUT AFTER SHE LEAVES, NOTHING IS THE SAME. AS ERIKA REMBERG'S CHARACTER PUTS IT, "WE START AND FINISH IN THE DARK. IN BETWEEN IS JUST A GAME OF HIDE AND SEEK!"

IT'S A RELEASE THAT HAD VARYING CRITICAL RECEPTION IN THE EARLY SEVENTIES, FROM A TRASHING BY ROGER EBERT ("THE MOVIE ISN'T GOOD ENOUGH TO SUCCEED ON THE LEVEL OF ITS AMBITION, AND IT DOESN'T EVEN TRY TO SUCCEED AS A SKIN FLICK.") AND A SCATHED SOURING BY THE VILLAGE VOICE ("SOPHOMORIC AND HOLLOW"), TO A BOISTEROUS THUMBS UP FROM VINCENT CANBY AT THE NEW YORK TIMES ("ENTERTAINING, BEAUTIFUL, RIPE WITH INCREDIBLE COLOR AND DECOR"), L.A. FREE PRESS ("A CLASSIC!"), AND PLAYBOY MAGAZINE ("ELEGANT EROTICISM").

WHILE THE SKIN ON DISPLAY IS PLENTIFUL ENOUGH, IT SHOULD BE NOTED THAT RADLEY WAS, FOR THE MOST PART, DISINTERESTED IN SHOOTING SEX AND NUDITY FOR THEIR OWN SAKE IN THIS MOVIE, INSTEAD EMPLOYING UNIQUE ATMOSPHERE IN THE MANNER OF SET DESIGN (AN AMAZING LIBRARY WITH THE FLOOR PAINSTAKINGLY INSCRIBED WITH VARIOUS WORDS FOR FUCKING AND GENITALS) OR VISUAL WEIRDNESS (A UNIQUE MIRROR THAT PERVERTS AND DISTORTS REALITY). THAT SAID, THE MOVIE MANAGES TO BE LOFTY AND THEMATIC WITHOUT BEING SMUG OR OBNOXIOUS. IT TEASES WITH PRETENSION, BUT IS AWARE THAT IT EXISTS TO ENTERTAIN AND AROUSE. AS VOYEURS, WE'RE WATCHING A SEX MOVIE, BUT WE'RE ALSO WATCHING VOYEURS WATCHING A SEX MOVIE, AND THE DIRECTOR JOYFULLY REVELS IN THAT NARRATIVE ADVENTURE, AND TOYS WITH IT. I'M LEFT WISHING MORE PORNOGRAPHERS HAD SUCH AMBITION AND TOOK SUCH RISKS.

ACTOR FRANK WOLFF BEGAN HIS CAREER ON SEVERAL ROGER CORMAN FILMS ALONG WITH CLOSE FRIEND AND UCLA SCHOOLMATE MONTE HELLMAN, BUT EVENTUALLY WAS FORCED TO MOVE TO EUROPE IN ORDER TO FIND SUCCESS. WOLFF DID QUITE WELL IN THE SPAGHETTI WESTERN GENRE, AND WAS EVEN OFFERED ONE OF THE LEAD ROLES IN A FISTFUL OF DOLLARS BY SERGIO LEONE, BUT TURNED IT DOWN. SUFFERING FROM DEPRESSION, WOLFF COMMITTED SUICIDE IN A BATHTUB IN HIS ROOM AT THE HILTON HOTEL IN ROME A YEAR AFTER LICKERISH QUARTET PREMIERED.

THE LICKERISH QUARTET CAME AT THE TAIL END OF THE CAREER OF RAVEN-HAIRED AUSTRIAN STARLET ERIKA REMBERG. BORN IN INDONESIA TO AN AUSTRIAN TOBACCO FARMER IN 1932, ERIKA WAS A TALENTED ACTRESS WHO WORKED STEADILY THROUGHOUT THE 1950S AND '60S. SHE'S ALSO KNOWN TO HAVE HAD A TORRID SIX-MONTH AFFAIR WITH ACTOR KLAUS KINSKI IN 1955, AND IN THE MID TO LATE SEVENTIES DROPPED OUT OF ACTING TO OPEN A BOUTIQUE IN MUNICH AND TO WORK AS AN ENGLISH-TO-GERMAN BOOK TRANSLATOR. SHE THEN MARRIED BRITISH DIRECTOR SIDNEY HAYERS AND MOVED TO SPAIN.

GORGEOUS SILVANA VENTURELLI DIDN'T HAVE ANY STARRING TURNS BEFORE OR AFTER LICKERISH QUARTET, BUT SHE DID HAVE A SMALL ROLE IN METZGER'S CAMILLE 2000, AND A COUPLE OF VERY MEMORABLE UNCLOTHED LAYOUTS IN PLAYBOY MAGAZINE (IN MARCH 1986 AND MAY 1969).

CINEMA SEWER READERS POLL:
WHAT ARE YOUR 3 FAVORITE HONG KONG MARTIAL ARTS/ACTION FILMS?

THIS POLL TOOK PLACE IN JUNE OF 2016. ENTRANTS WERE ALLOWED THREE PICKS (EACH WITH EQUAL POINT VALUE). HERE ARE THE TOP 25 RESULTS:

WINNER WINNER, CHICKEN DINNER!

1. Hard Boiled (1992) 22 votes
2. The Killer (1989) 20 votes
3. Police Story (1985) 19 votes
4. Drunken Master 2 (1994) 15 votes
5. 36th Chamber of Shaolin (1978) 12 votes
6. 5 Deadly Venoms (1978) 11 votes
7. Iron Monkey (1993) 10 votes
8. Master of the Flying Guillotine (1976) 10 votes
9. Riki-Oh: The Story of Ricky (1991) 9 votes
10. Fist of Legend (1994) 8 votes
11. Full Contact (1992) 8 votes
12. Infernal Affairs (2002) 7 votes
13. Boxer's Omen (1983) 6 votes
14. Drunken Master (1983) 6 votes
15. Five Element Ninja (1982) 6 votes
16. Kung Fu Hustle (2004) 6 votes
17. Bullet in the Head (1990) 5 votes
18. Chinese Ghost Story (1987) 5 votes
19. City on Fire (1987) 5 votes
20. Prodigal Son (1981) 5 votes
21. Project A (1983) 5 votes
22. Tiger on Beat (1988) 5 votes
23. Duel to the Death (1983) 4 votes
24. Eastern Condors (1987) 4 votes
25. Wheels on Meals (1984) 4 votes
12 others with 3 votes each
16 others with 2 votes each

NO SHADOW KICK!

MY PERSONAL TOP 3 ARE:
1. Drunken Master 2 (1994)
2. Hard Boiled (1992)
3. Iron Monkey (1993)

I'M REALLY SATISFIED WITH THESE RESULTS OVERALL, WHICH PROVE YET AGAIN THAT CINEMA SEWER READERS REALLY KNOW THEIR STUFF. BUT THAT SAID, IT WAS REALLY QUITE WEIRD TO ME THAT THERE WAS NOT ONE SINGLE SOLITARY VOTE FOR:

Crouching Tiger, Hidden Dragon (2000)
Better Tomorrow 2 (1987)
Once Upon a Time in China (1991)
Armour of God 2: Operation Condor (1991)
Fong Sai Yuk (1993)
Shaolin Soccer (2001)

?

I MEAN, I KNOW SHAOLIN SOCCER IS CONSIDERED MORE OF A SPORTS MOVIE THAN AN ACTION MOVIE, BUT C'MON. THOSE OTHERS SHOULD HAVE BEEN IN THE MIX, FOR SURE, RIGHT? ESPECIALLY BETTER TOMORROW 2! THAT FINALE IS <u>RADNESS</u>!

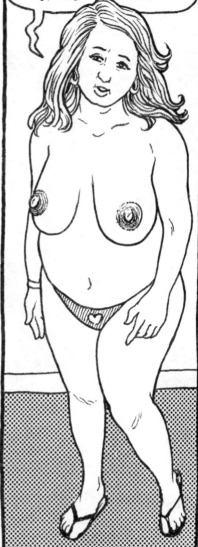

IN JUNE 2017 I WAS CHATTING WITH A COOL PROSTITUTE PAL OF MINE NAMED ANNA, AND THE TOPIC OF WHORES IN MOVIES CAME UP. SHE SAID SOMETHING I LIKED:

"HOW COME EVERY SEX WORKER IN MOVIES IS A SKINNY TWIG? WE'RE NOT ALL CRACK ADDICTS, AND THE LARGE MAJORITY OF WHORING DOES NOT TAKE PLACE IN PUBLIC OR STREET SIDE. THE INTERNET IS A THING, HOLLYWOOD. FEEL FREE TO CATCH UP WITH HOW SEX WORK ACTUALLY HAPPENS ANY TIME NOW. YEAH, NOTHING BUGS ME MORE THAN NEVER HAVING THE GORGEOUS PLUS SIZED GALS REPRESENTED. WE MAKE UP THE MAJORITY OF THE INDUSTRY!"

MAKING THE SCEEN

ANOTHER ROBIN BOUGIE JOINT ☆

MICHIGAN GAVE THE WORLD SO MANY THINGS. THE CAR, THE ASSEMBLY LINE, THE LEGENDARY MUSIC OF MOTOWN, BUT WHAT MANY PEOPLE DON'T KNOW IS THAT IT ALSO GAVE US THE VERY FIRST TRIPLE XXX DRIVE-IN MOVIE THEATER.

TODAY IT AIN'T MUCH MORE THAN A DILAPIDATED FORMER GOLF RANGE OFF OF INTERSTATE 69 IN DURAND (WHICH IS JUST WEST OF FLINT) BUT BACK IN THE 1970S, THE SITE OF THE SCEEN DRIVE-IN WAS GROUND ZERO FOR THE PORNO DRIVE-IN EXPERIENCE. AND IT WAS POPULAR ENOUGH OF AN IDEA TO NOT ONLY SPAWN 70 IMITATORS ACROSS THE COUNTRY, BUT ALSO LAUNCH THE LEGACY OF HARRY MOHNEY, ONE OF THE MOST SUCCESSFUL PORNOGRAPHERS FEW OUTSIDE OF MICHIGAN KNOW OF. FOR A TIME, HE BECAME ONE OF THE LARGEST DISTRIBUTORS OF ADULT MATERIAL IN NORTH AMERICA, OR AS STEVE MILLER, JOURNALIST AND AUTHOR OF "DETROIT ROCK CITY" CALLED HIM: "THE HOWARD HUGHES OF PORN, A MAN WHO HAS ECLIPSED EVEN LARRY FLYNT IN THE SKIN GAME".

HARRY IS THE FOUNDER OF THE EROTIC HERITAGE MUSEUM IN LAS VEGAS, THE DÉJÀ VU CHAIN OF 132 STRIP JOINTS/DIRTY BOOK STORES, THE CO-FOUNDER OF LARRY FLYNT'S $40 MILLION DOLLAR, 70,000 SQUARE FOOT EROTIC EVENTS CENTER, AND THE MOVIE PRODUCER WHO BROUGHT US QUENTIN TARANTINO'S FAVOURITE HARDCORE MOVIE OF ALL TIME, HOT SUMMER IN THE CITY (1976). BUT HE COULDN'T HAVE DONE ANY OF IT WITHOUT INITIALLY DIPPING HIS TOE IN THE POOL OF THE JIZZ-BIZZ WITH A VERY INAUSPICIOUS BEGINNING.

"IN 1960, AS A JUVENILE DELINQUENT TEENAGER, MOHNEY WAS ARRESTED ON CHARGES OF BREAKING AND ENTERING INTO THE CONCESSION STAND, MULTIPLE TIMES, AT A DRIVE-IN THEATER IN BATTLE CREEK", NOTED PETER ALILUNAS, PORN HISTORIAN AND AUTHOR OF "SMUTTY LITTLE MOVIES: THE CREATION AND REGULATION OF ADULT VIDEO".

"HE WAS SENTENCED TO A YEAR AT A YOUTHFUL OFFENDERS CAMP IN TRAVERSE CITY. PROBABLY NOT THAT LONG AFTER HE WAS RELEASED FROM THE CAMP, MOHNEY STARTED WORKING FOR FLOYD BLOSS AT THE STARDUST DRIVE-IN IN HASTINGS, NEAR BATTLE CREEK. BLOSS WAS A REAL CHARACTER, AND I BELIEVE A BIG INFLUENCE ON MOHNEY IN TERMS OF A PARTICULAR REBELLIOUS SPIRIT. BLOSS OWNED THE DRIVE-IN AND A FEW OTHER ADULT THEATERS AND WAS ARRESTED A LOT ON OBSCENITY CHARGES. HE ALSO FOUGHT THE CITY OF BATTLE CREEK PRETTY INTENSELY FOR THE RIGHT TO SHOW THE FILMS. VERY SADLY, BLOSS'S 19-YEAR-OLD DAUGHTER DEBRA WAS MURDERED IN OCTOBER, 1970 WHILE WORKING AS A CASHIER AT HIS EASTOWN CAPRI THEATER IN BATTLE CREEK. SHE WAS STABBED TO DEATH, AND DESPITE THERE BEING A TRIAL, NO ONE WAS EVER CONVICTED. BLOSS RETIRED SOON AFTER THAT AND MOVED TO HAWAII."

WORKING AS A SEXPLOITATION PROJECTIONIST AND THE MENTORSHIP OF FLOYD BLOSS HAD GIVEN HARRY THE CONNECTIONS AND THE KNOW-HOW SO HE COULD RUN A VENUE ON HIS OWN AND AT THE TENDER AGE OF 24 THAT'S EXACTLY WHAT HE DID, HE BOUGHT A STRUGGLING DRIVE-IN THAT NO ONE ELSE WANTED TO BUY, A PLACE THAT HAD PREVIOUSLY BEEN CALLED THE HI-VUE AND HE

RENAMED IT "THE SCENE" IN 1966. 10 MONTHS LATER HE TWEAKED THINGS, CHANGING THE SPELLING TO "THE SCEEN", AND THEN NEVER LOOKED BACK.

THERE WERE EARLY STRUGGLES. HE ONLY REPORTED INCOME OF $60,000 THAT FIRST YEAR. BUT MAKE NO MISTAKE: WHEN MOHNEY BEGAN PROJECTING WHAT BECAME KNOWN REGIONALLY AS THE "DURAND DIRTIES," IT WAS A TURNING POINT FOR THE SMUT INDUSTRY. AT FIRST THESE WERE SOMEWHAT TAME TITS-AND-ASS SEXPLOITATION MOVIES LIKE SMELL OF HONEY, SWALLOW OF BRINE AND THE LUSTFUL TURK. BUT FULL-PENETRATION CHANGE WAS BREWING.

"THE DRIVE-IN ACTUALLY PUT OUR SMALL TOWN ON THE MAP", LAURIE BOWERS, THE LONG TIME PRESIDENT OF ONE OF HARRY'S COMPANIES, DEJA VU, TOLD THE WEBSITE EDPUBLICATIONS.COM IN 2012. "DURAND BOASTED ABOUT THE SAME NUMBER OF BARS AS IT DID CHURCHES. IT WAS A QUIET COMMUNITY WHERE EVERYONE KNEW YOU AND YOU KNEW THEM. AT THAT TIME, THE TALK AROUND TOWN WAS THE "SCEEN", AND I KNEW SOME FRIENDS AND ACQUAINTANCES THAT WOULD HIDE IN THE TRUNK OF THEIR FRIEND'S CAR SO THEY COULD SNEAK IN."

AFTER THE MASSIVE POPULARITY OF DEEP THROAT USHERED IN THE HARDCORE ERA IN 1972, HARRY'S REPORTED INCOME AT THE SCEEN SKYROCKETED. COMING UP WITH THE IDEA TO HIRE TOPLESS WOMEN TO SERVE HOTDOGS AND POPCORN CERTAINLY DIDN'T HURT, EITHER. FRANKLY, HARRY'S IDEA OF

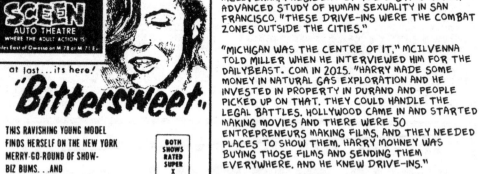

HARRY MOHNEY

SHOWING BIG-SCREEN SEX OUTSIDE OF A MAJOR POPULATION BASE WAS SMART AS FUCK. PORNOGRAPHERS WERE DRAWING WAY TOO MUCH ATTENTION FROM THE POLICE AT THE PORN THEATERS IN THE DOWNTOWN HUBS AROUND THE COUNTRY. PORN WAS STILL IN A GRAY AREA, LEGALLY SPEAKING, AND THE LAWMAKERS SENT THE COPS TO CRACK DOWN ON A REGULAR BASIS, CONFISCATING PRINTS, ARRESTING CUSTOMERS AND STAFF ALIKE, AND DOING WHAT THEY COULD TO REASSURE THE PUBLIC THAT THEY WERE FIGHTING OBSCENITY.

"PEOPLE WERE WORRYING ABOUT THE ADULT FILM INDUSTRY BEING IN THESE DOWNTOWNS AND

PEOPLE WANTED TO SHOW THEIR FILMS WITHOUT WORRYING ABOUT ENDLESS TRIALS," SAYS TED MCILVENNA, PRESIDENT OF THE INSTITUTE FOR ADVANCED STUDY OF HUMAN SEXUALITY IN SAN FRANCISCO. "THESE DRIVE-INS WERE THE COMBAT ZONES OUTSIDE THE CITIES."

"MICHIGAN WAS THE CENTRE OF IT," MCILVENNA TOLD MILLER WHEN HE INTERVIEWED HIM FOR THE DAILYBEAST.COM IN 2015. "HARRY MADE SOME MONEY IN NATURAL GAS EXPLORATION AND HE INVESTED IN PROPERTY IN DURAND AND PEOPLE PICKED UP ON THAT. THEY COULD HANDLE THE LEGAL BATTLES. HOLLYWOOD CAME IN AND STARTED MAKING MOVIES AND THERE WERE 50 ENTREPRENEURS MAKING FILMS, AND THEY NEEDED PLACES TO SHOW THEM. HARRY MOHNEY WAS BUYING THOSE FILMS AND SENDING THEM EVERYWHERE. AND HE KNEW DRIVE-INS."

HARRY THEN OPENED THE AMAZING CINEMA X IN LANSING, AND THE LOCAL PAPERS AT THE TIME CALLED THE CINEMA X THE "SUPERMARKET OF SEX", AS IT FEATURED MAGAZINE, MOVIE AND SEX TOY SALES, A GAMES ROOM WITH POOL AND PINBALL, NUDE SHOESHINES, A PORN THEATER AND LIVE BURLESQUE SHOWS. THEN CAME THE CREST, AND THE NEW ART THEATERS, WHICH ALL SHARED THE SAME COOL LOGO FONT WHEN YOU SAW THEM LISTED TOGETHER IN MICHIGAN NEWSPAPERS.

FOLLOWING MOHNEY'S LEAD, DRIVE-IN OPERATORS ALL ACROSS THE MIDWEST STARTED SHOWING FILTH.

SOME CONVERTING THEIR VENUES TO BECOME FULL-TIME SMUT PEDDLERS, AND SOME WERE PART-TIMERS. THEY'D TREAT THE COMMUNITY TO JOHN WAYNE AND MARYLIN MONROE IN THE SUMMER MONTHS, AND JOHN HOLMES AND MARILYN CHAMBERS IN THE WINTER.

"THE BEL-AIR DRIVE-IN IN FONTANA, CALIFORNIA, WHERE I LIVED FOR YEARS, STARTED SHOWING PRETTY SEXY STUFF ON THEIR SCREEN THAT WAS CLEARLY VISIBLE FROM VALLEY BOULEVARD", RICHARD STEGMAN JR -- A LONG-TIME ADULT FILM FAN, "THERE WAS AN APARTMENT BUILDING NEARBY WHERE YOU WATCH THE SHOW AND IT WAS AROUND THE CORNER FROM THE HIGH SCHOOL."

MANY OF THE DRIVE-INS, WITH YEARS OF EXPERIENCE SHOWING G OR PG RATED FARE, HAD HUGE SCREENS THAT WERE EASILY SEEN BY MOTORISTS OR BY NEARBY LOCALS SITTING IN THEIR BACK YARDS. WHEN PORNO HIT AMERICA LIKE A TSUNAMI, DRIVE-IN OWNERS CLEARLY HADN'T GIVEN MUCH THOUGHT TO HOW JARRING THAT MIGHT BE. BUT THEY FOUND OUT IN A HURRY WHEN COMMUNITY OUTRAGE FROM INDIGNANT FINGER-WAGGERS MEANT COURT SQUABBLES APLENTY. TREMENDOUS PROFITS, HOWEVER, MEANT THOSE WERE

BATTLES WORTH FIGHTING.

"MOHNEY'S EMPIRE WAS VAST", PETER ALILUNAS TOLD ME IN 2018. "IT STRETCHED ALL ACROSS NORTH AMERICA AND INTO CANADA, WHERE HE MADE EARLY EFFORTS TO BREAK THE CENSORSHIP STRUCTURES IN TORONTO TO SHOW HARDCORE FILMS. THAT DIDN'T WORK, BUT HE DEFINITELY HAD A THRIVING TRADE TO THE BOOKSTORES THERE. ALL OF THIS WAS RUN OUT OF THE WAREHOUSES AND OFFICES IN DURAND OUT OF DOZENS OF SHELL COMPANIES, WHICH IS INCREDIBLE. HAVING BEEN TO DURAND AND PHOTOGRAPHED THESE PLACES, I CAN ATTEST TO WHAT A TRULY SMALL, OUT-OF-THE-WAY TOWN IT IS."

LIKE CARLOS TOBALINA, ALEX DE RENZY, AND SO MANY OTHER PORN THEATER OWNERS OF THE 1970S, MOHNEY EVENTUALLY DECIDED TO START CREATING HIS OWN CONTENT TO SHOW ON HIS SCREENS. SAVVY PORNOGRAPHERS WERE ALWAYS LOOKING FOR A WAY TO CUT OUT THE MIDDLE MAN AND MAXIMIZE PROFITS. THAT'S WHEN HE STARTED CARIBBEAN FILMS IN 1976, AND MADE HIS BEAUTIFUL YOUNG GIRLFRIEND, GAIL PALMER (A CURLY HAIRED CHEERLEADER FROM WESTERN MICHIGAN UNIVERSITY IN KALAMAZOO) THE PUBLIC FACE OF THE PRODUCTION COMPANY, AND CLAIMED THAT SHE WAS DIRECTING ALL THE MOVIES. IT WAS REVEALED DECADES LATER THAT HARRY WAS ACTUALLY HIRING TALENTED ESTABLISHED DIRECTOR (AND THE INSPIRATION FOR BURT REYNOLD'S CHARACTER IN BOOGIE NIGHTS) BOB CHINN TO DIRECT MOST OF THEM, AND IN A BRILLIANT MARKETING MOVE HAD GAIL POSING NUDE IN PLAYBOY AND TALKING ABOUT HOW

EMPOWERING IT WAS TO BE THE ONE BEHIND THE CAMERA.

THE NATIONAL MEDIA, ASTOUNDED AT THE VERY NEW CONCEPT OF A SEXY YOUNG WOMAN DIRECTING PORN INSTEAD OF STARRING IN IT, ATE THE STORY UP. GAIL PALMER BECAME A CELEBRITY EVEN OUTSIDE OF PORN, WITH MULTIPLE TALK SHOW INTERVIEWS WITH TOM SNYDER AND OTHERS. GAIL WASN'T SIMPLY A PRETTY FACE THOUGH. SHE DID MANAGE THE CINEMA X IN LANSING AND WORK ON SOME OF THE MOVIE SCRIPTS, AND SHE'D LATER SUE HARRY IN 1984 FOR ENTIRELY EXCLUDING HER FROM THE PROFITS OF THEIR FILMS. SHE WAS ALSO SADLY PHYSICALLY ABUSED BY HUNTER S. THOMPSON, FOR WHICH HE WAS ARRESTED.

IT'S RATHER IRONIC AND SAD THAT A WOMAN LIKE SHARON MCNIGHT THAT ACTUALLY DID DIRECT HARDCORE FEATURE FILMS AT THE SAME TIME (AND DID A REALLY IMPRESSIVE JOB OF IT WITH THE EXPLICIT 1976 COSTUME DRAMA KNOWN AS AUTOBIOGRAPHY OF A FLEA), GOT ZERO

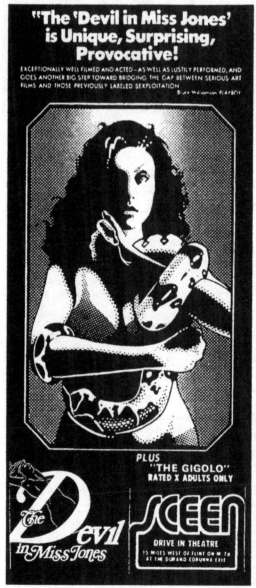

INTEREST FROM THE MEDIA. IT JUST GOES TO SHOW THAT SELLING THE SIZZLE IS OFTEN MORE IMPORTANT THAN HOW AUTHENTIC THE STEAK ACTUALLY IS. IT'S WORTH MENTIONING THAT MCNIGHT WASN'T ALONE, EITHER. THERE WAS ALSO ROBERTA FINDLAY, ANN PERRY, CLAIR DIA, AND JOANNA WILLIAMS, AND THEY ALL GOT NEARLY ZERO MEDIA ATTENTION COMPARED TO MISS GAIL PALMER.

HARRY HIMSELF STEPPED BEHIND THE CAMERA (AND BEHIND THE ODD MONIKER OF "THE HARE") TO DIRECT HOT SUMMER IN THE CITY, ONE OF THE MOST RACIALLY INCENDIARY PORN MOVIES OF THE 1970S. HE ALSO PRODUCED THE EROTIC ADVENTURES OF CANDY, WHICH MADE ITS LEAD ACTRESS, CAROL CONNORS (THORA BIRCH'S MOM), AN EROTICA SUPERSTAR. GETTING HIS GRUBBY MITTS ON THE RIGHTS TO AN OLD NEW YORK SEXPLOITATION FILM CALLED THE PARTY AT KITTY AND STUDS WAS A CASH COW, BECAUSE HE BRILLIANTLY RELEASED IT AS THE ITALIAN STALLION AFTER SLY HIT IT BIG WITH ROCKY. THE WORLD WOULD NOW SEE A VERY FLESHY SIDE OF SYLVESTER STALLONE THAT THEY'D NEVER SEEN BEFORE, IN WHAT BASICALLY AMOUNTS TO THE FIRST BIG TIME CELEBRITY SEX-TAPE.

FOR HIS PART, MOHNEY SUCCESSFULLY FOUGHT OFF 39 ARRESTS OR INDICTMENTS FOR OBSCENITY, ACCORDING TO FLINT JOURNAL NEWSPAPER FILES, WAS CAUGHT UP IN THE MIPORN INVESTIGATION (THE BIGGEST AND MOST ELABORATE ATTEMPT TO SHUT DOWN THE PORNOGRAPHY INDUSTRY IN AMERICAN HISTORY), AND CAME OUT THE OTHER SIDE UNSCATHED. BUT CAVORTING WITH KNOWN MOB FIGURES PUT EVEN MORE SCRUTINY ON HIM, AND EVENTUALLY HE WENT TO PRISON FOR TAX EVASION-RELATED CHARGES IN 1992, WHERE HE SERVED TWO YEARS BEHIND

BARS. IN ADDITION, MOHNEYS CLUBS WERE HIT WITH A $14 MILLION DOLLAR LIEN. GAIL PALMER WAS THE KEY WITNESS TESTIFYING AGAINST HIM IN THAT TRIAL.

AMAZINGLY, THAT AND THE GUTTING OF THE PORN INDUSTRY'S PROFITS DUE TO FREE ONLINE CONTENT DIDN'T EVEN REMOTELY SLOW HIM DOWN. BECAUSE TODAY HE'S MORE SUCCESSFUL THAN EVER WITH HIS CHAIN OF HIGH-END STRIP CLUBS. THE SCEEN DRIVE-IN, HOWEVER DIDN'T FARE AS WELL. IT WAS CLOSED IN THE MID 1980s, AND EVEN THOUGH THE BIG GREEN SCREEN TOWER HAS A FRESH COAT OF PAINT AND STILL STANDS, THE REST OF THE VENUE CURRENTLY LOOKS LIKE A GIANT UNUSED PARKING LOT -- A GHOST TOWN, RIPE WITH SENTIMENTAL VALUE. MOHNEY STILL OWNS THE PROPERTY AND CERTAINLY ISN'T HURTING FOR MONEY ENOUGH TO NEED TO SELL IT, BUT IT'S BEEN OVER 30 YEARS SINCE AN ADULT MOVIE FLICKERED ACROSS THAT FIVE STOREY HIGH SCREEN.

THE 'E' EVENTUALLY FELL OFF THE SIGN.

A SPECIAL THANKS TO PETER ALILUNAS AND STEVE MILLER FOR THEIR INVALUABLE RESEARCH PUT INTO THIS SUBJECT, WITHOUT WHICH THIS PIECE WOULD NOT HAVE EXISTED.

— BOUGIE 2018

THIS RIGHT HERE IS ONE OF MY PERSONAL FAVE "ON SET" PHOTOS IN XXX HISTORY. IT'S MISS SHARON MITCHELL WHO WAS NOT ONLY A PERFORMER, BUT ALSO A DIRECTOR. IT WAS TAKEN IN THE LATE 1980s, AND AS YOU CAN SEE, SHE'S TOPLESS ASIDE FROM A PAIR OF SUSPENDERS. SHE'S RIGHT IN THE MIDDLE OF DIRECTING A SCENE IN THE FILM.

THIS MOMENT SUBVERTS EXPECTATION. IT IS NOT WHAT MOST PEOPLE THINK OF WHEN THEY THINK OF HOW PORN IS MADE. BUT THIS IS WHAT IT IS. I'VE BEEN ON A PORN SET. NO ONE IS GAWKING AT NUDITY THERE.

EVERYONE HAS A JOB TO DO. PEOPLE USUALLY THINK ABOUT EXPLOITATION AND BIMBOS, BUT I WISH PEOPLE WOULD OCCASIONALLY THINK OF STRENGTH AND AUTONOMY WHEN THEY THINK OF WOMEN MAKING SMUT.

ON THE RECORD! WITH AARON LANGE

HOWARD THE DUCK, 1986
GOTHIC, 1987
THOMAS DOLBY

IN 1985 BRITISH NEW WAVER THOMAS DOLBY APPEARED IN A SEGMENT ON CLEVELAND'S NEWS CHANNEL 5 ABOUT THE NEW CROP OF MUSICIANS USING SYNTHESIZERS AS INSTRUMENTS. WELL, "NEW" IS A MATTER OF OPINION AS SYNTHESIZERS HAD BEEN IN USE FOR SOME TIME, AND DOLBY HIMSELF HAD ALREADY COME TO PROMINENCE DUE TO HIS SUCCESSFUL 1982 SINGLE, "SHE BLINDED ME WITH SCIENCE". BUT THIS WAS LOCAL NEWS AND NOT EXACTLY THE VANGUARD, SO LET'S BE FORGIVING.

THE NEXT YEAR SAW THE RELEASE OF THE NOTORIOUS LUCAS-PRODUCED FLOP, **HOWARD THE DUCK**. THE BIG BUDGET STINKER CONCERNS HOWARD (A CREEPILY ANTHROPOMORPHIC DUCK) SUDDENLY BEING TRANSPORTED FROM HIS HOME PLANET TO GLAMOUROUS CLEVELAND, OHIO, ALTHOUGH THE **PSYCHOTRONIC VIDEO GUIDE** (WRITTEN BY CLEVELANDER MICHAEL WELDON) NOTES THAT "IT WAS OBVIOUSLY MADE IN LA".

UPON LANDING IN THE "MISTAKE ON THE LAKE" HOWARD MEETS LEA THOMPSON, A BIG-HAIRED NEW WAVY ROCKER THAT FRONTS THE BAND CHERRY BOMB. IN REALITY, THOMAS DOLBY WROTE CHERRY BOMB'S TUNES UNDER THE GUISE OF HIS STUDIO ONLY SIDE PROJECT, DOLBY'S CUBE. THESE SONGS OCCUPY SIDE A OF THE SOUNDTRACK, WHILE JOHN BARRY'S SCORE TAKES UP SIDE B, OF WHICH LESS SAID THE BETTER. DOLBY SELECTED THE MEMBERS OF CHERRY BOMB (ONE MEMBER PLAYS KEYBOARD GUITAR) AND CHOREOGRAPHED THE GROUP'S STAGE MOVES. MOST IMPRESSIVE, LEA THOMPSON'S VOCALS WERE SOLID ENOUGH THAT THE ORIGINAL PLAN TO OVERDUB THEM WAS SCRAPPED.

THE ALBUM'S OPENING TRACK, "HUNGER CITY", IS THE STANDOUT. THOMPSON DELIVERS AND THE TUNE IS IN LINE WITH '80s POWER ROCK LIKE PAT BENATAR. IT WON'T FLOOR YOU, BUT IT'S NOT BAD. I SUSPECT THE SONG COULD HAVE SEEN SOME CHART ACTION HAD THE FILM NOT BEEN A KERPLUNK BOMB-O. STILL, IT IS WELL REMEMBERED BY SOME, WITH ONE YOUTUBE COMMENTATOR WRITING, "HUNGER CITY IS CLEVE-LAND". OR MAYBE THEY MEANT THAT AS AN INSULT? NOW I'M NOT SURE.

NEXT UP IS THE THEME SONG, "HOWARD THE DUCK", CO-WRITTEN BY DOLBY AND GEORGE CLINTON, THE THEME IS SERVICEABLE AND FITS WELL IN THE FILM'S ON-STAGE FINALE. THE GUITAR WORK WAS DONE BY FORMER JAMES GANGER AND CLEVO GUITAR HERO, JOE WALSH, AND CLINTON HIMSELF CONTRIBUTES BACK-UP VOCALS. A STRAIGHT-FACED THOMPSON MANAGES LYRICS LIKE "HICKORY DICKORY DUCK" WITH HER DIGNITY INTACT.

THE RECORD CAME WITH A "LIMITED SOUVENIR COLOR POSTER" FEATURING HOWARD IN MARTY MCFLY GEAR, GUITAR IN HAND, AND HIS BACK TURNED TO THE CAMERA, WIGGLE-WAGGLING HIS CUTE BUTT/TAIL. IF THAT IMAGE DOESN'T DISTURB YOU, FLIP THE POSTER OVER FOR A COLLAGE OF FILM SCENES, ONE OF WHICH DEPICTS HOWARD AND THOMPSON IN BED TOGETHER—AND YOU THOUGHT HER SCENES IN **BACK TO THE FUTURE** WERE ICKY.

FAR FROM CLEVELAND, WE NOW HEAD TO LORD BYRON'S SWISS VILLA, WHERE KEN RUSSELL WEAVES A FICTIONALIZED VERSION OF MARY SHELLEY AND CO.'s INFAMOUS VISIT IN THE UNDER-LOOKED **GOTHIC**. RUSSELL EXCELLED AT JUXTAPOSING HIGH WITH LOW BROW, AND DOLBY'S SCORE, WHICH MIXES CLASSICAL ELEMENTS ALONGSIDE FUNHOUSE SPOOK EFFECTS IS A PERFECT FIT. THE FILM, MOST FAMOUS FOR ITS BLINKING EYEBALL/NIPPLE GROTESQUERIE, IS NOT RUSSELL'S BEST WORK, BUT IT DEFINITELY MERITS A VIEWING. IN SPITE OF THE FILM'S SHORTCOMINGS, DOLBY'S SOUNDTRACK STANDS UP INCREDIBLY WELL ON ITS OWN, PERFECT FOR BONG-RIPPING OR HALLOWEEN PARTYING.

THE DISC ANNOUNCES ITS MOOD AND INTENTIONS WITH THE OPENING CUE, TITLED "FANTASMAGORIA", AND, LIKE A BAROQUE JOHN CARPENTER, PROCEEDS FROM THERE. OCCASIONALLY INTERRUPTED BY DIALOGUE FROM THE FILM, THE MANY CUES HAVE TITLES LIKE "BYRONIC LOVE", "SHELLEY/MANIA", "SIN AND BUGGERY", "IMPALEMENT", AND (MY FAVORITE), "SKULLPULSE". THE FINAL TRACK, "THE DEVIL IS AN ENGLISHMAN" IS A HORROR NOVELTY THROWBACK, LIKE "PURPLE PEOPLE EATER", OR "WEREWOLVES OF LONDON". CREDITED TO SCREAMIN' LORD BYRON (THAT'S A SCREAMIN' LORD SUTCH GAG, FOLKS) THE SONG IS IN FACT SUNG BY FREQUENT MIKE LEIGH COLLABORATOR TIMOTHY SPALL.

I STUMBLED ON THIS RECORD BY CHANCE AND, AS IT WAS ONLY 8 BUCKS, PURCHASED IT ON A WHIM. IF SUCH FORTUNE FAVORS YOU WHILE CRATE DIGGING, I SUGGEST YOU DO THE SAME.

STAY GROOVY!

CLEVELAND CAN SUCK AN EGG!!

THE PRINCE OF PORN (and son)

☆ ARTICLE AND INTERVIEW BY: ROBIN BOUGIE ☆

IT'S NOT TOO OFTEN THAT FANS OF THE 1980S HOUSE OF DISREPUTABLE NEW YORK SLEAZE, AVON PICTURES GET A NEW DVD RELEASE TO REVIEW AND SLOBBER OVER, BUT THAT DAY CAME IN 2015 WHEN AN AVON TRIPLE FEATURE RELEASE CAME FROM VINEGAR SYNDROME. RATHER THAN A SHORT SYNOPSIS REVIEW OF EACH OF THE THREE FILMS (SAVAGE SADISTS, DEN OF DOMINANCE, AND DAUGHTERS OF DISCIPLINE) ALL DIRECTED BY SMUT MAVEN, PHIL PRINCE, I'M GOING TO INSTEAD GO IN-DEPTH INTO ONE OF THE MOVIES AND LEAVE THE OTHER TWO FOR YOU TO DISCOVER ENTIRELY ON YOUR OWN. SOUND GOOD? OK! HERE WE GO:

Daughters of Discipline (1983 USA. Dir: Phil Prince)

OPENING WITH A PANORAMA SHOT OF NEW YORK CITY, THE HIGHLY IMMORAL DAUGHTERS OF DISCIPLINE QUICKLY SETTLES INTO ITS FIRST LOCATION, A BED IN THE CORNER OF A TEENAGE GIRL'S BEDROOM. YOU DON'T NEED TO WORRY ABOUT BLINKING AND MISSING IT -- THIS AND A COUCH IN THE LIVING ROOM OF A NEW YORK HOME ARE THE ONLY TWO LOCATIONS THAT THE MOVIE EVEN HAS.

SITTING ON THE SMALL BED ARE TWO SISTERS, RHODA (ROBIN THORN) AND GLENDA (VICTORIA SANDS). THEY'RE SUPPOSEDLY JUST HOME FROM COLLEGE, BUT THEY HONESTLY BOTH LOOK LIKE THEY'RE ABOUT 30-SOMETHING YEARS OLD. THESE BORED, HAGGARD SIBLINGS HAVE JUST DISCOVERED ONE OF THEIR DAD'S BDSM MAGAZINES (ONE THAT I RECOGNIZE! IT'S ISSUE 2 OF "FANTASY WORLD" FROM 1981 PUT OUT BY HOLLY PUBLICATIONS OF NORTH HOLLYWOOD, CALIFORNIA) AND FLIPPING THROUGH ITS FILTHY SIN-SOAKED PAGES PROMPTS RHODA TO EXCLAIM "I DON'T BELIEVE THIS STUFF! IT SURE IS MAKING ME HORNY!".

I CAN'T BE POSITIVE, BUT I'M PRETTY SURE MISS ROBIN THORN NEVER STUDIED UNDER STANISLAVSKI, ADLER, OR STRASBERG. ANYWAY, AFTER STRIPPING DOWN TO NOTHING BUT THEIR STRIPED SPORTS SOCKS, GLENDA LEANS BACK IN BED AND INVITES HER SISTER TO LAP CLAM, AND IT'S QUITE A HAIRY ONE TO WADE THROUGH. NOW, THIS ISN'T LIKE MODERN PORNO WHERE THEY LITERALLY CHANGE POSITIONS EVERY TWO MINUTES, THIS IS NEW YORK GRINDHOUSE SMUT SPECIFICALLY MADE TO PLAY IN THE SMALL AVON THEATER CHAIN IN TIMES SQUARE, AND WHEN A GIRL GOES DOWN ON A GIRL, SHE JUST SADDLES ON UP TO THE OL' HAIR-PIE AND CHOWS DOWN FOR THE NEXT 14 MINUTES. YOU KNOW, JUST LIKE ONE EATS PUSSY IN REAL LIFE! OR AT LEAST IT'S HOW I DO IT, ANYWAY.

SISTERS SHOULD BE FISTERS!

AFTER EXCHANGING THEIR POSITIONS FROM LICKER TO LICKEE, GLENDA BECOMES AROUSED ENOUGH TO NOT ONLY SLOBBER ALL OVER RHODA'S PUFFY LABIA FOLDS, BUT TO FIST HER SISTER AS WELL. IT'S A KIND GESTURE THAT COMES MUCH APPRECIATED BY RHODA, AND THE STAR OF CHARLES IN CHARGE, SCOTT BAIO, SEEMS TO APPROVE OF THE SISTER FISTING (SISTING?) AS WELL. WHAT'S THAT? YOU NEED TO READ THAT AGAIN TO MAKE SURE YOU DIDN'T IMAGINE IT? GO AHEAD! THAT'S EXACTLY WHAT I'M SAYING HERE, THOUGH: MAKING A GUEST APPEARANCE OVER THE BED IN QUESTION IS A SCOTT BAIO POSTER, AND THE CAMERA PANS UP TO SCOTT AND HIS LEERING SMILING FACE MORE THAN A COUPLE TIMES. DIRECTOR PHIL PRINCE SEEMED QUITE TICKLED AT THE IDEA OF THE HAPPY DAYS ALUM BEING AN UNOFFICIAL CAST MEMBER OF HIS DISREPUTABLE LITTLE CRANK-YANKER, AND SO AM I CONSIDERING HE'S A STAUNCH TRUMP-LOVING REPUBLICAN THESE DAYS.

"LET'S CALL JOHN." THE GIRLS DECIDE AFTER REALIZING THAT FEMININE MOUTHS AND FISTS JUST AREN'T GOING TO CUT IT. "WE NEED SOME OF THAT COCK". WHILE WAITING, THEY FLIP THROUGH THEIR ISSUE OF FANTASY WORLD AND GET SOME IDEAS FOR LATER.

JOHN IS PLAYED BY DAVID CHRISTOPHER, AND SHORTLY AFTER HE ARRIVES HE SUCKS ON SOME TITS AND INFORMS THE GIRLS THAT THEIR BOOBS TASTE "AWFULLY GOOD". THEN HE GOES AHEAD AND INSTRUCTS THEM ON HOW TO GOBBLE HIS COCK AND BALLS, ALL WHILE SCOTT BAIO SEEMS MOSTLY BEMUSED BY HIS INSTRUCTIONS. WHEN I INTERVIEWED DAVID IN 2013 AND ASKED HIM ABOUT HIS STINT IN AVON'S OUTPUT, HE HAD ONLY FOND MEMORIES.

"(AVON'S FILMS) WERE LIKE AN ENSEMBLE", HE NOTED. "THEY WERE WILD, KINKY, SORT OF B-MOVIES WITH ALL KINDS OF FETISH ACTION, VIOLENCE AND HOT SEX. THEY HAD A THEATRE CALLED THE AVON WHICH SHOWED THE MOVIES, AND HAD THE STARS PERFORM THEIR SCENES LIVE ON STAGE. ALWAYS STANDING ROOM ONLY... NO PORN THEATRES IN THOSE DAYS WERE STANDING ROOM ONLY, EXCEPT FOR SCREENINGS OF THE CLASSICS LIKE DEEP THROAT, AND BEHIND THE GREEN DOOR. THE IDEA WAS TO MAKE OUTLANDISH, WILD SEX MOVIES."

AFTER FUCKING THE TWO SISTERS FOR AWHILE, JOHN GETS SLEEPY AND PASSES OUT. THAT MEANS IT'S TIME FOR US TO LEAVE THAT SMALL SINGLE BED IN THE CORNER OF THAT ROOM AND HEAD OFF TO THE COUCH IN THE LIVING ROOM -- THE EXCITING AFOREMENTIONED SECOND LOCATION! BY THIS TIME 30 MINUTES HAVE PASSED (WITH LITTLE TO NO SADOMASOCHISM OR DEGRADATION DISPLAYED WHATSOEVER -- VERY UNUSUAL FOR AN AVON RELEASE), SO YOU'RE MORE THAN READY FOR THE CHANGE OF SCENERY, ALTHOUGH LEAVING SCOTT BAIO BEHIND IS SORT OF A BUMMER. NOT TO WORRY THOUGH, BECAUSE HANGING OVER THE COUCH IS YET ANOTHER HIGHLY OBTRUSIVE AND SCENE-STEALING POSTER!

WHY, LOOKEE THERE, IT'S NASTASSJA KINSKI — KLAUS KINSKI'S DAUGHTER, AND SHE'S NAKED AND ALL WRAPPED UP AND INTERTWINED WITH A GIANT BOA CONSTRICTOR. THIS WAS A POPULAR BEST-SELLING POSTER OF THE ERA ENTITLED "NASTASSJA AND THE SERPENT". IT OFTEN HUNG IN TEENAGE BOYS' ROOMS AND IT WAS ORIGINALLY PHOTOGRAPHED BY RICHARD AVEDON (ONE OF THE FOREMOST FASHION AND PORTRAIT PHOTOGRAPHERS IN THE WORLD) IN 1981 FOR AN ISSUE OF VOGUE MAGAZINE. I DON'T MIND TELLING YOU THAT A LIMITED EDITION PRINT OF THE PHOTO SOLD FOR OVER $74,000 AT AN AUCTION AT CHRISTIE'S IN 2009. NASTASSJA'S BLANK STARE AS THE CONSTRICTOR LICKS HER EAR IS BETTER SUITED FOR WHAT IS ABOUT TO TRANSPIRE THAN BAIO'S STUPID GRINNING PUSS WAS, SO PERHAPS IT IS FOR THE BEST.

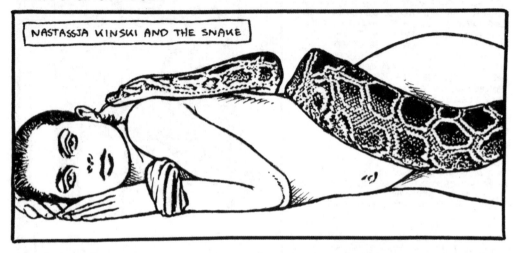

NASTASSJA KINSKI AND THE SNAKE

YES, PHIL PRINCE SAVED THE BEST FOR LAST AS THE KINK FACTOR GETS CRANKED UP A FEW MORE NOTCHES WHEN JOHN IS AWOKEN FROM HIS SLUMBER AND TIED TO A GIANT X-FRAME "ST ANDREW'S CROSS" BY THE TWO GIRLS, WHO HAVE NOW DECKED THEMSELVES OUT IN LEATHER FETISH GEAR AND STOCKINGS. "DID YOU THINK YOU WERE THE ONLY ONE THAT WAS GOING TO HAVE ANY FUN?" RHODA SNARLS. AFTER WHIPPING JOHN'S DICK, PUTTING CLIPS ON HIS NIPPLES, AND GENERALLY MAKING HIM BEG FOR ABUSE, SUDDENLY MOM (NICOLE BERNARD) AND DAD (DAVE RUBY) BARGE IN! FURIOUS, DAD HOLLERS: "WHAT THE FUCK IS GOING ON? YOU KIDS COME HOME FROM COLLEGE AND YOU'RE USING ALL MY STUFF?"

"IF IT'S SEX GAMES YOU WANT, THEN YOU'RE GONNA PLAY A LITTLE SEX GAME WITH ME!" DAD BARKS AS HE SHOVES HIS COCK IN RHODA'S MOUTH. MOM GETS IN THE ACT TOO, AND BEFORE YOU KNOW IT A BONDAGE AND DEGRADATION THEMED INCESTUOUS GANG BANG HAS BUSTED OUT ALL OVER THAT POOR COUCH. ANY DISTRESSING ELEMENTS ARE TOTALLY DEFUSED AND SOFTENED BY DAVE RUBY'S FUNNY PERFORMANCE (HE'S CACKLING MADLY ONE SECOND — BORED LOOKING THE NEXT) AS HE NONCHALANTLY PAUSES FROM HIS HUMPING OF RHONDA SO HE CAN SLAP THE CHAINED UP GLENDA ACROSS THE FACE.

NOW NORMALLY I DON'T REALLY LIKE TO GIVE AWAY THE FINAL SCENE IN ANY MOVIE REVIEW I DO, BECAUSE I FIND THAT IT SPOILS THE PLOT FOR FIRST-TIME VIEWERS AND DOESN'T LEAVE ENOUGH FOR PEOPLE TO DISCOVER ON THEIR OWN. IT'S JUST BAD FORM. BUT LET'S FUCKING FACE IT, THERE IS HONESTLY SO LITTLE PLOT TO SPEAK OF HERE AND THE FINAL FEW MOMENTS OF DAUGHTERS OF DISCIPLINE REALLY IS THE *MOST* NOTEWORTHY PART OF THE ENTIRE MOVIE, SO IT FEELS TOTALLY FUCKING WRONG TO LEAVE IT OUT OF THIS REVIEW.

IN THE SCENE WHICH TAKES PLACE AFTER DAVID CHRISTOPHER AND DAVE RUBY FINALLY UNLOAD THEIR BALLS ALL OVER THE PLACE, THINGS ARE WRAPPING UP AND RUBY LOOKS AT CHRISTOPHER AND BLUNTLY EXCLAIMS "DERELICT! GET OUT". NOW I'M PRETTY EASY TO PLEASE, SO THIS HILARIOUS BIT OF LINE-READING WOULD BE ENOUGH TO MAKE THE SCENE A FAVOURITE, BUT THEN DAVE STARES DIRECTLY INTO THE CAMERA AND LAUGHS LIKE A LITTLE KID PLAYING A BAD GUY IN A 3RD GRADE SCHOOL PLAY. THIS LAUGH GOES ON FOR AN UNCOMFORTABLE PERIOD OF TIME UNTIL WE ACTUALLY HEAR DIRECTOR PRINCE CALLING OUT FROM OFFSCREEN, "OKAY, LET'S TRY THAT AGAIN" BEFORE THE SCREEN FADES TO BLACK. IT'S LITERALLY ONE OF THE GREATEST MOMENTS IN THE ENTIRE AVON FILM CATALOG, AND A PERFECT PLACE FOR BOTH THIS REVIEW AND THIS SCABBY LITTLE STAIN OF A MOVIE TO STOP.

KEITH PRINCE

WHAT DOESN'T STOP IS THE SEARCH FOR THE MAN WHO MADE THIS MOVIE, AND SO MANY OF THE OTHER AVON FEATURES -- WHICH BASICALLY ACCOUNT FOR MOST OF MY FAVE XXX MADE IN NEW YORK IN THE 1980S. FOR MANY YEARS, IT WASN'T EVEN KNOWN IF PHIL PRINCE WAS STILL ALIVE. THEN, AROUND 2009, WHILE I WAS FREQUENTING A NOW-DEFUNCT MOVIE NERD MESSAGE BOARD CALLED AVMANIACS, SOMEONE CLAIMING TO BE PHIL'S SON WAS MENTIONED BY ONE OF THE OTHER POSTERS. HE WAS AN UP AND COMING DJ IN NEW YORK, AND WHILE I WAS SKEPTICAL, IT WAS CERTAINLY THE FIRST CONCRETE LEAD IN THE SEARCH FOR THE PRINCE OF PORN, SO I MOST CERTAINLY WAS GOING TO FOLLOW UP ON IT.

NOT LONG AFTER I WAS EMAILING BACK AND FORTH WITH KEITH PRINCE, AND THEN WE WERE FOLLOWING EACH OTHERS LIVES ON FACEBOOK. IT TURNED OUT HIS LEGENDARY DAD WAS STILL ALIVE AND LIVING IN THE NEW YORK AREA, AND HE WAS CONVINCING ENOUGH THAT I CERTAINLY BELIEVED THAT HE WAS WHO HE CLAIMED TO BE. (HE LOOKS LIKE HIS DAD, FOR ONE THING.) HE WAS FRIENDLY AND FORTHCOMING, BUT UNFORTUNATELY AFTER MANY TRIES TO CONVINCE HIS FATHER TO TALK TO ME (EVEN A COAXING OF $500 FOR AN INTERVIEW PAID BY THE LADS OVER AT VINEGAR SYNDROME), HIS ADMITTEDLY GRUMPY OLD MAN WAS ENTIRELY UNINTERESTED — MUCH TO MY FRUSTRATION AND KEITH'S.

"SORRY", KEITH WROTE TO ME. "I'M ALL FOR IT, HONESTLY, BUT IT'S MY DAD WHO NEEDS CONVINCING."

THIS WENT ON FOR YEARS, WITH KEITH ALWAYS PATIENTLY HEARING OUT MY GEEKY PLEADING, DOING HIS BEST TO GET HIS RECLUSIVE DAD TO GIVE HIS FIRST INTERVIEW IN MANY DECADES, AND THEN 8 TO 12 MONTHS WOULD PASS BEFORE WE'D TRY IT ALL OVER AGAIN -- ALWAYS WITH THE SAME PREDICTABLE DECLINE FROM POPS. EVENTUALLY I JUST GAVE UP, AND ASKED KEITH IF HE'D LIKE TO DO AN INTERVIEW INSTEAD SO I COULD AT LEAST GET SOMETHING ON PAPER. HE WAS GAME, AND HERE IS WHAT WAS SAID:

CS: SO LET'S SETTLE SOMETHING ONCE AND FOR ALL: DID YOUR DAD SETTLE A DEBT BY KILLING A GUY AFTER HE DID TIME FOR THE HOLD-UP OF THE FROZEN YOGHURT PLACE?

KP: FROM WHAT I KNOW, NO. FOR THE PEOPLE WHO THINK HE DID, OR SAY THEY KNOW HE DID... HOW DO THEY KNOW, BUT THE POLICE DON'T? STRANGE. MY DAD IS NOT IN JAIL OR SERVING TIME FOR MURDER SO I AM GOING TO SAY HE DIDN'T.

CS: YEAH, AS THE STORY GOES HE DID 20 YEARS IN PRISON FOR THIS KILLING. I THINK YOU WOULD HAVE NOTICED THAT. IF YOU'RE WONDERING WHERE THIS STORY ORIGINATES, IT ALL COMES FROM THE OLD SLEAZOID EXPRESS ZINE THAT BILL LANDIS DID. HE WAS PRETTY MUCH THE ONLY SOURCE OF NON-MAINSTREAM NEWS ABOUT VINTAGE NEW YORK PORN IN THE LATE '80S, SO EVERYONE TOOK WHAT HE WROTE ABOUT THAT TIME AS FACT. HE WAS ACTUALLY IN THE VERY FIRST PORNO I EVER SAW, ALONG WITH HIS ROOMMATE GEORGE PAYNE.

KP: DO YOU KNOW IF GEORGE PAYNE IS DEAD OR ALIVE?

CS: HAHA! FUNNY YOU SHOULD ASK. HE IS INDEED. CHECK OUT THIS PICTURE. THAT IS A PHOTO OF GEORGE I FOUND ON FUCKING GOOGLE EARTH! HAHA! HE'S STANDING IN FRONT OF HIS HOUSE. THAT'S HIM IN THE STRIPED SHIRT.

KP: HAHAHA! WHAT THE HELL ARE THE ODDS?!

PHIL PRINCE

CS: I KNOW! CHECK THIS OUT: IT'S A VIDEO CALLED "NO PAYNE, NO GAIN!" THAT GEORGE PUT UP ON YOUTUBE A FEW YEARS AGO. HE'S WORKIN' OUT TO CAMEO'S "WORD UP"! A TOTALLY RIPPED SENIOR CITIZEN, MAN! HE LOOKS DAMN GOOD FOR HIS AGE! IS PHIL HOLDING UP AS WELL?

KP: THE YEARS HAVE BEEN UNKIND TO MY FAMILY, IN TERMS OF HEALTH.

CS: SUCKS, MAN. BEEN HEARING THAT A LOT LATELY

KP: AS I AM SURE YOU ARE AWARE FROM FACEBOOK, MY MOM DIED IN THE PAST LAST YEAR. THAT HIT MY DAD

HARD, AND HE HAS HIS OWN MEDICAL SHIT GOING ON.

CS: YEAH, MY CONDOLENCES. THAT'S REALLY HARD TO TAKE, MAN.

KP: PAT RODGERS, MY FATHERS CLOSE FRIEND, DIED IN THE MID 1990S.

CS: AH YEAH, HE WORKED FOR AVON AS WELL.

AVON IS THE GNARLIEST!

KP: HE HAD TB WHEN THEY GOT ARRESTED FOR THE HOLD-UP, WHICH TURNED TO THROAT CANCER, WHICH IS WHY HE GOT LET OUT EARLIER THEN MY DAD, WHO SERVED 6 YEARS, NOT 20 YRS IN JAIL. I WOULD LOVE TO MEET THE JACKASS WHO MADE ALL THOSE STORIES UP.

CS: YOU CAN'T, HE DIED TOO. BILL LANDIS WAS A HEROIN JUNKIE BACK WHEN HE WAS DOING HIS ZINE AND WROTE THAT STUFF, AND YOU KNOW WHAT THEY SAY ABOUT JUNKIES.

KP: AND YET FOR SOME REASON THESE SO CALLED FANS OF MY FATHER'S WORK TAKE HIS WORD FOR GOSPEL.

CS: HEY, I DID TOO...NONE OF US KNEW ANY BETTER. THIS WAS BEFORE THE INTERNET, AND WE WERE JUST DESPERATE FOR ANY SCRAP OF INFO. DOESN'T HELP THAT ALPHABLUEARCHIVES STILL KEEPS THE MISINFO UP ON THEIR WEBSITE, THOUGH.

KP: EH, I DON'T BLAME YOU. YOU WERE HIS FLOCK AND SOME ASS WHO NEEDED A DIME FOR HIS NEXT BAG OF DOPE LEAD YOU ASTRAY.

CS: LANDIS WAS THERE, YOU KNOW? LIKE I SAID HE WAS IN SOME OLD PORNOS UNDER THE NAME "BOBBY SPECTOR", AND HE WAS TIGHT WITH GEORGE PAYNE, SO PEOPLE BELIEVED WHAT HE HAD TO WRITE ABOUT THESE MOVIES. EVERYONE GRABBED ONTO EVERY LITTLE SHRED OF INFO THAT HE LAID OUT FOR YEARS. I MEAN, WHO KNOWS? MAYBE LANDIS DID TELL THE TRUTH AS HE KNEW IT AND GEORGE PAYNE WAS THE ONE WHO TOLD HIM ALL THAT MADE UP SHIT ABOUT YOUR DAD. HE WAS A HEROIN JUNKIE TOO. I KINDA DOUBT IT THOUGH, CONSIDERING ALL OF THE OTHER FACTUAL DISCREPANCIES THAT HAVE TURNED UP IN SLEAZOID.

KP: YOU KNOW, I SAW DOCTOR BIZARRO WHEN I WAS 5 OR 6. MY MOM, GOD BLESS HER... WELL, WHEN MY DAD GOT PINCHED WE HAD TO GET RID OF SOME TAPES SHE HAD IN THE GARAGE IN STATEN, SO SHE DUBBED OVER THEM WITH CHILDREN'S MOVIES! HAHA! WELL, HALF WAY THROUGH THE RACCOONS — IF YOU RECALL THAT CARTOON — IT SUDDENLY GOES INTO DR. BIZARRO AND THERE IS MY DAD ON THE TV. IT WAS HORRIFYING FOR A 6-YEAR-OLD KID. I FREAKED.

CS: NO DOUBT! I SAW IT AS A 26-YEAR-OLD FOR THE FIRST TIME, AND I FREAKED TOO! IT'S A CRAZY MOVIE! HAHA!

KP: I GOT IN TROUBLE FOR WATCHING IT TOO. LIKE, WHAT THE FUCK! I DIDN'T DUB OVER PORN WITH CARTOONS! I HAD NO IDEA WHAT I WAS WATCHING. MY DAD LOVES THAT STORY, SICK FUCK.

CS: THE SICKEST OF FUCKS!

KP: HAHA! HE IS SO FUCKING COMPETITIVE. HE DOESN'T MAKE SHIT ANYMORE BUT HE KNOWS DAMN WELL HIS WAS THE RAUNCHIEST. COMPETITIVE PRICK UNTIL HE DIES. AND EVEN THEN HE WILL PROBABLY ASK US TO MAKE SURE HE HAS HIS MIDDLE FINGERS AND ARM EXTENDED TO ANY MORBID FUCK THAT WANTS TO PAY THEIR RESPECTS. I CALL HIM "SIR" SOMETIMES JUST TO PISS HIM OFF. IT'S "DAD", "POP" OR "PHILLY". NOTHING ELSE IS ALLOWED. I GUESS IT'S LIFE'S WAY OF PAYING IT FORWARD. YOU PAY PEOPLE TO PISS ON EACH OTHER, AND IN RETURN YOU GET KIDS THAT PISS YOU OFF. IT'S A FUNNY, FICKLE THING THIS THING CALLED LIFE IS.

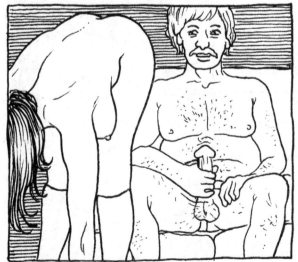

CS: AND SO IT GOES. HEY, I WROTE A REVIEW OF DAUGHTERS OF DISCIPLINE. CAN YOU SHOW IT TO HIM?

KP: SURE. (A DAY LATER) HIS INTERNET IS FUCKED. I READ IT TO HIM. HE SAID: "LET HIM KNOW THAT HE WRITES WELL, AND THANK HIM FOR TAKING SUCH A LIKING IN MY WORK. DOES HE KNOW THAT DAUGHTERS OF DISCIPLINE WAS ACTUALLY SHOT IN THE SAME LOCATION AS THE DEVIL IN MISS JONES?"

CS: WOW, THANKS FOR SHOWING IT TO HIM! NO, I DIDN'T KNOW THAT! THAT'S SO COOL THAT HE READ IT. OR HEARD IT, I GUESS.

☆ Postscript ☆

SO THAT RIGHT THERE IS WHERE THINGS STOOD AS OF 2016. PHIL PRINCE WAS STILL ALIVE, HIS SON KEITH WAS NOW MARRIED AND KEITH'S

106

LOVELY WIFE HAD A BABY GIRL. BUT THAT OH-SO EVER ELUSIVE INTERVIEW CONTINUED TO EVADE ME AND EVERY OTHER PORN HISTORIAN THAT WANTED TO KNOW THE TRUE, NO-BULLSHIT, STORY OF AVON FILMS.

THAT IS, UNTIL 2018, WHEN ASHLEY WEST AND APRIL HALL FINALLY REELED THAT FISH IN - THANK GOD - JUST MONTHS BEFORE PHIL PASSED AWAY AT THE AGE OF 65. TO NEVER HAVE HEARD PHIL'S STORY FROM HIS OWN FOUL MOUTH BEFORE HE SHUFFLED OFF THIS MORTAL COIL -- TAKING ALL THAT HISTORICAL INFORMATION TO DIE WITH HIM -- WOULD HAVE REALLY BROKEN MY HEART. ASHLEY AND APRIL WOULD GO ON TO PUBLISH THAT IN-PERSON INTERVIEW IN BOTH TEXT AND PODCAST FORM ON THEIR WEBSITE WWW.THERIALTOREPORT.COM AND IT FINALLY LAID TO REST MANY QUESTIONS ABOUT BOTH AVON AND PHIL PRINCE. IT WAS SOME GODDAMN BEAUTIFUL WORK, AND I HIGHLY RECOMMEND THAT Y'ALL CHECK IT OUT. I DO HOPE IT GETS TRANSLATED INTO BOOK FORM AT SOME POINT.

WE FOUND OUT SO MUCH THAT I CAN'T EVEN GO INTO IT ALL RIGHT HERE. WE FOUND OUT ABOUT HIS LOSING HIS PARENTS AT AGE 12, OF GROWING UP IN THE LATE '60S IN THE TOUGH NEW YORK NEIGHBOURHOOD OF HELL'S KITCHEN, OF GETTING DEEPLY EMBROILED WITH THE INFAMOUS IRISH MOB KNOWN AS THE WESTIES, HUSTLING AND RUNNING SCAMS, AND THEN PARTNERING UP WITH A MADE MAN IN THE GAMBINO CRIME FAMILY.

WE FOUND OUT THAT HE FIRST STARTED IN THE WORLD OF 'ADULT' AS THE MUSCLE IN TIMES SQUARE BURLESQUE STRIP CLUBS LIKE THE PSYCHEDELIC BURLESQUE (670 8TH AVE), THE LOCATION OF THE VERY FIRST LIVE SEX SHOW IN MANHATTAN. IT WAS HIS JOB TO MAKE SURE NO ONE WAS BOTHERING THE GIRLS OR THE EMPLOYEES, AND BY THE TIME HE WAS 20 IN 1973, HE'D GRADUATED TO DATING ONE OF THE STRIPPERS AND DOING A REGULAR LIVE SEX SHOW WITH HER AT VARIOUS VENUES ON THE DEUCE. A WOMAN WHO HE WOULD GET PREGNANT, AND WHO WOULD BE HORRIFICALLY KNIFED TO DEATH BEFORE SHE COULD GIVE BIRTH. PHIL FOUND HER AND HER FRIEND DEAD IN HIS APARTMENT, AND HE BECAME A SUSPECT.

"I KNEW WHO DID IT," PHIL SAID TO THE RIALTOREPORT.COM. "HE WAS PART OF THE COCAINE COWBOYS IN NEW YORK THAT MARIE AND I HAD BEEN DEALING WITH. MARIE WAS A HARD CHARACTER, AND THIS GUY RODRIGUEZ, WHO WAS IN THE COLOMBIAN MOB, EVIDENTLY DIDN'T APPRECIATE DEALING WITH A STRONG WOMAN. IT WAS SOME SORT OF MACHISMO SHIT. HE DECIDED TO FUCK WITH HER, SO HE SENT A GUY TO MY APARTMENT WHEN I WAS OUT, AND THIS GUY WHACKED BOTH THE GIRLS. TERESA WAS INNOCENT. SHE JUST HAPPENED TO BE THERE. I DON'T KNOW HOW ANYBODY COULD DO THAT TO TWO WOMEN."

PHIL WOULD TALK ABOUT THE PEOPLE HE MADE HIS FILMS WITH, HOW MUCH THEY COST, WHERE THEY WERE SHOT, AND WHO REALLY RAN THINGS AT AVON. HE TALKED ABOUT HOW HIS FILMS WERE BLAMED FOR INSPIRING SERIAL KILLER STEVEN PENNELL, AND THE TIME HE ROBBED A HAAGEN DAZ ICE CREAM PLACE WITH PAT RODGERS AND GOT SENTENCED TO 15 YEARS IN PRISON, AND THEN BECAME A TRUCK DRIVER AFTER HE GOT OUT IN 1988.

AT ONE POINT THEY BEGAN TO TALK ABOUT CURRENT US PRESIDENT DONALD TRUMP, AND THE SMILE WAS WIPED RIGHT OFF PHIL'S FACE. "DON'T COMPARE ME TO HIM", PHIL SAID STERNLY. "LET ME TELL YOU SOMETHING: COMPARED TO THAT GUY, I'M A SAINT. I'M TELLING YOU. I'VE DONE NOTHING COMPARED TO THAT FUCKING CLOWN. TAKE TRUMP UNIVERSITY: IF I DID WHAT HE DID, THEY WOULD'VE HAD ME ON A FUCKING RICO VIOLATION. HE DEFRAUDED ALL THOSE PEOPLE, MAN. HE HAD A SCHEME TO CHEAT PEOPLE. HE CONSPIRED IN AN ILLEGAL, FRAUDULENT WAY, YOU KNOW? AND GIULIANI!? 'THE TRUTH ISN'T THE TRUTH?' WE SHOULD'VE WHACKED HIM WHEN WE HAD THE CHANCE."

RIP PHIL PRINCE.

☆ - BOUGIE 2019

HAHA! YESSS!

RIALTOREPORT, YOU'VE DONE IT AGAIN!

HERBIE

LADIES AND GENTLEMEN, BOYS AND GIRLS:
DYIN' TIME'S HERE!
☆ ☆ ☆ BY: RINGO STALIN ☆ ☆ ☆

COULD THERE BE ANYTHING BETTER THAN SQUEEZING YOURSELF INTO YOUR FINEST SILVER JUMPSUIT OR WRAPPING UP IN YOUR FILTHIEST RAGS AND HEADING OVER TO THE CENTRE OF TOWN TO JOIN YOUR FELLOW CITIZENS IN CHEERING THE INEVITABLE SLAUGHTER OF A COCKY GLADIATOR OR BEDRAGGLED POLITICAL PRISONER? IT WOULD SURE TAKE YOUR MIND OFF OF HOW LITTLE PERSONAL FREEDOM YOU ALL HAVE UNDER THE YOKE OF THE OMNIPRESENT DICTATORSHIP OR CORPORATE CONCERN THAT RUNS THE STATE/COUNTRY/CONTINENT/WORLD (DELETE WHERE APPLICABLE).

LUCKILY, IN THE FUTURE, WE HAVE A HUGE RANGE OF SPECTATOR SPORTS TO CHOOSE FROM THAT WILL CATER TO YOUR BLOODLUST. TO HELP YOU DIFFERENTIATE YOUR STALKERS AND SCHOOLKIDS FROM YOUR JOX AND JUGGERS, HERE'S YOUR GUIDE TO JUST A HANDFUL OF THE BLOODSPORTS THAT OUR FUTURE HAS TO OFFER.

TO NARROW THE VAST FIELD SOMEWHAT, THE GAMES WERE CHOSEN BY USING THE FOLLOWING CRITERIA:

THERE MUST BE SOME KIND OF AUDIENCE.
THE COMPETITORS MUST INCLUDE AT LEAST ONE SENTIENT BEING
THERE MUST BE THE THREAT OF PHYSICAL INJURY OR DEATH.
THE GAME MUST TAKE PLACE WITHIN SOME KIND OF ARENA OR SET BOUNDARY.

OK, NOW THAT YOU KNOW THE RULES, LET'S PLAY. <u>GAME</u> <u>ON</u>!!

ROLLERBALL (DIR. NORMAN JEWISON, 1975)
GAME: ROLLERBALL
COMPETITORS: TWO TEAMS OF TEN, EACH TEAM COMPRISED OF SEVEN SKATERS AND THREE BIKERS
EQUIPMENT REQUIRED: MOTORBIKES, STUDDED GLOVES, METAL BALL.
VENUE: A BANKED CIRCULAR TRACK, SEPARATED INTO ZONES, SURROUNDED BY SPECTATOR SEATING, WITH

AN INNER BARRIER PROVIDING AN AREA FOR BENCHED PLAYERS, TRAINERS, COACHES, AND MOST IMPORTANTLY, FIRST AID.
PRIZE: SOCIETAL COHESION, CLASS PRIVILEGE AND, IN EXTREMELY RARE CASES, INDIVIDUALITY.

UNDER THE WATCHFUL EYE OF THE TOTALITARIAN GLOBAL CORPORATIONS, ROLLERBALL SERVES A DEFINITE SOCIAL PURPOSE --TO LIMIT INDIVIDUAL ENDEAVOUR. HOW THE CORPORATIONS THOUGHT THIS WOULD WORK IS BAFFLING, CONSIDERING THAT THERE HAVE BEEN STAND-OUT SUPERSTARS IN EVERY SPORT EVER.

A COMBINATION OF AMERICAN FOOTBALL, SPEEDWAY, ROLLER DERBY AND SKEE BALL, THE PLAYERS SCORE POINTS BY TRAVELLING AROUND A CIRCULAR TRACK ON ROLLERSKATES OR MOTORBIKES AND THROWING A METAL BALL INTO ONE OF THE TWO MAGNETIC GOALS SET INTO EITHER SIDE OF THE TRACK. THE BALL, ABOUT THE SIZE OF A REGULATION SOFTBALL, IS FIRED FROM A PNEUMATIC CANNON INTO THE GAME AREA, MIMICKING A CASINO'S ROULETTE BALL. PLAYERS ARE REQUIRED TO PICK UP THE BALL BEFORE IT REACHES THE GUTTER OF THE INNER BARRIER, OR IT BECOMES 'DEAD' AND THE PROCESS BEGINS AGAIN.

ON POSSESSION OF THE BALL, THE TEAM NEEDS TO COMPLETE ONE FULL REVOLUTION OF THE TRACK WITH THE BALL BEFORE THEY ARE ABLE TO MAKE AN ATTEMPT ON GOAL. THE OPPOSING TEAM CAN USE ANY TACTIC AVAILABLE TO THEM TO GAIN POSSESSION OF THE BALL, INCLUDING, BUT NOT LIMITED TO, KICKING, PUNCHING, SHIRT PULLING AND RUNNING DOWN PLAYERS WITH A MOTORBIKE.

MORE THAN JUST A BASIC SLUGFEST, THERE IS A FRAMEWORK OF RULES THAT KEEP IT FROM BECOMING AN ALL OUT BRAWL, SUCH AS PENALTIES, SUBSTITUTIONS AND TIME LIMITATIONS. BUT SHOULD THE CORPORATIONS FEEL THAT MAYBE THERE'S NOT QUITE ENOUGH BLOOD ON THE TRACKS, THESE RULES CAN BE AMENDED OR DISCARDED ACCORDINGLY.

ROLLERBALL CAN ALSO BE A GAME FOR STATS FREAKS-- THE GREATEST NUMBER OF POINTS SCORED IN A SINGLE GAME: 18, THE HIGHEST SPEED OF THE BALL WHEN FIELDED BY A PLAYER: 120MPH (ENOUGH TO TAKE YOUR ARM OFF), MOST PLAYERS PUT OUT OF ACTION IN A SINGLE GAME: 18, MOST DEATHS: NINE, ROME V PITTSBURGH.

FUTURESPORT (DIR. ERNEST DICKERSON, 1998)

GAME: FUTURESPORT
COMPETITORS: TWO TEAMS OF FIVE, EACH COMPRISED OF TWO FLYERS, ONE FLYING BLOCKER, ONE BLADE BLOCKER, ONE STOPPER.
EQUIPMENT REQUIRED: METAL BALL, THREE HOVERBOARDS PER TEAM, ONE PAIR OF ROLLERBLADES, ONE STOPPER'S NET, BLOCKER'S METAL STAFFS, PADS AND HELMETS.
VENUE: OVAL SKATE BOWL WITH A RAISED PLATFORM IN CENTRE.
PRIZE: INCREASED PI (POPULARITY INDEX), CHAMPIONSHIP TROPHY.

CREATED BY OBIKE FIXX IN 2015, AND THEREBY MAKING ITS NAME COMPLETELY REDUNDANT, 'FUTURESPORT' (OR, MORE ACCURATELY, 'SPORT') HAS SUPPLANTED BASKETBALL AS THE GLOBAL GAME OF CHOICE, FOLLOWING A DISASTROUS POINT SHAVING SCANDAL. ORIGINALLY A COMBINATION OF HALF-PIPE SKATEBOARDING AND BASKETBALL PLAYED BY THE IMPOVERISHED YOUTH OF THE DOWN ZONE, AND THEREBY CAUSING A REDUCTION IN GANG WARFARE, THE SPORT RECEIVED SOME ATTENTION FROM THE PRESS AND GREW INTO A SLICK PRODUCTION WITH HOVERBOARDS AND CUSTOM-DESIGNED ARENAS.

THE GAME IS PLAYED OVER FOUR QUARTERS (LASTING 15 MINUTES EACH) BY TWO TEAMS, COMPRISED OF FIVE PLAYERS EACH. IT TAKES PLACE IN AN ELONGATED BOWL, WITH A SMALL HOLE SET IN A METAL PLATE SERVING AS A GOAL AT EACH END. EACH TEAM HAS TWO FLYERS, A FLYING BLOCKER, A BLADE BLOCKER AND A STOPPER. THE FLYERS ACT AS OFFENCE, USING HOVERBOARDS COUPLED WITH GYMNASTICS TO SCORE, BLOCKERS ARE ARMED WITH METAL STAFFS WITH THE FLYING BLOCKER ATOP A HOVERBOARD, AND THE BLADE BLOCKER ON ROLLERBLADES. THE STOPPER STANDS IN A SMALL ALCOVE SET AT THE END OF THE BOWL, JUST UNDER THE GOAL, WITH A SMALL NET ON A STICK; THE STOPPER HAS A THANKLESS AND MOSTLY INEFFECTUAL ROLE AND IT SEEMS LIKE THE POSITION WAS CREATED AFTER ONE PLAYER'S MOTHER INSISTED THEIR LITTLE BROTHER BE ALLOWED TO PLAY.

AT THE OUTSET OF THE GAME, A METAL BALL IS SHOT INTO THE AIR FROM A HYDRAULIC PUMP SET INTO A RAISED PLATFORM IN THE CENTRE OF THE BOWL. ONCE A PLAYER GAINS POSSESSION OF THE BALL, THEY HAVE FIVE SECONDS TO PASS IT ON TO ANOTHER PLAYER, OTHERWISE THE BALL WILL BECOME ELECTRIFIED. IF A PLAYER POSSESSES THE BALL DURING THIS TIME, THEY ARE SAID TO BE 'RIDING THE LIGHTNING' OR 'GRIPPING THE ZAP'. THE PLAYER MUST PUT THE BALL IN THE GOAL TO SCORE AND WILL GET ONE POINT FOR A THROW AND THREE FOR A 'SLAM' (SIMILAR TO A SLAM DUNK IN BASKETBALL).

PLAYING FUTURESPORT COULD RESULT IN A FEW SCRAPES AND BRUISES BUT IF ONE OF YOUR TEAMMATES MAKES A DEAL WITH A STATE-SPONSORED TERRORIST CELL OVER THE FATE OF AN ISLAND NATION, STAKES CAN BE CONSIDERABLY HIGHER.

THE RUNNING MAN (DIR. PAUL MICHAEL GLASER, 1987)

GAME: THE RUNNING MAN
COMPETITORS: RUNNERS (CONVICTED CRIMINALS AND ENEMIES OF THE STATE) AND STALKERS.
EQUIPMENT REQUIRED: RUNNERS – PERSONALISED ADIDAS JUMPSUIT, STALKERS – CHARACTER-RELEVANT PARAPHERNALIA.

VENUE: 400 SQUARE MILES IN EARTHQUAKE-DEVASTATED CALIFORNIA.
PRIZE: TRIAL BY JURY, SUSPENDED SENTENCE, FULL PARDON.

DO YOU HAVE TALENT, CHARISMA AND (FIGURATIVE, NOT LITERAL) BALLS? DO YOU HAVE A COURT-
APPOINTED TALENT AGENT? DO YOU HAVE A GRUDGE AGAINST THE GOVERNMENT? IF SO, THEN YOU'VE GOT
WHAT IT TAKES TO BE A STAR IN THE RUNNING MAN, THE MOST POPULAR TELEVISION PROGRAM IN
HISTORY!

HOSTED BY ITS CREATOR, DAMON KILLIAN, AND PRESENTED BY THE STATE-CONTROLLED ICS NETWORK,
ALONG WITH OTHER GREAT PROGRAMMES INCLUDING 'THE HATE BOAT', 'CONFESS', AND 'CLIMBING FOR
DOLLARS', THE RUNNING MAN IS A HIGH-GLOSS, SEXUALLY-CHARGED PROPAGANDA TELEVISION PHENOMENON,
DESIGNED TO KEEP THE PROLES DISTRACTED. OUTSIDE THE STUDIO, GIANT SCREENS HAVE BEEN ERECTED
FOR THE MASSES TO HUDDLE AROUND, WHILE INSIDE THE STUDIO, THE AUDIENCE PARTICIPATE FOR
PRIZES OF CONSUMER GOODS AND HOME VERSIONS OF THE GAME. THIS ALL SERVES TO KEEP THEM IN
FRONT OF THE TV AND OUT OF THE PICKET LINES.

THE GAME TAKES PLACE ON 400 SQUARE BLOCKS OF CALIFORNIA THAT WERE DEVASTATED IN THE
MASSIVE EARTHQUAKE IN 1997, WHICH IS THEN SPLIT INTO FOUR QUADRANTS. THE UNARMED COMPETITORS,
MADE UP OF DANGEROUS CRIMINALS AND POLITICAL PRISONERS, MUST TRAVEL THROUGH ALL FOUR QUADS
IN THREE HOURS, WITHOUT BEING KILLED BY THE STALKERS, WHO ARE SPECIALIST GLADIATORS EMPLOYED
BY ICS. EACH OF THE STALKERS HAS A SPECIFIC SCHTICK, SIMILAR TO WRESTLERS OF THE LATE 20TH
CENTURY, AND FEATURE CHARACTERS SUCH AS 'SUBZERO' WHO DRESSES IN ICE HOCKEY GARB AND WIELDS
A RAZOR-SHARP STICK AND EXPLOSIVE PUCKS, 'DYNAMO' WHO IS CLAD IN BLINKING CHRISTMAS LIGHTS
AND CAN MANIPULATE ELECTRICITY, AND 'FIREBALL' WHO CARRIES A FLAMETHROWER (NATCH). AS FAR AS
RULES OF ENGAGEMENT BETWEEN THE STALKERS AND THE COMPETITORS ARE CONCERNED, ANYTHING GOES.

IF THE COMPETITORS CAN SOMEHOW MAKE IT PAST THE STALKERS, THEY MAY WIN PRIZES INCLUDING A
TRIAL BY JURY, SUSPENDED SENTENCE, OR EVEN A FULL PARDON. HOWEVER, BEHIND THE SCENES, THE
CHANCES ARE SLIM, WITH ALL SORTS OF SLIMY HANDSHAKE DEALS AND DIGITAL MANIPULATION
CONSPIRING TO KEEP THE COMPETITORS FROM EVER BECOMING ANYTHING OTHER THAN QUIVERING PILES
OF MEAT AND GOO ON THE STUDIO FLOOR.

ENDGAME (DIR. JOE D'AMATO, 1983)
GAME: ENDGAME
COMPETITORS: THREE HUNTERS VS ONE PREY.
EQUIPMENT REQUIRED: ONE FIREARM AND TWO WEAPONS OF CHOICE.
VENUE: WITHIN DESIGNATED ZONES OF THE CITY FILLED WITH CLOSED CIRCUIT TELEVISION.
PRIZE: STAKES PUT UP BY THE THREE HUNTERS.

SPONSORED BY LIFEPLUS, THE HIGH ENERGY PROTEIN TABLET, THE 'GREAT INTERNATIONAL SPORT' OF
ENDGAME IS BASICALLY THE RUNNING MAN WITHOUT THE WACKY WEAPONS, FLASHY OUTFITS, DECENT BUDGET
OR ANYTHING RESEMBLING CHARISMA. THE COMPETITORS DO GET TO WEAR SOME SNAZZY FACEPAINT
THOUGH, WHICH IS NICE.

THE POST-NUCLEAR ARMAGEDDON HAS LEFT THE CITY A PERFECT STAGE ON WHICH TO HOST A TELEVISED
GAME OF CAT AND MOUSE, IN WHICH THREE HUNTERS STALK THEIR PREY. EACH COMPETITOR, INCLUDING
THE PREY, IS KITTED OUT WITH ONE FIREARM, E.G. SHOTGUNS, MACHINE PISTOLS OR TOMMY GUNS, AND
TWO OTHER WEAPONS OF THEIR OWN CHOICE, WHICH COULD INCLUDE WHIPS, MACES OR KNIVES. THERE'S
NOTHING OVERLY COMPLEX ABOUT THE CHOSEN WEAPONRY, AND HUNTERS CAN OFTEN FIND THEMSELVES IN

A HAND-TO-HAND SITUATION, SO A DECENT REPERTOIRE OF MARTIAL ARTS OR BRAWLING SKILLS IS ALSO RECOMMENDED. ANYONE FOUND WITH ADDITIONAL WEAPONS IS AUTOMATICALLY DISQUALIFIED. THERE ARE NO LIMITATIONS IN REGARDS TO CLOTHING OR ARMOUR. ONCE THE WEAPONS HAVE BEEN CHECKED AND APPROVED, THE PREY IS THEN ALLOWED INTO THE GAME AREA, WHICH ARE SPECIFIC ZONES OF THE RUINED CITY. 30 MINUTES LATER, THE THREE HUNTERS ARE RELEASED.

IF THE PREY HAS SURVIVED THE FIRST SIX HOURS OF GAMEPLAY, THEY THEN HAVE AN OPTION TO SURRENDER, HOWEVER, IN DOING SO, THEY WILL BE PENALISED IN THE CHAMPIONSHIP STANDINGS AND WILL NOT RECEIVE THE PRIZE MONEY FOR THAT ROUND, WHICH IS COMPRISED OF THE STAKES PUT UP BY EACH OF THE HUNTERS. SHOULD THE PREY DISPATCH ALL THREE HUNTERS, THEY WILL RECEIVE THE PRIZE. IF A HUNTER KILLS THE PREY, THEY WILL RECEIVE THE PRIZE. A DRAW IS CALLED IF THE GAME TIME RUNS OUT AND THE PREY IS STILL ALIVE.

THE GAME IS RELAYED TO THE AUDIENCE (ESTIMATED TO BE AT ROUGHLY FIVE MILLION VIEWERS WORLDWIDE) VIA FIXED AND REMOTE-CONTROLLED CAMERAS AND COMPERED BY AN UNNAMED HOST WHO, UNLIKE THE RUNNING MAN'S KILLIAN, IS COMPLETELY DEVOID OF PERSONALITY. DESPITE ITS BLAND PRESENTATION AND FULL RUNNING TIME OF 12 HOURS, IT IS SAID THAT NOT EVEN ANOTHER NUCLEAR ATTACK COULD DISTRACT THE HOME VIEWERS FROM THE GAME.

ARENA (DIR. BY PETER MANOOGIAN, 1989)
GAME: THE ARENA
COMPETITORS: ONE VS ONE, TRAINED FIGHTERS.
EQUIPMENT REQUIRED: SOME FIGHTERS MAY WEAR PADS.
VENUE: RECTANGULAR MAT, SURROUNDED BY SEATED SPECTATORS.
PRIZE: CHAMPIONSHIP TITLE, PRIZE MONEY.

THE ARENA IS ONE OF THE MORE RESTRAINED AND REGULATED SPORTS ON THIS LIST AND ONE OF THE FEW THAT DOESN'T HAVE AN ULTERIOR MOTIVE OF KEEPING THE GENERAL POPULACE BEGUILED, SEDATE AND/OR MINDFUL OF THE CONSEQUENCES OF DISRUPTING THE STATUS QUO. MAYBE WE'VE MOVED PAST THOSE SORTS OF SHENANIGANS BY 4038AD.

SET ON A SPACE STATION FILLED WITH SPECIES FROM AROUND THE UNIVERSE, THE ARENA BEARS A STRONG RESEMBLANCE TO EARTH'S SUMO WRESTLING, WITH UNARMED FIGHTERS ATTEMPTING TO PUSH OR KNOCK EACH OTHER OUT OF THE ELECTRONIC BOUNDARIES OF THE RECTANGULAR MAT FOR POINTS. IN ORDER TO ADDRESS THE WIDE PHYSIOLOGICAL DIFFERENCES AND STRENGTH VARIANCES OF THE COMPETITORS, THERE IS A SOPHISTICATED SEIKO 3000 HANDICAPPING SYSTEM IN PLACE, WHICH CREATES A STRENGTH-ALTERING ENERGY FIELD AROUND EACH FIGHTER, TO ENSURE THAT THE FIGHTERS ARE EVENLY CLASSED. FIGHTERS MAY NOT USE WEAPONS BUT MAY HAVE APPENDAGES OR ANATOMICAL MECHANISMS SPECIFIC TO THEIR SPECIES, SUCH AS LARGE TALONS OR PNEUMATIC PISTONS; DESPITE THIS, THE ARENA REMAINS RELATIVELY BLOODLESS AND FREE OF GORE.

EACH FIGHTER COMES FROM A STABLE COMPLETE WITH MANAGERS AND TRAINERS AND PROGRESSES THROUGH A TOURNAMENT ROSTER TO BECOME CHAMPION OF THE ARENA. AS SHOULD BE EXPECTED IN MOST COMPETITIVE SPORTS, THERE ARE THOSE WHO ATTEMPT TO MANIPULATE THE OUTCOMES OF THE MATCHES BY BENDING THE RULES AND USING PROHIBITED PERFORMANCE-ENHANCING SUBSTANCES. SOME MAY EVEN ATTEMPT TO SNEAKILY RECALIBRATE THE SEIKO 3000 FOR THEIR OWN ENDS.

MAD MAX BEYOND THUNDERDOME (DIR. GEORGE MILLER/GEORGE OGILVIE, 1985)
GAME: THUNDERDOME.
COMPETITORS: ONE VS ONE, OPEN TO ALL.
EQUIPMENT REQUIRED: BUNGEE CORD HARNESSES, VARIETY OF WEAPONS.
VENUE: A ROUND ENCLOSED STEEL CAGE.
PRIZE: UNEQUIVOCAL DISPUTE RESOLUTION.

NOT SO MUCH A GAME AS A JUDICIAL SYSTEM IN WHICH DISPUTES ARE RESOLVED, BARTERTOWN'S 'THUNDERDOME' IS FAIRLY STRAIGHTFORWARD: 'TWO MEN ENTER, ONE MAN LEAVES.' THERE ARE EXPLICITLY NO RULES AND ANYTHING IS POSSIBLE WITHIN ITS CONFINES, WITH DEATH TAKING THE FIRST MAN THAT SCREAMS. EVEN THOUGH THAT WELL-WORN ADAGE PERTAINS TO 'MEN SPECIFICALLY', IT IS ASSUMED THAT

ANY TWO PEOPLE WITH GRIEVANCES CAN ENTER THUNDERDOME TO SETTLE THEIR HASH, WITH NO GENDER, AGE OR DISABILITY RESTRICTIONS.

THE PLAINTIFF AND DEFENDANT ARE STRIPPED OF ANY WEAPONS (THOUGH SOMETHING SMALL, SUCH AS A WHISTLE, MIGHT GET PAST THE BAILIFFS) AND ARE STRAPPED TO BUNGEE CORD HARNESSES ATTACHED TO THE CEILING OF THE THUNDERDOME, WHICH IS BASICALLY A ROUNDED CAGE, APPROXIMATELY 30 METRES ACROSS, MADE FROM SCAFFOLDING AND CHICKEN WIRE. THE BUNGEE CORDS ALLOW FOR SOME NIFTY AERIAL ACROBATICS THAT WOULDN'T USUALLY BE POSSIBLE IN MOST GLADIATORIAL ARENAS, AS WELL AS ALLOWING ACCESS TO THE NUMEROUS WEAPONS ATTACHED TO THE ROOF OF THE CAGE, INCLUDING, BUT NOT LIMITED TO, GIANT HAMMERS, SPIKED MACES AND GUANDAO (CHINESE POLEARMS). WHILE IT SEEMS THAT THESE WEAPONS ARE CHOSEN FOR THE LARGE AMOUNT OF DAMAGE THEY CAN DEAL TO THE HUMAN BODY, THEY MAY NOT ALWAYS BE ALL THAT USEFUL, ESPECIALLY IN THE CASE OF WEAPONS THAT REQUIRE FUEL, SUCH AS CHAINSAWS.

THE SPECTATORS ARE CLOSE TO THE ACTION, CLINGING ONTO THE SCAFFOLDS THAT ENCIRCLE THE THUNDERDOME, CHANTING FOR BLOOD. WITHOUT ANY PROTECTIVE SCREENS OR SAFETY NETS TO BLOCK WEAPONS OR LIMBS FROM FLYING OUT OF THE ARENA, THE UNLUCKIEST ONES MAY SOMETIMES FIND THEMSELVES ON THE WRONG END OF A PARTICULARLY POINTED STATEMENT FROM THE DEFENSE.

IT'S WORTH NOTING THAT THUNDERDOME ISN'T THE ONLY GAME IN TOWN -- THERE'S ALSO 'BUST A DEAL, FACE THE WHEEL', BASED ON THE OLD TELEVISION SHOW, 'WHEEL OF FORTUNE'; THOSE FOUND TO HAVE BROKEN AN AGREEMENT MAY FIND THEMSELVES SPINNING THEMSELVES A SENTENCE THAT COULD RESULT IN LIFE IMPRISONMENT, AMPUTATION OR DEATH.

DEATHSPORT (DIR. NICHOLAS NICIPHOR/ALLAN ARKUSH, 1978)
GAME: DEATHSPORT
COMPETITORS: CONVICTS SENTENCED TO DEATH, STATE-OPERATED MILITIA.
EQUIPMENT REQUIRED: DEATH MACHINE BIKES, WHISTLERS (CRYSTAL SWORDS), HAND BLASTERS, SENSOR BOMBS.
VENUE: LARGE SAND-FILLED STADIUM WITH HIGH TIERED SEATS FOR SPECTATORS.
PRIZE: FREEDOM.

CLOSELY MIRRORING THE SCENES IN THE COLOSSEUM OF ANCIENT ROME, DEATHSPORT'S MASSIVE STADIUM IS USED PRIMARILY FOR THE EXECUTION OF THOSE WHO THREATEN OR RESIST LORD ZIRPOLA, AN INSANE DESPOT WITH A PENCHANT FOR TORTURING NAKED WOMEN WITH LOW-HANGING DISCO TUBES (NOT A EUPHEMISM).

LORD ZIRPOLA IS PARTICULARLY PROUD OF HIS 'DEATH MACHINES', MOTORCYCLES FITTED OUT WITH DISINTEGRATION RAYS, AND USES DEATHSPORT AS AN OPPORTUNITY TO TRAIN HIS STATESMEN SOLDIERS IN THEIR USE BEFORE TAKING ON LARGER TARGETS, SUCH AS NEIGHBOURING CITY-STATES. THE DISINTEGRATION RAYS, REFERRED TO AS 'HAND BLASTERS', ARE LETHAL, COMPLETELY OBLITERATING ANYTHING THAT GETS IN ITS WAY. IN A SURPRISINGLY SPORTING TURN OF EVENTS, THE PRISONERS THAT ARE FORCED TO COMPETE ARE PROVIDED WITH WHISTLERS, A TYPE OF CRYSTAL OR CLEAR PLASTIC SWORD, THAT ARE UNEXPECTEDLY EFFECTIVE AND CAN LOP OFF NOGGINS WITH ONE STROKE.

THOSE SENTENCED TO DEATHSPORT WILL MOST LIKELY FIND THEMSELVES ON FOOT AGAINST WAVES OF ENEMIES RIDING DEATH MACHINES AND SUCCESS GENERALLY RELIES ON HOW STUPID THE OPPONENTS ARE, RATHER THAN ANY PARTICULAR INBORN SKILL. A COMMON TACTIC INVOLVES HIDING BEHIND THE ARENA'S SAND DUNES AND SLASHING AT THE OPPONENT WITH A WHISTLER WHEN THEY DRIVE PAST, SIMILAR TO HOW A MATADOR DEALS WITH A BULL. CONSIDERING THOSE ON FOOT ARE REQUIRED TO PLANT THEMSELVES IN A POSITION TO SWING THEIR WHISTLERS, IT SEEMS THAT THOSE RIDING THE DEATH MACHINES SHOULD ABLY SEE THE INTENT OF THE OPPONENT AND REACT ACCORDINGLY BUT THIS IS RARELY THE CASE.

SO THAT NOT ALL OF THE WORK DEPENDS ON THE INEPT STATESMEN, THE GROUND OF THE STADIUM IS LITTERED WITH SENSOR MINES THAT CAN BE DETONATED REMOTELY OR WILL GO OFF WHEN TRIGGERED BY NEARBY PRESSURE. UNFORTUNATELY, THESE CAN DISPATCH STATESMAN AS READILY AS THE PRISONERS.

SALUTE OF THE JUGGER (aka THE BLOOD OF HEROES, DIR. DAVID PEOPLES, 1989)

GAME: THE GAME.
COMPETITORS: TWO TEAMS OF FIVE JUGGERS, EACH TEAM COMPRISED OF THREE BLOCKERS, ONE SLASH, AND ONE QWIK.
EQUIPMENT REQUIRED: HEAVY DUTY PADDING, BLOCKERS' STAFFS, SLASH'S CHAIN, DOG'S SKULL.
VENUE: THE GENERAL SETTING AND PITCH SIZE CAN VARY SLIGHTLY FROM MATCH TO MATCH, BUT EACH PITCH REQUIRES A SHORT STAKE AT EITHER END.
PRIZE: TROPHIES (DOG SKULLS), TRIBUTES, ELEVATION TO ELITE STATUS.

ON AN EARTH GOING THROUGH A NEW DARK AGE, THE GAME'S ORIGINS ARE A MYSTERY; IT IS AS MUCH A SERIES OF WELL-WORN RITUALS AS IT IS A SPORT. FROM THE STRAPPING ON OF THE RUBBER AND BAMBOO PADS TO THE THROWING OF THE STONES THAT MARK THE PASSING OF TIME IN EACH GAME, ALMOST EVERY ACTION IS PURPOSEFUL AND SOLEMN.

BUT DON'T BE FOOLED; ONCE THE FIRST STONE IS THROWN, THE ACTION COMES HARD AND FAST. A DOG'S SKULL IS PLACED IN THE MIDDLE OF A CIRCLE IN THE MIDDLE OF THE PITCH, AND THE NIMBLE QWIKS NEED TO GAIN POSSESSION OF IT AND IMPALE IT ON THEIR TEAM'S STAKE, SET AT EITHER END OF THE PLAY AREA. ONCE A QWIK HAS THE SKULL, THEY BECOME THE TARGET OF EVERY OFFENSIVE PLAYER ON THE PITCH WHO WILL DO EVERYTHING POSSIBLE TO DISABLE THEM. BLOCKERS ARE EQUIPPED WITH PADDED STAFFS, SOME WITH CROOKS AT ONE END, THAT CAN BE USED TO BLUDGEON, HOOK OR PIN AN OPPONENT, WHILE SLASHES WIELD INTRICATE LENGTHS OF CHAIN THAT ARE PART NET, PART FLAIL, AND ARE SUPERB AT RAISING WELTS, BREAKING LIMBS OR PROVIDING A PROTECTIVE BARRIER AROUND A QWIK. IF A PLAYER SUFFERS AN INJURY, THERE IS THE OPTION TO CONTINUE PLAYING WITH THE INJURY, WHICH COULD BECOME A WEAK POINT FOR THE OPPOSITION'S ATTACKS, OR THE TEAM MAY MAKE A SUBSTITUTION, IF THERE IS SOMEONE WILLING TO FILL THE ROLE.

WHILE THERE ARE NUMEROUS TEAMS IN THE DOGTOWNS AND WANDERING THROUGH THE WASTELAND, IT'S THE NINE CITIES LEAGUE THAT MANY AMATEUR JUGGERS DREAM OF PLAYING IN, WHERE THE LEAGUE

PLAYERS ARE TREATED TO LUXURIES SUCH AS SILKS, FRAGRANT OILS AND CANDIED FISHES. TO JOIN THE LEAGUE, ONE MUST FIRST CHALLENGE THE LEAGUE TO A GAME. IF THE CHALLENGE IS ACCEPTED, THE GAME IS SET FOR 100 STONES, THREE TIMES. THE LEAGUE IS SO FORMIDABLE THAT THE RECORD GAME LENGTH STOOD AT ONLY 26 STONES, UNTIL BROKEN BY A PARTICULARLY NOTABLE TEAM. IF THE CHALLENGERS CAN PROVE THEMSELVES AS BEING ABLE TO STAND AGAINST THE LEAGUE, THEY HAVE A CHANCE AT BEING INVITED TO JOIN. FAILURE WILL MEAN THE TEAM WILL NEED TO REGROUP AND REBUILD THEIR REPUTATION OUT IN THE WASTELAND.

ROBOT JOX (DIR. STUART GORDON, 1989)

GAME: NO SPECIFIC NAME, BUT REFERRED TO AS 'TERRITORIAL DISPUTES' OR 'THE GAMES'.
COMPETITORS: TWO SPECIALLY-TRAINED JOX.
EQUIPMENT REQUIRED: GIGANTIC ROBOT SUITS.
VENUE: VAST CLEARED AREAS OF LAND.
PRIZE: LAND ACQUISITION.

50 YEARS AFTER THE HOLOCAUST, ONLY TWO NATION STATES REMAIN: THE CONFEDERATION AND THE MARKET, DUKING IT OUT OVER WHO GETS THE REMAINING BITS OF LAND AND THE VALUABLE RESOURCES THEREIN. WAR HAS BEEN OUTLAWED AND THESE LAND DISPUTES ARE RESOLVED BY SCHEDULED SINGLE COMBAT BETWEEN REPRESENTATIVES FROM EACH NATION. THANKS TO A QUESTIONABLE DECISION MADE SOMEWHERE IN THE MISTS OF TIME, THESE TWO REPRESENTATIVES, KNOWN AS 'JOX', ARE HOUSED IN THE COCKPITS OF GIGANTIC ROBOTS THAT MIMIC THEIR MOVEMENTS, AND ARE LOADED FOR BEAR WITH AN ARSENAL OF IMPRESSIVE WEAPONRY, INCLUDING LASERS, CANNONS, GATLING GUNS AND ROCKET FISTS.

THE JOX, MOUNTED IN THEIR MECHSUITS, RISE FROM UNDERGROUND BUNKERS INTO A LARGE OPEN SPACE, CLEARED OF BUILDINGS AND PEOPLE (APART FROM SOME STADIUM SEATING FOR SPECTATORS) AND IMMEDIATELY RAIN DOWN FIRE ON EACH OTHER WITH THEIR MISSILES, CANNONS AND LASERS, UNTIL THE REFEREES REMOTELY SHUT DOWN THE LONG-RANGE WEAPONS AND THE MECHS PROCEED WITH ROBOT-HAND-

TO-ROBOT-HAND COMBAT. THE BRAWL COMPONENT OF THE BATTLE IS NOT JUST GIANT METAL FISTICUFFS; BOLA SAWS, ARC TORCHES AND EXTREMELY FREUDIAN CROTCH-SAWS ADD SOME UNIQUE FLAVOUR TO THE DUST-UPS.

THE STADIUM SEATING PROVIDES SOME PROTECTION TO THE AUDIENCE BUT MAY SUCCUMB TO THE FULL WEIGHT OF A POORLY PLACED MECH. SOME OF THE PROLETARIAT MAY BE BETTER OFF VIEWING, AND BETTING THEIR MARKET SHARES ON, THE ACTION SHOWN ON MASSIVE SCREENS WITHIN THE CITY LIMITS.

JOX ARE SPECIALLY-TRAINED, AND IN SOME INSTANCES, SPECIALLY-BRED, FIGHTERS, BUT THE GAME ISN'T DOWN TO THEM ALONE-- A HIGHLY SOPHISTICATED CONTROL ROOM FULL OF A TEAM OF EXPERTS ARE ON HAND TO ASSIST THE JOX. HOWEVER, WITH A LARGER TEAM, THERE COMES A HIGHER RISK OF TREACHERY -- MORE GAMES HAVE BEEN LOST TO LEAKED INFORMATION SUCH AS WEAPONRY AND ARMOUR WEAKNESSES THAN THE SUPERIOR SKILL OF THE OPPONENTS.

BATTLE ROYALE (DIR. KINJI FUKASAKU, 2000)
GAME: BATTLE ROYALE
COMPETITORS: ONE HIGH SCHOOL CLASS (APPROX. 40 STUDENTS).
EQUIPMENT REQUIRED: FOOD, WATER, MAP, COMPASS, FLASHLIGHT, ASSORTED WEAPONRY, PERSONAL EFFECTS, MONITORING NECKLACES.
VENUE: REMOTE UNINHABITED 10KM2 ISLAND, SEPARATED INTO 1KM2 SECTORS.
PRIZE: NOT DYING

NOT ALL BLOOD SPORTS ARE FOR GROWN UPS! YOU GOTTA HAVE SOMETHING FOR THE KIDS! JAPAN HAS COLLAPSED, BURDENED WITH HIGH UNEMPLOYMENT RATES AND A SOARING RISE IN JUVENILE CRIME. THE MILLENNIUM EDUCATIONAL REFORM ACT - AKA "THE BR ACT" - HAS BEEN INTRODUCED IN AN EFFORT TO DISCIPLINE THE YOUTH WHO ARE RUNNING WILD IN THE STREETS, MOSTLY BY REDUCING THEIR NUMBERS THROUGH STATE-SANCTIONED MURDER. JUVENILE DELINQUENT ETHNIC CLEANSING, IF YOU WILL.

THE GAME OF BATTLE ROYALE IS PLAYED OVER THREE DAYS ON A 10 KM UNINHABITED ISLAND, MAINTAINED AND MANAGED BY THE MILITARY. THE COMPETITORS OF BATTLE ROYALE, APPROXIMATELY 40 SCHOOL STUDENTS AGED 14 TO 15 YEARS, ARE NOT WILLING PARTICIPANTS IN THE GAME. THEIR INTRODUCTION TO THE GAME IS COMPRISED ENTIRELY OF ONE SCREENING OF 'THE CORRECT WAY TO FIGHT IN BATTLE ROYALE', A VIDEO PRESENTED BY THE BR LAW PROMOTION COMMITTEE. SHOULD THEY ARGUE OR REFUSE TO PARTICIPATE IN THE GAME, THEY MAY BE EXECUTED ON THE SPOT BY THE 'TEACHER', ALTHOUGH THIS IS GENERALLY FROWNED UPON BY THE BIGWIGS IN CHARGE. IT IS NOT UNCOMMON FOR RINGERS FROM OTHER SCHOOLS TO BE BROUGHT IN TO A CLASS; THESE RINGERS CAN EITHER BE VOLUNTEERS OR COERCED, DEPENDING ON THE INDIVIDUAL'S SITUATION.

EACH STUDENT IS PROVIDED WITH A BAG OF PROVISIONS: FOOD, WATER, MAP, COMPASS, FLASHLIGHT AND A 'WEAPON'. THEY ARE ALSO PERMITTED TO TAKE WITH THEM THE SCHOOLBAG THEY BROUGHT WITH THEM ONTO THE ISLAND (UNDER THE ASSUMPTION THAT THEY WERE GOING ON A FIELD TRIP) AND THESE MAY CONTAIN USEFUL UNIQUE COMPONENTS, SUCH AS FRESH CLOTHES, LAPTOPS OR ANARCHIST GUIDEBOOKS. THE WEAPONS PROVIDED TO THE STUDENTS VARY IN PRACTICALITY, WITH SOME STUDENTS RECEIVING SHOTGUNS, HATCHETS OR CROSSBOWS, WHILE OTHERS MAY RECEIVE GPS TRACKERS, BINOCULARS OR SAUCEPAN LIDS. EACH STUDENT IS ALSO FITTED OUT WITH AN ELECTRONIC NECKLACE, WHICH RELAYS THEIR PULSE RATE, POSITION AND VOICE TO THE MILITARY MONITORS AT THE CENTRAL BASE.

THE NECKLACES ARE AN ESSENTIAL COMPONENT IN MAINTAINING A HIGH LEVEL OF COMPLIANCE AMONG THE COMPETITORS; THEY ARE RIGGED WITH AN EXPLOSIVE THAT CAN BE DETONATED REMOTELY, SHOULD THE STUDENTS' ACTIVITY BE DEEMED AS 'NAUGHTY' -- IT SHOULD BE NOTED THAT MURDER IS NOT CONSIDERED 'NAUGHTY' IN THIS INSTANCE AND IS ACTIVELY ENCOURAGED. AS FAR AS GAME RULES, ANYTHING GOES, PROVIDED THE STUDENTS REMAIN ON THE ISLAND AND DO NOT ATTEMPT TO DISRUPT OR HARM THE AUTHORITIES OVERSEEING THE OPERATION. THE NECKLACES ALSO PREVENT PASSIVE RESISTANCE; IF A SINGLE SURVIVOR ISN'T DETERMINED BY THE TIME THE GAME IS OVER, ALL THE NECKLACES WILL AUTOMATICALLY EXPLODE.

THE ISLAND IS SEPARATED INTO 1 KM SECTORS AND EVERY SIX HOURS, SEVERAL OF THESE SECTORS ARE DEEMED DANGEROUS; IF A STUDENT IS LOCATED IN, OR ENTERS, A DANGEROUS AREA, THEIR NECKLACE WILL BE DETONATED.

WHILE THE GAME ITSELF ISN'T TELEVISED, THE NATION EAGERLY AWAITS NEWS OF THE RESULTS, WITH MEDIA CLAMOURING OVER ONE ANOTHER TO REPORT THE WINNER FIRST (AND THEREBY NUDGING IT TO JUST WITHIN THE PARAMETERS SET OUT IN THE INTRODUCTION OF THIS ARTICLE).

SPECIAL MENTIONS:

SOLARBABIES (DIR. ALAN JOHNSON, 1986)
SKATEBALL -- A STYLE OF LACROSSE PLAYED ON ROLLERBLADES BY ORPHANS UNDER THE CARE OF THE STATE. THE EXACT RULES ARE UNCLEAR BUT SHOVING IS NOT ALLOWED. MOSTLY HARMLESS.

QUINTET (DIR. ROBERT ALTMAN, 1979)
QUINTET -- A TABLETOP GAME FOR SIX PLAYERS THAT SERVES AS A DISTRACTION FROM THE PACKS OF FERAL ROTTWEILERS IN THE FROZEN WASTELAND OUTSIDE. SIMILAR TO BACKGAMMON AND ABOUT AS VIOLENT.

-RINGO STALIN · 2016

Mother's Wishes (1973)

What's That?

IT'S TIME FOR A GAME OF "WHAT'S THAT?", AND TODAY OUR CONTESTANT WILL BE THE 1973 INCEST-THEMED XXX STROKER, MOTHER'S WISHES! GIVE IT A HAND, FOLKS! ALL RIGHT, LET'S PLAY!

AUNT NANCY (NANCY MARTIN) IS SITTING AROUND THE BREAKFAST TABLE IN A TYPICALLY SUBURBAN LOOKING CALIFORNIA HOME, BUT INSTEAD OF DRINKING HER COFFEE, READING THE PAPER, AND DOING HER NAILS, SHE'S READING A PLAYBOY MAGAZINE (THE NOVEMBER 1972 ISSUE) AND RUBBING HER SLOPPY PUMPHOLE. TABLE MANNERS AND PROPER ETIQUETTE? WHAT'S THAT?

CYNDEE SUMMERS IS WALKING HOME FROM SCHOOL, THINKING ABOUT HOW HER SEX EDUCATION CLASS WENT, HER TEACHER'S MONOTONE VOICE STILL ECHOING HER TEENAGE EARS. "THE ERECT MALE PENIS IS ABSOLUTELY NECESSARY FOR COITUS", THE VOICE BOOMS. "WHEN FLACCID, INSERTION CANNOT TAKE PLACE, IN THE HEAT OF PASSION, THE VULVA LUBRICATES ITSELF." SHE'S A BEAUTIFUL STRAWBERRY RED HEAD WITH HER HAIR IN PIGTAILS AND SHE'S WEARING A GORGEOUS YELLOW BLUE AND WHITE TARTAN SKIRT THAT WOULD FETCH A GOOD PRICE IN A VINTAGE CLOTHING SHOP IF YOU COULD FIND IT TODAY. SHE'S PLAYING WAY YOUNGER THAN SHE IS, WHILE NANCY MARTIN IS PLAYING WAY OLDER THAN SHE IS, BUT THE FACT IS THEY LOOK EXACTLY AS OLD AS THEY ACTUALLY ARE -- WHICH IS ABOUT 22 YEARS OLD. PROPER CASTING, WHAT'S THAT?

WHEN CYNDEE ARRIVES AT HOME, SHE GETS GRILLED ON HOW CLASS WENT. WHEN AUNT NANCY HEARS ABOUT SEX ED, SHE DECIDES TO DO A LITTLE OF HER OWN, SHOWING HER NIECE HOW ONE MASTURBATES TO A PORN MAGAZINE. "DO YOU WANT TO DO WHAT I'M DOING WITH MY HAND?" SHE COOS, AS SHE PLACES CYNDEE'S HAND ON HER TWAT AND INVITES HER TO DO SOME MUFFIN BUFFING. IT REALLY DOESN'T TAKE LONG BEFORE THE TWO OF THEM ARE HAPPILY CHOWING DOWN ON EACH OTHER'S FLAPPY MEALS. ANY AND ALL ADHERING TO THEIR ASSIGNED CHARACTERS IS TOSSED OUT THE WINDOW WHEN THE SEX BEGINS. ACTING? WHAT'S THAT?

WHEN DAD (KEITH ERICKSON) WALKS IN THE ROOM, AT LEAST HE'S PLAYED BY A GUY WHO IS THE RIGHT AGE. ALTHOUGH HIS FIRST REACTION IS TO QUICKLY YANK OUT HIS COCK AND START PLAYING WITH IT. AFTER JIZZING IN HIS HAND, THE CAMERA PULLS BACK AND WE SEE THAT MOM (PENNY KING) HAS ALSO BEEN SPYING ON THE ENTIRE TURGID BREAKFAST NOOK SCENE FROM ANOTHER PART OF THE ROOM AS WELL. REALISM? WHAT'S THAT?

CUT TO A LATER SCENE AND BEFORE YOU KNOW IT, DAD IS ENJOYING THE "EDUCATION" OF HIS DAUGHTER BY BANGING HER DOGGY STYLE AND BLOWING HIS GOOF JUICE ON HER LITHE LITTLE BACK. WE ALSO FIND OUT LATER THAT MOM HAS TOSSED HER SISTER OUT OF THE HOUSE BECAUSE OF THE WHOLE "MOLESTING MY DAUGHTER" THING. APPARENTLY BLOOD IS NOT THICKER THAN PUSSY JUICE. DOING A PORN REVIEW WITHOUT AN OFF-PUTTING REFERENCE TO BLOOD? WHAT'S THAT?

WE FIND THIS BIT OF INFO OUT BECAUSE SHE TELLS HER BEEFY SON (TOM CANTRELL) WHILE SHE'S IN THE SACK WITH HIM. HE CONSOLES HER, AND THEN ROLLS HER OVER AND PROCEEDS TO FUCK HER IN THE ASSHOLE WHILE DOODLY-DOODLY-DOODLY SURF ROCK PLAYS ON THE SOUNDTRACK. THEY AWKWARDLY GET HER POOP ALL OVER EVERYTHING, AND IT'S DISGUSTING. HE ALSO DOUBLE DIPS, PLOWING HER PUSSY WITH HIS WOMB WEASEL AFTER HIS COCK IS ALL SHIT-ENCRUSTED, WHICH MADE ME WINCE AND DRY HEAVE A LITTLE. PROPERLY PREPPING FOR AN ANAL SCENE WITH AN ENEMA? WHAT'S THAT?

AS SO MANY OF THESE TYPES OF 1970S ADULT FILMS DO IT, THE WHOLE THING COMES TO A CLOSE IN A GIANT SWEATY, HAIRY ORGY. HEY, THE FAMILY THAT LAYS TOGETHER, STAYS TOGETHER! (SLIDE WHISTLE)

THAT'S ALL FOR NOW, FOLKS! THANKS FOR TUNING INTO (AUDIENCE SHOUTS IN UNISON) "...WHAT'S THAT ??!" THIS EPISODE BROUGHT TO YOU BY:

French "Flugina" massage glove

IMPORTED FROM FRANCE / NEW DEEP DOWN ACTION FITS FIRMLY TO STIMULATE AND INVIGORATE

SPANKS FOR THE MEMORIES:
HITTING LADY BUTTS IN CLASSIC HOLLYWOOD FILMS

(IT WOULD TAKE AN ENTIRE ISSUE OF CINEMA SEWER TO RECOUNT ALL THE SPANKINGS THAT HAVE TAKEN PLACE IN X AND XXX FILMS, SO FOR THIS PIECE I WILL FOCUS EXCLUSIVELY ON VINTAGE MAINSTREAM HOLLYWOOD FARE, WHICH AS YOU WILL READ, ARE EXTENSIVE SPANK-FESTS IN THEIR OWN RIGHT. -- BOUG)

"THE BEST POSITION FOR SPANKING GIRLS IS OVER THE KNEES IN SUCH A WAY THAT YOUR FINGERTIPS AND TOES JUST TOUCH THE GROUND AND YOUR BOTTOM IS AT AN ANGLE THAT MAKES IT EASY FOR THE SPANKER TO MAINTAIN A METRONOME BEAT. WHEN THE HAND COMES DOWN, THE STING IS QUICKLY FOLLOWED BY A PRICKLING NUMBNESS. THE PAIN VANISHES AND THE HEAT GENERATED FROM THOSE SLAPS SENDS LINES OF ELECTRIC FIRE THROUGH ALL THE TISSUES AND NERVE ENDINGS, RIPPLES OF WARMTH THAT GATHER IN A WAVE OF SENSATIONS." -- CHLOE THURLOW, A GIRL'S ADVENTURE (CHIMERA BOOKS. 2006)

BACK IN THE EARLY DAYS OF CINEMA, JUST GLIMPSING THE SHAPELY BARE LEG OF A COMELY LASS WAS AN EROTIC VIEWING EXPERIENCE FOR LESBIANS AND STRAIGHT BROS, SO YOU CAN RIGHTLY IMAGINE THAT SEEING THAT SAME FEMALE GETTING HER CURVY DERRIERE SPANKED BY HER CO-STAR WAS LITERALLY ENOUGH TO HAVE SOME OLD-TIMEY MOVIEGOERS BLOWING LOADS AND GOOING THEIR VAGINAS ALL OVER THEIR SEATS. THIS WAS A TIME, SHORTLY AFTER THE TURN OF THE 20TH CENTURY, WHEN REPRESSIVE SOCIAL NORMS DECIDED THAT EVEN THE WORD 'SEX' WAS DIRTY, AND CENSORSHIP OF ANY TOO-OBVIOUS DEPICTION OF A LEWD ACT HAD FILMMAKERS RESORTING TO SYMBOLISM IN ORDER TO GET SOMETHING ONTO THE SCREEN THAT WOULD MAKE YOU BLUSH. A ROUGH-AND-TUMBLE SPANKING WAS ONE OF THEIR MOST POPULAR GO-TO'S.

NO DIRECTOR HAD TO SIT DOWN AND EXPLAIN TO JOHN WAYNE HOW TO SPANK A WOMAN. THE DUKE REPORTEDLY SPANKED AT LEAST TWO OF HIS WIVES, AND WARMED MORE LADY BUNS ON-SCREEN THAN ANY MAINSTREAM ACTOR IN HOLLYWOOD HISTORY. HIS MOST MEMORABLE AND TALKED ABOUT BUM-WHACKING CAME IN MCLINTOCK! (1963). HERE, HE ENTHUSIASTICALLY SLAPPED THE REAR-END OF HAUGHTY, RED-HAIRED MAUREEN O'HARA WHILE THE WHOLE GODDAMN TOWN LOOKED ON WITH FRANKLY ODD EXPRESSIONS OF RESOLUTE JOY. "MY FATHER WOULD BE PROUD OF YOU!" A MAN SHOUTS.

O'HARA CO-STARRED WITH WAYNE IN FIVE FILMS, AND GOT HER POSTERIOR OR SOME OTHER PERKY PART OF HER ANATOMY PLAYFULLY PUNISHED BY THE DUKE IN EVERY ONE OF THEM. DESPITE HER RAVISHING ADULT BEAUTY, MAUREEN GREW UP A TOMBOY, AND RELISHED IN HER ABILITY TO GIVE AS GOOD AS SHE GOT, EVEN GOING BLOW-FOR-BLOW IN A FIST FIGHT WITH DIRECTOR JOHN FORD AT A HOLLYWOOD PARTY. NO WONDER WAYNE ONCE CALLED HER "MY KIND OF WOMAN" AND EXPLAINED: "SHE'S A GREAT GUY. I'VE HAD MANY FRIENDS, AND I PREFER THE COMPANY OF MEN. EXCEPT FOR MAUREEN O'HARA."

NEXT TO WAYNE, THE MOST FAMOUS SERIAL SPANKER AT YE OLDE PICTURE SHOWS WAS PROBABLY CLARK GABLE. IN ACROSS THE WIDE MISSOURI (1951) GABLE SITS ON A TREE STUMP NEAR A STREAM, PUTS HIS YOUNG INDIAN WIFE OVER HIS KNEE, AND WAILS ON THAT CUTE LIL' ASS LIKE A HORSE JOCKEY. HE DISHES OUT ON A WRIGGLING JOAN CRAWFORD WITH A HAIRBRUSH IN 1934'S FORSAKING ALL OTHERS, AND BY THE END OF THE FILM SHE PLEDGES HER DEVOTION TO HIM -- NOT WITH A KISS-- BUT BY HANDING HIM THE HAIRBRUSH. THIS SAME GESTURE OF KINKY SUBMISSION OCCURS AT THE END OF TAMING THE WILD (1936), WHICH FEATURES MAXINE DOYLE'S ASS GETTING BRUTALIZED BY SAID HAIRBRUSH RIGHT ON THE POSTER FOR THE MOVIE!

BUT WHAT WAS THIS ALL ABOUT, ALL THIS HITTING OF WOMEN? WHAT DID IT MEAN, AND WHY DID MAINSTREAM AUDIENCES WANT TO SEE IT SO BADLY?

HOMER

"I know Morse Code, Dear—and I love you, too!"

FAR FROM FINDING THESE SCENES PROBLEMATIC, 1940S, 1950S AND '60S AUDIENCES -- BOTH WOMEN AND MEN -- ALMOST UNANIMOUSLY LOVED GETTING TO SEE ACTORS LIKE WAYNE THROW ACTRESSES LIKE O'HARA OVER THEIR KNEE. THEY SAW "DOMESTIC DISCIPLINE" AS EITHER FUNNY, EROTIC, RESPONSIBLE, LOVING, OR IN SOME CASES EVEN BIBLICAL (EVANGELICAL WOMEN, FOR INSTANCE, BELIEVE WOMEN ARE CALLED UPON BY GOD TO SUBMIT TO THEIR HUSBANDS) ALL WHILE VIEWING DOMESTIC ABUSE AS JUST THAT - VILE, INDEFENSIBLE ABUSE.

EVERYONE KNEW THEN, AS WELL AS TODAY, THAT ONLY A CAD -- A REAL FUCKIN' LOWLIFE -- PUNCHES/KICKS/ABUSES A WOMAN. THERE WAS A DISCONNECT AND A SEPARATION BETWEEN SPANKING AND ABUSE THAT DOESN'T SEEM TO EXIST ANYMORE. IF YOU SPANK YOUR WIFE TODAY IN ANY CAPACITY OUTSIDE OF SEXUAL ROLEPLAY (AND EVEN THAT IS FROWNED UPON BY SOME), THAT IS CUT-AND-DRY SPOUSAL ABUSE. BUT BACK THEN? MAN, THE JURY WAS DEFINITELY STILL OUT.

IN EARLY 1946, A WOMAN FROM CARMEL, CALIFORNIA WROTE THE HOLLYWOOD FAN MAGAZINE 'SCREENLAND' TO SAY HOW MUCH SHE APPRECIATED SEEING THE RECENT CHRISTMAS RELEASE FRONTIER GAL WITH HER HUSBAND, BECAUSE IT HAD SAVED HER MARRIAGE BY TEACHING HER HUSBAND THE VALUE OF SPANKING HER TUSH, THEREBY GIVING THE TWO OF THESE REPRESSED SOULS THE GATEWAY TO PHYSICAL INTIMACY THEY HAD PREVIOUSLY BEEN LACKING.

NOW I SHOULD SAY THAT THE MINUTE-LONG SPANKING SCENE OF STARLET YVONNE DECARLO IN FRONTIER GAL (1945) IS A MEMORABLE ONE EVEN IN A YEAR WHEN FIVE OTHER MAJOR HOLLYWOOD MOVIES FEATURED ADULT WOMEN BEING SPANKED, BECAUSE IT IS DONE RIGHT IN FRONT OF HER CHARACTER'S 5-YEAR-OLD DAUGHTER. BEFORE ROD CAMERON EVEN MEETS YVONNE DE CARLO IN THE MOVIE, SHE'S EYEBROW-RAISINGLY DESCRIBED AS A "LIVELY FILLY" WHO IS "WELL WORTH STABLE ROOM ONCE SHE'S BROKEN FOR THE BRIDLE", AND WHILE YVONNE'S CHARACTER IS INITIALLY UPSET AND CONFUSED BY THIS DEGRADING HUMILIATION, THE LITTLE GIRL IS DEPICTED AS BEING GREATLY SATISFIED BY WHAT SHE'S SEEN.

"DADDY, YOU SPANKED MAMA!", THE GIRL HAPPILY BLURTS WHILE HER GRIMACING AND DISHEVELED MOTHER IS DRAPED OVER HIS KNEE. "THAT MEANS YOU LOVE HER!"

"IN DESPERATION, AFTER SEEING THE SHOW, HE TRIED LITTLE BEVERLY'S PHILOSOPHY," WROTE MRS. J.B. M TO SCREENLAND ABOUT HOW CORRECTIVE DISCIPLINE HAD WORKED FOR HER AND HER HUBBY. "DADDIES SPANK MAMAS BECAUSE THEY LOVE THEM. WHILE THIS OLD-FASHIONED APPROACH PROBABLY WOULDN'T WORK IN ALL CASES, IT DID FOR US, AND I WOULD APPRECIATE AN OPPORTUNITY TO PUBLICLY THANK UNIVERSAL AND FRONTIER GAL."

WAS THIS A SEX THING IN THEIR RELATIONSHIP? AN ABUSE THING? A FAKE LETTER DESIGNED TO SUPPLY COVERT JOLLIES TO REPRESSED READERS? WE'LL NEVER KNOW FOR SURE, BUT WHAT WE DO KNOW IS THAT THIS WASN'T AN ISOLATED CASE BY ANY MEANS. MANY LETTERS ON THIS TOPIC WERE SENT TO MOVIE MAGAZINES AND TABLOIDS. "IT'S TRUE THAT IF AMERICANS FEARED LIBERATED WOMEN, THERE WERE SURELY NONE MORE FRIGHTENING THAN THESE RICH, YOUNG, PROMISCUOUS STARS" WROTE JOURNALIST ANDREW HEISEL FOR JEZEBEL.COM. "FAN MAGAZINES FREQUENTLY REPORTED THEIR ANTICS AND NOTED HOW MUCH THEY DESERVED A GOOD SPANKING IN REWARD, AND FANS IN TURN WROTE TO SAY WHO THEY WOULD LIKE TO TURN OVER THEIR KNEE."

"This will show you I can take matters into my own hands!"

THE MESSAGE IN EVERY SINGLE SEQUENCE, WITHOUT EXCEPTION, IS THAT THESE WOMEN HAVE IT COMING TO THEM, AND THE BLOWS THAT RAINED DOWN ON THEIR PROTRUDING HEINIES WERE ALL THE MORE FORCEFUL IF THEY WERE PORTRAYED AS BEING HARD AND DOMINANT AT A TIME WHEN SOCIAL MORES WOULD HAVE EXPECTED RESPECTFUL, GRACEFUL, LADY-LIKE SUBMISSION FROM THEM. IN THE MOVIES THESE SCENES WERE ALL ABOUT TEACHING A LESSON VIA HUMILIATION. THE WOMAN IS ALWAYS SHOWN AS BEING UPPITY, BACK-TALKY, UNFEMININE, OR LACKING IN RESPECT FOR OTHER PEOPLE -- IN PARTICULAR, MEN.

TAKE KATHARINE HEPBURN IN 1949'S ADAM'S RIB. SHE MADE A CAREER OUT OF PLAYING MOUTHY BITCHES, SO WHEN SPENCER TRACY'S RUGGED AND MACHO CHARACTER WENT AHEAD AND LAID HER ON A MASSAGE TABLE AND BRUISED UP HER BISCUITS, AUDIENCES OF THE DAY PRACTICALLY STOOD AND CHEERED. THEY REACTED AS IF THEY HAD BEEN WAITING TO SEE THIS PUNISHMENT FOR TWO DECADES, AND PERHAPS THEY HAD. "I'D LIKE TO SPANK HER FOR HER

AN OLD-FASHIONED SPANKING WITH SCREAMS, SQUEALS, AND THEN HEARTFELT SOBS!

ATTITUDE TOWARD FANS," A FORMER ACQUAINTANCE OF HEPBURN WROTE TO A CELEBRITY RAG IN 1934. HER CHARACTER'S FURIOUS REACTION IN THE FILM ONLY TITILLATED THEM ALL THE MORE. "YOU HIT ME!" SHE STORMED. "AS THOUGH YOU THOUGHT YOU HAD THE RIGHT!"

THE MAINSTREAM POPULARITY OF THIS SHIT GOT SO OUT OF HAND, THAT FOR A TIME, PHOTOGRAPHS OF SPANKING BETWEEN MALE AND FEMALE LEADS OF A PICTURE WERE OFTEN TAKEN ON SET TO PROMOTE A FILM - EVEN WHEN THEY DIDN'T EVEN TAKE PLACE DURING THE RUNTIME OF THE FILM ITSELF! I MEAN, HONESTLY - IT'S CLEAR THAT PORNOGRAPHY DESPERATELY NEEDED TO BE LEGALIZED, ALREADY.

IT'S IMPORTANT TO NOTE THAT ALL-TOO-OFTEN THE SPANKER -- THE HUSBAND OR BOYFRIEND -- IS MEANT TO BE A SURROGATE FATHER. IN COW-CATCHER'S DAUGHTER (1931), A FATHER TIRES HIMSELF OUT SPANKING HIS DAUGHTER OVER "50 TIMES", FINALLY DECLARING THAT HE'S REALLY GLAD SHE'LL SOON HAVE A HUSBAND TO TAKE OVER PATERNAL RESPONSIBILITIES. THE MESSAGE WAS ABUNDANTLY CLEAR: WOMEN WERE NOTHING BUT GROWN UP LITTLE GIRLS, PASSED IN OWNERSHIP FROM FATHER TO HUSBAND, AND WOULD NOT PROPERLY BEHAVE IF THEY WERE NOT KEPT IN LINE. TO 'SPARE THE ROD SPOILS THE CHILD', AND SPANKING WAS A WAY OF RECLAIMING THE NEW LIBERATED WOMAN BY INFANTILIZING HER.

BEFORE SEXUAL LIBERATION AND SECOND WAVE FEMINISM IN THE MID-TO-LATE '60S, POLITE SOCIETY WAS MUCH MORE OPEN TO AT LEAST CONSIDERING THE POSSIBILITY THAT SPANKING ADULT WOMEN WAS NOT ONLY ACCEPTABLE, BUT NEEDED. JUDGES CONTINUALLY RULED IN FAVOUR OF THE SPANKER IN THE FEW CASES THAT ACTUALLY MADE IT TO COURT, AND ADVICE COLUMNISTS CONTINUALLY RETURNED TO THE TOPIC THROUGHOUT THE 1940S AND '50S. DOROTHY DIX FAMOUSLY DECLARED THAT "BAD WIVES ARE JUST AS MUCH THEIR HUSBANDS' FAULT AS BAD CHILDREN ARE THEIR PARENTS", AND FREQUENTLY RAN LETTERS FROM WOMEN CLAIMING THEY WERE SAVED FROM THE DEPRESSED LIFE OF THE "MISERABLE DIVORCEE" BY A TIMELY SPANKING. IT WAS SIMPLY ANOTHER WAY THAT OLD FASHIONED CONSERVATIVE VALUES WERE EXPRESSED IN A GOD-FEARING SOCIETY.

THE SEXUAL DYNAMIC OF SPANKING IS CLEAR AND OBVIOUS, BUT I THINK THE FETISHIZATION COMES FROM THE FACT THAT SO MANY OF US ARE PHYSICALLY DISCIPLINED AS CHILDREN, AND I SAY THAT EVEN IN THIS MODERN ERA WHEN SO MANY MORE PEOPLE FROWN ON SPANKING AS A MEANS OF TRAINING CHILDREN OR CORRECTING THEIR BAD BEHAVIOUR. A STUDY DONE IN 2010 FROM THE UNIVERSITY OF NORTH CAROLINA AT CHAPEL HILL, INDICATES THAT 80 PERCENT OF CHILDREN AGES 3 TO 5 YEARS ARE SPANKED, AND ANOTHER PROMINENT STUDY BY ELIZABETH GERSHOFF OF COLUMBIA UNIVERSITY REPORTED THAT MORE THAN 90 PERCENT OF AMERICANS WERE SPANKED AS CHILDREN.

THAT'S A BUILT-IN AUDIENCE FOR DEPICTIONS OF POWER-PLAY, AND I HAVEN'T EVEN GOTTEN INTO HOW HUGELY POPULAR IT IS IN THE UK. SPANKING FETISHISTS HAVE STRENGTH IN NUMBERS, AND IN PARTICULAR SIMPLY ADORE THE OCEAN-SIDE WALLOPING THAT ELVIS PRESLEY DISHES OUT ON A 20-YEAR-OLD (HER CHARACTER IS 16) JENNY MAXWELL IN BLUE HAWAII (1961). AND I'LL TELL YOU PRECISELY WHY.

"YOU KNOW WHAT YOU NEED?" A STERN-FACED ELVIS SAYS TO THE SOBBING BLONDE AFTER BEING FACED WITH AN EMOTIONAL OUTBURST AFTER SAVING THE UPSET GIRL FROM DROWNING. "A GOOD OLD FASHIONED SPANKING".

"MAYBE I DO" SHE SAYS WHILE WEEPING. "NOBODY EVER CARED ENOUGH ABOUT ME, EVEN FOR THAT." AND WITH THAT HE GRABS HER AND WHACKS THE SHIT OUT OF HER ASS WHILE THE SPOILED GIRL IN HER PINK PARTY DRESS WAILS. SHE REALLY DOESN'T LOOK LIKE SHE'S WEARING PANTIES UNDER THERE, AND THE 15 SMACKS WE SEE LAND SQUARELY ON A FRESH-OUT-THE-OCEAN ASS, WHICH ANY SPANKING FETISHIST WILL TELL YOU IS 10X MORE DELICIOUSLY PAINFUL THAN BEING HIT ON A DRY HEINIE.

SHE'S SHOWN IN CLOSE-UP AS SITTING ON TWO CUSHIONS THE

YALE STUDENT SPANKED WIFE

WIFE SPANKING UPHELD BY COURT IF IT ISN'T CRUEL

SPANKING WITH HAIR BRUSH NOT BEATING WIFE, JUDGE RULES

JUDGE ORDERS WIFE SPANKED

105 WALLOPS
Tired of Spankings, Wife Asks for Divorce

NEXT DAY. THIS GETS ACROSS THE POINT THAT WHAT WE SAW WAS EXACTLY WHAT WE THOUGHT WE SAW: A HARDCORE THRASHING AND NOT JUST A FEW TOKEN SWATS. WHILE IT ISN'T SPOKEN OF IN POLITE CONVERSATION, ALL 6 OF THE OTHER PEOPLE AT THE BREAKFAST TABLE SEEM TO KNOW PRECISELY WHAT HAS TRANSPIRED -- WE SUPPOSE BECAUSE OF HER LOUD YELLING DURING HER BEACHFRONT BEATING.

WHEN JENNY SNEEZES, HER TEACHER SAYS "I HOPE YOU DIDN'T CATCH A HEAD COLD LAST NIGHT." TO WHICH JENNY REPLIES WITH A CUTE SMIRK "NO, MAAM. JUST THE OPPOSITE". JENNY IS CLEARLY THANKFUL FOR HER TRANSFORMATIVE EXPERIENCE - AND THAT A MAN CARES ENOUGH TO BEAT HER. THERE IS NO PRIVACY FOR THIS GIRL, AND SHE'S MADE TO TELL EVERYONE ABOUT WHAT THEY HEARD WITH A KNOWING GLANCE EXPRESSING GRATITUDE TO THE MAN WHO ADMINISTERED IT. IT'S SO FUCKING CRAFTY HOW VANILLA IT ALL IS ON A SURFACE LEVEL, WHILE ALSO UNDERPINNING AS AN ENTIRELY SEXUALIZED BDSM FETISH-FEST. WHAT SHE'S DONE IS THE VERBAL VERSION OF TURNING AROUND, LOWERING HER PANTIES, LIFTING HER SKIRT AND SHOWING THE RED MARKS THAT PROVE SHE'S BEEN PROPERLY CORRECTED. EVERYONE AT THE TABLE SEEMS PLEASED.

IN REAL LIFE, HOWEVER, MR "DON'T BE CRUEL" COULDN'T EVEN BRING HIMSELF TO SPANK HIS YOUNG DAUGHTER, LISA MARIE. ELVIS LOVED THEM TENDER, BUT APPARENTLY DIDN'T LOVE TO TENDERIZE. "THE ONE TIME HE DID, IT DIDN'T EVEN HURT, BUT I WAS JUST HEARTBROKEN THAT HE DID IT", SHE TOLD ENTERTAINMENT TONIGHT IN 2003. "HE FELL APART. HE COULD NEVER DISCIPLINE ME AFTER THAT." HE'D TRIED TO RUN AWAY FROM HOME AT AGE 4 AFTER HIS FATHER SPANKED HIM, AND HE VOWED HE WOULDN'T MAKE THE MISTAKE OF HURTING HIS OWN CHILDREN.

THAT'LL TEACH YOU!

IN CLASSIC-ERA HOLLYWOOD, THERE WAS HARDLY A BIG NAME ACTOR THAT DIDN'T BEAT THE BUTTOCKS OF A FEMALE IN AT LEAST ONE OF HIS PICTURES, IF NOT MORE. WILLIAM POWELL SPANKED MYRNA LOY IN AFTER THE THIN MAN (1936), FREDRIC MARCH SPANKED CAROLE LOMBARD IN NOTHING SACRED (1937), GUY MADISON SPANKED A 17-YEAR-OLD SHIRLEY TEMPLE IN HONEYMOON (1947), JOHN CARROLL SPANKED SUSAN HAYWARD IN HIT PARADE (1943), HOWARD KEEL SPANKED KATHRYN GRAYSON IN KISS ME KATE (1953).

IT MAY NOT SIT WELL WITH AUDIENCES TODAY, BUT FROM THE BEGINNINGS OF CINEMA RIGHT UP THROUGH THE 1960S, A GOOD HARD SPANKING WAS JUST A ROUTINE PART OF AN AMERICAN BIG SCREEN ROMANCE.

BUT DON'T JUST TAKE MY WORD FOR IT. GO ON AND MAKE A VISIT TO INFORMATIVE WEBSITES LIKE MAINSTREAMSPANKING.WORDPRESS. COM OR SPANKINGART. ORG AND YOU'LL START TO REALIZE THAT SPANKING THROUGHOUT HOLLYWOOD HISTORY HAS BEEN EXHAUSTIVELY CATALOGED AND ARCHIVED BY SPANKING NERDS ONLINE. ONE SITE HAS 615 ON-SCREEN SPANKING LISTINGS IN THEIR DATABASE -- AND THAT ISN'T EVEN INCLUDING ALL THE SPANKING ON CLASSIC TV OR THE MANY SCENES FROM KINKY ADULT MOVIES.

-ROBIN BOUGIE · 2019·

HOW ABOUT SOME RANDOM TRIVIA?

AT ONE POINT IN 1975'S LIFESPAN, (DIRECTED BY SANDY WHITELAW) TINA AUMONT IS PUT INTO SOME "DNA HELIX" BONDAGE AS PART OF A SEX SESSION WITH DR. LAND. MANY BONDAGE ENTHUSIASTS BELIEVE THIS IS THE VERY FIRST APPEARANCE OF ELABORATE JAPANESE SHIBARI BONDAGE IN A MAINSTREAM WESTERN FILM.

VALERIE PERRINE BECAME THE FIRST WOMAN TO DISPLAY HER NIPPLES ON PURPOSE (THERE WERE PRIOR TO THIS A COUPLE ACCIDENTAL NIP-SLIPS) IN AN AMERICAN-MADE TELEVISION SHOW DURING THE 4 MAY 1973 US BROADCAST OF A TV MOVIE CALLED STEAMBATH, WHICH AIRED ON PBS' HOLLYWOOD TELEVISION THEATER. IN THE SCENE, VALERIE PERRINE IS SEEN TAKING A SHOWER. ONLY A FEW STATIONS WERE ADVENTUROUS ENOUGH TO ACTUALLY AIR IT.

MARY TYLER MOORE ONCE TOLD DAVID LETTERMAN IN ONE OF HER APPEARANCES ON HIS LATE NIGHT TALK SHOW THAT HER NICKNAME FOR DICK VAN DYKE WHEN THEY WERE MAKING THE DICK VAN DYKE SHOW TOGETHER IN THE EARLY 1960S, WAS "PENIS VON LESBIAN".

MICHAEL KEARNS, WHO IS CREDITED AS "MALE PORN STAR" IN HIS BIT PART IN DE PALMA'S BODY DOUBLE (1984) ACTUALLY STARRED IN THE GAY PORN THEATRICAL FEATURE L.A. TOOL & DIE (1979). DE PALMA AND THE CASTING DIRECTOR DID NOT KNOW THIS WHEN THEY GAVE HIM THE ROLE, BUT THEY FOUND OUT SOON AFTER.

PORSCHE LYNN

"I WAS USUALLY ABLE TO ORGASM EASILY, ON OR OFF-CAMERA" REDHEADED AND FRECKLED VINTAGE PORN STAR PORSCHE LYNN WRITES IN HER RECENT AUTOBIOGRAPHY THAT DOCUMENTS HER YEARS IN XXX.

"I CAN'T SAY THAT I DID EVERY SINGLE TIME, BUT WHEN I COULDN'T GET OFF IT WAS USUALLY DUE TO EXTREME SET CONDITIONS. FOR INSTANCE, MAKING PORN IN THE CALIFORNIA DESERT WITH BLAZING TEMPERATURES IN THE 100'S, WITH SAND BLOWING INTO EVERY ORIFICE, EATING A CUP OF SAND WHILE YOU GIVE A BLOWJOB. THOSE ARE CONDITIONS THAT MAKE IT NOT SO EASY TO GET OFF. SOMETIMES IT WAS JUST AN UNCOMFORTABLE POSITION, LIKE HAVING SEX IN THE KITCHEN SINK OR HANGING FROM A POLE. SOMETIMES IT WAS JUST THE END OF A LONG DAY, CALL TIME 7 A.M. AND FINALLY DOING YOUR DOUBLE PENETRATION SCENE AT 2 AM? FUCK, YOU HAVE GOT TO BE KIDDING ME! ALL I CAN SAY IS, THANK GOD I DIDN'T HAVE TO GET MY COCK HARD."

IN AUGUST 2014, ON THE EVE OF THE RELEASE OF THAT BOOK (ENTITLED THE GIRL WITH THE MILLION DOLLAR LEGS) I INTERVIEWED PORSCHE, A MEMBER OF THE ADULT MOVIE HALL OF FAME. HERE'S WHAT WAS SAID:

ROBIN BOUGIE: HEY, PORSCHE LYNN! THANKS FOR TALKING WITH ME. SO, LETS GET RIGHT INTO IT. YOU STARTED IN ADULT MAGAZINES AND DOING STRIPPING IN 1983, AND THEN BEGAN IN ADULT MOVIES IN 1985. AND I SAY MOVIES HERE, BUT THIS WAS WHEN SHOT-ON-VIDEO WAS JUST TAKING OVER THE INDUSTRY FROM SHOT-ON-FILM. XXX RELEASES WERE MADE QUICKER AND FOR FAR LESS MONEY, AND LESS AND LESS PEOPLE WERE WATCHING ADULT MOVIES IN PUBLIC IN THEATERS, AND FAR MORE IN THE PRIVACY OF THEIR OWN HOMES. BEING THERE AT THE BEGINNING OF A NEW ERA FOR SMUT, WHAT SORT OF MEMORIES COME TO MIND?

PORSCHE LYNN: IT IS A VERY UNIQUE TIME IN PORN. BY 1985 THE VIDEO REVOLUTION WAS COMPLETELY ON, AS IN: GAME ON! PORN IS, WAS AND WILL ALWAYS BE DRIVEN BY TECHNOLOGY. EVERY TIME THE TECHNOLOGY OF DELIVERING A PICTURE, ESPECIALLY A MOVING PICTURE WITH SOUND, IS IMPROVED, PORN WILL CHANGE TO ACCOMMODATE IT AND THAT'S EXACTLY WHAT HAPPENED WHEN VIDEO HIT XXX FILMS. FOR THE FIRST TIME PORN WAS BEING DELIVERED TO THE PRIVACY OF YOUR HOUSE, TELEVISION, WHERE YOU COULD ENJOY IT, OVER AND OVER AGAIN IF YOU WANTED.

RB: OH, I WANTED.

PL: HAHA! I CAN'T TELL YOU HOW MANY PEOPLE WORE OUT THEIR REWIND OR PAUSE BUTTONS ON THEIR VHS PLAYER! WE HAD AN INTIMATE CONNECTION WITH THE FANS; THEY KNEW WHAT WE WORE IN OUR LAST MOVIE, WHO WE LIKE TO WORK WITH AND WHO WE DIDN'T LIKE TO WORK WITH. WE WERE LIKE A FAMILY, WHO SAW EACH OTHER A COUPLE OF TIMES OUT OF THE YEAR, AT CONVENTIONS, USUALLY IN VEGAS & CHICAGO.

RB: AND THE CONVENTIONS ARE WHERE YOU WOULD MEET YOUR FANS.

PORSCHE, WITH ANGEL KELLY'S TIT BETWEEN HER ASSCHEEKS.

PL: YES. THE FANS WERE EXCITED BECAUSE THEY WERE MEETING THEIR FAVORITE PORN STARS, WHO THEY HAD JUST WATCHED ON TV THE NIGHT BEFORE. AND THE PORN STARS WERE EXCITED BECAUSE WE WERE MEETING PEOPLE WHO ACTUALLY WATCHED OUR MOVIES AND WHO THOUGHT WE WERE MOVIE STARS.

RB: IT'S AN EGO STROKE FOR BOTH PARTIES.

PL: YES IT IS. WE ALL ENJOYED A RATHER INTERESTING FORM OF FAME. I WAS VERY LUCKY WITH THE TIMING OF MY XXX DEBUT. I MADE MY FIRST MOVIE, DECEMBER 1985. LIKE YOU SAID, VIDEO/VHS WAS JUST STARTING TO GO CRAZY. XXX-VHS TAPES WERE SELLING FOR $99.99 AND PEOPLE WERE BUYING THEM LIKE STARBUCKS COFFEE. VHS DECKS WERE STILL KIND OF EXPENSIVE BUT THEY WERE COMING DOWN IN PRICE EVERY YEAR. PORN WAS LITERALLY EVERYWHERE IN AMERICA; YES, THERE WERE STILL SOME STATES THAT DIDN'T WANT IT AND TRIED IN VAIN TO KEEP IT OUT. THE MOVIE PRODUCERS WERE STILL COMING FROM A FILM MENTALITY, EVEN THOUGH THE SHOOTING TIME WAS MUCH SHORTER, THEY WERE STILL USING WRITTEN SCRIPTS, MAKEUP & WARDROBE PEOPLE, CATERERS, ETC, AND TREATING THE SHOOT AS IF IT WAS BIG BUDGET. SHOOTING ON FILM COULD COST UP TO $750,000.00 WHILE SHOOTING ON VIDEO COULD COST YOU $60,000.00. THE PRODUCTION COMPANIES WERE CRANKING OUT THE PRODUCT. THERE WAS ABOUT 20 COMPANIES THAT RELEASED ANYWHERE FROM 2-6 TITLES A MONTH. NOWADAYS THEY PROBABLY RELEASE THAT IN AN HOUR.

RB: YEAH. THAT'S A LOT OF CONTENT. SO YOU GOT A LOT OF WORK. BONERS SWOOPING IN FROM EVERY DIRECTION.

PL: A PORN STAR COULD WORK AS MUCH AS THEY WANTED, SOMETIMES TWICE A WEEK. I WAS BLESSED TO WORK WITH SOME WONDERFUL MEN AND WOMEN, LIKE JOHN LESLIE, NINA HARTLEY, SHARON MITCHELL, JAMIE GILLIS, ERICA BOYER AND SO MANY MORE. IT WAS A WONDERFULLY MAGICAL TIME.

PETER NORTH KISSES ASS.

RB: THOSE ARE SOME OF MY PERSONAL FAVES THAT YOU JUST MENTIONED. TERRIFIC PERFORMERS. WHICH DIRECTORS DID YOU LIKE TO WORK WITH?

PL: FRED LINCOLN, BRUCE SEVEN & HENRI PACHARD WERE SOME OF MY FAVORITES TO WORK WITH. THEY WERE ALL VERY RELAXED AND EASY GOING ON A SET. THEY WERE ALL VERY SUPPORTIVE OF THEIR VARIOUS PERFORMERS. THEY ALL HAD INTEGRITY, EXPERTISE AND WISDOM WHICH ALWAYS FLAVORED THEIR MOVIES. I ALWAYS KNEW THAT I WAS IN GOOD HANDS WHEN I WORKED WITH ANYONE OF THESE DIRECTORS. LATER ON I GREW TO LOVE JOHN STAGLIANO AS A DIRECTOR; BEING AN ACTOR HIMSELF, HE HAD COMPASSION FOR THE PERFORMERS AND HE KNEW HOW TO BE SUPPORTIVE OF THE PROCESS.

RB: WHO WAS THE HARDEST TO WORK WITH? ANY PRIMA-DONNAS?

PL: I HONESTLY DO NOT REMEMBER ANY DIRECTORS THAT I DID NOT ENJOY WORKING WITH. I WAS ALWAYS TREATED WITH PROFESSIONAL RESPECT AND DIGNITY BY EVERYONE ON A SET, INCLUDING THE DIRECTOR.

RB: THAT'S GOOD TO HEAR. SPEAKING OF DIGNITY, HAVE YOU EVER HAD A BAD EXPERIENCE WITH THE PUBLIC BECAUSE OF YOUR JOB WORKING IN THE ADULT INDUSTRY?

PL: IN ALL HONESTY YES, BUT NOT THAT OFTEN. I HAVE EXPERIENCED THE OCCASIONAL COMMENTS LIKE 'WE DON'T CATER TO PEOPLE LIKE YOU.' IN THE LATE '80S, WE WOULD HAVE THE EXPERIENCE OF WALKING THROUGH THE RELIGIOUS PICKET LINES TO ENTER AN EVENT LIKE XRCO AWARDS. THERE WOULD

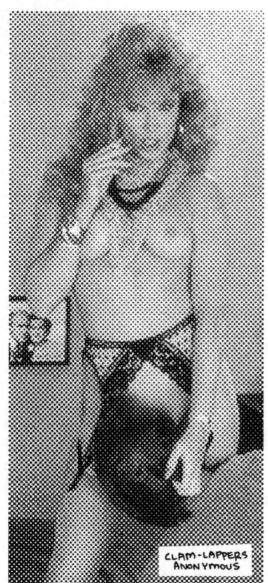

CLAM-LAPPERS
ANONYMOUS

BE PEOPLE WITH THEIR SANDWICH BOARDS ON DISPLAYING SIGNS THAT SAID THINGS LIKE, 'PORN IS A HIGHWAY TO HELL, PORN STARS WILL ROT IN HELL, REMOVE PORN FROM THE PLANET', ETC. THESE PEOPLE WERE VERY VOCAL AND SOMETIMES THEY WOULD THROW ROTTEN VEGETABLES. THEY WOULD BE SHOUTING AT US AS WE WALKED INTO THE VENUE, SO IT WAS MORE MENTALLY CHALLENGING THAN ANYTHING.

RB: DAMN. WHAT ABOUT WHEN YOU WERE WORKING AS A STRIPPER OR DOING BURLESQUE? NO ROTTEN FRUIT THEN, I HOPE.

PL: I DID HAVE ONE EXPERIENCE MANY YEARS AGO, ABOUT 1992. I WAS PERFORMING IN HOUSTON, TEXAS AT A WELL-KNOWN CABARET. I ARRIVED ON SUNDAY EVENING, PLACED MY LUGGAGE IN THE DRESSING ROOM OF THE CLUB AND TOOK A QUICK TOUR OF THE CLUB. ON MONDAY MORNING, I RECEIVED A CALL FROM THE OWNER OF THE CLUB SAYING, 'MISS LYNN WE HAVE HAD A TERRIBLE ACCIDENT AT THE CLUB, YOU MUST COME IN RIGHT AWAY.' AS I ARRIVED AT THE CLUB, THE TERRIBLE ACCIDENT BECAME OBVIOUS, THE BEAUTIFUL CABARET HAD BEEN SET ON FIRE.

RB: HOLY SHIT.

PL: IT STOOD A SHADOW OF ITSELF, HALF BURNED, CHARRED; SPRAY PAINTED ON THE OUTSIDE OF THE BUILDING WERE STATEMENTS LIKE, 'PORN STAR GO HOME, WE DON'T WANT PORN HERE'. THIS WAS A WAKE UP FOR ME. PERSONALLY, I KNEW THAT MANY PEOPLE FELT THIS WAY, I JUST NEVER THOUGHT THEY WOULD DO SOMETHING SO DESTRUCTIVE TO MAKE THEIR POINT. BURNING DOWN A BUSINESS JUST TO HURT ME OR STOP ME FROM WORKING SEEMED POINTLESS. THEY WERE REALLY HURTING ALL OF THE LOCAL PEOPLE WHO WORKED IN THE CLUB, THE BARTENDERS, WAITRESS, DJ'S AND OTHER STAFF. IT JUST SEEMED LIKE SUCH A WASTE.

RB: YEAH, THAT'S JUST IDIOCY. AND CRIMINAL IDIOCY ON TOP OF THAT! SO YOU DID A BOOK WITH BRIAN WHITNEY THAT WAS PUBLISHED BY BEAR MANOR CALLED THE GIRL WITH THE MILLION DOLLAR LEGS. DID YOU HAVE SOMETHING IN PARTICULAR THAT YOU WANTED TO GET ACROSS TO THE READER?

PL: I DON'T KNOW THAT I HAD A CONSCIOUS MESSAGE THAT I WANTED TO GET ACROSS BUT I AM CERTAIN THAT THE BOOK DOES DELIVER SEVERAL MESSAGES. I HAD WANTED TO WRITE A BOOK ABOUT MY WONDERFUL LIFE FOR MANY YEARS BUT KEPT PUTTING IT OFF. THE RIGHT TIMING OPENED UP ABOUT A YEAR AGO SHORTLY AFTER TURNING 51 YEARS OLD. I SAT DOWN AND PUT MY LIFE IN BURLESQUE, PORN AND KINK ON PAPER, OR MORE ACCURATELY ON COMPUTER. MY FIRST INTENT WAS TO SIMPLY GET MY STORY OUT, IN MANY WAYS, A WALK OR RECAPITULATION OF GRATITUDE THROUGH MY LIFE. VERY PERSONALLY HEALING. I ALSO HAD LISTENED FOR MANY YEARS TO DIFFERENT PEOPLE IN THE ADULT BIZ WHO TOLD WOEFUL TALES OF THEIR EXPERIENCES, FROM CHILDHOOD TO XXX-STARDOM. IT WAS OFTEN TOLD AS THE 'POOR ME: THE VICTIM OF CIRCUMSTANCE' PERSPECTIVE. AND THAT MAY VERY WELL HAVE BEEN TRUE FOR THEM, BUT MY EXPERIENCE WAS COMPLETELY DIFFERENT.

RB: YEAH, I'VE HEARD A FEW STORIES HERE AND THERE LIKE THAT. COMPLAINTS ABOUT BEING EXPLOITED BY LADIES LIKE LINDA LOVELACE, STACY DONOVAN, PENNY FLAME, AND SHELLEY LUBBEN.

PL: I NEVER ALLOWED MYSELF TO BE EXPLOITED. ANYTIME I WOULD SNIFF OUT AN INDIVIDUAL THAT LACKED INTEGRITY, I WOULD SIMPLY NOT WORK WITH THEM. I HAVE NEVER FOUND PORN FOR THE MOST PART TO BE DEGRADING TO WOMEN. MY STORY WAS ONE OF EXPLORATION, EVOLUTION, EMPOWERMENT, SELF-RESPONSIBILITY AND ULTIMATELY HEALING. I GUESS I WANTED PEOPLE TO KNOW THAT THERE ARE DIFFERENT STORIES THAN THE ONES THEY MAY BE ACCUSTOMED TO HEARING. I WAS NEVER A VICTIM OF PORN, I NEVER FELT DEGRADED OR EXPLOITED, NOT ONCE. I ACCEPTED THE JOBS, WITH MY EYES WIDE OPEN AND WITH FULL AUTONOMY OF MY ACTIONS AND I HAD A WONDERFUL TIME. I GUESS THAT'S THE REAL MESSAGE.

RB: THAT'S A STORY THAT NEEDS TO BE HEARD TOO, ESPECIALLY BY PEOPLE WHO DON'T KNOW ANYTHING ABOUT THE INDUSTRY, AND ALWAYS SEEM TO ASSUME THE WORST ABOUT IT. WHAT IS SOMETHING PEOPLE CAN FIND IN THIS BOOK THAT THEY MIGHT NOT HAVE KNOWN ABOUT YOU BEFORE?

PL: THAT I AM A VERY PRAGMATIC PERSON. I AM SUPER SARCASTIC, AND SOMETIMES DOWNRIGHT FUNNY.

RB: AND WHAT MOTIVATED YOU TO WRITE AN AUTOBIOGRAPHY?

PL: HONESTLY? OLD AGE AND DEATH.

RB: YEAH, THAT WOULD DO IT. SO IN THE MID '90S YOU SWITCHED FORM BEING A VANILLA PORN STAR TO GETTING INVOLVED WITH FEM-DOM STUFF WHERE YOU DOMINATE GROVELING SLAVES. IS THAT SOMETHING THAT STEMS FROM YOUR OWN SEXUAL INTERESTS?

PL: I MOVED FROM VANILLA SEX FILMS TO BDSM IN ABOUT 1992-ISH. TO BE HONEST WITH YOU, I WAS GETTING REALLY BORED WITH THE VANILLA SEX BIZ. THE HEALTH ISSUES WERE RISING, THE MOVIES WERE MOVING INTO GONZO TYPE SHOOTING WITH THE A DIRECTOR YELLING JUST GIVE ME A COUPLE OF POSITIONS AND A POP SHOT, SO WE CAN FINISH THIS THING. NOW THAT'S REALLY HOT, RIGHT? NO, I WAS BORED LOOKING FOR SOMETHING TO LIGHT THE FIRE BETWEEN MY LEGS AGAIN.

RB: BOREDOM WAS THE CULPRIT?

PL: I KNOW TO MANY OF YOU IT SEEMS IMPOSSIBLE THAT ANYONE WOULD GET BORED MAKING XXX-MOVIES, BUT IT WAS TRUE. THERE IS ONLY SO MANY TIMES YOU CAN FUCK ON THE HOOD OF A CAR, GET GANG BANGED BY 3 MEN AND 3 WOMEN AT THE SAME TIME, AND SO ON. AT THAT TIME I HAD ABOUT 7 YEARS INTO THE XXX BIZ, SO CALL IT THE 7-YEAR ITCH. AT THE TIME I HAD SEVERAL FRIENDS THAT WERE INTO BDSM, WHO WERE INVITING ME TO PARTIES AND CLUBS. I WILL NEVER FORGET THE FIRST TIME I WALKED INTO THE HELLFIRE CLUB IN NYC. I FELT LIKE I HAD FOUND A MAGICAL WORLD. EVERYTHING WAS KINKY AND UNUSUAL, THE CLOTHES, THE FURNITURE, THE PEOPLE. IT CREATED A SENSATION BETWEEN MY LEGS AND IN MY MIND, WHICH IS WHERE ALL THE SEXUAL DOORS MUST OPEN FIRST. SO, YES, MY GOING INTO BDSM WAS SPAWNED FROM MY OWN DESIRES AND INTERESTS.

RB: OK, COOL. AND WHAT SORT OF TRAINING AND LEARNING GOES INTO TAKING ON A NEW ROLE LIKE THAT?

PL: THERE IS A FAIRLY RIGOROUS TRAINING PROCESS THAT GOES INTO LEARNING TO PLAY SAFE, SANE AND CONSENSUAL IN THE SCENE. THERE IS A LOT OF PHYSICAL TRAINING TO USE THE EQUIPMENT, AND

LOOKING MORE LIKE ILSA AS THE YEARS GO BY...

PORSCHE AS A DOMINATRIX AT THE AGE OF 50.

EXPERIENCING AND FEELING. I WAS TRAINED VERY OLD SCHOOL, FIRST LEARNING TO BE A SUBMISSIVE BEFORE EVER BEING ALLOWED TO BE A DOM. THE ADVANTAGE TO THIS IS THAT ONE LEARNS HOW THE FEELING OF POWER EXCHANGE AFFECTS THEM EMOTIONAL, MENTALLY, PHYSICALLY, SPIRITUALLY, AND SEXUALLY. THE OLD SAYING THAT 'YOU DON'T KNOW HOW IT FEELS UNTIL YOU'VE DONE IT' IS CERTAINLY TRUE. I QUITE ENJOYED BEING SUBMISSIVE, ALL I HAD TO DO IS SURRENDER AND ENJOY THE EXPERIENCE. THE DOM WAS THE ONE WHO HAD TO DO EVERYTHING. I HAD SEVERAL MENTORS, APPRENTICE GUIDES, FRIENDS, LOVERS, SLAVES, SUBMISSIVE AND MASTERS WHO TAUGHT ME MANY THINGS ALONG THE WAY, WHICH IS PROBABLY THE MAIN REASON THAT I AM STILL ACTIVE IN THE SCENE TODAY.

RB: GREAT! IS THERE ANYTHING YOU WOULD LIKE TO PROMOTE ASIDE FROM THAT BEFORE WE SIGN OFF AND GO OUR SEPARATE WAYS?

PL: YES, AS A MATTER OF FACT... I OWN AND OPERATE THE DEN OF INDOMITUS, LOCATED IN PHOENIX, ARIZONA, WHERE I INVITE YOU TO VISIT THE CAVE OF THE UNTAMED/UNCONQUERABLE. READERS CAN REACH ME AT MISTRESLYN@AOL.COM AND AT **WWW.DOIAZ.COM**

CLASSIC PORN'S MISSING FISTING
WHERE DID IT GO?

FIST-FUCKING EMERGED AS A SEX PRACTICE POPULARIZED BY GAY MALE SUBCULTURE IN THE LATE 1960S, WITH SOME HISTORIANS SURMISING THAT IT MAY NOT HAVE EXISTED IN ANY WIDESPREAD CAPACITY UNTIL THE TWENTIETH CENTURY. SEX EDUCATOR, ROBERT MORGAN LAWRENCE, HOWEVER, BELIEVES THE PRACTICE DATES BACK THOUSANDS OF YEARS. EVEN THOUGH YOU WON'T SPOT THEM ON THE HISTORY CHANNEL ANYTIME SOON, THERE ARE ROMAN FRESCOES THAT CLEARLY ILLUSTRATE THE PRACTICE.

I DO REMEMBER FOR MANY YEARS FISTING, FOOTING AND STUMPING WAS BANNED IN CANADA (WHERE I LIVE) IN PARTICULAR, UNTIL THEY REMOVED IT FROM THEIR "OBSCENE" LIST IN AUGUST OF 2003. THEIR DEFINITION OF FISTING UP UNTIL THAT POINT WAS 4 FINGERS OR MORE INSERTED INTO A BODY CAVITY AT ONCE, AND OF COURSE ONCE THAT THUMB WENT IN THERE IT WASN'T EVEN UP FOR DEBATE. I DID NOT GET MUCH JOY FROM HAVING MY MAIL OPENED, AND MOVIES I'D ORDERED DESTROYED, BUT I DID ALWAYS LIKE TO IMAGINE CENSORS WORKING AT CANADA CUSTOMS, SITTING THERE WATCHING SMUT AND COUNTING FINGERS LIKE FOOLS.

"A CLENCHED FIST SALUTE" TO ONE OF THE TRUE ORIGINATORS -- SHAUN COSTELLO'S LOVE BUS.

AWW YEAAH

I'VE NEVER BEEN FISTED OR FISTED ANYONE ELSE, BUT SOME OF MY FRIENDS HAVE AND WHEN I'VE ASKED THEM ABOUT IT, THEY'VE NOTED THAT ONCE SOMEONE IS INSIDE YOU IN THAT WAY, THEY DON'T EVEN REALLY NEED TO PUMP OR THRUST. "FIST FUCKING" IS A MISNOMER FOR THE MOST PART, BECAUSE FOR ALL BUT THE MOST EXTREME PRACTITIONERS, THERE ISN'T MUCH NEED FOR ACTUAL FUCKING. THE SHEER INTENSITY OF STRETCHING YOURSELF WIDE OPEN ENOUGH TO LET ANOTHER PERSON DEEP INSIDE YOUR BODY IS MORE THAN ENOUGH STIMULATION.

"NO, FISTING WILL NOT MAKE YOUR PUSSY LOOSE," COURTNEY TROUBLE WROTE ON HER BLOG IN 2011, AS SHE WAS ADDRESSING ONE OF THE BIGGEST CONCERNS SHE HEARS ABOUT IT FROM WOMEN. "YOUR VAGINAL WALLS WILL STRETCH ONLY ENOUGH TO FORM TIGHTLY AROUND THE HAND INSIDE IT -- AND ONCE THE FISTING IS OVER, YOUR MUSCLES WILL GRIP QUICKLY, LIKE IMMEDIATELY GO BACK TO WHERE THEY WERE BEFORE. I CAN USUALLY GRIP ONE FINGER FIRMLY ABOUT A MINUTE AFTER BEING FISTED... IT'S MY FAVOURITE KIND OF SEX TO HAVE WITH MY BOYFRIEND."

IN THE US OF A, FISTING HAS BEEN SORTA LINGERING IN A LEGAL GRAY AREA. IT'S NEVER BEEN SPECIFIED AS OBSCENE UNDER THE LAW, BUT IT DID SHOW UP IN AN INFAMOUS ADULT INDUSTRY MEMO NOW KNOWN AS THE "CAMBRIA LIST" IN 2000.

KY

'YOLO' FOR FISTING SOLO!

124

THIS WAS A LIST FROM INFAMOUS LOS ANGELES LEADING FIRST AMENDMENT LAWYER, PAUL CAMBRIA, DETAILING XXX NO-NOS THAT COULD FEASIBLY TRIGGER OBSCENITY CHARGES IN THE WAKE OF THE ELECTION OF ONE GEORGE W. BUSH. THIS WAS A PRESIDENT WHO, DURING HIS INITIAL CAMPAIGNING, NOTED THAT ERADICATING OBSCENITY WOULD BE HIS MAIN JOB AS LEADER OF THE FREE WORLD -- THAT IS UNTIL TERRORISTS BROUGHT DOWN THE WORLD TRADE CENTER IN SEPTEMBER 2001 AND GAVE HIM AND HIS REPUBLICAN LEADERSHIP A WHOLE OTHER FOCUS.

THE DISASTER IN MANHATTAN TOOK THE HEAT OFF AMERICAN SMUT PEDDLERS TO SOME DEGREE, BUT IT DIDN'T PUT THEM IN THE CLEAR. EVER SINCE THEN PORNOGRAPHERS HAVE HAD THEIR LAWYERS TELLING THEM TO STAY AWAY FROM FISTING, AND THE FEW THAT HAVE IGNORED THIS ADVICE HAVE PUT THEIR COCKS AND TITS ON THE CHOPPING BLOCK.

IN 2002, SEYMORE BUTTS WAS SUCCESSFULLY PROSECUTED FOR DEPICTIONS OF VAGINAL AND ANAL FISTING IN A TERRIFIC SCENE BETWEEN ALISHA KLASS AND NOTED SQUIRTER CHLOE. THIS WAS IN SEYMORE'S DVD TAMPA TUSHY FEST PART 1. FISTING WAS ALSO PART OF THE OBSCENITY CHARGES THAT LANDED PERVERT PROVOCATEUR MAX HARDCORE IN PRISON IN 2009.

IRONICALLY, SOME OF THE SAME COMPANIES THAT WON'T SHOOT FISTING FOR FEAR OF BEING BUSTED DO SHOOT STUFF LIKE: DOUBLE ANAL PENETRATIONS, AND WILD PENETRATIONS FEATURING GIANT TOYS THAT ARE FAR BIGGER THAN A PERSON'S FIST. BUT A HAND? THEY WON'T DO IT BECAUSE OF THE HISTORY OF PORNOGRAPHERS BEING BUSTED FOR IT.

THAT SHOULDN'T BE TOO MUCH OF A SHOCK, THOUGH. MOST CENSORSHIP AND LIMITATION OF WOMEN'S REPRODUCTIVE RIGHTS IS CLEARLY HETERONORMATIVE AND PATRIARCHAL IN CONTEXT. FISTING IS A SEX ACT THAT DOESN'T REQUIRE A PENIS, AND CAN BE DONE BY PERFORMERS OF ALL GENDERS, AND THAT HAS ITS ROOTS IN GAY AND LESBIAN SEXUALITY. THAT MAKES IT RIPE FOR CENSORSHIP. "FAG STUFF" IS GROSS AND INDECENT IN THE EYES OF LEGISLATORS, AND ALWAYS HAS BEEN.

JIZ LEE AND THE AFOREMENTIONED COURTNEY TROUBLE FOUNDED INTERNATIONAL FISTING DAY IN 2011, WHEN TROUBLE'S PRODUCTION COMPANY SHOT A PORN VIDEO WHERE LEE WAS FISTED BY VETERAN SMUT LEGEND NINA HARTLEY. BUT WHEN TROUBLE BEGAN EDITING THE RELEASE, SHE FOUND HERSELF IN A DISPUTE WITH HER DISTRIBUTORS. THEY WERE CONCERNED THAT AN EXPLICIT FISTING WOULD LEAD TO AN OBSCENITY LAWSUIT.

"MAINSTREAM PORN COMPANIES RARELY SHOOT VAGINAL OR ANAL FISTING. THIS CENSORSHIP IS SELF-IMPOSED AND COMES STRAIGHT FROM ADULT INDUSTRY LAWYERS" TRISTAN TAORMINO NOTED IN 2011. "WHEN I SHOT THE EXPERT GUIDE TO ADVANCED ANAL SEX, I DECIDED TO SHOOT SOME ADDITIONAL FOOTAGE. AFTER WE SHOT THE "WORKSHOP" PORTION OF THE MOVIE (WHERE I GIVE LESSONS ON ANATOMY, HYGIENE, LUBE, TOYS, TECHNIQUES, ETC.), I SHOT A LITTLE BIT OF ME TALKING ABOUT ANAL FISTING. THEN, WHEN I SHOT THE SCENE WITH KYLIE IRELAND AND JAMES DEEN, I DECIDED I WOULD SHOOT A LITTLE EXTRA. IT SEEMED PERFECT. I MEAN, KYLIE LOVES ANAL FISTING. SHE DOES IT IN HER PERSONAL LIFE, SHE HAS ORGASMS FROM IT, AND SHE SPEAKS ARTICULATELY AND ALSO QUITE ENTHUSIASTICALLY ABOUT IT ON CAMERA. DURING THE SCENE, THEY GOT TO FIVE-FINGERS-BUT-NOT-QUITE-FISTING. I DIDN'T SHOOT THE WHOLE 'HAND-CHILADA,' BECAUSE I, TOO, COULD BE AT RISK OF PROSECUTION."

FFFFUUHH

GRONK HHULL

YOU CAN TELL BY THE CARNAL ANIMAL NOISES THAT IT IS GOING WELL!

BUT PRIOR TO ALL OF THIS LEGAL MESS, THE HETERO PORN INDUSTRY HAPPILY PRODUCED FISTING PORN FOR A DECADE OR SO THROUGHOUT THE 1970S AND EARLY 1980S, UNAWARE OF WHAT WAS TO BE CONSIDERED OBSCENE IN THE FUTURE. THIS HAS MEANT THAT

WHAT HAPPENS WHEN A BROTHER AND A SISTER BREAK THE ULTIMATE TABOO?

FIREWORKS WOMAN

Starring
SARAH NICHOLSON

MUCH OF THIS CONTENT HAS BEEN NOW ALTERED, WITH MOST FISTING SCENES REMOVED AND DESTROYED. SUCH A GOOD JOB HAS BEEN DONE IN THE DVD/BLU AGE OF CENSORING THIS STUFF, THAT MANY PORN FANS DON'T EVEN REALIZE THAT MANY OF THEIR FAVOURITE VINTAGE XXX EVEN HAD FISTING.

WELL, HERE'S A TASTE OF WHAT YOU'RE MISSING: THE LOST FISTING FOOTAGE OF CLASSIC PORN.

LOVE BUS (1974)
ALLEGEDLY THE FIRST FISTING SCENE IN FEATURE-LENGTH THEATRICAL PORN HISTORY. THIS WAS SOMETHING OF A LOST ONE UNTIL IT WAS PRESERVED IN ITS ENTIRETY BY VIDEO-X-PIX ON THEIR RECENT DVD RELEASE. THIS SCENE IS PLAYED FOR LAUGHS -- WITH JAMIE GILLIS DOING A SCENE WITH RITA DAVIS. HER FRENZIED MANTRA OF "I WANT YOUR WHOLE ARM UP ME" IS ONE THING, BUT THEN HE GETS HIS HAND STUCK. CUE THE KNEE-SLAPS! THERE ARE A HANDFUL OF OTHER FILMS THAT HAVE RECENTLY HAD THEIR LOST FISTING SCENES FINALLY REINSTATED, SO I WON'T BOTHER WITH THEM AND WILL INSTEAD FOCUS ON THOSE THAT REMAIN MIA IN THE FOLLOWING LISTINGS.

THE FIREWORKS WOMAN (1975)
THE UNCUT VERSION OF THIS MOVIE HAS BEEN REPORTEDLY LOST FOR SOME TIME. THE LONE XXX RELEASE BY HORROR DIRECTOR WES CRAVEN,

THERE IS SAID TO BE A PRINT OR TWO REMAINING BUT NO ONE SEEMS TO HAVE THE BALLS TO RELEASE IT TO DVD, ALTHOUGH A CENSORED BOOTLEG VERSION IS FLOATING AROUND WHICH I NABBED. JENNIFER JORDAN AND HELEN MADIGAN'S FISTING SCENE IS NOT THE ONLY THING CUT. THERE'S ALSO A MISSING FISH INSERTION, URINATION, AND A RAPE THAT TAKES PLACE ON A WHARF.

DEVIL'S PLAYGROUND (1976)
NOT TO BE CONFUSED WITH THE FRED SCHEPISI FILM WITH THE SAME TITLE, AND FROM THE SAME YEAR. WE GET WHAT SEEMS TO BE THE REMNANTS OF A FISTING SCENE, HERE. ODDBALL KELLY GUTHRIE (AS LUCIFER) STICKS 4 FINGERS INTO BONNIE HOLIDAY, BUT WE DON'T SEE HIM GO PAST THE KNUCKLES. IT'S JUST WAY TOO MUCH BUILDUP HERE FOR A SCENE THAT DIDN'T HAVE SOME KIND OF FISTING, SO I'M LEFT TO ASSUME THERE ORIGINALLY WAS FULL INSERTION FOOTAGE THAT HAS SINCE BEEN DUMPED.

STORY OF ELOISE (1976)
PORN HISTORIAN JIM HOLLIDAY ONCE CALLED THIS "THE LONGEST FIST SCENE ON RECORD". BOBBY ASTYR SPENDS A FULL FIVE MINUTES WITH HIS FIST IN THE GREASED-UP COOCH OF AN UNCREDITED BLONDE GIRL WHO NEVER SEEMS TO HAVE SHOWN UP IN ANYTHING EVER AGAIN. INFAMOUSLY GROUCHY IMDB PORN REVIEWER "IOR" SURMISES THAT SHE'S PROBABLY A GIRL THAT DIRECTOR SHAUN COSTELLO PICKED UP OFF THE STREET FOR THE FILM, AND WHEN I ASKED HIM ABOUT IT, HE AGREED THAT WAS PROBABLY THE CASE.

LITTLE ORPHAN DUSTY (1978)
THIS ONE FEATURES THREE FISTING SCENES. THE SCENE WHERE MING JADE FISTS RHONDA JO PETTY ON AN OL' MOTORCYCLE IN THE DESERT DURING A RAPE BY SOME DIRTY BIKERS, A SELF-FISTING SCENE THAT RHONDA JO PETTY DOES, AND ANOTHER WHERE JOHN HOLMES FISTS HER ON THE COUCH. SHE PLAYS A RUNAWAY THAT GETS CONTINUALLY TAKEN ADVANTAGE OF, AND GETTING YOUR HANDS ON AN UNCUT VERSION WAS REALLY HARD FOR A GREAT MANY YEARS. YEAH, EVENTUALLY VCX PUT OUT AN 84 MIN VERSION ON DVD IN 2002 WHICH HAD ALL THREE FISTING SCENES, BUT THE QUALITY IS SO LOUSY I'M STILL CONSIDERING THIS LOST TO SOME DEGREE UNTIL SOMEONE PUTS OUT A PROPER EDITION.

LOVE COUCH (1978)
"SOME PEOPLE THINK THERE WAS A CUT ASHLEY BROOKS BATHTUB SELF-FISTING SCENE FROM MY MOVIE

IT'S HOTTER THAN HELL

HEAVENLY DESIRE

starring
SERENA
JOHNNIE KEYES
introducing **SEKA**
guest starring
JAMIE GILLIS

COLOR

X

TINSELTOWN", PORN DIRECTOR CARTER STEVENS TOLD ME IN 2016. "I DON'T KNOW WHERE THAT COMES FROM. THERE NEVER WAS ONE. BUT IN MY MOVIE LOVE COUCH, HOWEVER, THERE WAS. FLUFFY LA BUSCHE HAD A FISTING SCENE IN THAT MOVIE WHICH WAS CUT OUT IN MANY VIDEO TAPE VERSIONS."

CANDY STRIPERS (1978)
TWO OF THE MOST NOTORIOUS FISTING SCENES COME IN THIS MOVIE. FIRST WE HAVE ROCK STEADY FISTING HIS GIRLFRIEND, AMBER HUNT. AND THEN LATER WE HAVE THE SMALL AND LITHE NANCY HOFFMAN PUTTING BOTH OF HER FISTS INTO EILEEN WELLES AT THE SAME TIME! BOTH SCENES APPEARED IN THE 2002 ARROW DVD RELEASE OF THIS MOVIE, BUT OTHERWISE HAS BEEN EDITED OUT IN EVERY OTHER HOME FORMAT VERSION UP TO NOW. YOU CAN ACCESS THEM ON THE MAIN MENU BY HIGHLIGHTING "PLAY MOVIE", AND THEN PRESSING THE FOLLOWING KEYS: RIGHT, DOWN, RIGHT, LEFT, AND ENTER. WHEN RETAILERS FOUND OUT ABOUT THIS EASTER EGG, MANY OF THEM PULLED IT OFF THE SHELF.

HEAVENLY DESIRE (1979)
MOST VERSIONS OF HEAVENLY DESIRE ARE MISSING PART OF THE SERENA/HILLARY SUMMERS AND DANI WILLIAMS SCENE IN WHICH SERENA STICKS FIVE FINGERS INTO SUMMERS AND FIVE FINGERS INTO WILLIAMS AT THE SAME TIME. THIS CUTE DUAL FISTING SCENE WHERE SERENA WEARS HER CO-STARS LIKE A PAIR OF MITTENS DID SHOW UP IN THE EARLIEST VHS VERSION OF THE MOVIE, AND THEN WENT MISSING IN EACH SUBSEQUENT VERSION. THE PLOT OF THIS IS PRETTY WICKED. JOHNNY KEYES PLAYS A PIMP FROM THE NETHERWORLD, WHO DEAD PROSTITUTES (SEKA AND SERENA) MUST APPEASE BEFORE HE'LL ALLOW THEM TO ENTER INTO HELL.

MS. MAGNIFICENT (AKA SUPERWOMAN 1979)
JESSIE ST. JAMES AND SHARON KANE HAVE A FISTING SCENE TOGETHER, BUT IT'S ONLY SHOWN OBSCURED IN A MEDIUM SHOT. THE EXPECTED CLOSEUPS OF THIS TABOO ACT ARE MISSING IN ACTION.

TAXI GIRLS (1979)
"I SAW TAXI GIRLS IN A PUSSYCAT THEATRE HERE IN LA WHEN IT CAME OUT IN 1979", A READER BY THE AKA OF MONOHAN, REPORTED. "TAKES PLACE IN A SEX SCENE IN A JAIL. ONE OF THE BABES GOT FISTED AND MY REACTION AT THE TIME WAS: 'WHY WAS THAT DONE? AND, BOY, IT MUST HURT'. THEN WHEN IT WAS AVAILABLE ON VIDEOTAPE, I RENTED IT BECAUSE I WAS IN LOVE WITH MS. NANCY SUITER (WHEREVER SHE MAY BE) AND NOTICED THAT THE FISTING ELEMENT WAS NO LONGER THERE." THE LOST FISTING SCENE WAS BETWEEN NANCY HOFFMAN AND HILLARY SUMMERS.

NEVER A TENDER MOMENT (1979)
THIS 29-MINUTE MITCHELL BROTHERS RELEASE PLAYED IN THEIR THEATER CHAIN ON A DOUBLE BILL WITH ANOTHER 30-MINUTE DOC CALLED BEYOND DE SADE. WHO NEEDS AN EXTENDED RUN TIME WHEN YOUR SELLING POINT IS THE FAMOUS MARILYN CHAMBERS DOING CRAZY, KINKY S&M SHIT? THIS ENTERTAINING DOCUMENTARY (WITH AN OVER-THE-TOP JAZZ SCORE) DOCUMENTED ONE OF THE WILD LIVE SEX SHOWS CHAMBERS WOULD DO FOR HER FANS IN THE "ULTRA ROOM" AT THE O'FARRELL THEATER IN

SAN FRANCISCO, WHICH IS STILL THERE EVEN TODAY. THIS SHOW FEATURED MISS CHAMBERS GETTING HER ASS, TITS AND PUSSY BEATEN BY A COUPLE OF MEAN, FOXY LESBIANS (ERICA BOYER AND TARA ROBINSON), ONE OF WHICH IS A BLACK GIRL IN A WHITE WIG THAT DILDOS AND THEN FISTS MARILYN'S PUCKERED POOP CHUTE. LATER INTERVIEWED ABOUT THE SESSION, CHAMBERS DULY NOTED THAT "PEOPLE SAY 'ARE YOU JUST ACTING?' WELL YOU CAN'T ACT WHEN YOU'VE GOT A FIST UP YOUR BUTT." THIS MOVIE HAS NEVER SEEN A HOME FORMAT RELEASE ASIDE FROM A RARE VHS EDITION.

BOO FANTASY LANE (1979)
ONLY THE FIRST VHS VERSION BY COLLECTOR'S VIDEO HAS THE SCENE WITH DESIREE COUSTEAU SHOVING ALL FIVE OF HER PRETTY FINGERS INTO LOVELY, LITHE SERENA -- A SCENE THAT TAKES PLACE EARLY ON IN THIS FEATURE. CAL VISTA'S VERSION HAS THE SAME RUNNING TIME AS THAT OF THE UNCUT VERSION -- BUT THAT SHIT IS VERY MISLEADING. THEY'VE SPLICED OUT THE OFFENDING MATERIAL AND PADDED THE SCENE IN QUESTION WITH REPEAT FOOTAGE TO RE-ESTABLISH THAT ORIGINAL RUN TIME. SNEAKY ASSHOLES THOUGHT NO ONE WOULD NOTICE... PPFFT! SADLY, EVEN THE EXPENSIVE, FANCY REMASTERED WILD SIDE DVD EDITION IS THAT DAMN EDITED VERSION. DANG NABBIT.

FANTASY (1979)
POINTY-NOSED JANE LINDSAY LIGHTLY SPANKS SHARON KANE'S ASS WITH A HAIR BRUSH, LICKS HER BUTTCHEEKS, AND THEN THE TWO LEZ OUT FOR AWHILE, HAPPILY LAPPING CLAMS. IF YOU'RE UNLUCKY ENOUGH TO OWN THE EDITED VERSION, THAT'S WHERE THE SCENE ENDS, BUT SOME TAPES HAVE EXTENDED FOOTAGE WHERE LINDSAY SHOVES SOME PEARLS IN KANE'S BOX, PULLS THEM OUT WITH HER TEETH, AND THEN PROCEEDS TO FIST THE DICKENS OUT OF HER BLONDE HAIRPIE FOR ABOUT 3 MINUTES. GERARD DAMIANO KNEW WHAT HE WAS DOING.

TIGRESSES (1979)
AT ONE POINT DURING THE 30-MINUTE-LONG ORGY SCENE THAT VANESSA DEL RIO STARS IN, HER CO-STAR JANE LINDSAY LAYS HER DOWN ON A BED AND PASSIONATELY FISTS HER WHILE MICHEAL GAUNT FLICKS HIS PENIS AT HER NIPPLES. SHE REALLY GETS INTO IT.

BUT THAT FOOTAGE IS GONE FROM ALL OF THE MODERN RELEASES OF THIS FEATURE. "VANESSA DEL RIO'S FISTING SCENE IS NO BIG DEAL", TRIPLE-XXX FAN MARMAC1 STATED IN HIS 2005 RAME REVIEW, CAUSING ME TO WONDER IF HE HAD ACTUALLY EVEN EVER SEEN IT. "I DOUBT SHE COULD FEEL MUCH", HE SNIPED. "SHE'S GOT THE BIGGEST PUSSY I'VE SEEN IN ALMOST 30 YEARS OF WATCHING PORN FLICKS." ODDLY ENOUGH, THE REAL LIFE LESBIAN INCEST SCENE IN THIS, FEATURING THE SLOAN TWINS, ISN'T CENSORED. YOU WOULD THINK THAT WOULD BE THE MORE TABOO ACT, BUT WHAT DO I KNOW?

INSATIABLE (1980)
A MEMORABLE ENCOUNTER FOR BOTH WOMEN, SERENA FISTED MARILYN CHAMBERS IN THE SWIMMING POOL SCENE, BUT AT THE LAST MINUTE IT WAS CUT FROM THE MOVIE BEFORE IT WAS RELEASED. "A FIST IS ABOUT TO PLUNGE INTO MY PUSSY AND THEN THE FILM CUTS," MARILYN COMPLAINED TO SWANK MAGAZINE IN 1981. "THE ATTORNEYS FELT IT WOULD BE TOO HOT. (FISTING) REALLY TURNS COUPLES OFF. A WIFE DOESN'T WANT TO HAVE TO PROVE THAT SHE CAN DO SOMETHING LIKE THIS AT HOME."

PLATINUM PARADISE (1981)
IN A MEMORABLE SCENE FEATURING ERIC EDWARDS AND VANESSA DEL RIO

MISTER, YOU CAN CALL ME MISS FISTER!

HA HA!

GOOSH!

THERE IS A NOTICEABLE CUT. ERIC IS FINGERING MISS VANESSA, AND THEN IT SWITCHES KINDA SUDDENLY TO FOOTAGE OF INTERCOURSE WITH THE MUSIC ON THE SOUNDTRACK ALREADY IN PROGRESS. NOW, ACCORDING TO MANY SOURCES WHAT WE MISSED HERE WAS A FISTING SCENE THAT GOT CUT, ALTHOUGH WHEN ERIC HIMSELF WAS ASKED ABOUT IT, HE COULD NOT RECALL HAVING FISTED DEL RIO.

SATISFIERS OF ALPHA BLUE (1982) MOST PRINTS OF THIS ONE ARE CENSORED. BILL MCKEAN (THE GUY FROM PANDORA'S MIRROR AND TWILITE PINK THAT DRIES VERMEULEN LIKED TO CALL "WEASLEY LOOKING") FISTS TIFFANY CLARK WHO LOOKS HIGH AS SHIT. ANOTHER SCENE FROM SATISFIERS THAT ALWAYS GETS CUT IS ANNIE SPRINKLE IN THE ACT OF SPRINKLING ALL OVER A GUY BEFORE SHE STUFFS A DILDO IN HIS BUMHOLE.

WORLD PREMIERE
The **CHERYL LADD**
Look·Alike
OUI Cover Girl
NANCY SUITER stars in
TAXI GIRLS X

also starring **JOHNNY WADD**
SERENA   NANCY HOFFMAN
Adults Only

10:00, 11:40, 1:05, 2:50, 4:30, 5:55, 7:40, 9:20, 10:45, 12:30 Late Show Fri. & Sat.

SWEETHEART'S
CIRCUS CINEMA
THE GREATEST ADULT SHOWS ON EARTH!
B'way at 49th St. 489-9290

SWEETHEART'S
EAST **WORLD** 59th ST
59th St. E. of 3rd Ave. 688-1717

PEEPHOLES (1982)
THIS GREAT AND OVERTLY SLEAZY VINCE BENEDETTI MOVIE IS HARD TO FIND IN GENERAL FOR SOME REASON, NEVER MIND FINDING IT UNCUT. BOBBY ASTYR HAS A SCENE WHERE HE FISTS THE VAGINA OF GINGER JAYE (PLAYING "READY ROSIE"), AND FROM WHAT I HEAR, HE ALSO KILLS HER. FISTING IS ONE THING, BUT MIXING IT WITH VIOLENCE IS THE ULTIMATE NO-NO. WHEN IT PLAYED IN THEATERS, ADULT CINEMA REVIEW NOTED THAT: "ASTYR'S CHARACTER IS ANGRY, WOMAN-HATING, AND WILL STOP AT NOTHING TO DEFILE THEM. THE BRUTAL FIST-FUCK MURDER SCENE AT THE FILM'S END IS NOT FOR THE SQUEAMISH -- NOR IS IT EROTIC IN ANY SENSE -- BUT IT IS A FINE PIECE OF ACTING."

—BOUGIE · 2016·

◆ THE MUTHERS ◆

(1976 Dir: Cirio Santiago)

AFTER CO-PRODUCING SEVERAL OF JACK HILL'S EXCELLENT WOMEN-IN-PRISON FEATURES (THE BIG DOLL HOUSE, THE BIG BIRD CAGE, AND WOMEN IN CAGES), WHICH PRODUCER ROGER CORMAN SET IN THE PHILIPPINES TO GET THE MOST BANG FOR HIS BUCK, FILIPINO FILMMAKER CIRIO SANTIAGO THEN PICKED UP THE MANTLE AND STARTED PUTTING HIS OWN ENTRIES IN THE GENRE ON CELLULOID. THIS BEGAN WITH THE VERY FUN EBONY, IVORY AND JADE, AND THEN PARLAYED ON INTO THIS MOVIE, THE MUTHERS.

WHAT I LOVE ABOUT THE MUTHERS IS THAT IT'S ONE OF THE VERY FEW TIMES -- NOT ONLY IN EXPLOITATION AND BLAXPLOITATION HISTORY, BUT FILM HISTORY IN GENERAL -- WHERE WE AS AN AUDIENCE ARE PRESENTED WITH FOUR BLACK FEMALE STARS IN A MOVIE, WHO ARE UNDENIABLY STRONG CHARACTERS. FINDING A MOVIE FROM THIS GENRE WITH THE LEAD BEING PLAYED BY AN AFRICAN-AMERICAN WOMAN NOT NAMED PAM GRIER IS RARER THAN IT SHOULD BE, AND GETTING FOUR AT ONCE IS VIRTUALLY UNHEARD OF. THESE PISSED-OFF SISTERS ARE NO SHRINKING VIOLETS, NOR DO THEY TRIP AND FALL AND NEED TO BE PICKED UP AND DRAGGED AWAY FROM DANGER BY A MAN. THEY HAVE ADVENTURES ON SEA AND ON LAND, THEY GO TOE-TO-TOE WITH WORTHY, HEAVILY ARMED ADVERSARIES, KICK SERIOUS MOTHERFUCKING ASS, AND THEY DO IT ALL ON THEIR OWN TERMS.

JAYNE KENNEDY IS "SERENA", JEANNIE BELL -- BEST KNOWN AS TNT JACKSON ("SHE'LL PUT YOU IN TRACTION!") -- IS "KELLY", ROSANNE KATON (PLAYBOY PLAYMATE OF THE MONTH FOR SEPTEMBER 1978) PLAYS "ANGIE", AND TRINA PARKS ("THUMPER" FROM DIAMONDS ARE FOREVER, AND THE STAR OF THE AMAZING DARKTOWN STRUTTERS) TURNS IN A GOOD PERFORMANCE AS "MARCIE". THESE WOMEN ROCK STEADY, AND ARE EASILY THE REASON TO CHECK THIS 1976 EFFORT OUT. NOT ONLY ARE THEY SASSY BLADE-WIELDING PIRATES WHO ROB WHITE TOURISTS ON THE ASIAN SOUTH SEAS, BUT THEY ALSO END UP IN A VILE JUNGLE PRISON/PLANTATION WHILE ON THE HUNT FOR A MISSING 16-YEAR-OLD YOUNGER SISTER OF ANGIE'S. AND OF COURSE, NO WOMEN'S PRISON MOVIE WOULD BE COMPLETE WITHOUT A VIOLENT BREAK-OUT SCENE AND A SHOWER OR TWO!

Out of the steaming slave markets come the ravaging sea-savages... The Muthers!

CIRIO SANTIAGO'S MOVIE SEEMS OVERTLY PROUD OF ITS LEADING LADIES, AS IT GRANDSTANDS THEIR PRESENCE, GRACE AND POWER-- WHICH MAKES IT ALL THE MORE CONFUSING THAT JAYNE KENNEDY WAS PORTRAYED AS WHITE ON THE ORIGINAL POSTER (WHICH WAS REUSED FOR THE DVD COVER). THIS CAN BE EXPLAINED TO SOME DEGREE BY A SCENE IN THE 2010 DOCUMENTARY MACHETE MAIDENS UNLEASHED, WHERE TRINA PARKS NOTED THAT THE ROLES WERE NOT ORIGINALLY WRITTEN TO BE FOUR BLACK WOMEN. WHEN THE POSTER ART WAS DONE, I'M BETTING THAT JAYNE'S CHARACTER WAS ACTUALLY SLOTTED TO BE PLAYED BY A REDHEAD.

I'D ALSO LIKE TO MAKE NOTE THAT THIS MOVIE CONTAINS ONE OF MY ALL TIME FAVOURITE LINES IN FILIPINO/AMERICAN EXPLOITATION FILM HISTORY. IT TRANSPIRES AFTER THE GROUP HAVE GAMELY ATTEMPTED TO ESCAPE FROM THE PRISON-PLANTATION HELL HOLE, AND ARE RESTING IN THE JUNGLE WHILE TRYING TO STAY ONE STEP AHEAD OF THEIR PURSUERS. TRINA PARKS IS THE UNFORTUNATE VICTIM OF A

THE MUTHERS

SNAKE BITE, AS A COBRA SNEAKS
UP ON HER AND LATCHES ON TO
HER TIT, INJECTING A DEADLY
PORTION OF POISON. JUST BEFORE
JAYNE KENNEDY LEANS IN TO SUCK
THE VENOM OUT OF HER ABUSED
BOOB, TRINA VOICES HER DISGUST
AT SUCH AN INTIMATE ENCOUNTER
WITH AN UNWANTED CARNIVOROUS
REPTILE: "JUST LIKE EVERY OTHER
SNAKE I EVER MET", PARKS
GROWLS. "CAN'T LEAVE MY TITS
ALONE!".

ALONG WITH PARKS, THE OTHER
REAL STAND OUT FOR ME HERE
WAS ROSANNE KATON. SHE'S
STUNNING, GETS SOME GOOD LINES,
IS ADEPT WITH KICKING
ASS/FIRING A MACHINE GUN, AND
LOOKS LIKE SHE'S HAVING A
FUCKING BLAST ALL THE WAY
THROUGH. "THE CIRIO SANTIAGO
FILMS WERE GREAT FUN", ROSANNE
TOLD DAVID WALKER IN BADAZZ
MOFO ZINE, ISSUE 5. "IT WAS VERY
EMPOWERING FOR ME. I HAD A LOT
OF FUN MAKING MOVIES. I LOVED
THE TRAVELLING... AND DOING
THESE MOVIES IN THE PHILIPPINES
I GOT ALL INVOLVED WITH FILIPINO
POLITICS. IT WAS A WONDERFUL
SORT OF CROSS-TRAINING FOR MY
POLITICAL ACTION IN THE US. IT
WAS A WONDERFUL WAY TO GET
AWAY FROM THE POLITICAL PLIGHT
OF AFRICAN AMERICANS IN THE US,

FEB. 5 1976/60¢ A JOHNSON PUBLICATION

JET

JEANNE BELL:
PIN-UP MODEL
TO FILM STAR

AND SEE WHAT WAS HAPPENING IN THE PHILIPPINES. IT GAVE ME A NEW LEASE ON HOW TO WORK MORE
EFFECTIVELY IN THE US, AND SO I ALWAYS LOOKED AT DOING A LOT OF THESE MOVIES AS A FREE
TICKET."

IT'S NOT LIKE THE MOVIE IS WITHOUT ITS FAULTS, THOUGH. THE ACTION SCENES ARE OFTEN CLUNKY,
CHARACTERS ARE WEAKLY WRITTEN (HOW ABOUT SOME INDICATION AS TO WHERE THESE WOMEN CAME
FROM AND WHY THEY DO THE THINGS THAT THEY DO?), THE PLOT MECHANICS DON'T SEEM TO WORK FROM
TIME TO TIME, AND THERE ARE SOME BASIC FILMMAKING MISTAKES. LIKE WHERE SCENES ARE LACKING AN
ESTABLISHING SHOT, AND OTHER ODDLY PACED MOMENTS WHEN IT WASN'T CLEAR WHAT HAD TRANSPIRED.
THERE WERE ALSO A FEW SLOPPY SPOTS WHERE THINGS NEEDED DESPERATELY TO BE EDITED DOWN TO
MAKE THINGS A LITTLE MORE LEAN AND MEAN. NONE OF THESE WERE DEAL BREAKERS FOR ME (AND
QUITE FRANKLY MOST FANS OF VINTAGE EXPLOITATION CINEMA ARE RATHER USED TO IGNORING THESE
TYPES OF ERRORS) BUT IT WAS FRUSTRATING TO SIT THROUGH THEM AND KNOWING THAT A FEW
TWEAKS HERE AND THERE WOULD HAVE MADE THIS A MUCH MORE SATISFYING MOVIE OVERALL. SO CLOSE,
AND YET SO FAR FROM GENRE FILM GREATNESS. HOW MANY TIMES HAVE WE SEEN THAT BEFORE, RIGHT?

ROSANNE KATON ♡

"THE MOVIE WAS MADE WITHOUT A SCRIPT!" ROSANNE
KATON REVEALED, THIS TIME IN AN INTERVIEW THAT RAN
IN THE 25TH ISSUE OF SHOCK CINEMA ZINE. "THEY SENT US
A SCRIPT, BUT WHEN WE GOT THERE THEY SAID 'WE'RE
THROWING THAT OUT'. EVERY COUPLE OF DAYS THEY'D GIVE
US SOME PAGES. WE WERE JUST TRYING TO KEEP IT
COHERENT IN OUR OWN HEADS. PEOPLE WERE THROWING IN
LINES ABOUT NAIL POLISH -- IT WAS ABSOLUTELY ABSURD.
BUT THE FUN PART WAS THE FOUR OF US RUNNING
THROUGH THE JUNGLE, AND WE HAD A REALLY GREAT TIME.
MY GIRL SCOUTS LOVED THAT MOVIE."

SPEAKING OF SUITABLE VIEWING FOR GIRL SCOUTS, IT'S
ALSO WORTH NOTING THAT THIS PICTURE IS LIGHT ON THE
SLEAZE FACTOR THAT FANS OF THE GENRE WANT TO SEE.
THERE ARE A COUPLE OF SHOWER/BATHING SCENES WHERE
JEANNIE BELL GETS TOPLESS, AND COUPLE OF SHORT TORTURE
SCENES IN THE WORK CAMP, BUT THEY ARE FLEETING -- AS
IS THE BLOOD SPILLED IN THE OTHERWISE COPIOUS ACTION
SCENES. BUT THERE ARE SOME OTHER MOMENTS THAT I
HAVEN'T REALLY SEEN IN THE GENRE, SUCH AS THE
SADISTIC VILLAIN SUBTLY REVEALED AS BEING BISEXUAL,
THE AFOREMENTIONED REVOLUTIONARY PIRACY ANGLE, THE
WILD SCENE WHERE SUDDENLY THE GIRLS ARE SWINGING
THROUGH THE JUNGLE ON VINES LIKE TARZAN, AND THE
GREAT SILLY ADVENTURE RIDE FEEL TO THE WHOLE THING.
FUN STUFF.

—BOUGIE '16

FAITH TO FAITH WITH JOEL WYNKOOP

BY ROBIN BOUGIE

IT'S BEEN A REAL "SCREWED UP WEEK" FOR STEVE, AS HE TELLS US, EMPHATICALLY..."THE VCR FRIES ITSELF, THE CABLES TURNED OFF, THE CAR BREAKS DOWN, AND TO TOP IT OFF NOW DONNA GOES MISSING!"

MO' 1980S PROBLEMS, EH STEVE? WELL, HANG LOOSE PAL, CAUSE YOU'RE THE LEAD CHARACTER IN JOEL WYNKOOP'S CHRISTIAN 1988 KUNG-FU CULT-CLASSIC, LOST FAITH, AND SHIT IS ABOUT TO GET CRAY-ZAAAY!

LOST FAITH WAS THE FEATURE LENGTH DIRECTORIAL DEBUT FOR WYNKOOP, AND JOEL ALSO STARRED, WROTE, PRODUCED, CHOREOGRAPHED THE FIGHT SCENES, WROTE THE MUSIC, AND PRETTY MUCH DID EVERYTHING ON A FILM THAT A SINGLE STRESSED-OUT GOD-FEARING PERSON CAN DO WHILE FLYING BY THE SEAT OF THEIR PANTS. BEFORE 1988 HE'D ACTED IN A FEW FILMS FOR CULT DIRECTOR TIM RITTER (TRUTH OR DARE: A CRITICAL MADNESS, KILLING SPREE), BEFORE DECIDING HE WANTED TO MAKE A FEATURE FILM ON HIS OWN SO THAT HE COULD GIVE HIMSELF A BEEFY LEAD ROLE. HEY, SOMETIMES YOU GOTTA MAKE YOUR OWN BREAKS, RIGHT?

THE MOVIE BEGINS WITH A RATHER BUXOM BLONDE LASS BEING CHASED BY SOLDIERS IN THE WOODS. A "SIMPLE KIDNAPPING" ACCORDING TO A DIRTY POLICE DETECTIVE NAMED SHIELDS -- A MAN WHO CONTINUALLY AND EMPHATICALLY "DEMANDS RESPECT". BUT WHAT IS THIS? ANOTHER BUXOM BLONDE LASS RUNNING AWAY FROM SOLDIERS IN THE WOODS! THIS MOVIE IS CHOC-FULL OF LADIES IN PERIL. SHE WON'T GET FAR THOUGH, AND IS ESCORTED BACK TO A CAMP ON AN ISLAND WHERE SHE AND A BUNCH OF VERY MULTI-ETHNIC WOMEN RESIDE AS THEY WAIT TO BE SOLD INTO A LIFE OF SLAVERY AS PORN SLUTS. DID YOU KNOW THAT PORN PERFORMERS COME FROM NEFARIOUS SLAVE CAMPS? I GUESS IT IS KIND OF LIKE AN ILLEGAL PUPPY MILL, BUT WITH MORE VAGINAS. LOST FAITH IS HERE TO EDUCATE.

"ARRANGE THE WOMEN, I WISH TO SPEAK TO THEM NOW!" YELLS A GIANT DOUCHE-NOZZLE THAT SHALL BE REFERRED TO THROUGHOUT THE REST OF THE MOVIE AS "THE MASTER". THIS IS OUR LEAD VILLAIN, AND HE'S PLAYED BY DAVID BARDSLEY, AN ACTOR WHO LIKES TO ENUNCIATE ALL OF HIS STILTED SYLLABLES AND THEN LAUGH MIGHTILY IN THE GRAND TRADITION OF MARTIAL ARTS MOVIE VILLAINS. HONESTLY, IT'S ALMOST AS IF DAVID WAS IN AN OLD SHAW BROS. MOVIE, AND HIS VOICE WAS BEING DUBBED IN BY VOICE ACTORS.

"I COULD USE AN ATTRACTIVE YOUNG LADY LIKE YOU FOR MY OWN PURPOSES," THE MASTER LEWDLY INTONES, RIGHT BEFORE SHOVING HIS TONGUE DOWN THE THROAT OF A HORRIFIED MAIDEN.

"DAVID WAS A STAGE ACTOR", JOEL WYNKOOP INFORMED ME WHEN I ASKED HIM ABOUT HIS FILM AND ITS CAST. "IT WAS HARD TO BREAK HIM FROM BEING A STAGE ACTOR, AND I FINALLY GAVE UP...IN STAGE ACTING YOU HAVE TO AMPLIFY YOUR VOICE, KIND OF THROWING IT OUT THERE AND ENUNCIATING, BUT IN THE MOVIES YOU DON'T HAVE TO DO THAT, AND IT IS VERY HARD FOR SOME STAGE ACTORS TO DO MOVIES JUST FOR THAT REASON. HE DID A GOOD JOB, BUT IF I COULD HAVE BROKE HIM OF THAT STAGE ACTING, HE WOULD HAVE BEEN MUCH BETTER."

BUT NEVER MIND ALL OF THAT -- THIS IS A MOVIE ABOUT STEVE AND HIS SHITTY, GODLESS WEEK FROM HELL. STEVE IS PORTRAYED BY WYNKOOP HIMSELF, AND HIS KIDNAPPED WIFE DONNA IS ONE OF THE MANY INNOCENT GALS THAT PATIENTLY AWAIT THEIR LIFE OF PORNOGRAPHIC SERVITUDE. STEVE IS BESIDE HIMSELF WITH RIGHTEOUS FURY UPON FINDING OUT ABOUT HER KIDNAPPING. YES, HE WANTS SOME ANSWERS, AND HE WANTS SOME ANSWERS RIGHT NOW! STEVE POINTS AT EVERYONE AGGRESSIVELY WHEN HE SPEAKS TO THEM, AND WATCH OUT BUDDY, BECAUSE HE HASN'T BEEN TO CHURCH IN WEEKS! STEVE ANNOUNCES THAT HE DOESN'T NEED TO PRAY. HE DOESN'T HAVE TIME FOR THAT.

HIS ELDERLY PAL WALT IS WORRIED ABOUT HIM AND THE RECKLESS WAY HE'S BEEN HANDING OUT

ELLEN McDUFFIE AS THE MOUTHY GANG LEADER

BOOTY-WHOOPINGS, AND HE CALLS UPON THE GOOD LORD TO SHOW STEVE THE WAY. IN FACT, WALT GETS ALL UP IN STEVE'S GRILL IN A COUPLE OF SCENES, AND JUST WON'T SHUT THE HECK UP ABOUT PRAYING AND ALLOWING GOD INTO ONE'S LIFE. SURE HE'S A NAGGING PASTOR JUST DOING HIS JOB, BUT DOESN'T WALT REALIZE THIS IS AN ACTION MOVIE? THERE ARE MANY BUTTS TO IMPLODE WITH THE FORCE OF YOUR SAVAGE KICKINGS, AND LAST TIME I CHECKED IT WAS PHYSICALLY IMPOSSIBLE TO KICK A BUTT WHEN YOU'RE KNEELING.

WHILE YOU'VE BEEN THINKING ABOUT THAT PUZZLE, STEVE HAS JUST BEING RUN OFF THE ROAD BY A GANG OF CRAZY FLORIDIAN REDNECKS THAT THINK HIS NAME IS 'THRASHER'. THESE CARTOONISH TOUGHS CALL THEMSELVES 'SATAN'S DEVIL DOGS', AND THEIR LEADER IS THE SCARIEST GODDAMN PERSON IN THIS WHOLE MOVIE. SERIOUSLY, I HAD TO PULL THE COVERS RIGHT UP TO MY CHIN WHEN I SAW THIS WOMAN. YOU WON'T BE ABLE TO TAKE YOUR PEEPERS OFF THIS WILD, WHITE-TRASH CROSS BETWEEN DEE SNIDER FROM TWISTED SISTER AND MIMI FROM THE DREW CAREY SHOW. SHE CACKLES AND MUGS LIKE A MANIAC FOR THE CAMERA, CHEWING THE SCENERY SO HARD, IT REMAINS SEVERELY CHEWED LONG AFTER STEVE UNCEREMONIOUSLY HIGH KICKS HER RIGHT IN HER PUG NOSE, SENDING HER STRINGY BLONDE HAIR SHOOTING AROUND HER GRIMACING FACE LIKE AN EXPLOSION OF CRUSTY, BUDWEISER-SOAKED FIREWORKS. IT'S A MEMORABLE DISPLAY.

"THAT WAS HELEN McDUFFIE", RECALLED WYNKOOP, FONDLY. "SHE CAME WITH HER DAUGHTER TO THE AUDITION AND I TOLD HER I WANTED HER TO TRY OUT FOR THE PART OF THE GANG LEADER, AND SHE DID. I THOUGHT SHE WAS AWESOME! LATER, AFTER THE MOVIE CAME OUT, SHE TOLD ME SHE WAS VERY EMBARRASSED AND ASKED IF I WOULD TAKE THE MOVIE OFF THE SHELVES, OR TAKE HER OUT OF IT. I COULDN'T. I WANTED HER IN THE SEQUEL (WHICH I STILL WANT TO DO) BUT WHEN I ASKED HER, SHE SAID SHE DIDN'T WANT ANYTHING TO DO WITH IT."

AFTER WE WITNESS STEVE GET INTO SOME ZANY BENNY HILL-STYLE SPED-UP CAR CHASES, WE'RE TAKEN BACK TO THE ISLAND OF LOST SOULS, WHERE THE MASTER IS LOUDLY LECTURING HIS LOWLY MINIONS ON THE PROPER CARE OF FEMALE SEX SLAVES. A GOOFY BLACK GUARD NAMED BARNES (DAVID LURRY) IS THE COMIC RELIEF -- THAT IS IF YOU THINK A CLASSIC, STEREOTYPICAL STEPIN FETCHIT CHARACTER IS FUNNY. I ESPECIALLY LIKED WHEN HE EXCLAIMED "I FELL BOSS! DIDJA SEE? I FELL RIGHT OUTTA DA TREE!" HAHAHA, OH BARNES! WILL YOU EVER WIN?

"DAVID LURRY GOT THE PART OF 'BARNES' BECAUSE HE HAD ON THE SAME KIND OF BOOTS I WAS WEARING WHEN HE AUDITIONED", WYNKOOP SAID. TALK ABOUT RANDOM. GOD WORKS IN MYSTERIOUS WAYS, I GUESS.

IN ONE OF THE MOVIE'S ODDEST SCENES, STEVE GOES BUCKWILD AND BEATS UP A RANDOM CHUBBY MIDDLE-AGED GUY IN A STRIPED SHIRT, AND THEN GETS YELLED AT BY A VERY YOUNG N' SASSY BLACK ACTRESS IN A TINY BIKINI. AFTER TEARING A STRIP OFF STEVE FOR BEING SUCH A BULLY, SHE RETURNS TO THE FAT OL' LOSER WHO IS LAYING IN THE DIRT, RUBBING HIS FLATTENED JAW.

"YOU'LL BE OK NOW, BABY BOY", SHE COOS AS SHE CONSOLES THE GROANING TUB OF GUTS. THE AUDIENCE CAN'T HELP BUT RAISE THEIR COLLECTIVE EYEBROW, CONSIDERING THIS EBONY JAILBAIT IS CLEARLY YOUNG ENOUGH TO BE HIS GRANDDAUGHTER. "WE'LL GO HOME.. AND TO CHEER YOU UP, I'LL LET YOU TAKE OFF MY BIKINI!"

"OH BOY!" HE EXCLAIMS. "SEX!"

"THAT WAS MAURICA JOHNSON", SAID WYNKOOP. "SHE WAS 13 YEARS OLD AT THE TIME. HER MOTHER HAD TO SIGN THE RELEASE." (AWKWARD)

THE LOCAL CAPTAIN OF POLICE WAS A FELLAH NAMED CHUCK JOHNSON, AND WYNKOOP TO THIS DAY FONDLY REMEMBERS WHAT A TRUE

WEIRD STRIPED-SHIRT FATSO AND HIS 13-YEAR-OLD BLACK GIRLFRIEND

HELP HE WAS TO THE MAKING OF HIS HUMBLE MOVIE. "HE WAS AWESOME", JOEL RECALLED. "HE LET ME USE HIS OFFICE, HIS GUN, HIS OFFICERS AND A PATROL CAR. THE POLICE OFFICERS EVEN TOOK MY CAST BACK TO (THE STATION) AND TOOK BOOKING PHOTOS OF THEM, AND SHOWED THEM WHAT IT WAS LIKE TO GO THROUGH THE PROCESS OF BEING ARRESTED. HE EVEN ASSIGNED OFFICERS TO ME."

NONE OF THAT SHOULD COME AS TOO MUCH OF A SURPRISE THOUGH, SINCE WYNKOOP COMES OFF AS A SWEET AND HUMBLE GUY, EVEN WHILE HIS CHARACTER STEVE IS GOING BALLS DEEP. SERIOUSLY, EVERY TIME YOU THINK THIS MOVIE IS GOING TO HIT A DEAD SPOT AND FALL INTO A LULL, WYNKOOP NUTS UP, GRABS THE BULL BY THE HORNS, AND RUNS THE RIPPING, SNORTING BEAST RIGHT INTO A DISMAYED CROWD. CASE IN POINT: A SCENE WHERE STEVE GETS REAL PISSED OFF WHILE POWER LIFTING AND THROWS THE BAR (LOADED DOWN WITH TWO MASSIVE WEIGHTS) RIGHT OUT OF FRAME!

"I BUILT THAT WHOLE SCENE AROUND WANTING TO THROW 110-POUND WEIGHTS ACROSS THE ROOM" JOEL TOLD ME. "SO I WENT TO WALMART IN FORT PIERCE AND ASKED THE MANAGER IF I COULD BORROW HIS DISPLAY, WHICH WEIGHED ABOUT FIVE POUNDS. HE LET ME TAKE IT TO USE AS LONG AS I BROUGHT IT BACK, WHICH I DID. WHEN I THREW THEM, SEAN MCCARTHY, MY ASSISTANT DIRECTOR, WAS OFF CAMERA AND HE CAUGHT THEM AND THEN PROCEEDED TO KICK MY MOM'S GARAGE DOOR TO MAKE THE SOUND OF THE WEIGHTS HITTING IT. ONLY HE PUT A DENT IN THE GARAGE DOOR, SO I HAD TO EXPLAIN THAT."

NO GUNS ARE ALLOWED AT THE DINING TABLE AT MOM'S HOUSE, AND NO GUNS ARE ALLOWED IN THIS CHUCK NORRIS FLAVOURED WORLD, EITHER. TO PROVE THAT POINT, STEVE TRIES TO BRING A HANDGUN TO THE MASTER'S ISLAND AS A TOOL TO HELP SAVE HIS WIFE. A WISE PLAN, FRANKLY, WHEN DEALING WITH EVIL BAD-GUYS -- BUT THEN SOMEONE HAS TO GO AND SAY "WHERE DID YOU GET THAT?", AND THEIR ODD MONOTONE VOICE IS ENOUGH TO STARTLE STEVE INTO DROPPING HIS PISTOL INTO TWO FEET OF WATER. THERE IT REMAINS AS HE RUNS OFF TO SAVE HIS LADY, SUBSEQUENTLY IMPOSSIBLE TO RETRIEVE FOR SOME REASON. OH WELL, I GUESS HIS FISTS OF STEEL AND HIS WHIRLING ROUNDHOUSE FACE-KICKS WILL HAVE TO SUFFICE.

YOU KNOW WHAT ELSE RULES ABOUT LOST FAITH? THE MUSIC. IF THERE EVER HAD BEEN A LOST FAITH NINTENDO GAME, THEY COULD HAVE JUST USED THE SOUNDTRACK AS IT IS. WYNKOOP REVEALED THAT IT WAS A LITTLE PLACE IN VERO BEACH FLORIDA (THAT HE FOUND WHILE HE WAS WORKING AS A BOTTLED WATER DELIVERY MAN) CALLED "TRAXX RECORDING" THAT HELPED HIM ROCK SOCKS ON THIS SCORE.

"I ASKED THEM IF THEY WOULD BE INTERESTED IN DOING SOME MUSIC", SAID JOEL. "BEFORE YOU KNEW IT THEY WERE MAKING THE SOUNDTRACK, AND I RECORDED THE SONG 'PHOTOGENIC WOMAN' IN THEIR RECORDING STUDIO".

JAM-PACKED WITH NUTTY FIST-SWINGIN' SOUND FX, THE MAJORITY OF LOST FAITH WAS SHOT IN SOUTH FLORIDA TOWNS CALLED FORT ST LUCIE AND FORT PIERCE IN 1988 -- ALTHOUGH IT WASN'T ACTUALLY RELEASED ONTO VIDEO UNTIL 1992. "RIGHT IN THE MIDDLE OF WORKING ON LOST FAITH, MY WIFE AT THE TIME HAD AN AFFAIR WITH A CO WORKER", WYNKOOP SAID. "WE GOT BACK TOGETHER AND WORKED THINGS OUT, BUT SHE WENT RIGHT BACK TO SEEING THE GUY AND WE ENDED UP GETTING A DIVORCE, WHICH JUST ABOUT KILLED ME...AT ONE POINT I GOT MY CAR UP TO 85 AND WAS GOING TO ROLL IT, BUT THE CALM VOICE OF GOD CAME OVER ME AND SAID 'EVERYTHING WILL BE ALRIGHT'. I SLOWED MY CAR DOWN. SHE WASN'T WORTH KILLING MYSELF."

"BECAUSE OF MY BREAKDOWN AND DIVORCE, ALMOST A YEAR WENT BY WITH NOTHING BEING DONE ON THE MOVIE. BY THE TIME I RECOVERED AND WAS READY TO GET BACK TO WORK, IT TOOK TIME...ONCE THE MOVIE WAS FINALLY DONE IT JUST SAT THERE TILL WE WERE ABLE TO GET TOGETHER AGAIN AND ADD SCENES THAT WE THOUGHT WERE NECESSARY. SO HERE IT WAS, ALMOST 3 YEARS LATER AND WE

STEVE NEKODA HAULS ASS IN A MUSCLE CAR

WERE RE-SHOOTING SCENES, THEN IN 1992 WE FINALLY FINISHED THE MOVIE, BUT THEN I HAD TO MAKE THE BOXES, MAKE TAPES AND START TO MARKET IT."

BUT WHAT ABOUT THE FACT THAT LOST FAITH IS SHOT ON VIDEO? WELL, THE LATE 1980S WAS THE 'DIRECT TO VIDEO' ERA -- A TIME WHEN MANY INDIE FILMMAKERS REALIZED THAT THEY COULD AFFORDABLY MAKE FILMS WITHOUT SELLING OFF THEIR HOMES TO PAY FOR INSANELY EXPENSIVE FILM STOCK AND PROCESSING, AND DID SO WITH SUPER VHS CAMERAS. FRANKLY, IT LOOKS FUCKING HORRIBLE IN COMPARISON TO FILM, BUT YOU HAVE TO ADMIRE THE BALLS-OUT, GET 'ER DONE ATTITUDE OF THOSE MEN AND WOMEN WHOSE BURNING PASSION TO GET THEIR WORK TO THE CONSUMER FOUND THEM USING WHATEVER AFFORDABLE MEANS THEY COULD MANAGE. ANYONE WHO HAS EVER COMPLETED A CREATIVE PROJECT OF ANY KIND WILL TELL YOU THAT IT IS FAR BETTER TO ACCOMPLISH SOMETHING AND NOT HAVE IT BE PERFECT, THAN TO NEVER HAVE FINISHED IT AT ALL.

THE LATE 1980S WAS ALSO A TIME WHEN LOW BUDGET INDIE FILMMAKERS GOT THE IDEA TO UTILIZE XXX STARS IN ORDER TO GET DISTRIBUTION OR FUNDING. IT WAS A WIN-WIN, USUALLY. THE GIRLS WERE TICKLED TO NOT HAVE TO SPREAD HAIR-PIE FOR A DAY'S PAY, AND THE FILMMAKERS GOT THE ONLY AFFORDABLE FAMOUS NAMES AVAILABLE TO THEM. THE MICRO-BUDGETED CANADIAN PRODUCTION, THINGS (1989) FOR INSTANCE, BROUGHT IN AMBER LYNN TO PLAY A NEWSCASTER. WYNKOOP, HOWEVER, WOULDN'T BE PLAYING THAT SINFUL GAME.

"AFTER THE MOVIE WAS FINISHED WE WERE SHOPPING IT AROUND, AND ONE GUY WANTED TO THROW MONEY INTO IT AND SHOOT NEW SCENES WITH NINA HARTLEY, THE PORN STAR. SHE WAS ALL READY TO COMMIT, BUT I TOLD THE GUY 'NO THANKS'. THAT WAS NOT WHAT I WAS GOING FOR."

"SOME ACTORS THAT I DIDN'T GIVE PARTS TO CALLED MY APARTMENT AND LEFT HATE MESSAGES ON MY ANSWERING MACHINE", WYNKOOP TOLD ME, "STUFF LIKE 'FUCK YOU ASSHOLE' AND 'YOU SHOULD HAVE HIRED ME, YOU'LL BE SORRY YOU DIDN'T GIVE ME THE PART.'" EVEN MAKING IT INTO THE FINISHED MOVIE WASN'T ENOUGH TO PLEASE SOME OF WYNKOOP'S WHITE-TRASH EXTRAS. "ONE OF THE GIRLS IN THE MOVIE THREATENED TIM AND I", HE ALLEGED. "SHE SAID SHE WAS GOING TO KILL BOTH OF US, AND BLOW UP OUR HOUSES."

WHEN I ASKED JOEL ABOUT THE BUDGET UTILIZED, HE SIMPLY SAID THAT THE THINGS HE NEEDED TO SHOOT WERE PAID FOR WITH WHATEVER SPENDING MONEY HE HAD SITTING AROUND THAT DAY. "(IT WAS) BASICALLY NOTHING. MY CAMERAMAN PUT UP THE TAPES AND HIS CAMERA AND TIME...ALL THE ACTORS WORKED FOR FREE, AND IF I ABSOLUTELY HAD TO BUY SOMETHING IT CAME FROM MY POCKET. THE BIGGEST THING WAS I HAD TO BORROW $3,000.00 FROM MY MOM TO GET THE ART WORK DONE AND MADE INTO THE BOXES, BUT I MADE THAT MONEY BACK IN TWO WEEKENDS JUST DRIVING FROM VIDEOSTORE TO VIDEOSTORE, MOST PLACES WOULD BUY 6 COPIES, BECAUSE EVERYONE WAS COMING INTO THE STORES ASKING FOR IT. I SO CAREFULLY RELEASED IT AT THE SAME TIME I WAS DOING ARTICLES AND INTERVIEWS IN THE LOCAL PAPER, AND TV APPEARANCES. BY THE TIME I WALKED INTO THE STORES, THEY WERE SAYING 'WE'LL TAKE SIX COPIES!'. IT WAS GREAT!"

REGARDLESS OF YOUR OWN PERSONAL FAITH OR IF YOU THINK THIS FILM IS ANY GOOD OR NOT, YOU JUST CAN'T HELP BUT ROOT FOR IT. ORDER A PIZZA AND WATCH LOST FAITH WITH SOME FRIENDS, AND JUST TRY TO KEEP YOUR FISTS FROM PUMPING AND YOUR TOOTSIES FROM HIGH-KICKING. TO BE AGAINST IT IS NOT UNLIKE BEING MAD AT AN ADORABLE WET KITTEN WHO JUST SNEEZED, BECAUSE DESPITE ITS TECHNICAL AND BUDGETARY LIMITATIONS, LOST FAITH SIMPLY CANNOT BE LABELED AS A "BAD MOVIE". THERE IS NOTHING BORING OR UNMEMORABLE ABOUT IT, AND WHAT JOEL WYNKOOP'S MOVIE LACKS IN PRETENSION OR CLASS, IT MAKES UP FOR WITH BOUNDLESS ENERGY AND HEARTFELT EARNESTNESS. THERE IS A TRUE HONESTY ABOUT THIS SHOT-ON-VIDEO PRODUCTION THAT ENDEARS IT TO EVEN THE MOST BITTER AND JADED CINEASTES.

AND BESIDES...WHO HASN'T HAD A "SCREWED UP WEEK"? BEEN THERE AND DONE THAT, MAN! WHOOP THEIR ASSES AND LET GOD SORT IT OUT!

-BOUGIE

SYLVIA

The real horror story behind
THE GIRL NEXT DOOR (2007)
and
AN AMERICAN CRIME (2007)

THE MORNING AFTER I SAW 2007'S THE GIRL NEXT DOOR (WHICH WAS A NEW RELEASE TO DVD AT THE TIME) I WROTE THIS LIVEJOURNAL ENTRY: "HOLY CRAP, THAT WAS THE MOST GENUINELY DISTURBING MOVIE I HAVE SEEN IN YEARS. I ACTUALLY HAD TROUBLE SLEEPING LAST NIGHT BECAUSE OF IT -- AND I DON'T REMEMBER THE LAST TIME THAT HAPPENED TO THIS JADED HORROR FAN."

IT'S NOT SO MUCH THAT THE MOVIE IS GRAPHIC, IT'S THE CONCEPT OF WHAT YOU'RE SEEING THAT REALLY HITS YOU WHERE YOU HURT. WE'VE ALL BEEN YOUNG, AND REMEMBER WHAT IT WAS LIKE TO FEEL HELPLESS AND AT THE MERCY OF THE ADULTS WHO HAD FULL CONTROL OF US. WE ALL REMEMBER WHAT IT WAS LIKE TO BE BULLIED BY OUR PEERS. THE GIRL NEXT DOOR TAPS INTO WHAT MAKES THOSE THING SCARY, AND THE END RESULT IS A CHILLING STUDY IN UNDERAGE MOB MENTALITY, CROSSING LORD OF THE FLIES WITH LAST HOUSE ON THE LEFT.

THE STORY IS BASED ON THE GENUINELY STARTLING AND DEPRESSING NOVEL OF THE SAME NAME BY JACK KETCHUM, WHICH IS ONE OF THE MOST HARROWING HORROR NOVELS IV'E EVER READ. IT, IN TURN, IS BASED DIRECTLY ON THE NEARLY UNFATHOMABLE TRUE STORY OF WHAT HAPPENED TO A 16-YEAR-OLD GIRL WHO LIVED IN INDIANAPOLIS IN THE 1960S NAMED SYLVIA LIKENS.

THE FILM STARS A YOUNG BLYTHE AUFFARTH IN THE ROLE OF SYLVIA (HERE NAMED "MEG"), AND SHE'S REALLY DECENT. I REMEMBER THINKING AT THE TIME OF THAT FIRST VIEWING THAT EVEN THOUGH SHE'D ONLY DONE SOME SMALL ROLES ON TV UP TO THAT POINT, THIS WOULD LIKELY BE THE FIRST IN MANY NOTEWORTHY FILMS FROM THIS TEENAGE ACTRESS. SADLY THAT HASN'T BEEN THE CASE. THE MOVIE DID NOT CATCH THE EYE OF CRITICS OR AUDIENCES, AND BLYTHE WENT BACK TO TOILING IN SMALL TV ROLES IN THE DECADE SINCE THE MOVIE HIT THEATERS.

INTERESTINGLY, THE OTHER YOUNG ACTRESS TO PORTRAY SYLVIA, IN A MOVIE CALLED AN AMERICAN CRIME THAT CAME OUT THE SAME YEAR, DID GO ON TO BIG SUCCESS IN HOLLYWOOD. THAT WAS ELLEN PAGE, AND IT'S SORT OF AMAZING HOW MUCH HER FACE LOOKS LIKE SYLVIA'S. IT'S UNCANNY. THIS TOMMY O'HAVER MOVIE STICKS CLOSER TO THE TRUE STORY, BUT DESPITE PAGE'S TERRIFIC PERFORMANCE AND GREAT DIRECTION AND EDITING, THE MOVIE DIDN'T CREEP ME OUT NEARLY AS BAD AS THE GIRL NEXT DOOR DID. THAT COULD HAVE A LOT TO DO WITH THE FACT THAT IT TRIED TO BE MORE OF A TRUE CRIME MELODRAMA, AND DIDN'T GO FOR THE JUGULAR.

WHAT I COULD DO IS EXPLAIN WHAT DID AND DIDN'T WORK WITHIN THE RUNTIME OF THESE TWO FILMS, BUT RATHER THAN GO INTO DETAIL ABOUT THEIR RESPECTIVE PLOTS, I FEEL I'D DO FAR BETTER TO SIMPLY RECOUNT THE FACTS OF WHAT HAPPENED TO THE REAL LIFE SYLVIA IN 1965. TO REALLY GET THE HORROR OF THESE FILMS, YOU MUST KNOW THE TRUE STORY THEY'RE BASED ON, BECAUSE NEITHER OF THEM COME CLOSE TO DEPICTING THE TRUE DEPRAVITY OF WHAT TOOK PLACE A HALF CENTURY AGO — AND I BELIEVE IT IS IN UNDERSTANDING INHUMANITY THAT WE LEARN HOW TO FIND OUR OWN HUMANITY. I SHOULD NOTE THAT I WROTE BRIEFLY ABOUT THIS CASE BACK IN CINEMA SEWER VOL. 4, BUT A COUPLE OF PARAGRAPHS DOESN'T REALLY GET ACROSS JUST WHAT AN UNSETTLING CRIME THIS TRULY WAS.

WHAT WAS PERPETRATED UPON POOR SYLVIA MARIE LIKENS (JANUARY 3, 1949 – OCTOBER 26, 1965) WAS DESCRIBED BY THE PROSECUTOR IN THE TRIAL OF HER ATTACKERS AS "THE MOST TERRIBLE CRIME EVER COMMITTED IN THE STATE OF INDIANA." SYLVIA'S PARENTS, CARNIVAL WORKERS NAMED LESTER AND BETTY, HAD LEFT LIKENS AND HER POLIO-SUFFERING SISTER JENNY IN INDIANAPOLIS FOR

THREE MONTHS, UNDER THE FULL, TRUSTED CARE OF THE BANISZEWSKI FAMILY IN EXCHANGE FOR TWENTY DOLLARS A WEEK. IN THAT TIME, SYLVIA WAS MALICIOUSLY ABUSED AND TORTURED TO DEATH BY NOT JUST THE PSYCHOTIC DIVORCEE GERTRUDE BANISZEWSKI, BUT ALSO BY GERTRUDE'S YOUNG CHILDREN, AND OTHER KIDS FROM THEIR NEIGHBOURHOOD. I WASN'T KIDDING WHEN I REFERENCED LORD OF THE FLIES AND LAST HOUSE ON THE LEFT IN THE SAME BREATH, Y'ALL.

"WE [HE AND GERTRUDE] GOT TO TALKING" LESTER TOLD THE COURT DURING THE LIKENS MURDER TRAIL, "SHE SAID SHE WOULD TAKE CARE OF THE CHILDREN AND TREAT THEM LIKE HER OWN." DURING SEVERAL SUBSEQUENT VISITS TO THE HOUSE (THE LAST OF WHICH TOOK PLACE ON OCTOBER 5, JUST WEEKS BEFORE HIS DAUGHTER'S DEATH) HE NOTICED NOTHING UNUSUAL. UNFORTUNATELY FOR LESTER, THE ONLY PART OF THE BANISZEWSKI HOUSE HE EVER SET FOOT IN WAS THE LIVING ROOM. HE TRUSTED MRS. BANISZEWSKI -- A HAGGARD ASTHMATIC DRUG ADDICT - FAR, FAR TOO READILY FOR SOMEONE WHO WAS A TOTAL STRANGER.

THE CHAIN-SMOKING GERTRUDE WAS 37, AND HAD LIVED THROUGH SEVERAL FAILED MARRIAGES, 13 PREGNANCIES AND SIX MISCARRIAGES. SHE HAD SEVEN OF HER OFFSPRING LIVING IN HER HOUSE WITH HER. THE ELDEST, PAULA, 17, WAS UNMARRIED AND PREGNANT, AND THE YOUNGEST WAS JUST AN INFANT. GERTRUDE'S HOME AT 3850 E. NEW YORK ST, WAS THE HANGOUT OF MANY OTHER NEIGHBOURHOOD CHILDREN, WHO CALLED HER "GERTY". THE KIDS LIKED GERTY BECAUSE SHE LET THEM COME IN HER HOUSE, AWAY FROM PRYING EYES, AND ENCOURAGED THEM TO OPENLY SMOKE, SWEAR, AND DRINK BOOZE. HER FAVOURITE OF THE BUNCH WAS A 14-YEAR-OLD BOY NAMED RICKY HOBBS, WHO LIVED A COUPLE HOUSES OVER. EXPERTS ON THE CASE HAVE SURMISED HE WAS LIKELY HAVING A ROMANTIC RELATIONSHIP WITH GERTRUDE.

IN AUGUST 1965, INFURIATED THAT HER $20 PAYMENT FOR BOARDING THE TWO GIRLS HAD ARRIVED LATE IN THE MAIL, BANISZEWSKI BEGAN TO VERBALLY AND PHYSICALLY ABUSE SYLVIA. GERTY HAD SERIOUS OBSESSIVE ISSUES ABOUT WOMEN AND THE CONCEPT OF BEING SLUTTY, AND SHE INCORRECTLY ACCUSED LIKENS OF BEING A PROSTITUTE (IN FACT, SYLVIA WAS STILL A VIRGIN), AFTER OVERHEARING SYLVIA SPEAK ABOUT HOW SHE'D ONCE MADE OUT WITH A BOY.

GERTY HAD LONG BEEN GATHERING THE CHILDREN IN HER HOME TOGETHER SO SHE COULD DELIVER "SERMONS" ABOUT THE FILTHINESS OF PROSTITUTES AND WOMEN IN GENERAL. BUT THINGS REALLY WENT SIDEWAYS WHEN SHE MADE UP A STORY ABOUT THE TWO LIKENS SISTERS STARTING RUMOURS AT SCHOOL ABOUT HER TEENAGE DAUGHTERS, PAULA AND STEPHANIE, BEING PROSTITUTES. THIS ENRAGED PAULA AND STEPHANIE, AND TURNED THEM AND THE OTHER KIDS AGAINST SYLVIA. STEPHANIE'S BOYFRIEND, COY HUBBARD, AND SEVERAL OTHER OF HIS CLASSMATES WERE THEN BROUGHT IN TO ASSIST IN A BRUTAL RETALIATORY BEATING OF SYLVIA. GERTY EVEN FORCED YOUNG JENNY TO HIT HER OLDER SISTER. LATER, SYLVIA VOMITED, AND IN A RAGE GERTY FORCED HER TO SCOOP UP THE VOMIT AND EAT IT.

IN AUGUST THE VACANT HOUSE NEXT DOOR WAS BOUGHT BY A MIDDLE-AGED COUPLE NAMED PHYLLIS AND RAYMOND VERMILLION. PHYLLIS, SEEING THE NUMBER OF CHILDREN AROUND THE BANISZEWSKI HOUSE, DECIDED GERTY WOULD MAKE A GOOD BABYSITTER FOR HER TWO YOUNG KIDS. THAT FIRST WEEKEND, THE VERMILLIONS ARRANGED A BACKYARD BARBECUE SO EVERYONE COULD GET TO KNOW EACH OTHER. THERE, PHYLLIS NOTICED SYLVIA WANDERING AROUND THE YARD WITH A BLACK EYE AND BRUISES. 17-YEAR-OLD PAULA WALKED UP AND PROUDLY ANNOUNCED TO PHYLLIS THAT SHE'D BEEN THE ONE TO BESTOW SYLVIA WITH THOSE MARKS. THEN, IN FRONT OF BOTH GERTY AND MRS VERMILLION, PAULA APPROACHED SYLVIA WITH A GLASS OF STEAMING WATER AND THREW IT IN HER FACE.

TWO MONTHS LATER, PHYLLIS WENT NEXT DOOR TO BORROW SOMETHING. IN THE FEW MINUTES SHE WAS THERE, SHE NOTICED SYLVIA IN A DAZE WITH BIG SWOLLEN LIPS AND AN EYE THAT HAD SWOLLEN TIGHTLY SHUT. WHEN SHE ASKED

A
TRUE
STORY

JACK KETCHUM'S
THE
GIRL
NEXT DOOR

"This is the dark-side-of-the-moon version of Stand By Me."
Stephen King

137

PAULA HOW THIS HAD HAPPENED. PAULA AMICABLY TOOK OFF HER BELT OFF AND BEGAN TO BEAT SYLVIA WITH IT AS A DEMONSTRATION. PAULA WAS FRUSTRATED THAT SHE'D BROKEN HER OWN HAND (WHICH WAS NOW IN A CAST) BY PUNCHING SYLVIA, SO SHE NOW STUCK TO USING BELTS AND OTHER IMPLEMENTS TO EXERCISE HER DOMINATION. ASTOUNDINGLY, NEITHER OF THE VERMILLIONS EVER REPORTED THESE ALARMING INCIDENTS TO THE AUTHORITIES.

A FEW DAYS LATER, GERTRUDE PULLED SYLVIA OUT OF SCHOOL, AND AGAIN ACCUSED THE 16-YEAR OLD GIRL OF SPREADING RUMOURS ABOUT SOME OF THE OTHER CHILDREN'S MOTHERS BEING WHORES. SHE EVEN USED THIS TACTIC TO TURN SYLVIA'S BEST FRIEND AGAINST HER. THIS TIME AS PUNISHMENT SHE FORCED THE GIRL TO STRIP NAKED AND ENCOURAGED THE CHILDREN TO TORMENT LIKENS BY PUTTING CIGARETTES OUT ON HER SKIN, FORCING HER TO DO STRIPTEASES AND INSERTING A COKE BOTTLE UP INTO HER VAGINA FOR THE GROUP'S ENTERTAINMENT. THE PRACTICE OF PUTTING CIGARETTES OUT ON SYLVIA AND KICKING HER IN THE GENITALS NOW BECAME COMMONPLACE IN THE HOUSEHOLD, AND SHE WAS OFTEN KEPT NAKED, TIED UP, AND RARELY FED. THE 13 CHILDREN (THE 7 THAT LIVED IN THE HOUSE, AND 6 THAT WERE ROUTINE VISITORS) THAT TOOK PART IN SYLVIA'S TORTURE REPORTEDLY BEGAN DOING IT AT THEIR OWN DISCRETION AT THIS POINT, OFTEN NO LONGER NEEDING PROMPTING FROM GERTY.

NOT ONE OF THEM REPORTED WHAT THEY SAW OR DID TO ANYONE, WITH THE SOLE EXCEPTION OF A NEIGHBOURHOOD CHILD WHO HAD VISITED -- A TWELVE-YEAR-OLD NAMED JUDY DUKE. JUDY, FINDING THE SITUATION ODD, WENT HOME AND TOLD HER MOM THAT THE BANISZEWSKI FAMILY "WERE BEATING AND KICKING SYLVIA." JUDY'S MOTHER REPLIED THAT IT WAS NOTHING TO WORRY ABOUT, AND THAT THIS WAS "WHAT HAPPENS WHEN SOMEONE IS PUNISHED". JUDY DIDN'T BRING IT UP AGAIN.

AS A RESULT OF THE TRAUMA OF THE ABUSE SHE'D SUFFERED UP TO THIS POINT, A TERRIFIED SYLVIA BEGAN INVOLUNTARILY URINATING ON A REGULAR BASIS, AND WAS, AS A RESULT, LOCKED IN THE BASEMENT. A DAILY BATHING REGIME TO "CLEANSE" SYLVIA BEGAN, INVOLVING DOUSING HER WITH SCALDING WATER AND RUBBING SALT INTO THE BURNS. AT TIMES, BANISZEWSKI AND HER TWELVE-YEAR-OLD SON JOHN WOULD FORCE LIKENS TO EAT HER OWN SHIT AND DRINK HER OWN PISS, WHILE TELLING HER IT WAS AN OPPORTUNITY TO PAY PENANCE FOR HER DISGUSTING SLUTTY BEHAVIOUR. COY HUBBARD, IT WAS REVEALED IN COURT, OUTSIDE OF THE COMMUNAL ABUSE OF THE GIRL, ALSO STARTED USING SYLVIA AS A PRACTICE DUMMY FOR JUDO FLIPS, PUNCHES, AND CHOKE HOLDS. BANISZEWSKI'S CHILDREN ALSO TURNED THEIR PRISONER INTO A MONEY-MAKING OPPORTUNITY, CHARGING KIDS FROM AROUND THE HOOD A NICKEL TO GAWK AT HER NAKED, SCARRED BODY.

PAULA BANISZEWSKI

AROUND THIS TIME, JENNY LIKENS MANAGED TO CONTACT HER OLDER SISTER, DIANNA LIKENS, CLEARLY OUTLINING THE HORRORS THAT THE TWO SISTERS WERE EXPERIENCING, AND DESPERATELY BEGGED DIANNA TO CONTACT THE POLICE. DIANNA, A NEWLY MARRIED 18-YEAR-OLD, IGNORED THIS LETTER FROM HER LITTLE SISTER, BELIEVING THAT JENNY WAS SIMPLY UNHAPPY ABOUT BEING DISCIPLINED, AND THAT SHE WAS MAKING UP OUTRAGEOUS, HARD-TO-BELIEVE STORIES.

WHEN DIANNA LATER DECIDED TO PAY HER YOUNGER SIBLINGS A VISIT, SHE BEGAN TO REALIZE SOMETHING WASN'T KOSHER. GERTY REFUSED TO ALLOW HER INSIDE, TELLING HER THAT THE GIRL'S FATHER, LESTER, HAD SAID DIANNA WAS NOT TO BE ALLOWED INTO THE BUILDING. WHEN DIANNA SAID THAT WAS BULLSHIT, GERTY THREATENED TO CALL THE COPS, PROMPTING DIANNA TO HIDE NEARBY UNTIL SHE FINALLY SAW YOUNG JENNY OUTSIDE ON HER OWN. BUT JENNY (PREVIOUSLY COACHED BY GERTRUDE THAT SHE'D SUFFER THE SAME FATE AS SYLVIA IF SHE SNITCHED) TOLD HER OLDER SIBLING THAT SHE WAS NOT ALLOWED TO TALK, BEFORE RUNNING BACK INTO THE HOUSE.

UNDERSTANDABLY CONCERNED, DIANNA CONTACTED SOCIAL SERVICES, AND WHEN A SOCIAL WORKER ARRIVED AT THE HOME, SHE WAS ALSO REFUSED HER ENTRY. GERTY ANNOUNCED SHE'D KICKED SYLVIA OUT OF THE HOUSE FOR BEING A PROSTITUTE, AND THAT SYLVIA HAD SINCE RUN OFF TO DO HER WHORING ELSEWHERE. THE SOCIAL WORKER THEN FILED A REPORT STATING THAT NO MORE VISITS NEEDED TO BE MADE TO THE HOUSE ON NEW YORK STREET, AND TOLD DIANNA THAT SHE WAS TO STOP HARASSING THE BANISZEWSKI FAMILY.

ON OCTOBER 21, GERTY HAD JOHN, COY, AND STEPHANIE BRING LIKENS UP FROM THE CELLAR AND TIE HER TO A BED UPSTAIRS. THE MATRIARCH OF THE HOUSEHOLD BECAME ENRAGED WHEN SYLVIA PREDICTABLY WET THE BED, AND AGAIN FORCED HER TO PERFORM A STRIP TEASE AND COKE BOTTLE MASTURBATION SHOW FOR HER SONS AND SOME NEIGHBOURHOOD BOYS. THEN SHE

CARVED THE PHRASE "I'M A PROSTITUTE AND PROUD OF IT" INTO HER ABDOMEN WITH A RED-HOT SEWING NEEDLE, WHICH WAS SUGGESTED BY HER 14-YEAR-OLD LOVER, RICKY HOBBS. WHEN GERTRUDE WAS TOO TIRED TO FINISH THE BRANDING, SHE ENLISTED RICKY TO FINISH THE JOB. BANISZEWSKI'S DAUGHTERS, MARIE (11) AND SHIRLEY-ANNE (10) WERE ALSO GIVEN SEWING NEEDLES AND ENCOURAGED TO CUT WORDS INTO SYLVIA. THEY GOT AS FAR AS CARVING "I'M A JOE" INTO HER STOMACH BEFORE THEY LOST INTEREST AND WENT OUTSIDE TO PLAY.

THE NEXT DAY, BANISZEWSKI WOKE LIKENS, AND THEN DICTATED A LETTER FOR HER TO WRITE, INTENDING IT TO LOOK LIKE A 'GOODBYE' LETTER TO HER PARENTS. THE SHITTY SOCIAL WORKER HAD BOUGHT IT, SO WHY NOT? GERTRUDE WAS FORMULATING A PLAN TO HAVE SYLVIA TIED UP, TAKEN TO A NEARBY GARBAGE DUMP, WHERE SHE WOULD BE BURIED ALIVE AND LEFT TO DIE. SYLVIA OVERHEARD GERTRUDE TELLING ONE OF HER KIDS OF THE PLAN, AND MADE ONE LAST DITCH ATTEMPT TO ESCAPE, BUT WAS JUST TOO WEAK AND SLOW FROM MALNOURISHMENT. SHE WAS CAPTURED ON THE FRONT PORCH BY THE SADISTIC WITCH GERTRUDE, TOSSED DOWN THE BASEMENT STAIRS, AND LOCKED IN.

3 DAYS LATER, GERTY AND SOME OF THE CHILDREN CAME DOWN TO THE BASEMENT FOR ONE OF THEIR ROUTINE TORTURE SESSIONS WITH SYLVIA. WHEN THE 37-YEAR-OLD DIVORCEE ATTEMPTED TO BLUDGEON LIKENS WITH A WOODEN PADDLE, SHE MISSED HER AND ACCIDENTALLY STRUCK HERSELF. SEEING THIS ENRAGED YOUNG COY HUBBARD, WHO STEPPED IN AND VICIOUSLY BEAT LIKENS REPEATEDLY ON THE HEAD WITH A BROOMSTICK HANDLE, LEAVING THE GIRL UNCONSCIOUS. GERTY CLIMBED ATOP OF HER PRONE BODY, AND SMASHED HER HEAD INTO THE CONCRETE BASEMENT FLOOR.

SHE SIMPLY COULDN'T TAKE ANY MORE. SYLVIA DIED OF HER WOUNDS A FEW HOURS LATER.

THUS CAME TO A CLOSE ONE OF THE MOST HORRIBLE CRIMES EVER COMMITTED AGAINST A SINGLE VICTIM IN AMERICAN HISTORY. THE OFFICIAL CAUSE OF DEATH WAS EXTREME MALNUTRITION, BRAIN SWELLING, INTERNAL HAEMORRHAGING OF THE BRAIN, AND SHOCK FROM SEVERE AND PROLONGED DAMAGE TO HER SKIN (THERE WERE LARGE AREAS WHERE HER OUTER LAYER OF SKIN HAD PEELED OFF). IN HER DEATH THROES, SYLVIA BIT THROUGH HER OWN LIPS, NEARLY SEVERING EACH OF THEM. HER EMACIATED CORPSE HAD OVER 150 WOUNDS ON IT.

UPON FINDING THEIR VICTIM DEAD, STEPHANIE BANISZEWSKI WAS PANIC-STRICKEN, AND YELLED AT HOBBS TO CALL THE POLICE. WHEN THEY ARRIVED, GERTRUDE TOLD THE INVESTIGATING OFFICER,

GERTRUDE BANISZEWSKI

MELVIN DIXON, THAT A GANG OF SLUTTY SYLVIA'S JOHNS HAD COME AND RAPED HER TO DEATH AND STASHED HER BODY IN THE BASEMENT WHILE THE FAMILY WAS OUT FOR THE DAY. ALL THE CHILDREN (INCLUDING JENNY LIKENS) REPEATED GERTY'S STORY WORD FOR WORD. DIXON WAS BAFFLED BY THE STATE OF SYLVIA'S BATTERED BODY, BUT TOOK THEM AT THEIR WORD FOR THE TIME BEING. JUST AS HE WAS ABOUT TO LEAVE, LITTLE JENNY MANAGED TO WHISPER TO HIM: "GET ME OUT OF HERE AND I'LL TELL YOU THE WHOLE STORY". THE STATEMENT SHE THEN GAVE AT THE PRECINCT PROMPTED THE INDIANAPOLIS POLICE DEPARTMENT TO ARREST GERTRUDE, PAULA, STEPHANIE AND JOHN BANISZEWSKI, AS WELL AS RICHARD HOBBS, AND COY HUBBARD FOR MURDER.

DURING THE HIGHLY-PUBLICIZED TRIAL, GERTRUDE WENT ABOUT DENYING RESPONSIBILITY FOR THE MURDER, EVENTUALLY PLEADING NOT GUILTY BY REASON OF INSANITY. THE TURNING POINT IN THE TRIAL CAME WHEN MARIE, GERTRUDE'S 11-YEAR-OLD DAUGHTER, WAS CALLED TO THE STAND AS A WITNESS FOR THE DEFENCE, AND BROKE DOWN CRYING AS SHE ADMITTED THAT SHE'D BEEN THE ONE TO HEAT THE NEEDLE WITH WHICH HOBBS HAD CARVED UP SYLVIA'S SKIN.

ON MAY 19, 1966, GERTRUDE WAS CONVICTED OF FIRST-DEGREE MURDER, BUT SPARED THE DEATH PENALTY AND SENTENCED TO LIFE IN PRISON. HER DAUGHTER PAULA WAS CONVICTED OF SECOND-DEGREE MURDER AND ALSO GIVEN A LIFE TERM. DESPITE TRYING TO ESCAPE FROM PRISON TWO YEARS LATER, SHE WAS RELEASED IN 1971.

15-YEAR-OLD STEPHANIE, SECOND-OLDEST OF THE BANISZEWSKI CHILDREN, WAS GRANTED A SPECIAL TRIAL WHERE ALL CHARGES AGAINST HER WERE DROPPED BECAUSE SHE TURNED STATE'S EVIDENCE AGAINST HER FAMILY. SHE REPORTEDLY CHANGED HER NAME, MARRIED, HAD CHILDREN, AND GOT A JOB AS A TEACHER IN FLORIDA. SHE REPORTEDLY ABUSED SLYVIA THE LEAST OUT OF THE BANISZEWSKI FAMILY, AND WAS REMEMBERED FOR REGULARLY SINGING WITH SYLVIA DURING THE EARLY PART OF HER STAY AT THE HOUSE. SHE WAS ALSO THE ONLY ONE WHO TRIED TO RESUSCITATE THE PRONE GIRL WITH MOUTH-TO-MOUTH AFTER SHE STOPPED BREATHING, BUT WAS ORDERED BY GERTY TO STOP, BECAUSE LIKENS WAS "ONLY FAKING".

THE BOYS, JOHN, COY AND RICKY, WERE CONVICTED OF MANSLAUGHTER AND GOT 21 YEARS EACH, BUT WOULD SPEND ONLY 2 YEARS EACH IN REFORMATORIES AND PRISONS. SOME POETIC JUSTICE WAS SERVED WHEN RICKY HOBBS WOULD DIE OF LUNG CANCER AT THE UNLIKELY AGE OF 21, ONLY 4 YEARS AFTER GOING FREE.

THE ONLY ONE OF SYLVIA'S TORTURERS THAT HAVE EVER EXPRESSED GUILT OR ACCEPTED RESPONSIBILITY FOR THEIR ACTIONS WAS JOHN BANISZEWSKI, WHO WAS 12 AT THE TIME, AND MADE NO ATTEMPT TO HIDE HIS PAST -- UNLIKE HIS SIBLINGS. HE BECAME A CHURCH DEACON AND A REAL ESTATE AGENT BEFORE DYING OF CANCER IN 2005. COY HUBBARD WAS TRIED IN 1982 FOR MURDERING TWO 20-YEAR-OLD MEN 5 YEARS EARLIER, BUT WAS ACQUITTED WHEN HIS FORMER WIFE SAID COY HAD BEEN WITH HER AT THE TIME OF THE SLAYINGS.

IN 1985 GERTRUDE WAS PAROLED (DESPITE 40,000 PEOPLE IN INDIANA SIGNING A PETITION TO KEEP HER IMPRISONED), CHANGED HER NAME TO NADINE VAN FOSSAN, AND MOVED TO IOWA TO LIVE WITH HER DAUGHTER PAULA, WHO NOW HAS TWO ADULT SONS. GERTRUDE DIED FIVE YEARS

RICKY HOBBS AND GERTRUDE BANISZEWSKI WITH THEIR LAWYERS DURING SENTENCING

LATER OF LUNG CANCER, AND CROAKED WITHOUT EVER APOLOGIZING TO THE FAMILY OF THE VICTIM. IN FACT, WHEN SHE WAS PAROLED, SHE TOLD THE PAROLE BOARD "I'M NOT SURE WHAT ROLE I HAD IN IT . . . BECAUSE I WAS ON DRUGS. I NEVER REALLY KNEW HER." SHE ALSO CLAIMED SHE WAS TOO DISTRACTED TO CONTROL HER OWN CHILDREN, BECAUSE SHE WAS DEPRESSED.

IN OCTOBER 2012, PAULA, WHO HAS ALSO NEVER PUBLICLY ACCEPTED ANY BLAME DESPITE BEING ONE OF SYLVIA'S PROUDEST AND MOST FLAGRANT ABUSERS, WAS DISCOVERED UNDER A FAKE NAME AND OUTED ON FACEBOOK FOR HER ROLE IN THE CRIME, AND AS A RESULT LOST HER JOB AS A TEACHER'S AID.

DESPITE THE COLD INDIFFERENCE OF PHYLLIS VERMILLION AND OTHERS THAT TURNED A BLIND EYE (TWO NEIGHBOURS HAD BEEN KEPT UP ON A REGULAR BASIS BY SYLVIA BANGING A SHOVEL AGAINST THE CONCRETE WALL IN THE BASEMENT), ONE OF THE MYSTERIES OF THE CASE IS WHY NEITHER JENNY NOR SYLVIA EVER SOUGHT DIRECT HELP FROM TEACHERS OR NEIGHBOURS BEFORE THINGS ESCALATED. BUT WHY WOULD YOU SEEK HELP IF YOU HAD NEVER BEEN TAUGHT THAT YOU HAVE A RIGHT TO COMPASSION?

"I SPECULATE THAT THERE WAS NEVER ANY EXPERIENCE IN SYLVIA'S LIFE, UP TO THE TIME SHE WENT INTO GERTIE'S HOUSE, WHEN SHE LEARNED THAT PEOPLE WOULD COME TO HER AID," SAID FORREST BOWMAN JR, COY HUBBARD'S ATTORNEY. "SHE WASN'T CONDITIONED TO BELIEVE THAT ANYONE WOULD HELP HER."

WHEN ASKED BY HER FELLOW INMATES WHY SHE'D TREATED SYLVIA THE WAY SHE HAD, GERTY

WOULD ONLY RESPOND: "I HAD TO TEACH HER A LESSON". HEARING OF THIS PROMPTED RADICAL SECOND WAVE FEMINIST KATE MILLETT TO WRITE IN HER PRESUMPTUOUS-YET-COMPELLING 1979 BOOK, THE BASEMENT: MEDITATIONS ON A HUMAN SACRIFICE, "GERTRUDE SEEMS TO HAVE WANTED TO ADMINISTER SOME TERRIBLE TRUTHFUL JUSTICE TO THIS GIRL: THAT THIS WAS WHAT IT WAS TO BE A WOMAN."

IN MILLETT'S WORDS, THE ANTI-SEXUAL GERTRUDE'S WHORE-HATING ACTIONS WERE NOT JUST OF AN ABUSIVE MURDERER, BUT OF A REPRESSED DICKLESS RAPIST. A FRUSTRATED MOLESTER "PERFORMING A SEXUAL ACT UNDER THE PRETEXT OF SOMETHING PERMISSIBLE, AS SEDUCTION WOULD NEVER BE. NO MATTER HOW EAGER THE CHILD, NO MATTER HOW TENDER AND LOVING, HOW PASSIONATE OR KINDLY OR SUBTLE THE SEDUCER, FOR SUCH IS A SIN. TO STROKE IS TO MOLEST. WHEREAS TO BEAT IS NOT... THE HAND MUST NOT TEACH PLEASURE, ONLY SUFFERING."

SYLVIA WAS BURIED AT OAK HILL CEMETERY IN LEBANON, INDIANA, WHILE HER LITTLE SISTER, JENNY, DIED IN 2004 AT THE AGE OF 54. THE ABANDONED HELL-HOUSE AT 3850 E. NEW YORK STREET (WHICH RATHER IRONICALLY, ONCE ABANDONED, BECOME A HAVEN FOR DRUG-ADDICTED STREETWALKERS) WASN'T DEMOLISHED UNTIL APRIL 2009.

IT'S UNSETTLING TO THINK THAT CHILDREN ARE CAPABLE OF HORRENDOUS VIOLENT CRIMES. YOU KNOW, I ALMOST WROTE "CAPABLE OF EVIL" OUT OF HABIT, JUST NOW. BUT I THINK THAT'S REALLY THE WRONG STANCE TO TAKE WHEN SPEAKING ABOUT THIS STUFF. EVIL SHOULD BE RELEGATED TO FICTION, IN MY OPINION. SYLVIA'S REALITY WAS NOT A BIBLE STORY, AND NOT A HORROR MOVIE. AS SOON AS YOU SAY SOMEONE IS "EVIL", SUDDENLY YOU'RE LETTING THEM OFF THE HOOK. ALL OF A SUDDEN YOU'RE NOT TAKING INTO ACCOUNT THAT MENTAL ILLNESS, CORRUPTION, PEER PRESSURE, AND PROLONGED ABUSE ARE ALL THINGS THAT HAVE INCREDIBLE POWER OVER HUMAN PSYCHOLOGY. IT'S NOT A MATTER OF INNOCENCE, IT'S A MATTER OF THE FACT THAT CHILDREN ARE ESPECIALLY VULNERABLE TO BEING MANIPULATED BY ALL THOSE THINGS, BECAUSE THEY LACK THE MATURITY, POWER AND SOCIETAL AGENCY TO COUNTERACT OR STAND AGAINST THEM.

IN RESEARCHING HER CASE OVER THE YEARS, I'VE FOUND THAT I FEEL PROFOUNDLY PROTECTIVE OF SYLVIA, MOSTLY BECAUSE IT ANGERS ME THAT NO ONE ELSE WAS. IT SEEMS ODD TO SAY THAT, ESPECIALLY SINCE SHE DIED 8 YEARS BEFORE I WAS EVEN BORN. BUT "PROTECTIVE" SEEMS LIKE THE BEST WORD FOR HOW I FEEL. PERHAPS HER SAD AND BRUTAL STORY HOLDS GREAT SWAY OVER ME BECAUSE MY OWN AUNT WAS MURDERED AS A TEENAGE GIRL YEARS BEFORE I WAS BORN. I'LL NEVER ACTUALLY KNOW ADELE BOUGIE, AND I'LL NEVER KNOW SYLVIA LIKENS, BUT THAT WON'T KEEP ME FROM REMEMBERING THEM, AND AS LONG AS WE'RE REMEMBERED, WE NEVER TRULY DIE.

-ROBIN BOUGIE (OCTOBER 11TH 2018)

GIIRRRRRRLFIIIGHTS!!!

SO, YEAH... I FEEL A LITTLE GUILTY DELIGHTING IN THE STRESS AND FURY OF OTHERS, BUT I CAN'T ARGUE THAT THERE IS AN UNDENIABLE SEXUALIZED THRILL MANY STRAIGHT DUDES AND LESBIAN GALS DEVELOP WATCHING WHAT IS KNOWN AS "CATFIGHTING". THE MORE RAW AND FILLED WITH THE RIPPING OF CLOTHES, THE PULLING OF HAIR, AND THE YELLING OF DEROGATORY LANGUAGE, THE BETTER! AT LEAST FOR ME, ANYWAY. MOST AFICIONADOS OF THIS VIOLENT FETISH HAVE THEIR OWN PREFERANCES.

IT'S A TYPE OF PORN THAT OFTEN ISN'T EVEN FOUND ON PORN SITES, BUT RATHER PRESENTED AS VIRAL VIDEO CONTENT AND DISTRIBUTED THAT WAY. NO ONE REALLY GETS HURT (ASIDE FROM THAT ONE INFAMOUS CLIP WHERE A TEENAGE GIRL GOT NAILED IN THE BACK OF THE HEAD WITH A FLYING SHOVEL) ASIDE FROM A FEW BRUISES AND SUCH. IT ALL TIES INTO THE POWERPLAY THAT CAN SOMETIMES BE A PART OF FUCKING, ESPECIALLY IN BDSM. SUBMISSION HOLDS, SWEATY SKIN, AND HAIR PULLING ARE KEY AS WELL!

FUCKIN' WHORE!!

FUCK U, BIITCH!!

BOUG 2018

DANGEROUS MEN (2005. DIR: JOHN RAD)

IN 1979, AN IRANIAN FILMMAKER WHO
GAVE HIMSELF THE MONIKER "JOHN RAD"
MOVED HIS FAMILY TO AMERICA SO HE
COULD BEGIN SHOOTING HIS DREAM
MOVIE: AN EXPLOITATION AND VIOLENCE
FILLED ACTION/CRIME/REVENGE/BIKER
DRIVE-IN MOVIE THAT NEVER GOT A
PROPER THEATRICAL RUN, MUCH LESS A
SCREENING IN A DRIVE-IN. DESPITE VERY
LITTLE FILMMAKING EXPERIENCE OR
MONEY TO SPEND, RAD COMMITTED
HIMSELF TO 26 ARDUOUS YEARS OF
SACRIFICE TO GET DANGEROUS MEN IN
THE CAN. YES, 26 YEARS.

FOR YEARS IT WAS RUMOURED THAT
ONLY ABOUT A DOZEN PEOPLE HAD SEEN
THE MOVIE DURING TWO SPARSELY
ATTENDED AND BARELY ADVERTISED 2005
SCREENINGS, AND SO IT'S GREAT TO SEE
ON THE DRAFTHOUSE FILMS BLU/DVD
COMBO RELEASE THAT ONE OF THE
SPECIAL FEATURES IS SOMETHING MADE
BY TWO OF THE PEOPLE WHO SAW THE
MOVIE THAT NIGHT. THE DOCUMENTARY,
WHICH IS GOOD TO WATCH BEFORE
WATCHING DANGEROUS MEN ITSELF, SHOWS
THEM TRAVELING AROUND AMERICA TO
FIND AND INTERVIEW AS MANY OF THE
OTHER PEOPLE WHO WERE THERE TEN
YEARS EARLIER WHEN JOHN RAD RENTED
OUT A THEATER SO HIS MOVIE COULD
FINALLY SEE THE LIGHT OF DAY.

THAT'S RIGHT. JOHN RAD "FOUR WALLED"
HIS MOVIE. MEANING: NOT ONLY DID HE
NOT MAKE ANYTHING EVEN RESEMBLING A
PROFIT, HE ACTUALLY HAD TO PAY PEOPLE
TO WATCH IT. DAMN.

THE PLOT OF DANGEROUS MEN IS TOTALLY
UNCLEAR, AND ON TOP OF THAT, IT
CHANGES ABRUPTLY TOWARDS THE MIDDLE
OF THE FILM. THAT'S BECAUSE STAR
MELODY WIGGINS (MINA) WAS INJURED
WHILE MAKING IT, AND NOT ONLY DID
THE NOTORIOUSLY CHEAP JOHN RAD NOT
OFFER TO PAY ANY MONEY FOR HER
HOSPITAL BILLS, HE ALSO WOULDN'T
SPRING FOR FOOD TO FEED HIS CAST
AND CREW. THERE ARE STORIES ABOUT
HOW HE WOULD SQUIRT KETCHUP INTO
WATER, AND SERVE THE REVOLTING LOW-
RENT CONCOCTION TO THEM AS "TOMATO
JUICE".

WITH YOUR PISSED-OFF STAR WALKING
OFF, NEVER TO RETURN, WHEN ONLY HALF
THE FILM HAD BEEN SHOT, MOST
DIRECTORS WOULD EITHER REWRITE THE
MOVIE AND EDIT HER PART OUT, OR
START AGAIN. RAD DID NEITHER. HE
SIMPLY STARTED RANDOMLY FOLLOWING
ANOTHER CHARACTER, AND NOW MADE THE
MOVIE ABOUT THEM. IN THE FINAL
ACTION CLIMAX OF THE FILM, 3 OF THE 4
CHARACTERS IN THE SCENE HAVE ONLY
BEEN IN THE MOVIE FOR THE PREVIOUS
FEW MINUTES. THAT'S WHAT KIND OF
FUCKING BONKERS SHIT THIS MOVIE IS.

"IT'S A COMPLETELY UNFILTERED VISION
FROM SOMEONE WHO OBVIOUSLY
APPROACHED MOVIES IN THE MOST
UNIQUE POSSIBLE WAY," SAID
DRAFTHOUSE FILM'S ZACK CARLSON. "IT'S
FEARLESS. HE JUST LET HIS IMPULSES

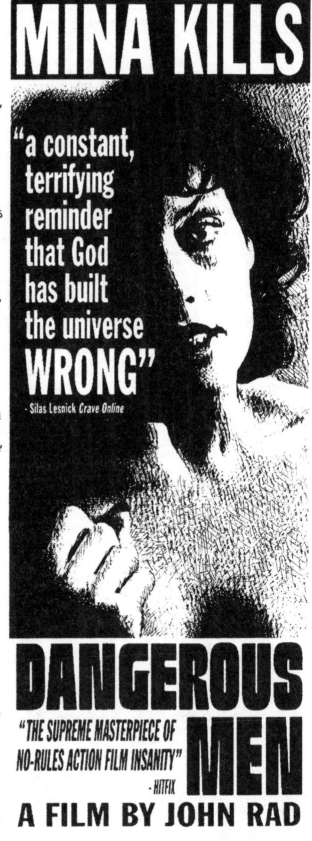

MINA KILLS

"a constant, terrifying reminder that God has built the universe WRONG"
- Silas Lesnick *Crave Online*

DANGEROUS MEN

"THE SUPREME MASTERPIECE OF NO-RULES ACTION FILM INSANITY"
- HITFIX

A FILM BY JOHN RAD

142

AND IDEAS UNFOLD, AND WHAT HE ENDED UP WITH IS INFINITELY MORE FASCINATING THAN ANY MOVIE DELIBERATELY MADE TO BE UNUSUAL." CARLSON KNOWS HIS OUTSIDER FILMMAKERS. HE'S THE GUY WHO DISCOVERED THE ONLY REMAINING 35MM PRINT MIAMI CONNECTION, WHICH HE BLIND-BOUGHT ON EBAY FOR $40, AND THEN PROCEEDED TO INTRODUCE TO FLABBERGASTED FILM FANS AROUND THE WORLD. IF YOU HAVEN'T SEEN IT, DO THAT ASA FUCKING P. MIAMI CONNECTION AND DANGEROUS MEN MAKE THE MOST EXQUISITE DOUBLE BILL.

"THE FIGHT SCENES RECALL TWO FIVE-YEAR-OLDS THROWING SIMULTANEOUS TANTRUMS", READ JASON NEWMAN'S REVIEW IN ROLLING STONE. "DIFFERENT ACTORS PLAY THE SAME ROLE, PRESUMABLY DUE TO THE YEARS-LONG SHOOTING SCHEDULE, WHILE TANGENTIAL SUBPLOTS APPEAR AND DISAPPEAR WITH NO RESOLUTION. THERE APPEARS TO HAVE BEEN A ONE-TAKE-MAXIMUM RULE FOR EACH SHOT. THE JOY OF DANGEROUS MEN, FOR A CERTAIN TYPE OF FILM LOVER, IS THAT THERE ARE MORE QUESTIONS THAN ANSWERS. WHY DOES A BIKER BAR HAVE AN ESPRESSO MACHINE? WHY IS THERE ROMANTIC MUSIC (COMPOSED BY RAD HIMSELF) PLAYING DURING A TENSE SCENE BETWEEN A KIDNAPPED BIKER AND A VIGILANTE COP? AND WHY DOES ONE CHARACTER HIDE A KNIFE IN HER ASS?"

— BOUGIE 2017

THE CLOWN PRINCE AND THE SCORPION

THE LATE GREAT JODY MAXWELL (RIP, MY FRIEND) TOLD ME THIS IN 2012 WHEN I ASKED HER ABOUT FELLOW 1970S PORN ACTRESS SAMANTHA FOX AND THEIR CONNECTION TOGETHER. AS IS OFTEN THE CASE WHEN SAMANTHA'S NAME COMES UP, HER TRUE LOVE — THE CLOWN PRINCE OF PORN — BOBBY ASTYR, ALSO CAME UP. LET'S LISTEN IN, SHALL WE?

"SAMANTHA FOX IS AN AWESOME LADY AND ONE OF MY CLOSEST FRIENDS. SHE WAS SO TALENTED, HAD SO MUCH FUN DOING WHAT SHE DID, AND WE HAD A HOT BALL DOING OUTLAW LADIES TOGETHER. HER PARTNER WAS FELLOW ADULT FILM PERFORMER, BOBBY ASTYR, WHO HAS PASSED AWAY NOW, BUT HE WAS ONE OF MY DEAREST, CLOSEST FRIENDS ALSO. BOBBY AND I BONDED EARLY ON AND HE ALWAYS HAD MY BACK. YOU KNOW, HE RESCUED ME A COUPLE OF TIMES FROM SITUATIONS — NOTHING TO DO WITH ADULT FILMS OR THE BIZ, MIND YOU — BUT THINGS THAT WERE POTENTIALLY HARMFUL TO ME."

"HERE'S A STORY ONLY FAMILY AND CLOSE PERSONAL FRIENDS KNOW: WHEN FILMING GUMS IN FLORIDA, I PICKED UP A LARGE BEAUTIFUL CONCH SHELL FROM A DESERTED ISLAND SOUTHWEST OF KEY WEST WHERE WE DID SOME SCENES. I TOOK IT TO MY HOTEL ROOM AND TOOK IT WITH ME THE REST OF THE TRIP. I CARRIED IT ON THE PLANE, AND I SLEPT WITH IT IN BOTH KEY WEST AND IN MIAMI. WHEN I RETURNED TO NYC, I TOOK IT OVER TO BOBBY'S APARTMENT TO GIVE IT TO HIM."

"HE WAS ADMIRING IT AND HE SUDDENLY SAYS 'HEY, I SEE SOMETHING MOVING IN THERE.' SO BOBBY SETS IT ON THE FLOOR AND, LO AND BEHOLD, THIS SCORPION — IN ALL ITS GLORY — WALKED RIGHT OUT OF THE SHELL LIKE HE WAS ABOUT TO UNPACK HIS BAGS! CITY BOY BOBBY FREAKED OUT AND I CAN TELL YOU THAT I WASN'T FEELING TOO GREAT EITHER, KNOWING I HAD BEEN CARRYING IT AROUND WITH ME EVERYWHERE. BOBBY IMMEDIATELY GOT ON THE PHONE CALLED THE NEW YORK CITY HEALTH DEPT, AND THEY SAID "KILL IT", SO HE STOMPS DOWNSTAIRS AND FINDS A TWELVE FOOT LONG 2X4. I JUMPED UP ON A CHAIR WHERE I'D BE SAFE, AND BOBBY STOOD 12 FEET BACK AND — WHACK WHACK WHACK ! HIT THAT SCORPION 3 TIMES!"

"THEN HE THREW AWAY MY BEAUTIFUL SHELL AND WE LAUGHED SO HARD. I HAD NEVER SEEN ANYTHING SCARE HIM BEFORE LIKE THAT, AND I NEVER DID AGAIN. HE SAID TO ME, 'MAX, HOW COULD YOU HAVE BROUGHT ME THIS FROM FLORIDA!?' I REMINDED HIM WE WERE BOTH SCORPIOS, BUT BOBBY NEVER LET ME FORGET THAT ONE! SO MANY MEMORIES OF A REALLY GOOD MAN."

Red Heat (1985. Dir: Robert Collector)

LINDA BLAIR PLAYS TOURISTY CHRISTINE CARLSON, A PRETTY AMERICAN COLLEGE CO-ED ON HER WAY TO WEST GERMANY TO VISIT HER US ARMY FIANCÉ MIKE, WHO IS STATIONED THERE. UNABLE TO CONVINCE HIM TO MARRY HER, (HE WANTS TO WAIT UNTIL AFTER HE DOES ANOTHER TOUR OF DUTY) CHRISTINE GETS PISSY AND TAKES A LATE-NIGHT STROLL. THERE, SHE WITNESSES A KIDNAPPING BY THE EAST GERMAN SECRET POLICE AND GETS NABBED HERSELF. SPIRITED AWAY TO GOD-KNOWS-WHERE, SHE IS BRUTALLY INTERROGATED BY THE COMMIES, FORCED TO ADMIT TO SOME ESPIONAGE BULLSHIT SHE NEVER TOOK PART IN, AND TOSSED INTO A NASTY-ASS EAST GERMAN WOMEN'S PRISON. <u>WHAT</u> IS <u>A</u> <u>GAL</u> <u>TO</u> <u>DO</u>?

WHILE HER SERVICEMAN BOYFRIEND ATTEMPTS TO ORGANIZE A RESCUE MISSION, CHRISTINE MUST TRY TO SURVIVE A RUN-IN WITH REDHEADED SOFIA (SYLVIA KRISTEL), WHO ANNOUNCES HERSELF AS "TOP BITCH", AND EXERTS CONTROL OVER THE PRISON POPULATION. THE WARDEN OF THE JAIL IS A SADISTIC DEVIANT. BUT KEEPING THE LESBIAN WARDEN IN THE PALM OF HER HAND, IS SOFIA, WHO OFFERS A SEETHING ADMISSION THAT SHE MURDERED HER DAD BECAUSE HE ATE HER PET SNAKE. (?!?) KRISTEL CAN'T REALLY PULL OFF THE TOUGH GAL THING, BUT DANG -- DOES SHE GIVE IT A GOOD EFFORT, ESPECIALLY WHEN SHE'S HOLDING HER HAND OVER BLAIR'S MOUTH AND RAPING HER, AND THEN ORDERING A MALE GUARD TO DO THE SAME. "YOU'LL DO MY BIDDING, OR THIS WILL HAPPEN AGAIN AND AGAIN AND AGAIN." SHE TELLS THE SOBBING GIRL.

WHILE CHAINED HEAT IS THE BETTER KNOWN LINDA BLAIR WIP FILM, I BELIEVE THAT THE DARKER AND DECIDEDLY JOYLESS RED HEAT WOULD BE EVERY BIT ITS EQUAL IF ONLY IT HAD MORE THAN ONE BRIEF SHOWER SCENE AND MORE SLEAZE. IT'S A VERY WELL MADE MOVIE, THOUGH, AND IT'S KIND OF A BUMMER THAT IT'S SO RESOUNDINGLY DESPISED BY ITS STAR, LINDA BLAIR, WHO WASN'T AT ALL SHY ABOUT HEAPING SCORN UPON THE MOVIE WHEN SHE RECORDED AN AUDIO COMMENTARY FOR ITS CANADIAN DVD RELEASE. I MEAN, SURE, SHE BROKE HER LEG DURING FILMING IN AUSTRIA AND DIDN'T SEEM TO GET ALONG WITH ANYONE ON THE TOTALLY UNHYGIENIC SET (SHE CALLS KRISTEL "OVER SENSITIVE"), BUT MAN, DOES IT EVER GET TIRING LISTENING TO HER WHINING ABOUT IT FOR AN HOUR AND A HALF.

DIRECTED BY ROBERT COLLECTOR (I WONDER HOW BIG HIS COLLECTION OF ROBERTS IS?) AND FEATURING A COOL/WEIRD SCORE BY TANGERINE DREAM, RED HEAT IS A SOUL-CRUSHING VIEWING EXPERIENCE FOR WIP AND LINDA BLAIR FANS ALIKE. MILAGE WILL VARY DEPENDING ON HOW CRUSHED YOU LIKE YOUR SOUL, BUT PERSONALLY I PREFER MINE HAMMERED FLAT AND PISSED ON.
— BOUGIE

ARNOLD KOPELSON and TAT FILMPRODUCTIONS GMBH Present 'RED HEAT' Starring LINDA BLAIR and SYLVIA KRISTEL

Produced by ERNST R. VON THEUMER Written by ROBERT COLLECTOR AND GARY DRUCKER Directed by ROBERT COLLECTOR

BIG PUSSY

THE WORLD OF PORN IS <u>OBSESSED</u> WITH BIG DICKS. STRAIGHT PORN, GAY PORN, PRETTY MUCH EVERY KIND OF PORN ASIDE FROM LESBO STUFF SPENDS MUCH OF ITS RUNTIME LETTING THE VIEWER KNOW THAT OVERSIZED COCKS ARE WHERE IT'S AT. BUT WHY NO LOVE FOR THE BIG VAGINAS? THE SAME WAY NO MAN IN OUR SOCIETY WANTS TO BE SADDLED WITH AN UNDERSIZED PENIS, IT SEEMS RARE FOR ANY WOMAN TO WANT HER PUSSY TO BE CONSIDERED BIG OR OVERSIZED. IT'S CONSIDERED UNSEXY, OR A SIGN OF WORTHLESSNESS.

BUT I'M HERE TO LET YOU KNOW THAT A BIG PUSSY IS NOT ONLY SOMETHING YOU SHOULDN'T BE ASHAMED OF, IT'S ACTUALLY REALLY FUCKING <u>HOT</u>. AND I'M NOT THE ONLY ONE WHO THINKS SO.

"DESTROYED-HOLES", "PRINCESS-STRETCH", "LOOSEPUSSYLAND", "HUGETOYS", "FATGREEDYPUSSY", "STRETCHITGOOD", "MONSTERGAPES", "LOOSECONNOISSEUR", "PUSSY-IS-HUGE" ARE TUMBLR ACCOUNTS BELONGING TO WOMEN WHO ARE PROUD TO HAVE BIG LOOSE PUSSIES, AND THE MEN WHO ADORE THEM. THERE ARE DOZENS AND DOZENS OF THEM, AND IT'S A WHOLE COMMUNITY. THEY POST IMAGES AND VIDEOS OF THEMSELVES TAKING BIG INSERTIONS OF OVERSIZED DILDOS, 'KONG' BRAND DOG TOYS (A BIG FAVOURITE AMONGST SIZE QUEENS, BECAUSE OF THEIR LARGE SIZE AND RUBBERY RIBBED SHAPE), AND FISTS (BOTH THEIR OWN, AND THEIR PARTNERS').

THE PHOTOS AND VIDEOS ARE DISPLAYED AS EVIDENCE OF THE WORK EACH WOMAN HAS BEEN DOING TO "RUIN", "WRECK", OR "DESTROY" THEIR VAGINAS, AND LET'S TAKE A MOMENT TO LOOK AT THAT TERMINOLOGY COMMONLY USED IN THIS KINK. THOSE BARBED TERMS ARE USED EMPHATICALLY BY THE WOMEN AND THEIR FANS, NOT AS A NEGATIVE PUT-DOWN, BUT AS A SUBVERSION OF SOCIETAL NORMS OF WHAT A VAGINA IS EXPECTED TO BE. IT'S A BIG TURN ON FOR MANY OF THEM TO USE THOSE WORDS TO DESCRIBE THEIR GENITALS, TO BE SEEN AS SLUTTY, AND TO GET COMMENTS OF ADORATION AND SUPPORT, SUCH AS "KEEP WORKING AT IT", "NOW THAT'S A BEAUTIFULLY RUINED TWAT", AND "PERFECTLY WRECKED! MY DICK WOULDN'T EVEN TOUCH THE SIDES OF IT, I BET."

CUNT LOOSENESS IS A SUBJECT FRAUGHT WITH MISINFORMATION. WHEN A WOMEN IS WORKED UP, THE VAGINAL AREA BECOMES ENLARGED, WHICH IS KNOWN AS VAGINAL TENTING. THE MORE TURNED ON YOU ARE, THE LARGER YOUR VAG COULD POTENTIALLY GROW. NORMAL INTERCOURSE SIMPLY DOES NOT PERMANENTLY STRETCH A PUSSY. THE VAGINA STRETCHES A GREAT DEAL DURING CHILDBIRTH BUT IT DOES USUALLY RE-TIGHTEN IF WE'RE TALKING ABOUT YOUNG MOTHERS IN THEIR LATE TEENS TO MID TWENTIES. WITHIN SIX MONTHS AFTER DELIVERY, THE TYPICAL YOUNG WOMAN'S CLAM WILL FEEL THE SAME AS IT DID BEFORE SHE GAVE BIRTH. THAT'S A FACT.

WHERE YOU CAN START SEEING PERMANENT CHANGE IS IF YOU STRETCH PAST THE NORMAL SIZE OF YOUR VAGINA A GREAT DEAL, AND OVER A LONG PERIOD OF TIME. AT THAT POINT IT NO LONGER SNAPS BACK ENTIRELY. THIS HAPPENS WITH YOUNG WOMEN AFTER MULTIPLE BIRTHS, WOMEN IN THEIR THIRTIES (OR OLDER) AFTER ONE BABY, FEMALES WHO HIT MIDDLE AGE, AND WITH WOMEN WHO STRETCH THEMSELVES WITH BIG DILDOS AND FISTS. THE VAGINAL MUSCLES THEN FATIGUE AND WILL NO LONGER FULLY CONTRACT.

ONE "GAPER" WHO POSTS CONTENT ON TUMBLR UNDER THE USER NAME "WRECKEDBITCH", TOOK TIME FROM PROUDLY (YET ANONYMOUSLY) SHARING SELFIES OF HER STRETCHED OUT BEAVER TO ELOQUENTLY ANSWER A FEW QUESTIONS ABOUT WHY SHE DOES WHAT SHE DOES:

DURING THE YEARS WHEN I FIRST BECAME SEXUALLY ACTIVE IN GRADE 12 AND MY FIRST YEAR IN COLLEGE, I WAS EXTREMELY TIGHT. UNCOMFORTABLY SO. MY EARLY BOYFRIENDS TOLD ME I'D LOOSEN UP OVER TIME, AND THAT I'D NEED MORE PENETRATIONS TO OPEN ME UP. OF COURSE, THEY WANTED TO BE THE ONES TO DO IT. I WAS QUITE SEXUALLY ACTIVE DURING THIS TIME BECAUSE I LOVED

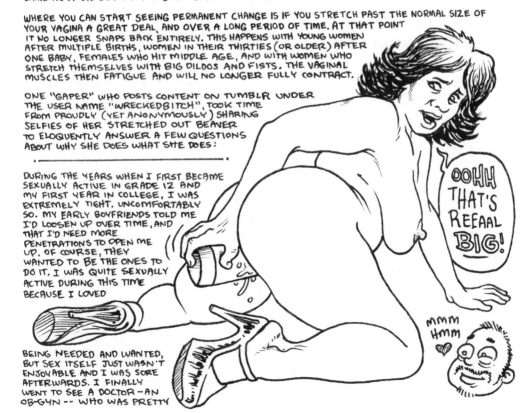

BEING NEEDED AND WANTED, BUT SEX ITSELF JUST WASN'T ENJOYABLE AND I WAS SORE AFTERWARDS. I FINALLY WENT TO SEE A DOCTOR – AN OB-GYN -- WHO WAS PRETTY

UNSYMPATHETIC, AND HE TOLD ME I WAS JUST BORN THAT WAY. HE REALLY DIDN'T HAVE SUGGESTIONS AS TO WHAT I COULD DO TO ALLEVIATE THIS PROBLEM AND BASICALLY TOLD ME THAT IT WAS JUST SOMETHING THAT I'D HAVE TO LEARN TO LIVE WITH, AND THAT I'D FIND IT EASIER IN 15 YEARS OR SO.

AFTER I GOT OUT OF COLLEGE I STARTED DATING A CHARMING GUY WHO I REALLY LIKED AND EVENTUALLY, ONE NIGHT, HE GOT ME IN BED TO SEDUCE ME AND THAT'S WHEN I FOUND OUT HE WAS VERY WELL HUNG. WE TRIED TO HAVE SEX, BUT IT WAS JUST TOO PAINFUL. HE WAS TOO BIG TO COMFORTABLY DEEP THROAT (WHICH IS SOMETHING I'D GOTTEN REASONABLY GOOD AT, BECAUSE OF MY ISSUES DOWNSTAIRS) SO I GOT WORRIED RIGHT AWAY THAT I'D NEVER BE ABLE TO MAKE HIM HAPPY. WHEN HE LATER SUGGESTED THAT WE DO SOME VAGINAL STRETCHING SO THAT HE COULD FIT, I WAS OPEN TO THE IDEA PROVIDING IT WAS SAFE.

I WAS NOT THE FIRST GIRL WHO HAD EXPERIENCED DIFFICULTIES TAKING HIM VAGINALLY. TURNS OUT HE'D DONE IT WITH TWO OTHER GIRLFRIENDS, AND HE EVEN OWNED A UNIVERSITY TEXT BOOK THAT HAD A WHOLE SECTION ON GENITAL MODIFICATION. I WAS JUST AMAZED BY THIS BOOK, IT DISCUSSED LABIA STRETCHING AND ELONGATION, NIPPLE PIERCING, CLIT HOOD PIERCING, CLIT HOOD REDUCTIONS, ETC ETC. I WAS AMAZED. I WASN'T EVEN AWARE THIS SORT OF STUFF WAS EVEN A THING. HAHA I WAS REALLY NAIVE BACK THEN.

I WAS GETTING SERIOUS ABOUT HIM, THOUGH. I THOUGHT THAT I WAS FALLING IN LOVE, SO I WANTED TO PLEASE HIM IN ANY WAY IN COULD AND HE WAS ADAMANT THAT DOING A SERIOUS STRETCHING ROUTINE WAS THE ANSWER. PLEASING MY MAN WAS A TOP PRIORITY FOR ME, SO THE DEDICATION IT TOOK AT FIRST WASN'T THAT HARD. I'D THOUGHT CAREFULLY ABOUT THE PERMANENCE OF IT AND I'D TALKED IT OVER WITH A FEW GIRLFRIENDS, AND I COULDN'T SEE HOW IT COULD BE A BAD THING SINCE HE HAD SUCCESSFULLY STRETCHED OUT TWO OTHER GIRLFRIENDS WITH NO ADVERSE EFFECTS.

"WRECKED BITCH" SHOWS OFF FOR HER FANS...

HIS PROGRAM CONSISTED OF ME WEARING A PANTY GIRDLE WHEN I WENT TO BED AT NIGHT, AND INSERTING AT FIRST A 4" DILDO FOR A MONTH WHILE I SLEPT, AND THEN GOING UP IN 2" INCREMENTS UNTIL UNTIL HE GOT ME TO 12", WHICH WAS THE SIZE WE DECIDED WOULD HAVE ME ADEQUATELY OPENED UP. EACH DILDO THAT WAS LONGER WAS ALSO THICKER WITH THE 12" DILDO BEING 2 INCHES THICK. I COULDN'T EVEN GET MY HAND ALL THE WAY AROUND IT, JUST TO GIVE YOU AN IDEA HOW BIG THAT IS. DURING THE EARLY MONTHS (UP TO 4 INCHES) I OFTEN WORE THEM WHEN I WENT TO MY JOB, AND WE OFTEN WORKED THE INSERTIONS INTO OUR SEX PLAY.

SOME NIGHTS IT WOULD BE UNCOMFORTABLE AND KEEP ME FROM SLEEPING, BUT I GOT USED TO IT AND THREE MONTHS IN WE BEGAN TO GET REALLY GREAT RESULTS. FUCKING HIM WAS BECOMING A BREEZE. NO PAIN, AND I WAS EASILY ABLE TO TAKE HIM FOR LONG VIGOROUS SESSIONS. FUCKING ME WITH BIG DILDOS ALSO BECAME ONE OF HIS FAVOURITE PASTIMES. HE WAS SO HAPPY, I WAS SO HAPPY, AND THERE WERE NO SIDE EFFECTS REALLY WORTH COMPLAINING ABOUT. WHAT IS WORTH COMPLAINING ABOUT IS HOW WE BROKE UP UNDER LESS-THAN-IDEAL TERMS WHEN HE CHEATED ON ME WITH A STUPID BITCH – BUT THE LESS SAID ABOUT THAT, THE BETTER.

IGNORING THE SAD ENDING TO THE STORY, I'M PLEASED THAT I TOOK THE INITIATIVE TO DO THIS, AND STRETCHING, FISTING, AND LARGE DILDO PLAY SOON BECAME MY FAVOURITE WAY TO GET OFF. SHOWING OFF WHAT I CAN DO ONLY MAKES IT BETTER. I THINK I'M BECOMING MORE AND MORE OF AN EXHIBITIONIST AS I GO.

SOME OF YOU GUYS ASK ME IF I HAVE ANY REGRETS ABOUT WRECKING MY PUSSY, AND I HAVE NONE. VAGINAS ARE MAGIC. THEY CAN DO SO MUCH MORE THAN MOST PEOPLE EVEN REALIZE. THIS IS MY BODY, AND MODIFYING IT WITH TATTOOS, PIERCINGS AND STRETCHING IS HOW I CHOOSE TO LIVE IN IT. WRECKED IS BEST!!

—BOUGIE 2017

The death of Tumblr and the Rise of SESTA/FOSTA

TUMBLR WAS MY GO-TO MASTURBATION SITE FOR ABOUT 8 YEARS. THE PLATFORM MADE IT RELATIVELY EASY TO FIND JUST WHAT KIND OF PORN YOU WANTED, WHILE ALSO INTRODUCING YOU TO NEW CONTENT. IT WASN'T LIKE GOING TO REDTUBE OR YOUPORN, BECAUSE YOU WEREN'T SEARCHING, YOU WERE JUST CHECKING YOUR FEED LIKE ON SOCIAL MEDIA. HERE YOU FOLLOWED BLOGGERS WHO CURATED PHOTOS, GIFS, AND VIDEOS THAT THEY THEMSELVES LIKED OR HAD MADE, WHICH PERFECTLY PERSONALIZED THE WHOLE THING. EVERY TIME YOU LOGGED ON, IT WAS LIKE A FRIEND HAD MADE YOU <u>A SMUT MIXTAPE.</u>

IT WAS GLORIOUS. YOU COULD TAILOR-MAKE YOUR TUMBLR EXPERIENCE, FROM THE MOST VANILLA AND CLASSY OF EROTICA, ALL THE WAY TO THE NASTY-ASS, DEGRADATION-THEMED, SUBMISSIVES-GONE-WILD, SEMEN-SOAKED BDSM STUFF I ENJOY. AND IT WAS SO MUCH BETTER THAN THE MAINSTREAM SITES, BECAUSE IT WAS ALL AMATEURS-- JUST REGULAR PEOPLE EXPLORING WHAT TURNS THEM ON. THAT'S HOT.

I WOULD FOLLOW A CERTAIN TYPE OF DOMINANT, AND A CERTAIN TYPE OF SUBMISSIVE. WHEN YOU SCROLLED THROUGH THEIR POST HISTORY, THE SUBS I LIKED (USUALLY THE INTELLIGENT ONES WITH SOME CHUB AND A TASTE FOR DEGRADATION) SAW THE SAME KIND OF NATURAL PROGRESSION TO THEIR TUMBLR EXPERIENCE, OVER AND OVER:

✳ FIRST SHE WOULD DISCOVER WHAT OTHER PEOPLE WERE UPLOADING AND SHARING, AND TEXT A FEW THINGS ABOUT 'OH ISN'T THIS DIRTY, I CAN'T BELIEVE I'M A FEMINIST BUT ALSO INTO THIS PROBLEMATIC STUFF', AS SHE GOT COMFORTABLE WITH HER EMBARRASSING FANTASIES SHE NORMALLY WOULDN'T TELL ANYONE.
✳ SHE'D POST HER FIRST NUDES -- ALWAYS TASTEFULLY POSED AND WITH FACE OBSCURED OF COURSE. BABY STEPS.
✳ THEN SOME SLIGHTLY DEGRADING ONES THAT DIDN'T TRY TO HIDE HER FAT ROLLS. ENCOURAGING USERS TO LEAVE DEGRADING COMMENTS AS SHE TOYS WITH MASTURBATING TO EXPOSURE AND BEING DEGRADED.
✳ NEXT, SOME GIFS THAT WOULD FEATURE ANY COMBINATION OF KISSING HER TOILET SEAT, DRINKING HER OWN PISS, WEARING A BUTT PLUG TO WORK, WRITING DEGRADING NAMES ON HER BODY IN LIPSTICK, OR BEATING ON HER TIED-UP PIG-TITTIES.
✳ THE ARC WOULD COMPLETE WHEN SHE'D MEET A LESBIAN DOMME OR MALE DOMINANT TO HELP HER EXPLORE, AND THEY WOULD HAPPILY POST CONTENT THEY'D MADE TOGETHER.

FANTASY BLURRED WITH REALITY, AND FOR THE MOST PART-- WITH SAFE WORDS AND BOUNDARIES HAPPILY RESPECTED-- I WAS SEEING CONSENSUAL ADULTS ENJOYING THE THRILL OF SEXUAL EXPLORATION.

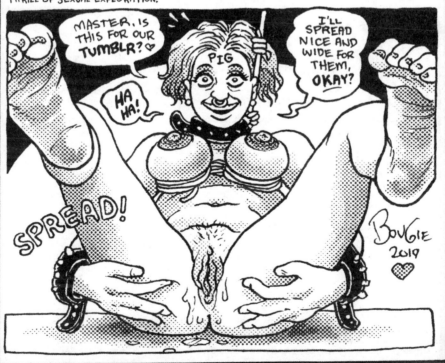

147

I MEAN REALLY, A PERVERT PARADISE, AND CHECKING IN ON THEM EVERY OTHER DAY LET YOU FEEL LIKE YOU WERE FOLLOWING AMATEUR-SMUT SOAP OPERAS. THEY WOULD EXPRESS THEIR JOYS, THEIR DISAPPOINTMENTS, INTERACT IN ENTERTAINING WAYS WITH THEIR FOLLOWERS AND FELLOW BLOGGERS, TALK FREELY 'BOUT WHAT WAS OR WASN'T A TURN-ON, GO ON LITTLE SEX-MISSIONS, AND JUST GENERALLY BE FUCKING AMAZING. HUMBLEDCUNT, PIG9137, SAMMIE LOUISBURG, LOOSE FAT PIG, HEATHER WEATHERGIRL326, MIZZPORKER, VERONICA OWLGLASS, SLAVE PIG KAREN, CUMSLUT ALLIE, HISRACHELLE, BETH AKA THIRSTYPISSWHORE, ANAL ONLY JESSICA, WORTHLESSWOMAN30. IN ALL HONESTY, SOME OF THESE AMATEUR SLAVE SEXPIGS BECAME LIKE <u>CELEBRITIES</u> TO ME.

BUT THEN ON DECEMBER 17TH, 2018, TUMBLR STARTED THE PROCESS OF REMOVING ALL ADULT CONTENT FROM THE SITE, AND ALL THE PERVY RATS ABANDONED THE SINKING SHIP. WHY DID THE SITE COMMIT SUICIDE?

IT WAS THE FAULT OF A SET OF BRAND NEW LAWS CALLED SESTA AND FOSTA THAT CAME INTO PLACE ONLY MONTHS BEFORE, WITH NARY AN EYEBROW RAISED BY THE DONALD TRUMP-CONSUMED MEDIA. THESE US LAWS AFFECT FAR MORE THAN JUST MY CHUBBY FUCKPIGS ON TUMBLR, BECAUSE THEY MAKE ANY WEBSITE RESPONSIBLE FOR THIRD PARTY CONTENT RELATED TO SEX WORK. THAT MEANS ANY US SITE (THAT'S MOST OF THE BIGGEST ONES) CAN BE SUED AND BROUGHT TO THEIR KNEES IN LIABILITY IF A SINGLE SEX WORK SOLICITATION SHOWS UP ON THEIR PLATFORM, EVEN IF THEY HAD NO IDEA IT WAS THERE.

SESTA/FOSTA WERE CREATED AS A REACTION TO SOME ADS THAT SHOWED UP ON THE NOW DECEASED BACKPAGE.COM (A CRAIGSLIST-TYPE SITE) WHERE UNDERAGE GIRLS WERE SELLING SEX. BUT AS PER USUAL WITH GOVERNMENT CENSORSHIP, THE LAWS SIMPLY DON'T DO WHAT WE WERE TOLD THEY WOULD DO, AND STAND SIMPLY AS A REPUBLICAN ATTEMPT TO LIMIT NOT ONLY ONLINE SEX WORK, BUT ALSO QUEER CULTURE (WHICH IS SEEN BY CONSERVATIVES AS INHERENTLY SEXUAL) AND ANY KIND OF ONLINE SEXUAL EXPRESSION.

THIS MUCH IS OBVIOUS: SESTA/FOSTA DOES NOTHING TO STOP SEX TRAFFICKING, AND ACTUALLY MAKES IT FAR HARDER FOR POLICE TO CATCH PREDATORS AND TO HELP THEIR VICTIMS. THE LAWS VICTIMIZE SEX WORKERS, SINCE KILLING THEIR ABILITY TO SOLICIT ONLINE NULLIFIES THEIR ABILITY TO SCREEN CLIENTS (INCREDIBLY IMPORTANT), HAVE AUTONOMY (AKA BE YOUR OWN BOSS) SO THEY CAN STAY CLEAR OF PIMPS, AND IT ALSO KEEPS THEM OFF STREET CORNERS. THE WORLD'S OLDEST PROFESSION IS GOING NOWHERE, AND LEGISLATORS FORCING PROSTITUTES BACK OUT ONTO THE STREET UNDER THE CLAIM THEY ARE "PROTECTING THEM", SHOULD NEVER BE SEEN AS ANYTHING OTHER THAN DISINGENUOUS.

BUT I NEED TO BE PAINFULLY CLEAR THAT SEX WORKERS WEREN'T THE ONLY ONES FUCKED BY THIS. THE LAWS ARE SO BROADLY WRITTEN, THEY PUSH WEBSITES TO DELETE ANY KIND OF LEWD CONTENT, AND TRAINING AN ALGORITHM TO SPOT LEWD SOLICITATIONS AND LEAVE OTHER TYPES OF TALK/IMAGERY ABOUT SEX ALONE IS OBVIOUSLY NEARLY IMPOSSIBLE. THE ALREADY CENSORIAL FACEBOOK BEGAN OVERZEALOUSLY BANNING THE DISCUSSION OF ANYTHING RELATED TO SEX, THE CAM SITES BEGAN TO REALIZE THAT THEY WERE AT RISK, AND BANKS CAME UNDER INCREASED PRESSURE TO STOP PROCESSING PAYMENTS OF INVOLVED PARTIES AS WELL.

THIS ANTI-SEX CENSORSHIP BILL COULDN'T JUST BE LAID AT THE FEET OF REPUBLICANS ALONE, THOUGH. LIBERALS WERE JUST AS MUCH AT FAULT, AND IN FACT IT WAS LIBERAL CELEBRITIES LIKE COMEDIAN AMY SCHUMER AND TALK SHOW HOST SETH MEYERS WHO WERE SESTA/FOSTA'S BIGGEST BOOSTERS, EVEN BLATANTLY APPEARING IN ADVERTISING DESIGNED TO DRUM UP PUBLIC SUPPORT FOR THEM. IT WAS HONESTLY ONLY SEX WORKERS WHO WERE UP IN ARMS ON SOCIAL MEDIA ABOUT SESTA/FOSTA BEFORE THEY PASSED, AND NO ONE FUCKING LISTENED. AS PER USUAL, SEX WORKERS WERE IGNORED WHEN THE SOCIETAL IMPLICATIONS OF SEX CENSORSHIP LAWS WERE DISCUSSED.

SO HERE WE ARE IN 2020. I'M NOT SURE WHERE SHIT WILL BE BY THE TIME YOU READ THIS, BUT MY PREDICTION IS THAT ELECTED OFFICIALS WON'T OVERTURN THIS IDIOTIC LEGISLATION, AS THEY WILL CERTAINLY BE ACCUSED OF BEING "SOFT" ON SEX TRAFFICKING AND CHILD ENDANGERMENT IF THEY DO. I DARE SAY THIS SHIT IS HERE TO STAY. — BOUGIE '20

☆ SEE IT OR BE IT: THE LAST AMERICAN VIRGIN ☆

(WARNING: WATCH THE MOVIE FIRST — THIS ESSAY INCLUDES PLOT SPOILERS - YOU'VE BEEN WARNED!)

THE TALE OF THE LAST AMERICAN VIRGIN STARTS WITH A SERIES OF FILMS FROM ISRAEL CALLED LEMON POPSICLE. THIS CYCLE OF ZANY HIGH-SCHOOL SEX-BASED ADVENTURES SET IN THE FIFTIES BECAME A WORLDWIDE HIT IN THE 1970S, PACKING THEATERS IN EUROPE AND JAPAN IN PARTICULAR. THERE WERE 8 MOVIES MADE FROM 1978 TO 1988, AS WELL AS A TV SERIES IN 2001, WHICH WAS INSTEAD REFORMATTED AS YET ANOTHER FEATURE FILM.

AND SO WHEN MENAHEM GOLAN AND YORAM GLOBUS (A PAIR OF ISRAELI COUSINS WHO MADE CANNON FILMS THE BIGGEST INDEPENDENT FILM STUDIO IN HOLLYWOOD IN THE 1980S), ADAPTED THE POPULAR FRANCHISE, AND WENT SO FAR AS TO HIRE ON THE ORIGINAL DIRECTOR (BOAZ DAVIDSON) TO REMAKE HIS FILM, THEY ASSUMED THEY'D HAVE A HIT ON THEIR HANDS.

"(LEMON POPSICLE) WAS A TRUE STORY ABOUT ME GROWING UP IN TEL AVIV, ISRAEL", DIRECTOR BOAZ DAVIDSON TOLD INTERVIEWER ART EDDY IN 2012. "THE MOVIE WAS A BIG HIT ALL OVER THE WORLD. THIS WAS THE FIRST TIME A SMALL ISRAELI MOVIE WENT PLACES."

THE PROJECT WAS MARKETED CORRECTLY. THE RETITLING IS PERFECT, ITS EXCELLENT WELL-ADVERTISED SOUNDTRACK IS LITTERED WITH POPULAR ROCK BANDS OF THE ERA, AND THE THEATRICAL POSTER DID MORE THAN JUST HINT AT THE DEBAUCHERY TO BE EXPECTED. SUCCESS WASN'T IN THE CARDS, HOWEVER. THE LAST AMERICAN VIRGIN DIDN'T BUST ANY BLOCKS WHEN IT OPENED IN LATE JULY 1982, OBSCURED BY THE WAKE OF THE HIT TEEN SEX COMEDY PORKY'S.

BUT A FUNNY THING HAPPENED AS THE MOVIE SLOWLY BEGAN BUILDING A CULT FOLLOWING BY BEING REDISCOVERED VIA CABLE TV AIRINGS AND VHS COPIES FLOATING AROUND IN THE '80S AND '90S. EVEN CELEBRITIES SUCH AS DIRECTOR ELI ROTH NAMED IT "THE MOST UNDERRATED TEEN COMEDY EVER MADE", AND ESPN'S BILL SIMMONS WENT ONE FURTHER, CITING IT AS "THE MOST UNDERRATED AMERICAN FILM OF ALL TIME".

THE PLOT, AS CRASS AND POLITICALLY INCORRECT AS IT IS, IS PROPELLED BY THREE TEENAGE BOYS WHO SHARE A COMMON SINGULAR GOAL OLDER THAN RECORDED TIME: TO JAM THEIR BONERS INTO SOME TEENAGE VAGINA. AND GOSH DARN IT, DO THEY GET INTO SOME CRAZY MISADVENTURES DURING THEIR BEST EFFORTS TO DO SO.

"THE LAST AMERICAN VIRGIN IS ESSENTIALLY TWO FILMS", WROTE LOS ANGELES AUTHOR KEVIN KOEHLER IN 2007 FOR THE WEBSITE IDENTITYTHEORY.COM. "THE FIRST IS YOUR STANDARD TEEN COMEDY FARCE.., THE SECOND IS A SUBLIME PIECE OF SUBVERSIVE GENIUS; COMING-OF-AGE AS PASSION PLAY, HUMPING AS HOBSON'S CHOICE!"

"VIRGIN'S MESMERIC FINAL MOMENTS, FEATURING GARY'S ULTIMATE CUCKOLDING/CASTRATION AT A BIRTHDAY PARTY, ARE REALLY WHAT ELEVATE THE PICTURE FROM MERE CULTURAL CURIOSITY TO UNHERALDED SUBVERSIVE BRILLIANCE... A DECIDEDLY MICHAEL HANEKE-ESQUE BIT OF GUT-PUNCH AUDIENCE SADISM, MADE ALL THE MORE POWERFUL BY HOW ANACHRONISTIC IT IS; AMERICAN MULTIPLEX PICTURES JUST DO NOT HAVE THE COURAGE TO END LIKE THIS. NOT ANY MORE!"

YES, THE GUT-PUNCH ENDING. THERE WAS SOMETHING JUST SO BITTER AND UNFORGIVING ABOUT IT-- A TONE THAT WOULDN'T HAVE BEEN OUT OF PLACE OR NOTEWORTHY IN A DRAMA OR ART-HOUSE FEATURE, BUT IS BREATHTAKING IN THE UNFAMILIAR SURROUNDING OF A TEEN SEX COMEDY. EXPECTATION IS EVERYTHING IN CINEMA.

WHEN GARY (LAWRENCE MONOSON) HELPS POOR KAREN (DIANE FRANKLIN) BY PAYING FOR HER ABORTION, HE'S PAWNING MOST OF HIS MEAGRE POSSESSIONS AND GOING INTO DEBT BY BORROWING MONEY. HE'S DOING WHAT THE FATHER OF THE UNWANTED CHILD, HIS BEST FRIEND RICK (STEVE ANTIN) IS TOO MUCH OF A SELFISH DICKHOLE TO DO. HE KINDLY STEPS UP TO THE PLATE WHEN SHE NEEDS IT THE MOST, BRAVELY CONFESSES HIS LOVE, AND IS THE ONLY ONE THERE TO CARE FOR KAREN WHILE SHE RECOVERS BOTH FROM THE TRAUMA OF THE ABORTION AND THE HEARTBREAK OF RICK'S ABANDONMENT. GARY IS THE ONE DEVOTED TO HER, AND FINELY TUNED TO THE ANGUISH INVOLVED IN SUCH A PAINFUL EXPERIENCE.

MERE DAYS LATER, AT KAREN'S 18TH BIRTHDAY PARTY, WE BEAR WITNESS TO THE SEVERING OF GARY'S DREAMS OF A MEANINGFUL ROMANCE WITH THIS GORGEOUS YOUNG WOMAN. WE SEE THE MOMENT ON HIS FACE WHEN HE IS UTTERLY SHATTERED AFTER WALKING IN ON KAREN MAKING OUT WITH RICK. SOON AFTER, THE CREDITS ROLL.

IT'S THIS BITTER "NICE GUYS FINISH LAST" FINALE THAT IS GROUND LIKE SANDPAPER IN THE FACE OF ANYONE WATCHING WHO EMPATHIZED WITH GARY, WHO FOR ALL HIS GOOD INTENTIONS, IS AT THE MERCY OF THE CRUEL WHIMS OF A SILLY TEENAGER. TEENS ARE KNOWN TO MAKE STUPID DECISIONS WITH NO REAL CONSIDERATION FOR HOW IT MIGHT HARM THEMSELVES OR OTHERS, BUT BEING ONE HIMSELF, GARY ISN'T REMOTELY PREPARED.

THE MORE FANCIFUL ASPECTS OF THE FILM ARE THE ONES THAT KOEHLER REFERRED TO AS "STANDARD TEEN COMEDY FARCE", BUT I THINK THEY'RE EVERY BIT AS IMPORTANT TO VIRGIN'S WATCHABILITY. THE DRIVING OF CARS INTO THE OCEAN, THE AWKWARD REMOVAL OF BRAS AND BARING OF BREASTS, THE MEASURING OF DICKS IN LOCKER ROOMS, AND THE FUCKING OF OVERSEXED MIDDLE-AGED MEXICAN HOUSEWIVES AND DEPRESSING STREETWALKERS.

"WHEN WE WERE DOING THAT SCENE WHERE WE BANGED THAT HOOKER, WE WERE DOWN IN A BASEMENT OF AN ABANDONED RESTAURANT!" ACTOR JOE RUBBO TOLD MRSKIN.COM IN 2007. "THERE WERE RATS IN THERE. THEY SENT EXTERMINATORS ON THE DAY OF THE SHOOT, AND, DURING FILMING, YOU COULD HEAR THE RATS SCREAMING AND DYING. IT SCARED THE SHIT OUT OF ME."

IT WAS THE FIRST MOVIE FOR MOST OF THE TEENAGE CAST. STAR LAWRENCE MONOSON WAS AN INTENSE TEEN WHO, ACCORDING TO HIS CO-STARS, HAD A REALLY HARD TIME LOOSENING UP AND RELAXING ON SET BECAUSE HE FELT SO STRESSED AND OUT OF HIS ELEMENT. "I WAS A YOUNG ACTOR

AT THE TIME" LAWRENCE EXPLAINED. "I DO REMEMBER WORKING SO HARD BECAUSE I HAD TO LEARN...
I DID NOT HAVE THAT SORT OF TECHNICAL ACUMEN, WHICH YOU GOT FROM WORKING ON FILMS. SO I
TOOK IT VERY SERIOUSLY."

"HE FUSSED OVER EVERYTHING" CO-STAR KIMMY ROBERTSON (A HIGHLY UNDERRATED ACTRESS KNOWN
FOR HER HIGH-PITCHED VOICE AND QUIRKY COMEDIC TIMING) SAID OF WORKING WITH MONOSON WHEN
INTERVIEWED BY MRSKIN.COM. "HE WOULD TAKE HIS MAKEUP OFF IN BETWEEN SCENES. IN THE CAR
SCENE WHEN WE WERE KISSING, HE CUT MY LIP BECAUSE HE NEVER KISSED ANYONE BEFORE. HE WAS
AWKWARD LIKE THAT."

"I USED TO HANG WITH HIM AFTER SHOOTING THE MOVIE WAS OVER. I SAW MY ONLY PORN MOVIE
EVER, INSATIABLE, WHEN I WAS IN BED WITH LAWRENCE WATCHING IT. HE WAS EIGHTEEN, I WAS
TWENTY-NINE. WE WERE DRESSED UNDER THE COVERS. I THINK HE WAS TRYING TO FIGURE OUT WHO
HE WAS... I THINK I ASKED HIM IF HE WANTED A BLOW JOB. HE SAID NO."

"THE TWO THINGS I'M KNOWN FOR, THE TWO THINGS THAT I'VE BEEN IN THAT WERE GOOD IN MY
WHOLE CAREER -- WERE THE LAST AMERICAN VIRGIN AND TWIN PEAKS", KIMMY SAID AT THE NEW
BEVERLY CAST REUNION IN 2007. "AND THE BOTH OF THEM -- IT WAS BECAUSE THE DIRECTOR WAS
BEING OBSERVANT, AND WAS WATCHING ME. AND WHEN HE THOUGHT SOMETHING WAS NEAT, HE'D SAY 'CAN
YOU DO WHAT YOU WERE DOING 10 MINUTES AGO?'. BOAZ WAS THIS COOL GUY, AND HE WOULD WATCH
AND PICK OUT OF PEOPLE WHAT WAS OBVIOUSLY GREAT ON SCREEN, THINGS WE DIDN'T KNOW WERE
COOL."

IN 2011, GERRI ANN IDOL (WHO PLAYED THE SEXY 'ROXANNE') TOLD INTERVIEWER JAMES M. TATE THAT
SHE GREW UP IN DETROIT, WHERE BY CHANCE IN 1979 SHE ENDED UP MEETING DAVID LEE ROTH (LEAD
SINGER OF VAN HALEN) AT THE OLD WABX RADIO STATION. IN TRUE ROCKSTAR FASHION, HE LITERALLY
PICKED HER OUT OF A PARKING LOT OF SCREAMING YOUNG GIRLS, BEGINNING A DRUNKEN WHIRLWIND
EVENING THAT ENTIRELY CHANGED HER LIFE.

THE MOMENT THAT GARY'S LIFE IS METAPHORICALLY SMASHED INTO A THOUSAND LITTLE PIECES.

"(WE) WENT BACKSTAGE, AND I HELPED HIM PICK OUT HIS OUTFIT, AND DID SOME STRETCHING AND
DANCING WITH HIM... FOR A YOUNG GIRL OF 16, THAT WAS VERY EXCITING AT THE TIME. HE WAS THE
BEST IN THE BUSINESS, AND CERTAINLY THE SEXIEST. IT WAS MEETING HIM THAT BROUGHT ME TO
CALIFORNIA, AND MY BEAUTIFUL BELOVED MOTHER AND DADDY -- THEY DIDN'T KNOW WHAT TO THINK."

"MANY YEARS WERE SPENT IN HOLLYWOOD WITH MEN OF INFLUENCE AND POWER, THAT WHOLE SCENE OF
TRYING TO DO SOMETHING WITH MY YOUNG TALENTS. THERE WERE ALWAYS OTHER THINGS INVOLVED:
THE BOYFRIENDS, THE SEX, THE DRUGS, THE ROCK AND ROLL. THAT IS WHAT BROUGHT ME TO WORKING
ON (THE LAST AMERICAN VIRGIN)."

"I REMEMBER THAT THERE WAS AN IMMEDIATE CONNECTION BETWEEN TESSA, WINNIE, AND I. WE HAD
SO MUCH FUN DOING THOSE SCENES. IT WAS VERY SPONTANEOUS, AND A LOT OF FUN... WE DIDN'T HAVE
REHEARSALS AT ALL. THE SCENES THAT WE SHOT IN THE OLD DINER IN WEST HOLLYWOOD ON BEVERLY
BLVD, AND WE HAD JUST MET EACH OTHER FOR THE FIRST TIME!"

"IT WAS ON BEVERLY BOULEVARD AT A PLACE CALLED BIRD'S" ACTOR BRIAN PECK SAID ABOUT THE
LOCATION TO MRSKIN.COM. "(IT WAS) A FAST FOOD FRIED CHICKEN RESTAURANT. THEY MADE IT LOOK
HIP, LIKE A TEEN HANGOUT. I REMEMBER THE NIGHT A CREW MEMBER OFFERED THE CAST COCAINE TO
KEEP US AWAKE. IT WAS LATE AT NIGHT, AND I GUESS HE THOUGHT WE WERE GETTING A LITTLE
SLUGGISH. I MYSELF DID NOT TAKE HIM UP ON IT. I WOULD TELL YOU IF I DID. BUT HOW
QUINTESSENTIAL 1981: 'HEY, HAVE SOME COKE AND WE'LL FILM ALL NIGHT!'"

"WE ALL BECAME VERY CLOSE WHEN WE MADE THE MOVIE", SAID ACTOR JOE RUBBO. "WE WERE ALL

SEVENTEEN, EIGHTEEN YEARS OLD, AND IT WAS NEW TO ALL OF US. (DIANE FRANKLIN) DIDN'T MIND TAKING HER CLOTHES OFF. THERE WERE NO DRESSING ROOMS OR ANYTHING, AND THERE SHE WAS, TAKING HER CLOTHES OFF. I COULDN'T BELIEVE IT."

WHY LOVELY DIANE FRANKLIN DIDN'T BECOME A 1980S SUPERSTAR IS BEYOND ME. SHE HAD IT ALL: TREMENDOUS LOOKS (INCLUDING THOSE FULL DARK EYEBROWS THAT HER CHILDHOOD FRIEND, BROOKE SHIELDS, MADE POPULAR), A BEGUILING VOICE, AND A WINSOME SMILE THAT THE CAMERA LOVED. SHE'D GO ON TO MEMORABLE ROLES IN BETTER OFF DEAD AND BILL AND TED'S EXCELLENT ADVENTURE, BUT SHE NEVER BECAME THE HEADLINER THAT SHE SHOULD HAVE BEEN.

IN LATE 2011, PRODUCER BRETT RATNER ANNOUNCED THAT HE'D BE PRODUCING A REMAKE OF THE FILM. "THE GIRL IN THAT WAS SO BEAUTIFUL, CURLY HAIR, GORGEOUS EYES, I WAS TWELVE YEARS OLD AND I THINK I JERKED OFF TO HER AT LEAST TWO HUNDRED TIMES," HE TOLD HOWARD STERN, REFERRING TO DIANE FRANKLIN.

"BRETT RATNER CAME TO US AND WE WERE TALKING ABOUT SOME OTHER MOVIE", DIRECTOR BOAZ DAVIDSON REVEALED TO INTERVIEWER ART EDDY IN 2012. "HE SAW IN MY OFFICE THE POSTER FOR THE LAST AMERICAN VIRGIN. HE WAS EXCITED AND HE ASKED ME 'DO YOU LIKE THIS MOVIE TOO?' I SAID 'WHAT DO YOU MEAN? I DID THIS MOVIE!'"

NEEDLESS TO SAY, BRETT RATNER IS A CLUELESS ASSHOLE, AND I'M PLEASED TO NOTE THAT HE DIDN'T END UP PRODUCING THE REMAKE THAT HE HOPED TO.

"WHEN I GO OUT AND I GET RECOGNIZED, IT'S ALWAYS SHOCKING TO ME" DIANE FRANKLIN TOLD INTERVIEWER JEFF CRAMER IN 2012. "WHEN I WAS 18, I THOUGHT, 'OH, YOU KNOW, I DON'T KNOW IF THIS WILL EVER -- IF ANYONE WILL EVEN SEE THIS MOVIE.' SO IT IS SO SHOCKING TO ME THAT PEOPLE NOT ONLY HAVE SEEN IT, BUT THEY ALSO REMEMBERED, AND THEY ALSO PASSED IT ON TO THEIR KIDS. THE ENDING MAKES IT SO DISTINCTIVE THAT I DON'T KNOW IF THEY CAN MAKE A REMAKE OF IT, TODAY. ENDINGS LIKE THAT HAPPEN AND IT'S REALITY, BUT I DON'T KNOW IF THEY COULD MAKE THAT SAME MOVIE TODAY."

JEFFREY: DRESSED TO THRILL

IN THE MARCH 1987 ISSUE OF EROTIC X-FILM GUIDE, REPORTER/PERFORMER ANNIE SPRINKLE LANDED A CUTE INTERVIEW WITH SOMEONE USUALLY IGNORED IN THE SMUT INDUSTRY: THE CREW. IN THIS INSTANCE, IT WAS COSTUME DEPARTMENT AND PRODUCTION DESIGNER JEFFREY WALLACH, AND I NOW QUOTE SOME OF THE MORE INTERESTING TIDBITS FROM THAT TALK:

"MY JOB AS COSTUME PERSON INVOLVES ALL KINDS OF ODD JOBS ON SET. THERE ARE LOTS OF TIMES THE MAKE UP ARTIST IS REALLY BUSY, SO I MIGHT HAVE TO COVER UNSIGHTLY PIMPLES AROUND THE GENITAL AREA. I MIGHT HAVE TO MOP UP CUM SO EVERY THING LOOKS PRETTY AGAIN. I ALSO GET ASKED TO BABYSIT THE ACTRESSES. LIKE MAKE SURE THEY DON'T STAY OUT ALL NIGHT IN NIGHTCLUBS OR DRINK TOO MUCH IF THEY'RE FROM OUT OF TOWN, AND SEE TO IT THAT THEY GET TO SET ON TIME. OR DURING A SHOOT WHEN THEY AREN'T NEEDED FOR A COUPLE HOURS, I HAVE TO MAKE SURE THEY DON'T FORGET TO COME BACK AND FINISH THE MOVIE."

JEFFREY, I DON'T THINK THIS SHIRT FIIIITS...

"GLORIA LEONARD OWNS A REALLY BEAUTIFUL WARDROBE, BUT MOST OF THE YOUNGER, NEWER GIRLS HAVEN'T THE FOGGIEST IDEA OF HOW TO DRESS, AND THEY BRING ME THE TACKIEST, UGLIEST STUFF."

"LEE CAROL WAS REALLY HORRIBLE AND OBNOXIOUS. JOHN LESLIE IS TALENTED, BUT HE'S A CHAUVANIST. DAVID SCOTT IS REAL OBNOXIOUS TO WORK WITH. THERE ARE SOME GIRLS THAT I DON'T THINK ARE HAPPY DOING PORN, LIKE SUE NERO."

LADY TERMINATOR

(1988. Indonesia. Dir: Jalil Jackson)

CONNOISSEURS OF WORLDWIDE TRASH CINEMA RECOGNIZE THE FILMS THAT COME OUT OF INDONESIA AS SOME OF THE WILDEST HUMAN EYES CAN WITNESS. PACKED WITH OUTRAGEOUS VIOLENCE, STARTLING NUDITY AND SEX, GOOFY DIALOGUE AND LARGER THAN LIFE CHARACTERS, AND A SPECIAL SOUTHEAST ASIAN QUALITY THAT NO OTHER COUNTRY CAN DUPLICATE, INDONESIAN CINEMA IS ALWAYS SURPRISING AND NEVER DULL.

A SNARLING INSATIABLE QUEEN OF THE OCEAN (WITH HAIRY ARMPITS) KEEPS BUSY BAGGING AS MANY HORNY LOCAL MEN AS POSSIBLE, AND WHEN THEY CAN'T SATISFY HER, SHE CASTRATES THEM WITH HER LOVETRAP! "IS THERE ANY MAN WHO CAN SATISFY ME?" SHE ASKS, DARING THE AUDIENCE TO ANSWER. ONE BRAVE MUSCULAR WHITE GUY DECIDES TO TAKE THAT CHALLENGE, AND JUST BEFORE SHE CAN WHACK HIS WIENER OFF, HE PULLS A SNAKE FROM BETWEEN HER LEGS, WHICH BECOMES A KNIFE (?!). SHE VOWS VENGEANCE ON THE HERO'S GREAT-GRANDDAUGHTER AND VANISHES INTO THE OCEAN.

YEARS LATER, IN THE PRESENT (THE AWESOME 1980s), TANYA, A BEAUTIFUL YOUNG ANTHROPOLOGY STUDENT ("I'M NOT A LADY! I'M AN ANTHROPOLOGIST!") RESEARCHING THE LEGEND OF SAID SOUTH SEA QUEEN, GOES SCUBA DIVING TO FIND HER UNDERWATER CASTLE AND IS POSSESSED BY THE BLOODTHIRSTY SPIRIT OF THE QUEEN! EMERGING FROM THE SEA FULLY NUDE, SHE HAS SEX WITH TWO DRUNK GUYS (WHO JUST FINISHED PISSING LIKE RACEHORSES NEAR THEIR CAR!), CASTRATING BOTH OF THEM, SENDING BLOOD SPURTING INTO THEIR SCREAMING FACES. HER MISSION: KILL THE GREAT-GRANDDAUGHTER OF THE NOW-DEAD HERO AND SLAUGHTER ANYONE STANDING IN HER WAY,... AND OH YEAH: HAVE AS MUCH SEX AS POSSIBLE!

WORDS CANNOT DESCRIBE JUST HOW INSANE, EXCITING AND DOWNRIGHT BRILLIANT LADY TERMINATOR REALLY IS. EVERY LINE OF DIALOGUE IS A CAMP CLASSIC GEM, BADLY DUBBED INTO ENGLISH (THOUGH IT SEEMS THE FILM WAS SHOT IN ENGLISH, EVEN BY THE INDONESIAN CAST), THE OH-SO-80s SYNTHESIZER SCORE IS PERFECT, TONS OF THE ACTION SCENES FEATURE FLAMETHROWERS, MACHINE GUN BLASTS, EXPLOSIONS, AND TONS OF DEAD BODIES DROPPING LIKE FLIES (MASSACRES AT A MALL, A DISCO, A POLICE STATION, AND AT AN AIRFIELD ARE HIGHLIGHTS).

ON TOP OF THAT, THERE'S A GREAT POP MUSIC NUMBER, PLENTY OF BIG HAIR, BIG GUNS, BIG EXPLOSIONS, BIG BREASTS, WAY MORE REFERENCES TO THE ORIGINAL TERMINATOR (INCLUDING THE FAMOUS "COME WITH ME IF YOU WANT TO LIVE" LINE) THAN COULD POSSIBLY BE LEGAL, AND OF COURSE THE CONTROVERSIAL SEX SCENES RESULTING IN DISMEMBERED DONKEY DONGS.

BARBARA ANNE CONSTABLE

THE BUSTY AND BEAUTIFUL BARBARA ANNE CONSTABLE SHOWS NO FEAR AT DROPPING HER TOP, MOWING DOWN HUNDREDS OF INNOCENT PEOPLE WITH HER TRUSTY MACHINE GUN, AND INDULGING IN PANTING SEX SCENES -- ALL FOR THE PLEASURE OF THE AUDIENCE. WHAT A DEDICATED ACTRESS! SHE ALSO HAS A GREAT SCENE WHERE SHE CARVES HER EYEBALL OUT (!) THEN REPLACES IT AFTER FISHING A NECKLACE OUT OF THE SOCKET.

– REVIEW BY **CASEY SCOTT** ☆

BOUG SAYS:

I ♥ LADY TERM-INATOR SO MUCH!

SOOOO MANY A+ **WICKED** SCENES! THIS FILM IS MUCHO FUNNO, MAN!

HA HA!

SO MUCH ACTION!

WHIP!

WHOOSH!

AUGH I PULLED A MUSCLE IN MY BUTT! *

* THIS REALLY HAPPENED

the 4 most memorable three-ways in film history

THE THREESOME. ONE OF THE MOST COMMON SEX FANTASIES FOR BOTH MEN AND WOMEN, AND WHAT IS CINEMA IF NOT WISH FULFILMENT? MOST OF YOU PROBABLY WON'T EVER GET TO SCRATCH THIS ONE OFF YOUR BEDROOM BUCKET LIST, BUT HERE ARE THE FOUR THAT I THINK STOOD OUT ON THE BIG SCREEN. KEEP IN MIND THAT THIS IS A LIST OF NON-XXX RATED FILMS.

4. WILD THINGS (1998)
A TRIO OF CRIMINALS (PLAYED BY MATT DILLON, DENISE RICHARDS AND NEVE CAMPBELL) CELEBRATE (WHAT THEY THINK IS) A SUCCESSFUL CON SCHEME THAT WILL MAKE THEM ALL WILDLY RICH, AND DO SO BY POPPING CORKS, POURING CHAMPAGNE ALL OVER EACH OTHER, AND INTENSELY GRINDING IN A NIGHT OF PASSION THAT HAPPENS IN A FLORIDA MOTEL. TAKING THE CELEBRITY STAR POWER INTO ACCOUNT, THIS IS ONE OF THE MOST LEGENDARY HOLLYWOOD MENAGE-A-TROIS' IN CINEMA HISTORY.

3. SUMMER LOVERS (1982)
PETER GALLAGHER, DARYL HANNAH AND GORGEOUS FRENCH ACTRESS VALERIE QUENNESSEN (WHO WOULD DIE ONLY 7 YEARS LATER IN A TRAGIC CAR ACCIDENT) VACATION IN GREECE AND SPEND SO MUCH OF THE MOVIE SUNBATHING NAKED TOGETHER, THAT WHEN THE TRYST FINALLY HAPPENS, IT DOESN'T MATTER THAT THE SEX HAPPENS OFF SCREEN. THAT'S BECAUSE WHEN THE THREE OF THEM TENDERLY TAKE TURNS STARING INTO EACH OTHERS EYES AND KISSING EACH OTHER, ITS ENOUGH TO MAKE THE CROTCH OF YOUR PANTS EXPLODE. PROOF THAT TAKING THE TRIP CAN BE MORE IMPORTANT THAN REACHING THE DESTINATION.

2. Y TU MAMA TAMBIEN (2001)
OSCAR-WINNING DIRECTOR ALFONSO CUARON'S CRITICALLY ACCLAIMED ROAD TRIP MOVIE COMES TO A HEAD (HEH HEH) WHEN TWO YOUNG MALE FRIENDS MEET A PERCEPTIVE AND SEXY OLDER WOMAN NAMED LUISA, WHO, UPON WITNESSING THE MEN'S FRIENDSHIP UNRAVEL, COAXES THEM INTO A SINFUL MÉNAGE A TROIS, CULMINATING IN THE GUYS ENGAGING IN A PASSIONATE SLO-MO KISS WHILE SHE KNEELS AND SUCKS AND NIBBLES ON THEIR CEMENT-HARD WANGERS. MOSTLY WHAT MAKES THIS SO FUCKIN' HOT IS THAT THE SEX IS ENTIRELY IN SERVICE TO THE NEEDS OF THE STORY, AND OPERATES AS GREAT CHARACTER DEVELOPMENT. GOOD STUFF.

1. KEN PARK (2002)
LARRY CLARK'S DISTURBING FOLLOW UP TO KIDS (1995) FEATURES A STEAMY THREE-PERSON-ORGY (A "THORGY"?) TOWARDS THE END OF THE MOVIE. IT TAKES PLACE WHEN A TRIO OF YOUNG FRIENDS, SHAWN (JAMES BULLARD), CLAUDE (STEPHEN JASSO), AND PEACHES (TIFFANY LIMOS) DECIDE TO LET IT ALL HANG OUT. WHILE MOST BIG-SCREEN THREE-WAYS FEEL POSED AND FAKE, THIS MONTAGE OF VARIOUS SEX ACTS BETWEEN THE THREE OF THEM ARE BASICALLY HARDCORE AND PERFECTLY ENCOMPASS THE BLISSFUL FEELING OF JUST LAZILY LAYING AROUND AND BEING SEXUALLY CASUAL AND RELAXED WITH TWO OTHER PEOPLE AT THE SAME TIME. THIS IS THE THREESOME PINNACLE. A+.

BOUG SEZ:

REALITY: 3 IS USUALLY A CROWD. EVEN THE MOST SEASONED THREESOME LOVER WILL AGREE.

POSITIONING IS **VERY** IMPORTANT!

MMPH

OoHHH OH. OH. OH. GOHD

BOUGIE '17

1993: The year it all went to shit

NO WORDY INTRO OR SET-UP NEEDED FOR THIS ARTICLE, AS THE FILMOGRAPHIES SPEAK FOR THEMSELVES. SURE, THERE ARE A FEW GEMS SPRINKLED AMONGST THE VAST POST-1993 FIELDS OF DOGSHIT, BUT THEY COME TOO FAR TOO INFREQUENTLY FOR FILMMAKERS OF SUCH AN UNMISTAKABLY PROVEN CALIBRE. MY SIMPLE POINT WITH THIS PIECE BEING: PRE 1993, MANY DIRECTORS MADE FAR BETTER WORK THAN THEY MADE POST 1993. WHY THAT IS, I WILL LEAVE FOR YOU, THE READER, TO PONTIFICATE UPON. I JUST FIGURED IT WAS WORTH THINKING ABOUT. (LIST MADE IN 2017)

Brian DePalma
Career achievements pre 1993:
SISTERS, PHANTOM OF THE PARADISE, OBSESSION, CARRIE, THE FURY, DRESSED TO KILL, BLOW OUT, SCARFACE, BODY DOUBLE, THE UNTOUCHABLES, CASUALTIES OF WAR, RAISING CAIN, AND CARLITO'S WAY

Career achievements post 1993:
MISSION IMPOSSIBLE, SNAKE EYES, MISSION TO MARS, FEMME FATALE, THE BLACK DAHLIA, REDACTED, AND PASSION

Sam Raimi
Career achievements pre 1993:
THE EVIL DEAD, CRIMEWAVE, EVIL DEAD 2, DARKMAN, AND ARMY OF DARKNESS

Career achievements post 1993:
QUICK AND THE DEAD, A SIMPLE PLAN, FOR LOVE OF THE GAME, THE GIFT, SPIDER-MAN 1, 2, AND 3, DRAG ME TO HELL, AND OZ THE GREAT AND POWERFUL

Dario Argento
Career achievements pre 1993:
BIRD WITH THE CRYSTAL PLUMAGE, CAT O' NINE TAILS, FOUR FLIES ON GREY VELVET, DEEP RED, SUSPIRIA, INFERNO, TENEBRE, PHEONOMENA, AND OPERA

Career achievements post 1993:
TRAUMA, THE STENDHAL SYNDROME, THE PHANTOM OF THE OPERA, SLEEPLESS, MOTHER OF TEARS, GIALLO AND DRACULA 3D

Craig R Baxley
CAREER ACHIEVEMENTS PRE 1993:
ACTION JACKSON, DARK ANGEL (AKA I COME IN PEACE), AND STONE COLD

Career achievements post 1993:
SNIPER 2, LEFT BEHIND: WORLD AT WAR, BAD DAY ON THE BLOCK (AKA UNDER PRESSURE)

John Carpenter
Career achievements pre 1993:
ASSAULT ON PRECINCT 13, HALLOWEEN, THE FOG, ESCAPE FROM NEW YORK, THE THING, BIG TROUBLE IN LITTLE CHINA, PRINCE OF DARKNESS, AND THEY LIVE

Career achievements post 1993:
IN THE MOUTH OF MADNESS, VILLAGE OF THE DAMNED, VAMPIRES, ESCAPE FROM LA, GHOSTS OF MARS, THE WARD.

John Hughes (as producer)
Career achievements pre 1993:
FERRIS BUELLER'S DAY OFF, SIXTEEN CANDLES, PRETTY IN PINK, BREAKFAST CLUB, UNCLE BUCK, HOME ALONE, CAREER OPPORTUNITIES, AND PLANES TRAINS AND AUTOMOBILES

Career achievements post 1993:
BABY'S DAY OUT, REACH THE ROCK, HOME ALONE 3, DENNIS THE MENACE, MIRACLE ON 34TH STREET (REMAKE), 101 DALMATIONS (REMAKE), AND FLUBBER (REMAKE)

John Woo
Career achievements pre 1993:
HEROES SHED NO TEARS, A BETTER TOMORROW 1 AND 2, THE KILLER, BULLET IN THE HEAD, ONCE A THIEF, HARD BOILED, AND HARD TARGET

Career achievements post 1993:
BROKEN ARROW, FACE/OFF, MISSION IMPOSSIBLE 2, WINDTALKERS, PAYCHECK, RED CLIFF 1 AND 2, THE CROSSING 1 AND 2

James Cameron
Career achievements pre 1993:
TERMINATOR, ALIEN, THE ABYSS, T2

Career achievements post 1993:
TRUE LIES, TITANIC, AVATAR (AND ITS VARIOUS SEQUELS)

Wes Craven
Career achievements pre 1993:
LAST HOUSE ON THE LEFT, THE FIREWORKS WOMAN, THE HILLS HAVE EYES, A NIGHTMARE ON ELM STREET, SERPENT AND THE RAINBOW, SHOCKER, THE PEOPLE UNDER THE STAIRS

Career achievements post 1993:
NEW NIGHTMARE, VAMPIRE IN BROOKLYN, SCREAM 1, 2, 3, AND 4, MUSIC OF THE HEART, CURSED, RED EYE, MY SOUL TO TAKE

The Zucker Brothers
Career achievements pre 1993:
AIRPLANE, TOP SECRET, RUTHLESS PEOPLE, GHOST, NAKED GUN 1 AND 2 1/2

Career achievements post 1993:
FOR GOODNESS SAKE, BASEKETBALL, MY BOSS'S DAUGHTER, FIRST KNIGHT, SCARY MOVIE 3, 4, AND 5, AN AMERICAN CAROL, RAT RACE

John Landis
Career achievements pre 1993:
KENTUCKY FRIED MOVIE, ANIMAL HOUSE, BLUES BROTHERS, AN AMERICAN WEREWOLF IN LONDON, TRADING PLACES, TWILIGHT ZONE: THE MOVIE, SPIES LIKE US, THREE AMIGOS, AMAZON WOMEN ON THE MOON, COMING TO AMERICA, INNOCENT BLOOD

Career achievements post 1993:
BEVERLY HILLS COP 3, THE STUPIDS, BLUES BROTHERS 2000, SUSAN'S PLAN, MR WARMTH, DEER WOMAN, FAMILY, BURKE AND HARE

Paul Schrader
Career achievements pre 1993:
BLUE COLLAR, HARDCORE, CAT PEOPLE, MISHIMA, LIGHT OF DAY, PATTY HEARST, THE COMFORT OF STRANGERS, LIGHT SLEEPER

Career achievements post 1993:
TOUCH, AFFLICTION, FOREVER MINE, AUTO FOCUS, DOMINION, THE WALKER, ADAM RESURRECTED, THE CANYONS, DYING OF THE LIGHT, DOG EAT DOG

WOW! LOOKIT HOW MUSCULAR I AM! HAHA!

George Romero
Career achievements pre 1993
NIGHT OF THE LIVING DEAD, MARTIN, DAWN OF THE DEAD, CREEPSHOW, DAY OF THE DEAD, MONKEY SHINES

Career achievements post 1993
BRUISER, LAND OF THE DEAD, DIARY OF THE DEAD, SURVIVAL OF THE DEAD

Alex DeRenzy
Career achievements pre 1993:
PORNOGRAPHY IN DENMARK, HISTORY OF THE BLUE MOVIE, FANTASY GIRLS, THE PLEASURE MASTERS, FEMMES DE SADE, LONG JEANNE SILVER, BABYFACE 1 AND 2, PRETTY PEACHES 1, 2 AND 3, GIRLFRIENDS

Career achievements post 1993:
THE BOOTY BANDIT, BOOTY HO, ASSY SASSY 1, 2 AND 3, A BUNCH OF CUNTS, ANAL BOOTY BURNER 1 AND 2, ANAL CRACK ATTACK, GANG BANG JIZZ QUEEN

Ivan Reitman
Career Achievements pre 1993
MEATBALLS, STRIPES, GHOSTBUSTERS, TWINS, GHOSTBUSTERS 2, KINDERGARTEN COP

Career Achievements post 1993
DAVE, JUNIOR, FATHER'S DAY, SIX DAYS SEVEN NIGHTS, EVOLUTION, MY SUPER EX GIRLFRIEND, DRAFT DAY, NO STRINGS ATTACHED

Anthony Spinelli
Career achievements pre 1993:
SEX IN THE COMICS, THE SEDUCTION OF LYN CARTER, PORTRAIT OF SEDUCTION, NIGHT CALLER, CRY FOR CINDY, CONFESSIONS, EASY, SEX WORLD, HIGH SCHOOL MEMORIES, AUNT PEG, TALK DIRTY TO ME, THE DANCERS, NOTHING TO HIDE, VISTA VALLEY PTA, DIXIE RAY: HOLLYWOOD STAR

Career achievements post 1993:
WHITE MEN CAN HUMP, REVENGE OF THE PUSSYSUCKERS FROM MARS, PULP FRICTION, CLIFF BANGER, IN THE BUSH, HARD SQUEEZE, DOUBLE LOAD 2, WHACKERS, PUMP-HOUSE SLUT.

Brian Trenchard Smith
Career achievements pre 1993:
THE MAN FROM HONG KONG, DEATH CHEATERS, STUNT ROCK, TURKEY SHOOT (AKA ESCAPE 2000), BMX BANDITS, DEAD END DRIVE-IN, AND DANGERFREAKS

Career achievements post 1993:
NIGHT OF THE DEMONS 2, LEPRECHAUN 3 AND 4, ATOMIC DOG, PIMPIN' PEE WEE, AZTEC REX, ARCTIC BLAST, ABSOLUTE DECEPTION, AND DRIVE HARD.

Tsui Hark
Career achievements pre 1993:
WE'RE GOING TO EAT YOU, ZU: WARRIORS FROM THE MAGIC MOUNTAIN, PEKING OPERA BLUES, I LOVE MARIA (AKA ROBOFORCE), THE BIG HEAT, A BETTER TOMORROW 3, SWORDSMAN, ONCE UPON A TIME IN CHINA 1, 2, AND 3.

Career achievements post 1993:
THE LOVERS, THE BLADE, TRI-STAR, DOUBLE TEAM, KNOCK OFF, TIME AND TIDE, BLACK MASK 2, SEVEN SWORDS, ZU WARRIORS, DETECTIVE DEE: THE MYSTERY OF THE PHANTOM FLAME, THE TAKING OF TIGER MOUNTAIN.

1993 NEVER CAME AROUND AGAIN AFTER THAT. YOU KNOW, I HEARD FROM A FEW OTHER PEOPLE THAT IT HAD BEEN ASKING ABOUT ME -- TESTING THE WATER, I GUESS? THEY SAID IT SEEMED NERVOUS AND AGITATED. IT MADE ME WONDER IF I'D BEEN TOO HARD ON 1993. MAYBE I COULD HAVE BEEN MORE MORE UNDERSTANDING OF WHAT IT HAD BEEN THROUGH, BUT I JUST GET SO PROTECTIVE WHEN IT COMES TO DEFENCELESS MOVIES. WE ALL HAVE OUR OWN ROAD TO TRAVEL, MAN.
                                                                    — BOUGIE

THE 20 MOST UNDERRATED AND UNDISCOVERED MUST-SEE MOVIES OF THE 1990S

I SHIT ON THE 1990S A LOT. I DO. IT'S MY LEAST FAVOURITE DECADE WHEN IT COMES TO MOST FORMS OF ENTERTAINMENT AND POP CULTURE, WHICH IS A BUMMER BECAUSE THAT JUNCTURE IS WHERE I SPENT THE TIMEFRAME BETWEEN THE AGES OF 17 TO 27. THAT'S ALSO KNOWN AS THE YEARS WHEN A SIMPLE GEEK SUCH AS MYSELF IS REALLY EATING UP A LOT OF MOVIES, MUSIC, TV, BOOKS AND COMICS -- AND DECIDING WHAT HE/SHE PREFERS. IT'S WHEN I WAS FIGURING OUT WHICH MEDIA WOULD DEFINE ME AS A CONSUMER IN THIS CONSUMER SOCIETY. KEY YEARS.

AND NOW THAT I THINK ABOUT IT, I BET A LOT OF THE REASON I GOT SO OBSESSED WITH THE CINEMA SEWER-ESQUE ENTERTAINMENT OF 1960S, '70S, AND '80S DURING THAT TIME IS DIRECTLY ATTRIBUTABLE TO THE FACT THAT I WAS SO FLATLY UNIMPRESSED WITH MOST OF WHAT WAS BEING SERVED UP IN THE TEN YEARS LEADING UP TO Y2K. I'M SPEAKING IN GENERALIZATIONS HERE OF COURSE, BUT THEY ARE BASED ON PERSONAL EXPERIENCE. WHEN YOU ACTUALLY LOOK AT INDIVIDUAL THEATRICAL RELEASES OF THE NINETIES, THERE WERE A DECENT AMOUNT OF GREAT MOVIES MADE, JUST NOT THE MOUNTAIN OF AWESOMENESS WE'D BEEN SO SPOILED BY IN PREVIOUS DECADES.

WITH THAT IN MIND, I'D LIKE TO FOCUS ON SOME OF THE STUFF THAT DIDN'T SEEM TO MAKE IT OUT OF THE DECADE AND INTO THE CONSCIOUSNESS OF GENRE FANS. ANYONE WORTH A DAMN HAS FIGURED OUT HOW GREAT RESERVOIR DOGS, JACKIE BROWN, THE BIG LEBOWSKI, MILLER'S CROSSING, TRAINSPOTTING, GLENGARRY GLEN ROSS, SE7EN, CRUMB, HOOP DREAMS, CARLITO'S WAY, GROUNDHOG DAY, BOOGIE NIGHTS, THE USUAL SUSPECTS, RUSHMORE, CHUNGKING EXPRESS, GOODFELLAS, AND PRINCESS MONONOKE ARE. BUT LET'S FORGET ABOUT THOSE LANDMARK FILMS AND TALK ABOUT THE 1990S MOVIES THAT DON'T GET CELEBRATED EVEN THOUGH THEY DESERVE THEIR PROPS. SOME OF THEM ARE OBSCURITIES STILL WAITING TO BE DISCOVERED, AND OTHERS ARE FAIRLY WELL KNOWN BUT DISREGARDED BECAUSE OF AUDIENCE IGNORANCE ("WHAT THE HELL IS THIS? IT LOOKS LAME"), INTOLERANCE ("IT STARS THAT GUY I HATE, AND IT'S IN THAT GENRE I DON'T LIKE"), OR THE WORST ENEMY OF THE COMMON FILM-GOER: EXPECTATION ("HATED IT. IT WASN'T WHAT I WAS HOPING FOR").

THERE'S NOTHING SCIENTIFIC AT ALL ABOUT THIS LIST-- IT'S SIMPLY BASED ON MY OPINION. I'VE LEFT OUT DETAILED DESCRIPTIONS OF THE PLOT-LINES IN THE INTERESTS OF BREVITY AND BECAUSE I HAVE A SOMEWHAT EGOTISTICAL FANTASY THAT YOU'LL JUST TAKE ME AT MY WORD THAT THESE MOVIES FUCKING RULE. ANYWAY, HERE THEY ARE IN ALPHABETICAL ORDER SINCE I COULDN'T FIGURE OUT A BETTER WAY TO RANK THEM. OH, AND BECAUSE I'M BORED OF JUST HAVING ADVERTISING AD-MATS AND STUFF, I'M GONNA DRAW BUNNIES ACTING OUT THE MOVIES TO USE AS ILLUSTRATIONS.

Beyond the Law (1993 USA)

I WOULD HAVE LOVED TO INCLUDE BRIAN BOSWORTH'S STONE COLD (IT'S ONE OF MY ALL-TIME FAVES) BUT IT RANKED #1 IN A RECENT CINEMA SEWER POLL OF FAVOURITE ACTION MOVIES OF THE 1990S, SO THAT TELLS ME THAT IT'S NOT ALL THAT UNDERRATED. SO INSTEAD OF STONE COLD (WHICH YOU MUST FUCKING SEE), I'M INCLUDING THIS -- THE SECOND MOST AWESOME 1990S BIKER ACTION FILM. ALSO KNOWN AS FIXING THE SHADOW, IT STARS MICHAEL MADSEN AND A BEARDED CHARLIE SHEEN. ONE IS A GOOD GUY, AND THE OTHER IS THE BAD GUY, BUT THEY'RE BOTH TOTAL MENTAL CASES. I THINK A LOT LESS PEEPS KNOW ABOUT THIS ONE AND IT'S ALMOST AS GOOD AS STONE COLD. CERTAINLY NOT AS GOOD, BUT IN THE SAME BALLPARK ENOUGH TO WARRANT INCLUSION ON THIS LIST, AT LEAST.

COMING THROUGH, ASSHOLES!

BRUM BRUM

HARLE

Caged Heat 2: Stripped of Freedom (1994 Philippines)

WHAT'S THAT YOU SAY? YOU CAN'T BELIEVE THEY WERE STILL MAKING WOMEN-IN-PRISON CINEMA AS LATE AS 1994? WELL, THEY WEREN'T, BUT CIRIO SANTIAGO WAS. THE KING OF FILIPINO EXPLOITATION HAD ONE LAST KICK AT THIS GENRE'S CAN, AND HIS AIM WAS TRUE. IN FACT, THE BEST COMPLIMENT I CAN GIVE THIS MOVIE IS THAT IT LOOKS LIKE IT WAS MADE IN THE 1970S OR 1980S. IF YOU SQUINT YOUR EYES YOU CAN'T REALLY TELL AT ALL. OBVIOUSLY IF YOU'RE NOT INTO W.I.P., DON'T EVEN BOTHER WITH THIS, BUT IF YOU ARE YOU SHOULD KNOW THAT IT HAS ALL OF THE DEBAUCHERY, CATFIGHTING, WHIPPING, NUDITY, MEAN GIRLS, LESBIANS, AND RUTHLESS PRISON GUARDS THAT YOU WOULD EXPECT. SPEAKING OF PRISON GUARDS, GOOD OL' VIC DIAZ PLAYS THE WARDEN, AND HIS FAT, SWEATY ASS HAS NEVER LOOKED MORE SINISTER OR DERANGED IN HIS ENTIRE CAREER OF PLAYING PERVERTED PRISON OFFICIALS. STRIPPED OF FREEDOM IS WORTH HUNTING FOR, BUT THE MOVIE DOES NOT, HOWEVER, HAVE ANYTHING TO DO WITH THE FIRST CAGED HEAT MOVIE. CIRIO JUST USED THE TITLE, AND YOU CAN'T REALLY BLAME HIM FOR TRYING TO WRANGLE A LITTLE MORE CASH VIA NAME RECOGNITION. IT'S AN EXPLOITATION TRICK AS OLD AS THE GENRE ITSELF.

LEMME OUT!

The Cat (1992 Hong Kong)

THIS IS THE FIRST OF A FEW HONG KONG MOVIES ON THIS LIST, AND I

FEEL LIKE THERE EASILY COULD HAVE BEEN EVEN MORE.
DESPITE A LULL DURING THIS TIME OF QUALITY CINEMA
COMING OUT OF NORTH AMERICA, THE 1990s (SPECIFICALLY
1986 TO 1994) WAS ONE OF THE MOST CREATIVE AND HIGH
IMPACT ERAS OF HK GENRE MOVIE-MAKING. MANY FANS
KNOW OF THE EXCELLENT JACKIE CHAN, JOHN WOO, JET LI
AND CHOW YUN FAT MOVIES MADE THEN, BUT AREN'T AS
AWARE OF THE AMAZING SHIT COMING FROM OTHER ACTORS
AND FILMMAKERS. REMEMBER LAM NAI CHOI? HE'S THE RAD
MOTHERFUCKER THAT BROUGHT US 1991'S THE STORY OF RICKY,
WHICH WOULD HAVE MADE THIS LIST IF IT WASN'T SO BELOVED
(AND DESERVEDLY SO) BY FILM FANS WITH A TASTE FOR THE WILD
AND EXTREME. THE YEAR AFTER THAT MOVIE CAME OUT, HE FOLLOWED
IT UP WITH THIS ULTRA-WEIRD HORROR/SCI-FI/ ACTION FILM THAT
MIXES JAMES CAMERON'S TERMINATOR WITH DISNEY'S THE CAT FROM
OUTER SPACE -- AN ABSURD MELDING THAT WOULDN'T HAVE OCCURED TO
MOST FILMMAKERS, I'M SURE. CHECK THIS ONE OUT, IF ONLY FOR THE
INCREDIBLE DOG VS CAT JUNKYARD FIGHT THAT IS SO BALLS-OUT, IT ALMOST FEELS LIKE YOU
ARE WATCHING A CARTOON.

AWWW! CUTE LITTLE FELLA IS HAVIN' A NAP.

ZZZ

Freeway (1996 USA)

BASICALLY THIS IS LITTLE RED RIDINGHOOD FOR CINEMA
SEWER FANS. A WHITE TRASH TEENAGE GIRL (REESE
WITHERSPOON) GOES IN SEARCH OF HER ESTRANGED
GRANDMOTHER, AND ON THE WAY GETS PICKED UP ON THE
FREEWAY BY THE DERANGED SCHOOL COUNSELOR AND
SERIAL KILLER, BOB WOLVERTON (KIEFER
SUTHERLAND). SHE ESCAPES AND SERIOUSLY FUCKS HIS
ASS UP, BUT OL' WOLFY IS JUST GETTING STARTED!
FANS OF TASTELESS JUVENILE DELINQUENT
EXPLOITATION CINEMA CAN'T MISS THIS EFFORT BY
DIRECTOR MATTHEW BRIGHT, WHO GREW UP WITH
DANNY ELFMAN, AND WAS AN ORIGINAL MEMBER OF THE
MYSTIC KNIGHTS OF THE OINGO BOINGO, A DARK TWISTED
CULT FILM COMEDY WITH LOTS OF GRIT AND POIGNANCY.

MMN

BLAH MMRF

BLL

Godzilla VS. Destoroyah (1995 Japan)

THERE HAVE BEEN AS MANY GODZILLA MOVIES AS THERE ARE
DAYS IN A CALENDAR, AND IT'S GENERALLY CONSIDERED THAT THE
ORIGINAL 1950s AND '60s GODZILLA FILMS ARE THE BEST.
I, HOWEVER, AM A FIRM BELIEVER THAT THE 1990s ENTRIES
INTO THE GOJIRA MYTHOS ARE SUPERIOR THAN THOSE
IN ANY OTHER DECADE THUS FAR -- AND HERE ARE THE
THREE REASONS WHY: 1. THEY WERE MADE BEFORE IT
DAWNED ON ANYONE TO TRY AND USE CGI SPECIAL EFFECTS,
SO YOU GET AWESOME UNADULTERATED PUPPETS, MODELS,
AND JAPANESE GUYS IN SUITS SMASHING SAID MODELS
AND PUPPETS! 2. THEY HAD BIGGER BUDGETS THAN THE
GODZILLA FILMS THAT CAME BEFORE, AND IT SHOWS. 3.
THEY BEGAN TO REALIZE THAT IF YOU WERE ALWAYS
GOING TO ADD A LENGTHY AMOUNT OF RUNTIME ABOUT
THE HUMAN CHARACTERS, YOU BETTER MAKE THEM
SOMEWHAT INTERESTING. THE BEST OF THIS BUNCH IS GODZILLA VS. DESTOROYAH, WHICH IS
CONSIDERED TO BE THE FINAL FILM IN WHAT IS CALLED "THE HEISEI SERIES", WHICH SPANNED
FROM 1984 TO 1995. THIS IS, IN MY OPINION, THE MOST MENACING AND IMAGINATIVELY
DESIGNED MONSTER THAT TOHO EVER DEVISED TO GO UP AGAINST THEIR STAR REPTILE, AND
THAT'S NO SMALL FEAT CONSIDERING HOW FLIPPIN' COOL MECHAGODZILLA AND KING GHIDORA
ARE. PLUS THE MOVIE HAS A RATHER SHOCKING ENDING WHICH IS A REALLY NICE CHANGE FROM
THE STANDARD "GODZILLA RETURNS TO THE SEA" FINALE.

RAAR

Boom!

A Gun for Jennifer (1997 USA)

DON'T FUCKIN' CALL ME SWEETIE!!

THAT'S MY FAVE LINE OF DIALOG IN THIS LOW
BUDGET INDIE RAPE-REVENGE SHIT
DISTURBER MADE BY DIRECTOR TODD MORRIS IN
NEW YORK IN THE MID 1990s. STARRING
THE TALENTED AND PERSONABLE
DEBORAH TWISS AS THE TITULAR
JENNIFER, THIS ONE SADLY HAS NOT
BEEN MADE AVAILABLE ON A HOME
FORMAT OUTSIDE OF EUROPE AS OF THIS
WRITING, AND IT'S A SHAME BECAUSE I FEEL LIKE
IT WOULD BE FAR MORE TALKED ABOUT IF IT WERE
EASIER TO SEE. A BASIC SUMMATION OF THE PLOT
HAS TWISS' CHARACTER, AN ABUSED YOUNG WOMAN FROM
OHIO, GOING TO MANHATTAN, AND BY CHANCE, MEETING
UP WITH A GROUP OF FEMME FATALE VIGILANTES
WHO WORK IN A GO-GO STRIP BAR AND CASTRATE
AND/OR MURDER THE MEN WHO GET TOO TOUCHY
FEELY, OR WHOM THEY SUSPECT OF BEING RAPISTS.
GREAT DIALOG, PLENTY OF BAD-ASS BITCHES, GORE AND BLOOD SQUIBS
AND A GUY GETTING FORCE-FUCKED WITH A POOL CUE AWAIT

YOU! MORRIS HAS DONE SOME KEEN WORK TAPPING INTO WHAT MADE 1970s RAPE-REVENGE CINEMA SO COMMANDING AND POWERFUL, AND WHAT HE ENDED UP WITH IS IN THE SAME VEIN AS ABEL FERRARA'S MS.45, BOB KELLJAN'S RAPE SQUAD AND MEIR ZARCHI'S I SPIT ON YOUR GRAVE.

Hard Hunted (1992 USA)

A CONVINCING ARGUMENT COULD BE MADE THAT I AM A MORON AND THAT THE FILMS ANDY SIDARIS MADE IN THE 1990s ARE RATED AND CONSIDERED EXACTLY AS THEY SHOULD BE. BECAUSE IT'S TRUE THAT THESE RELEASES AREN'T 'GREAT CINEMA', AND YOU ARE INDEED LAUGHING AT THEM JUST AS MUCH AS YOU'RE LAUGHING WITH THEM, BUT ANDY'S STRING OF SOMEWHAT INTERCHANGEABLE TITS-AND-ASS BUBBLEGUM GUN-PLAY MOVIES (FILLED WITH SNARLING ASSASSINS AND LUSTY, BUSTY BIMBOS) DON'T GET ENOUGH LOVE IN MY OPINION. THERE IS A DUNGLOAD OF GOOD TIMES TO BE HAD WITH A PIZZA, SOME BOOZE, SEVERAL PALS, AND ONE OF THESE CORNBALL FILMS, (WHICH WERE ALMOST ALWAYS SHOT IN HAWAII) AND EVEN THOUGH THEY WERE CLEARLY MADE FOR GUYS, I'VE NOTICED THAT A SURPRISINGLY LARGE PERCENTAGE OF MY FEMALE FRIENDS DIG ON THE SIDARIS ACTION-SLEAZE ONCE THEY'VE BEEN TURNED ON TO IT. HARD HUNTED FROM 1992 IS A GOOD PLACE TO START WITH THESE, BUT AS MENTIONED, THEY'RE FAIRLY INTERCHANGEABLE, SO JUMP IN WITH WHICHEVER ONE YOU FEEL LIKE.

High Risk (1995 Hong Kong)

ALSO RELEASED IN NORTH AMERICA AS MELTDOWN, THIS IS A DIRECT REMAKE OF DIE HARD (WITH A COUPLE NODS TO SPEED), BUT WITH THE CRAZY FACTOR DIALED UP A FEW MORE NOTCHES. OK, A LOT MORE NOTCHES. FOR INSTANCE, IMAGINE IF JOHN MCLEAN HAD DRIVEN A COMPACT CAR INTO THE NAKATOMI PLAZA LOBBY, SHOT A PILE OF TERRORISTS THROUGH THE WINDSHIELD WHILE DRIVING, ALL WHILE HE WHIPPED THAT SHIT AROUND THE ROOM -- AND THEN DROVE HIS LITTLE CLOWN CAR INTO THE ELEVATOR SO HE COULD DRIVE IT OUT ON A HIGHER FLOOR AND CONTINUE HIS RAMPAGE OF BLOOD-SOAKED, BULLET-SPITTING! FUCK, YES!! CREATIVE MAESTRO OF BAD-ASSERY, COREY YUEN (ONE OF JACKIE CHAN, SAMMO HUNG, AND YUEN BIAO'S BEST PALS DURING THEIR CHILDHOOD TENURE IN THE CHINESE PEKING OPERA SCHOOL) SERVED AS THE MOVIE'S FIGHT CHOREOGRAPHER, AND IT SHOWS. THERE ARE SOME FLAT PARTS HERE AND THERE, BUT OVERALL THIS MOVIE FUCKING RULES THE SCHOOL. MOST OF THE BEST JET LI MOVIES (DID I FORGET TO MENTION THAT HE STARS IN THIS? I DID, DIDN'T I? WELL HE STARS IN THIS) WERE REDISCOVERED BY GENRE FILM FANS AND PROPERLY CELEBRATED, BUT THIS WAS NOT ONE OF THEM FOR SOME REASON.

King of Comedy (1999 Hong Kong)

WHEN STEPHEN CHOW FINALLY HIT BIG OUTSIDE OF ASIA WITH HIS FANTASTIC SHAOLIN SOCCER (2001) AND KUNG FU HUSTLE (2004), I WAS ANTICIPATING THAT NORTH AMERICAN AUDIENCES (AND DISTRIBUTORS) WOULD GET THE SMART IDEA TO VENTURE BACK THROUGH HIS FILMOGRAPHY AND DISCOVER THAT HE WAS ALSO IN A SHITLOAD OF OTHER GREAT FILMS -- YOU KNOW, LIKE THEY DID WITH JACKIE CHAN WHEN HE FINALLY BROKE INTO THE AMERICAN MARKET. MOVIES LIKE KING OF BEGGARS (1992) LOVE ON DELIVERY (1994), FORBIDDEN CITY COP (1996) AND THE SPLENDID GOD OF COOKERY (1996) --ALL MOVIES THAT EASILY COULD HAVE MAKE THIS LIST, EVEN AMONGST THE FEW NON-CHINESE CINEPHILES THAT WENT THERE AND REPORTED BACK, NONE OF THEM SEEMED TO HAVE HAD THE GOOD FORTUNE TO UNCOVER THE INSANE BRILLIANCE THAT IS 1999's KING OF COMEDY. NOT TO BE CONFUSED WITH THE FAR MORE FAMOUS MARTIN SCORSESE FEATURE STARRING ROBERT DENIRO, THIS PICTURE PLACES STEPHEN AS A DOWN-ON-HIS-LUCK ACTOR WHO TEACHES ACTING CLASSES AT THE LOCAL RUNDOWN COMMUNITY CENTER. WHEN A LOCAL PIMP CAN'T GET ONE OF HIS GIRLS TO ACT LIKE SHE'S REALLY INTO HER JOB, HE DROPS HER OFF AT STEPHEN'S CLASS, AND A VERY UNUSUAL LOVE BLOSSOMS BETWEEN THEM. TRUST ME, THIS ISN'T YOUR USUAL ROMANTIC COMEDY, AND IT IS A MUST-SEE IF YOU'VE ENJOYED ANY OF CHOW'S OTHER MOVIES.

Kite (1998 Japan)

ANIMATOR YASUOMI UMETSU IS A GUY WHO JUST ISN'T VERY WELL KNOWN IN NORTH AMERICA, AND WHILE HIS MEZZO FORTE IS THE SLIGHTLY MORE RECOMMENDABLE RELEASE -- IT'S FROM 2001, AND SO DOESN'T QUITE QUALIFY FOR THIS ARTICLE. NO MATTER, BECAUSE KITE IS FUCKING AWESOME AS WELL. IT'S AN ANIME THAT DETAILS THE ORIGINS OF A LOVELY YOUNG 'LA FEMME NIKITA' STYLE CHARACTER... A TEENAGE GIRL WHOSE PARENTS ARE BRUTALLY MURDERED, AND IS TAKEN UNDER THE CONTROL OF NEW GUARDIANS WHO TRAIN HER TO BE A RUTHLESS ASSASSIN. HER VICTIMS RANGE FROM RAPISTS, TO CORPORATE SLEAZEBALLS, AND EVEN TO ANOTHER YOUNG ASSASSIN NAMED OBURI. ABSOLUTELY

ESSENTIAL STUFF FOR ANIMATION FANS, AND YET I'VE HARDLY EVER MET ANYONE WHO HAS SEEN IT. BOTH KITE AND MEZZO FORTE WERE RELEASED IN NORTH AMERICA IN DVD VERSIONS WITH THE GRAPHIC SEX SCENES (WHICH ARE FLIPPIN' AWESOME) BOTH INTACT, AND EDITED OUT. I'M SURE I DON'T NEED TO TELL YOU WHICH VERSIONS ARE SUPERIOR.

Last Action Hero (1993 USA)

YOU CAN'T HAVE A LIST OF UNDERRATED 1990s FILMS AND NOT MENTION LAST ACTION HERO, SIMPLY FOR HOW IT WAS RECEIVED BACK WHEN IT CAME OUT (WOE TO ANY MOVIE THAT OPENED AROUND THE SAME TIME AS JURASSIC PARK, SUCH AS THIS DID), AND HOW IT STILL HAS NEVER BEEN EMBRACED BY THE FILM-FANS WHO LOVE ACTION MOVIES. I THINK WHAT THREW OFF CRITICS AND MOVIEGOERS BACK IN 1993 WAS THAT THEY COULDN'T GET COMFORTABLE WITH THIS ARNOLD SCHWARZENEGGER MOVIE UNTIL THEY COULD CATEGORIZE IT. WAS IT A COMEDY? AN ACTION MOVIE? A SATIRICAL SPOOF OF THE HOLLYWOOD ACTION GENRE ITSELF? TO BE HONEST, IT WAS ALL OF THOSE THINGS -- AND A DAMN SIGHT BETTER THAN PEOPLE HAVE TOLD YOU IT WAS. IT'S A PICTURE THAT DIDN'T SIT WELL IN 1993, BUT HAS CERTAINLY GOTTEN EASIER TO DIGEST AS THE YEARS HAVE GONE BY -- WHICH IS THE VERY DEFINITION OF A MOVIE AHEAD OF ITS TIME. ARNOLD ONCE STATED THAT HE THOUGHT IT HAD NOT ONLY THE BEST SCRIPT OF ANY OF HIS MOVIES, BUT WAS ONE OF THE BEST SCRIPTS HE'D EVER READ. EVEN IF YOU ALREADY SAW THIS BACK IN THE DAY, GO BACK AND GIVE IT A REAPPRAISAL. I'M BETTING YOU'LL BE A LOT MORE INTO IT THIS TIME AROUND.

Last Night (1998 Canada)

DON MCKELLAR IS ONE OF THOSE CANADIAN MOVIE AND TV PERSONALITIES WHO IS SOMEWHAT KNOWN TO CANADIANS WHO LIKE COOL CHARACTER ACTORS, BUT SEEMS TO BE MOSTLY UNKNOWN OUTSIDE OF HIS COUNTRY. HE WAS FANTASTIC IN THE WEIRDO 1990s TV SERIES TWITCH CITY (WHICH WAS FAR AHEAD OF ITS TIME), AND WAS EVEN BETTER IN THIS SLOW BURNER ABOUT THE LAST DAY BEFORE THE APOCALYPSE COMES IN THE FORM OF A MYSTERIOUS AND UNEXPLAINED NATURAL DISASTER. WITH THE WORLD COMING TO AN END, A GROUP OF CHARACTERS LED BY MCKELLAR, INCLUDING SANDRA OH, DAVID CRONENBERG (IN A RARE PERFORMANCE IN FRONT OF THE CAMERA), AND CALLUM KEITH RENNIE (WHO I SOMETIMES SEE DRINKING COFFEE AT A PLACE DOWNSTAIRS FROM MY ART STUDIO) TRY TO GET THE THINGS DONE THAT THEY NEED TO DO BEFORE THEY DIE. WITH PANIC AND CHAOS ERUPTING EVERYWHERE AROUND THEM, IT'S INTERESTING TO SEE WHAT THESE CHARACTERS THINK IS IMPORTANT TO ACCOMPLISH BEFORE LIFE ON EARTH IS WIPED OUT. SPOILER: ONE OF THEM HAS AS MUCH SEX AS POSSIBLE. I'D BE PRETTY TEMPTED TO GO OUT LIKE THAT, I GOTTA SAY. LAST NIGHT IS A REALLY COOL LITTLE MOVIE, AND THE ENDING IT'S GOT IS SO DEPRESSING AND YET TOTALLY BEAUTIFUL AT THE SAME TIME.

The Love Prophet and the Children of God (1998 Canada)

IF YOU'RE INTO DOCUMENTARIES ABOUT UNUSUAL AND SECRET SECTS (I TOTALLY AM!), YOU'RE GOING TO ENJOY THIS DISTURBING LOOK INTO THE 'CHILDREN OF GOD' CULT PRODUCED AND DIRECTED BY ABBEY JACK NEIDIK. IT'S PRETTY FAR FROM ERROL MORRIS TERRITORY, AS IT ISN'T SHOT ON FILM AND DOESN'T HAVE A PARTICULARLY ARTISTIC LOOK ABOUT IT, BUT IT'S WELL RESEARCHED AND BRINGS THE AUDIENCE INTO A TROUBLING RELIGIOUS ORGANIZATION MOST WOULD NEVER HAVE KNOWN ABOUT OTHERWISE. DYING IN 1994, DAVID BERG WAS SEEN AS A BIBLICAL PROPHET AND SOCIAL REVOLUTIONARY BY A QUARTER OF A MILLION PEOPLE AROUND THE WORLD, BUT TO EVERYONE ELSE HE WAS A VILE BEARDED SCUMBAG WHO OVER THE COURSE OF DECADES USED THE NAME OF JESUS TO JUSTIFY THE WIDESPREAD SEXUAL ABUSE OF CHILDREN. ON TOP OF THAT, HE PUSHED FOR HIS DISCIPLES TO COMMIT INCEST AND PROUDLY PIMPED OUT THE YOUNG WOMEN OF HIS CULT (WHAT BERG REFERRED TO AS "HOOKERS FOR JESUS") EVEN WHILE DISCOURAGING BIRTH CONTROL. AMAZINGLY, DAVID BERG NORMALIZED SUCH OUTRAGEOUS BEHAVIOUR AMONGST THE TENS OF THOUSANDS OF FAMILIES ENSCONCED IN HIS DOCTRINE, MAKING IT ALL SEEM HEALTHY UNDER THE MANTLE OF HIPPIE-FLAVORED SEX-POSITIVITY, WHICH HE DEEMED "THE POWER OF LOVE". THE LOVE PROPHET AND THE CHILDREN OF GOD IS A BIZARRE TRUE STORY THAT SHINES A BRUTAL LIGHT ON HOW POWER CORRUPTS AND HOW IMPORTANT IT IS TO THINK FOR ONESELF. TRIVIA: YOU

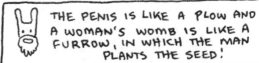

THE PENIS IS LIKE A PLOW AND A WOMAN'S WOMB IS LIKE A FURROW, IN WHICH THE MAN PLANTS THE SEED!

A PLOW

SOIL

KNOW HOLLYWOOD ACTORS ROSE MCGOWAN, RIVER PHOENIX AND JOAQUIN PHOENIX? YEAH, WELL THEY GREW UP IN THIS CULT BEFORE BEING PULLED OUT OF IT. THAT EXPLAINS A LOT.

Mousehunt (1997 USA)

THE LEE EVANS FILM TO PICK FOR THIS LIST COULD EASILY HAVE BEEN 1995'S FUNNY BONES, BUT I'M GOING WITH MOUSEHUNT FOR ITS SHEER REWATCHABILITY AND THE FACT THAT IT IS A MOVIE THAT HAS BEEN TOTALLY DISREGARDED, (FOR WHICH THE KID-FOCUSED MARKETING AND DUBBING FROM THE CRITICS AT THE TIME OF ITS RELEASE IS MOSTLY TO BLAME). IN FACT, THE WHOLE IDEA FOR THIS ARTICLE CAME FROM ME PUTTING THE MOVIE ON IN THE VIDEO STORE WHERE I WORK, AND EVERY THIRD PERSON STOPPING IN FRONT OF THE TV AND GOING "WHAT IS THIS??". AND WHEN I WOULD TELL THEM, THEY'D SAY "I THOUGHT THIS WAS A MOVIE FOR LITTLE KIDS. THIS ACTUALLY LOOKS PRETTY COOL." SO I FILED THAT AWAY IN MY HEAD UNDER: "PEOPLE DON'T REALIZE THAT MOUSEHUNT IS FUCKIN' AWESOME UNTIL SOMEONE SHOWS IT TO THEM". HELL ANY MOVIE THAT CAN MAKE NATHAN LANE WATCHABLE DESERVES AT LEAST A MOUSE-SIZED MORSEL OF RESPECT, AND THIS ONE IS STILL WAITING FOR SOME. I ESPECIALLY LOVE THE CINEMATOGRAPHY AND EDITING, WHICH ARE BOTH IMPRESSIVE AS HELL.

Oleanna (1994 USA)

"HE SAID IT WAS A LESSON. SHE SAID IT WAS SEXUAL HARRASSMENT. WHICHEVER SIDE YOU TAKE, YOU'RE WRONG." WILLIAM H. MACY PLAYS A UNIVERSITY PROFESSOR, AND DEBRA EISENSTADT (IN HER FIRST-EVER ROLE) PLAYS ONE OF HIS STUDENTS -- AND THEY SPEND THE WHOLE MOVIE JUST TALKING TO ONE ANOTHER. SOUNDS BORING, RIGHT? WRONG. OLEANNA IS EXCITING AND ENTERTAINING FROM BEGINNING TO END. IT WAS A SPECIAL EXPERIENCE FOR ME, BECAUSE I'VE NEVER SEEN A MOVIE THAT SO PERFECTLY AND APTLY ENCAPSULATES WHAT IT FEELS LIKE TO HAVE YOUR WORDS AND ACTIONS TAKEN OUT OF CONTEXT AND USED AGAINST YOU IN WAYS THAT MAKE YOU FEEL HELPLESS AND FRUSTRATED. THIS, OF COURSE, IS SOMETHING MANY PEOPLE HAVE BECOME FAR MORE FAMILIAR WITH IN THE ONLINE SOCIAL MEDIA AGE THAT IMMEDIATELY FOLLOWED THIS CONTROVERSIAL 1994 FEATURE. IT DOES AN AMAZING JOB AT ADDRESSING THE POWER DYNAMIC (AS WELL AS THE ABUSE OF THAT POWER) THAT CAN TAKE PLACE BETWEEN STUDENT AND TEACHER, MAN AND WOMAN, AND THE EXPERIENCED AND THE NOVICE -- ALL WHILE IT DISPLAYS HOW EACH CAN VIEW THE EXACT SAME EVENTS THROUGH AN ENTIRELY DIFFERENT PRISM. THE MOVIE PROVOKES SELF EXAMINATION, TELLS A GRIPPING STORY, AND DOES BOTH WITHOUT RESORTING TO GETTING PREACHY OR CONVOLUTED. IT WAS MOSTLY MISUNDERSTOOD BY CRITICS WHO REALLY SHIT ON IT BACK IN 1994 (MAMET WAS ACCUSED OF WRITING A SEXIST SCRIPT), BUT I'VE NEVER WATCHED THIS MOVIE AND NOT HAD IT INSPIRE A GREAT AND THOUGHTFUL CONVERSATION OR DEBATE.

Party Doll-A-Go-Go (1991. USA XXX)

IT'S CINEMA SEWER, SO YOU JUST KNEW THERE HAD TO BE SOME PORN ON THIS LIST. THE 1990s IS UNSURPRISINGLY NOTEWORTHY AS MY PERSONAL LEAST FAVOURITE DECADE FOR HARDCORE SMUT RELEASES, BUT THAT DOESN'T MEAN THAT THERE WEREN'T A FEW STANDOUTS! PARTY DOLL-A-GO-GO, FOR INSTANCE, IS ONE OF THE BEST SHOT-ON-VIDEO ADULT TITLES OF ITS ERA, AND YET MOST MASTURBATORS HAVE NEVER HEARD OF IT. DIRECTED BY RINSE DREAM (THE MAN WHO BROUGHT US THE OUTSTANDING AND DARKLY COMEDIC CAFE FLESH IN 1982 AND NIGHTDREAMS IN 1981) WHO ALSO GOES BY THE NAME STEPHEN SAYADIAN, THIS BIZARRE AND LURID ARTSPLOITATION XXX IS FULL OF ODD DIALOG, STRANGE MUSIC VIDEO VISUALS, AND INTERESTING SOUNDTRACK CHOICES. OH, AND SOME RAGING HOT SEX THAT WILL BLISTER YOUR PINK PARTS, TOO! CAN'T HAVE TERRIFIC PORN WITHOUT THAT, NOW CAN YOU? ^_^

LET'S DO IT BUNNY STYLE!

Super Lady Cop (1992 Hong Kong)

I LOVE THIS MOVIE, BUT EVEN HONG KONG ACTION FILM FANS DON'T EVER SEEM TO KNOW ABOUT IT WHEN WE GET TO CHIN-WAGGING ABOUT THE SWEET CHINESE SHIT. THAT'S WHY I HAD SCENES FROM IT INCLUDED IN THE VIDEO MIXTAPE THAT MY PAL ROEL AND I PUT OUT, ENTITLED RETARD-O-TRON 3. THAT COMPILATION OF RANDOM AWESOME CLIPS WENT VIRAL ONLINE, AND AN OFT-ASKED QUESTION WAS: "WHERE WERE THOSE INSANE FIGHT SCENES FROM -- THE ONES WHERE PEOPLE WERE FLYING AROUND AND SPINNING OFF STREET

LIGHTS AND SHIT?" WELL, IT WAS THIS CYNTHIA KHAN MARTIAL ARTS
VEHICLE, DIRECTED BY WELLSON CHIN -- WHO WAS ALSO RESPONSIBLE
FOR THE COOL 'INSPECTOR WEARS SKIRTS' FILMS. KHAN GETS WILD
AS A GENETICALLY ENHANCED "SUPER LADY COP" BY THE NAME
OF CHUN LI (YES, WELLSON INCLUDED VARIOUS FUN
REFERENCES TO THE WILDLY POPULAR STREET FIGHTER
VIDEO GAME OF THE EARLY 1990s, WHICH WAS ALSO
PARODIED IN JACKIE CHAN'S CITY HUNTER) WHO IS
TRACKING THREE MARTIAL ARTS SUPER VILLAINS LED
BY THE ALWAYS ENTERTAINING YUEN WAH. WHAT
FOLLOWS IS A SERIES OF OVER-THE-TOP COMIC BOOK
STYLE WIRE-FU SEQUENCES, CULMINATING IN A
CRAZY FINALE THAT IS WELL WORTH WAITING THROUGH
THE BORING TALKY BITS TO GET TO.

Swimming with Sharks (1994 USA)
WHEN KEVIN SPACEY HIT BIG WITH SE7EN A YEAR
LATER IN 1995, I THOUGHT FOR SURE PEOPLE WOULD
RETURN TO THIS BRILLIANTLY SAVAGE HOSTAGE
DRAMA ABOUT LIFE BEHIND-THE-SCENES IN
HOLLYWOOD, AND GIVE IT THE ATTENTION IT
SERIOUSLY DESERVED. YOU KNOW, WHAT WITH
SPACEY BEING THE MAIN CHARACTER AND TOTALLY
STEALING THE SHOW WITH ONE OF THE BEST
PERFORMANCES OF HIS CAREER. BUT IT DIDN'T AND IT
CERTAINLY DIDN'T RESULT IN MUCH OF ANYTHING FOR TALENTED FIRST
TIME FILMMAKER, 27-YEAR-OLD GEORGE HUANG, WHO ONLY EVER GOT TO DIRECT ONE
MORE MOVIE -- THE FORGETTABLE 1997 JENNIFER LOVE HEWITT TEEN ROMANCE FILM,
TROJAN WAR. MIND YOU, THE REASON FOR HUANG'S CAREER BEING DEAD-ON-ARRIVAL COULD
HAVE A LOT TO DO WITH THE PLOT OF THIS ACERBIC AND CYNICAL BLACK COMEDY, WHICH
WAS INSPIRED BY HUANG'S OWN DECADE OF DEALINGS AS AN UNDERLING FOR 1980s
MEGA-PRODUCER, JOEL SILVER. SPACEY'S BOSS-FROM-HELL CHARACTER OF "BUDDY
ACKERMAN", AN UTTER PIECE OF SHIT FILM PRODUCER WHO ABUSES HIS HARD-WORKING
EMPLOYEES WHILE SPORTING A SLY GRIN, IS BASED LOOSELY ON SILVER, WHO WAS APPARENTLY
NOT ONE BIT AMUSED ABOUT BEING PUBLICLY ROASTED. ACCORDING TO ENTERTAINMENT
WEEKLY, HUANG HAD TO MOVE BACK INTO HIS PARENTS HOUSE NOT LONG AFTER MAKING THIS,
ONE OF THE BEST MOVIES OF 1994. FUCKING WITH ONE OF THE BIGGEST PRODUCERS IN
HOLLYWOOD APPARENTLY CAN HAVE GRAVE REPERCUSSIONS IN TERMS OF GETTING WORK IN
THAT SAME INDUSTRY! WHO KNEW?!

Whore (1991 USA)
JUST LIKE WHORES IN REAL LIFE, WHORE HAS NEVER BEEN GIVEN ANY RESPECT AT ALL. IT'S ALWAYS
BEEN LOOKED DOWN UPON, SPIT ON, AND MALIGNED. LACKING STUDIO SUPPORT FROM THE OUTSET,
THIS KEN RUSSELL DRAMA STARRING THERESA RUSSELL (NO RELATION) AS THE TITULAR
STREET-WALKING WHORE (WHO SPEAKS TO US, THE AUDIENCE, DIRECTLY AS SHE GOES
ABOUT HER DAILY ROUTINE OF TRACKING DOWN AND SERVICING CUSTOMERS)
WAS MADE FOR A LOW BUDGET. IT WAS BASED ON A STAGE PLAY BY LONDON
TAXI CAB DRIVER, DAVID HINES, WHO ADAPTED THE STORY FROM A
CONVERSATION HE HAD ONE NIGHT WITH A PROSTITUTE SITTING IN
THE BACK OF HIS CAB. RUSSELL, RATHER DISGUSTED WITH THE HIGHLY
ROMANTICIZED, "SAFE", AND UNREALISTIC PORTRAYAL OF
SEXWORK IN 1990's PRETTY WOMAN, MADE THE MOVIE HOPING
TO PROVIDE A MORE SEAMY COUNTERPOINT TO THE JULIA
ROBERTS HOLLYWOOD BLOCKBUSTER. IN MY OPINION, HE
SUCCEEDED, AND THE CENSORS AGREED -- RATING THE MOVIE
NC-17 AND RELEGATING IT TO A MINOR RELEASE IN VERY FEW
THEATERS. ACCORDING TO THE LA TIMES IN 1992, WHEN THE
VHS DISTRIBUTOR, VIDMARK, RETITLED A CUT VERSION OF THE
MOVIE AS "IF YOU CAN'T SAY IT, JUST SEE IT", THE LAME-ASS
SCHEME ONLY ACCOUNTED FOR ABOUT 4% TO 5% OF THE
MOVIE'S ALREADY UNDERWHELMING SALES. DESPITE BEING
LABELLED AND MARKETED AS A SEQUEL, 1994'S WHORE 2,
WRITTEN AND DIRECTED BY AMOS KOLLEK, IS UNRELATED
AND UNCONNECTED.

Falling Down (1993. USA)
WHOOPS. FORGOT TO INCLUDE THIS ONE ALPHABETICALLY, BUT
I THINK THERE IS SOME POETIC IRONY IN IT "FALLING DOWN"
THE LIST TO THE BOTTOM WHERE IT NOW RESIDES.

THIS GREAT THRILLER CENTERS ON MICHAEL DOUGLAS AS HIS
CHARACTER GOES ON A VIOLENT ROAD-RAGE INSPIRED
RAMPAGE THROUGH THE STREETS OF LOS ANGELES. FIRST TIME
SCREENWRITER EBBE ROE SMITH TOLD THE LOS ANGELES
TIMES IN 1993 THAT HE WANTED TO WRITE ABOUT LA THROUGH
THE EYES OF WHITE MIDDLE-CLASS MEN THREATENED BY THE
URBAN SPRAWL BECAUSE, "TO ME, LA IS THE FUTURE OF
EVERYWHERE ELSE IN THE UNITED STATES".

"THE MAIN CHARACTER REPRESENTS THE OLD POWER
STRUCTURE OF THE US THAT HAS NOW BECOME ARCHAIC AND
HOPELESSLY LOST", SMITH SAID. "AND THAT WAY, I GUESS

YOU COULD (THE MAIN CHARACTER) IS LIKE LOS ANGELES. FOR BOTH OF THEM, IT'S ADJUST-OR-DIE TIME."

IT'S A MOVIE BORN OUT OF THE RACIALLY TENSE TIME AND PLACE THAT ALSO GAVE US THE RODNEY KING RIOTS, AND ONE THAT JUST SEEMS TO GET BETTER AS WE GO ALONG, REGARDLESS IF YOU FEEL SYMPATHY FOR DOUGLAS AS AN EVERYMAN WHO RAGES AGAINST A MODERN MULTICULTURAL WORLD, OR VIEW HIM AS A HATEFUL, SELF-PITYING MEMBER OF A SO-CALLED OPPRESSED MAJORITY. OFTEN APTLY DESCRIBED AS THE DEFINITIVE EXPLORATION OF THE "ANGRY WHITE MALE" AS HE APPROACHED THE CURRENT MILLENNIUM, FALLING DOWN PUTS A VERY HUMAN FACE ON WHAT IT IS TO BE BOTH A VICTIM AND A VILLAIN, WHICH SIDE OF THE COIN DOUGLAS'S CHARACTER ULTIMATELY LANDS ON DEPENDS ON YOUR POINT OF VIEW, AND I LOVE THE RARE MOVIE (SUCH AS THIS ONE) THAT IS SECURE AND CONFIDENT ENOUGH TO LEAVE THAT DISTINCTION IN THE HANDS OF EACH INDIVIDUAL VIEWER.

NOMINATED FOR THE PALME D'OR AT THE 1993 CANNES FILM FEST, THIS MOVIE SEEMS TO HAVE BEEN LEFT BEHIND AS TIME HAS GONE ON, AND IS FAR-TOO-RARELY CITED AS ONE OF THE DECADE'S BEST BY CRITICS AND FILM FANS THAT HAVE EITHER FORGOTTEN ABOUT IT OR WERE UNFORTUNATE ENOUGH TO NOT HAVE KNOWN ABOUT IT IN THE FIRST PLACE.

Cinema Sewer readers poll:

What are your 3 favorite Women-in-Prison movies?

IN JUNE OF 2016, I DID AN INFORMAL POLL OF CINEMA SEWER READERS, TO SEE WHAT THEY LIKED IN THE WOMEN-IN-PRISON GENRE. EACH PARTICIPANT WAS ALLOWED THREE PICKS (EACH WITH EQUAL POINT VALUE). MOVIES THAT DID NOT FIT THE GENRE CRITERIA CLOSE ENOUGH WERE NOT TABULATED, ALTHOUGH SOME "REFORM SCHOOL" AND "NAZISPOITATION" MOVIES WITH STRONG WIP GENRE ELEMENTS WERE ALLOWED. HERE ARE THE RESULTS:

1. Chained Heat (1983) 20 votes
2. Big Doll House (1971) 18 votes
3. Big Bird Cage (1972) 17 votes
4. Reform School Girls (1986) 15 votes
5. Female Convict 701: Scorpion (1972) 14 votes
6. Bare Behind Bars (1980) 10 votes
7. Caged Heat (1974) 9 votes
8. Ilsa: She Wolf of the SS (1975) 8 votes
9. Naked Cage (1986) 7 votes
10. Sweet Sugar (1972) 6 votes
11. Female Convict Scorpion: Jailhouse 41 (1972) 5 votes
12. Ilsa: The Wicked Warden (1977) 5 votes
13. Sadomania (1981) 5 votes
14. Women's Prison Massacre (1983) 5 votes
15. Barbed Wire Dolls (1976) 4 votes
16. Born Innocent (1974) 4 votes
17. House of Whipcord (1974) 4 votes
18. Caged (1950) 3 votes
19. Escape from Hell (1980) 3 votes
20. 99 Women (1969) 3 votes

11 other films with 2 votes each
16 other films with 1 vote each

MY OWN PERSONAL TOP 5, IN CASE ANYONE IS CURIOUS, IS AS FOLLOWS:

1. Female Convict Scorpion: Jailhouse 41 (1972)
2. Sweet Sugar (1972)
3. The Big Bird Cage (1972)
4. Female Convict 701: Scorpion (1972)
5. The Naked Cage (1986)

I'M THE BAD GUY?

GET DRESSED, INMATE. WARDEN WANTS TO SEE YOU.

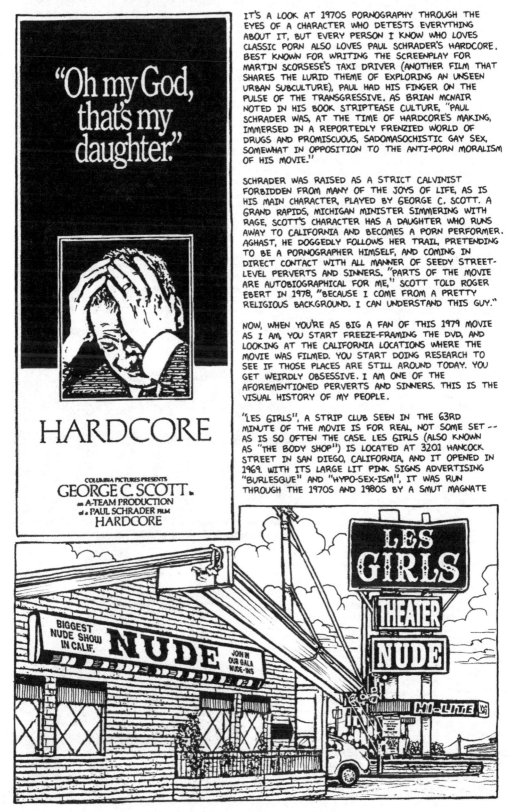

"Oh my God, that's my daughter."

HARDCORE

COLUMBIA PICTURES PRESENTS
GEORGE C. SCOTT in
an A-TEAM PRODUCTION
of a PAUL SCHRADER FILM
HARDCORE

IT'S A LOOK AT 1970S PORNOGRAPHY THROUGH THE EYES OF A CHARACTER WHO DETESTS EVERYTHING ABOUT IT, BUT EVERY PERSON I KNOW WHO LOVES CLASSIC PORN ALSO LOVES PAUL SCHRADER'S HARDCORE. BEST KNOWN FOR WRITING THE SCREENPLAY FOR MARTIN SCORSESE'S TAXI DRIVER (ANOTHER FILM THAT SHARES THE LURID THEME OF EXPLORING AN UNSEEN URBAN SUBCULTURE), PAUL HAD HIS FINGER ON THE PULSE OF THE TRANSGRESSIVE. AS BRIAN MCNAIR NOTED IN HIS BOOK STRIPTEASE CULTURE, "PAUL SCHRADER WAS, AT THE TIME OF HARDCORE'S MAKING, IMMERSED IN A REPORTEDLY FRENZIED WORLD OF DRUGS AND PROMISCUOUS, SADOMASOCHISTIC GAY SEX, SOMEWHAT IN OPPOSITION TO THE ANTI-PORN MORALISM OF HIS MOVIE."

SCHRADER WAS RAISED AS A STRICT CALVINIST FORBIDDEN FROM MANY OF THE JOYS OF LIFE, AS IS HIS MAIN CHARACTER, PLAYED BY GEORGE C. SCOTT. A GRAND RAPIDS, MICHIGAN MINISTER SIMMERING WITH RAGE, SCOTT'S CHARACTER HAS A DAUGHTER WHO RUNS AWAY TO CALIFORNIA AND BECOMES A PORN PERFORMER. AGHAST, HE DOGGEDLY FOLLOWS HER TRAIL, PRETENDING TO BE A PORNOGRAPHER HIMSELF, AND COMING IN DIRECT CONTACT WITH ALL MANNER OF SEEDY STREET-LEVEL PERVERTS AND SINNERS. "PARTS OF THE MOVIE ARE AUTOBIOGRAPHICAL FOR ME," SCOTT TOLD ROGER EBERT IN 1978, "BECAUSE I COME FROM A PRETTY RELIGIOUS BACKGROUND. I CAN UNDERSTAND THIS GUY."

NOW, WHEN YOU'RE AS BIG A FAN OF THIS 1979 MOVIE AS I AM, YOU START FREEZE-FRAMING THE DVD, AND LOOKING AT THE CALIFORNIA LOCATIONS WHERE THE MOVIE WAS FILMED. YOU START DOING RESEARCH TO SEE IF THOSE PLACES ARE STILL AROUND TODAY. YOU GET WEIRDLY OBSESSIVE. I AM ONE OF THE AFOREMENTIONED PERVERTS AND SINNERS. THIS IS THE VISUAL HISTORY OF MY PEOPLE.

"LES GIRLS", A STRIP CLUB SEEN IN THE 63RD MINUTE OF THE MOVIE IS FOR REAL, NOT SOME SET -- AS IS SO OFTEN THE CASE. LES GIRLS (ALSO KNOWN AS "THE BODY SHOP") IS LOCATED AT 3201 HANCOCK STREET IN SAN DIEGO, CALIFORNIA, AND IT OPENED IN 1969. WITH ITS LARGE LIT PINK SIGNS ADVERTISING "BURLESQUE" AND "HYPO-SEX-ISM", IT WAS RUN THROUGH THE 1970S AND 1980S BY A SMUT MAGNATE

NAMED BIG JIM MORGAN, WHO ALSO OWNED TWO OTHER STRIP CLUBS IN SAN DIEGO.

PORN STAR KRISTINA MUNROE (STAR OF 2007'S BLACK DICKS IN LATIN CHICKS 2) WORKED AT THE LES GIRLS THROUGH THE 2000S UNDER THE STRIPPER NAME "APRIL", AND YES IT'S STILL THERE TODAY AND LOOKS SOMEWHAT THE SAME: A LARGE SINGLE FLOOR BRICK BUILDING WITH AN A-FRAME ROOF, GIVING IT THE OUTWARD APPEARANCE OF A MIDWESTERN PANCAKE HOUSE OR MOTEL. WITH A LOT OF CRACK COCAINE ABUSE HAPPENING IN THE LIGHT INDUSTRIAL AREA SURROUNDING THE VINTAGE BUILDING, LES GIRLS HAS, BY ALL REPORTS, FALLEN ON HARD TIMES.

THERE HAVE ALSO BEEN A NUMBER VIOLENT CRIMES THAT HAVE TAKEN PLACE ON THE PROPERTY INCLUDING AN INCIDENT IN 2015 WHERE AN OFFICER ROLLED UP AT NIGHT ON A HOMELESS MAN WALKING DOWN THE ALLEYWAY BEHIND LES GIRLS, AND WITHIN SECONDS HAD SHOT AND KILLED HIM. HE SAID HE DID SO BECAUSE THE MAN HAD A KNIFE, BUT LES GIRLS' SECURITY CAM VIDEO SHOWED THAT RAWSHAN NEHAD WAS HOLDING A PEN AND WAS NOT MAKING ANY THREATENING GESTURES. NEHAD'S FAMILY IS CURRENTLY SUING THE SAN DIEGO POLICE DEPARTMENT FOR $20 MILLION DOLLARS.

"(LES GIRLS) CAN ONLY BE DESCRIBED AS A DUNGEON OF SIN", BENNETT L. FROM PORTLAND, REPORTED. "IMAGINE A FEW ROWS OF BENCHES COVERED IN WHAT FEELS LIKE CARPET. IF YOU'RE NOT LUCKY ENOUGH TO SCORE ONE OF THOSE PRIME SPOTS, PARK YOURSELF IN A PLASTIC CHAIR MUCH LIKE YOU'LL FIND ON YOUR BACK PORCH. EACH DANCER DOES TWO STAGE SONGS. ONCE CLOTHED, THE NEXT TIME FULLY NUDE, AND ONE OF THE STRIPPERS USUALLY PULLS DOUBLE DUTY AS THE DJ. GENERALLY, THE CROWD IS ONE-THIRD ILLEGAL IMMIGRANT, ONE-THIRD CREEPY, OLD MEN, AND THE OTHER THIRD A MIX OF YOUNG DUDES. IF YOU REALLY WANT SOMETHING UNIQUE, GET A PRIVATE DANCE. IT'S ONLY, LIKE, 10 BUCKS A POP, AND YOU'RE TAKEN INTO THIS ROOM (THAT LOOKS LIKE IT WAS) DESIGNED FOR AUSTIN POWERS IF HE WERE A 16-YEAR-OLD GIRL. AND TO KILL IT, SHE'S GOT A CASSETTE MIX TAPE SHE POPS INTO A BARELY-WORKING BOOMBOX TO PLAY WHILE SHE GRINDS ON YOU. THAT'S SOLID."

"THIS PLACE IS FUNNY", KENDRA M. SAID ON YELP.COM. "YOU WALK IN, PAY TEN BUCKS TO AN OLDER MADAM SORT OF LADY AND THEN GO SIT ON THE BENCHES WHICH LOOK LIKE CHURCH PEWS MORE THAN ANYTHING ELSE. THE STAGE LOOKS LIKE SOMETHING THE HIGH SCHOOL THEATER DEPARTMENT MADE. BETWEEN DANCERS, LESBIAN PORN BLASTS ON THE SCREENS. SITTING BEHIND YOU THERE WILL BE: STRANGE COUPLES ON AN EROTIC NIGHT ON THE TOWN, HOMELESS/TOOTHLESS WANDERERS, AND WANNABE PIMPS. THE GIRLS ARE MEDIOCRE, AND THAT'S BEING GENEROUS. THE PRETTIEST ONE WAS A GIRL NAMED FOX OR SOMETHING LIKE THAT, HOWEVER SHE MADE ONLY 15 DOLLARS IN TIPS AND THAT WAS THE LARGEST AMOUNT OF ANYONE. THE OTHERS MADE AN AVERAGE OF 4 BUCKS. PRETTY SAD MONEY FOR STRIPPERS."

"NEVER COME HERE ALONE, ESPECIALLY IF YOU'RE COMING HERE AT NIGHT." 22-YEAR-OLD ANGELA D. WARNED. "THERE'S ALWAYS A LOT OF GUYS IN THE PARKING LOT THAT ARE TRYING TO SELL YOU THEIR CDS AND WHATEVER. EW."

"THE PLACE HAS A RUNDOWN RETRO LATE '80S POOL HALL LOOK", SUGAR L. REPORTED. "WHICH I GUESS MAKES SENSE SINCE THEY HAVE POOL TABLES, BUT IF YOU'RE LOOKING FOR SOMETHING MORE MODERATE AND A NICE CLEAN ATMOSPHERE, THIS IS REALLY NOT FOR YOU. JUST A MINUTE INTO HAVING A SEAT, DESIREE APPROACHED ME WHO WAS A TALL BLACK GIRL WITH A SO-SO BODY, AND MAN -- WAS SHE AGGRESSIVE. I MANAGED TO GET DESIREE TO BACK OFF, BUT SHE STARTED TO RAISE HER VOICE AND KEPT TELLING ME SHE WOULD BE BACK AS SHE WALKED OFF."

SELENE G. HAD A SIMILAR EXPERIENCE. "AFTER THEIR SHOW, THE GIRLS GET OFF THE STAGE AND WALK AROUND AND ASK EVERYONE IN THE PLACE FOR TIPS. IT'S WEIRD AND AWKWARD, AND IF YOU CHOOSE NOT TO, THEY WALK AWAY BEFORE YOU EVEN FINISH ANSWERING. RUDE. MOST OF THEM LOOK LIKE THEY'RE FROM THE HOOD. I MEAN, I'M GHETTO, BUT IF YOU'RE GOING TO SELL A SHOW, AT LEAST CLEAN IT UP. COMB YOUR HAIR AND LOOK LIKE YOU TOOK A SHOWER."

"THE ONLY PLACE YOU'RE SAFE FROM THESE PANHANDLERS-IN-PANTIES IS WHEN YOU'RE PLAYING POOL", GARY P. NOTED. "THAT'S WHAT YOU LEARN WHEN YOU'RE A REGULAR. OTHERWISE, THE GIRLS

LITERALLY LINE UP TO HARASS YOU FOR POCKET CHANGE. I'VE NEVER BEEN TO A CLUB IN MY LIFE THAT FEATURES STRIPPERS THAT ARE THIS PUSHY, BUT CLEARLY IT MUST WORK, BECAUSE THEY'RE OBVIOUSLY INSTRUCTED BY MANAGEMENT TO PRESSURE AND BERATE EVERYONE WHO WALKS IN."

BUT HARD-ASS DRAMA FROM THE GALS ISN'T THE ONLY SELLING POINT. IN ORDER TO GET PEOPLE TO COME ON DOWN, LES GIRLS ADVERTISE THAT DRINKS ARE "ONLY 75 CENTS" ON THEIR BARE-BONES WEBSITE. "NO $2.50 SUCKER DRINKS!", THE SITE TRUMPETS. WHAT THEY DON'T MENTION IS THAT NO ALCOHOL IS SERVED, AND THE .75 CENT DRINKS ARE NOTHING MORE THAN WATER! HAHA!

IN RECENT YEARS, THE LATEST CO-OWNER OF LES GIRLS, A 65-YEAR-OLD POET NAMED KATA PIERCE MORGAN (A FORMER STRIPPER, HERSELF), HAS BEGUN TAKING THE CLUB IN UNPREDICTABLE DIRECTIONS. IN PARTICULAR, SHE'S MADE IT A VENUE FOR HER OWN "ADULT" PLAYS TO BE PERFORMED FOR THE LOCAL SAN DIEGO FRINGE FEST -- A FESTIVAL OF THE PERFORMING ARTS. ONE SUCH PLAY SHE DID THERE IN 2015, ENTITLED "HOOKER P.I." WAS DESCRIBED BY MORGAN AS SUCH:

"VIA LIVE ELECTRONICA, POLE-DANCING AND SINGING, BE TRANSPORTED TO A WORLD MUCH LIKE OUR OWN. ONE STORMY NIGHT, SEX WORKER KATE MCGREW TAKES A CLIENT FOR ONE HOUR OF ILLEGAL ILL-REPUTED TRANSACTIONAL SEX. WHEN HE KICKS THE BUCKET DURING THE ACT, MCGREW IS FACED WITH THE TASK OF HIDING FROM A PACK OF RADICAL FEMINISTS WHO ROAM THE STREETS, HELL-BENT ON ENSLAVING HOOKERS AND EATING THEIR CLIENTS FOR STRENGTH. SHE DEVISES A PLAN TO TRAP AND SCHOOL THE RAD-FEMS ONE-BY-ONE. WILL CROSS-DRESSING SAVE HER LIFE? CAN SHE END THE HORROR ONCE AND FOR ALL?"

"NUDITY IS ART," MORGAN TOLD THE LOCAL PAPER. "THERE'S THE STIGMA OF LES GIRLS -- IT ALWAYS GETS A LITTLE BIT OF A SNICKER. BUT THAT THEATER IS UNIQUE TO SAN DIEGO HISTORY. MY SHOWS SHOULD BE APPEALING TO BOTH MEN AND WOMEN, BUT THEY HAVE TO BE OPEN MINDED. THEY CAN'T BE MY RELATIVES FROM OKLAHOMA OR THE BIBLE BELT."

OR A CALVINIST MINISTER FROM GRAND RAPIDS, MICHIGAN, SEARCHING FOR HIS PORN STAR DAUGHTER, I WOULD IMAGINE.

—BOUGIE '16

(THE FOLLOWING IS A SHORT EXCERPT FROM THE 2012 BOOK 'GOLDEN GODDESSES', (BEAR MANOR MEDIA) WHICH IS A TERRIFIC SET OF INTERVIEWS AND DETAILED PROFILES ON 25 OF THE MOST LEGENDARY WOMEN OF CLASSIC ADULT CINEMA. IT IS 950 HEFTY PAGES, WRITTEN BY THE TALENTED JILL C. NELSON, AND WORTH ORDERING FOR FANS OF VINTAGE XXX – ROBIN)

JULIET ANDERSON IS ONE OF THE MOST FEROCIOUSLY SEDUCTIVE TEMPTRESSES TO HAVE ENTRANCED GOLDEN AGE AUDIENCES. ANDERSON MOVED SWIFTLY UP THE ECHELON OF ADULT PERFORMERS IN HER FORTIETH YEAR AFTER ACCEPTING THE ROLE OF A HOUSEKEEPER IN

JULIET ANDERSON the star of the Swedish Erotica series . . . Now in her FIRST full length motion picture as . . .

AUNT PEG

WORLD PREMIERE

with SERENA
SHIRLEY WOOD
ANGELA HART
Special Appearance by
JOHNNY WADD

xXx

100%
AL GOLDSTEIN

PUSSYCAT 2   B'WAY AT 48th ST. ● 582-0883
BOX OFFICE OPENS 9:45 A.M.
CONT. TILL 2:00 A.M.

ALEX DE RENZY'S PRETTY PEACHES (1978). WITH THE SUBSEQUENT UNVEILING OF HER ALTER EGO, THE INSATIABLE, SHOOT-FROM-THE-HIP, "AUNT PEG" NORTON, JULIET BECAME AN INSTANT SENSATION AND RECURRING SCREEN CHARACTER FOLLOWING A SCENE WHEREBY ANDERSON INSTRUCTED HER VIRGINAL "NIECE" (SHARON KANE) ON THE FINER POINTS OF SEXUAL GRATIFICATION DURING A MÉNAGE à TROIS WITH JOHN C. HOLMES.

THE ELDEST OF TWO DAUGHTERS, JULIET ANDERSON WAS BORN JUDY CARR, RAISED IN BURBANK, CALIFORNIA BY A BIG BAND TRUMPETER AND HIS WIFE. MONEY WAS SCARCE FOR THE SMALL FAMILY, BUT LOVE AND AFFECTION WAS BOUNTIFUL. JULIET SPOKE WITH HUMOUR AND AWE WHEN RECOUNTING HER PARENTS' UNINHIBITED SEXUAL COMPATIBILITY, VIVIDLY RECALLING HOW THEY WOULD OFTEN SNEAK AWAY AND MAKE LOVE. SHE CREDITED HER MOTHER AND FATHER FOR INSTILLING IN HER A CAREFREE AND HEALTHY ATTITUDE ABOUT HER OWN SEXUALITY.

CONTRARY TO HER LATER YEARS AS AN INDOMITABLE BLONDE COUGAR, JULIET'S CHILDHOOD WAS OFTEN LONELY AND ISOLATED AFTER SHE WAS DIAGNOSED WITH CROHN'S DISEASE. THE ILLNESS PRODUCED DEBILITATING SYMPTOMS THAT SENT HER TO HOSPITALS AND PREVENTED HER FROM PARTICIPATING IN REGULAR GIRLHOOD ACTIVITIES. VOWING TO NOT ALLOW THE CONDITION TO CONSUME HER, JULIET EVENTUALLY STUDIED ART AND ENGLISH IN COLLEGE, AND

TAUGHT CONVERSATIONAL ENGLISH ABROAD TO FOREIGN STUDENTS FOR SEVERAL YEARS BEFORE SETTLING IN SAN FRANCISCO. THERE, SHE PROCEEDED TO HOOK UP WITH A FRIEND FOR SOME CASUAL SEX AND THE ENCOUNTER BECAME THE IMPETUS FOR HER JOB SEARCH. SHORTLY AFTER ANSWERING AN ADVERTISEMENT IN A NEWSPAPER SEEKING TO HIRE NUDE PERFORMERS, ANDERSON MADE THE ACQUAINTANCE OF DIRECTOR ALEX DE RENZY AND HER FATE WAS SEALED.

"[DE RENZY] SAID, "YOU'RE DEFINITELY HIRED FOR THE SHOW, AND BY THE WAY, I'M SHOOTING A FILM AND THERE'S A PART THAT HASN'T BEEN CAST YET," WHICH WAS TRUE. HE WASN'T MAKING IT UP. HE TOLD ME, "I WAS WONDERING IF YOU MIGHT LIKE TO BE IN IT. IT'S NOT DIFFICULT OR ANYTHING. IT'LL ONLY TAKE A SHORT TIME AND IT'S JUST FOR ONE DAY, BUT I'LL GIVE YOU TWO HUNDRED DOLLARS." NOW, SEE THAT WAS A LOT OF MONEY. ANYWAY, [DE RENZY] SAID, "HERE'S THE SCRIPT. YOUR PART WOULD BE THAT OF THE MAID. IT'S NEAR THE BEGINNING." UP TO THAT POINT, I'D NEVER BEEN WITH A WOMAN. I READ THAT PART. I SCREAMED, AND ALEX COVERED HIS MOUTHPIECE OF THE PHONE AND SAID, "I'LL BE RIGHT WITH YOU.""

"MY HEART WAS POUNDING AND I SAID TO HIM, "OH, MY GOD, WHAT IS THIS?! DO YOU MEAN TO TELL ME THERE ARE MOVIES LIKE THIS?" I'D NEVER HEARD OF THE X-RATED FILM BUSINESS IN MY WHOLE LIFE. I'D BEEN LIVING ABROAD. HE WAS VERY PATIENT AND EVENTUALLY I SAID, "WELL, I BELIEVE I WAS GIVEN THIS OPPORTUNITY FOR A REASON AND IT WOULD BE REALLY FOOLISH OF ME TO PASS IT UP BECAUSE I LIKE TO LEARN NEW THINGS.""

"JOHN LESLIE WAS MY FIRST MAN I WORKED WITH AND THROUGHOUT MY ENTIRE CAREER; HE WAS MY FAVORITE. WE HAD THE MOST INCREDIBLE CHEMISTRY. WE ABSOLUTELY HAD A BALL. I WENT ON TO MAKE DOZENS OF FILMS AND I WAS IN THE INDUSTRY FOR SIX AND A HALF YEARS, BUT JOHN LESLIE WAS MY VERY FAVORITE. HE WAS INTELLIGENT AND FUNNY, A GOOD ACTOR, AND WE JUST HAD SO MUCH FUN; IT WAS EXTREMELY OBVIOUS ON SCREEN.""

"I TOLD MY PARENTS HOW IT HAPPENED AND THAT IT COMPLETELY SURPRISED ME. THEY LOOKED AT EACH OTHER AND LOOKED BACK AT ME—I CAN SEE IT RIGHT NOW—WITH BIG SMILES ON THEIR FACES. THEY SAID, "WE KNOW IT ALREADY." SOMEBODY THEY KNEW CAME TO THEM AND TOLD THEM. THEY HAD ACTUALLY GONE TO A THEATER. IN THOSE DAYS, YOU HAD TO GO TO A MOVIE THEATER. IT WAS BEFORE VIDEO. MY PARENTS TOLD ME THAT SOME FRIENDS OF SOME PEOPLE THEY KNEW WENT AND SAW ME. I SAID, "OH NO! I'M SORRY." THEY JUST STARTED LAUGHING. THEY SAID, "DON'T WORRY ABOUT IT. YOU'RE A GROWN-UP GAL AND IF YOU CAN'T TAKE CARE OF YOURSELF AT THIS POINT THEN IT'S TOO LATE.""

"I WANTED TO DISPEL THE MYTH THAT THERE WAS ANY SEPARATION BETWEEN BEING SEXY, AND INTELLIGENT, AND FUNNY, AND OLDER. THAT'S WHAT I DID IN THE FILMS—DISPEL THOSE MYTHS. IF WOMEN LET THEMSELVES BE EXPLOITED, I IMAGINE THEY WERE. I CAN'T REALLY SPEAK FOR THE OTHER WOMEN; I JUST KNOW THAT I NEVER WAS. I NEVER ALLOWED MYSELF TO BE. THE DIRECTORS WHO WANTED TO DO THAT DIDN'T HIRE ME BECAUSE I HAD A REPUTATION FOR BEING INDEPENDENT AND NOT PUTTING UP WITH NONSENSE. I DID A VERY GOOD JOB WHEN I WAS IN FRONT OF THE CAMERA AND I MADE IT EASY FOR EVERYBODY BECAUSE MY SCENES COULD OFTEN BE DONE IN JUST ONE TAKE.""

☆ HERE'S THE THING, YOU GUYS: ☆

TOXIC ONLINE GEEK BEHAVIOUR. IT'S BEEN A BIG TOPIC IN 2018 AMONGST MY CIRCLE OF FRIENDS. I DON'T KNOW HOW TO SOLVE SOME OF THE BIGGER AND MORE SERIOUS ISSUES LIKE HARASSMENT CAMPAIGNS, BUT I DO KNOW HOW TO SOLVE ONE OF THE MAJOR THINGS THAT HAS PEOPLE TURNING ON FILM NERDS. HEED THIS ADVICE, FILM FANS:

THE SAFEST RULE IS TO NOT WHINE ABOUT CASTING BEFORE A FILM IS RELEASED, AND NEVER COMPLAIN ABOUT A MOVIE (OR ANY OTHER FORM OF MEDIA) YOU HAVE YET TO SEE. IF NERDS WOULD ADHERE TO THOSE BASIC TENANTS IT WOULD ERADICATE LIKE 50% OF THEIR ONLINE GARBAGE *OVERNIGHT*. I STOPPED DOING IT WAY BACK IN 2003 WHEN VAL KILMER WAS ANNOUNCED TO PLAY JOHN HOLMES IN WONDERLAND. I SHIT ALL OVER THAT AND THEN HE ENDED UP DOING AN INCREDIBLE JOB. I FELT LIKE AN IDIOT. NEVER AGAIN. THAT'S 15 YEARS OF NO ONE HAVING TO LISTEN TO ME BITCH ABOUT PRECASTING: ONE OF MY GREATEST GIFTS TO THE INTERNET.

"VAL KILMER IS INSANE. . .HOW COULD YOU EVER DOUBT HE COULD PULL OFF HOLMES?", COMMENTED MY FRIEND, ROBERT LUNA.

THE SAME REASON EVERYONE GOES OFF ABOUT THIS STUFF. THE SAME REASON EVERYONE WHINED ABOUT HEATH LEDGER AS THE JOKER BEFORE THEY SAW THAT. THE SAME REASON EVERYONE STAMPED THEIR FEET ABOUT ELIJAH WOOD BEING CAST IN THE REMAKE OF MANIAC. WE JUST COULDN'T IMAGINE THE TRANSFORMATION BEFORE IT HAPPENED. SHORTSIGHTEDNESS.

-BOUGIE

THE LUSH EXCESS OF CAMILLE 2000

⊢ REVIEW BY ROBIN BOUGIE • 2015 ⊣

A FILM ADAPTATION OF THE ALEXANDRE DUMAS FILS NOVEL, "THE LADY OF THE CAMELLIAS" BY SCREENWRITER MICHAEL DEFORREST, CAMILLE 2000 IS QUITE A NOTEWORTHY ACHIEVEMENT IN THE HISTORY OF EROTIC CINEMA, AND IT CERTAINLY DIDN'T HURT THE FINAL PRODUCT TO COME FROM SUCH A SOLID LITERARY SOURCE. BUT WHILE CAMILLE 2000 IS A FILM THAT HAS ALMOST UNANIMOUSLY POSITIVE REVIEWS FROM CRITICS AND FILM HISTORIANS TODAY, AT THE TIME OF ITS RELEASE IT WAS RUTHLESSLY SAVAGED BY MANY MEMBERS OF THE MEDIA. IN THE SAME YEAR THAT HE WROTE THE SCRIPT FOR BEYOND THE VALLEY OF THE DOLLS, A YOUNG ROGER EBERT HAD NOT A SINGLE POSITIVE WORD TO SAY ABOUT HIS VIEWING EXPERIENCE, HAM-FISTEDLY CLAIMING THAT DIRECTOR RADLEY METZGER HAD BEEN, WITH EACH NEW FILM IN HIS FILMOGRAPHY, DIRECTING "THE WORST MOVIE OF ALL TIME".

"DANIELE GAUBERT IS PRESENTED IN THE NUDE", THE REVIEWER WOULD ANNOUNCE TO CHICAGO SUN-TIMES READERS, "BUT WITH ABOUT AS MUCH EROTIC EFFECT AS AN ARRID AD".

EBERT SO DISLIKED THE FILM, THAT HE'D GO ON TO REPRINT THE SCATHING REVIEW IN HIS 2000 BOOK "I HATED HATED HATED THIS MOVIE". NOW, WHILE I'D CONCEDE THAT CAMILLE 2000 TAKES FAR TOO LONG TO GET GOING (IT'S NEARLY 25 MINUTES BEFORE A SINGLE OVERTLY GROOVY, SEXY, OR HEDONISTIC THING TAKES PLACE ON SCREEN), THE FILM MORE THAN MAKES UP FOR ITS PLODDING FIRST REEL ONCE IT ROCKETS INTO ITS FULL 1960S EUPHORIC PHANTASM OF SEX-SOAKED RADNESS. AS MUCH EROTICISM AS A DEODORANT ADVERTISEMENT, ROGER? REALLY? THIS IS RADLEY METZGER'S HAPPENING, AND IT FREAKS HIM OUT!

♡ DANIELE GAUBERT

MORE OF A SENSUOUS AND TWISTED ROMANCE THAN LUSTY EROTICA, THIS IS A MOVIE THAT IS BOUND TO DISAPPOINT THE CASUAL VIEWER EXPECTING EITHER A FUTURISTIC CAMP FEST (THE TITLE IS SOMEWHAT MISLEADING) OR AN OVERT CAVALCADE OF FREAKY BUMP N' GRIND. AS ODD AS IT IS FOR FANS TO ADMIT, THE SEX SCENES IN CAMILLE 2000 AREN'T EVEN ALL THAT GOOD -- WHICH IS A TRUE TESTAMENT TO JUST HOW EXCELLENT THE REST OF THE MOVIE IS. IT'S FUNNY THAT THIS MOVIE WAS CONSIDERED "PORNOGRAPHY" BY THE MAINSTREAM WHEN IT WAS RELEASED, BECAUSE THERE IS FAR MORE GAZING AND YEARNING THAN LEGIT SEXING GOING ON, AND I FOR ONE DON'T EVEN MISS IT.

THE STORY TAKES PLACE IN ROME, WHERE WE'RE INTRODUCED TO A WEALTHY AND HANDSOME YOUNG MAN NAMED ARMAND (NINO CASTELNUOVO) WHO LIKES TO HORNDOG WITH HIS PAL GASTION (ROBERTO BISACCO). ONE NIGHT AT THE OPERA ARMAND SPOTS THE GIRL OF HIS DREAMS (DANIELE GAUBERT) IN THE AUDIENCE, ALTHOUGH GASTION GIVES HIM FAIR WARNING OF THE BEAUTIFUL MARGUERITE'S REP FOR BEING A DRUG AND MONEY ADDICTED SLUT WHO SEEMS TO EXIST ONLY TO LEECH AND BREAK MEN'S HEARTS.

"THE HILLS ARE FULL OF BODIES OF THE MEN SHE'S RUINED", ARMAND IS TOLD.

SAPPY MELODRAMA HAS ITS PROS AND CONS, BUT WHEN IT IS DONE RIGHT, VIEWERS ARE HELPLESS TO RESIST THE CAPTIVATING CHARMS OF THE CHARACTERS. THE THEME OF "LOVE FOUND AND THEN LOST" NEVER GETS OLD, BECAUSE IT IS SOMETHING EVERY SINGLE ONE OF US CAN IDENTIFY WITH. WE'VE ALL FALLEN FOR, OR HAD A CRUSH ON, AN INDIVIDUAL WE CAN'T CONTROL, AND CAN NEVER HAVE.

IT LOOKS AS THOUGH THAT MAY BE THE OUTCOME FOR ARMAND FROM THE GET-GO, AS THE GORGEOUS MARGUERITE IS INITIALLY RATHER HESITANT TO ABANDON THE ORGY-FILLED PARTY ANIMAL LIFESTYLE AND SETTLE FOR ONE COCK, EVEN IF IT'S ATTACHED TO A DEVOTED GUY SHE'S WILDLY IN LOVE WITH. THOUGH SHE IS A KEPT WOMAN (WITH THE KEYS TO BOTH THE HOUSE AND TO THE DOG COLLAR AROUND HER NECK BELONGING TO A SMIRKING DUKE), HER DEEP LOVE FOR ARMAND LEADS HER TO RUN OFF WITH HIM — OR FLOAT OFF WITH HIM, AS IT WERE, IN A YACHT. WHAT THE TWO STAR-CROSSED LOVERS DON'T KNOW, HOWEVER, IS THAT THEY WILL SOON BE VISITED BY A MAN WHO, WITH JUST A FEW WORDS TO MARGUERITE, WILL CHANGE THE COURSE OF THEIR LIVES FOREVER.

OUTLANDISHLY STYLISH, THIS MOD MELODRAMA IS A LUSH FEVER-DREAM EMBROILED IN THE PHILOSOPHY OF HEDONISM, BUT ULTIMATELY PARLAYS THE HEARTBREAKING FACT THAT TRUE LOVE IS NO MATCH FOR MEDDLING AND SOCIAL OBSTACLES. DESPITE THE SEXY AND TALENTED ACTORS AND ACTRESSES WHO TAKE UP MUCH OF THE SCREEN-TIME, THE TRUE STAR OF CAMILLE 2000 IS UNQUESTIONABLY ENRICO SABBATINI, THE MAN RESPONSIBLE FOR SET AND COSTUME DESIGN FOR THE PRODUCTION.

TRULY, SABBATINI'S SUCCESS IS METZGER'S SUCCESS. IN ADDITION TO SOME WICKED SEE-THROUGH OUTFITS, THE MOVIE IS LITTERED WITH OTHERWORLDLY TECHNICOLOR INTERIORS THAT ARE SOMEHOW ALL AT ONCE FUTURISTIC AND BORN OF THE 1960s. LUCITE, PLASTIC AND MIRRORED WALLS, ART DECO FRAMES, VINYL BEDSHEETS, CHAIN METAL AND MESH BATHING SUITS, LUXURIOUS COCKTAIL GOWNS, DRESSES MADE OF MIRRORS, GLOWING CHAIRS THAT DOUBLE AS LAMPS, AND MOST AMAZING OF ALL: TRANSLUCENT INFLATABLE FURNITURE.

INTERESTINGLY, IT WAS THESE OUTRAGEOUS CLEAR PLASTIC COUCHES, MATTRESSES AND PILLOWS THAT PROVIDED METZGER WITH HIS GREATEST TECHNICAL CHALLENGE. RADLEY WOULD COMPLAIN THAT THE HEAT FROM THE PERFORMERS BODIES WOULD MAKE THE SEE-THRU SET SLOWLY DEFLATE, AND EVERYTHING WOULD GRIND TO A HALT WHILE THE CREW WENT ABOUT RESETTING IT. I WOULD IMAGINE THAT THIS PROBABLY EXPLAINS WHY NO FILMMAKER BEFORE OR SINCE HAS UTILIZED THE GIMMICK, BUT WHAT ENDS UP ON SCREEN CERTAINLY MAKES ME FEEL IT WAS WORTH THE TROUBLE.

PIERO PICCIONI HAS BEEN RESPONSIBLE FOR MANY OUTSTANDING SOUNDTRACKS (MANY OF THEM BEING SPAGHETTI WESTERNS), BUT THIS ONE THAT CRITIC TIM LUCAS CALLED "ONE OF THE MOST VISIONARY EUROCULT SOUNDTRACKS EVER", STANDS AS HIS BEST. FROM THE OPENING TITLE MUSIC, TO TRACKS LIKE "ECHOES", "CHAINS OF LOVE" AND "FUNKY LOVERS", PICCIONI'S MASTERPIECE DOES A GREAT SERVICE TO THE VISUALS, AND HAS PRETTY MUCH EVERYTHING ONE COULD WANT FOR A 1960s SEX FILM SCORE.

ITALIAN ACTOR NINO CASTELNUOVO, BEST KNOWN FOR STARRING AS GUY FOUCHER IN THE 1964 FRENCH MUSICAL THE UMBRELLAS OF CHERBOURG, ALSO APPEARED IN SOME SPAGHETTI WESTERNS, SUCH AS LUCIO FULCI'S MASSACRE TIME (1966) AND FIVE MAN ARMY (1969). HORROR FILM FANS WILL RECOGNIZE NINO FROM HIS STARRING ROLE IN THE SKIN-FILLED GIALLO STRIP NUDE FOR YOUR KILLER (1975).

"camille 2000" "camille 2000" "camille 2000"

the 'now' child
"camille 2000"

PERSONS UNDER 17 WILL NOT BE ADMITTED

"camille 2000" "camille 2000" "camille 2000"

LOVELY SILVANA VENTURELLI WOULD GO ON TO STAR IN METZGER'S THE LICKERISH QUARTET, BUT SHE WASN'T THE HEADLINER THIS TIME OUT. IN CAMILLE 2000, THE STAGE BELONGS TO DANIELE GAUBERT. A KNOCKOUT WHO BECAME A FRENCH SEX SYMBOL AT THE AGE OF 15, GAUBERT WAS A REASONABLY POPULAR ACTRESS IN FRANCE IN THE LATE SIXTIES AND EARLY SEVENTIES, AND DIED ALL TOO YOUNG DUE TO CANCER IN 1987 AT THE AGE OF 44. FROM 1963 TO 1968 SHE WAS MARRIED TO RHADAMES TRUJILLO MARTINEZ, A SON OF THE DOMINICAN DICTATOR RAFAEL TRUJILLO, WHO SPORTS ILLUSTRATED CALLED "EVIL-TEMPERED" AND "SUPER RICH", WHILE STATING THAT TRUJILLO "KEPT HER A VIRTUAL PRISONER".

SEEKING A MAN THAT WOULD TREAT HER RIGHT, DANIELE MARRIED THREE TIME OLYMPIC GOLD MEDAL-WINNING SKIER JEAN-CLAUDE KILLY ON NOV. 2, 1973. IT WAS A SOLID RELATIONSHIP THAT WOULD LAST UNTIL HER PASSING, WITH GAUBERT AND KILLY APPEARING NUDE TOGETHER IN AN 8-PAGE LAYOUT IN OUI MAGAZINE IN SEPTEMBER 1974. "SHE WAS THE LOVE OF MY LIFE, THE GIRL OF MY LIFE FOR 20 YEARS," JEAN CLAUDE WOULD WRITE AFTER GAUBERT'S DEATH. "WE ARE NOT HERE FOR LONG. THERE ARE FIVE, SIX BILLION OF US ON THE EARTH, AND NONE OF US ARE HERE FOR LONG."

—FIN—

Blood Rage a.k.a. Nightmare at Shadow Woods (USA. 1987)

Written and illustrated by Seth Goodkind

I'VE NEVER BEEN MUCH FOR SLASHER FILMS MYSELF, PREFERRING MORE NON-HUMAN MONSTERS, BUT I AM A SUCKER FOR A LUSH AND BLOODY NUGGET OF RETRO CINEMA THAT REALLY LOOKS AND FEELS LIKE ITS MOMENT IN TIME, AND BLOOD RAGE IS HACKED LIMB-FROM-LIMB STRAIGHT OUT OF 1983. WHILE IT WAS SHOT THAT YEAR BY DIRECTOR JOHN GRISSMER AND CINEMATOGRAPHER RICHARD BROOKS, IT WAS HELD BACK UNTIL '87 BEFORE A CRIMINALLY BRIEF THEATRICAL RUN AND SUBSEQUENT VHS OBSCURITY. BY THAT TIME SLASHERS WERE VERY NEARLY PASSÉ, AND BY ALL ACCOUNTS BLOOD RAGE WAS LOST TO THE AGES BEFORE ARROW DECIDED TO GIVE IT A DELUXE BLURAY RE-RELEASE IN 2016.

THE FILM OPENS AT A DRIVE-IN THEATER WHERE A MIDDLE AGED WOMAN IS NECKING IN THE FRONT SEAT OF A STATION WAGON WHILE HER TWIN SONS SIT IN THE BACKSEAT. SENSING THE ANXIETY IN THE FRONT, THE BOYS SNEAK OUT AND FOR NO IMMEDIATELY APPARENT REASON ONE OF THEM BURIES A HATCHET IN THE FACE OF A DIFFERENT GUY FUCKING HIS GIRLFRIEND IN A NEARBY CAR. HE THEN WIPES BLOOD ALL OVER HIS BROTHER'S FACE, PUTS THE HATCHET IN HIS HAND AND LETS HIM TAKE THE BLAME. THE REMAINDER OF THE FILM TAKES PLACE 10 YEARS LATER DURING THANKSGIVING AT A CABIN RESORT. MOM HAS FINALLY MET BRAD, WHOM SHE IS GOING TO MARRY. MEANWHILE, A DISHEVELED, CONFUSED LOOKING TODD ESCAPES FROM THE ASYLUM TO WARN EVERYONE THAT TERRY IS THE REAL KILLER. TERRY CASUALLY INFORMS EVERYONE OVER DINNER OF TODD'S ESCAPE AND PROCEEDS IN FINE FASHION TO EXPLOIT THE SUBSEQUENT CONFUSION CAUSED BY THEIR IDENTICAL APPEARANCE TO HACK THE SECONDARY CAST TO GRUESOME KIBBLE. FORTUNATELY, THERE ARE A NUMBER OF GUESTS STAYING IN THE OTHER NEARBY CABINS TO GIVE TERRY PLENTY TO WORK WITH...

WITH SOME PARTICULARLY VISCERAL AND CREATIVE GORE EFFECTS FROM ED FRENCH, BLOOD RAGE DOES NOT SHY AWAY FROM THE BLOODSHED, OR THE PRECIOUS '80S CULTURAL TOUCHSTONES. FEATHERED BRO-MULLETS, PRIMITIVE VIDEO GAMES AND PASTEL SWEATERS ABOUND. IT IS EVERY BIT A PRODUCT OF A VERY PARTICULAR MOMENT IN MOVIE HISTORY. A MOMENT THAT I CONFESS TO BEING VERY MUCH ENAMORED WITH BOTH CULTURALLY AND CINEMATICALLY.

AS WITH ANY GENRE FILM THOUGH, THERE'S ALWAYS SOMETHING MORE GOING ON BENEATH ALL THE BAD BUSINESS. IN A TELLING INTRODUCTION, MOM'S INITIAL HOSPITAL VISIT TO SEE TODD TEETERS PRECARIOUSLY ON HER OWN MENTAL STATE AND HER ABILITY, 20 YEARS HENCE, TO GRASP THE DIVERGENT NATURE OF HER SON(S) AND WHAT HAD OCCURRED. FOR ALL INTENTS, SHE SEEMS TO CONFLATE THE TWO BOYS IN HER MIND. SHE CONTINUES TO SEE TODD AS THEY WERE, AND TERRY AS THEY SHOULD HAVE BEEN, FULLY UNABLE TO GRASP THAT THIS IS NOT IN FACT THE CASE. TWINS ARE NEVER A GOOD SIGN IN A HORROR FILM. THEY ALWAYS INDICATE SOMETHING SINISTER AND WHILE BLOOD RAGE MAKES MINOR COMEDY OF TERRY AND TODD'S IDENTICAL APPEARANCE, AND MUCH HORROR OF THEIR DIVERGENT PERSONAS, I BELIEVE THAT MOM'S INABILITY TO DISTINGUISH CONFIRMS THAT THEY ARE REALLY ONE IN THE SAME PERSON. BOTH LITERALLY, THE SAME ACTOR (MARK SOPER), AND METAPHORICALLY, TWO SIDES OF THE SAME COIN. FOR AS MUCH AS BLOOD RAGE CONCERNS ITSELF ON THE SURFACE WITH THE BROTHERS, IT IS FAR MORE FERVENTLY WORRYING AT THE EDGES OF MOTHERHOOD.

THE FIRST MURDER IS SET OFF BY MOM HOOKING UP AT THE DRIVE IN. TERRY IS THEN "RESTARTED"

10 YEARS LATER BY THE NEWS THAT MOM IS SHACKING UP AGAIN. TODD'S ESCAPE AT THIS RATE APPEARS TO BE ENTIRELY COINCIDENTAL. IT'S ALMOST AS IF THE FUNDAMENTAL SLASHER RULE OF SEX = DEATH HAS BEEN NARCISSISTICALLY FOISTED BACKWARDS A GENERATION. THE KIDS AREN'T KILLED FOR TRYING TO "DO ADULT STUFF." INSTEAD THE ADULTS ARE KILLED FOR NOT STICKING WITH "KID STUFF." TERRY'S ANGER IS ENTIRELY NARCISSISTIC TO THE POINT THAT IT APPEARS GENUINELY OEDIPAL, AND LACKING A "REAL" DAD, (AT LEAST UNTIL BRAD) HIS COMPLEX REMAINS UNRESOLVED. THIS POINT OF TENSION IS CONFIRMED BY THE BRIEF APPEARANCE OF ANOTHER WOMAN, A SINGLE WOMAN WITH A BABY, WHO COMES HOME WITH HER DATE AND IS MURDERED WHILE SEDUCING HIM.

TERRY ALSO SEEMS QUITE "INNOCENT" HIMSELF, REFUSING ALCOHOLIC BEVERAGES AND HAVING NEVER HAD SEX WITH HIS GIRLFRIEND WHOM AT ONE POINT DECLARES (ALTHOUGH, MISTAKENLY TO TODD) THAT SHE THINKS IT'S ABOUT TIME THEY TRIED SEX. THE FAILURE OF THE TRADITIONAL 1950S BETTY-CROCKER FAMILY, OR AT LEAST, MOM'S UNFORTUNATE DEVIATION FROM THAT IDEAL HAS CREATED TWIN MONSTERS, ONE UTTERLY IMPOTENT, THE OTHER A VIOLENT SOCIOPATH, BOTH OF WHICH AT ONCE WISH TO ELIMINATE AND REPLACE DADDY. FOR ALL OF TERRY'S BLOODY SHENANIGANS, THE MONSTER HERE IS VERY CLEARLY MEANT TO BE A "BAD MOTHER," THUS, BY THE TERMS OF BLOOD RAGE, MEN'S PROBLEMATIZED RELATIONSHIPS ARE THE FAULT OF WOMEN WHO HAVE THEIR OWN IDENTITIES.

AS THE SON OF A SINGLE MOTHER, AND A CHILD OF THE '80S I CAN SAY THAT WHETHER YOU CARE TO LOOK BEHIND THE CURTAIN OR NOT, BLOOD RAGE IS A GLORIOUS CLASSIC OF EARLY SLASHER CINEMA THAT HAS AT LAST BEEN MADE READILY AVAILABLE ON A HOME FORMAT SO A FRESH AUDIENCE CAN APPRECIATE IT.

Quentin's Dick Destruction

By Gilbert R. Smith

Quentin Tarantino movies where a guy gets shot in the dick:
-PULP FICTION
-INGLOURIOUS BASTERDS
-DJANGO UNCHAINED
-THE HATEFUL EIGHT
-TRUE ROMANCE

Tarantino movies where a guy is merely threatened with dick-shooting:
-JACKIE BROWN

Tarantino movies where a guy gets shot WITH a dick:
-FROM DUSK TILL DAWN

CONSIDER THIS: FOUR OF TARANTINO'S NINE (AS OF THIS WRITING) DIRECTORIAL EFFORTS FEATURE A DICK SHOOTING, AND MORE THAN HALF OF THE MOVIES HE'S WRITTEN FEATURE SOME CONFIGURATION OF DICK-RELATED GUN VIOLENCE, OR THE THREAT OF IT.

THERE'S NO DICKSHOT IN DEATH PROOF, BUT IF YOU TAKE GRINDHOUSE AS A WHOLE YOU WITNESS TARANTINO PLAYING A RAPIST WHOSE DICK MELTS OFF FROM THE ZOMBIE VIRUS. BESIDES, OL' STUNTMAN MIKE GETS AWAY WITH NOT HAVING HIS DICK SHOT OFF BECAUSE HE'S IMPOTENT, HIS CAR IS A STAND-IN FOR HIS DICK, AND THEY DEMOLISH IT. SO EVEN THOUGH NO DICKS ARE LITERALLY SHOT, SYMBOLICALLY DEATH PROOF IS THE MOST <u>SPECTACULAR</u> DICK-DESTRUCTION TARANTINO HAS FILMED TO DATE.

* HE IS SO! LOOK AT HIS LITTLE ARMS, THERE.

BOUGIE '17 + GHASTLY GILBERT

THE ABUSE OF MEG

©ROBIN BOUGIE · 2017 ·

FAMILY GUY, LENA DUNHAM, AND COLDPLAY ARE THE THREE MODERN THINGS THAT EVERYONE WHO EVEN MILDLY DISLIKES THEM MUST MAKE A BIG DEAL ABOUT TELLING YOU HOW TERRIBLE THEY ARE IF THEY EVER SEE YOU MENTION THEM ON SOCIAL MEDIA. THEY ARE THREE THINGS THAT RILE IMPASSIONED LEVELS OF OFTEN INEXPLICABLE ANNOYANCE AND ANGER FROM THOSE WHO DON'T SEEM TO USUALLY GET RILED ABOUT SUCH THINGS. NOTE I SAID "GOOD" REASON. THEY OFTEN GIVE YOU REALLY DUMB REASONS.

COLDPLAY IS JUST WAY TOO WELL KNOWN FOR THEIR OWN GOOD (U2 HAS THE SAME ISSUE), THE LEFT SEES EVERYTHING THEY DON'T LIKE ABOUT THEMSELVES IN LENA DUNHAM (AND TAKE IT OUT ON HER FOR IT), AND FAMILY GUY? WELL, I'VE OFTEN SEEN FAMILY GUY ROUTINELY CATEGORIZED AS "INDEFENSIBLE", "NOXIOUS", AND "CRUEL" COMEDY, AND THE MAIN REASON GIVEN FOR THAT IS THE UNENDING ABUSE OF THE 'MEG' CHARACTER--A TEENAGE GIRL WHO NEVER GETS A BREAK.

IN THE FIRST TWO SEASONS MEG WAS PRESENTED AS THE SWEET AND SOMEWHAT INNOCENT DAUGHTER, BUT AS THE SEASONS WENT ON, ESPECIALLY INTO SEASONS 3 AND 4, THE WRITERS BEGAN TO SET HER CHARACTER UP AS A BLACK SHEEP OF THE FAMILY. THE LOWEST RUNG ON A VERY UNIMPRESSIVE LADDER THAT GETS MISTREATED THE MOST, ESPECIALLY FROM HER FATHER, PETER, WHO MAKES IT ABUNDANTLY CLEAR THAT HE DOESN'T CARE ABOUT HER OR RESPECT HER. THIS IS OFTEN DEPICTED BY PETER SHOVING HER FACE INTO HIS ASSCRACK, AND FARTING WHILE SHE STRUGGLES TO FREE HERSELF. THIS HAS TAKEN PLACE IN MULTIPLE EPISODES, INCLUDING "THE TAN AQUATIC WITH STEVE ZISSOU", "BANGO WAS HIS NAME OH" AND IN "CALL GIRL" WHEN PETER'S PARTING GIFT TO MEG IS A VERY REPELLANT "SAD SOUNDING" FART DIRECTLY ON HER FACE.

MEG'S MOTHER, LOIS, DOESN'T CARE FOR HER MUCH EITHER, AS WE SEE IN "STEW-ROIDS", WHEN THE GIRL IS GIVEN FOOD WASTE FOR HER SCHOOL LUNCHES -- SUCH AS PEELS, CRUSTS AND A TAUNTING PICTURE OF LOIS EATING A TURKEY LEG. HER SIMPLETON BROTHER, CHRIS, GIVES HER THE LEAST AMOUNT OF MISTREATMENT, BUT THAT IS MORE BECAUSE HIS CHARACTER IS SO MENTALLY SLOW AND UNOBSERVANT, ALTHOUGH IT IS WORTH NOTING THAT HE DOES COME TO HER FOR ADVICE, AND EVEN ONCE THREATENED TO QUIT HIS JOB IN "MOVIN' OUT (BRIAN'S SONG)" IF HIS BOSS DIDN'T RE-HIRE MEG, WHO HAD BEEN LET GO.

WHEN CRITICS OF THE SHOW ANNOUNCE THAT THEY DON'T APPROVE OF THE WAY MEG IS TREATED, I THINK THEY ARE MISSING A CRUCIAL POINT. MEG'S ABUSERS ARE NOT DEPICTED AS HEROES, BUT RATHER BUFFOONS. THEY ARE NOT SHOWN AS BEING IN THE RIGHT OR HELD UP AS SOME KIND OF ROLE MODEL. WE ARE INVITED TO LAUGH AT HER ABUSE, YES, BUT ALSO WHAT WE ARE ASKED TO DO AT THE SAME TIME IS ACKNOWLEDGE IS HOW HORRIBLE HER FAMILY IS. THE UNFAIRNESS OF IT IS LAID NAKED AND BARE. THERE IS A SENSE OF COMMISERATION THAT IS ENCOURAGED, AND AS THE BLACK SHEEP OF <u>MY</u> FAMILY, I CAN TELL YOU THAT IT IS A KNOWING LAUGH THAT I LAUGH.

WE CAN LAUGH BECAUSE IT'S TRUE: SIBLINGS SOMETIMES PUSH ONE OF THEIR OWN TO THE SIDE. FATHERS AND MOTHERS OFTEN DO HAVE FAVOURITE SONS AND DAUGHTERS, AND OTHER ONES THAT THEY DON'T QUITE CONNECT WITH. PARENTS DO SOMETIMES ABUSE THEIR KIDS, IN WAYS THAT BECOME NORMALIZED TO THEM, BUT SEEM UTTERLY HORRIFIC TO OUTSIDERS. FAMILY GUY ISN'T AFRAID TO GO FOR THE LOWEST COMMON DENOMINATOR, BUT IT'S ALSO NOT AFRAID TO REFERENCE COLD, CRUEL, COMPLICATED REALITY. AND I LIKE THAT, BECAUSE THERE IS MATERIAL DOWN THERE THAT CAN BE MINED EVEN WHILE YOU'RE UNABASHEDLY SURROUNDING IT WITH FART AND DICK JOKES.

THERE'S SOMETHING ELSE INTERESTING ABOUT MEG'S MISTREATMENT.

PETER FARTS ON HIS DAUGHTER'S FACE

PPBBTT FFFRRRTT HONK

EEEEK!!

174

MEG IS DEPICTED AS UNPOPULAR AT SCHOOL, DESPERATE, EMOTIONALLY FRAGILE, AND ABOVE ALL: HOMELY. A BUTTERFACE. EYE BROCCOLI. A WOOFER. A SWAMP DONKEY.

IN OUR SOCIETY (AND ESPECIALLY OUR MEDIA) WOMEN WHO AREN'T BEAUTIFUL BY THE CURRENT STANDARDS ARE CONSIDERED GARBAGE AND DISPOSABLE. THEY'RE INVISIBLE, AND TOLD OVER AND OVER AGAIN THAT THEY HAVE NO VALUE. THE LESSON FOR THEM IS THAT IF YOU'RE NOT ATTRACTIVE, YOU'VE FAILED YOURSELF AND YOU'VE FAILED US. I THINK A LOT OF WHAT FAMILY GUY IS DOING WITH MEG IS SHINING A LIGHT ON THAT INJUSTICE, AND AMPLIFYING IT USING EXAGGERATION (PEOPLE BURN THEMSELVES ALIVE AFTER ACCIDENTALLY CATCHING A PEEK AT MEG IN HER UNDERWEAR IN ONE EPISODE) AND ABSURDISM. IN REALITY, MEG IS NO MORE QUANTIFIABLY CUTE OR UGLY THAN ANY OF THE OTHER FEMALE CHARACTERS ON THE SHOW, AND YET SHE IS TREATED AS A THING OF MONSTROUS, LOVECRAFTIAN REPULSIVENESS. IT'S A META-JOKE ABOUT THE ARBITRARINESS OF FEMALE BEAUTY PERCEPTIONS.

REGARDLESS IF YOU BUY INTO THAT OR ANY OF MY OTHER THEORIES ON THIS TOPIC, I FEEL COMPELLED TO IMPRESS UPON YOU THAT THE DEBASEMENT OF MEG IS NOT TO BE TAKEN AT FACE VALUE, BECAUSE SHE'S A CYPHER. SHE'S A REPRESENTATION. AS YOKO ONO AND JOHN LENNON ONCE SANG, "WOMAN IS THE NIGGER OF THE WORLD", AND YET FAMILY GUY'S BIGGEST CRITICS ARE OFTEN MY FELLOW FEMINISTS. "FAMILY GUY HATES WOMEN, SO I HATE FAMILY GUY" ONE OF MY FRIENDS TOLD ME RECENTLY.

AS THE SEASONS HAVE GONE ON, SETH MACFARLANE AND THE SHOW'S WRITING ROOM HAVE ACTIVELY TRANSFORMED MEG MORE THAN ANY OTHER CHARACTER. HER MORALS HAVE GOTTEN WORSE AND WORSE, AND SHE'S GONE FROM BEING FAIRLY SWEET AND KIND TO DOING THINGS THAT ARE JUST AS CRUEL AND APPALLING AS HER PARENTS. THIS DARK PROGRESSION IS THERE FOR A REASON, AND IT'S NOT TO SHOW THAT HER ABUSE WAS RETROACTIVELY JUSTIFIED. THE ONLY REAL TAKEAWAY THAT MAKES ANY KIND OF SENSE IS THAT THE GRIFFINS ARE TERRIBLE PARENTS WHO ARE RUINING THEIR KID.

ALL OF THIS COMES TO A HEAD IN THE SECOND EPISODE OF SEASON 10, ENTITLED "SEAHORSE SEASHELL PARTY". IT IS HERE, DURING A HURRICANE THAT HAS THE GRIFFINS TRAPPED TOGETHER AND HOUSEBOUND, THAT MEG, FINALLY, ANGRILY STANDS UP FOR HERSELF AND REFUSES TO TAKE IT ANY MORE. FOR THE FIRST TIME, MEG IS GIVEN THE FLOOR FOR AN ENTIRE EPISODE TO AIR OUT HER GRIEVANCES AGAINST THE REST OF HER FAMILY. AND IT AIN'T PRETTY.

PREVIOUSLY OBLIVIOUS, HEARING POINT BLANK ABOUT WHAT HIS BEHAVIOUR HAS DONE TO HIS DAUGHTER REDUCES PETER TO THE MENTAL STATE OF A CHILD, AND SUDDENLY WITHOUT A PASSIVE MEG TO BULLY, THE FAMILY TURNS ON ITSELF AND CAN NO LONGER COPE. WITH EVERYONE CRYING AND YELLING AT EACH OTHER AND UNABLE TO COME TO TERMS, MEG GETS TO THE REALIZATION THAT BY ALLOWING HER CLAN TO RELENTLESSLY INSULT HER, SHE ALONE HOLDS THE FABRIC OF THE FAMILY TOGETHER. PETER, LOIS, AND CHRIS NEED A "LIGHTNING ROD TO ABSORB ALL THE DYSFUNCTION," AND MEG IS THAT VERY IMPORTANT PERSON.

WHEN SHE FINALLY REALIZES THAT THERE IS VALUE IN BEING A MARTYR, SHE HEROICALLY DECIDES TO CONTINUE TAKING THE ABUSE IN ORDER TO RETURN TO "NORMALCY". SHE EATS SHIT IN ORDER TO GET BY. IS THIS FAIR? IS IT HEALTHY? NO, OF COURSE NOT, BUT ONCE AGAIN — IT'S REAL. THIS IS HOW ACTUAL VICTIMS OF ABUSE CONTEXTUALIZE WHAT IS HAPPENING TO THEM, AND IT'S HOW THEY COPE. WE ALL EAT SHIT IN THIS LIFE, TO VARYING DEGREES. WE ALL TAKE OUR LUMPS, AND HOPE WE'RE STRONG ENOUGH TO COME OUT THE OTHER END WITH A THICKER SKIN, AND SOME HARD-EARNED WISDOM OF HOW TO BE A BETTER PERSON.

-BOUGIE '17

WHAT HAPPENED TO Q?

ONE SNOWY WINTER EVENING IN NEW YORK CITY, IN 1985, DIRECTOR JONATHAN DEMME STEPPED INTO A WAITING CAB SO HE COULD GET TO WHERE HE NEEDED TO GO--JUST LIKE HE HAD SO MANY OTHER TIMES BEFORE AND SINCE. DEMME WENT ON TO BECOME A STAR DIRECTOR (AND PASSED AWAY AT THE AGE OF 73 IN APRIL 2017), BUT UP TO THAT POINT HE WAS FAMOUS FOR DIRECTING CRAZY MAMA, FIGHTING MAD, SWING SHIFT, AND THE LEGENDARY WOMEN IN PRISON FILM, CAGED HEAT.

HIS CAB DRIVER WAS A FRIENDLY, SASSY BLACK WOMAN IN HER MID 20S. SHE WAS FROM NEW JERSEY, WORE DREADS IN HER HAIR, CALLED HERSELF Q, AND JONATHAN FOUND HER EASY TO TALK TO. AS THEY SPOKE, HE ENDED UP TELLING HER WHAT HE DID FOR A LIVING, AND SHE EXCITEDLY ASKED HIM IF MOVIE DIRECTORS HAD CONNECTIONS TO THE MUSIC INDUSTRY, TO WHICH JONATHAN REPLIED 'NOT REALLY'. UNDETERRED, Q SLIPPED A CASSETTE TAPE INTO THE CAB'S PLAYER AND TOLD THE DIRECTOR TO LISTEN. IT WAS HER DEMO TAPE, AND AS THE CAB DROVE THROUGH A BLIZZARD, THE FIRST FEW NOTES OF "GOODBYE HORSES" RANG OUT. THEN Q'S SINGING VOICE FILLED THE TAXI ...

You told me I've seen it all before
Been there. I've seen my hopes and dreams
lying on the ground
I've seen the sky just begin to fall
And you say, "All things pass into the night"

IT'S AN ABSOLUTELY AMAZING SONG, AND DEMME WAS BLOWN AWAY BY IT AND THE ODD CIRCUMSTANCES THAT HAD TAKEN PLACE TO BRING IT TO HIM. "OH MY GOD," HE SAID, "WHAT IS THIS AND WHO ARE YOU?"

Q, WHO HAD GROWN UP AS A CHOIR SINGER, MARRIED YOUNG TO A DOMESTIC ABUSER (INSPIRATION FOR HER SONG "TEARS OF FEAR"), AND HAD TO FLEE BOTH NEW JERSEY AND HER MARRIAGE TO GET HER ASS TO NEW YORK--THE PLACE WHERE DREAMS COME TRUE, AND GO TO DIE. THERE IN CHELSEA SHE BECAME A NANNY FOR A WELL-OFF ENGLISH DUDE NAMED SWAN, AND SPENT HER FREE TIME TRYING TO GET HER MUSIC CAREER OFF THE GROUND.

BUT SWAN DIDN'T THINK HIS EMPLOYEE WAS ANYTHING SPECIAL, AND TOLD HER TO GIVE IT UP, ACTIVELY DISCOURAGING Q WITH THE HOPES THAT SHE WOULDN'T BECOME YET ANOTHER DIME-A-DOZEN BROKE NEW YORKER ARTIST/MUSICIAN. TAKING SWAN'S ADVICE OF FOCUSING ON A "PRACTICAL OCCUPATION", Q DECIDED TO DRIVE A TAXI, BUT LOVED MAKING MUSIC SO MUCH, SHE COULDN'T HELP BUT KEEP IT GOING AS A HOBBY WITH HER BAND, THE RESURRECTION.

DEMME WAS BOTH HALTED AND ASTOUNDED BY Q'S TOTALLY UNIQUE VOCAL TALENTS, WHICH HAD A DELICATE BUT ALSO A DEEP AND HUSKY TONE, GIVING HER A UNUSUAL SOUND THAT WAS HARD TO PLACE AS EITHER MALE OR FEMALE. HE GATHERED HER UP AND TOOK HER TO HOLLYWOOD, WHERE HE DID HIS BEST TO CONVINCE RECORD COMPANIES TO TAKE A CHANCE ON HER. EACH ONE OF THEM REFUSED, SAYING SHE WAS TOO WEIRD, AND "COULDN'T BE MARKETED".

Q AND DEMME WERE UNDETERRED. SHE WOULD FORM A NEW BAND CALLED Q LAZZARUS, AND DEMME WOULD USE HER IN HIS MOVIE SOUNDTRACKS, AND RECOMMEND HER TO ANY OTHER FILMMAKER THAT WOULD LISTEN. ONLY ONE DID, ADAM HOLENDER, WHO THAT YEAR IN 1986 USED ONE OF Q'S SONGS IN HIS NOW-FORGOTTEN CHRISTIAN SLATER FILM, TWISTED. ALSO THAT YEAR DEMME WOULD PUT OUT SOMETHING WILD (STARRING MELANIE GRIFFITH AND JEFF DANIELS) WHICH WOULD BE HIS FIRST FILM TO USE A Q NUMBER ("CANDLE GOES AWAY"), AND THEN TWO YEARS LATER, HE'D FINALLY FEATURE "GOODBYE HORSES" IN "MARRIED TO THE MOB".

DESPITE BEING MOURNFUL AND TRANSCENDENT, THE SONG DIDN'T GRAB ANYONE, AND HIS EFFORTS TO MAKE Q INTO A STAR HAD

GOODBYE HORSES

STALLED. IT WASN'T UNTIL DEMME AGAIN TOOK IT UPON HIMSELF TO USE 'GOODBYE HORSES' IN HIS BIGGEST-EVER FILM, 1991'S THE SILENCE OF THE LAMBS, THAT IT MANAGED TO GRAB PEOPLE'S ATTENTION AND CATAPULT Q'S DISTINCTIVE VOICE INTO THE POP CULTURE PANTHEON.

YOU REMEMBER IT, RIGHT? IT'S ONE OF THE FILM'S MOST ICONIC SCENES. BUFFALO BILL IS PUTTING ON MAKE-UP, GETTING ALL ANDROGYNOUS BY TUCKING HIS COCK BETWEEN HIS LEGS, AND TWEAKING HIS NIPPLE RING WHILE CREEPILY ASKING THE MIRROR: "WOULD YOU FUCK ME? I'D FUCK ME. I'D FUCK ME SO HARD".

DESCRIBED BY MUSIC JOURNALIST THOMAS GORTON AS "EUPHORIC AND DESPONDENT, FUTURISTIC AND ANCIENT" THE SONG "GOODBYE HORSES" WAS EXPLAINED BY THE MAN WHO WROTE IT, WILLIAM GARVEY (A MEMBER OF Q'S FIRST BAND, WHO DIED IN 2009) AS BEING "ABOUT TRANSCENDENCE OVER THOSE WHO SEE THE WORLD AS ONLY EARTHLY AND FINITE. THE HORSES REPRESENT THE FIVE SENSES FROM HINDU PHILOSOPHY AND THE ABILITY TO LIFT ONE'S PERCEPTION ABOVE THESE PHYSICAL LIMITATIONS AND TO SEE BEYOND THIS LIMITED EARTHLY PERSPECTIVE."

THE WAY MUSIC ROYALTIES WORK IS THAT THE PERSON WHO WROTE THE SONG GETS ALL THE $ $$, SO Q NEVER REALLY SAW ANYTHING MUCH FOR WHAT LITTLE FAME SHE EVER GOT. IT ALL WENT TO GARVEY, WHO REPORTEDLY DIDN'T MUCH CARE FOR Q. "HONESTLY, HE NEVER HAD A GOOD THING TO SAY ABOUT HER AND SAW HER AS AN INSTRUMENT," ARABELLA PROFFER, A CLOSE FRIEND OF GARVEY'S, TOLD THOMAS GORTON. "HE WROTE AND PERFORMED THE MUSIC AND THOUGHT SHE HAD TAKEN ADVANTAGE WAY PAST WHAT WAS NECESSARY. HE HINTED SHE WAS A DRUG ADDICT, AND ASIDE FROM THAT HE NEVER MUCH TALKED ABOUT HER."

"GOODBYE HORSES" WAS PLAYED AT GARVEY'S FUNERAL. ACCORDING TO ARABELLA, HE DIED A WEEK BEFORE HE WAS SCHEDULED TO SIGN ALL ROYALTIES TO THE SONG OVER TO HIS BEST FRIEND AND COLLABORATOR VERONICA RED, "HIS ESTRANGED SISTER NOW GETS ANY MONEY FROM THAT SONG, AND WE'VE SEEN RELEASES HAPPEN THAT HE IN NO WAY WOULD HAVE WANTED," ARABELLA TOLD GORTON IN 2018.

GORTON NOTES: "DURING HIS LIFE, GARVEY WAS FASTIDIOUS IN CLAIMING ROYALTIES, SUING MGM WHEN FAMILY GUY USED THE SONG WITHOUT PERMISSION – AN EPISODE WHERE CHRIS GRIFFIN PARODIES THE FAMOUS BUFFALO BILL SCENE. BUT Q WASN'T, AND ACCORDING TO PEOPLE THAT KNEW HER, SHE'S OWED A LOT OF MONEY. MON AMIE RECORDS IS THE LABEL THAT RELEASED THE SONG AND ITS FOUNDER MONA HAS ALSO BEEN LOOKING FOR Q 'FOR MANY YEARS, BUT TO NO AVAIL'. GARVEY SUSPECTED THAT SHE WAS DEAD AND HAD LAST TRIED TO FIND HER IN THE MID-90S WITHOUT LUCK, BUT WAS CONTACTED BY SOMEONE CLAIMING TO REPRESENT HER IN 2007."

JONATHAN DEMME, CIRCA 1985

SO WHAT HAPPENED TO Q? AT SOME POINT SHE MOVED TO THE UK TO PUT A BAND TOGETHER, BUT THAT APPARENTLY DIDN'T GO ANYWHERE, AND SOME HAVE SAID SHE MOVED BACK TO THE US. FRIENDS FEAR SHE AGAIN GOT INVOLVED WITH AN ABUSIVE MAN WHO ISOLATED HER, SINCE THOSE WERE THE TYPE SHE WAS ATTRACTED TO, OTHERS FEAR SHE COULD ONLY BE DEAD, SINCE IT WASN'T LIKE HER TO CUT OFF ALL CONTACT.

IN AUGUST OF 2018, SOMEONE CLAIMING TO BE Q CONTACTED ONE OF HER FANS TO REVEAL THAT SHE'S NOW A BUS DRIVER IN STATEN ISLAND. THAT HAS NEVER BEEN CORROBORATED, AND HAPPENS TO ALSO BE SOMETHING HYPOTHESIZED ONLY A MONTH EARLIER ON A WIDELY READ MESSAGE BOARD POST. IT COULD BE TRUE, BUT I FIND IT FISHY THAT WHOEVER THIS WAS, THEY FELT THE NEED TO DELETE THEIR TWITTER ACCOUNT RIGHT AFTER SENDING SOME RANDOM FAN A MESSAGE AS THEIR FIRST CONTACT IN DECADES.

-BOUGIE '18

Conversations with a Killer: The Ted Bundy Tapes (2019. Dir: Joe Berlinger)

IN EARLY 2019, A TERRIFIC NETFLIX DOCUMENTARY CALLED CONVERSATIONS WITH A KILLER: THE TED BUNDY TAPES WAS DROPPED, AND I WAS VERY IMPRESSED WITH HOW DIRECTOR JOE BERLINGER (FAMOUS FOR HIS PARADISE LOST, BROTHER'S KEEPER, AND METALLICA: SOME KIND OF MONSTER DOCS) USED EDITING AND VINTAGE FOOTAGE/CLIPS TO REFRAME INFORMATION I ALREADY KNEW INTO A WHOLE NEW INDEPENDENTLY ENJOYABLE PIECE OF ART. THIS NEW ERA OF DOCUMENTARIES FROM THE LAST 5 OR 6 YEARS IS GIVING US MORE AND MORE OF THIS KIND OF INVENTIVE FILMMAKING, AND SO MUCH LESS OF THAT BORING "TALKING HEADS" INTERVIEW EDITING STYLE, AND KEN BURNS-ESQUE NARRATION. I'M SO FUCKING PLEASED ABOUT THAT. THE FILM IS NOT ONLY GOOD, IT'S GOOD ENOUGH TO REWATCH.

A LOT OF OTHER PEOPLE WATCHED IT TOO, AND IT PUT TED BUNDY'S STORY BACK INTO THE SPOTLIGHT ON SOCIAL MEDIA FOR A WHOLE NEW GENERATION. A WEEK LATER, TWO HEAVILY SHARED ARTICLES BY SUZANNE MOORE AT THE GUARDIAN ("TED BUNDY WAS DEEPLY MEDIOCRE – SO WHY ARE WE ROMANTICISING HIM?") AND ASHLEY ALESE EDWARDS WERE DISCUSSED AMONGST MANY OF MY FRIENDS. THE PIECE EDWARDS PENNED WAS READ BY MILLIONS OF READERS, AND WAS A HOT TAKE BLATANTLY NAMED FOR CLICK BAIT PURPOSES: "TED BUNDY WASN'T SPECIAL OR SMART. HE WAS JUST WHITE." IT DISPUTED THE DECADES-OLD NARRATIVE THAT BUNDY WAS AN EXCEPTIONAL KILLER, AND IT QUESTIONED WHY HE SHOULD BE AS FAMOUS AS HE IS.

"BUNDY WAS NOT SPECIAL. HE WAS NOT SMARTER THAN THE AVERAGE PERSON: HE DID NOT HAVE A PERSONALITY SO ALLURING THAT HIS FEMALE VICTIMS COULD NOT HELP BUT SIMPLY GO OFF WITH HIM. HE DID NOT HAVE A SUPERHUMAN SKILL TO BE ONE STEP AHEAD OF THE POLICE. WHAT BUNDY DID HAVE WAS THE POWER OF BEING A WHITE MAN IN A SOCIETY THAT REVERES THEM AND HAS IMPLICIT FAITH IN THEIR ABILITIES ... BUNDY ISN'T EVEN EXCEPTIONAL WHEN COMPARED TO OTHER AMERICAN SERIAL KILLERS. SO WHY IS HIS LEGACY TREATED WITH FASCINATION AND TWISTED ADMIRATION RATHER THAN CONDEMNATION?"

IT'S A WELL-WRITTEN PIECE, BUT THE GENERAL CONCEIT THAT ONE OF AMERICA'S MOST FAMOUS SERIAL KILLERS IS ONLY THAT BECAUSE HE WAS WHITE AND MALE DOESN'T REALLY HOLD WATER. OF COURSE BUNDY HAD READY ACCESS TO PRIVILEGES THAT WHITE MALES HAVE -- BUT SO DO MANY MILLIONS OF OTHER PEOPLE.

THIS REMINDS ME A LOT OF WHEN BILL MAHER HAD HIS TV SHOW CANCELLED IN 2002 BECAUSE HE REFUSED TO STATE THAT THE 9/11 TERRORISTS WERE COWARDS, AND INSISTED THAT NO MATTER WHAT YOU THINK ABOUT THE TRAGEDY AND THE HORRIBLENESS OF THE ACT, FLYING A PLANE INTO A BUILDING TAKES BRAVERY. BUNDY WAS ARROGANT, POMPOUS, AND NARCISSISTIC, BUT TO DIMINISH HOW EXCEPTIONAL IT IS TO MANAGE TO (ALMOST) GET AWAY WITH MURDERING OVER 30 OTHER PEOPLE IN THE SPAN OF ONLY 5 YEARS AND ESCAPE FROM PRISON TWICE AFTER GETTING CAUGHT IS UNREALISTIC. IT'S NOT A CELEBRATION OF THOSE ACTS TO ACKNOWLEDGE THEY WERE NOTEWORTHY AND BEYOND THE PALE. IT IS SIMPLY STATING FACTS.

HE WAS A PSYCHOPATH, A FACT FAR, FAR MORE RELEVANT TO HIS FAME THAN HIS SKIN COLOUR. HE WASN'T NEARLY AS SMART AS HE THOUGHT HE WAS, BUT THEN THAT IS WHAT YOU SHOULD EXPECT FROM A NARCISSIST (VISIT THE ACTIONS OF MR DONALD TRUMP FOR MORE) AND IT'S PRECISELY WHY HE GOT CAUGHT.

—BOUGIE '19

ANTI-CENSORSHIP FEMINIST MARIANA VALVERDE HAD A REALLY INTERESTING STATEMENT ABOUT ORAL SEX IN PORNOGRAPHY IN HER BOOK: "SEX, POWER AND PLEASURE" (1985)

SHE WRITES: "A PHOTO OR VIDEO OF A WOMAN KNEELING DOWN TO PERFORM FELLATIO ON A MAN HAS A VERY DIFFERENT SOCIAL MEANING THAN A PICTURE OF A MAN KNEELING TO PERFORM CUNNILINGUS ON A WOMAN. THE FIRST PICTURE IMPLIES SUBORDINATION WHILE THE SECOND MERELY IMPLIES THAT A MAN IS GIVING A WOMAN PLEASURE. THE MAIN DIFFERENCE IN THE CONNOTATIONS IS NOT DUE TO ANYTHING IN THE PHOTOS THEMSELVES, BUT RATHER TO THE 'USUAL' CONNOTATIONS OF WOMEN'S BODIES VS. MEN'S BODIES."

SHOW AND TELL
The Story of Jamie Gillis and Show World

WITH THE POPULARITY OF HBO'S THE DEUCE (A SERIES ABOUT THE 1970S TIMES SQUARE PROSTITUTION, PEEP SHOW, AND PORN STAR SCENE) WHICH AS OF THIS WRITING HAS JUST FINISHED ITS 2ND SEASON, I FEEL LIKE IT IS AGAIN TIME TO WRITE ABOUT THAT PLACE AND TIME. BUT WITH THIS OUTING I'D LIKE TO SPECIFICALLY FOCUS ON THE CORNER OF 42ND AND 8TH, WHERE ONE OF THE MOST LEGENDARY PORN PALACES TO EVER EXIST RESIDED: SHOW WORLD.

I WENT TO MANHATTAN FOR THE FIRST AND ONLY TIME IN 2006, AND I WAS IN SEARCH OF GHOSTS. I SPEAK OF THE SLEAZE AND DEPRAVITY HISTORY HAD TAUGHT ME ABOUT THIS PLACE THROUGH WORD, VERSE, AND CUM-SOAKED PORNO HOUSE FILM STOCK. THE TIMES SQUARE OF YESTERYEAR. I KNEW IT WAS NO LONGER, THANKS TO THE CRASS DISNEYFICATION OF THAT SECTION OF THE ISLE, BUT MY TRAVELLING COMPANION, DIRTYBIRD AND I, CAME TO HUNT FOR EVEN JUST A LINGERING SMELL OF JIZZ-COATED ASS. IF ONLY JUST TO SAY THAT WE'D BEEN THERE, AND TAKEN A LOVING WHIFF.

THE HUNT FOR FREAKY FUN BEGAN IN A STRIP CLUB ACROSS FROM THE EMPIRE STATE BUILDING CALLED RICKY'S. RICKY'S HAD AN AMAZING THREE COURSE LUNCH MENU (WHERE ELSE CAN YOU GET A STEAK, SALAD, SIDE OF MASHED POTATOES AND ICE CREAM ALL FOR $10??) BUT DIDN'T HAVE ANY PUSSY ON DISPLAY. THE STRIPPERS WERE ALL HALF DRESSED, WHICH LEFT US WITH BEMUSED AND UNIMPRESSED EXPRESSIONS. EVEN IN MODEST VANCOUVER, WHERE WE WERE VISITING FROM, THE 'PEELER BARS' HAVE TITS, CUNT AND ANUS PROUDLY WAVING AROUND IN YOUR FACE. WHAT WE DIDN'T KNOW, AND AS I'LL SPEAK ABOUT LATER IN THIS PIECE, THE HOMOGENIZATION OF RICKY'S WAS STRICTLY COURT-MANDATED.

ROUNDING THE CORNER OF 42ND STREET AND 8TH AVE, I WAS RELIEVED TO FIND THAT THE FAMOUS HALLOWED GROUND OF DEPRAVITY KNOWN AS THE SHOW WORLD CENTER WAS STILL IN EXISTENCE. THAT GAVE ME A HUGE SMILE AND LITTLE BIT OF HOPE. I'LL ADMIT IT, MY HEART SKIPPED A BEAT AS I SCRAMBLED IN THE FRONT DOOR, CHASING A DREAM, BARING DOWN ON THOSE AFOREMENTIONED GHOSTS. WHAT I FOUND COULDN'T QUITE LIVE UP. IT WAS 3 FLOORS OF TRUNCATED FUCK-SUCK AND . . . . CROSSWORD PUZZLE MAGAZINES? THE XXX ACTION WAS STILL ON HAND, BUT THE SENSE OF DANGER AND DELIRIOUS SEXUAL ENERGY WAS GONE. I SEARCHED EVERY INCH OF SHOW WORLD LOOKING FOR IT.

ENTERING A PEEPSHOW BOOTH IN THE BASEMENT (THE SAME BASEMENT WHERE PSEUDO-SNUFF RAPE PEEPS AND SAVAGE BESTIALITY CLIPS WERE SHOWING IN 1980) I FOUND ONLY A VIDEO SCREEN DECLARING "GOD BLESS AMERICA" BEFORE LAUNCHING INTO SOME DECIDEDLY BORING WHITE-ON-BLACK CUM GUZZLING. WE WALKED AROUND A LITTLE, POKING OUR NOSES HERE AND THERE, AND TOOK NOTE OF HOW EMPTY THE PLACE WAS. IT WAS OK I GUESS, BUT NOTHING LIKE WHAT I'D READ PENNED BY PORN JOURNALISTS OF YESTERYEAR.

BUT GHOSTS HAVE A FUNNY WAY OF CONTACTING YOU FROM THE DEAD. I WAS A FOOL TO COUNT NEW YORK OUT SO EARLY, BECAUSE AS I WAS STANDING RIGHT THERE IN THE ENTRANCEWAY OF SHOW WORLD, DIRTYBIRD'S CELL RANG OUT WITH A 'DEETLE-DOOTLE' SOUND. HE ANSWERED THE PHONE, LOOKED CONFUSED, AND HANDED IT OVER TO ME.

"HELLO?", I SAID INTO IT. "HI, ROBIN, IT'S JAMIE GILLIS", A VOICE REPLIED.

WOW. JUST: **WOW**. DESPITE EMAILING PORN ACTOR JAMIE GILLIS A WEEK EARLIER AND ATTEMPTING TO SET UP A MEETING, I HAD NOT HEARD BACK FROM HIM AND HAD ASSUMED NOT MUCH WOULD COME OF IT. BUT NOW HERE I WAS, TELLING JAMIE HOW AMAZING IT WAS THAT I WAS VISITING *THE* SHOW WORLD FOR THE FIRST TIME. THE SYNCHRONICITY OF IT HONESTLY NEARLY KNOCKED ME RIGHT OFF MY FEET.

"OH SHOW WORLD... YEAH!" GILLIS CHUCKLED IN THAT WAY I'D HEARD HIM CHUCKLE IN SO MANY OF HIS FILMS. "IF ONLY IT WAS THIRTY YEARS AGO, I COULD HAVE TAKEN YOU IN THERE AND SHOWN YOU THINGS THAT WOULD JUST BLOW YOUR MIND. THERE WERE NAKED GIRLS IN THE BASEMENT. FOR $5 BUCKS YOU COULD DO WHATEVER YOU WANTED. IT WAS GREAT. I TOOK SEKA THERE ONE TIME AND FUCKED HER IN A PEEPSHOW BOOTH."

AND THOSE WERE THE FIRST WORDS I SHARED WITH MY FAVOURITE MALE ADULT FILM ACTOR OF ALL TIME. FOR THOSE OF YOU COMING IN LATE, OR WHO ARE TOO SENILE TO REMEMBER HIM, GILLIS IS ONE OF THE MOST IMPORTANT PERFORMERS IN XXX HISTORY, EITHER IN FRONT OF THE CAMERA, OR IN THE DIRECTOR'S CHAIR. IN 1971 GILLIS WAS WORKING WITH AN OFF-BROADWAY REPERTORY COMPANY, DOING CLASSICAL PLAYS, AND TO SUPPORT HIMSELF, WAS DRIVING CAB. HE'D DRIVE THAT CAB ALL DAY, THEN PLAY HAMLET AT NIGHT, ALL THE WHILE DESPERATE FOR ANOTHER JOB TO PAY THE BILLS. ONE DAY, GILLIS ANSWERED AN AD FOR "NUDE MODELLING" IN THE VILLAGE VOICE THINKING HE WAS GOING TO PROVIDE INSPIRATION FOR A LOCAL NYC ARTISAN, BUT AS IT TURNED OUT THE MODELLING GOING ON WAS IN A GROTTY BASEMENT ON 14TH STREET WHERE SOME STINKY GUY SHOT FUCK MOVIES.

"I SHOWED UP THERE, WORKED FOR ABOUT AN HOUR, HAD A GOOD TIME, MADE AS MUCH MONEY AS I WOULD DRIVING CAB, AND THAT'S HOW I STARTED." GILLIS ONCE TOLD XXX JOURNALIST ANTHONY PETKOVICH. "ACTUALLY, A LOT OF PEOPLE STARTED THERE IN THAT DIRTY BASEMENT-- LINDA LOVELACE, ERIC EDWARDS, ME ... BUT THERE WERE NO STARS IN THOSE DAYS, NO INDUSTRY. IT WAS ALL UNDERGROUND."

HIS DIRECTORIAL DEBUT ON THE PROWL BACK IN '89 WAS THE FIRST OF ITS KIND TO TAKE SOME AVERAGE DUDE OFF THE STREETS, PUT HIM IN THE BACK OF A LIMOUSINE, AND LET 'EM WILDLY FUCK AWAY AT SOME SEXED UP YOUNG ADULT VIDEO STARLET. IT ORIGINATED THE "GONZO" REALITY STYLE OF PORN THAT CURRENTLY HAS A STRANGLEHOLD ON THE MODERN PORN WORLD, AND WAS THE OBVIOUS INSPIRATION FOR THE LIMO SEX SCENE IN P.T. ANDERSON'S BOOGIE NIGHTS, WITH BURT REYNOLDS TAKING ON THE ROLE OF GILLIS.

JAMIE GILLIS

IN THE LATE '80S, JAMIE BECAME KNOWN IN UNDERGROUND PORN CIRCLES FOR HIS OUTLANDISH SCAT AND DEGRADATION-THEMED HOME MOVIES THAT MADE THE ROUNDS AMONGST PERVERTS IN THE KNOW. THESE WERE TOTALLY AMATEUR TAPES FEATURING SUBMISSIVE FEMALE FRIENDS JAMIE WOULD SHIT ON AND RACIALLY DEGRADE -- CONSENSUALLY, I ASSURE YOU. GILLIS WAS ALL ABOUT CONSENT WHILE SURROUNDING HIMSELF WITH FELLOW DEGENERATES. THEN IN THE EARLY '90S HE KICKED THE PRO-AM CRAZE INTO FULL GEAR BY CO-PRODUCING THE INFLUENTIAL AND LONG RUNNING DIRTY DEBUTANTES SERIES WITH ED POWERS, WHO THEN WENT ON TO STEAL THE SERIES FROM GILLIS AND TURN IT INTO A MASSIVE HIT.

IN MY OPINION JAMIE IS BASICALLY XXX ROYALTY AND DESERVES PROPS FOR HIS VARIOUS SLEAZY ACHIEVEMENTS IN SMUT, BUT I'D QUICKLY LEARN THAT THE MAN WAS ADMIRABLY MODEST ABOUT HIS ACCOMPLISHMENTS WHEN HE MET US LATE THAT EVENING AT A FANCY GREASY SPOON IN THE WEST VILLAGE.

WE WERE FLANKED BY OUR TALENTED/PRETTY NEW YORK PAL WENDY CHIN, WHO, ALONG WITH HER HUSBAND/BANDMATE JASON, DIDN'T WANT TO MISS OUT ON A MEETING WITH SUCH A LEGENDARY FIGURE. WHEN GILLIS WALKED IN AND SAW US, ONE OF THE FIRST THINGS OUT OF HIS MOUTH WAS "HEY, I HAVEN'T BEEN IN HERE IN YEARS. THIS IS JUST AROUND THE CORNER FROM THE SHIT HOLE WHERE LINDA LOVELACE SCREWED THE DOG IN THAT OLD PORNO LOOP."

I WAS LIKE AN EXCITED PUP MYSELF AS GILLIS DROPPED LITTLE NUGGETS OF PORN TRIVIA SUCH AS THAT ALL THROUGH THE EVENING AS WE ALL GOT PROGRESSIVELY DRUNKER. I WAS LIKE A DOG WITH ITS HEAD HANGING OUT OF THE WINDOW OF A FAST MOVING CAR, IT'S TONGUE BEING WHIPPED AROUND BY THE WIND. I WAS HAVING A FUCKING BLAST, AND IT'S STILL ONE OF THE BEST NIGHTS OF MY LIFE, EVEN ALL THESE YEARS LATER. WENDY WAS VOCALLY DISAPPOINTED IN HINDSIGHT THAT GILLIS DIDN'T ATTEMPT A GROPE, BUT EVEN PERVERTS CAN BE GENTLEMEN.

ANECDOTES ABOUT THE KINKY ORIGINATOR OF STUMP FUCKING: LONG JEANNE SILVER (WHO I LATER BEFRIENDED – HI JEANNE!), A TALE ABOUT SHOVING A CIGAR UP HIS OWN ASS IN ORDER TO SUCCESSFULLY WOO A FEMALE NEIGHBOUR THAT WAS CONTINUALLY PEEPING IN HIS WINDOW, FUNNY STORIES ABOUT WHERE CERTAIN PORN STARS FROM YESTERYEAR HAD ENDED UP...THEY FLOWED OUT OF JAMIE LIKE A LEAKY FAUCET, AND IT BECAME A TORRENT AFTER WE ENDED UP AT A LOVELY MEXICAN RESTAURANT OVER ON THE WEST SIDE OWNED AND OPERATED BY JAMIE'S MAIN SQUEEZE, MISS ZARELA. WE MET UP THERE WITH DRUMMER CHESTER THOMPSON (NOT TO NAME DROP TOO OBNOXIOUSLY, BUT THIS DUDE PLAYED DRUMS FOR GENESIS, FRANK ZAPPA, PHIL COLLINS, AND NEIL DIAMOND) AS GILLIS EFFORTLESSLY HOOKED US UP WITH SUPER-TASTY FREE MARGARITAS AND INTERESTING DRINKING COMPANIONS.

WHEN I GOT HOME, I BLOGGED A LITTLE ABOUT THIS OVERWHELMING EXPERIENCE, AND WHEN MY DEAR FRIEND, CLASSIC PORN STAR JODY MAXWELL, SAW WHERE I'D BEEN AND WHO I'D BEEN HANGING OUT WITH, SHE CHIMED IN WITH HER OWN SHOW WORLD ANECDOTE.

"I WAS THE FIRST TRUE PORN STAR TO DO A STAGE SHOW AT THE SHOW WORLD, OTHER THAN PERHAPS STRIPPERS WHO GOT INTO PORN AND STRIPPED THERE", JODY SAID WITH A CONTEMPLATIVE SIGH. "I APPEARED THERE OFF AND ON, DOING MY BOWL SHOW UNTIL I LEFT PORN. MANY OF THE OTHER STARS AND DIRECTORS THEN WOULD COME TO MY SHOW BECAUSE OF ITS UNIQUENESS AND HUMOR.

I MADE HOT, SEXY, AND HUMOUR WORK WELL TOGETHER. THEY USED TO RUN A CLIP OF ONE OF MY MOVIES IN THE OUTSIDE WALL OF THE BUILDING, ON THE STREET. I USE TO BE AMAZED TO STEP OUTSIDE AND SEE ME SITTING ON JAMIE GILLIS, FUCKING, WITH MY BREASTS BOUNCING UP AND DOWN AS I WAS RIDING HIM. YOU DIDN'T SEE THE ACTUAL INSERTION, BUT YOU SAW ENOUGH TO KNOW WHAT YOU WERE SEEING. YOU CERTAINLY SAW MY BARE BREASTS AND ME GOING AT IT HARD! HAHA! I WAS ALWAYS AMAZED THAT PEOPLE WALKING DOWN THE STREET COULD SEE THAT. IT ALSO MADE ME WEAR A HAT AND SUNGLASSES OUTSIDE A LOT!"

SADLY, BOTH JAMIE AND JODY HAVE SINCE PASSED AWAY IN THE YEARS SINCE I VISITED SHOW WORLD, BUT THEIR ENIGMATIC LEGENDS LIVE ON, AND SO DOES THE PLACE AND THE TIME IN WHICH THEY AND SHOW WORLD THRIVED.

IT'S AN INTERESTING HISTORY. MARTY HODAS (THE ORIGINATOR OF THE PEEP BOOTH MACHINE, AND WHO HAD A MONOPOLY ON ALL THE PEEPS IN NYC UNTIL HE RETIRED) GAVE WAY TO JOE BROCCHINI (WHO I WROTE ABOUT AT LENGTH IN CINEMA SEWER VOL. 5) AND RICHARD BASCIANO, WHO BOTH HAD MOB TIES TO THE GAMBINO CRIME FAMILY AND BECAME, INDEPENDENTLY, THE NEW UNDISPUTED KINGS OF XXX IN TIMES SQUARE. BROCCHINI HAD BLACK JACK BOOKS AND 3 OTHER SHOPS, AND IN 1977 BASCIANO OPENED SHOW WORLD CENTER, THE BIG APPLE'S LARGEST SMUT EMPORIUM. IT WOULD BE A GAME CHANGER.

LOCATED AT 669 EIGHTH AVENUE, SHOW WORLD INITIALLY TOOK UP FOUR STORIES OF A TWELVE-STORY BUILDING, AND HAD AN ASTOUNDING 22,000 SQUARE FEET OF FULL COLOR IMAGERY OF SPLAYED THIGHS, MOIST AND ERECT GENITALS, AND HEAVING BREAST MEAT. BUILT AT A COST OF $400,000, SHOW WORLD FEATURED ITS OWN FULL SIZE THEATER, AND EACH DAY, NEARLY 100 WOMEN WORKED A ROTATING SEX DISPLAY THAT WAS LOCATED ON THE SECOND FLOOR. IT WAS ONE STOP SHOPPING FOR ANYTHING AND EVERYTHING THAT WAS LEGALLY AVAILABLE AT THE TIME IN ADULT ENTERTAINMENT: MOVIES, LOOPS, BOOKS, MAGAZINES, SEX TOYS, PEEPSHOWS, LIVE SEX PERFORMANCES OF EVERY BIZARRE VARIETY, AND REGULAR IN-STORE SIGNINGS BY FAMOUS PORN STARS.

"WHEN SHOW WORLD WAS JUST OPENING I RAN A FEATURE STORY ON IT FOR A JAPANESE PUBLICATION", ELDERLY SMUT REPORTER R. ALLEN LEIDER TOLD ME IN 2018. "I MET (BASCIANO) SEVERAL TIMES, AND HE WAS A NICE GUY TO ME. SHOW WORLD WAS TO BE A MAJOR PROJECT AT THE OUTSET. IT WAS SUPPOSED TO HAVE A BURLESQUE THEATER AND A RESTAURANT WITH LIQUOR AND TOPLESS WAITRESSES, TO GO ALONG WITH THE PEEP SHOW BOOTHS, LIVE PERFORMERS, AND THE MAGAZINE AND TOY STORE. THE ORIGINAL MANAGER WAS A GUY NAMED BOB GREEN WHO WAS INEPT, AND SOME OF THE BIG PLANS NEVER CAME TO BE. THE BURLESQUE SHOW WAS FIRST RUN BY ROD SWENSON WHO LATER FORMED THE PLASMATICS PUNK ROCK GROUP WITH STRIPPER WENDY O. WILLIAMS."

A CIRCUS CARNIVAL STYLE BARKER STOOD OUTSIDE ON THE WALKWAY AND IN A LOUD HUCKSTER VOICE PROMISED EXPLICIT, EXPLOSIVE SEX PERFORMED RIGHT IN FRONT OF YOUR NOSE BY SWEDISH MODELS, FATHER/DAUGHTER DUOS, A LIVE APE, VAMPIRES — ASIDE FROM CHILDREN OR CORPSES, THE SKY WAS THE LIMIT. "MOST LIKELY, YOU'D SEE A COUPLE OF NAKED JUNKIES ONSTAGE TRYING TO HAVE SEX," SAID TIM CONNELLY, WHO PERFORMED IN THE LIVE SHOWS DURING THE LATE 1970S. "AND IF YOU WERE DUMB ENOUGH TO BELIEVE THE BARKER, YOU HAD A LOT OF NERVE ASKING FOR YOUR MONEY BACK."

CONNELLY TOLD NY POST REPORTER MICHAEL KAPLAN IN MAY OF 2017 ABOUT AN AUDIENCE MEMBER WHO BECAME IMPATIENT AND FRUSTRATED WITH HIS PERFORMANCE WHEN HE DECIDED TO TRY TO WARM THE CROWD UP WITH SOME COMEDY WHILE HIS PARTNER WAS WAITING TO BE PENETRATED BY HIM: "HE WALKED TO THE STAGE AND SAID, 'FUCK THE BROAD!' I TOLD HIM TO SHUT UP, THEN I SAW HIS GUN. I WAS BUCK-NAKED AND THE GUY HAD A PISTOL ON ME! EVERYBODY STARTED GOING CRAZY; I GRABBED THE WOMAN I WAS WITH AND WE WALKED OFF STAGE. THE GUY PUT THE GUN BACK IN HIS COAT AND LEFT. MEANWHILE MY KNEES WERE WEAK AND THE AUDIENCE MEMBERS WERE STOMPING THEIR FEET, WANTING US TO COME BACK OUT AND FINISH."

AND UPSTAIRS FROM THIS FILTH MECCA? BASCIANO'S MASSIVE 3-STOREY LUXURY APARTMENT OVER LOOKING IT ALL, COMPLETE WITH A PRIVATE GYM AND A FULL SIZE BOXING RING — SOMETHING RICHARD COULD NEVER DREAM OF BEING ABLE TO AFFORD IN HIS YOUTH WHEN HE WAS A BOXER TRYING TO MAKE IT. BUT EVEN THOUGH RICHARD WAS MOSTLY THE OWNER OF SHOW WORLD, THE BUILDING ITSELF THAT IT WAS HOUSED IN BELONGED TO THE GAMBINOS — IN PARTICULAR, A NEW YORK CRIME LORD NAMED ROBERT DIBERNARDO. UNLIKE THE OTHER 'MADE MEN' IN THE GAMBINO CLAN, 'DB' WAS INFAMOUS FOR HANDLING HIS BUSINESS WITHOUT RESORTING TO VIOLENCE, SOMETHING THAT ENDEARED HIM TO NEW YORK PORNOGRAPHERS WHO NEEDED A SILENT INVESTOR AT A TIME WHEN BANKS WERE CERTAINLY NOT INTERESTED IN FUNDING XXX.

"IT'S ONE OF THE MOST VALUABLE PIECES OF REAL ESTATE ON THE PLANET", 1970S ADULT FILM DIRECTOR SHAUN COSTELLO NOTED WHEN I TALKED TO HIM IN 2018. "BUYING THAT PROPERTY WAS DIBERNARDO'S FIRST MAJOR ACHIEVEMENT, AFTER SWITCHING FROM THE DECAVALANTE'S TO THE GAMBINOS. BASCIANO HAD A PIECE OF SHOW WORLD, BECAUSE THAT WAS THE WAY THESE GUYS DID BUSINESS. HE WAS THE 'ON SITE' GUY, PRETTY MUCH THE WAY MICKEY ZAFFARANO WAS THE 'ON SITE' GUY AT THE PUSSYCAT THEATER, WHICH WAS ACTUALLY OWNED BY THE BONNANO FAMILY. CIVILIANS THOUGHT MICKEY OWNED THE PLACE, BUT OF COURSE, HE DIDN'T."

UNLIKE HODAS AND BROCCHINI (WHO WAS LATER WHACKED BY THE GAMBINOS), BASCIANO PLAYED IT SMART, AND KEPT A LOW PROFILE. NO TALKING TO THE PRESS, NO FLAUNTING A PLAYBOY LIFESTYLE IN PUBLIC, AND RARELY EVEN LEAVING HIS LUXURY APARTMENT AT ALL. THIS KEPT THE HEAT OFF HIM, AND MADE IT VERY HARD FOR THE AUTHORITIES TO EVER BUST HIM ON OBSCENITY CHARGES, DESPITE THEIR MANY EFFORTS. HIS OPERATION WAS METICULOUS, AND ALWAYS OPERATED JUST BARELY INSIDE WHAT WAS ALLOWED BY LAW. THE UNDERAGE PROSTITUTES STREETWALKING RIGHT OUTSIDE THE DOOR? DIDN'T HAVE ANYTHING TO DO WITH HIM, HE INSISTED. THAT WAS THE CITY'S PROBLEM.

"YOU DID NOT TALK TO RICHARD BASCIANO: YOU DID NOT MAKE EYE CONTACT," REMEMBERS JOSH ALAN FRIEDMAN, THE AUTHOR OF ONE OF MY FAVOURITE BOOKS OF ALL TIME, TALES OF TIMES SQUARE (FERAL HOUSE PRESS). "THE LESS YOU KNEW ABOUT HIS OPERATION, THE BETTER OFF YOU WERE. HE EMPLOYED BOXERS FROM HIS ULTRA-PRIVATE GYM UPSTAIRS, TO SERVE AS QUARTER CASHIERS. THEY WERE TOUGH GHETTO GUYS AND FUNCTIONED AS BASCIANO'S ARMY. THEY WERE VERY GOOD AT THROWING OUT ANYONE WHO MISBEHAVED. PIMPS CAME IN TO RECRUIT GIRLS AND THEY GOT BOUNCED VIOLENTLY."

HE MADE SO MUCH MONEY FOR THE GAMBINOS, BASCIANO BEGAN TO OPEN UP NEW LOCATIONS AROUND TIMES SQUARE. THERE WAS SHOW PALACE THEATER AT 670 EIGHTH AVENUE AND SHOW FOLLIES THEATER AT 713 SEVENTH AVENUE, AND IN EACH: LOVELY YOUNG WOMEN WERE THE GREASE THAT OILED THE ENGINE OF THE BUSINESS. FOR A QUARTER, CUSTOMERS WATCHED THEM GYRATING NAKED, RUBBING THEMSELVES, 30 SECONDS PER QUARTER, BEFORE A METAL SHUTTER SLAMMED DOWN, BLOCKING THE VIEW UNTIL MORE QUARTERS WERE PONIED UP. SHIT TRULY EXPLODED AND PROFITS WENT INSANE WHEN BASCIANO TOOK THE MEASURE OF REMOVING THE PEEP-SHOW WINDOWS IN 1978, WHICH ALLOWED THE GIRLS TO REACH IN AND TOUCH THE PATRONS, AND BE GROPED THEMSELVES. AGGRESSIVE GALS MADE SERIOUS BANK — HUNDREDS OF DOLLARS PER SHIFT.

THE ATTORNEY GENERAL'S COMMISSION ON PORNOGRAPHY SAID IN ITS 1986 REPORT THAT PEEP SHOWS -- BOTH OF THE LIVE AND THE 8MM FILM VARIETY -- WERE THE BIGGEST AND MOST PROFITABLE

TWO SIDES OF THE SAME COIN: SHOW WORLD PEEP SHOW TOKEN. CIRCA 1990

PORTION OF THE PORN INDUSTRY AT THE TIME, WITH ANNUAL NATIONWIDE PROFITS AT A STAGGERING TWO BILLION DOLLARS. ACCORDING TO WILLIAM P. KELLY, A FORMER FBI AGENT WHO INVESTIGATED PORN AND SERVED AS A CONSULTANT ON OBSCENITY FOR VARIOUS LAW ENFORCEMENT GROUPS, "THE BIGGEST SINGLE INCOME OF ANY OF IT IS THE 25-CENT COIN OR THE TOKEN DROPPED IN THE PEEP SHOW MACHINE IN THE BACK OF THE DIRTY BOOK STORES."

BUT THE PROFITS EVERYONE INVOLVED AT SHOW WORLD SAW FROM DIRECT CUSTOMER INTERACTION CAME AT A GRAVE PRICE. ON MARCH 24TH 1991, A 21-YEAR-OLD YVONNE HAULSEY WORKED A ONE-ON-ONE FANTASY BOOTH, WHICH WERE BETTER KNOWN AS "CONFESSIONALS" BY INSIDERS. SHE'D JUST GOTTEN MARRIED TO HER HUSBAND LEO THE YEAR BEFORE. THEY WERE TRYING TO MAKE A GO OF IT, BUT SHE NEVER CAME HOME THAT NIGHT. SHE WAS STABBED TO DEATH IN HER CONFESSIONAL BY A PSYCHO, AND LAY SLUMPED IN HER BOOTH FOR HOURS BEFORE ANYONE NOTICED.

EVENTUALLY A CONSERVATIVE NEW YORK JUDGE CREATED THE "60/40" ZONING RULE, WHICH MEANT THAT ANY PORN SHOP OR STRIP CLUB'S SPACE HAD TO BE CONVERTED TO 60% NON-SEX MATERIAL, WHICH IN THE CASE OF SHOW WORLD BECAME KUNG FU TAPES, CROSSWORD PUZZLE BOOKS, AND I LOVE NY SHIRTS AND TOTE BAGS FOR THE TOURISTS, AND IN THE CASE OF NEW YORK STRIP CLUBS MEANT MOST OF THEM WOULD NOW ALSO HOUSE STEAK HOUSES.

BEGINNING IN 1998, SHOW WORLD WOULD GROW INCREASINGLY MORE DIMINUTIVE. AFTER NEIGHBOURHOOD PROPERTY VALUES SOARED AND CLEANUP EFFORTS WERE UTILIZED WITH TRANSFORMATIVE RESULTS, MUCH OF SHOW WORLD'S SPACE WAS SUBLET. THE THEATER WOULD NOW STAGE ALL-AGES PRODUCTIONS LIKE "THAT PHYSICS SHOW" AND "DRUNK SHAKESPEARE", AND NEXT DOOR A CASTRATED SHOW WORLD WAS NOW BUT A TINY, SAD, RUN-DOWN ISLAND OF SMUT IN A SOULESS SEA OF G-RATED COMMERCIALISM.

RICHARD BASCIANO'S LAST YEARS WERE NOT GOOD ONES. IN 2013 A FOUR-STOREY PROPERTY AT 2136 MARKET STREET IN PHILADELPHIA HE BOUGHT TO HAVE DEMOLISHED SO HE COULD MAXIMIZE PROFITS FELL AWKWARDLY WHILE IT WAS BEING KNOCKED DOWN, AND CRUSHED A SALVATION ARMY THRIFT STORE NEXT DOOR. 7 DIED AND 12 WERE INJURED, AND RICHARD WAS FOUND LIABLE IN THE $227 MILLION DOLLAR SETTLEMENT.

HE DIED A FEW YEARS LATER IN 2017 AT THE AGE OF 91, JUST COMING UP SHORT TO BE ABLE TO LIVE TO SEE A DECADES-LONG LEGAL BATTLE COME TO AN END. IN JULY OF THAT YEAR CITY LAWYERS FINALLY PREVAILED IN THEIR EFFORT TO KILL "SEXUALLY FOCUSED BUSINESSES" WHEN THE NEW YORK COURT OF APPEALS REINSTATED A 2001 LAW, WHICH BANNED STOREFRONTS WITH "LIVE PERFORMANCES CHARACTERIZED BY AN EMPHASIS ON CERTAIN SPECIFIED ANATOMICAL AREAS OR SPECIFIED SEXUAL ACTIVITIES" FROM MOST COMMERCIAL AND RESIDENTIAL HOODS IN THE CITY. IRONICALLY, DESPITE IT BEING NOW LEGAL FOR WOMEN TO BARE THEIR BREASTS IN PUBLIC IN NEW YORK STATE, THEY WOULD NOT BE ALLOWED TO EXPOSE THEM IN PRIVATE -- IN PLACES FREQUENTED BY ADULTS EXCLUSIVELY.

IN APRIL 2018, SHOW WORLD SHUTTERED ITS DOORS, AND TURNED OFF THE PEEP SHOW BOOTH VIDEO SCREENS FOR THE LAST TIME. IN HIS WAKE BASCIANO LEFT BEHIND HIS SPOUSE, LOIS, AND THREE ADULT DAUGHTERS, ALL FROM A PRIOR MARRIAGE.

"I TALKED TO THE NUTS 4 NUTS GUY WHO WORKS OUTSIDE", JEREMIAH MOSS, THE AUTHOR OF VANISHING NEW YORK REPORTED. "HE TOLD ME THAT THE BUILDING WILL NOT BE TORN DOWN. A SECURITY GUARD CONFIRMED THAT INFORMATION, SAYING THE PLACE WILL BE RENOVATED INSTEAD. WE'LL PROBABLY GET A CHAIN STORE OF ONE KIND OR ANOTHER BECAUSE THAT'S WHAT THE NEW TIMES SQUARE DESERVES. BUT SOME WILL REMEMBER THAT FOR 40 YEARS, SHOW WORLD WAS HERE, SMELLING OF BLEACH AND ORANGE-SCENTED MOP WATER, DOING ITS SERVICE FOR NEW YORKERS, COMMUTERS, AND TOURISTS ALIKE."

· 2018 · — ROBIN BOUGIE

index

(Note: Entries in **bold** refer exclusively to illustrations.)

index

index

index

index

The Complete Cinema Sewer Book Collection is Published by FAB Press

CINEMA SEWER VOLUME 1
The Adults Only Guide to History's
Sickest and Sexiest Movies!

ISBN: 978-1-903254-45-5
Pages: 192
UK Price: £14.99
US Price: $19.95

"What sets Cinema Sewer apart is that even
though the coverage is of the most insane,
repellent smut around, Robin's writing never
seems to pander... it's a refreshing approach."
Neon Madness magazine

CINEMA SEWER VOLUME 2
The Adults Only Guide to History's
Sickest and Sexiest Movies!

ISBN: 978-1-903254-56-1
Pages: 192
UK Price: £14.99
US Price: $19.95

"Prepare to veer wildly between curiosity,
arousal, disgust, laughter, embarrassment,
disbelief, confusion and uncontrollable glee.
Such is the power of Cinema Sewer."
The Nerve magazine

CINEMA SEWER VOLUME 3
The Adults Only Guide to History's
Sickest and Sexiest Movies!

ISBN: 978-1-903254-64-6
Pages: 192
UK Price: £14.99
US Price: $19.95

"Overwhelmingly positive in outlook. Intelligent,
relaxed and unpretentious, the book has a DIY
aesthetic that screams punk chic while the
text offers an unrelenting renegade attitude."
Sex Gore Mutants website

CINEMA SEWER VOLUME 4
The Adults Only Guide to History's
Sickest and Sexiest Movies!

ISBN: 978-1-903254-74-5
Pages: 192
UK Price: £14.99
US Price: $19.95

"Cinema Sewer is the direct heir and foremost
survivor of decades of mayhem-trash-film
fanzines, and Bougie has proven there's still
meatballs to be pulled out of the gravy."
www.quimbys.com

CINEMA SEWER VOLUME 5
The Adults Only Guide to History's
Sickest and Sexiest Movies!

ISBN: 978-1-903254-83-7
Pages: 192
UK Price: £14.99
US Price: $19.95

"Bougie and his contributors really know their
stuff, possessing a dizzying array of cinematic
knowledge, the likes of which should impress
even the most jaded and diehard film fan."
George Pacheco, Examiner.com

CINEMA SEWER VOLUME 6
The Adults Only Guide to History's
Sickest and Sexiest Movies!

ISBN: 978-1-903254-91-2
Pages: 192
UK Price: £14.99
US Price: $19.95

"There's no elitist attitude. These people love
movies, know their history, and like anyone
who truly loves anything, they want you to be
as stoked about is as they are."
Razorcake magazine

For further information about these books and others in the acclaimed FAB Press line, visit our online store, where we
also have a fine selection of excellent cult movie magazines and other items of interest from all over the world!

www.fabpress.com